Semi-Invisible Man

Julian Evans is the author of *Transit of Venus*, the account of a journey to the heart of the US nuclear-missile testing programme in the Pacific Ocean. He lives in south-west England.

www.julianevans.com

semi invisible man

the life of Norman Lewis

Julian Evans

PICADOR

First published 2008 by Jonathan Cape

First published in paperback 2009 by Picador
an imprint of Pan Macmillan Ltd
Pan Macmillan, 20 New Wharf Road, London N1 9RR
Basingstoke and Oxford
Associated companies throughout the world
www.panmacmillan.com

ISBN 978-0-330-42708-1

The author gratefully acknowledges funding support during the writing
of this book from Arts Council England, the Authors' Foundation
and the Oppenheim–John Downes Memorial Trust

1 3 5 7 9 8 6 4 2

A CIP catalogue record for this book is available
from the British Library.

Printed and bound in the UK by
CPI Mackays, Chatham ME5 8TD

Visit www.picador.com to read more about all our books
and to buy them. You will also find features, author interviews and
news of any author events, and you can sign up for e-newsletters
so that you're always first to hear about our new releases.

For Michel Déon,
the godfather

CONTENTS

PRELUDE:
THE RELUCTANT BIOGRAPHER

I must be frank. I didn't want to write this book.

In July 1983, twenty years before he died, Norman Lewis had lunch at Covent Garden, London, with his new British publisher. The restaurant where the lunch took place, the Grange, is long gone, but in the 1980s it had an English name, a good, mainly French menu and a discreet oriental atmosphere. It could have passed for a luxury Chinese restaurant, in fact, the kind of place where diners eat imperceptibly and seem not to talk at all, and that confusion of styles could well have been responsible for its failure to continue to attract enough customers. Norman's hosts were waiting for him towards the back of the deep, darkly furnished room. He arrived a few minutes after one, a tall, stooping silhouette against the light, wearing spectacles and an unpronounced moustache, his straight hair combed obediently back; a man in his seventies but ageless by virtue of the impression of a kind of austerity of appearance. The chair-scraping and introductions over, everyone sat down. A silence followed, and was broken by a burst of warm words from one of Norman's hosts about his writing and his most recent books, including his new novel. Norman responded shortly, his gaze on the tablecloth. Silence returned. Norman's new publisher and the publisher's editor both tried to engage their guest. How was his new book going? Was he happy with the editorial comments he'd had about his novel? With each shot at conversation, each short answer, the silence recoiled more strongly. At one point, as Norman speechlessly gazed at the tablecloth, the publisher raised his eyebrows at the editor across the table.

Drinks arrived, lunch was ordered: flurries of activity that released the tension temporarily. Norman's speechlessness, however, was lasting.

It went through the editor's mind that his silence might be due to thoughtfulness or to a physical distraction (was he perhaps feeling unwell?). It was not until much later, after the lunch was long over and Norman had gone home to Finchingfield, the Essex village where he had lived for more than twenty years, that the editor realised his muteness had been more like wariness: like the cautious immobility of an animal as it weighs up potential predators, or the vigilance of a man calculating another sort of threat, a boredom that would prey on him equally horribly.

For a good twenty minutes, it was as if Norman was there but was *pretending not to be there*.

Quite suddenly, without any kind of signal, it was over. He seemed to decide that these people were all right and that the situation could be trusted, and stories – his preferred form of conversation – started to pour out, about the lunacy of his commanding officer in north Africa during the war, about an evening he had spent in a bar in upland Guatemala in the 1950s operating the jukebox for three drunken bandits addicted to a song called "Mortal Sin" (a situation from which he'd been saved by an earthquake), about his summers in a Catalonian fishing village in the early 1950s, about his role as an Intelligence NCO in the repatriation of several thousand Cossacks by the British in 1944.

"And by the way," he would say in his glasspaper north London voice, and the narrative would bifurcate into another continent.

I know all this, incidentally, because I was the editor. The impressions follow on from the facts. And then time transforms and refines things. Long after this first meeting with Norman, his silence acquired more importance than it had had at the time. In retrospect, I treasured it. It was as though, by not speaking, he was compelling the world in his immediate vicinity – his audience of myself and Christopher Sinclair-Stevenson, the publisher of Hamish Hamilton – to his pace, his mood, his atmosphere. It was a sort of conquest. And having imposed acceptance of his idea of who he was, nothing could have been less wary than the letter he sent the following day.

15.7.83
Dear Christopher,
It was delightful to meet you and Julian Evans yesterday, and thank you for the lucullan lunch. Such rare and invigorating occasions are all the more memorable when one lives, as I do, in the intellectual tundra of Essex, condemned

on festive outings to an eating house – the only one within five miles – appositely named The Nosebag.

I will now cerebrate over the new title [of his novel], while awaiting André [Schiffrin, his US publisher]'s suggestions for reducing the Americans' tooth-grating impact, and incorporate these with other small changes. Let us hope that these turn up before my departure on the annual family holiday, which looms close. I dearly need an excuse for slipping away from those threatening beaches.

With best wishes,
Sincerely,
Norman

At the time the letter's first line, in which he perfectly recalled the name of the other person at lunch, seemed just an example of his extreme courtesy. Yet rapidly, in the space of not more than a few months, Norman and I became friends. This happened unexpectedly and in an oddly formal way. I can talk with some precision about the occasion, another lunch in November of that year, at El Vino's, the one-time journalists' bar in Fleet Street, because during my twenties I kept a diary that records many of my meetings with Norman. Before I do, though, I want to revert to our first meeting (which is not in my diary). I started this prelude with an account of that occasion not for the obvious reason, but because 1. I wanted to tell it from memory and 2. it also seems to offer some perspectives on the practice of biography that interest me. Forgive this change of gear. If it seems abrupt or disruptive or undesirable, feel free to move straight to the next chapter where events will be less mediated.

The first observation, then. Since the account of our meeting above is from memory, everything you have read, apart from Norman's thank-you letter, which is in the Hamish Hamilton archive at the Special Collections of the Arts and Social Sciences Library, Bristol University, is made up. Made up from an often taken-down-and-examined memory, perhaps, but still fabricated. Was the Grange, for instance, really decorated in a Chinese style? Was Norman really silent for "a good twenty minutes"? Did Christopher Sinclair-Stevenson raise his eyebrows? Were those particular stories the ones Norman told? All of which is only to point out at this stage the very obvious matter of memory's subjectivity, mine and everyone else's. The observer's subjectivity was a question that was of intense interest to Norman himself, as I want to show:

Akira Kurosawa's *Rashomon*, released in Britain in 1952 and one of the great artistic treatments of how markedly individuals' accounts of events will always differ, was among his favourite films. So however sure I can be that I haven't retro-injected details into my account of our meeting to make it more curious and emblematic of Norman than it was in reality, it is for ever made up. (Just to be clear. Another possibly strange, subjective way of putting things – that "twenty years before he died" in the opening lines – is not in fact to do with subjectivity but perspectivity. How could anybody in 1983 have known that Norman had another twenty years, no more or less, to live? That hindsight, however, is an equal part of the biographical problem, one that I want to talk about later.)

The second observation: in supplying the barest sketch of Norman Lewis the writer as he was when away from his desk, my description of meeting him presents, I hope, among other things the picture of one kind of outsider's temperament. In a radio interview a few years after the lunch in Covent Garden, Norman was asked if he felt he was an outsider. "A total one, yes," he said, "I am actually slightly better than I used to be. Taking a long time to improve, but I am less of an outsider. That is to say, with extreme effort now I can sort of produce a sort of creditable small talk, not very much of it, but a few sentences."[1] One aspect of outsiderness was that he disliked personal publicity. John Hatt, who republished several of Norman's works in his Eland Books imprint in the 1980s, says, "He was absolutely dead against publicity," although Hatt succeeded in persuading him to give his first magazine interview at the age of seventy-five. Even after "improving" he still armed himself with the isolation of his Essex tundra and a serene courtesy by which he evaded the personal intrusions of his interviewers. I once asked him how many times he had been married. "Can we leave that one out?" he answered. "I like to remain a mystery to my family."

Which leads on to the third observation, that in the media-ubiquitous climate of our time, which also embraces two decades' unflagging output of literary biography, we have become accustomed to believing (at so deep a level of assumption that we hardly think about it) that "personality" is an essential and true key to every stratum of revelation about ourselves. Is it? Perhaps. I suspect nevertheless that if we wonder about the details of a writer's life (and we do with reasonable curiosity; as Graham Greene, for instance, writes about Joseph Conrad, "The domestic background *is* of interest: to know how a writer with the peculiar sensitivity we call genius compromises with family life"), we find it difficult to accept that what is most interesting about a writer is the one thing that makes him or her different from most people – that a writer sits or stands at a desk or table or lies in bed for hours at a time, tapping at a keyboard or scratching on pieces of paper. Or rather, that the most interesting thing about a writer is the product of their tapping and scratching: their books. As Jonathan Coe puts it in his re-creation of the novelist B S Johnson's life, *Like a Fiery Elephant*, "If they did not do it, none of the other, superficial, gossipy stuff that fills up books like this would matter in the slightest."

That activity – those hours when writers do what they do best – may still be the route by which their work, and name, are published, but it is no longer the route by which they are *known*. To be known as a writer, with some (ironically well-known) persistent exceptions (Salinger, Pynchon, Süskind) is to be the product of a parallel industry of epiphenomena, in which it is the writer's "personality" that is recorded on private and public sofas in hotel rooms and radio studios, over notebooks and Minidisc recorders, through the medium of questions chosen by an interviewer and answers organised by him or her into a story of his or her choosing. Milan Kundera in *The Art of the Novel* has collated this submission of the work to the personality into an interesting comparison between eastern and western Europe:

Official propaganda in the Communist countries began to pummel elitism and elitists at that same time [1967]. It used the terms to designate not captains of industry or famous athletes or politicians but only the cultural elite: philosophers, writers, professors, historians, figures in film and the theatre.

An amazing synchronism. It seems that in the whole of Europe the cultural elite is yielding to other elites. Over there, to the elite of the police apparatus. Here, to the elite of the mass media apparatus. No one will ever accuse these new elites of elitism.[2]

What does this have to do with the practice of modern biography? One answer can, I think, be found in the late sixteenth and early seventeenth centuries, when, cultural historians tend to agree, something of a mutation in human nature took place. Throughout the falsity, manoeuvring and power play of the sixteenth century, dissimulation had ruled Europe to an extraordinary degree. The ensuing reaction, and the rebirth of sincerity, had something to do with the rise of the Protestant Church and, in England at least, the conviction that the only requirement for speaking out was the belief that one had the Word to say. This grasping and championing of personal sincerity, and the modern-sounding Calvinist doctrine of the human being's "inner space", amounted to the emergence of what we now think of as the individual. The change went hand in hand, both as cause and effect, with the dissolution of feudalism and the onset of urbanisation. Its literary consequence was a sudden, widespread flowering of autobiography. The new genre's popularity was particularly remarkable, Paul Delany writes in his study *British Autobiography in the Seventeenth Century*, in the context of new geographical and social mobility: more than half of the secular autobiographers he found had travelled to London, and one Lancashire lad nicely summarised the connection between autobiography and mobility. "We would often tell what a fine thing it was to travel."[3]

Three hundred years later the twentieth-century concept of "personality" looks to have done something similar for biography. As a citizen I can see that the polymorphous ubiquity of the term, used today to account for everything from a socio-psychological notation to a subset of celebrity, might be due to a subconscious need to give us, as humans, an escape route from the horizons of conformity implied by mass culture and the political control that goes with it. If we have personalities, we cannot be drudges and minions.

Yet in my more specialised role as a reader, it seems to me that the prevalence of "personality" has been something of a negative inspiration in the context of biography, sowing the ground for the luxuriant growth of a curious literary genre of simultaneous elevation and contempt, of admiration followed, via revelations of fallibility, by a thorough dismantling. We have been through a long stage of being less familiar with Larkin's poetry than with his attachment to pornography, less familiar with Eliot's poetry than with his anti-Semitism, less familiar with Graham Greene's novels than with his affairs with the tricky Catherine Walston and others. A cultural historian might seriously have said in 1967 that "we know how little we know about human beings, and how little of the evidence we have would satisfy a psychologist interested in . . . character and motives".[4] The boom in literary biography-writing that began with Richard

Ellmann's testamentary *Oscar Wilde* twenty years later cheerfully asserts the opposite.

Why should this crisis of over-confidence make me uneasy? One reason is that what one could call biography's invitation – what it offers in its glimpses of the otherness of others – seems at best limited. Fiction, the novel, describes a world of ambiguity and complexity. Its spirit whispers to the reader, in Kundera's words, that "Things are not as simple as you think"; its wisdom is the wisdom of uncertainty. Its interest is, as Greene noted, quoting Browning, "on the dangerous edge of things. The honest thief, the tender murderer, The superstitious atheist."

Biography on the other hand, with its dedicated clue-gathering, seeks explanation, certainty, the categorical. An example (which I quote because it shocks me): the number of accounts of novelists' lives that are preoccupied with identifying the real-life models for the writer's created characters. At best this betrays an ignorance of the novelist's craft: in asserting who, in Graham Greene's "real life", was Querry the architect ("Querry is Greene"), Bendrix the writer ("basically Greene"), Morin the recluse ("Morin is Greene"), Greene's biographer is denying his characters life, denying their author authorship. It is, if you like, a kind of applied postmodernism. Isn't the truth the contrary, that characters live because their creator *lives their life for them*, occasionally at some cost to his or her own? But in its dedication to scene-of-crime forensic means, biography wrestles blindfolded with the subjective internal life.

Where there is "personality" there is always, not very far away, a belief in the harmonious entity that Hegel categorised as "the honest soul". (Such belief refuses Hegel's opposing concept of the disintegrated consciousness, that we must all become if we are to be truly free.) But even if we *are* honest souls, we remain restless beings. Why? Possibly because subconsciously we know that we are failures, that the honest soul is a mask, a construct, not the real thing. Much current biography seems to be an expression of our desire to see that no one else, not even the writer, that once admired figure of the cultural elite, has succeeded in being that "honest soul" either. Read the biography, and the thought strikes, consciously or not, that there is now no need to read the writer. Kundera again:

The novelist destroys the house of his life and uses its stones to build the house of his novel. A novelist's biographers thus undo what a novelist has done, and redo what he undid. All their labour cannot illuminate either the value or the meaning of a novel, can scarcely even identify a few of the bricks. The moment Kafka attracts more attention than Joseph K, Kafka's posthumous death begins.[5]

How can biography's invitation be improved? There is no reason, outside Milan Kundera's partisan dislike, why it should not exist. There is no reason why it should not be an inquiry; but perhaps an inquiry like the novel: an attempt not to judge or dismantle, but to re-create, understand, breathe life into. A literary form in search of itself. In one sense or more, it can perhaps best be the pursuit of fiction by other means. A novel may be a biography that could take place. Biography may be a novel that took place in a fully physical world, a novel in which the biographer, also from that world, imagines themselves in the living persona of their subject.

What raises these matters more sharply in Norman Lewis's case is that, as writer and traveller, his life and work are inseparable. The body of the writer, his live self, is the blade of the knife, putting himself in the middle of the experience he relates. The writer does not have to be so self-abnegating, so detached, so purely observational as his readers imagine. Norman is an ideal subject to illustrate how false, in biography, is the distinction between life and work. Both need to be described and imagined.

As for biography – it needs, I think, to resist itself. To resist its assumptions. The biographing of a writer like Norman Lewis should not have the purpose of cross-questioning his motives or his fidelity to truth or his privacy, as a route to proclaiming "here is the real Norman Lewis". This is surely secondary. The real Norman Lewis is the one who stood apart from the other children on the Forty Hill Freehold, who went into business, travelled, wrote and spent summers in Spain, decided he was a novelist, then that he was not, then that he was again, organised his *Sunday Times* journalism to coincide with the coldest part of the English winter, was terrified of frogs, fond of poaching and red wine, cooking and spear fishing and fast cars, detested cats and Christmas and organised religion: the Norman he himself, and only he, knew. The primary offering here is, instead, one view – mine – of a writer with an inimitable voice who, resisting the epiphenomena of the writer's world, achieved an unusually high measure of freedom. It occurs to me that possibly, just possibly, that is the key to the relationship between this biographer and his subject: that this is a biography by someone who dislikes biography about someone who disliked exposure, a kind of double reluctance.

This reminds me of the occasion of the consecration of our friendship. It was a cold Tuesday in November 1983. In El Vino's on Fleet Street Norman was his usual engaging self, a reservoir of stories, a highly enjoyable ancient mariner (to my diary he seemed like "a reformed civil servant who has decided to make up for his loss of living"), and at the same time he was a reticent companion where more reciprocal conversation was concerned. As a combination this made for a slight tension, in which every remark, observation or gesture seemed to be extended on an invisible spring, ready to be jerked back if his listener was not interested.

As we ate the sandwiches and drank the good-sized glasses of El Vino's red bordeaux I realised he had extended his careful friendship to me when, after a moment's silence, he asked me what "my situation" was. It felt like a question of considerable magnitude, coming from him. Afterwards, with neither of us either drunk or sober, as we separated outside the Tube he clasped my forearm tight, in what struck me as a Sicilian way, to say goodbye. At that moment I understood, with a concurrent feeling of being immensely flattered, that some kind of bond existed between us. This was all, I emphasise, Norman's generosity. It was certainly not my doing. I had no idea how to make friends with writers of stature in their seventies.

In conclusion: to go back to my first confession. I didn't want to write Norman's life. I declined the suggestion twice while he was alive. Why did I eventually agree? To stop someone else from doing it. This may seem a trivial reason. But given my intense dislike of some of the ways in which biography is written maybe it will be understood if I say that the prospect of receiving, as a book reviewer, a biography of Norman written by another writer was intolerable. This has a good deal to do with having been Norman's friend for more than fifteen years.

Having agreed in principle to write the book, and secured his family's generous agreement, I found myself (of course) rapidly caught in the snare. I was the reluctant biographer, compelled to be engaged. The form in search of itself became a personal search for a form. I wanted the trajectory of the book to begin with Norman's work – why did he write? – and to finish with it. There is no other reason for me to chronicle his extraordinarily eventful life. So when readers finish reading this book, as I hope they will having started it, I also hope they will want to go immediately (back) to his books. At which point, instead of being the excuse for not reading a writer's work, the biography can disappear, its work done. Writing is not so much about what you make as what you make happen.

In the decision to write Norman's biography I also decided that I was fortunate in some ways. This imposed, as good fortune should, responsibilities. Norman Lewis is not just a remarkable and important subject. Because I knew him, talked to him, listened to him, thought about many things as a result of knowing him, he existed for me not as a phantom to be tracked through papers and writings, but as a reality. I not only know my own way, its progress and frustrations, rather better for knowing his. I also remember the paths of thought and pleasure he has taken me down. All this of course is the coincidence and randomness of friendship; which raises the next question. How to relate the coincidence and randomness of his life? Because Norman's path was very far from preordained. He grew up at the distant edge of north London's apparently endless suburbs, the lower-middle-class son of a pharmacist. He won a scholarship to the local grammar school, and left when he was seventeen. He did not go to university. Few would have predicted in the caste-bound 1920s that he would establish himself as a significant writer from such an entry level. Yet as a stylist (apart from any other thing) he succeeded not just at the highest level but as a revolutionary – a class hero, entirely self-taught. "Human behaviour is a series of lunges, of which, it is sometimes sensed, the direction is inevitable," as Patrick White says of *Voss*. That was half Norman's case, half not. Which brings us back to the question of perspective.

I remember reading one of Norman's first notebooks, a tiny, red, water-stained book, covering his arrival at Salerno as part of the invasion force of the Italian mainland in September 1943. In it is an episode in which an Australian officer suggests to a soldier that he murder an Italian civilian. In the version of the episode recounted in Norman's memoir, *Naples '44*, where he describes it as the "most revolting episode I have seen since joining the forces", the officer is unnamed. In his notebook the officer is named. The exchange goes: "Horsefall to Hampshire pvt [private]. 'Would you like to shoot this man?' 'I don't mind if I do sir' (spitting on his hands)." It could be argued that those two lines are, in Norman's writing them down, a retelling of something already gone. But when I handle these small, ancient notebooks, their pages falling out (good paper) and their ink spreading and lightening, it isn't just the minuscule nearly illegible notes that fascinate. I think also of the days before they were written: when the notebooks were empty, the days unlived, when the world was waiting to happen on clear pages that we know now (and only know) as history: concluded, settled.

Should we be interested in what "actually" happened? Those researches (Salerno, landings, casualties, General Clark's incompetence) are essential at the time-line level. At the same time they obscure the level at which life is lived. Worse even than that: by painting life as a tunnel of chronology, they are useless in what the historian Greg Dening calls the tease of describing *process* – how we tell, to ourselves, to others, the stories that part the tunnel's darkness. Life is not lived from the future to the past (despite our liking for stories to which we, as narrators, already know the ending). So I feel compelled not just to give a subjective, personal perspective of Norman and of his writing, but also to attempt, in Dening's words, to return to the past the qualities of the present that it once possessed.

And maybe these two concerns – the vitalness of subjectivity and the vitalness of attempting to experience the past as we experience the present, not as if it was over and done with but with its possibilities intact – rough out an idea of what the poetics of biography might be. Only an idea, because, whatever it is, biography is (as novels are) a mongrel form: history, fiction, anthropology, sociology, philosophy, prosody, criticism etc. etc. And because to focus on a life is also to focus on what it means to be alive. Although my first and spontaneous reason for writing Norman's biography was to stop anyone else from doing the same (at least for a while), that form and that focus deserve their own poetics.

INTRODUCTION

TURN left at the top of Goat Lane and within twenty seconds you find yourself breathing in the proximity of London. Forty Hill, unrolling in front of you, seems to set itself straight at the capital's great, incoherent skyline, and then, as it runs out of downhill momentum and passes the last of the old houses (a handsome early Georgian Hermitage, with white-hooded windows), to buckle and lose its nerve, forking right and left at the village green in an attempt to ward off the encounter. It is too late. Re-entry into the world of urbanity, its landmarks and emblems, is abrupt and complete as you reach the filled-in village pond, the boarded-up Goat Tavern, the local-authority flats of beige 1960s brick, the long road of 1930s houses that leads to a later pair of low-rise blocks going by the inspirational, though possibly misunderstood, names of Purcell and Bliss House, in whose shadow two Enfield Council workers in reflective waistcoats are serenely scrubbing the sprayed tags off the brickwork of the bridge over the New River.

A boy who grew up here during and after the First World War would recognise none of the modern parts of this description, but the area's future was already being shaded in. Between 1913 and 1935, the borough maps show, the first suburban building boom to provide small family homes for the city's workers began to obliterate the tracts of nurseries and orchards, replacing them with the leafless regularity of massed bay-windowed semis. "Do you know the road I live in – Ellesmere Road, West Bletchley?" George Bowling asks in George Orwell's *Coming Up for Air* (1939). "Even if you don't, you know fifty others exactly like it." The boy himself would have lived in one of the forerunners of those semis, on a piece of early development land known locally as the Freehold. Of the Freehold a girl named Gwen Nicholls who grew up here at the same time says, "The roads were not made up, there was no lighting, and people who could find a little spot of land built a few houses. And so we had all these open spaces between ... we were always out in the Freehold, playing feverishly."

But now go back to Goat Lane and turn right instead of left, onto the hill, away from the city, upwards to a different world, a world whose appearance succeeding waves of the twentieth century have barely altered. Rising gently, tree-shaded on the left side and lined on the right by the walls and locked gates, softened by hedges and ivy, of individual Georgian houses, Forty Hill dismisses the city: a frieze of propertied wealth that once bespoke the Tory party at home, its half-and-half town-and-country houses owned by those who, having land interests to the north and business interests to the south, preferred in their domestic life to avoid the mundane details of both.

Forty Hill (I'm talking about the hill itself rather than the district to which it gives its name) was a kind of select early suburb, an exemplar of the utopian pleasantness of life detached from the odorous chaos of city and country. Its apotheosis comes at the brow of the hill in the grandiloquent but oddly heavy shape of Forty Hall, built by Inigo Jones for Sir Nicholas Raynton, sometime Lord Mayor of London, in the grounds of what was once Queen Elizabeth's palace of Elsynge. Past the gates of Forty Hall the road drops away again, leaving the houses behind and narrowing between the dark trees to turn past the ugly Victorian front of Jesus Church and Forty Hill primary school and cross another bridge, rather older than the one crossing the New River. This is Maidens Bridge. The story of Walter Raleigh spreading his "new plush coat" on the wet ground so that Queen Elizabeth could walk over it has little basis in fact, but to it belongs the plausible detail that it happened at Maidens Bridge. (Elizabeth visited Elsynge frequently before it fell into neglect and was left to her spymaster Sir Robert Cecil.) A privately published memoir of Forty Hill describes Maidens Bridge in the 1920s having "three waterfalls and the brook ran round to form what was known as Bluebell Island. In the spring it was a beautiful sight with masses of bluebells and the waterfalls tumbling down. ... It was on Bluebell Island that the boys would go to swim in the brook." The memoir's author does not mention one boy who had a bicycle and also played there in the early 1920s, but eighty years later Gwen Merrington, the former Gwen Nicholls, remembers him well. "He rode over Maidens Bridge on the parapet. The parapet was about eighteen inches or two foot wide, and flat ... [it was] a very brave thing to do, because it would be a fall of fifteen to sixteen feet into the river."

These were the two halves of Forty Hill and still are: downhill to the city and the democratic sweep of north London suburbia, uphill to the grounds of Forty Hall and Maidens Bridge and beyond, to green places with more than enough wilderness for an adventurous boy, but all owned by someone else. The boy who balanced his way along the capstones of Maidens Bridge was also suspended between the opposing ways at the end of Goat Lane, where the cut-through of tied cottages inhabited by Forty Hall workers opened out onto the hill: he could turn left to domesticity, repetition, the attractions of urbanity, or right to undiscovered places and (class-compromised) pastorality.

Anyone familiar with the books he wrote will know which way he preferred; but the choice is not quite as simple as that. To explore is to find and to lose: yourself, boredom, tormentors at home. All of these were elements of his desire to escape. And growing up, always a matter of going one way rather than another, is also, for some, a question of going one way so far that they are obliged to look for the edge. Where does that impulse come from? It's an impossible question to answer, there being no control experiment, no double-blind test available for a life, yet I think one can say, at least, that this boy's life began in edges and oppositions: the edge of the capital, the edge of a wilderness; he was the explorer who returned nightly to the protection of his suburban home, the fugitive adored by his mother, the only son, privileged and smothered in the wake of family tragedy (he was the only survivor of four sons). That protective embrace is enough to make a boy want to wriggle out and run away, and he did. And it was here at the start of the incline of Forty Hill, a couple of hundred metres from his front door, that he worked out what a getaway was. Not swimming idyllically in the brook, but riding the length of the parapet, disdaining the stony riverbed.

PART ONE

BECOMING

A Youth in Eight Tendencies

Exclusion, madness, mistrust, boredom,
escape, dandyism, hedonism, speed

"Par quels moyens cherchez-vous à plaire?" ("By what means do you aim to please?")

Joseph Conrad: "By making myself scarce."

Question 2 of a questionnaire in "Album de Confidences", 1888, printed in Gérard Jean-Aubry, *Vie de Conrad*

1

ARABIA

"O my house, my dear little house,
hider of my little failings!"
Arabian saying

IN spring 1937 Norman Lewis spent two months in southern Arabia. He was twenty-eight years old and had travelled to Aden at the suggestion of the Foreign Office. Until March 1937 Aden had been an anomalous pocket of British India on the Arabian peninsula, but on 1 April the settlement became a full colony controlled directly from London. The change was dictated by the urgent refashioning of British strategy. The Foreign Office was actively looking for ways to protect Britain's interests in Arabia, particularly the Yemen, after Italy's conquest of Abyssinia (Ethiopia) in 1936 and was highly nervous of where Italy's gaze would fall next. The context of this nervousness was the widely held British belief that most of Arabia, including its emerging oil wealth, was its personal fief. The writer and traveller Freya Stark beautifully demonstrates British anxiety in a slightly neurotic but prophetic (in the sense that it lays out British worries for the next three-quarters of a century) letter she wrote from Baghdad that spring to her friend Lord Halifax: "I can't tell you how urgent I think the Arabian problem has become, now with the discovery of oil: as if the Bank of England were dumped unguarded in the middle of Chicago! I hope we may provide a guard . . . and then we can talk afterwards about dividing raw materials!"[1]

Norman's Arabian journey was a spying mission. He had been selected informally for his photographic ability and tasked with documenting the Yemen and the comings and goings of its Italian suitors at first hand. In the event he spent six weeks at Aden, unable to find a way into the country, though his travelling companion, a Hungarian adventurer named Farago, did get across the border for a brief reconnaissance (without telling Norman or his British minders). Norman's greatest success on the journey was a trip he eventually made by dhow from Aden along the Indian Ocean and up the Red Sea along the coast of the Yemen. Back in England he turned the photographs he had taken into an album with his own commentary, published the following year under the pedestrian (there's no other word) title *Sand and Sea in Arabia*. Later he dismissed this book as a "deadly secret". But his unexpected Arabian adventure – until then he had been a businessman dealing in an implausible range of goods, from lost umbrellas to photographic supplies – lodged deep in his memory. "The fact of the matter was," he said nearly sixty years later, "having got there I remember thinking that what I would really like to do would be to get out there and stay there, just drop all my responsibilities."[2]

Yet this was not the first time Arabia had inspired him. At the age of fourteen or fifteen Norman had come across the idea of Arabia somewhere – in his reading perhaps, at a time when books can powerfully vaccinate their readers against the tedium of reality – and been so struck by it that he had imported it into the scenery of suburban Enfield. His first step was to dress like an Arab. At weekends and during the holidays he "often had a knife in his belt . . . a long camel-haired coat, a tied scarf, a knife", one of the other Forty Hill children remembers.[3] "The girls, the children in the village, rather struggled for notoriety to know Lewis. He became that kind of figurehead." He also claimed to be of Arab origin through his mother (who was from Carmarthen). This self-identification was not a passing enthusiasm. A girl who used to see him on the bus from Forty Hill to Enfield Chase station in the morning describes him in his early twenties as "a sight to behold. He was very striking [with a] sallow complexion, Levantine . . . dark hair, very dark eyes, narrow cheekbones and aquiline nose. He wore a long belted camel overcoat to his ankles."[4]

The Arab figure evolved into a more diffuse Latin, Spanish, Mediterranean identity but its association with his childhood self stayed with him. On the first page of his autobiography *Jackdaw Cake*, describing his perplexity at being sent to stay with three severely eccentric aunts in Wales, he likens his acceptance of this twist in his life to that of "an Arab child stuffed with the resignation of his religion". And there is, surprisingly, a further perspective: he may actually have been right. Despite the deep vein of self-reinvention in this first impulse to dissociate himself from his Forty Hill and Enfield surroundings, his "Arab roots" and his Welshness may have been more connected than they seem. Welsh has similarities with the Celtiberian language (as does Irish), and Celtiberian culture, about whose origins archaeologists remain at the several-theories stage, is at least connected, as Gerald Brenan points out, to the microlith-making of the Saharan Capsians and the round-bellied pots of the Libyan or Tunisian early Mediterraneans.[5]

Real or mock, whatever the genetic soup in which the fourteen-year-old Norman cooked and served himself, his future attraction to the shores of southern Europe and north Africa and the islands of the Mediterranean, to the Spanish islands of the Caribbean and the totality of Latin America, and his attraction to Spanish, Italian and Arabic languages, make him without doubt an honorary Mediterranean or Levantine, even if "Arabia" in the context of early 1920s Enfield was only a teenage boy's emblem of romance, the farthest place he could think of. His first edge.

Norman's feelings of emotional displacement were also not exclusively his. In an unpublished essay, "Blessing the squire and his relations", which is really about his father, he describes Richard Lewis too as "a stranger in a foreign land".

Everything about England and the English mystified him, and he was handicapped in his contacts by a poor English vocabulary. ... Father found his surroundings alien and uncomfortable. [His birthplace of] Carmarthen was set among the green hills, littered with ruined castles and abandoned chapels. It was a place of half-forgotten martyrdoms where Christian zealots from overseas had wrestled with sophisticated pagans, where a great Celtic epic – the Black Book of Carmarthen – had been composed. Forty Hill, where he lived in exile, had no past to speak of, and no great vestiges of power or faith. From my father's bedroom window he saw a flat landscape without surprises, drawn to a dry, powdery horizon, on which the dome of St Paul's Cathedral sat like a grey bubble, fourteen miles away.[6]

The details of Richard Lewis's exile differ in the telling. In *Jackdaw Cake* Norman describes his father as being driven to England by irreconcilable clashes with his grandfather, in the unpublished essay by economic circumstances attendant on Carmarthen's decline as a small port on the Tywi. In a published piece with a similar title, "God bless the squire", his father is referred to more positively as starting his working life "promisingly enough in London as an analytical chemist".[7] But in all his son's accounts Richard Lewis is the same model of a lonely estranged Welshman, his situation and character one-part English suburban absurdity to three-parts Welsh tragicomedy. Instead of becoming, as his son variously suggests he wanted to, an artist, a preacher, a lawyer or a doctor, Richard Lewis trained as a pharmacist, stepping up from managing a north London branch of the Timothy White chemist's chain to opening his own chemist's shop in Southbury Road in the centre of the prospering, still semi-rural Enfield Town.

His first Enfield address was 3 Hampton Villas in Sydney Road, now part of the town's choked one-way system, its villas replaced by a bombsite car park on one side and a lowering shopping mall on the other. By the time of Norman's birth in 1908 the Lewises, Richard and Louisa and their sons David, fifteen, and Montague, nine, had removed themselves from the expanding town centre and been living in the village calm of Forty Hill, a couple of miles to the north, for five years.

Richard Lewis was a diminutive man, nothing like his son's future height, and easily excited. His limited English vocabulary, the result, according to Norman, of a psychological block instigated by a mild thrashing for being caught speaking Welsh at Pentrepoeth primary school in Carmarthen, was the launch pad for a ritual of incomprehension. "He tried to cover up the frequent gaps where the words were missing by speaking very rapidly and filling in with a quick meaningless gabble, and often a word or two of dog-Latin from his pharmaceutical studies. Usually an intelligent listener got the gist of what he was talking about, but breakdowns in communication were frequent."[8]

Norman's father embarrassed him. The other Forty Hill children found Richard Lewis a target for laughter. Gwen Nicholls, born the year after Norman and one of the few Forty Hill children he was close to, remembers that on 5 November

we would go round to see Norman's firework display. Whereas we had ours in the street and Norman would come, Norman had to have a special one in his garden, and his father used to entertain us far more than the fireworks.

He would start talking and he'd get so excited that he'd go off and do a foreign sort of language which I imagine must have been [Welsh]. And Norman used to get so embarrassed . . . he was half in our world and then had this incredibly contrasting world . . . we were the only family who would respond to him. All the other children rejected him.[9]

Later, as the years and the Lewis parents' unhappinesses intensified Richard Lewis's discomfort, he started drinking, and Norman's embarrassment gave way to practical action, steering the Beckettian figure of his father home and keeping him as far as he could from harm and ridicule.

His mother Louisa was the clown's foil. In the way of spouses, she matched her husband's excitability with a balancing earnestness, his capering with an obsidian coolness. She was tall and is remembered as oppressively mysterious, possibly the least at home of all the family in the makeshift domesticity of Forty Hill. "While growing up," Gwen remembers, "there were parties on [Norman's] birthday with a selected choice of local children – very basic scene and fare – Mrs Lewis was a poor cook, a sad heavy-laden person. I remember Lewis whispering to me, 'I've spat in the custard', and having to spare Mrs Lewis and the children by my silence, and leaving an uneaten trifle."[10]

Writing about Richard and Louisa Lewis, whom I didn't know, I feel divided between the rational task of listing their oddities and an irrational concern for narrative adequacy. How can their lives, living through what they lived through, be fairly told, giving reasonable latitude to Norman's often very funny reactions to them *and* to the possible reasons behind their many failings? Why ought we to worry in any case? Perhaps we should start with the facts, which are simple. When Norman was born, on 28 June 1908, he had two brothers, David and Monty. Less than fifteen months later, he had one. Just over six years after that, before he reached the age of eight, he was alone. David Rae Douglas Lewis died of tubercular peritonitis and exhaustion, aged sixteen, in the Lewises' home at Carterhatch Lane in September 1909. Less than seven years later, in January 1916 Montague Richard Warren Lewis also died, aged seventeen, at home of chronic nephritis. Monty, who had talent as a musician, was in poor health, and the winter of 1915–16 was a notably wet one. "I remember seeing him," Gwen Nicholls says – she would have been five – "I remember my mother and aunt [saying] with awe in their voices, 'There goes poor Monty.'"

So from before his eighth birthday Norman was an only child. As if two deaths were not enough, there had also been a third brother who, "dropped as an infant by a girl who was looking after him, was carried off by meningitis".[11] One reason, then, that we might worry about how adequately the Lewis parents' story can be told is that, even allowing for the unforgiving child mortality rates of a century ago, the grief of parents is irremediable. Richard and Louisa may have been eccentric, and increasingly so. They must also be allowed not just their sorrow, but some long-term derangement at the death of two teenage sons – the younger of whom Norman too was very attached to, and stayed so in memory. (In hospital at Saffron Walden ninety years later, as his lucidity left him, it was Monty he called out for.)

From 1916, the year of Monty's death, oddities small and great cropped up in Norman's parents' behaviour: the smallest, that after his brother died Norman was known alternately as "Normie" and "Monty" by his mother; the greatest that they put up a spiritualist chapel in their back garden to be able to contact the astral bodies of their dead sons. (Its successor, the unpoetic redbrick Beacon of Light spiritualist church on the corner of Carterhatch Lane and Layard Road – motto "Life After Death Proved" – still welcomes congregations for clairvoyance and spiritual healing on Mondays and Thursdays.) Despite the alleged contemporary appeal of spiritualism – a combination of mumbo-jumbo and coping mechanism in the face of the carnage of the First World War – it did not enjoy much popularity among the working class who made up most of Forty Hill's population. There were plenty in Forty Hill whose sympathy for Mrs Lewis's grief did not extend to her repeated recruitment drives for her seances, and who failed to find the Lewises' new-found serenity as rich a well of comedy as Norman did in his later ruthlessly satirical portrait of home life at Carterhatch Lane in *Jackdaw Cake*.

The effect on Norman of losing Monty was deep. He had loved his serious, dutiful older brother. The effect on him of his parents' loss would have been, one imagines, added oppression at the concentration on him of all their affection and protectiveness. They were, in addition, middle-aged: Louisa was forty-three when Norman was born, Richard forty-one, so in 1916 they would have been fifty and forty-eight. Norman was their last hope. The silent fear that their youngest son too would fail to outlive them must have sensitised all three. In Norman's case it honed his need to flee their dependency, however benevolent.

In *Jackdaw Cake* Norman remembers his pleasure as a small boy in his father's company.

I saw as much as I could of my father at weekends, or on Wednesday afternoons when he was free from business, and I hurried home from school. He was an excellent companion for a child, because his personality was childlike, and he was strikingly immature in his enthusiasms.[12]

It was a short-lived idyll. When grief and spiritualism took hold of mother and father and adolescent self-consciousness took hold of the son, embarrassment and distance replaced it.

Views are important. The flat landscape all the way to St Paul's seen from his father's bedroom contrasted with the rise of cow-grazed meadowland from the back bedrooms of their house in Carterhatch Lane (now a car-packed access route to the Great Cambridge Road), and Norman's description of "Clifton", later 343, Carterhatch Lane as a "quiet, rather dismal little house tucked away behind the orchards" cannot be entirely trusted. One of a pair of semi-detached houses standing in large, lush gardens, it was a cut above the terraced houses in neighbouring Bridgenhall and Layard Roads. But Norman's feelings about almost everything in Forty Hill were conditioned by his deep vulnerability to boredom there. When he says that the area "had no past to speak of, and no great vestiges of power or faith", he is wrong: it had kings and queens, spymasters and grandees, estates owned by invisible knights and other *capi* of church and state, including Field Marshal French, leader of the British Expeditionary Force in the First World War, and Sir Dudley Orr-Lewis, maker of the Lewis gun. But for Norman then and later it was the wrong kind of past, scattered with the palaces of the monarchy and the *latifundias* of the nobility, and the wrong vestiges of power. There were no struggles, no martyrdoms, no Black Books, no rebellion against the tyranny of facts; only feudal servitude.

Gwen Nicholls (now Merrington) sees his situation differently. "He lived just round the corner in a slightly nicer house, but facing a beautiful cherry orchard which stretched for two miles, so you could either walk the cherry orchard way to Enfield or cut along Baker Street. It was rutted, it was puddly, you know, it was natural. He was most scathing about it."

The area of houses where Norman and the Nicholls children lived, known as the Freehold, was part of an estate that had been sold in the 1860s for building, but development was sluggish. To Gwen the semi-wilderness of gravel pits and rutted roads was a child's paradise for play. "It was just sort of grown up out of the earth. . . . It was not lighted. The roads were not surfaced. . . . We could see right across to Epping Forest from behind." Norman, however, lived in the Freehold "much to his disgust. He didn't want to be attached to anything, I suppose."[13]

Forty Hill, in short, was boring because he found it boring. But there was another factor to his boredom and disgust. The Lewises' marginal economic superiority to other Freehold families, and Richard and Louisa's failings that began as marginal and grew not to be, made the family stand out. Forty Hill had no middle class; Norman, nowhere near upper-class and only just outside working-class, had no place. In the subtle tribalism of the English class system, and its even subtler variant, the English class system as understood by children, he was immediately marked.

"He was different from our point of view because he was in a better position than we were," Gwen says. "We were definitely poor, working-class kids, and to be a chemist's son was one stratum, two, three strata above."[14] Norman stayed on the edge of whatever game or group activity was going on, never joining in. Later he had a bicycle, which few working-class children had, and a collie and an air rifle, gifts from his parents: the possession of such obvious status signs increased his social difference. There was also his Welshness. "In the case of my own family," he wrote, "class divisions remained an enigma never fully understood. . . . The social complexities of Forty Hill were wholly foreign to rural Wales."[15] And there was, increasingly, the rather public fact of his father's, and later mother's, idiosyncrasies of behaviour.

Norman – John Frederick Norman on his birth certificate – was enrolled at Forty Hill Church School on 19 May 1913, a month before his fifth birthday. His immediate destiny as a junior denizen of Forty Hill, about to acquire experiences he would later use both as urgent reasons to escape and rich material to dismantle, comically, the place where he was forced to spend most of his childhood, was confirmed. The first few weeks of school passed by, I would think, in a blur of not entirely unpleasant novelty. On 11 June the School Sports were held in Town Park, and there was a holiday for all the schools in the parish. A week later, on the 18th, Enfield Carnival resulted in another half-day holiday, and ten days later it was Norman's fifth birthday. On 4 July the Forty Hill School children bought a "cross of flowers" to be placed on the coffin of Elizabeth Hardwick, an ex-pupil who had just left school at fourteen and had died of unknown causes on 30 June. On 16 July the annual Primrose League Fête was held in Forty Hall Park, and on the 21st the school closed again, this time for the Forty Hill Church Choir annual excursion to Eastbourne. On 1 August the summer holidays started.

School and church were indissolubly linked. This was a fact Norman later reserved particular sarcasm for. You can see his point. Levels of Christian oppressiveness were high in English suburban society, and the parsimonious silhouette of the neo-Gothic Jesus Church with its mean grey towers and crosses at both ends peering down at the school across a paddock must have seemed authoritarian, if not baleful, to the children. Frederick Eastaugh, Forty Hill School's headmaster, was the church clerk, and the vicar of Jesus Church, Reverend E W Kempe, was school manager. Organised religion, to the adult Norman, was generally "diabolical", "a hugely successful political thing, but successful for those who take the spoils of the world ... the school I went to was a Church of England school and we used to start with the creed in the morning at assembly, 'To do our duty in that sphere of life unto which it has pleased God to call us', over and over and over."[16] Knowing your station in life and sticking to it, a theme drummed into the children early on, was another focus for Norman's scorn. Yet when the children went to church on Ash Wednesday and Ascension Day, half-holidays followed; there were also half-holidays for the "Sunday School annual Treat", the "Coronation Treat", when all the children would salute the Union Jack before marching to Myddelton House, and for several other occasions, from Empire Day to the "Enfield Tradesmen's Cycling Club School Singing Competition". There was a full holiday for the king's birthday.

And Frederick Eastaugh, for all his trailing clouds of Victorian starch – he had become head teacher in 1878 and did not retire until 1920 – may have noted with disapproval the slumps in attendance that coincided with the arrival of Sangers Circus in Enfield or the annual fêtes in Cherry Orchard Lane and Baker Street, but he never made serious attempts to counter them. We know about his disapproval from his entries in the Forty Hill School Log Book that he kept as headmaster until his retirement.[17] The pages of the log cover fifty-six years in all, including the years before and after Eastaugh's headship, and Eastaugh himself comes out as the most informative of its three keepers, more human – and sometimes unintentionally revealing – than his predecessor or successor. Despite Norman's mockery, he is unlikely to have been worse than most members of the black-winged brotherhood of the late Victorian teaching profession.

And despite condemning Eastaugh's apparent snobbery (when Eastaugh's nephew was admitted to the school Mrs Eastaugh instructed the children to address him not as "Thomas" but "Master Thomas") and his liking for caning the girls, Norman enjoyed learning. "I learnt very easily indeed, and I had an excellent memory so that pretty well if I read a poem I could almost speak it back."[18] It was not the arbitrary subjugation of school authority that would threaten his happiness and stability at school, as it later turned out, but his own intelligence and facility.

Before that happened, the stability of most of Europe was to be threatened. As war against Germany was declared in the summer holidays of 1914, the Forty Hill School log records only that on 9 October Mr Eastaugh "received from the E[nfield] E[ducation] C[ommittee] another pamphlet for distribution among the teachers on 'Why we had to go to War'". A few days later, the children sang "naval songs" on the anniversary of Nelson's death and the older ones wrote an epitome of his life; but Gwen Merrington remembers that generally "We young children were by no means borne down by [the war] . . . it was life slowly unfolding, so while Europe inflicted terrible suffering on its adult population, we were adjusting to the new ideas it brought to our games – mock battles for the boys, nursing their wounded for the girls." Gwen's brother Bill, two years older than Norman, who later became his friend and political mentor, heard the declaration of war on a hot summer's day on his way home from Enfield Town Baths. In his description of the war's early impact on the people of Forty Hill, in the noise of clinking spurs and young men singing, the sounds of doomed anachronism and misjudgment are clearly to be heard.

I was with Len Parker, a neighbour of twelve or thirteen years of age. I was eight years old. His first reaction was an excited "I bet we'll win, I bet we'll win". I remember exactly where we were, nearing Ridler Road, not far from the spot where I'd seen Buffalo Bill about three years previously.

There was great excitement and a feeling of release and escape, I believe. People felt that they could get off from the deadly grind, the treadmill of ordinary living, and raise their sights to new horizons.

... I can remember hundreds of cavalry-men and their horses bivouacking in Fish's Field near our school shortly after the outbreak of war. And Aunt Marge having a taciturn soldier billeted on her at her home. Also regiments of soldiers marching and training. Spurs were much in evidence, every other soldier seemed to wear jingling spurs and riding breeches. Some men flocked to join up in the early days and patriotic songs were sung. Ebullient cheerfulness was the order of the day.[19]

School life continued its metronomic pace. The rhythm of lessons, illnesses – there was whooping cough, measles and diphtheria in 1915 – church attendance and sports days went on. A girl named Nora Cracknell, who had won a prize for regular attendance and good conduct at Christmas, died at the beginning of June. In September the Zeppelin raids that had started in east Anglia at the beginning of the year affected school attendance, and Frederick Eastaugh was warned to economise on fuel and gas. The week before Christmas he was absent from school in London, finding out what had happened to his wounded son, who had emigrated to Australia and enlisted in the Australian army. He had also taken on a new member of staff named Lewis – also from Carmarthen, and probably a cousin of Norman's – and after the Christmas holiday a pimple of displeasure at Lewis's repeated absences from school on various excuses began, even filtered through the disciplined tone of the school log, to swell into a boil of annoyance. On 16 March 1916 "Mr Lewis has permission from the Clerk E[nfield] E[ducation] C[ommittee] to go to South Wales on business." Six days later, on 22 March, "Mr Lewis returned this morning having exceeded his leave of absence by two days." By November, serious anger management had taken over as "Mr Lewis received a telegram this afternoon [the 21st] requesting him to go down to Carmarthen at once. He saw Mr Hepworth (Clerk to the Enfield Education Committee)" who, clearly unwisely, "gave him leave of absence till Thursday evening". On Friday 24 November, through gritted teeth, Eastaugh recorded "Mr Lewis not at school" and hardly mollified on the 27th noted that "Mr

Lewis returned to school (Monday)". Paris and London were being bombed by Zeppelins, Verdun and the Somme were reaping their harvest of dead, but the greatest tragedies and controversies imply no cessation of the least. Sometimes the opposite is true, and war is a distraction.

On 3 September 1916 there occurred the most potent incursion of the war into the lives of Forty Hill's civilians, the shooting down of a Zeppelin at the village of Cuffley five miles away. The high, throbbing tone of the Zeppelin airships had regularly been heard over the village. "In a way I enjoyed the Zeppelin raids," Gwen's brother Bill said.

It was different and exciting to be wakened in the middle of the night, bundled downstairs, the kitchen table dragged to the wall with us children tight underneath, an eiderdown pinned up to the window against flying glass. . . . Cousin Jack Tofts from Braintree was staying with us at the time of the Cuffley Zepp. It seemed to arrive in our vicinity unheralded. We were tumbled out of bed and downstairs in a silent hurry, teeth chattering . . . with Dad in and out of the front door reporting progress. We'd hear the droning of the engines. "It's right overhead now," Dad reported, "God help us if they drop a bomb. Here comes a bomb." We waited, crouched [there] for ages, it seemed, before we heard the explosions. The bombs fell a couple of miles away. No doubt the Zepp, realising it was under attack, released its bombs to gain mobility. We heard the rattle of machine-gun fire and then saw the brilliant glow as the gas-filled monster burst into flames and slowly fell out of the sky.[20]

In an unpublished manuscript that was part of an intended novel, Norman describes the airship's fall.

When the airship caught fire all the people ran out of their houses and started to shout. The sound of the shouting was all round us, and went on and on. The whole sky had gone red, with the airship burning almost overhead and fire trickling from it all the way down to the earth. In the garden it was hard to believe [the] leaves and branches of the trees weren't on fire. The light was as strong as at midday, except that it was red. I saw my mother's eyes wide open for the first time, with the tight wrinkles all round them lit up by the flames, and the pink reflections in them, and to my surprise I saw that she was weeping.

I expected the airship to come plunging down, to fall like a stone. Instead it tilted as it drifted away from us and a glowing mass began to drip from it in the way wax drips from a tilted candle. I was surprised that half the airship still in the sky kept its shape, although it was slowly sinking away from us towards the horizon, emptying fire into the night. With all the shouting still going on it was hard to hear each other speak: I asked my mother among all these shouts of joy why she was crying, and she said, "It's all those poor men up there being burned to death."[21]

The flaming airship sailed on to its doom, and people set out on foot from Forty Hill to the scene. Annie Nicholls, Gwen and Bill's mother, joined the crowds, "only to be most horrified at seeing twelve very young Germans laid out in death in the little village church of Cuffley".[22]

The eight-year-old Norman's state of mind in 1916 cannot be known, but it would be unusual if Monty's death at the start of the year hadn't left him feeling stranded and anxious, as children often feel after calamity, about what bad thing might happen next. He was an only child now, with parents helplessly different from the other parents they lived among. An easy target for animosity, he made things worse by being academically clever. Other children called him names, Gwen remembers, and apart from the Nicholls children he wasn't close to anyone in the neighbourhood. A few weeks after the Cuffley Zeppelin was shot down, on 2 November, his name appears in the Forty Hill School corporal punishment book. Almost all the recorded punishments – mostly a stroke of the cane on the hand – were for offences that would go unremarked today, "Calling out unnecessarily", "Inattention", "Impudence", "Silly answer", "Rudeness", "Swearing in school", and the perennial (till desks were modernised) "Playing with the inkwells". The most serious infractions were truanting, stubbornness and cheeking a teacher in public; these could earn the offender two strokes on the seat. But Norman's punishment, two strokes on his hand, was for the rare offence of "Fighting" with a boy named Charles Prior, who got the same.

We don't know what he and Prior were fighting about, but there is a suggestion of a boy under pressure. Despite his later insistence on the dismalness of his Enfield background (in which he wasn't alone: an anonymous writer in the *Enfield Tatler* in 1905 considered it "suburban to the core"), it was not that Forty Hill as a place was entirely gross and unpleasant. It was that *Norman didn't fit*. The contrast between Norman's life and that of the Nicholls children, for instance, was very great. Gwen's father, a builder who had to give up work because of ill health, brought in just enough to keep his family and, labouring in conditions of insecurity and overwork familiar to most working-class men, suffered and died young. The Nicholls' life was far more straitened than the Lewises' – William Nicholls earned £3 if he succeeded in working a five-and-a-half-day week – yet their memories are sweeter. Gwen recalls

fiendish crazes for bowling hoops, whipping tops, skipping and best of all was our golf craze when, with one golf club between us and a ball each, we boys and girls would play each other with such concentration and zest, our golf course stretching from one open green to another, across the road and back again – there was no traffic then to impede our activities. And there was never to be forgotten the occasions during the frequently severe winters when we would skate or slide on the village pond, during one such winter being allowed free access to Sir Henry Bowles' beautiful lake [at Forty Hall], my brothers and I taking and cooking our breakfast on the brink of this sparkling frozen scene and skating as skilfully as we could with skates that had been used by our parents in their young days. All this before going to school.[23]

Her brother Bill Nicholls describes a Forty Hill simultaneously thrilling and opiate, a childhood that glows with remembered light, the sunshine dripping off its days like paint, its ingredients recognition of the seasons, disdain for the automobile, an apparently permanent but unintrusive war, and life out of doors.

The horse was still the motive power, pulling the drays and carts and carriages along. Motor cars were an expensive joke, mainly for the wealthy to toy with. In those days the great majority of roads were not surfaced with tarmac. They were very muddy in winter and dusty in summer. A motor car passing when it was dry would be followed by a giant cloud of dust and would usually frighten the horses. On the rare approach of one, we would try to take refuge in a gateway off the road, out of harm's way, to avoid the shying and bolting of the frightened horses. Otherwise the roads were not dangerous, we used to play football on them on the way to school, passing the ball from side to side as we went along, or play legalong marbles along the gutters. . . .

There were often fighter aircraft practising over the Bowles estate [at Forty Hall], diving, looping and stunt-flying over the parkland. . . . One hit the top of a tree and crashed in fragments. The pilot was unhurt. I went to the scene of the crash and proudly brought home half of the propeller which was a great prize. The planes of those days, being so much smaller, could be far more acrobatic, with their tight turns and twists, loops and falling-leaf dives, opening up and shutting off their engines. . . . It was our intrepid uncle [Harry, stationed at Chingford aerodrome] who caused such excitement in the Freehold when he persuaded a pilot to land with him in nearby Cracknell's Field so that he could dash home and surprise Aunt Marge, while the boys of the village,

Norman Lewis included, looked on at the unusual sight of an aeroplane light-landing in our back yard. . . .

For us children the war went on for ever. Four and a half years is a long time, almost a lifetime, to a child. . . . We carried on as best we could. . . . We were outdoor children, playing in the street and open spaces. There was always the rat-tat-tat of machine-gun fire, especially if the wind was easterly from Enfield Lock, where small arms production and testing was at full stretch. But we took little notice of it, it was a backdrop to everyday living and we didn't realise its significance. War scenes invaded our drawing books. I can still draw a passable Zeppelin, surrounded by shellbursts.[24]

Others' contentment, of course, didn't better Norman's perspective. (Perhaps large families – there were six Nicholls children – offer better insurance against unhappiness than small ones.) There is no direct trace of what his life was like during the following year; in biographical terms he was lying low, and may also have been lying low in reality, a lonely, clever young misfit apprehensive of the future. He shared one interest with his father: they went birdwatching together or, more accurately, bird-nesting, which was not the taboo it now is (though taking certain eggs, like the robin's, was). Orchards that by 1935 had been obliterated by a dozen of George Bowling's West Bletchley avenues ran the full two miles to Enfield Town. You could walk the Baker Street highway, or the twitchel path over a stile that ran between hedges through cherry orchards as far as Southbury Road, Enfield, where R G Lewis the chemist's was. The thousands of fruit trees supplied constant opportunities for watching finches, woodpeckers and robins. A couple of years later Norman would break his leg in the orchards, going after robins' eggs. "He was very proud of his collection of eggs, and with the orchard opposite there was always a temptation," Gwen says.[25] Richard Lewis put an aviary in the back garden at Carterhatch Lane and imported Japanese robins to fill it. Louisa too did her earnest best to stop Norman from being bored, and possibly from escaping. "Lewis's mother used to say, 'Could Gwen play with Normie?' and I'd go to his garden. He had a lot of beautiful toys he never played with, and he had an aviary, but we didn't play, he just chased me round the garden and frightened the wits out of me."[26]

Through the spring of 1917, the novel experience of enemy air raids provided diversions and affected school attendance. Norman's namesake, Lewis the teacher, had joined up as a special constable. Frederick

Eastaugh seems to have seen this as an excuse for more malingering.
"3 April: Received notice that Mr Lewis has leave of absence tomorrow
afternoon in order that he may attend to duties as a special constable."
"19 June: Mr Lewis has been called up to Mill Hill today for another
medical examination." On 2 July Eastaugh recorded that the fiancé of
Vida Cooke, his favourite teacher who had worked at the school since
1907, had been killed in France. The summer holidays were early that
year, and the children were back at their desks on 27 August. Ten days
later the head teacher was informed that the children "must be encouraged to harvest and gather horse chestnuts", and within two weeks he
reported that they were "busy gathering horse chestnuts, which are
said to be useful substitutes for grain which is used in certain industrial processes which are essential to the prosecution of the war". Night
air raids intensified over the winter, reaching a climax in the last week
of January 1918 and emptying the school, parents keeping their children at home because of lack of sleep and in some cases, including
Eastaugh's own daughter, panic attacks. It was not all grim: Gwen
Merrington remembers that "for Saturday afternoons and Sundays in
all weathers we would take long, rambling walks into the countryside.
Midwinter would be the time to have a better fire and push back the
kitchen table, make room for us all and in flickering firelight have a
family sing-song." But her family had sorrow to come: William Nicholls,
her father, died from pericarditis caused by rheumatic fever on 8 March.
He was forty-two. Five days later, as the Nicholls children got ready
for their father's funeral, all Enfield schools were given a holiday for
the children to witness a visit to the town by one of the army's new
tanks. This was a flag-waving portent of events later in the year, of the
motorised counter-attack in August by British Mark IV and Mark V
tanks and 120,000 men that was the overture to German defeat. In
April and May, however, the Germans' spring offensive was not near
being halted.

Yet on 31 May the war, I think, did seem a distraction to one pupil
at Forty Hill School. It took him eight decades to talk about the event.
It happened during the visit by the Diocesan Inspector, who came to
the school once a year to examine the children in their knowledge of
scripture.

"There was an inspector [who] called at the school," Norman said,
"and was talking to the headmaster in front of the other children ...
I realised I was condemned at that moment, [as] the headmaster said

to him, 'Of course we have a boy here who we don't teach at all, he teaches himself.'"²⁷ Frederick Eastaugh may have been fond or proud or both of Norman, but the impact of his foolish compliment on classmates who already regarded Norman as an outsider can be easily pictured. For most of his life Norman did not mention the sustained campaign that now started. In *Jackdaw Cake* he suppressed his Forty Hill schooldays entirely, putting his year with his grandfather and three aunts in Carmarthen down to "my grandfather's ambition to make a Welshman of me". In 1996, I began an interview with him for a newspaper feature by trying to draw him out about a period he hadn't written about. He unexpectedly started talking about this episode.

Forty Hill, he said, had a semi-rural roughness, "not wholly rustic because a number of the menfolk there used to go on their bicycles to a place called Brimsdown [to the Enfield small arms factory or the Brimsdown Lead Works] which was on the Lee and it was industrialised and they of course had a worse life than the semi-serfs who worked for the local landowners there. ... There were those people, and the ones that were under the landlords who had a slightly better time of it, but they too were severely exploited. Therefore they were brutalised by their environment." Their children had few niceties of behaviour.

I was driven to go to Wales at the age of [ten] through bullying of such an intensive kind that it would have been the headlines in the papers today. ... For example, they would decide what would be likely to cause the maximum amount of pain in the minimum time, and I remember being thrown in deep beds of nettles – that would have been in summer – and I remember in winter the final example was that I was thrashed with sheets of ice, the cutting edges, and I was so covered with blood that I remember when these boys then went off and left me there, a woman was going past with a pram, trying to get me into the pram and take me home. This was the most awful thing, this was worse than the pain I had suffered. ...

They were exceedingly cruel. [There was] nothing the children used to like better than the times when the frogs came out in spring. They used to tie them up by their feet, throw stones at them. And the young birds, they would take them out of their nests and hang them. They were infatuated with cruelty.²⁸

Norman spoke matter-of-factly about this period eighty years later, but the prospect from the spring of 1918 to the summer of 1919 must have looked vile. Between dodging the dismal atmosphere at home and the boys waiting for him in Forty Hill's lanes, all he could do was develop ingenuity in survival and providing his own entertainment. 1918 was decisive for him (though its decisiveness was obviously not yet clear to anyone). It confirmed him as an outsider, bearer of Coleridge's description "Like one that on a lonesome road / Doth walk in fear and dread", and it gave him something – cruelty – to hate. He much later acknowledged that his career and temperament had been affected by the violence of those days, and insisted on the literary usefulness of a certain quotient of horror. "I always say that the more horrific things are for you, the more chance you've got of writing about them."[29] But violence is not the only key: Norman maintained an ironic fondness for the tedium of his upbringing too. "It filled me with a desire to seek out pastures new as soon as possible, to make for somewhere else that was as else as could be. You see, I had an exceedingly boring childhood."[30]

A curious side-story to this horrible turn in his life is that at the age of ten he was confronted by a fact that he later made a capital theme of his writing: the gulf between urban and rural poverty. The seeds of his later pastoralism, his hippy pursuit of the simple life, and his liking for indigenous peoples, were sown in Forty Hill, whose working class "were completely unlike people living at a very low financial level or a low level of possessions, say, in the Amazonian forests, who were very very kind". This hybrid village, neither suburb nor country, neither industrial nor rural, settled by a desensitised and deculturated proletariat, could not be belonged to, in his opinion. He may have been right: even the Nicholls children eventually moved away, although Gwen blamed Forty Hill's development for her departure. "We didn't leave Forty Hill. *It left us*. The cherry orchards, the twitchel path (where he and I so often walked), the open spaces, the village pond – *all gone*."[31] It is not that complicated to imagine now that it was out of Norman's complete failure to belong as a child that he turned belonging into the underlying object of all his adult quests. In a couple of unusually personal sentences he explained to his Indian guide in Orissa in 1990 his compulsion to travel. "I'm looking for the people who have always been there, and belong to the places where they live. The others I do not wish to see."[32]

Perhaps the predominant fact about Norman's childhood, with hindsight, is that his life was a *mess* – of considerable dimensions – and for most of his pre-adult years it would stay that way. As readers of his books, as students of his life we should remember how easy it is to see now that his career had a push from the past. As the lives of many people do. There is, so often, a turning point that makes *all* the difference to a life. But – *but* – we should remember too that it's almost never possible to know this *at the moment it happens*. Though we are very often partial to look back and rationalise, choose, a point at which we, or some other agency, "made" our life happen, and *that* then is fixed as the decisive moment, that self-chosen moment is almost always only true for the purpose of our own self-narration to the world. The self-chosen moment is also nearly always later than the unconscious turning point that preceded it. Norman fixed many turning points in his life. Most of them were to do with journeys and escape: Arabia ("what I would really like to do would be to get out there and stay there") was an important early one. But I'm inclined to think that 1918 was his real turning point, the year when he was cast out from the tribe with violence. I don't expect he knew it: in those days of his (at best) equivocal childhood, mostly what could have been going through his head was a feeling of twisting and turning, painful, fearful, bored, in the suburban-village straitjacket of Forty Hill, desperate to be released. And the other element he possessed – which children possess before they understand that there is any alternative to their rotten lives – was simple resignation.

The war had ended. Forty Hill School had reopened on the morning of 11 November after being closed since mid-October because of the influenza pandemic. (Most of the teachers had been ill. Inevitably Eastaugh's *bête noire*, Mr Lewis, was the last to come back to school, not returning until the following term.) Bill Nicholls, who attended the other Forty Hill school at Lavender Road, remembered that "We were let out of school without explanation during the morning of the 11th of November, and we heard the good news almost immediately. We built a huge bonfire in the middle of Bridgenhall Road. Fireworks appeared as if from nowhere, and high jinks went on for days and nights afterwards. Mr Fish [a Gypsy who grazed his horses at Forty Hill] magnanimously opened up the green, which he had earlier pinched from us, for our later-organised peace party. Thus ended the monumental outpouring of blood and treasure, the watershed from which there was no return."[33]

On the morning of 20 December Norman sat the General Knowledge exam, a precursor to entry to one of the secondary schools (he sat it with Frances Everett, who later became well known as a gardener under her married name of Frances Perry). He was thriving within the safety of academic halls, but outside school he was not allowed to forget children's capacity to mobilise overwhelmingly against someone they pick out as different. The winter was mild until January, when heavy snow fell and kept falling intermittently until the end of April. In many places in London there were 30 centimetres of level snow. Gwen and her brothers and sisters skated on the lake at Forty Hall, and Norman was abducted by a group of boys and attacked with sheets of ice.

In the Forty Hill School log there is an ironic confirmation of the fondness felt by Frederick Eastaugh – the architect of Norman's ordeal by ice – for his star pupil. On 13 March he records that he has "Received notice that Norman has passed the two preliminary examinations for the Free Scholarships to the Secondary Schools". The surname "Lewis" has been added later; nowhere else in the log book is any child referred to by his or her first name. On 6 May, as the snow thawed, the head teacher heard that Norman would be examined for a free place in a secondary school. Norman took the exam the following Monday afternoon at Enfield Grammar School. On 19 June Eastaugh writes triumphantly that "Norman Lewis has been awarded a Free Scholarship to the Enfield Grammar School". The last day of June, a Saturday, had been announced as Peace Day, and the children sang "O God our help in ages past" and the national anthem, and after a short address were dismissed. A further celebration, a Victory Fête held in Forty Hall park, took place a couple of days later, and Eastaugh notes that very few children are present at school that day either.

For Norman, Peace Day and the temporary carnival atmosphere can't have meant very much. His scholarship to Enfield Grammar was not going to be an instrument of *his* peace, or an end to the hostilities he faced; it was very likely the opposite. He had taken the scholarship exam as early as possible, to give him a chance to retake it if he failed first time. He now faced a year's wait before he would be admitted. His parents were, if anything, more panic-stricken than he was. They decided that their last son's best life expectancy lay well away from Forty Hill School. The decision to send Norman to live at his grandfather's house in Carmarthen may have seemed to them the best choice they could make. It may have seemed to Norman too, in prospect, exactly the escape he was looking for, despite the separation from his parents. In some ways it was an escape, from bullying, from Carterhatch Lane. In other ways he was about to understand that his capacity for resignation, and the experience of family failings that he had already gained, would both be useful.

He was always there. He was not with us, the Freehold children who went out and played every game under the sun, and some of our own imagination. He used to just be on the fringe, not deriding but always sort of analytical and looking on with amazement, rather than joining in. I don't know if you've grown up with brothers and sisters and cousins, but it was as natural as breathing, knowing Lewis was as natural as knowing yourself – he was there.

Gwen Merrington

Thereafter, almost immediately, at a certain moment when my parents thought I really would not survive, I was sent to Wales, where my family originally came from, to stay with my grandfather and three aunts, all three of whom were not really spectacularly mad, but they were fairly mad.

Norman Lewis

In the Wales of my childhood legend twined like a splendidly flowering weed through the prosaic fields of reality. ... People spoke seriously of local events which they believed to have taken place in the days of their great-grandfathers, quite unconsciously repeating folk tales of the dawn of Celtic history and still current in parts of Asia.

Unpublished typescript

The fact of the matter is that the people living in Wales are mentally, temperamentally, generally speaking very different from those living in England, you might say almost [as] different as the Chinese.

Norman Lewis

2

CHINA

"I was wise once. When I was born I cried"
Welsh proverb

NORMAN'S removal to the safe haven of south Wales was comparatively
successful. Safety came at a price. His world was safer, but there was
little improvement in its legibility. After the shock of arrival and his
mother's departure, he resigned himself to the situation. "I was nine years
of age [in fact just eleven]," he writes in *Jackdaw Cake*, "and the adults
peopling my world seemed on the whole irrational, but it was an irrationality I had come to accept as the norm." He had been dropped into
a place as foreign as China, and a household his parents must have
known to be eccentric – or perhaps not, given Norman's description of
the great temperamental divide between the English and the Welsh (and
the household Richard and Louisa Lewis came from in Enfield). If it was
completely normal for a Welshman at very slight cause to weep in public,
as Norman claimed, then possibly the house in Wellfield Road, Carmarthen
where his grandfather and three aunts lived was not much more than
very Welsh, with the additions of some chronic sibling rivalry and medium-
level neurological disorder. From the point of view of a ten-year-old boy,
however, required to live there for an unspecified length of time and
separated from his parents, such a description would be something like
describing the sinking of the *Titanic* as just a ship hitting just an iceberg.
Norman had been tipped from theatre of cruelty into theatre of the
absurd. The combination of people and circumstances produced a
Pinteresque domestic situation that was never stable for long and turned
out daily dark, histrionic climaxes. The household's structure didn't help
its instability: a strong hint of sexual starvation, reinforced by lack of

useful employment, informs Norman's portrait of his spinster aunts and alternates with the prowling sexuality of his widowed grandfather, whose tastes veered towards the conventionally libertine. If the bourgeoisie of Carmarthen actively encouraged public expressions of feeling, they were equally intolerant of any sign of sexual incontinence, in fact any reference at all to the sexual life.

Even allowing for the prevailing emotionality and piety of Welsh life at the time, then, it's difficult to picture the whole of Carmarthen as made up of establishments as eccentric as the one at Wellfield Road. When Norman arrived in July 1919, three of his five aunts – Polly, Annie and Li – still lived as unmarried sisters with their father, David Lewis. There were good reasons: the eldest aunt, Polly, was epileptic and according to her nephew "had suffered at least one fit per day since the age of fourteen, in the course of which she had fallen once from a window, once into a river and twice into the fire".[1] Annie, the second aunt, had decided to improve her life by spending her days dressed up as a variety of more glamorous figures, the kind of superior historical characters that believers in reincarnation often like to associate themselves with: a courtier of Queen Mary, a female Cossack, a flamenco dancer. Aunt Li, the youngest, was timid and tearful and very rarely addressed any words to anybody, though she raved quietly to herself. She and Polly apparently had not spoken to one another for years when Norman arrived, and they lived as far apart as possible in the house, using Annie as a go-between on the occasion when communication could not be avoided.

What united Norman's aunts more than their disorders was that daily reality was deeply problematic. To lay the whole blame for this at their father's feet might be unjust, but it is hard to avoid the conclusion that their alternately cowed and escapist worlds were shaped and influenced by David Lewis's overbearing, patriarchal manner. Norman only saw his grandfather at weekends because David Lewis stayed late at his business in King Street on weekdays, but he still succeeded, in Norman's memory, in filling "every corner of the house with his deep, competitive voice, and the cigar-smoke aroma of his personality". He had been a widower for twenty-five years and was by this time one of the leading citizens of the town, "a man with the face of his day, a prow of a nose, bulging eyes, and an Assyrian beard, who saw himself close to God, with whom he sometimes conversed in a loud and familiar voice largely on financial matters".[2] If one were looking for an analysis of the chief psychological trend in Lewis family life, it could easily be found in the impulse of almost every family member to escape David Lewis's presence. His wife, Charlotte Griffiths, the daughter of a wealthy farmer, may have died of natural causes, but she lost no time in doing so. Lewis's three daughters left at home, lost in their private worlds, ignored or occasionally attacked the one he had created. His only son Richard, Norman's father, had fled first to Scotland, then to Enfield, and of the last two of his five daughters one had settled for an arranged marriage in Canada after getting herself "into trouble" and the other had taken her first chance of marriage, to a schoolteacher, and rapidly swapped Carmarthen for Cardiff. One circumstantial indicator of just how fearful Norman's Wellfield Road aunts were is that of the five houses in the road canvassed for the 1901 census, number 3 was marked as "uninhabited" and also "in occupation" which, translated, meant that there were people living there but no one answered when the census-taker knocked. (The 1901 census was taken in the evening, when the aunts should have been home, but grandfather Lewis was working, and his daughters were too scared to answer the door.)

Norman had a different relationship with each of his aunts. Polly, in addition to the epilepsy that had left her badly scarred and hoarse from her burns, "extended a tyranny in small ways to all who had dealings with her", but by scrupulously following her hissed or whispered instructions on politeness, punctuality and personal hygiene Norman got on reasonably well with her. His memory for learning gave him added credit, as he recited to her the tedious collects he had to memorise at Sunday school. "When I showed myself as word perfect in one of these it was easy to believe that she was doing her best to smile, as she probably did when I accompanied her in my thin and wheedling treble in one of her harmonium recitals of such favourite hymns as 'Through the Night of Doubt and Sorrow'." Aunt Annie he remembered as hardly noticing him, she was so wrapped up in the demands and pleasures of her dressing-up complex – though it is Annie who provokes the first of Norman's oblique admissions in *Jackdaw Cake* of the state of fear he was in after the bullying he had suffered at Forty Hill. "Once, when later I went to school, and became very sensitive to the opinions of my schoolfriends, [Annie] waylaid me on my way home got up as a Spanish dancer in a frilled blouse and skirt, and a high comb stuck into her untidy grey hair." He was sent to the same Carmarthen primary school where his father had been punished forty years before for speaking Welsh, and his paramount ambition was not to shine but, foreshadowing his later adult strategy of self-effacement, do the opposite, deliberately putting himself in the background. "I was accepted on sufferance by the boys of the Pentrepoeth School who at best regarded me as harmless although not overbright, and above all *I was anxious not to be associated in any way with eccentric behaviour*" (my emphasis).

Unable to dissociate himself from his Wellfield Road connections, he found himself walking on eggshells. As the summer went on, it was Aunt Li he developed an alliance of sympathy and timid confidence with. They first joined forces in self-defence against the attacks of Norman's grandfather's fighting cocks. These Old English game fowl, bred for aggression, had a habit of getting out of their pens in the back garden, and Norman and Li were targeted as the smallest members of the household: "any king [cockerel] that had managed to break out had the habit of laying in wait well out of sight until either of us came on the scene, when he would rush to the attack, leaping high into the air to strike at our faces with his spurs". Because of David Lewis's pride in his birds they had to retaliate indirectly, deploying subterfuge to keep the menace under control. Li's tactic was worthy of a secret agent: she would take several eggs from a sitting hen, parboil them for a few seconds, and replace them. She also bought a wild cat, which she starved for three days and then let loose in the garden. This was less successful: the next morning three escaped game cocks still ruled the flowerbeds, and the cat had vanished. Later, when this bond of trust had been forged, Norman and his auntie often escaped the house, and town, and roamed the fields in a sad but safe pastoral, without witnesses, unthreatened by attack from cocks or bullies.

She would wet me with her tears, and I would listen to her sad ravings and sometimes stroke her hand. One day she must have come to the grand decision to tell me what lay at the root of her sorrow. We climbed a stile and went into a field and, fixing her glistening eyes upon me, she said, "What I am going to tell you now you will remember every single day of your life." But whatever she revealed must have been so startling that memory rejected it, for not a word of what was said remains in my mind.[3]

The silent war against the cocks reflected more than Li's fear of her father's hobby, because it was her elder sister who looked after the brooding hens and chicks. Every parboiled egg was a blow by Li against

Polly, one of the many surreptitious shots both aimed at each other. Polly, unfairly, was her father's favourite, while Li was his scapegoat. The only moment of harmony between the three sisters that Norman records was in their ritual, every Saturday morning, of baking the jackdaw cake. Carmarthen was glutted with jackdaws, and the garden at Wellfield Road, in its marginally damper location at the foot of Pen-lan hill, saw even more of them because of its cornucopia of snails which were their main diet. The jackdaws, for mercenary avian reasons, were friendly. "They would tap on the windows to be let into the house and go hopping from room to room in search of scraps." For years the aunts had responded in kind, and for once they collaborated peacefully:

the ingredients had to be decided upon and bought: eggs, raisins, candied peel and sultanas required to produce a cake of exceptional richness. Li did the shopping, because Polly was not supposed to leave the house and Annie was too confused to be able to buy what was necessary, put down her money, and pick up the change.

Each aunt took it in turn to bake and ice the cake and to decorate the icing. While they were kept busy doing this they seemed to me quite changed. Annie wore an ordinary dress and stopped laughing, Li ceased to cry, and Polly's fits were quieter than on any other day. While the one whose turn it was did the baking, the others stood about in the kitchen and watched, and they were as easy to talk to as at other times they were not.

. . . For some hours after this weekly event the atmosphere was one of calm and contentment, and then the laughter and weeping would start again.[4]

The sudden truce that broke out for as long as this communal activity lasted hints at another root of the Carmarthen Lewises' problems. Although they lived in clocks-and-mirrors opulence and their reception rooms had teak doors, their years of wealth were short. They were eventually compromised by a strain of shadiness that David Lewis never completely left behind. He had begun, respectably, as a maker of the clocks he later filled his house with. In his youth he was suspected of the mildly deplorable pastime of entering his game fowl in illegal cock fights, but in acquiring his fortune in a "single magnificent coup", buying up a cargo of ruined tea from a ship sunk in Swansea harbour and retailing it at "several thousand per cent" profit, something disreputable clung to him. He was one kind of model of a Victorian entrepreneur – the man who seeks social reinvention as well as money – at the gentler end of a spectrum whose other extremity would have included Trollope's Melmotte or his inspirations, George Hudson and John Sadleir. David Lewis was no railway speculator or seller of false prospectuses, but he was not content with reselling his tea as it was and repackaged it with a fraudulent royal crest. He then repackaged himself as David Warren Lewis, with a house in Wellfield Road and a device on his letterhead. He continued to labour at his tea-dealing business, but his concentration on commerce emerges as a form of neglect: his daughters' idleness must have contributed, you feel, to their respective disorders, and his preoccupation with his invented status – his false self – would be the eventual instrument of his downfall. The Warren Lewises were destined to decline from fortune to *fin de race* in ultra-quick time, within two generations.

Norman's summer was spent around Carmarthen and on the Tywi (Towy) river that leads to the sea at Llanstephan six and a half miles away. He was happy(ish) when he went for walks with Aunt Li, following the river as it threw "great, shining loops through the fields, doubling back on itself sometimes in a kind of afterthought to encircle some riverside shack or a patch of sedge in which cows stood knee-deep to graze". On Sundays there were formal, less enjoyable, trips to the seaside, where more Lewis relations lurked in Llanstephan's gingerbread cottages, overlooking the estuary and sandbanks of the Tywi. At the edge of this handsome breeze-swept wilderness of grass, sand and water, under the extravagant silhouette of the thirteenth-century castle, the inhabitants existed in a kind of frozen disapproval of anything that disturbed their peace: the worst offenders were the miners' families who descended by train throughout the summer from their dark valleys to Ferryside across the estuary, and then crossed over to occupy the sands and infuriate the villagers by rolling up their trousers, drinking beer and unforgivably enjoying themselves. Placards were put up, Norman remembers, saying "Remember the Sabbath Day, to keep it Holy". When the miners invited him to join their picnic, his aunt Williams screeched at him to come away. At the appearance of the miners' wind-up gramophone, apples and then stones were thrown. Inevitably these confrontations plunged Aunt Li into nameless sorrow once more, and she would leave before the bus, imposing on Norman an hour and a half's walk back to Carmarthen. His liking for the wild beauty of Llanstephan stayed with him. Living at Wellfield Road, his favourite relative was his aunt Margaret, who as an apprentice baker "had had the misfortune to marry into the Lewises, and thereafter waste her sweetness on the desert air"; warm, generous and dignified, she was occasionally allowed to invite him for tea, though she was never welcome at his grandfather's. When Margaret was widowed she moved to Llanstephan, and in the late 1920s Norman visited her and the village when he came to Wales to race motorcycles on Pendine Sands – but what he called his "fundamentalist Welsh Baptist upbringing", in which his Llanstephan cousins played their extremist part, was to be escaped at all costs and prejudiced him in adult life to "almost any form of fundamentalism".[5]

When the new school term started, he was sent to the local Pentrepoeth day school. He did not shine, on purpose, and was helped by being unable to follow lessons in Welsh (the pendulum having swung back since his father's time). The future Enfield Grammar scholarship boy was censured in front of his peers by the master – "'What is the name for him?' All the children would shout with delight, 'Dickie Dwl, sir' (stupid Dick). 'That's right, boys, and that's what his name shall be'"[6] – and sent down to the infants' school to force some Welsh into him, unsuccessfully. The severe early winter, its first sign a freak snowstorm on the night of 19 September, satisfactorily disrupted school life and produced distraction for him – as it did for his suddenly energised Aunt Polly. By November, with the hill farms snowed in and the town's electricity cut off, she was busy organising food and fuel supplies, the challenges to survival thrown down by the weather releasing her from the severity of the fits she suffered when life was calm. In *Jackdaw Cake* Norman writes sympathetically about his aunt's epilepsy, obliquely noting the pressure it placed on him, his grandfather and his two other aunts, only indirectly associating the good times at Wellfield Road with her periods of remission. The reality was that he, as most eleven-year-olds would,

went in mortal fear of seeing Aunt Polly's face when she was having a fit. Before entering any room I would push open the door, inch by inch, until I could see what was going on, and it always happened that if Polly was there and in trouble, I soon spotted her feet which were small and neat sticking out from behind the sofa or an armchair, whereupon I silently closed the door and slipped away.

With the thaw, and water, electricity and food supplies flowing again, Polly's fits revived and the good times were finished. They were also finished for David Lewis, though he might have thought they were just beginning, having, according to Norman, recently started a liaison with a French milliner thirty-five years his junior. He set her up in King Street, steps away from his own business, and possibly anticipated that his senior years would be sweetened by her favours. It was not to be. The town's chapels were electrified, and his daughters were outraged. Norman writes that he saw the unlucky young woman twice, once when Aunt Li rushed at a woman in King Street and tore the hat off her head, and on another occasion when she called at Wellfield Road, perhaps to attempt peace negotiations. From his place of concealment in the large hall of the house, he saw the diminutive Polly, still unsteady from a recent fit, walk up to the visitor and slap her face. Disgrace for David Lewis was progressive but total: talk ceased of his becoming mayor, his chapel functions shrank, and finally allegations were broadcast that an outbreak of gonorrhoea in the town had been traced to the Frenchwoman's presence. (Norman adds dolour to this episode by invoking the simultaneous downfall of his grandfather's friend and protector Lord Kylsant, chairman of the giant Royal Mail Steam Packet Company, "the greatest merchant sovereign of the seven seas", *Time* magazine called him.[7] After rumours spread about the City of unreliable dealings, Baron Kylsant of Carmarthen was eventually charged under the Larceny Act, found guilty of extensively misrepresenting the company's assets, and jailed. There is a problem, though, with rolling the Kylsant affair up with the slump in David Lewis's fortunes: it was not simultaneous but took place in 1931, more than a decade after Norman's visit. A curious fact about *Jackdaw Cake* is that when Norman wrote it, in his mid-seventies, he was anxious to understate his age both to his children and his critics. It suited his personal as well as his literary purpose to put the two episodes together; Kylsant's appearance is one of the numerous sleights of hand in the account of his first three decades that obscure the fact that he was ten years older than he claimed.)

If an artless young French milliner was Lewis's nemesis – one pauses to wonder, the tone of the story is a bit showy – was Carmarthen in any case the kind of town where an honest entrepreneur might succeed? It was Maridunum to the Romans, the two lines of the Julian Way met at it, it had been the capital of Wales until 877, and for the next thousand years ships of up to 300 tons had been able to navigate the Tywi as far as its quay. "The town has a head post office, a railway station with telegraph, two banking offices, and three chief inns; publishes two weekly newspapers; and is the capital of the county, the seat of assizes at both circuits, and of quarter sessions in April and Oct. Markets are held on Wednesday and Saturday. . . . Some manufacture is carried on in flannel, malt, ropes, and leather; much business is done in connexion with numerous copper and tin works, and coal and lead mines, in the neighbourhood," as the 1872 *Imperial Gazetteer of England and Wales* says. This is the last time its prosperity was posted. A sandbar at the Tywi's mouth had been recorded as early as the sixteenth century. In 1886, after the storms of a single extreme winter, the barrier of sand rose up from the sea – celebrated at first for its dramatic appearance and nicknamed "Cefn Sidan" ("Silk Back") – and blocked the river to shipping. The one industry that did not suffer was the salmon fishery, jealously guarded by local coracle men. They had fished for salmon and sewin (sea trout) since before the Romans. They now migrated downriver. When Norman arrived, there would still have been these mistrustful-featured men in beaten hats, with the stocky musculature of the oarsman, trudging the streets and the banks of the river, their half-walnut-shaped vessels strapped to their shoulders before they slipped bobbing into the stream. "The appearance in the streets of coracle men, carrying their prehistoric boats on their backs, confirmed that ruin was irreversible. These men never made their long communally-owned nets to spread across a river for sewin without the assurance of the special instincts of their trade that navigation was at an end."[8]

There were probably very few legitimate ways left to make large fortunes in this one-time seat of government. The world was elsewhere, in Tenby and Llanelli and Swansea. The "grey . . . milk-swilling, psalm-singing" prospect was made greyer, in the Lewis household, by the worsening of Polly's condition. Her fits intensified, the relationship between her and Li deteriorated, and when spring warmed to summer and Norman escaped with Li to go "fishing in the ponds and chasing butterflies on the top of Pen-lan" (today crowned with relay stations and mobile communication masts), the police arrived.

A rash of anonymous letter-writing had flared up in the town. After an apparent confrontation between David Lewis and the plainclothes officer about the possibility of Polly Lewis being a suspect – apparent because it is hard to imagine Norman, at eleven, being witness to his grandfather's account of the meeting to Annie and Li – the officer departed. The rest of this episode we can, I think, trust Norman on more easily. The following day or day after, Polly took her nephew shopping in town, an unheard-of kindness, and showered a football, a mouth organ – late birthday presents – and a gramophone record on him. She bought Jockey Club perfume for herself. At shop counters she chatted with the sales assistants. At the butcher's, a cousin's business which she had deserted in acrimony months before, she bought meat and made up the quarrel. She bought cakes for tea. Norman remembered that the afternoon "was an exceptionally pleasant one". He kicked his football in the garden, listened to his record and ate cakes. "It may have been the most relaxed day I spent at Wellfield Road."[9] That night in the bathroom his aunt tried to hang herself.

She failed – if it was a serious attempt. The doctor came with a straitjacket. But somehow inevitably, when the decision came to be made it was Li, the family scapegoat, whom it was decided to institutionalise. David Lewis could not bear to be parted from his favourite eldest daughter.

Two days later, Norman's mother came to fetch him. When he saw her, he felt let down.

During our separation she had changed slowly in my memory, becoming saint-like, calm, aloof and sedate. Now suddenly confronted with her in the flesh, she was a stranger, earthy and vigorous, but almost unrecognizable, and I was disappointed to find that I was less excited and pleased to see her again than I had expected to be, and unhappy with the self-sufficiency that I had developed.[10]

He went for his last sad walk on Pen-lan with Aunt Li. They held hands, he remembered, and she told him that she was being sent away "on holiday". "She clenched her lips until they disappeared," he writes, "and this, although she had ceased to cry while we were together, showed me that she was unhappy. ... I didn't want either aunt to be sent away, but it seemed unfair that it had to be her, and not Polly."[11]

It was the end of what he later called, in an unpublished piece, "the cloud cuckoo-land of my youth".[12]

Eight decades later, almost all that we can know about Norman's year in Carmarthen comes from Norman himself. To a biographer these are not the best periods to write about. This is not necessarily because the subject is unreliable, although it's true that Norman *is* unreliable: he was a writer after all, and a writer of the Romantic or at least subjective stamp that realises meaning and truth are a scattered dissemination of signifiers, and that the writer's job is to take advantage of that. It is because biographers like to have witnesses through whom they can compare, refute and confirm accounts on the way to documenting their own portrait. (If biographers have any rights, they surely have the right to scatter their own choice of signifiers.) A further reason I'm not drawn to write at great length about Norman's Carmarthen year is because he has written about it himself so sharply, so mercilessly, so shrewdly. The first twenty-five pages of *Jackdaw Cake* are, to paraphrase Scott Fitzgerald's phrase about youth's "eternal carnival by the sea", a marvellous carnival by the Tywi, though in a different register from Fitzgerald's dreams. The collage he creates of so many improbable parts – his grandfather's fighting cocks and scandalous affair, the miners stoned at Llanstephan, Li's devastating and immediately forgotten secret, the aunts' momentary truce as the jackdaw cake is baked, the episode of the poison-pen letters and the failed suicide attempt with its frozen instant of nocturnal human chaos and final detail, "the smell of Jockey Club and urine", before the writer turns away – is a small masterpiece of family dysfunction observed. No incident is without its ironic coda, no character without their luggage of ridicule or unwanted pathos waiting to pop its locks.

A last reason, perhaps, why Carmarthen doesn't really call for further interpretation than Norman's own is that it was not, in truth, much of a formative experience. Possibly the only thing Norman added to his character during this time was a honing of his talent for self-concealment. To his picture of Wales we could add that it strongly affected his idea of himself: he saw himself afterwards as Welsh, not English. He often came back to the area around Carmarthen to race motorcycles, to see his aunt Margaret, to birdwatch, after he left the army to seek, three years in a row, that cloud cuckoo-land of youth. He also developed a habit later in his writing of giving the name *Llanstephan Castle* to almost every ship he travelled on.

But all that happened to him in south-west Wales had already happened in Enfield: however teetering on the insane, it was a consolidating experience, an antechamber, a waiting room for his further youth in Enfield. It may, later on, have reminded him in distilled form of the great lesson of his childhood and adolescence: that almost nothing any adult did for him when he was young did him any good, which certainly contributed to his absolute insistence – as soon as he was old enough to insist – on managing his own life in every possible way.

And then he went on to the grammar school in Enfield, and when it got to the stage that they were to matriculate we all thought Lewis would shine. But he didn't, as so often with people I've noticed, people who get right, wherever they get in the end.

Gwen Merrington

I recall how he would relish certain phrases as if savouring them, roll them around his tongue. He once put me on the spot by asking, "Are you speaking, literally, metaphorically or figuratively?"

Gwen Merrington

When he came back from Wales he broke his leg, it was said, getting robins' eggs . . . in our village, you never touched a robin's egg or nest. But Lewis dared and broke his leg because he went too far.

Eric Nicholls

He was on his bicycle and he hooked himself onto a lorry to pull himself along and got dragged under the lorry and had a big chunk out of his heel.

Lesley Lewis

When Norman used to ride home, he'd come down Bridgenhall Road, which was an unmade road, choosing the grass verge which would take him right near the front gates of the houses, and of course that did annoy the grown-ups. You'd hear a terrific roar from the motorcycle.

Eric Nicholls

We hadn't walked more than ten minutes when the witch doctor stops us and he pulls out a Luger, and I think, This is it, we're finished. And Norman says to me, "Oh, he's very surprised I'm not carrying a gun because we're going into dangerous territory." So I think, This is really, I need this, you know. . . . The witch doctor gives Norman the gun and he points to a tree, and Norman says, "He wants to see if I'm a good shot", and Norman pegs this target and hits it. I mean, Norman didn't look like he could handle anything more than a ballpoint pen, you know, and he gets the gun and he shoots the thing.

David Montgomery

3

REJECTED WORLDS

"The treasure of a happy life can only be secured by desperate deeds"
Chinese proverb

WHEN, in February 1970, on a trail out of the Mexican village of San Andrès, Norman borrowed the shaman's handgun for target practice – a 9mm pearl-handled Star automatic by his description, not a Luger – he was at home. In England he owned a Star .22 automatic pistol with silencer and a semi-automatic Beretta .22 rifle, also silenced. He did not give them up until firearms legislation in Britain began to restrict gun ownership after the Hungerford massacre in 1987 (when a gun-obsessive with a legally licensed collection walked out one afternoon and shot sixteen people). In the 1950s and 1960s Norman used a rifle for poaching on Deeside, and in London, at parties at his flat in Orchard Street opposite Selfridges, one entertainment he offered was a shooting gallery, with a target set up on the sitting-room wall for guests to fire at from the dining room next door. (He was a keen diver and for variety sometimes offered a speargun instead.) He carried a pistol when he was travelling alone, and on holidays with his family. In the mid-1960s he began to leave it at home at Finchingfield, but there was always an air rifle behind the coats in the downstairs cloakroom. In autumn he would set up hides at the end of his long garden at Finchingfield and wait at dusk with his son Gawaine for the pheasants to come in off the fields. He was a passionate birdwatcher and signed up some of his children for membership of the Royal Society for the Protection of Birds, but he shot sparrows too for beheading his crocuses, and jays for attacking young birds and owls. Cats he regarded as his particular enemies. Their habit of killing for fun – he himself always had a reason for killing, he claimed: he was either hunting or he was keeping the natural balance – infuriated him. Local cats would be kept under surveillance, discouraged from straying into his garden, then, if other means failed to keep them away, bushwhacked with a silent shot from his first-floor bathroom window. He was not an unfailing marksman: one cat, after several efforts to scare it or otherwise keep it from killing ducklings, was designated for a bullet, dispatched and stuffed under a pile of grass cuttings for later burial. But when Norman came back to bury the animal, it had disappeared. Anxiety about his neighbours' reactions followed, until, a day later, the cat was seen in apparently perfect health ambling down the driveway. In the course of a tentative conversation its owner admitted her pet had been feeling "a bit peaky recently".

Why would a writer renowned for the pastoral urgency of his writing, and a pacifist attitude to the world, show such enthusiasm for guns? The answer probably lies in his early adolescence. Whatever else they represented, guns for Norman symbolised in their borderline lawlessness a version of freedom. As a youth cast out of the Forty Hill tribe, developing the marked identity of the insecure outsider, his hidden lack of confidence was beginning to be masked by a carefully displayed arrogance. Later, "there was a side to Norman," Lesley Lewis says, "that if he decided he wanted to do something, he would just do it. It didn't matter whether it was always strictly legal or not."[1] This side of his character chimed with his journalistic instincts, serving him effectively in his pursuit of interviews with Viet Minh fighters and Indian-hunting evangelical missionaries. In his adolescence it signalled the start of his insistence on managing his own life, and the first expression of a (sometimes dogmatic) sense of freedom and consciousness. In Cartesian terms, the writer whose public self would eventually be displayed in a combination of often comical self-deprecation and effacement and mandarin-like attention to good manners concealed a private self whose motto could be, I do absolutely what I like, therefore I am.

The first mention of a gun is in his early adolescence. "Norman always had extraordinary things," Eric Nicholls remembers. "His father bought him a very powerful airgun, and Norman became a crack shot with that. He would hit a lamp-post 200 yards away, and of course he was keen on demonstrating that to us."[2] Eric's sister Gwen remembers Norman being given the gun after breaking his leg when he got back from Wales, and how keen he was on taking potshots in the orchard. Back on his feet, with his bicycle, collie and air rifle, there would have been something of a saturnine William Brown about him, without the Outlaws. The one close friend Norman had at this time was another of the Nicholls children, Bill. Their friendship, Gwen remembers, "was mostly to do with reading, stimulating each other with reading at an age when they started thinking about things apart from just being children. Bill was a lovely contrast, steady and kind, to Lewis who was very much into promoting himself as different. [Norman] never joined in with our games, he would just appear, he was always there like a shadow, as an observer. He would appear with his collie dog on the fringe of what we were doing, obviously he was lonely."[3] She feels her brother modified Norman's view of the world. Bill Nicholls, who left Lavender Road school at fourteen to work as an apprentice dental mechanic, was left-wing and as a young working man precociously well read in the class polarities of the 1920s. Without his influence, Norman "would have been right-wing from his upbringing". Gwen herself had understood the situation that faced most working-class children. "When I was about thirteen, during the last year at school, the penny dropped. I remember realising that our stratum of society was really being sub-educated in readiness to be manual workers."

Norman, a couple of social calibrations above the Nicholls children, had had the benefit of his parents' relative prosperity and loving attention. At the price of a little immersion in the icy waters of rejection, those factors carried him across the barrier of social determinism and, with his intelligence, secured the one escape available, a scholarship to a secondary school where the ideals of education (at least for boys) were more sincerely observed. Enfield Grammar School has warm, russet-coloured Tudor architecture; its roots go back even further, to a chantry school established under licence in 1471 from King Edward IV. The chantry belonged to the parish church of St Andrew: it was a place where a few boys would be instructed by the priest in "grammar" – Latin not English – and enough plainsong to be able to assist in the responses at Mass. The grammar school that exists today was founded eighty-seven years later, in 1558. A year earlier, Francis Segar's *The Schoole of Vertue and Booke of good Nourture for Chyldren and Youth* had contained the reminder that

> Experience doth teche, and shewe to the playne,
> That many to honour by learninge attayne,
> That were of byrthe but simple and base.

When Norman arrived in September 1920, the shadow of religious influence at the school was remote. He benefited from its relatively liberal teaching, its large playing fields and leafy grounds, and its distance from Forty Hill (his attackers were unlikely to ambush him), but was never particularly partisan about the school that awarded him a scholarship. He admired the French master, Henri Le Bas, and never selected his Grammar School years as a satirical target except to mock lightly the school's motto, *"Tant que je puis"*, translating it as "I will give you as much as you can possibly take".[4] He was already an obsessive reader of both books and the world around him when he arrived: when children can't read the world emotionally through relationships with other children, they find other ways of reading it, violence, withdrawal and excessive rationality among them. Excellent, if eccentric, deconstructors of the world, children will read and read and read to try to discover why it is like it is.

Norman's permanent watchfulness and reticence slackened at the grammar school. His five years there were stamped by stability: they gave him a breathing-space, a chance to inspect the world, to begin to draw his place in it. He was prone to stammer and had become asthmatic, but both conditions gradually eased. If there was a recurrence of violence, he never mentioned it. The grammar school would have contained a less brutalised class of schoolboy, and with his home in the Forty Hill Freehold he was on the Enfield side of the village and didn't have to negotiate the class-ridden streets of two-up, two-downs to get to school. Growing taller, he was less easy to intimidate. And he knew how to keep his head down. "I had adopted a posture of non-commitment like a personal camouflage," he writes. "I never argued, seldom offered a point of view."[5] The end of persecution was a reprieve. He learned to stand back, to underplay himself, to detach himself now to his advantage. "He was a figurehead but not a ringleader," Eric Nicholls says. "Somehow nobody attached themselves to him. . . . He used to cycle to the grammar school in the gutter – between the kerb and the road there was the gutter way – he would cycle the mile and a half, mile and three-quarters without coming out of the gutter. [That was another] one of his stunts."[6] He underplayed his academic ability:

his scholarship was worth £60, "an incredible amount of money then. It should have paid for my education and books and things, but I bought a motorbike and scraped through everything else."[7] A truer picture is that while he had absorbed the lesson of showing too much intelligence, he was also putting down markers of his future interests, showing aptitude for French and German, winning a history prize. He later gave a typically surreal version of a conversation with the headmaster, Mr E M Eagles, when called to his study to be told about this prize:

Eagles: Lewis, do you read books?
NL: Occasionally, sir.
Eagles: What kind of books do you read?
NL: If I can get them, books of science.
Eagles: Why have you said that? You have no feeling for literature, have you? Your spelling is atrocious. Are there any books here [pointing to a row of books] that you perhaps like?
NL: Well I see a book of astronomy over there, sir, I think I would like to read that very much indeed.
Eagles: Well, we will see about that.

His eventual prize was a copy of Wordsworth's *Collected Works*. (He claimed that he took it immediately to a bookseller who told him nobody read poetry any more, and had to add a shilling of his own money to buy for himself – not much of a book of science – a hand-decorated copy of *Maria Marten or The Murder in the Red Barn*.)[8]

At home the scene was also calm, but newly irrational. Left to their devices and to the ghosts of three dead sons during his absence in Wales, Norman's parents had become spiritualists. Richard Lewis, as the result of his wife's ambitions more than his own, had even become a medium with a growing north London following. Norman's account in *Jackdaw Cake* of his parents' revelation of belief and his father's uncomfortable acceptance of fame is a comic sonata accompanied by a detailed anatomy of English suburban eccentricity: the peculiar English fusion of the exotic and bathetic that has bred generations of constructors of the Statue of Liberty from milk-bottle tops, and plumbers who claim to be Tibetan lamas. "Suddenly the quiet, rather dismal little house tucked away behind the orchards was full of hushed, soft-footed activity, and had acquired faint churchy scents. Gentle smiling people came and went, exuding sympathy and understanding; all of them extremely kind to me." Monty's death in 1916 had been the last straw for his parents. Losing their elder son when they might have thought they were beyond the reach of any more tragedy had propelled Richard and Louisa into the embrace of a belief system cushioned at every turn by soft furnishings, the softest and most comforting its conviction that the souls of the dead are always with us, only waiting for our contact. Spiritualism's doctrine was enjoying popular resurgence after a war that had bereaved most families in the nation and left the pro-war established Churches impotent to console. Few spiritualists took their beliefs as far as the Lewises and built chapels in their gardens, but spiritualism was far from being the mocked tendency it is today. Materialists and idealists were equally attracted to its rituals: several men of science who started by subjecting its phenomena to scrutiny ended up being converted, including the chemist and physicist Sir William Crookes and Darwin's brilliant but self-effacing co-theorist Alfred Russel Wallace, who believed that natural selection on its own could not explain artistic, musical or mathematical genius, or the higher consciousness of wit and philosophical reflection. Crookes too, in his 1874 study of several mediums, believed that he witnessed, among other events, the moving of bodies at a distance, levitation and the appearance of phantom figures.

Norman notes in his autobiography that he found it hard to reject out of hand the message of the kindly, soft-spoken visitors who tramped through his parents' front room. Nor, as a twelve-year-old in the second form at Enfield Grammar, could he refute the findings of top scientists or the endorsement of as illustrious a figure as Sir Arthur Conan Doyle. Even in his descriptions of the "phenomena" he witnessed he is unable to put every one down to fraud or conjuration. His main objection to the seances and other experiments he attended was their deadly mixture of embarrassment and dullness. He underwent an induction at the hands of a visiting clairvoyant, a Mrs Carmen Flint: he took an instant dislike to Mrs Flint for her abrupt and officious manner and her way of pouncing on the Welsh rarebit and cup-cakes. The main purpose of this gathering was to attempt a contact between the French master at the Grammar School, Henri Le Bas, and his wife, and their son Jean-Paul, tragically blown to pieces at Verdun. An experiment with the planchette, a small plank equipped with wheels and a vertically held pencil that was supposed to roll about and write under pressure, produced an almost illegible "*oui*" to Mr Le Bas's question, "*Jean-Paul, es-tu là?*" Mrs Flint's subsequent demonstration of clairvoyance produced a doubtful image of a young man with a limp, holding up a toothbrush, but the Le Bas were more than satisfied. "My son was very fastidious about his appearance. He cleaned his teeth three times a day."

The Lewises' renown grew, the number of seances increased. Norman's faith did not. When the Sunday congregations could not be accommodated in the house, they were moved into the garden while the service was broadcast from the kitchen. On one occasion, when Norman's belief "was weakening but before all my illusions had collapsed", the medium – Mrs Flint or possibly another – saw a boy about seventeen years old. "'He is wearing a peaked cap, and a short jacket, and is carrying what appears to be a musical instrument. Will someone claim him?'

"It was still hard for me to articulate in the presence of adults," Norman says, "but this was an occasion of such urgency that it was impossible not to speak up, and I forced the words to come. 'It's my brother,' I said. 'He used to play in a band.'"

"Have you a message for him?" the medium asked.

"I would like to ask him where he is," I said.

"He tells you he is in another place. He wishes you and his mother and father not to go to Lavender Hill to look for him. He is not there. There must be no more flowers."

My disappointment was crushing. My brother, once frank and open, had become guarded and evasive, sounding as I would have imagined like a prisoner answering a visitor's questions in the presence of a warder. Another issue came into this which I had already taken up with my mother. Why should my brother, who had been an excellent musician in life, and whose favourite composer was Bach, now be attracted, as she assured me he would be, by the simple and even sickly melodies of her musical box?[9]

So it went on. Louisa took a course in "psychic unfoldment", of which a feature was daily meditation in a front room-cum-temple that sounds strangely like a forerunner of modern suburban homes with New Age leanings: it contained a Tibetan prayer-flag, wind chimes, joss-sticks, and a lingam, "the purpose of which [my mother] was doubtful". There was not much constituency for the Lewises' ministry in the immediate vicinity, among the workers of Forty Hill. "When my father died in 1918," Eric Nicholls says, "Mrs Lewis came to mother and she said, 'Would you like to speak to your husband, I'll bring a medium and you'll be able to speak to him?' And mother had *nothing* to do with it, nothing at all."[10] But as word spread, 343 Carterhatch Lane became the twice-weekly destination of growing bands of followers, from Ruislip to Ilford. Norman's initial curiosity was rapidly replaced by a sense of duty and then deep boredom as he experienced the dullness of the dead and above all their lack of pagan spontaneity ("'Do the initials GHW mean anything to you?' 'They belong to my aunt Heather.' 'And the name "Rosedale"?' 'That was the house she lived in.' 'She asks if you remember Torquay, and the boat trip?'").

Many of the revelations from the other world were on the level of messages scribbled in haste on holiday postcards by writers who could think of nothing much to say. I soon discovered that the spirits of the dead had no sense of humour, and there was a terrible flatness, a lack of enthusiasm in their communications suggestive of convalescence, fatigue, even boredom. Sometimes messages from beyond the grave were fragmentary and meaningless like the random sentences of radio hams, intent only in testing their equipment. Once when a sitter put the point-blank question, "What is it like in the Beyond?", he received an answer Hemingway might have given. "It is good."[11]

Norman's experience of his parents' spiritualism estranged him from them and helped bring on his early independence. Spiritualism's saturating influence on family life, on his mother's outlook and behaviour and every decision, apparently, temporal as well as spiritual – her spirit guide "also advised her on household matters, and had been recently responsible for the redecoration of the middle room, which seemed to me to have been carried out in deplorable taste" – eventually annoyed him to the point of revenge. After his parents' discovery that he possessed a "glowing and vibrant" aura and their immediate subsequent attempts to induce him to become a medium himself, he took to sabotage. "Lewis used to get on the roof of the little chapel they'd got and make all sorts of appropriate noises. He got great pleasure out of that. . . . He would get up and rattle tin cans at the right moment."[12] But it was probably because it dismantled his relationship with his father that spiritualism later became a literary target. Despite Richard Lewis's becoming a medium, Norman clung to the thought that his father wanted somehow to stay aloof from the proceedings, particularly when they were under the control of his wife or another woman. Yet his father had not become just any kind of medium, but a trance medium, a bill-topping role in the spiritualist programme. In his description of his first experience of his father in a trance, the writer's usually bullet-proof sense of the absurd deserts him: the calamitous event left Norman nothing but "embarrassed, feeling myself in some way personally affected by my father's gross loss of dignity, and [I] longed for the strength of character that would have enabled me to get up and leave the room". Twelve participants were present, hands touching in a circle as usual. Monsieur and Madame Le Bas were again among them, hoping for a further sign from their son. The seance was conducted under controlled conditions of calm and low light, but something went wrong with Richard Lewis's channelling, connected to his excitable and inarticulate temperament.

Incense smoke curled from a joss-stick, the musical box had tinkled into silence, and my father mouthed and blabbered, watched by the sitters, of which little but expectant faces showed in the lamp-lit gloom. There was spittle on my father's lips and chin, he opened his mouth as if half-strangled, and an incoherent gush of words came from his throat: the voices of men, of women and young children, some calm, some shrill, some argumentative; the sound of drunken brawling, the snatch of a sea shanty, then the mixture of voices again, none separable from the other. . . .

Although my mother had explained to me that my father was highly esteemed for his gifts, his development was unsatisfactory, as he had no control over the spirits who spoke through him. Hence the chaos at this moment, the great disorderly queue of souls all demanding to be heard. . . .

Her method of dealing with this crisis was to stand over my father and wave her arms in his face with stern commands, whenever an unacceptable – and often ribald – voice became audible, of, "Step out, friend. Please step out." This took effect, the babel quietened leaving a residue of disconnected words, of sense and nonsense drifting into soft muttering, then silence.[13]

The lucid moment following his mother's arm-waving didn't last long before it was brushed aside by new invading voices and she had to step in again. Thirty years later, when he went to the Curzon cinema in Mayfair to see Kurosawa's *Rashomon* for the first time, he identified the sounds produced by Kurosawa's medium as the same "inhuman" sounds his father had made – although Richard Lewis's outpouring seems not so much inhuman as like Rabelais' "frozen words" left behind after the great battle between the Arimaspians and the Cloud-riders,[14] thrown down and melting, "barbarous sounds . . . some terrifying words, and others rather unpleasant to look at". The trance ultimately coalesced in a traumatic conclusion as "suddenly and with absolute clarity a voice called out, 'Papa! Où êtes-vous?'" Norman remembered the thin consolation of the moment sixty years later. "The only comfort it could offer to Le Bas and his wife seemed a cold one. Even if their son had reached them across the barrier of death, he seemed to have come as a wandering spirit, lost, displaced, searching as desperately for them as they for him. ... Mr and Mrs Le Bas had stolen away into the kitchen where they fell into each other's arms."

Norman's portrait of his father in his autobiography is comical, affectionate and acidic, coloured with the restraint of an unfulfilled relationship. Though Norman wanted to admire his father, and succeeded at first, he quickly overtook him in insight and discovered that his father had nothing to tell him about the adult world. Their relationship became distant in his early adolescence, a distance accentuated because until then Norman had had (apart from his year in Wales) a loving and indulgent father to himself. They had spent as much time together as they could, walking, identifying wildlife, hunting for birds' eggs, in summer going to the fairs from where, with his strangely constant good luck, Richard Lewis would come back loaded with cheap china prizes from the hoopla stalls. As Norman later wrote, his father's childlike personality made him an excellent companion for a child, but as soon as he was old enough to voice such insights to himself, his father as a figure of admiration dissolved until no father remained, only the unhappy figure who increasingly needed his son's protection.

In the odd way in which the public world lags behind the private, Richard Lewis remained a businesslike, if idiosyncratic, pharmacist. His Southbury Road shop in Enfield Town thrived. He was famous for his advice, and for forthrightness with his customers. If a customer irritated him, particularly if they had a remediable defect (body odour, halitosis), he would stonily order them out of his shop. (Norman inherited and on rare occasions fully displayed his father's ability to freeze out people.) Curiously Richard Lewis's scepticism about science, allied to his central belief that faith was the most important component of the bodily condition, increased his popularity. Barely interested in his business and uninterested in concealing the fact from customers, his attitude to proprietary medicines was summed up by a shop-window display that contained several dozen books on pharmacology and medicine, gathered around a box of Beechams Pills and a card printed with

the words "I read all these, to sell this". His answer to the thousands
of despised pharmaceutical products that stocked his shelves was his
own tonic, made of garlic-flavoured water and quinine. Produced for
next to nothing, bottled and sold to customers who insisted on leaving
his shop with some kind of remedy, even after he had laughed scorn
on their original prescription, Lewis's elixir generated a steady income
and ultimately a franchise request. It paid for the all too solid flesh of
the Beacon of Light church in the Lewises' back garden, for Norman's
many gifts from his father and for his trips to France in the school
holidays. He crossed the Channel several times on exchange visits:
Gwen Merrington remembers that when one of his exchange partners
visited Forty Hill, Norman told her he had brought the boy "to observe
the wildlife", i.e. the other children.

Richard Lewis's improbable business success, however, did not save
him from sheer incongruity, from a country, a profession, a language,
a material world in which he was increasingly out of place. Towards
the end of his life he was slipping into mental illness. Now, during
Norman's adolescence, his instability manifested itself mostly in shy
eccentricities. His reluctant trance seances were well known, and he
enjoyed hypnotising the birds in his aviary by stroking them until he
could lay them down immobile on their sides; once he carried out with
Norman's help a mass planting of mistletoe in Enfield, believing that
he would thus dispel the crucial emotional difference, caused by the
absence of mistletoe in England, between the Celts and (his expression)
"the Saxons". The result was a mass mystification of Enfield's residents, faced with an epidemic of mistletoe in their borough. His icy
dismissal of clients was part lifelong linguistic inadequacy, part defence
mechanism, as much as rudeness. For a long time his garbled speech
did not affect his professional reputation or his balance sheet, but by
the time Norman left Enfield Grammar his father was drinking heavily
and possibly self-medicating with other drugs.

The memories Norman gives of his father in *Jackdaw Cake* are
gentler than his remarks about him later in his life. "I went and worked
for my father [after leaving Enfield Grammar], which once again was
a grotesque experience," Norman said in a conversation about his
childhood. "He was an alcoholic and also a spiritualist healer. What
can you do with a father like that?"[15] Gwen Merrington remembers
that when Norman was in his teens his father went through an odd
phase. Norman would go to meet him and escort him home with

considerable embarrassment. His father would be talking wildly to himself and waving his arms. "The opinion generally held was that he was on drugs ... and I think his father must have dabbled in morphine. He didn't always have to come down Bridgenhall Road but did so often, with his father waving and gesticulating and talking to himself. Norman would just be leading him quietly down the road."[16] If he was embarrassed, he was also protective of his father. Gwen noticed his fondness for both his parents, despite their conspicuous capacity to produce embarrassment, particularly noticeable to the children at the Lewises' yearly firework display, where "we and he would be indulging his father, who would become peculiarly incoherent with excitement".

Although Norman maintained his spiky, slightly arrogant distance from the other Forty Hill children, she saw that "he had a compassionate side ... but perhaps at that time he didn't know he had it". Later, Norman compared his own life with his father's and concluded that boredom was the killer: Richard Lewis's mismatch of character and circumstances eventually left him without interests and fatally unengaged with life. "My father suffered from boredom so badly he used to groan with it. I used to say, 'What are you groaning about now?' and he'd say, 'I'm bored.'"[17] At the age of sixty-nine Richard Lewis retired from business and within a year was dead from cancer. His life, in the end, was almost tragicomically unfortunate. Louisa's equally ill-adapted character probably played a part in his tragedy: Norman's eldest son Ito remembers being told by his mother Ernestina, Norman's first wife, that one of the reasons Richard became an alcoholic was because his devoutly spiritualist wife "withheld his conjugal rights". (Louisa was reticent in every direction on sexual matters: she also insisted that Norman sleep with the window open, so that he would not become too comfortable and get "nasty thoughts".)

The becoming years are in a sense the most interesting in a life: the most unlikely when looked back on later, the most formative *and* the most enigmatic when all the possible futures are viewed through their lens. Norman's life between twelve and sixteen was crowded, at school, at home, in the holidays when he travelled to France or came back to entertain, as well as he could, his French exchange partner at home. At weekends he was busy helping his father bottle the R G Lewis elixir. But it was the wrong kind of crowded. He was too old to enjoy his father's arrested enthusiasms for walks and bird-nesting any more, and a few years too young to seek full-blown escape in the testosterone-influenced paths of young men.

Yet for all his complaints about the cruelty and tedium of Forty Hill life, at this stage it offered him a hinterland, physical and sociological, that he could explore freely and in the exploration fashion an outline for his later implacable passions: obsessive escape, the glorious surfaces of the natural world, and the politics of rich and underdog. Three people were instrumental. One of them was the younger Bill Nicholls, Gwen's brother, who argued with him and toned up his political sense. The other two were members of the Bowles family: Colonel Sir Henry Ferryman Bowles ("Ferrryman", Norman enunciated sarcastically later, rolling the rs), the owner of Forty Hall, and his younger brother, the famous gardener Augustus ("Gussie") Bowles who lived at Myddelton House at Bull's Cross, beyond Maidens Bridge. The two houses were adjacent with enough rolling Bowles land between them to keep them a couple of miles apart. Norman wandered at will. He had first met the Colonel before he went to Wales, by his own account trudging up the long drive to the Hall and ringing the bell, hoping to speak to the butler to ask permission to go bird-nesting on the estate. Sir Henry himself, coming to the door, had waved his butler away, confiding to Norman in a stammer that not only was bird-nesting allowed but that he would have liked to come with him and show him the best places, except that there was a meeting of the Primrose League[18] that afternoon which he was obliged to address.

At ten or eleven Norman may have confused the personal and political, but he disentangled them soon enough. He later wrote more on the subject of Sir Henry's repressive reign over Forty Hill than he did about any other English subject: as though he wanted to use him as a lightning-conductor for his dislike of the inhumanity and brutalism that were assumed components of the English class system in the first half of the twentieth century. Sir Henry's paternal kindness did not stop Norman from describing him later as "small and unimpressive" and "rather foolish". The Bowles family's rule over the class-ridden and static society of Forty Hill was catastrophically negative, the main reason why Forty Hill possessed no communal activities apart from Sir Henry's annual Primrose League fête and was devoid, as a place, of any joy, vitality, or sense of shared culture. The royal chase that the village had once been part of had been the first leveller, a great parkland purged of homesteads and hamlets. The deer that were introduced as targets could look after themselves but the pheasants could not, and the game-keepers culled everything that threatened their rearing for the gun. Victorian plant-hunters had then removed many of the botanical varieties – royal ferns, orchids, lilies of the valley – that lingered. "Here," Norman wrote, "we were watched by no unseen presences. Who could have imagined Arthur or the enchanter Merlin walking amongst these trees, or Druids working their magic in these fields?"[19] Fifteen thousand acres of stagnant uniformity remained, and Sir Henry Bowles and his class were guilty. A composite picture of the baronet from three descriptions by Norman shows the depth of his antagonism.

The land and its hamlets were owned and ruled by Colonel Sir Henry Ferryman Bowles, a sporadically benevolent tyrant who would not have been out of place in Tsarist Russia. . . . Isolation in relatively empty country, crossed with byroads going nowhere in particular, had never quite released the village from the previous century. An early photograph of it could have been of Russia in about 1913, with small houses of all shapes scattered about a ragged little prairie remaining deep in mud or dust according to the season. Livings in Forty Hill, too, had always been scraped, and this, added to its cut-off location, made the place a sort of museum of outworn social attitudes that could only be remedied by more freedom of movement and more cash in pockets.

Sir Henry owned everything down to the last rut in the road and the last tiny cabin perched over the cesspit at the bottom of narrow village gardens. . . .[20]

[He] was a phenomenon of English rural life hardly changed since the invention of the open-field system of agriculture. He had represented Enfield as a Tory MP longer than anyone could remember – although he had never made a speech in parliament – he wielded huge and uncontested power, paid the lowest wages in the county, and was understood to possess a harem of three young, gracious and well-bred girls. Nobody in the village begrudged him these. It was assumed that the ruling classes, compelled by custom to eat meat every day, suffered sexual desires from which the peasantry were spared by a diet which included meat only once a week and limited sexual activity to Saturday nights.[21]

The squire was a small, neat, fussy man, with a white moustache, sincere blue eyes, and a monocle hanging like a decoration from his lapel. . . . He was a barrister of the Inner Temple who had never held a brief, and an honorary colonel who had seen no service in the War. In manner, this representative of privilege and sterility of purpose was genial and conciliatory. He enjoyed praising those who served him and he took a paternal interest in their lives. Like some powerful Sicilian capo-mafia he kept order in the village by settling quarrels instantly and without cost to the disputants, who were simply called to the

Hall to state their cases and listen to his decision[,][22] although by comparison
Giuseppe Genco Russo, a much larger-scale landowner and head of the Sicilian
Mafia whose character and doings I had occasion to study at a much later
date, was a progressive and socially responsible man, and I cannot imagine
that Giuseppe would have recommended – as Sir Henry did, speaking on the
bench – the reintroduction of man-traps to put an end to poaching. Both men
rewarded their friends and dealt with their enemies after their own manner.
. . . If a man displeased [Sir Henry] – as for example in the case of a tenant
who put up an election poster for the Liberal candidate – Sir Henry's factor
paid him a visit, not armed in Sicilian style with a sawn-off shotgun but in
the English fashion of the period with the no less deadly threat of destitution.
Ninety-five per cent of the electors of Forty Hill, few of them believing in the
true secrecy of the ballot, cast their votes for Sir Henry. . . .[23]

There is no proof that Sir Henry kept a harem. His entourage
included a number of maidenly young women "visiters" who were,
according to Norman, the bane of Goat Lane's hard-pressed wives and
mothers. Accosted in their kitchens, they were forced to display their
poverty and tired hair to these unwanted do-gooders, and to endure
their vacuous small talk. An American attorney also remembers his
parents' account of meeting Sir Henry on travels in Europe before the
Second World War and subsequently visiting Forty Hall, where the
baronet made clear his attraction to the wife.[24] In an unpublished piece
impassioned by disapproval Norman went further, attributing to Sir
Henry an episode in which an orange tree, planted at the Hall and
tenderly nursed by the estate gardeners, had been persuaded to produce
a single, miraculous fruit. A few days later Sir Henry wanted to show
the tree to Norman's father, but its barely ripe fruit had gone, picked
by a village boy and, as they discovered, thrown down in disgust a few
yards away at the first bite. Caught, the terrified boy was asked gently
by Sir Henry if the orange was bitter, then sent on his way. "'What
can you expect?' he said to my father." By Norman's account this was
the moment when his father finally realised that Bowles had tricked
him (and by extension every one of his serfs) "into the belief that he
had to do with a foolish, but on the whole, loveable eccentric, but now
he began to suspect the cold intelligence and the calculation behind
this iron self-control, and he was chilled by its inhumanity".[25] In *Jackdaw
Cake* the orange tree episode, more plausibly, takes place between
Norman himself and Sir Henry's brother Augustus Bowles, the famous
gardener and indulgent patron of many Forty Hill boys.

Bowles had reinforced his fief by becoming Enfield's member of parliament in 1889 – in 1900 he won the seat with the slogan (how it would have amused Norman's sense of irony!) "Bowles, your Friend and Neighbour". Bowles lost in 1906 to a Liberal candidate, but regained the seat in 1918. He left parliamentary politics in 1922. It is unlikely that he retired because he saw change coming, and through the 1920s and 1930s he continued to be the grey eminence of Conservative candidates. But with Ramsay MacDonald's first Labour government in December 1923 and the election of Enfield's first Labour MP, William Henderson,[26] a chink of open resistance had appeared. A dozen years later, when Stanley Baldwin, a friend of Bowles's who had been at Harrow school with him, visited Forty Hill on the occasion of the Primrose League fête in the summer of 1935 having recently become prime minister for the third time, and delivered his dull but famous "Torch of Freedom" speech, hecklers chimed in with the next sentence whenever he paused for breath.

At the start of the 1920s, any such revolutionary action was only dreamt. The air of Forty Hill remained suffused with the heavy perfume of class, the rich man in his castle, the poor man at his gate, their estate ordered by God (Norman remembers Baldwin as having, on an earlier visit, quoted the whole verse to the villagers). Norman was in his early teens, but he was quietly accumulating a private lexicon of class dislikes that he carried around with him all his life. His son Ito describes his view of the upper-class English as "really venomous". Their meanness was a political act. "He used to say to me," Ito says, "'Why is it that they're so mean? These people have got masses of money and they're incredibly mean and avaricious.' This was a thing that always amazed him."[27] Asked in 1996 for his view on how history was made, Norman simply answered, "History is – these things have to be stated in a very succinct form, in a couple of sentences – the robbery of the poor by the rich."[28]

One member of the Bowles family was exempt from his horror. Sir Henry Bowles' younger brother, Augustus (E A) Bowles, is described by Norman instead as "Enfield's most interesting native … a good painter … a deeply thinking man". E A Bowles was England's most famous gentleman gardener; he was also known to every boy in Forty Hill. Norman's and the other boys' keenness to take refuge in the grounds of Myddelton House was the result of Augustus's eccentric benevolence. The younger Bowles, like his brother, was not a social innovator. "Philosophically committed to the existing order of things", in Norman's words, he had become a Sunday school teacher at Jesus Church at sixteen, and his chief concern was for the village boys' religious education – not the girls', and the distinction led later to assumptions about his sexuality – but in return for their attendance and companionship he was happy to allow them absolute liberty to roam on his land.

"He was ... very much liked by everyone despite his proclivities," Norman remembered later. "What was interesting was that they may have succeeded in not noticing that these things went on. So if anybody – rare – had anything to say against Augustus Bowles ... people would be very angry. They just wouldn't listen to the fact that he was always surrounded by small boys."[29] "Gussie" gave confirmation classes, and confirmands and choirboys were led on Sunday afternoon walks, followed by tea, along his "dead river" – a winding length of the New River that had been severed to straighten it – looking for wildflowers and wild birds. In midwinter there was skating on his lakes: Gussie possessed dozens of pairs of skates.

The set piece of Norman's own account of Gussie Bowles is the final confirmation class, dealing with the business of sex, in which as illustration Gussie would show the suddenly alert boys a pair of French dolls powered by a tiny spirit-fuelled engine to which he would put a match, setting them on their climactic journey. Norman, "almost noted for being heterosexual at a very young age",[30] did not attract Gussie, but his association with him was the start of his interest in botany. As an example of Bowles's achievement, a few years before he began collecting in the 1890s, there were sixty-five named species and varieties of crocus. By 1901, he was already growing the astonishing number of 135. Norman pays his generosity ungrudging tribute. "He was ... a man who saw deep into the minds of boys, offering in return for their companionship the run of his magnificent garden, fishing in the section of the New River running through it, a game of billiards at any time in his sports pavilion, and a Bank Holiday entertainment three times a year, with organized games, more fishing with rods and tackle provided, and a lavish tea."[31] There was always a party around Christmas. A letter Bowles wrote to one of his older "boys" on New Year's Day of 1925 (Bowles was then fifty-nine years old) shows the incredible lengths he went to in his involvement with them.

I have been working *hard* for a week . . . making paper insects for a children's party. It comes off tomorrow & I hope the study floor will get its last basketful of chips. The tea table will be a mass of crawly creepies of gorgeous colouring & flights of butterflies & spiders hanging from the ceiling. Some huge fire-flies with coloured glass balls of the Xmas-tree-fruit type for the fire – are really quite pretty, & a blue & tinsel cockchafer is a dazzling affair, & a 2-foot earwig enough to terrify an elephant.[32]

Whatever was happening day by day in Norman's life, it was marked by an obvious maturing. In realms material and immaterial he had grasped that the adult world was neither adult nor sane a lot of the time. Instead of an authority based on some humane sort of acquired wisdom, it relied on superstition, privilege and grotesquely coercive authority to impose its will. Now viewing his own solitude as a state-ment rather than a disadvantage, the prudently silent boy had more to say for himself. His scepticism deepened. A more self-sufficient ego was pushing at the edges of its world and its possibilities. If he had to play alone, he would play to impress. The outsider aligned himself as performer rather than observer in the staging of stunts on his bicycle, showing off his gunslinging, costuming himself in long coat and knife, and claiming desert origins. His character possessed a sharpness both defensive and offensive. "He had no sort of mission," Gwen Merrington remembers, "he wasn't an idealist [as] we were. We were more inspired to think that we, however poor we were, if we were upright and held to our principles the world would be a better place. But he was always sardonic. Whatever made him like that was in his growing-up years, in that incredibly divisive situation he was in."[33]

At home he still scorned the Freehold, though 343 Carterhatch Lane was built on its reasonable precincts, and continued to keep his distance from the other children and village functions, both of which he minimised in memory. Attendance at church roused his sharpest satirical instincts. He detested the canon of Jesus Church, Reverend William Carr-Smith, who "looked like an embittered Father Christmas" and treated the Forty Hill boys with authoritarian abruptness, stop-ping them to bellow in their ears, "Purge me with hyssop and I shall be clean." Seeing Revd Carr-Smith walk down the aisle at church and read the Bible in his flat tones with his nose just over the lectern, Norman would start mimicking him, "Do not believe ye brainwashed sheep all this rubbish," and send Gwen and her brothers and sisters in the next pew into fits of laughter.

But Gwen found his mischief testing her. When she was thirteen (and Norman fourteen), he threw a jumping cracker at her on Guy Fawkes' Night that landed in her coat pocket. "I didn't like the way you were taken along [with him]," she says, "and suddenly a can of worms would be opened. . . . While walking home from church one Sunday he insinuated that many of the village children would be indulging in incest, whereupon I whacked his legs with my umbrella."[34]

At home Norman's retaliation against his situation intensified. After one particularly poor fraud of a seance, his rejection of spiritualism was complete. A medium from Sydenham with an Indian woman assistant and a portmanteau of accessories turned up, there was a bat-squeak in the darkness and by Norman's scathing recall the sound of farting, tittering, a catcall and gibberish, and when the lights went up, the discovery of supposed "apports" from the beyond in the sitters' pockets and handbags, in fact badly made marbles with mystic signs painted on them. It was a wretched performance, and though his loyalty to his parents remained he was probably unable, from that point on, to take them seriously. He ridiculed their activities with practical action, hiding and moaning under the windows at Carterhatch Lane. His mother still threw gloomy birthday parties like the one where he told Gwen he had spat in the custard. Joyce Dale, a younger neighbour, says, "My sister . . . used to go to Mrs Lewis's parties. The garden was sort of sinister, thick with dark shrubs, they had to clear some of it to make the Beacon of Light. You never saw a flower, it was all dark shrubs and conifers. . . . Mrs Lewis used to put out two Jaffa oranges for [the dead brothers] on the piano . . . she told my mum that she used to come down and find the peel there because their spirits had come down and taken them. . . . it was young Norman playing around."[35] Gwen recalls that "From his early grown-up years he . . . enjoyed and deliberately [went] out of his way to flout the conventions that prevailed."[36]

Norman summed up his father's position (he seems to have accepted his mother's as passing all understanding) bluntly as "My father never ceased to be stunned by the credulity of others, although he lacked self-criticism in this matter." Deploring the gullibility of an English population addicted to the claims of the makers of yeast tablets or an object called the Wonder Worker, a talismanic spade-shaped bakelite contraption worn in the rectum to ward off all ills, Richard Lewis's search for proof of the spiritualist position led him in the direction of science via photography, in which otherwise unseen auras might be captured. He arranged a seance for those of his circle with Native American spirit guides, generally judged the most dependable (therefore easier to photograph). Norman describes with clinical seriousness the chosen sitter, a spirit attached to a Mrs Head, manager of the ABC cinema in Lower Edmonton: he was "a shaman of the Blackfoot tribe named Thunder Star, who in a feat of intense mental concentration had caused a small tributary of the Missouri river to run backwards, before passing on in about 1830. When Mrs Head, using my father as intermediary, had put this problem to him, explaining the photographic processes involved, he had readily agreed to assist, promising to put aside all his other duties to be present on the next Sunday evening seance."[37]

The resulting picture, of a chair surmounted by a headless halo, briefly provoked a sensation, until dissenters pointed out that the effect was produced by the reflection of the flash on the lens. It was the end of photography for his father – though curiously a first step for Norman in an interest and, even more curiously, an eventual respectably successful business that would underwrite his travelling and writing.

He continued to go to Myddelton House, more often accompanying Gussie Bowles on individual walks now, appreciating Bowles's learning and enthusiasm and the garden's rarities. This too he found had a political aspect. In writing about dodging, with Gussie, a disliked Bowles nephew and his girlfriend, he reiterates the peculiarly English connection that exists between beauty – the glorious surfaces of nature – and ownership.

. . . we suddenly heard the sound of ringing, jubilant voices . . . we ducked into some bushes. . . . From the glimpse I caught of them he was as handsome and dashing as I knew he would be, and she as beautiful, the pair of them differing not so much from natives of Enfield in their beauty and their dignity, but by the way in which they spoke, and for all who might be listening to their intimacies to hear. The fact was that Mr Bowles' village boys had no existence for them. They probably did not even register their presence. They were so splendid, but why had God given them the Earth?

When they were out of sight – although the gay lilting voices went on and on – Mr Bowles and I came out from behind the bushes and began our walk

back, and soon the summer house was in sight. Around us the birds kept up
their chorus. A shower came and went, bringing down a little sodden blossom
and pelting the surface of the lake with the heavy summer raindrops the drag-
onflies so effortlessly avoided. The smoke of burning sap from the gardener's
fire tickled the membranes of my nose, a dog barked, a fish splashed, the
swifts dived on us with their thin, delirious screeching. Even the rich could
possess no finer moment than this.[38]

There was background to this observation. A short post-war boom
had collapsed in 1921, with unemployment rising to 2.2 million; coal
was rationed, and a new left–right struggle began with the Rothermere
press vilifying war veterans as workshy, a farcical editorial spin that
set the tone for the *Daily Mail*'s more disgraceful publication of the
Zinoviev letter three years later.[39] Bill Nicholls, Gwen's elder brother,
had left school at fourteen and had to wear his sister's shoes with the
heels cut off because there was no money for shoes. He was his father's
son, a studious idealist who noticed events around him.

I remember in 1921 an ex-serviceman had been brought to court charged with
begging. He was a match-seller, which activity was seen as a form of begging. The
magistrate dismissed the case with some contempt. Almost immediately following,
I remember seeing the approaches to Liverpool Street station lined with hundreds
of bemedalled ex-servicemen with their trays of matches for sale. This [is] just to
illustrate some of the disillusioned bitterness of the early postwar years.[40]

Norman and Bill were friends at the level of discussion and reading.
Norman was not knowledgeable about politics, and Bill Nicholls should
be credited with changing his opinions and beginning to formalise his
political beliefs, drawing him towards socialism, directing him to Shaw's
plays and to the thinking of Wells and Russell. Norman respected Bill
because he was better read, an older, already manly figure. Sixty years
later Norman replied to a letter from Bill with a tribute and an interesting pairing of subjects.

Dear Bill,
Thank you for your long letter and for winding up the Bugatti for me all those
years ago. More still for introducing me – at the age of 15 – to the basic
concepts of socialism, to which I still adhere in a rather backsliding fashion.[41]

Bill Nicholls considered himself a democrat and socialist. Norman characteristically had to go one step further, claiming that he was a Communist. (No evidence exists that he ever carried a CP card, but the routine British fear of communism in the 1920s would have been enough for him to want to profess membership.) Characteristically, he was at the same time chasing riches by filling in the "bullets" in *John Bull*, the magazine owned by the lottery conman and popular hero Horatio Bottomley. Its selling slogan was, "If you read it in *John Bull*, it is so", an assertion that put Bottomley's readers in possession of vast realms of knowledge and in thrall to his various exploitations, one of which was his fund-raising idea (for himself) of offering attractive cash-prize competitions that readers had to pay to enter. The income from sixpenny entries vastly exceeded the prize money. The bullets were a word game that involved a phrase needing an answer which contained letters from it, and Norman won several of the competitions, often at £5 a time when £5 was enough to keep a working man for a fortnight.

In July 1925, after five years, he passed his matriculation exam and left Enfield Grammar. He had turned seventeen at the end of June.[42] He told one interviewer later that he had won a place at university but failed to take it up because his parents could not pay for his tuition.[43] It may be more likely that a combination of restlessness and his parents' indulgence meant that he was allowed to make his own decision and rejected academic study in favour of unformed terrain of his own.

Tall, long-faced, a bit jug-eared, with a thick lash of hair and deep, curiously lazy eyes, in photographs looking enthusiastic and lethargic by turns, he had a well-cared-for and well-dressed look: at fifteen his suit already had the fashionable unstructured cut of the 1920s. He had given up his bicycle for motorbikes (you could ride a motorcycle at fourteen), the first an American Reading-Standard v-twin followed by several slippy AJSes on which he used to wait for the fifteen-year-old Gwen outside the draper's in Enfield, where she was working an oppressive apprenticeship. "At the end of the day one would walk home, there were no buses then. And then his motorbike would be throbbing and he'd be drawing up. He had a wonderful way . . . like breathing, you were walking somewhere and here was this brrr-brrr coming up behind, it was Norman."[44]

At school he had never got out of second gear. It had been an excellent education – he said so several times later – but he was not interested in prolonging it. He had taken the full list of subjects, including German, science and maths. He spoke French fluently. He was not a scholar. (He already had the look of a rakish individual rather than a face in a school photograph. It is striking in photographs of the period that when not with his family, he is always alone.)

He was enjoying the usual territory of male adolescence – cash, motorbikes, girls (and guns) – and had wide interests for a youth of his background. But they were too wide for synthesis. He was well informed about science, photography, ornithology and botany, but the essential condition for study – the willingness to stay in one place for long enough to absorb deeper knowledge – was lacking. No one had ever shown him, and so far he had not found, any place that pleased him enough to stay there. He preferred physical mobility. Freedom. Escape. The question was, what was he going to do?

These boys would turn up on their bicycles, all Grammar School boys. They sought us out because our sisters were attractive, and it gained us some notoriety. I can remember a group of boys sitting on the bank of the orchard hedge, and being given a bag of sweets to go and tell my sisters they were there. We had boys from all round coming round. Gwen was very, very pretty at the time.

Eric Nicholls

He roughed up one young man who decided to walk home with me one evening. He was a young man who no doubt gazed at me getting on the bus. I'd seen him evening after evening and I thought, What does he queue up for if he doesn't get on the damn bus? Then one day he did and he asked if he could see me home – I'd been to the cinema or whatever – and I allowed him to walk home with me. And I said, "This where I live" when I got to the top of the road, and Norman lurched out from the dark and beat him up, knocked him to the ground. I fled and fetched my brother.

Next day I came out of Muldoon's and there were two throbbing motorbikes waiting. One was this chap, one was Lewis, and I regret to this day that I got on Lewis's bike.

Gwen Merrington

He was particular with his girlfriends and courted two of my sisters, but my elder sister [who was] not so attractive he gave rides to in his Bugatti to make it up to her.

Eric Nicholls

I didn't love him. Physically I was incredibly attracted to him and in every way, and being combative, I was always a challenge to him.

Even sixty years afterwards I might be dressing up to go out somewhere in the evening and put on a dress, and when I looked at myself in the mirror I'd say to myself, "I wonder what Lewis would think of me in this?"

Gwen Merrington

4

MRS ENGLAND'S DINING ROOMS

"You can't polish a turd"
Persian proverb

THE immediate answer, as often with precocious teenage rejecters, was that he had no idea. He went to the City to try for a job as a clerk in an insurance company, but competition for secure jobs combined with a mutual lack of interest thwarted him. Rapidly he found himself back in his father's shop, handing out medicines and bottling elixir.

He alleviated the "grotesque experience" of working for his alcoholic father by walking the short distance from the pharmacy in Southbury Road to Enfield's Carnegie Library. In the shop he was bored stiff but read every spare moment and eventually worked out a way to sub-contract his boredom: with his father paying him a generous £4 a week to manage it, he paid an assistant £1.50 a week to hold the fort while he sat in the back of the shop, reading and making plans. He wanted to read popular modern writers, but later claimed that other readers always got to the new novels quicker than he did. He was left with several shelves of an eccentric bequest made to the library of every Russian classic translated into English. "Shelf after shelf, there was no Russian author from Dostoyevsky and Pushkin and all the rest of it sufficiently obscure that it wasn't in this library." (This story has always had a whiff of the disingenuous about it. If he read at high speed as he also claimed, why couldn't he get to the library at high speed?) But there is nothing suspect about his satisfaction with the narrative naturalism of nineteenth-century Russian fiction.

I was dazzled by Chekhov, for example, [and] by comparison to the kind of the short stories that were being published in English magazines, they were extremely realistic . . . I would read a piece of Chekhov about somebody travelling in central Asia or somewhere . . . on a slow-moving Russian train, and Chekhov would describe the character's reactions to his surroundings, to the people he met on the train. Although this was a highly exotic situation, it struck me as eminently believable. . . . And this may have been beneficial . . . because at least what I read was about real life, the Russian form of real life.[1]

Chekhov's stories, one suspects, with their responsiveness to their characters' lives and their sheer "thereness", helped identify for Norman what real life might be like, burning away with their clarity the fog of Enfield existence, revealing its nowhereness and unreality.

Norman read, he said, a Russian classic a day (four days for *War and Peace*). When he came to the end of the bequest – well over 100 books, by his description – he started again. He later acknowledged the unintended influence of this enforced Russianism on his style – "As I never had the chance to read rubbish, I therefore couldn't obviously absorb the rubbish that went with the style of the popular writers of the day."[2] The King James Bible was another influence. Though he stopped considering himself a Christian at sixteen, he had discovered that it was written in superbly economical English and full of wonderful stories. He thought he might be one of the few non-Christians who had read it from beginning to end, several times.

Britain's economic slump in the mid-1920s, its politics marred by savage polarity, its commerce by loss of competitiveness abroad, its society by mass unemployment and a general strike, put a brake on the aspirations of Norman's generation. He saw his school friends, who had attended one of the dozen best grammar schools in the country, leave to do seasonal work in Enfield's orchards; the ones who found full-time work tended to become council rat-catchers, professional dance partners, and in one case a clown employed by a Soho restaurant to advertise its menu.

For all its grotesqueness, Norman's job at R G Lewis's in Southbury Road was a useful stop-gap. (It went on being one well into the 1930s, whenever, as periodically happened, his later income-generating schemes dried up.) He was in a sounder economic state than most of his contemporaries. He didn't greatly care (one might say he could afford not to care). Driven by boredom, he continually looked for more adventurous options for their own sake. Writing was one of them: he began entering literary competitions in *Answers*, *Titbits* and *John O'London's Weekly*, and occasionally winning cash prizes. He already had an ambition to write, Gwen recalls. "Norman did have an ambition at a very early age because I remember him going to night classes in London to master the art of writing and telling me that." He did not last long: other people's night classes were not *his* night classes. Out of this combination of hideous boredom and lonely individualism, an entrepreneurial vein started to surface in his character. Having first viewed the acquisition of physical mobility as a prerequisite of his freedom, via his AJS 348cc, he now started to see the acquisition of cash in the same light, although through 1925 and 1926 he continued to work at R G Lewis's, reading, entering competitions, doing seasonal work himself – working in the cherry orchards as a marksman, shooting with a twelve-bore some of the thousands of blackbirds and thrushes that descended on the ripe crop – and riding his motorcycles. Motorbikes were fashionable as a cheap and relatively glamorous way for young men to get around (and take girls with them). Groups of youths formed formal and impromptu clubs to ride together. Norman rarely joined.

An exception to his solitude was when he gave Gwen Nicholls a lift home from the draper's or offered her a ride somewhere. He was beginning to appear behind her on his AJS more often. At seventeen, after years of mocking her like a surrogate younger sister, he had woken up to her attractiveness. Two of the Nicholls girls – Gwen and her sister Nancy – were known in Enfield as good-looking and were sought out by the area's *vitelloni*. Gwen, brown-haired with a streak of fair, with soft pale skin and a quick spark of liveliness in her eyes and her habit of tilting her head to the right, was seen as a flirt by other girls. "She always had the latest fashions and she used to wear a rose tucked in her ear and that sort of thing, and she was quite a belle," Joyce Dale says.[3] (Even in 2003, when we visited her in Devon, my wife pointed out that Gwen was flirting with me at the age of ninety-four.)

When she gave up working at Pearson's, the draper's, having had enough of one senior male assistant who fastened "hot kisses" on her neck and shoulders whenever he found her in the stockroom, Gwen got a job as an usherette at Sidney Bernstein's newly redesigned Rialto cinema in Enfield town centre. She and Norman saw each other at lunchtimes and after the last performance. On Gwen's side, she felt close to Norman but stopped at friendship. The emotional deficit of her father's death when she was nine had left her looking for a man she could idealise. She knew Norman too well for that. Their relationship was still based on childish things. "When I was about seventeen years old, he dared me to go into a chemist's shop and ask a particular young male assistant for a catheter, knowing I hadn't the first idea of what a catheter was – he watched with devilish amusement."[4] On his part, under the mockery there was a serious intention (or at least a serious desire for pursuit). His long alliance with Gwen, since their earliest childhood, had led him to think of her as his. The problem was that he could now see her going *her* own way. In Gwen's mind "although there was constant contact, there seemed tacit agreement that it was to be so far but no further",[5] but in Norman's there was no question of contact on her part going further with anyone else. In the winter of 1926 it did. At the Rialto, the new usherettes "all in one accord fell in love from afar with the . . . stars, John Gilbert, Rudolph Valentino". They would all, however, according to Gwen, have settled for Stan Sims. Sims was a popular sportsman and the twenty-year-old captain of Enfield's football team. He had asked Gwen out once, and when she was stuck in bed ill for several weeks soon afterwards, he visited her one evening. They began to court properly. In the summer of 1927 she went on holiday to Devon with her sister Nancy and Nancy's husband, and Stan Sims joined them for a long August weekend. But Gwen was not to have her romance. Soon after the Devon holiday, on the weekend she was due to meet Stan Sims' parents, he was taken ill. His healthy constitution concealed the seriousness of the infection, and by the time it was acknowledged, an abscess had burst, poisoning his system. He was moved from the local hospital to a special unit in London, and Gwen never saw him again. He died several months later.

Gwen was "turned to stone". A few young men, she remembers, tried to console her. Norman saw his chance and stepped in. He was twenty, she was nineteen. He "became very persistent in his attentions, and because we knew each other so well I did not, as time passed, resist those attentions," Gwen says.[6] Wherever she went, she would hear his motorbike, and rapidly find herself racing down country roads with him, to home, to work, to the sea at weekends. Norman "haunted" her; Gwen felt that his happiness depended on being with her. She herself was only going through the motions. Her brother-in-law had taken a post as colonial officer at Jinja in British East Africa (Uganda) and offered to pay her fare out to join him and Nancy. The offer was partly made to raise Gwen's spirits; she was also aware that her sister was coping disastrously badly both as memsahib and wife. She considered and accepted. Having accepted, she felt she could not deceive Norman any more. Her passage was booked for November 1928, and she told Norman.

It came as a great shock to him. I now felt that, having accepted his constant overtures and companionship, while suffering my own loss, I had compromised myself and, by going away, was being quite cruel. He threw himself more deeply at my disposal, while hoping to dissuade me from leaving. He even gave me a motorcycle which, up until then, was an unthought-of acquisition for a female [and] which, after a few hair-raising efforts to master with the help of my brother Eric riding an ordinary bicycle while shouting directions, I decided was not for me.[7]

He sent Gwen poems too, pushing under her door calligraphed quatrains from *The Rubáiyát of Omar Khayyám* and poems of his own. The growing urgency of his courtship had not robbed him of his sense of humour or his territorial certainty that Gwen was his. He sent her one poem, written beautifully on orange paper and brush-stroked in black ink, called "If I were the caliph of old Baghdad".

> If I were the caliph of old Baghdad
> Or even the sultan of Turkistan,
> Into my hareem you would go
> With a pair of silken trousers on,
> Futility to call me mad if I were the caliph of old Baghdad.
> On Saturday night ey! wy! wolla! wo!
> To dance among silly young men you intend to go,
> Wouldn't their heads come off bedad,
> If I were the caliph of old Baghdad.[8]

He went further than poetry. Gwen was working as receptionist at Muldoon's, the hairdresser's on Church Street. One evening a young man called Knowles, a shy boy who had waited for her at the bus stop (the bus service had recently started) several nights in a row, worked up the courage to ask if he could see her home. Reaching the corner of Carterhatch Lane and Bridgenhall Rd, Gwen was telling him this was as far as he need escort her when Norman appeared out of the darkness and punched him to the ground.

The next day a Miss Knowles came into Muldoon's and told Gwen that her young brother had come home bruised and covered in mud. "I told her I was sorry, and that Lewis, who she knew [the Knowles hardware business was opposite R G Lewis], had no right to do what he did." Later that day, as Gwen left work, she was confronted by a pair of motorbikes in the road, their engines running. Knowles was on one, his brother standing beside him, Norman the other. "To this day, I regret not going up to young Knowles and saying how sorry I was for what had happened, and then walking away to my bus stop. Instead I got on Norman's bike, perhaps realising [that] had I got on Knowles' a duel on motorbikes could have been hair-raisingly dangerous."[9]

Norman had won. Gwen's passage was still booked. Ignoring the inevitable day (he translated it into German – "*der Tag*" – so he wouldn't have to say it in English), he took her out repeatedly. They made visits to the theatre, where he would suggest that they compared their opinions with those of the critics: he was surprised to find that her opinion tallied more closely than his. (Gwen remembers judging "Dance, dance, dance little lady" the best song from Noel Coward's *This Year of Grace*, which premiered in March 1928, and being pleased that the critic James Agate agreed.) Gwen was aware that he found these excursions difficult to afford. More was to come. The situation in both households was becoming more turbulent. Norman made no secret of his desire to seduce Gwen, whose mother was concerned for her and only half-jokingly called Norman "the son of Satan" to his face, "which he laughingly enjoyed". Louisa Lewis, who had been content for Gwen to play with "Normie" when the children were small, was alarmed. "When it got to the fact that he was falling in love with me, one could tell it was not what she had in mind." Gwen says that anyhow she "was determined not to weaken to his will, to be untrue to myself. I enjoyed the company, and, to be truthful, the blatant flattering desire of this unique individual, and the friendship, and have missed it ever since."[10] But she had "no intention of being seduced by" Norman.[11]

He did not give up. A habit of their childhood relationship had been the game of dare, and Norman dared Gwen to go with him for a weekend to Paris, knowing that she had her passport ready for Africa. She accepted.

He and I, I'm sorry to say, worked out what I could tell my mother to prevent her knowing and being worried, and off we went. As always, he went out of his way to make it an enriching – perhaps that's the wrong word – experience. He was an excellent guide.[12]

It was October 1928, a month before "*der Tag*". They left early on Saturday morning to catch the Channel ferry. Gwen had told her mother she was going to stay with a friend she had spent weekends with before. Between Saturday and Monday they climbed the Eiffel Tower, went to Notre Dame, had "delicious food", and Norman took Gwen to the Moulin Rouge *and* to see Mistinguett at the Folies Bergère "with her retinue of almost equally beautiful showgirls dressed, or rather undressed, in swirling feathered plumes". From somewhere he had found the money to pay for everything. Seventy-five years later, Gwen remembered how foreign Paris looked, and how they looked foreign to the Parisians. "People's heads turned to look at us, so we must have cut a dash which was different."[13] And seventy-five years later, talking about the events of the weekend for the first time, she could not remember how Norman persuaded her into bed. "I don't remember because I didn't want to remember, probably. As if detached from myself – which in the light of what had happened the previous year [Stan Sims' death], I suppose I was – I relented as if hypnotised."[14]

Gwen felt that Norman had every excuse for his actions, but she had little. She came back from Paris feeling divorced from her real self, her conscience most stricken because she had deceived her mother whom she had never lied to. Nor had she realised that her passport would be stamped. "And so I tore that little bit out and got away with it."[15] The sexual endgame having happened, she felt less guilty about Norman. Not proud of herself but not blaming him, she continued to see him. He invited her to go to Wales with him for a weekend – he needed to pay a duty visit to Carmarthen – and they went by motorcycle and sidecar, a wild 650-kilometre round trip on the roads of the 1920s. When they arrived Norman booked them into a pub with separate rooms (Gwen noticed hers had a double bed), and they rode to the seven-mile beach at Pendine Sands. There was a race meeting going on. (The sands were a magnetic racing venue, "the finest natural speedway imaginable" in *Motor Cycle* magazine's description. On their flat surface the previous year J G Parry-Thomas had flipped his 27-litre car at 180 mph in pursuit of Malcolm Campbell's land speed record and killed himself.) Norman, not content to watch, entered himself and Gwen in the combination category. "We . . . took part in hair-raising races – I hanging half out of the sidecar at given signals."[16] After a thin supper at the pub they parted, Norman to ride into Carmarthen to see his grandfather and aunts, Gwen to bed. Several hours later, she heard and ignored his tapping on her door. On Sunday, both tired from the last twenty-four hours, they left on the journey back to Enfield. Gwen fell asleep in the sidecar. She woke to savage jarring. The combination was tipped on its side in a ditch, and Norman, asleep at the handlebars a few seconds before, was lying in the road some distance away. He raised himself and limped back to her with a gash in his leg that would give him trouble for years afterwards.

On the evening before Gwen's departure, 9 November, Norman put a ring on Gwen's engagement finger and tactically extracted a promise from her that she would wear the ring for the duration of the journey and come home single. Covering all his options, he had also written her a poem, "Dawn comes up on the red hills breaking, All things living are all things waking, Only one day for me will dawn, The day my love when you return", which despite its intense cheesiness she kept for seventy-five years. She responded with the gift of a recording of "The song is ended but the memory lingers on" by the vaudeville singer Winnie Melville. Next morning, flanked by her mother, three brothers and older sister, she left in the cold fog to catch the bus to Enfield Town station. She would take the train to Liverpool Street and on to Tilbury to embark later that day for Mombasa on the Union-Castle Line's 11,000-ton *Llanstephan Castle* (the genuine *Llanstephan Castle* and probable origin of his later ship-naming habit). A lingering, dimly outlined figure watched her go.

Gwen's disappearance may have thrown Norman into confusion; probably the entire year of their doomed courtship had confused him. He had fully believed he could dissuade her from going to Africa. When he failed he may not have realised that it was not because he was without economic prospects or that his feelings were without reciprocation, but because he was having emotional dealings with a human being for the first time. Gwen had *her* reasons for escaping from Enfield that nothing *he* could offer her would change. (On board ship, seasick and homesick, she did announce that she was getting off at Marseille and coming home, but then changed her mind.) Later in his life, when another woman left him to travel on her own, Norman had the experience to know that a combination of patience and decisiveness can succeed better than gifts and a good time. (He waited, kept in touch, and eventually fetched her back.) If Gwen was, in some way, an heuristic experience, she may also have been an origin to which we can trace back his later trenchancy about relationships. He would have been, first of all, definite that he would not find himself again in the paralysing position of not knowing what to do to get what he wanted. And a painful parallel between Gwen's departure and the shape of his life up to that point may have occurred to him: that yet again, pleasure – of time spent together, of shared spirit, of another's welfare, of the sexual kind – was deserting him. They wrote to each other, "on and off, not too often" in her words. But with her gone he was again being ambushed by loneliness. Without her he had to fall back on his wide, but solitary, resources.

A curious aspect to Norman's life in his twenties is that he went through a prolonged period of discovery – his sense of adventure regularly sharpened and enlarged, his conviction of Enfield's ghastliness never softened – but until his twenty-seventh year his base remained there (he even returned regularly to stand behind the counter of his father's shop) and he offered no sign of the writing career that followed. The dream that the next valley would always be wilder was not the dream that was driving him yet – he situates it a bit too early in his own biography – because, in truth, the years that followed Gwen's departure, like his late teenage years, a decade altogether, were a long experimental phase during which he still breathed mostly suburban air. Maybe he remained mystified as to exactly how one *should* make a break: he was self-invented, he had no mentors, no tracks of middle-class privilege to follow, no Oxford or Cambridge or country-house upbringing to ease his way, unlike almost every writer who would become his contemporary. He considered his one recorded professional writing enterprise – the plagiarising of the content of German magazines in order to sell some of the sensational stories coming out of Germany at the time to magazines like *John Bull* – as proof of his ambition, and who could blame him? He had tried night classes, won small prizes for literary competition entries. He had decided that he wanted to be a writer. "[This] was a substantial part of my income. ... I think there's no doubt whatever that I had decided one way or another to commit myself to professional writing. I was not interested in doing anything else at all."[17] But in the late 1920s and early 1930s Norman was a sluggish, even non-existent *littérateur*, his literary activities generally mercantile.

Yet if there was no sign of the *kind* of writer he would become, why should there be? One of the most misjudged aspects of the past comes from our tendency to be complacent about its finishedness – it was never finished while it was happening. Conversely the best thing about the present (that the past once was) is its uncertainty, the blank sheet it pushes under the door, under our nose, for our energy and curiosity to work well, or badly, or somehow transformingly, on. If there was no writing to show for this phase of Norman's life, the years were, all the same, usefully packed with the kind of activity that writers miss because they sit on their backsides too long.

The overwhelmingly pressing need, since leaving school, had been to make some sense of the extreme dullness of life in Forty Hill. With the end of childhood and its scot-free irresponsibilities, Enfield's appeal fell to zero. E A Bowles was going blind, and Norman's one refuge at Myddelton House no longer had the same appeal. The town and its surroundings remained, in his eyes, appalling. Their suburban mixture of public virtue and private lunacy, their economic and class oppressions that boiled life down to a clinging to appearances, the sheer uneventfulness of daily existence, urged constant thoughts of flight, and vengeance. At R G Lewis's Norman was known for claiming that his father had enough poison in the shop to knock out the town's entire population. From a biographical point of view, naturally, Norman's unwillingness to talk about any positive influence Enfield could have had makes it interesting. He wrote only two (damning) articles about his childhood, and published only one. His autobiography too uses Enfield as a sort of ghastly and ghostly counterpoint, a bathetic benchmark and comic shadow that somehow casts the rest of the world into sharp relief. That was, personally, what it was like: definitely no one can object that it did not feel like that to him, and in my own experience it still feels something like that. (Generously, you could say, he also cloaked its brutality in comedy, and did not record his own persecution in its grim streets.)

In artistic terms, of course, Enfield was more valuable, even invaluable, a pearl of positivity. Within its circumference, between Enfield Town and Freezy Water, is his arsenal, the store he draws his firepower from, the negative principle he departs from to construct, by the usual process of trial and error, the life that seventy years later he will still be describing as heady.

At the time none of this was obvious, and he saw Enfield's insubstantiality and dreariness, reinforced by its magnification into a modern town, merely as potent causes for a reaction of disgust. In a passage of unusually charged eloquence – unusual even for him – he analyses his stranded situation in the late 1920s, at a time when he and his schoolfriends were attempting to locate the social pleasures of adulthood. Sidney Bernstein's new Rialto cinema, in the old marketplace, was in the process of consigning Enfield's original flea pit, the Queen's, to oblivion. The Rialto's opening presentation was Luigi Sapelli's *The Power of the Borgias*.

I saw *The Power of the Borgias* with an old schoolmate, Alexander Hagen, who had been good at maths and had set his sights on becoming an airship designer, then jettisoning the idea owing to the state of the world, and philosophically accepting employment at the sewage farm in Ponders End. A ritual Saturday night meal followed at Mrs England's Dining Rooms in the passage at the back of the station, where the tables were screened in such a way that patrons did not risk loss of face by being seen there, scuffling their feet in the sawdust. We began to ask ourselves if in fact we really existed or whether what we took to be life could not be a complex illusion, an endless, low-quality dream. These threadbare surroundings in which we sat hunched over a scrubbed table, our backs to the light, came very close to being nothing. Perhaps we too were nothing, had come from nothing, were journeying through nothing, towards a distant goal of nothingness. Enfield was nothing, the Rialto cinema nothing to the accompaniment of organ music, the Queen's nothing with fleas. We had come here to confront a supper of nothing, boiled, fried or scrambled, with or without chips, to be followed by custard if desired at no extra charge. After this it was back home to nothing, or down the town to pick up a couple of girls at the bottom of Church Street, and engage them in a lively conversation about nothing plus sex, or just nothing.

Christ stopped at Eboli, but he would have found people there who still had the spirit to sing and dance, and Mr Bowles mentioned that on the Greek island where he went to dig up plants, the impoverished peasantry got away with fifty days of what was supposed to be the working year and used them on parties, pilgrimages and processions. What had happened to us? Why had the lives of Sir Henry's serfs, and the workers at the Lock, been reduced to survival without distraction? Why had communal activities in the surroundings in which I was born come down to a couple of hours over a pint of sour ale in the Goat?[18]

This expression of existential repugnance is a good part of the explanation behind his generation's compulsion to reinvent themselves, to lie for all they were worth about who they were and where they came from.

No wonder we took refuge in make-believe, dealt in pretence and self-pretence, and half-believed the personal myths of our own creation. No wonder our pudgy-faced local beauties started life as Ethel, Gladys or Florence but ended as Esmée, Phoebe and Diane and inflicted upon themselves their soulless accents.[19]

Because no obvious escape presented itself, this refashioning was a slow process, and in many cases too tentative to break the spell of the suburbs. When his friend Alex Hagen left the sewage farm and set up as a wedding photographer, Norman went into partnership with him for a time, at first developing and printing the pictures in his parents' kitchen. (His father made a point of inspecting the prints closely for any signs, in the form of shadows or fogging, of other-worldly presences.) Hagen did well and made money, according to Norman. He began to ask his friends to call him Alexander rather than Alex and pronounce the "a" in Hagen "ah" rather than "ay", and he wore his homburg with a swagger, but, though intelligent, he "like the rest of us, was too cautious, too premeditated, too afraid at bottom of his own shadow . . . he gave the impression of listening to the noises of the pogrom in the next street".[20] Norman harvested insights from his alliances, with Bill Nicholls, Alex Hagen and others, never following his friends but instead either going further, or sideways. With Hagen he saw that there was money to be made from photography, gradually evolving his processing activities into a small business above his father's shop. He also grasped that his future did not lie in pretending or trying, as Hagen did, to be somebody else – in Hagen's case, a German Jew passing himself off as a member of the English upper class. Neither of these conclusions reduced Norman's desire for flight or his revulsion for Enfield. In his earliest writing[21] he had the rebuking eye of a young man who was clever and knew it. Later, after the war had shown him that stupidity, absurdity and tedium were ubiquitous and not just located north of the North Circular, he learned to be generous and to wrap dullness in comedy; but the transforming, forgiving quality of his satire that rarely ever slips in the face of a comic target, is noticeably exhausted in the adjectives he chooses for adult Enfield. The girls he meets have given themselves "soulless" accents, and the wedding guests whose pictures he prints put on "boozy, foolish smiles" and "inane grins". Where a prose style that is emblematically defined by tolerance and humanity can find no excuse for someone's behaviour even fifty years later, something must have been very seriously wrong.

We were not much older when we met, do you remember? A pair of graceless monsters passing harsh judgment on our parents. Could this bitterness have been the chief bond between us, *au fond*?

Ernestina Lewis, letter, 25 January 1958

When she was in a good mood she would say wonderful things about him – your father this, your father that – but when she was in a bad mood she would lose her temper and say, "You're just like him." It's an extraordinary thing that from a very early age on my mother used to say to me, "You're just like your father. How could it be that you've no contact with him, you're so much like him?"

Ito Lewis

5

SICILY

"Buy at the cost of four and sell at the cost of eight"
Sicilian proverb

THE alliance with Hagen branched out from photography to dealing in
a literally far-fetched range of goods. At Hagen's instigation, these were
at first mostly located at lost property depots run by the London railway
companies and so restricted to the kinds of items people forgot or jetti-
soned on train journeys. The Hagen–Lewis railway operation reached
its zenith in the snapping-up of several hundred umbrellas on which,
according to Norman, they trebled their outlay on the resale. The pair
then began to expand their activities to trade auctions across the city,
travelling to the farthest horizons of the suburbs and specialising in
motley lots in whose disposal they gradually developed an expertise:
photographic supplies, scientific and surgical instruments, anatomical
specimens and (Norman's area) motorcycles.

At one auction he bought a racing motorcycle that had been repatriated from the continent after its rider had been killed and, reluctant to
sell it on immediately, decided to try his luck at the new speedway courses
at Harringay and White City. He claimed afterwards – though since the
whole point of the claim is, as often with Norman, its self-deprecatory
value one can't be sure how true it is (in later conversation he insisted
he was not exaggerating) – that before the engine exploded he came last
in every race but one, "when two of the four contestants crashed".[1] The
craze for speedway racing, after its introduction from Australia in 1928,
was chiefly the result of the adrenalin rush for both audience and riders
of the speeds achieved over several laps on the oval cinder tracks. When
speedway evolved, winning machines were re-geared (for acceleration)

and so stripped down that they were unrealistic for road use, but as a new sport, barely regulated, it pulled in high levels of amateur participation. The popularity of motorbikes as the instrument and emblem of thrills and liberty for young working-class males in the 1920s reinforced its appeal. Between 20,000 and 30,000 people turned up to the first, virtually unadvertised meeting at High Beech in the middle of Epping Forest in Essex in February 1928, and the forty-two riders in the day's fifty-odd races rode the bikes they had turned up on, sometimes but not always stripping them of lamp, speedometer and horn before racing. Norman's entries (increasing his fortunes by a couple of pounds starting money a race) were always accepted by race organisers: in terms of crowd excitement they had nothing against a rider who, as he wrote, "could be relied upon to fall off in three races out of four". But other entrants could still beat him at the modesty game. His machine was at least an authentic racing motorcycle; in the early days of speedway some young men who could not afford motorbikes raced pushbikes instead.

Most of Norman's activities, mercantile, sporting or both, were now sporadic and nomadic; though he still lived at Carterhatch Lane, where he might be found at any moment was becoming less predictable. In March 1930 – he was twenty-one – he wrote to his parents from the French Riviera. The postcard from Nice followed the fashion of the day, a photograph of the sender by a professional photographer, rapidly processed on a printed card. Norman's reason for being in Nice was that he was in pursuit of a pretty French girl who had smitten him in London, a jeweller's daughter. She had gone back to her family at the end of her visit, Norman had followed. From Norman's portrait, the reaction of the girl's father on meeting him was the one most fathers of daughters would have. Taken on the blinding terrace of Frank Jay Gould's recently opened Palais de la Méditerranée, the photograph is of a hooded-eyed young man groomed to the nines, slumped rather than draped in his armchair, under an empyrean of pale scalloped parasols. He has the tailoring of a dandy with links to an activity only distantly respectable, the complexion of a Levantine swell, and a delinquent's gaze. His chivalric journey to Nice provides the first photographic record of him abroad as a young man aware of himself and his possible effect. In magnificent contrast to his later self, to the writer whose degree of self-erasure would be unmatched by his contemporaries, it is the photograph of a young man waiting to be seen, fully intending an impact, propelling himself to the centre of the frame.

Predictably, when he was seen by the jeweller the result was not the desired one. The daughter may have been very interested, the father's reaction was to bar her English suitor from his house.

The negative outcome was still in the future when he wrote optimistically to his parents,

[postmarked 9 March 1930]
Dear Lou & Rich, Having a grand time here. Sun always. Hot night & day. I am going to the alps by car tomorrow morning. Hope you got flowers alright. Lewis P.S Had a marvellous time today

When they drove up into the saxifrage and gentian slopes of the Alpes-Maritimes next day he and the girl, as many tourists do, got lost in the switchback country of villages crouched behind white crags and wedged into swooping valleys; they stopped to ask directions and were invited to a wedding party, where they finished the afternoon dancing on a table. Recounted exploits such as this probably added to the aura of danger sensed in this unknown Briton by the girl's father: some combination anyway of rakish looks, adventurousness and invisible prospects, plus the conservative provinciality of the Côte d'Azur bourgeoisie, made sure that Norman returned empty-handed to Enfield.

He seems at this stage to be most things, the dandy, the gambler, the seeker after excitement, that he later was not. But as the Protestant writer Søren Kierkegaard has noted, to the seeker the stages on life's way are measured in transformations, not degrees. Norman did not begin his life as a modest self-deprecating observer and become more so, but started out as the opposite, to be transfigured from dandy and rake to ascetic by depth or breadth, or both, of experience. Joyce Dale's memory at seventeen of her neighbour on the bus to Enfield Chase in the mornings, in a belted camel overcoat to his ankles and wearing a black wide-brimmed hat, carrying "a big book bound in leather, like a book you'd go and get out of a medieval library", draws a clear picture of the figure he wanted to cut. The only thing more foreign than him in the Enfield rush hour was the tooled folio book he carried. "You looked at that before you looked at him, and that took some doing, because to look at him, he was so striking. Everybody looked at him."[2]

In the early spring of 1931 Gwen Nicholls came home from two years in Uganda. She met Norman sitting alone on the verge of one of Forty Hill's dusty roads. He had grown a beard and was muttering to

himself. "When he did speak, he rose politely and he said that I looked
attractively weatherbeaten, meaning that I showed the wear and tear
of having lived in Uganda."[3] Although he had extracted a promise from
her to come back single, Gwen was engaged to a man named Frank
Varnals whom she had met in Africa. Wiser this time, Norman did not
try to pursue or dissuade her, as she had been afraid he would. He had
always had the power to frighten her. "I was frightened to go against
Lewis at times, he'd threaten all sorts of murderous [acts]."[4] When she
invited her fiancé to visit, she was terrified to find her mother's front-
room window open, thinking that Norman had broken in and would
waylay her fiancé and attack him (in fact it was her brother who had
climbed through the window to avoid introductions before he had
changed his clothes). But she also felt that "all his violence was a show,
because he couldn't find himself".[5] Meeting him again, she found him
changed enough – the beard, the muttering (she came across him several
times talking to himself like his father) – to make her think he might
be experimenting with the drugs in his father's shop. But her chief
feeling was the old one of his difference. "He was always creating
impressions, I suppose saying 'I'm different', which he was."[6] On 23
April Gwen married Frank Varnals in Jesus Church. It was the one
occasion when Norman expressed his emotion publicly. Possibly, given
his liking for causing a commotion in church, he just wanted to tease
Gwen in his dramatic fashion. "He came to the church uninvited and
when it got to the point 'Should any man . . .' he started shouting, and
my uncle had to go and sit with him."[7] Though frightened, Gwen was
flattered. "It was incredibly flattering in a way. I've missed it ever since,
for someone to be quite as enamoured."[8]

Soon after their wedding Mr and Mrs Varnals left for Dublin where
Frank Varnals had found work. What about Norman? Whether it
included drugs or not, his experimental phase went on intensively. He
leaves the impression of someone set on going, or getting, somewhere,
and probably, no, certainly, writing was constantly in his mind; but he
had no idea what his subject was, or style or tone. There was no indication that within four years he would publish his first book. All he
knew he had in the way of assets was an entrepreneurial streak and
an aggressively private feeling of what he wanted, and all he could do
with such assets was keep on combining them experimentally with life
to see if any one of his experiments would transform him and lead him
to his subject. The common factor of the experiments, of course, was

that they were all designed to give off intoxicating fumes of escape. Leaving Gwen's marriage and departure aside, 1931 did turn out to be a year of the transformation hinted at the previous year. His life was still a laboratory of random elements, and he had little idea where he was going, but at twenty-two Norman was, consciously and unconsciously, hunting down his next bid for freedom. One other thing: I'm inclined to think that it is that synchrony of conscious and unconscious – of action and appetite – rather than any categorical ambition "to be a writer" that led him eventually in the right direction. Writers do sometimes emerge from applied chemistry.

The Hagen–Lewis business ventures continued. Hagen, in his quest for elevation, had fallen for a girl named Zahra, "pretty and amazingly fair", who happened (so Norman writes) to be the daughter of the chief rabbi of Astrakhan, exiled with her family a few years earlier and sent to school in Highgate. Composedly she accepted Hagen's advances, though the liaison would be the high-water mark of his social aspirations. Ultimately doomed by his lapsed Jewishness and his unconvincing accent and tie, before the affair was over it had a momentous outcome. Zahra's family had agreed that meetings could take place between her and her prospective fiancé, so long as one of her friends was present. Hagen asked Norman if he would make up the fourth, an invitation that was heavily influenced by the fact that Norman had a car, the presence of which would inject useful mobility and helpful glamour. On Sunday 3 May, ten days after Gwen's wedding, the two men collected Zahra and her friend in central London at "the old Euston arch, just as a few small snowflakes began to fall". The car's hood needed putting up, a fiddly operation that "the girls . . . entered into in the spirit of fun . . . working with us and their hands like ours blue with cold".[9]

About the car: a digression. Norman's first car (as far as we know), it had surfaced through a business operation with another schoolfriend, Arthur Baron, a self-taught mechanic and engineer. The Baron family were garage owners in Surrey during the 1930s, with branches at Dorking, Brooklands and Shere. Baron's father indulged him, employing him as a race driver, but before he started racing he had found a gap as a specialist rebuilding crashed cars at the luxury end of the market. In the 1920s and 1930s, out of grief and superstition cars like these sold cheaply and, if someone had been killed, very cheaply. Norman's own vehicle was not technically a wreck, merely an aesthetic miscarriage, its coachwork, built in Paris by Lavocat et Marsaud, executed under the orders of the car's wealthy Indian owner to achieve a fusion of homage to the Hindu elephant god, Ganesh, and the back end of a yacht. Norman claimed that "an ivory plaque covering most of the instruments on the dashboard showed a pair of lovers in lascivious oriental intertwinings", though there is no proof of this nor that the rear of the car came with decking and portholes. It did have deck-like running boards, and the original elliptical radiator emblem had been replaced by one from the Sunbeam Motor Company. Crucially, for the masculine purpose of impressing young women, it was still a roadster adequate to the task of supplying adventurous transport: still, recognisably, a Bugatti, a straight-eight dual-cowl (four-seater) Type 30.

The story of the picnic in the Bugatti in Norman's autobiography – the drive to Epping Forest, the sandwiches and the "derelict sunshine", the different characters of the two girls, the political and philosophical discussions about love and the English class system, the undertone of Hagen's persistent interrogation by the Russian girl Zahra – has a bit of the quality of one of Ettore Bugatti's own cars, whose appeal was greatly in the artistry of their detail: the Cubist shape of the motor, the hand-brushed finish to the engine block, the lightening holes in every possible location, safety wires intricately laced through almost every bolt head. It looks right, and so it is: a memorable, serio-frivolous, uncalculated object catching the light. Except that, like the car, Norman's account has calculation and detachment to its design: this *is* an object, and Norman is not the participant but the narrator. What is striking about the telling, apart from the obvious extraordinary recall of details fifty years later, is how much it convinces, and yet it cannot, in reality, have been like that. At least, Norman at twenty-two could not have described it as Norman did at seventy-five: although at twenty-two he undoubtedly felt the subtle currents between the members of this strangely assorted group, he was too young to articulate them and did not have the perspective, either historically or experientially, to see what was happening. (We can never get a perspective on ourselves either, because we are our own perspective.) He wasn't exactly blundering through this event or others in his life at this time – he was too intelligent for that – but he had no idea where the events were leading. Perhaps I feel strongly about the telling of the episode because, as told by Norman, it is a perfectly caught moment. It is not misleading as such. It is just easy to be misled by it: it has all the timing and organisation of hindsight and composition. The girls are chilled but vivacious, everyone in the car shares a taste for adventure, ideal weather and an ideal location are happily exchanged for a compromise in which one of the girls finds the steely light of Epping Forest "Turneresque" and both are "enchanted" to sit by a lake dotted with half-submerged oil drums and bicycle wheels; only towards the end, with the unspoken question of where these couples will go next (if anywhere), does gaiety shade into prudence. Perhaps it really was like that. But although, in an arresting passage, Norman puts himself as participant into Zahra's mind to catch at her thoughts about Hagen, we know nothing of what Norman himself felt, spending this day caught between observation and experience, between what was happening around him and what was happening to him. Fifty years later his only description of himself is untruthful, as "dressed badly" and incurably untidy. In particular, we know nothing about *his* thoughts at the experience of discovering Zahra's friend Ernestina, whom he would marry less than five months later.

Ernestina, he writes, reminded him of Carmen Miranda "and sported a good deal of jewellery unsuited to the climate". She was Sicilian (in fact Swiss-Sicilian – her great-grandmother on her father's side was Swiss) and lived in Bloomsbury with her parents, having been educated in France and Spain. (The Corvaja family had seventeenth-century roots and purchased aristocratic origins in southern Spain.) She had "a most infectious laugh", and when the subject of love came up over the sandwiches she enjoyed shocking her girlfriend with the fact that in Sicily all married men who could afford to kept mistresses. If they were foolish enough to be found out, she said, their wives generally shot them.

"Would you shoot your husband?" I asked.
"No," she said, "but I won't marry a Sicilian. Just to be on the safe side."

Whatever Norman thought of Ernestina, it was enough for him to want to meet her again the following Saturday evening. Another foursome was arranged with Hagen and Zahra but by then, according to Norman, Zahra's cautious mind was made up. Ernestina arrived at Euston with a note from her claiming a cold, and Hagen stoically withdrew, leaving Norman and Ernestina to cement their friendship at the Corner House at St Giles Circus. Like the description of their first meeting (in truth, like all the events described in his autobiography), this second encounter has its glorious and its unrevealing side. The

Lyons Corner House, "Xanadu as far as either of us was concerned", was host to a playing-out of cosmopolitan gestures probably more convincing on her part than his, as she had seen something of Europe and the United States and studied at Madrid University. Norman all the same sensed that this was the first time she had been out alone with a man. What else did he think? Was he attracted to her? Did he feel any attachment to a young woman who was also a fugitive from her background? If it is impossible to say, which of course it is, there is still discernibly an undercurrent of protective affection in his memory of her (despite the fact that later he could not stand her). She is the decisive one, and he was thankful both for her vivacity and just possibly everything she represented to him as an escape route.

Allowing her to lead the way offered him a rapid series of discoveries and strangenesses. As a way of breaking out of "the intensely parochial life of the outer suburbs, the working day surrendered to sales patter for yeast tablets and the fraudulent elixir, the glum pick-ups in Church Street, Enfield and Hilly Fields Park, the teeth-baring bonhomie of the George and Dragon, and the Saturday night hop at the Oddfellows' Hall",[10] he could not have found better. Their relationship did not in any sense lead him where he expected it to in the end, but for now it was the *break* that was all-important. The possibility of breaking away was the final authority for his decisions (in this case his acceptance of Ernestina's decisions). If a new situation could get him out and away from his old situation, it was, a priori, good.

Norman claims that he was surprised that Ernestina, who could speak and read English, Italian, Spanish and French fluently enough to discuss European literature on the basis of having read its canon in the original, found his conversation adequate. She may have been more cosmopolitan, but he protests too much. He was a long way from being able to offer as accomplishments only a few sentences in Welsh and an experience of the world restricted to Forty Hill and "the soggy villages of south Wales", with his fluent spoken French, usable German and encyclopedic knowledge of Russian fiction, not to mention his (dubious) record as a motorcycle racer and worldly acquaintance with Pigalle and the promenade des Anglais. They swapped cultural references on more or less equal terms, though their real equality – and more importantly their emotional link – was all in their shared urgency to shed their background: in which she, predictably, was a good dozen steps ahead of him.

They had been going out for less than two months when, at one meeting, Ernestina decided without warning that he must meet her parents. The Corvajas resided at the most English of addresses, between Euston and the British Museum, but lived behind their front door in a state of Mediterranean idiosyncrasy. The island of Sicily, cut off from modern Italy, clings to habits of provincial elegance with a famished hankering for display traceable to its eighteenth-century glory days; Palermo's immense squares glitter without shadow. At number 4 Gordon Street, Sicily had come to Bloomsbury. The scene Norman came across as he stood in his, as he claims, "suit of inferior cloth, of trousers that were too short and sleeves too long" was that of a presentation from which there was no hiding place. Chandelier, powerful wall lamps, furniture, gilded chairs and doors, the glasses in which the wine was served, all either emitted a glare of light or scintillatingly reflected it. Signora Corvaja, Maria, spoke good English but Norman and Ernestina's father Ernesto restricted themselves to responding by guesswork to the other's speech. This however, as the essential encounter of the evening, depended more on its ambassadorial formality than any human comprehension, and seemed to pass off satisfactorily – though in an overheard aside Ernesto Corvaja allegedly muttered as he left the room, "Has she brought a ragpicker home?" Signor Corvaja was to become an admired figure in Norman's life, by his implacable loyalty and sense of fatalistic irony a tonal opposite to Norman's own anguished father.

He was dressed in a dark suit of conservative cut which he might have been wearing for the first time. His eyes were black and protruding, and his black hair was brushed close to his scalp and no expression showed in his face as he came towards us, taking short, shuffling steps. We shook hands, he gave me a quick, mechanical smile and said something incomprehensible in a language which I presumed to be Italian in a cracked, grating voice that managed in some way to be pleasant. "Daddy is welcoming you to our house," Ernestina said. "He asks you to make yourself at home." I bowed and, stricken momentarily with my old speechlessness, produced a faint, inarticulate gargling, before seating myself, still gripping my frayed parcel, on the edge of a small golden throne. Thus began my long acquaintance with Ernesto Giovanni Batista Corvaja, a singular man.[11]

Lacking any information from Norman about his feelings for Ernestina, one is inclined, forced might be more accurate, to see the next step in their relationship again as one of hers, with Norman improvising

compliantly in her wake. That would not be unusual as the prelude to
a marriage, except that this marriage was explicitly not to be any sort
of love match but, in Ernestina's view, a "working partnership" between
the two of them. Ernestina would keep her own name, they would
have separate rooms, each would be free to come and go as they
wanted. It would be an alliance steeped in the free-love doctrines of
Russell and the experimentalism of the 1930s – in the left-right political polarity of the time the amatory equivalent of a statement that if
one was not a Communist, one was at least an anti-Fascist in the private
arena as well as the public, holding established conventions in contempt.

The couple married on 15 September in a ritual of pronounced
nonchalance. The only witnesses at Henrietta Street register office were
Hagen and his latest girlfriend, the heiress to a Bombay rag-trade fortune.
After the ceremony, having thrown away the Woolworths ring, they
addressed themselves to "the ticklish problem" of telling Ernestina's
parents. Norman suspected that for Ernestina it was less of a problem
than for him, and he was right. When they arrived at Gordon Street
she marched into the electric blaze of the drawing room and with
triumphal élan delivered the fait accompli to her father –

. . . as Ernesto listened, a grey patina seemed to spread across his cheeks. In
silence he drew a hand across his face and the shadow was gone, and a defeated
looseness of the jowls was drawn tight.

"Show me the paper," he said in Italian, and Ernestina took the marriage
certificate from her handbag and gave it to him.

"*Non è uno scherzo, Papa*," she is said to have replied, and in
Norman's account the words clang with the echoes of a millennial
contest, an ancient generational struggle summarily ended by a winning
blow that ends years of paternal domination and in which the vanquished
father can only retain his dignity by redeploying the shreds of his
authority into a proud fatalism. Ernesto Corvaja sat in stunned silence,
and then "straightened and smiled at me, a little wolfishly, I thought",
Norman wrote. "What I was witnessing was a classic example of the
stoic Sicilian reaction to irretrievable calamity, known in their enigmatic island as 'swallowing the claws of the toad'." Standing, his
father-in-law stepped stiffly forward to embrace him. "I will give you
my blood."[12] (We should remember that this wasn't what Norman
witnessed at twenty-three – Norman aged twenty-three had nil expe-

rience of Sicilian proverbs – only what he saw in his memory's eye when he wanted to write about the moment half a century later. In fact "to swallow the claws of the toad" is not a Sicilian proverb at all: the *Italian* proverb meaning "to bite the bullet" is "*ingoiare il rospo*", "to swallow the toad". The curious thing is that Norman improves not only the scene in his re-creation of it but the proverb too, at least in English: in its rhythm it really should be "to swallow the claws of the toad".)

Norman had broken the bonds of Forty Hill. He had found the new base that he was looking for, the migration inwards to the city, and if it came with a complete new household, both suited him. The fundamental contrast between the traditional Sicilian background and "extraordinary openness of mind" of the Corvaja parents, compared with Enfield and his own parents' inflexible gloom, had raised his gaze to a horizon so expansive that it annihilated any question marks at closer range about his marriage. He was willing to make the social experiment with Ernestina work and felt that was all that was required. It was its own justification: it gave both of them everything they needed, chiefly a double escape from the suffocation of Sicilian patriarchy in Ernestina's case and in Norman's the desert thirst of the city's perimeter. In Bloomsbury he could drink from many cups at once: from the tangible attractions of the capital, and from the mysterious fusion of Italian life and the more primitive and obscure elements that Sicily represented. The senior Corvajas endeared themselves to him by having no religious belief, no class-consciousness and no national pride, and by apparently possessing only interesting eccentricities. Maria spent her spare time sewing shepherdesses' dresses and speed-reading classic novels, while Ernesto indulged himself in painting and gilding (and lighting) the interior of the Gordon Street house. His ceilings were his own inspiration, "of fat-limbed *putti* bouncing on haloed clouds" in the style of Michelangelo, and their illumination – never complete, always changing, lamps one day being replaced by theatre spotlights the next – demanded constant labour of improvement. The parents were, as Norman notes, as much fugitives as he and Ernestina were. They had abandoned Sicily and Italy to live in

London; in London they had enough money for their needs and time on their hands. The combination of displacement and slight boredom led them forwards, in search of new sensations, and back to extreme examples of Sicilian ways. Norman reserved his greatest gratitude for the Corvajas' complete acceptance of him, the *cenciauolo*, the rag-picker. (His punctilious father-in-law, always dressed in a blue pinstripe "as if attending at an important funeral", was universally disappointed by the reality of British dress standards.) Norman was instantly a member of the family, and more privileged than the Corvaja children in that neither of his in-laws "ever permitted themselves a criticism of me, except on the single occasion when, as we were about to visit a restaurant together, Ernesto suggested that I should smarten up my appearance. To this, as if inspired by an afterthought, he added, '– and always strive to develop character.'"

His bond with Ernestina was equally untroubled. She had partly selected Norman for what she perceived as Englishness, or an interesting streak of it. Beneath her conscious decision she was unaware that there was nothing English about Norman, and blunt judgment would insist that her choice of the Bugatti-owning, literature-talking, political-and-social-rebel kind of Englishman she thought she needed was a long way from the slow, stolid, prejudiced variety of Englishman she probably needed rather more: after an existence of such cosmopolitan rootlessness, what she most urgently needed was not to escape *from* her father, but a decisively anchored place to escape *to*, "a tradition, a sense of history, allegiances, attitudes and a firm point of view".[13] None of which Norman, the teenage-rejecter-turned-adult-improviser, was in any position to give her.

For now this did not matter. He and Ernestina were preoccupied with their coup's success and its new arrangements. In 1932 at Gordon Street he carried on business with Alexander Hagen in step with his partnership with his engineer friend, Arthur Baron. An escapist by reflex – arguably Norman's management of that reflex is the dominant theme of his life – his attraction to lively wheeled transport had become commercially valuable. Every vehicle he owned was a symbolic getaway car, but he and Baron found the means to turn escapism to profit, buying, restoring, driving and selling efficiently (and later racing not so efficiently) a series of cars that would make a heavily insured collection today. After his fancy Type 30 Bugatti with the Lavocat et Marsaud body came a road-race FWD (front wheel drive) Alvis, a vast two-seater with slab sides and a predatory wheelbase bought that year, followed by a Bugatti Type 40 roadster, an Alfa Romeo 1750 and another very quick Bugatti Type 55. These were touring cars that Norman owned one after another – he estimated that he covered 50,000 miles (80,000 kilometres) in the three highly reliable Bugattis – in addition to the race cars, an insanely over-powered supercharged Brescia Bugatti, a Grand Prix Type 51 and others, that he and Baron shared at the track.

Life in the Corvaja household did not stretch his resources – indulgence shown to the new family member made his domestic existence comfortable as never before – but its patina of gloriously strange novelty inevitably eroded, to reveal stranger depths. The face Ernesto Corvaja presented to the world was stoical, family-loving and attuned to gaiety, yet any curious observer might eventually have wondered if the lights that blazed even from the cupboards of 4 Gordon Street as soon as their doors were opened weren't a form of denial: a symbolic way of denying that his past possessed any doubtful corners. Officially on his passport Ernesto was a diamond dealer: Norman recounts the satisfaction his father-in-law took in periodically pouring a handkerchief full of stones onto a cloth beneath the drawing-room chandelier, and the "faintly watery sound" they made as they tumbled out: but Corvaja's professional manner was rather belied by the absence of any commercial activity. His exact route from Palermo to Bloomsbury, via New York, also remained mysterious, and to begin with there was no visible cause for Ernestina's apparently overwhelming desire to detach herself from her father either. "Life with the Corvajas", Norman wrote later, "had the effect in time of stifling natural curiosity"[14] – it is a Sicilian characteristic to seek safety in numbers and at the same time to guard privacy with fanatic composure – but it was impossible for him not to amass some insight into the family background over time and at unguarded moments. The obvious opportunity was at dinner, a prolonged, literally operatic meal eaten beneath the stage lighting to the accompaniment of Verdi and Puccini arias on the gramophone, when the consumption of a few glasses of Ernesto's black Sicilian wine, imported in cask and bottled at Gordon Street, ritually loosened Corvaja reserve. Every night animation slid into argument that became the prelude for violent screaming quarrels. These were practically always about ridiculous controversies – "the highest building in New York, or the number of children given birth to by Queen Victoria" – that everyone joined in with, including Ernestina's younger brother Eugene, peppering his interjections with strings of English swear words newly learnt at school (everyone swore in their preferred language). But the most frequent and noisy participants were Ernestina and her father, their ritual antagonism a front for a profounder conflict.

The truth as Ernestina eventually told it was twofold, though this too may have possessed some deeper and more anguishing, pre-existing cause. First, the nanny who had been taken on to look after her and her brother several years before had not been a nanny at all but her father's mistress (her mother, when she found out, had shot Ernesto as custom demanded and emptied a slop-bucket over the nanny, then afterwards been tearfully and noisily reconciled with her husband). Second, the emerald ring that he had bought Ernestina for her seventeenth birthday had turned out not to be a proper stone, just a chip. Coming to adulthood, jettisoning the pedestal she had placed him on, she had decided that her fallible father, guilty of both vicarious and personal betrayal, was to be thrown aside with great force.

Gradually other elements of Ernesto's past surfaced. He was, more by failure to confirm that he was not, a member of the mafia. One night Maria Corvaja got drunk and revealed that the day he left Sicily he had been shot at (not by her). He himself admitted that in his twenties he had been taken into custody for a serious crime in Catania, escaped from prison, and been smuggled out of Sicily to the USA. The family legend was that he had been sent with other fugitives, hidden in coffins with air-holes drilled in them. In America he had become a member of the Unione Siciliana, an organisation founded in the 1880s in New York's Italian Harlem to look after the welfare of newly arrived Sicilians and progressively overtaken by the mob. His legal training suggested that he was not a strategist or an enforcer, therefore only tainted by association as an adviser, but after a machine-gun ambush outside his New York apartment that carried away his hat, he and Maria decided to take ship for Europe. Mussolini's government had expanded his original arrest warrant to an order of permanent banishment from Italy, so it was England, and Bloomsbury, instead. Maria also revealed that he had to take care against the eventuality of another assassination attempt from America, which was the reason for the continued presence of both her useless pistol in her handbag and the loaded revolver that lay in the top drawer of her husband's desk.

In the almost febrile atmosphere of self-invention and escape at Gordon Street – every member of the household with getaways behind them, or in front, or both – Norman's and Ernestina's alliance bucked the trend for a time. Norman's wife was witty, highly articulate and cheerful, with an extraordinary memory for facts and languages, and "pretty", her son Ito says, "when she dressed up she was pretty. They made a very handsome couple."[15] Ito remembers that "she needed people and people needed her, and she had a vast crowd of friends wherever she went, my mother would pick up friends just like that".[16]

But Ernestina's wit and effervescence packaged a manic quality that Norman sometimes found tiring. Others' gaiety, unchecked, can be a form of coercion; and Norman's character, introspective, arrogant, with its own social modes of wanting either to impress his audience or to vanish and observe, reacted badly to coercion. Having gone along with Ernestina's determination for marriage, he had nevertheless been conscious and consented for his own reasons: to get himself out of Enfield, away from the horror. (There may also have been an element of retaliation against Gwen Nicholls, now Gwen Varnals, for her very recent marriage.) Later he summarised his first marriage as "an avenue of escape".[17] If he had not taken that avenue, he would have taken the next. So he was startled to find that, though theirs was supposed to be an absolutely open relationship to which either could call a halt, once he was in it Ernestina would not accept a halt. The Russellian justification that had validated it had not provided an exit strategy. Ernestina had committed herself emotionally more than she had expected to (or perhaps just hidden some of her real motives for marrying Norman); socially she also had nowhere to go if they divorced or separated and was dependent on Norman to keep her out of her father's fief. As a couple they were discovering that the moral progressiveness of the 1930s had limits (not even partly shed until the 1960s).

Ernestina was charming, but imperious and demanding and a bit mad, and as their "working partnership" went on Norman admired his wife's intellect but was unable to deal with her character. He might perhaps have agreed that it was an injustice that she gave him some of his best material by introducing him to some of the places that would take deepest root in his imagination (Sicily first, via Ernesto, and later Guatemala), and was eventually rewarded for it by being purged from his thoughts.

Elements of Norman's life in the 1920s and early 1930s reflect to a surprising degree the cultural colonisation of that era by the potent pairing of Surrealism and hedonism – the former attempting to capture the inter-war decades' absurdity, the latter to deal with their atmosphere of intractable futility. (There was a dash of Futurism thrown in too, in those decades' obsession with speed.) Few people in Britain believed in a long peace after the treacherous domestic politics of the 1920s and the war's aftershocks in Europe that had begun with German hyperinflation and by the first years of the 1930s had evolved into near-certainty that there would be another war. Evelyn Waugh's Jesuit Father Rothschild in his 1930 novel *Vile Bodies* is clairvoyant in his attempt to widen the dull conversational topics of "the younger generation" at Lady Anchorage's party.

Wars don't start nowadays because people want them. We long for peace, and fill our newspapers with conferences about disarmament and arbitration, but there is a radical instability in our whole world-order, and soon we shall all be walking into the jaws of destruction again, protesting our pacific intentions.

Lord Metroland's dismissive response – "'Anyhow,' said Lord Metroland, 'I don't see how all that explains why my stepson should drink like a fish and go about everywhere with a negress'" – suggests both the gulf between old and young and the failure to grasp that inter-war hedonism was a flight from, rather than into, instability: an instability papered over by repressive politics and conservative dullness.

"I think they're connected, you know," said Father Rothschild. "But it's all very difficult."[18]

Norman's brand of survival, as he negotiated the years from 1925 onwards, had been to push onwards: to seek, having effected the necessary escape from Enfield, the maximum of pleasure and sensation, to accept the need for solvency, and to nurse his literary ambitions without knowing for certain what he was looking for from a career as a writer. Put another way, he was neither purely a hedonist nor was he building anything permanent. There was nothing permanent to build. Yet in 1932, at twenty-four, he had already – if writing means having something to write *about* – put considerable social and literary space between himself and the blank tedium, the "nothing … with chips", of his starting point. The young fugitive from the perimeter was living in the middle of Bloomsbury, at the heart of the modernist establishment (Virginia Woolf's house was across the square at number 46), married to the daughter of a Sicilian *mafioso*, a businessman using a string of rare fast cars as personal transport. There is something of Paul Pennyfeather in Evelyn Waugh's *Decline and Fall* about him ("Paul was beginning to feel cosmopolitan, the Ritz to-day, Marseilles tomorrow, Corfu next day, and afterwards the whole world stood open to him"). Or if we catch at his feelings about life with the Corvajas, something too of Agatha Runcible:

D'you know, all that time when I was dotty I had the most awful dreams. I thought we were all driving round and round in a motor race and none of us could stop, and there was an enormous audience composed entirely of gossip writers and gate-crashers and Archie Schwert and people like that, all shouting to us at once to go faster, and car after car kept crashing until I was left all alone driving and driving – and then I used to crash and wake up.[19]

In the general dash for sensation or escape from Depression asperities, there is no sense that Norman rested idly on pleasure where he found it. If he was not an artist yet, or not a proven success at anything, he was not a social casualty either. The 1920s gossip columnist and partygoer Patrick Balfour summarised his generation's aspiration in the phrase "there was no particular object in anything that we did, but we were sensible of its full flavour as we did it".[20] Setting the Thames on fire was a "public demonstration against the dulness of social life".[21] That was not Norman's rationale. These were still becoming years; he carried on improvising, channelling his energy into something that *might* take him further. The sense that he wanted to do *something*, get *somewhere*, in these years is overwhelming. As an improviser he set high standards, even if much of the improvisation went into committed self-promotion: he drew attention to himself strenuously in the manner of clever outcasts: his view of the world, from his politics to his mode of dress, ranged against almost everyone else's. Gwen Varnals, who came back from Ireland with her husband in the winter of 1932 and found work in the City of London, remembers that his dandyism was unchecked. "It was nothing to see him with long hair and a cloak and a sombrero. And he grew a beard before anybody else."[22]

He still went back regularly to Forty Hill, racing the dust roads in whatever car he was driving at the time, to see his parents and manage the photographic processing business over his father's shop. He took charge of the business and made it a branch of the chemist's. Eric Nicholls, Gwen's brother, had an older sister Gertie "not so beautiful as Gwen or Nancy . . . he was kindhearted enough, when he would be passing Gertie on the way from Enfield town or whatever, to pick her up and give her a ride in the Bugatti. I know he did it out of kindness, because she would feel she wasn't [as] attractive [as] the other two."[23] Joyce Dale remembers that "there were hardly any cars on the road" and "he had this red Bugatti" that he drove "like mad around the village, terrifying the villagers".[24] He took Ernestina to meet his parents in the Alvis and drove the Corvaja parents out to meet Richard and Louisa too, a formality that was littered with hazards, among them Louisa's dislike of Ernestina, chiefly on the grounds that Ernestina was married to her son.

But the day went off successfully, despite the Corvajas' nervousness about leaving the security of the city, Louisa's decision to serve a bleached and rubbery *macaroni pomodori* in the belief that that was what Italians always ate, and Richard's descent into a trance. Norman's set-piece account describes the Forty Hill surroundings, his parents' house and garden and the neighbouring cherry orchards, appearing to the Corvajas as "encrusted with small wonders". The sun shone and the trees sagged under blossom, and even a chance contact with the villagers charmed the visitors. "A spotty local girl on the arm of her lover arrived to deliver a pot of cream, and Maria said that it reminded her of a scene from *Cavalleria Rusticana*. What could be greater tribute to Forty Hill, Enfield on a May morning than that it should be seen so closely to imitate the opera?"[25] At lunch, when Richard Lewis, with Norman watching aghast, began to mumble and then sweat and writhe in an uncontrolled trance, the ordeal turned out to have unexpectedly positive consequences. The "thin, and unearthly and troubled" voice of a small girl issuing from Richard's throat with a repeated appeal to "Mamma, mamma", was, Maria asserted, that of Ernestina's younger sister who had died ten years before. The Corvajas, Norman claimed, returned to the safety of Gordon Street entirely under the spell of life in Forty Hill: Maria became a secret spiritualist, and Ernesto installed a brood of a dozen Rhode Island Red chickens in their basement bedroom where they tottered around, miring the carpet and stricken with rickets.

By early 1933, however, the tension between Ernestina and her father had built up to a pressure that required practical release. Norman and

she left Gordon Street and set up home briefly at Manor House in a
Victorian mansion "built in prison style" with a view of a reservoir from
its back windows. Their street, Woodberry Down, had a good deal of
rented property and had arbitrarily attracted a knot of Caucasians and
Kazakhs who had fled Soviet collectivisation, whose numbers had swelled
as Stalin's drive to liquidate the kulaks intensified. (So barbaric were
Stalin's confiscations that in the spring of 1930 the writer Isaac Babel
had lost his faith in socialism when he travelled into the country to areas
of "socialist construction" and witnessed the devastation of Ukrainian
collectivisation.) The "Soviets" of Woodberry Down were country people,
Ingushes, Chechens and Kazakhs, who had improbably escaped to the
eventless urbanity of north London from a land of wolves, marals and
golden eagles where men slept fully clothed in case of attack, and who
socialised with a vividly un-English sense of occasion.

   There were heady months of drinking and party-going, all-night fireworks, furniture-burning, and interior redecoration in a central Asian
style. In the midst of the carousal Norman continued to look round
for ways to make money. In his autobiography he places the move to
Finsbury Park two years earlier, before his marriage to Ernestina, but
his business activity did not begin to focus and take off until 1933,
and it happened at Manor House when his photographic experience
identified a nascent boom in amateur photography. The German
company Leitz had marketed the first high-quality 35mm Leica camera
in 1925; in 1931 Henri Cartier-Bresson, Norman's exact contemporary, had bought his first Leica in Marseille. From 14 Woodberry Down
Norman began to buy and sell good-quality cameras, advertising in the
classified section of *Amateur Photographer*.

Zeiss Ikon Miraflex. Indistinguishable from new – Lewis, 14 Woodb'y Down,
Manor House, N4.[26]

In April and May he was selling in ones and twos. In May too the
Lewises' tenancy expired and, in view of their partying and interior
decorating, was not renewed. Business and home life reverted to 4
Gordon Street. The camera sales business developed slowly, with only
the odd Zeiss and Kodak for sale until September when Norman began
to put "Wanted" announcements – "cheap Leica or Contax cameras,
cheap for immediate cash" – in the classifieds. A few months later his
first trade advertisement appeared, containing the whole Lewis

business formula in embryo: high quality, best value, personal attention. "Before buying a Leica, Contax, Rolleiflex, etc., write to R G
Lewis, Miniature Camera Specialist, 5, Southbury Road, Enfield, who
will definitely offer the highest allowance in England on your old
camera."[27] The advertisement ran weekly, and by the following May
he had Leicas to sell, by July too many to list individually.

Business was accelerating, possibly with his father-in-law Ernesto's
help as a backer. (Help that Ernesto gave substantially later on.) Norman
was diversifying his sources and customers however he could. On a
later trip through Germany he is rumoured to have avoided paying
import tax on the Leicas he brought back from Wetzlar by stuffing
them in the spare wheel of his car and smuggling them through customs;
he is also said to have carried off a commercial coup by selling a
consignment of Leicas to Japan at a huge profit.

Whatever the success or probity (or truth) of such coups, he had
correctly foreseen the explosion in popularity of the small camera – the
Photographic Journal noting in 1937 that "There are in Britain alone
over five million amateur photographers" – and by the end of that same
year he would be not just selling Leicas from his first London shop but
writing promotional manuals for developing and printing, and holding
a Royal Photographic Society-sponsored "kinematograph exhibition" of
Ampro cine projectors. A curious angle to Norman's career in the 1930s
is that over and above his enthusiasm for the generally unwriterly matters
of business and motor sport, in commerce he instinctively involved
himself with two of the most iconic products – the Bugatti and the Leica
camera – of the twentieth century, much as later he showed literary originality and timing in the choice of places he travelled to.

The couple went on living at Gordon Street, and there were occasional welcome (I imagine) respites from Corvaja family pressures.
Norman taught Ernestina to shoot. They went to Paris, where they
were photographed at a shooting range. Ernestina aims with her leading
arm well up and her cheek against the stock of the rifle; her face – she
photographed well – shines with animation. Norman stands slackly
next to her, in a polka-dotted shirt with spotted tie and a moustache
and goatee beard for the first time, his gaze also on the target but with
that curiously watchful lethargy that seems to assert that he is far more
likely to score a bull, if she would only pass him the weapon.

Norman's embarrassment about his own family inevitably included
the distant madhouse of his grandfather and aunts in Wellfield Road,

Carmarthen. He tried to keep Carmarthen at a distance but his grandfather had recently died and family matters arose that needed to be settled. His father Richard, having reached a stage of unshakable boredom, refused to leave Enfield to deal with them. Norman was forced to make the visit in his place. He was worried, he wrote later, about the effect the journey would have on Ernestina, determined to accompany him. It was perhaps not his greatest worry. In his account of life at the time, periodic – as though necessary or even purgative – references to Ernestina's vivacity are nearly always followed by some veiled allusion to her instability: her laughing uproariously and inappropriately at an episode no English person would find funny, for instance, or bursting into noisy tears at a sentimental anecdote. His story of their planned visit to Carmarthen is really more about the curious fragility of their marriage than his anxiety about the impact it would have on her. (He also worried that her "unaccommodating personality" would make settling anything with his aunts difficult.) Within a year of getting married doubts had taken root in Norman's mind, communicated fifty years later in delicate analogies like this:

A central legend of the Celtic people is that of the Lady of the Lake: the union between a human being and a fairy who endows her human husband with all manner of material and spiritual benefits, but who leaves him when he objects to her irrational behaviour. There were times in our association when I was reminded of the legend. The fairy at Myddfai startled the human beings among whom she lived by exaggerated displays of feeling, and this sometimes happened with Ernestina too.[28]

The expedition to Wales turned out to be an unwelcome plunge back into the stark, uncomfortable medley of his childhood. Time had done its Daliesque work, leaving some aspects of what he had known still recognisable while it pulled and distended others into grotesque or barely readable shapes. Carmarthen had changed. It was "drained of all the magic it had had for me, even as a captive, when a child". In his elegy Norman privileges the irrecoverable pleasures over the pain.

There had been so many freedoms no one had been able to shut out: the little bright snails, pink, yellow and blue, that had come over the walls in their hundreds to deliver themselves into my eager collector's hands; the cackle of the knowing jackdaws awaiting their cake; the song of the linnets and goldfinches I trapped; even the freedom expressed in the smell of the country town itself, spreading through all the lanes and entering every window, which was of ferns and milk and freshly wetted earth. Above all I remembered with nostalgia the great freedom of escape with Aunt Li to the summit of Pen-lan, followed as we trudged up into the mists by the chiming every quarter-hour of the bells of St Peter's church. . . .[29]

Without the custodial protection of their father, Norman's aunts had completed their descent into seclusion. The imposing facade of the house had faded and cracked, and Aunt Li, seen in the front garden as Norman and Ernestina arrived, had dimmed to a "grey little wraith". The bright, immaculate state of the lawn, in contrast, looked shockingly refulgent against the greyness. (It had been part of his aunt's therapy during her hospitalisation to mow the lawns, which she continued frenziedly to do at Wellfield Road.) At the front door they found that one kind of patriarch had been substituted by another, a Baptist minister who "clearly had the run of the house" and somehow had acquired a power of attorney for the aunts. One purpose of Norman's visit was to try to win over his aunts to a more equitable distribution of their father's tea fortune, so that their sister-in-law, his aunt Margaret, might profit modestly from her late husband's (and their brother's) contribution to the business. John Lewis had worked for the old man all his life but his father had willed most of the profit to his sisters; the son had drunk himself into an early grave, and Margaret had been driven into exile on the seafront at Llanstephan. The involvement of the blandly sanctimonious minister, Reverend Emrys Davies, irritated Norman as it left him unable to mediate directly with his aunts, though the mental health of all three made it difficult to do so in any case. The epileptic Polly was almost catatonic, Annie was found, her pirate costumes discarded, sitting on the floor painting smilies on acorns, and Li continued to churn up and down outside with her lawnmower. Norman was made more uncomfortable by the continued existence – now more cracked, shrivelled, yellow and dusty – of every ugly thing he had disliked about his grandfather's house, including the "crackthroated piano" and the "ancient clocks, mysteriously kept wound, [that] still disputed the hour of the day". In the kitchen "a trick of memory brought back the faint bloody reek of pigs' intestines in a tin bath awaiting their transformations into chitterlings". Ernestina's unpredictable presence did not soothe him.

The confrontation that followed was inconclusive. Norman was forced to accept Reverend Emrys Davies's flourished power of attorney and let matters lie. Ernestina, shocked by what she had seen, fell silent as they left Wellfield Road to drive the few miles down the lush estuary road to the coast. Norman's liking for Llanstephan and his attachment to his aunt Margaret, dating from his exile and the warmth she had shown him, allowed him to ignore the village's sinister piety:

. . . they no longer stoned holiday-making miners, and ten years had gone since Mr Williams had put up his placard for the last time warning Sunday visitors to keep holy the Sabbath day, but a tight rein was still kept on religious belief, the social life of the village being firmly bound up with the chapel which took a hard-line fundamentalist approach in matters of faith. . . . No one here could drag themselves clear from the past.[30]

Ernestina cheered up at the sight of the castle and the wide, salty horizon. Ladies in broad Welsh hats passed them, eyeing the couple, and an illegally working fisherman wheeled his cartload of sewin and cockles by. But Margaret Lewis, as they found out when they arrived for tea, had already fallen foul of the local chapel, caught in the act of putting a vase of flowers at the base of the pulpit on the day of her induction: a pagan transgression that would have to be repented in public before she would have any chance of being accepted by her new neighbours.

Faced with another incident of Baptist fundamentalism so soon after the first, Norman and Ernestina retreated. They had planned the Welsh journey to be a basis for more sightseeing, as Ernestina had seen practically nothing of Britain outside Bloomsbury, but on the drive back to London both their intended inspection of Bath and any conversation about their Carmarthen experience were suppressed. Ernestina, Norman thought, was depressed by her immersion into yet another Lewis family reality. On their return to Gordon Square he watched her take herself off for a full day's visit to the news cinemas – there were several in central London, at Marble Arch, Piccadilly Circus, Leicester Square, and Waterloo and Victoria stations, showing a one-hour loop of British and American newsreels, cartoons and short comedy films – from which she came back to a prolonged communion with her collection of American comics until she had had enough of wild laughter and had decompressed sufficiently to deal with the world again.

Through 1933 and 1934 Norman had helped with the pharmacy side of his father's shop as Richard Lewis's depressions worsened. He was also spending time with Arthur Baron at his Dorking, Surrey garage, where Baron was developing his interest in Bugatti's race-winning Grand Prix cars. Baron is recorded as entering a Bugatti in a race at Brooklands as early as March 1934, and he later rebuilt and raced a Type 59 Bugatti that had killed its inexperienced driver at the 1936 Limerick Grand Prix. (The Type 59's driver, the Duke of Grafton, was twenty-two and died of his burns after he hit a convent wall on the first lap at Limerick. His family gave the car to his chauffeur, who sold it to Baron. Baron's aptitude for salvaging dead men's cars was impressive. The following year, 1937, Mervyn White crashed in practice for the Cork International Car Race on 20 May, dying of a brain injury four days later, and Baron and Norman jointly bought his wrecked Type 51.) In 1934 Norman and Ernestina joined Baron at several Brooklands meetings. The lure of race days at the Surrey circuit was held to be as much social as professional.

In 1934 another change, as sudden as his marriage, took place, in what seems afterwards like one of those movements when the camera speeds up – to the biographer gazing at the re-created film of Norman's life in his mind, the playback seems to accelerate to x2 or x4 – and takes over the person on the screen. In the next twenty years there would be several of these "alterations": unpredictable and rapid ruptures with the past and without any apparent stimulus, decisive points in an internal life leading to another self-conversion and all its consequences. Their internal provenance is obscure, though they seem in most cases to be brought on by a crisis of (unexpressed) frustration. (Norman's frustrations remained for most of his life so powerful that whenever they occurred he made extreme tactical efforts to conceal them.)

The source of the change is a mystery very probably connected to another mystery, of what kind of, and how much, literary activity was going on in the business-and-racing Lewis brain of the early 1930s. Writing does not always come from one place in the writer's mind, or two or three, and in Norman's case it probably comes from many conjecturable sources: displacement and isolation, rejection and loneliness, boredom and the outsider's enforced position of observation, intelligence, quick wit, the prison of the suburbs, the urge to flee, an embarrassing father, an over-protective mother, deficit of feeling, surfeit of passion, love of language(s), the desire to show off, the desire to understand the world in the way that children like to take clocks to pieces, to see how they work, the feeling about his generation that

Adam voices to Nina in *Vile Bodies*, "Nina, do you ever feel that things simply can't go on much longer?"

This synaptic and historical map of conjectural, interacting connections may seem obvious now, and curiously the only question that cannot be answered is the factual one. What writing was there? What had he written between the first *John Bull* bullets and plagiarised German news stories, and now? There are no notebooks, no letters, no living witnesses to say: all we have are a couple of certainties: literary ambition was not extinguished, and it was private. (He never spoke about it to Gwen Nicholls, his closest friend.)

Yet somewhere in the landscape, out of his escape reflex and his reading and his watchful lethargy and his dandyish glee at the possibilities of language for promoting himself ("Are you speaking, literally, metaphorically or figuratively?"), a new self-definition was emerging. Elements of his improvisation were beginning to react with each other. Unlike Adam, who fails to marry Nina because he hasn't got any money and he doesn't fight for her, or for anything, enough, Norman was striving for *something*. He *had* saved money from his various activities, or kept enough back from buying rare vehicles and other expenses. He had bought cheap and sold dear in several realms: cameras, cars, time. He had fought to liberate himself from parents and Mrs England's Dining Rooms. In the late summer of 1934 he decided that he needed to take himself off again.

On 5 September he advertised a "Special Seven Days' Clearance Sale" and on the 12th "Final cash clearance bargains" of camera stocks. Collecting funds, at the outset what he planned was unexpected: an expedition with Eugene, Ernestina's brother. (It was arranged that they would meet Ernestina somewhere on the way.) It was also an expedition that was intended to be literary from the start. Where it would lead, as they embarked on the ferry to France on Saturday 22 September 1934, both would probably have admitted that they did not have much idea, though Norman might have agreed that, as far as motive was concerned, at this point in his life and marriage to Ernestina he would echo Adam Fenwick-Symes' plea for complete change: "I'd give anything in the world for something different. . . . Different from everything."[31]

I went out and I saw that people were crossing the road and they were crawling across to get to the other side of the street and go wherever they were going. So I thought, well, English people don't do that, you see, so I started to walk. Well, there was a terrible sort of outburst of firing, so I got down on my hands and knees and crawled with the rest. The army were being shot at by revolutionaries on the roofs, wherever they were. And then suddenly there'd be an order, "Fuego!", boo-boo-boo-boo-boo.

Well, when I came back I wrote a book about this, a piece of juvenilia obviously.

Norman Lewis

Before the war as far as I can remember I wrote two books, both of which are deadly secrets. I don't think you'll find any examples round about. Amazingly enough, the first one I ever wrote Gollancz took like that. Straight away, no problem. I think it was an atrocious book. And then I wrote another one about this trip in the dhow – I found it really appalling. I suppose one has to feel like that about the early books. The first one was published by Gollancz, the second one by Routledge. I really keep them under wraps. They were a lot of rubbish.

Norman Lewis

I can at least vouch for the quality of the photography, being concerned with it professionally.

Norman Lewis, letter to Victor Gollancz Ltd, 27 April 1935

When I looked through the collection of photographs which accompany this manuscript – many of them superb, many of them fascinatingly unusual – I prayed that the text would be sufficiently tolerable to allow them to be published. And I believe my prayer has been answered.

They travel third class, they put up at cheap hotels, they visit the lowest cabarets and brothels, even in a cinema they take the cheapest seats. As a result, they have to endure some particularly nauseating experiences, and they must have ruined their digestions.

It should be a success.

JRE, Gollancz reader

6

SPAIN

"The house is burning. Let us warm ourselves"
Spanish saying

LITERARY, because he took notes from the start. Deliberate, closely detailed notes, in his curling, tiny handwriting with its crosses flying off the ts, filling page after page that would have to be reread with a magnifying glass. The notebooks he filled no longer exist, so those two sentences are in every sense a biographer's invention. But the book Norman wrote and published about his 1934 journey, *Spanish Adventure*, is so charged with attentiveness to facts and immediacy of impressions – impressions that in some cases seem to have struck him in the face, or at least with the intensity of Robert Louis Stevenson's "virginity of sense"[1] – that the journey just could not have been remembered afterwards with the thought that maybe, after all, it might make a book. Norman set out with the express intention of writing a substantial account, almost certainly something more than his notes. He wrote it fast and he was without modesty. Returning from his last stop at Casablanca in late November, he had an 80,000-word manuscript, with photographs, ready to send to a publisher four months later. The book he submitted to Victor Gollancz shows all the ambition of his arrogance, and all the imitation of his style. The tone he strove for gives obvious clues to who he might have been reading, apart from the Russians, in his twenties. *Spanish Adventure* lies halfway between Fleming (Peter), whose *Brazilian Adventure* was published the year before, and Wodehouse. (He did not go as far as imitating Peter Fleming's title. That was Gollancz's doing. Norman's own title was "The Spanish October".) With its incorporation of adventure and comic aloofness, the opening sentence willingly identifies its sources.

From the very first my attitude towards the canoe was tinged with distrust and condescension.[2]

The apparent plan was to combine a journey to southern Europe with an attempt to travel by the cheapest means of transport. The justification for the journey was – and it was a justification that he would often use afterwards – that very soon irrevocable change might make it impossible to see things as they were now. There is a curious stamp of the future writer, a youthful pomposity that with experience would become an entirely acceptable trope, as well as a prescience about future travellers in his explanation that "It merely was – and still is – my private opinion that if you want to see the world, now is the time. There are omnipresent signs of a wrath to come, embracing the possibility, at least, of a return to the Dark Ages. In such a case the only travellers will be refugees and the Hegira is likely to supersede the Pleasure Cruise."[3]

The objectives of the journey were vague. He admits to spending some time trying to dream up some kind of academic motivation, but apart from "wandering through southern Europe in contemplation of the spectacle of our civilisation faced with disruption", all he could come up with to "invest the journey with some slight claim to originality – to have something fresh to talk about on my return", was to cross to the Atlas mountains and see some of the areas of French pacification of the Maures in southern Morocco. The canoe was chosen as his and Eugene's form of transport because, once across the Channel, there were no fares, no hotel bills (they would pack a tent), and, if fortunate in their hunting of "fish, rabbits and wild ducks, and – prejudices permitting – rooks and moorhens too", no restaurant bills. Other writers and styles hover over his introductory chapter, the now revered polemicist and traveller Robert Byron for one, who had made a name for himself with *The Station* (1928) and *First Russia, Then Tibet* (1933), and a very obvious Jerome K. Jerome in a throwaway vaudevillian speech about the ultimate (and obviously soon to be confounded) benefits of the canoeist's way:

All you do is to paddle up a river as near as possible to the source, fold the canoe up, pack it away on your back and stride forward across the heath, moor or tableland that separates you from the next waterway that will carry you further in your direction.

Simplicity itself. In theory. Think about it long enough and your doubts and mistrusts begin to look unreasonable. In the end you work up a kind of enthusiasm and go about proclaiming the spiritual and physical benefits conferred by the open-air life.[4]

The first hitch came with the miniature rifle they were intending to hunt with. The French would allow only shotguns to be imported, the Spanish (despite the movement of arms by the crateload across the Pyrenees at the time) allowed no firearms at all, and strict licensing by the Portuguese made personal importation quasi-impossible. They left England without the rifle, resigned to a diet of fish, making for Alençon in southern Normandy as the place from which to launch canoe and story. They intended to use France's network of rivers and canals to reach Bayonne, then walk across to the Douro and, making for Porto, somehow reach the Tagus and Lisbon with a view to taking a cargo boat to north Africa. The second, minor inconvenience materialised at Alençon where, arriving at seven in the evening, they were unable to find the river Sarthe and instead found themselves the focus of mockery by sophisticated Norman sportsmen. Their payload of canoe and baggage, intended to be shouldered lightly by two energetic travellers, had worked up to more than 100 kilos and was being transported on a small cart: apparently it was all badly secured and each time the cart hit a pothole some piece of luggage flew off (though one can imagine the juvenile writer milking this scene for all it was worth). A facetious crowd gathered, holding up the traffic and a "lane of veteran Citroën cars conducted by prosperous Norman dairy farmers would pile up hooting and tooting like the Israelites before Jericho. At that time we were absurdly sensitive to publicity of this kind," he writes. "Dark of face and pale of knee" (another influence: an adaptation of Waugh's description of the Llanabba Silver Band in *Decline and Fall* as "low of brow, crafty of eye and crooked of limb") "we struggled silently at our task." Retreating to an hotel, the next morning they were up at dawn. One of the pleasures of *Spanish Adventure* for a reader today is recognising the earliest appearances of technique and tone for which Norman later became known: here, in rough outline, there is already the mixture of reportage and bubbling sweetness of expression. Reconnoitring, he and Eugene finally spotted a bridge, signalling water:

Rushing back we dragged out the trailer and dashed off in the direction of the river, desperately anxious to spare those citizens who were up and about the trouble of getting up a sending-off party.[5]

After several false starts, a broken wheel, and up to their knees in slime, they managed finally to launch. There is something quixotic about the idyll that follows, an escape into "the midst of plenty" from the troubles that have beset them, with the reader's sense of dread following close behind. Later, Norman's particular tonal fusion of elegy and absurdity, able to encapsulate a situation with visual precision and wit, would bring a place to life with a single unexpected phrase (one thinks of Epping Forest's "derelict sunshine") and sum up a moment in a sentence as nearly perfect and transient as the moment he was describing. His first published passage of description is an extended one, but he shows equal promise and an understanding that description is an exacting art (watch for the sequence of birds). "The sensation of being actually afloat partook to some degree of the miraculous," he begins.

Enthusiasm was undoubtedly high. The new world of the river through which we were passing was to us an almost elemental experience. We were privileged spectators at a pageant staged for our benefit by nature on its best behaviour. The river was black, silent and motionless. We slid forward over the surface without a sound except for the slight wash of the paddles. The sensation of smooth flight was soothing and luxurious. A faint exhalation of damp earth and decaying roots filled the air with an appropriate fragrance. Kingfishers, absorbed in voluptuous contemplation of the depths, remained insentient of our approach until we were almost upon them and then whirred away with tropical flashes of colour. Yellow wagtails bobbed and curtsied on the banks and made short, fluttering incursions over the water in search of the invisible flies for which fish competed with reiterated and amazingly athletic leaps from their natural element. Occasionally a heron minced away as if bored by our intrusion. The sudden flash of an uncorrodible salmon tin on the river bed reminded us that civilisation was still within easy distance.[6]

With the luxuriance of this account the reader imagines they must have made terrific headway. (In fact they had covered a kilometre.) The "black, silent" river Sarthe puts out its first hazards: shallows of pallid flags, then reeds and bulrushes, then a watermill. The watermills, which multiply, are, as in Quixote's case, not-watermills; but where the knight saw enchanted castles holding captive Dulcinea,

Norman and Eugene faced progressively greater ruins and dilapidation, making their passage increasingly taxing. Before sunset they had to carry the canoe over, then around, six progressively steeper and rustier weirs. The river had shrunk to a creek (the summers of 1933 and 1934 were two of the driest of the century so far). The canoeists pitched their tent next to a farmyard and went to sleep without food and exhausted (or in the tyro author's version, "courted sleep and after an arduous wooing succeeded, in fact, in relapsing into a kind of chilly torpor"). The next day things got worse. The river plunged through forested gullies strewn with rocks, in an area known as the Alpes-Mancelles. It poured with rain. They still had no food, apart from some fish they stole from a fisherman's trap and some blackberries. The weirs got steeper and more desolate, the rocks "coated with chromatic, odoriferous slime". They spent more time carrying the canoe than paddling it and that evening camped in the first meadow they found. Eugene returned from a farm where the family had nothing but bread and cider in the pantry but had managed to come up with a scrape of butter to fry the stolen fish in. They slept in all the clothes they had, "not forgetting our bathing costumes".

On the morning of the third day they met a genial fisherman, a holidaying civil servant from Paris flicking trout from the shrunken river, who assured them there was practically no water between where they stood and Le Mans.

(I take all this as read, from the text of Norman's French chapters. The narrative sequence, at any rate: as his first published book, the story has an artlessness – a youthful breeziness cloaking its lack of shape – that shows he didn't know everything he did later about forming his material.)

By midday the subdued pair were ready to concede to each other their private disgust with the river (their feelings probably in line with the drenched, beaten Quixote's at his watermill: "God help us, for the entire world is nothing but tricks and deceptions opposing one another. I can do no more"[7]). They packed up, dragged their cart over the hill to the main road, and booked into the Lion d'Or at the village of Saint-Céneri le Gérei where they had their first proper meal for three days. "I remember," Norman writes, "experiencing a gush of almost sensual pleasure at the sight and touch of the rich glaze on the soup bowl." The hotel was run by a woman who, "even for a Norman peasant, was an unsmiling old lady": his criticism is slightly unfeeling given that her grimness was, "in part at least, attributable to the recent annihilation by a sporting motorist of her only daughter". (It was also well known as a rendezvous of painters who, trapped inside by bad weather or indigence, decorated its walls, though Norman seems to have been unaware of this, commenting severely about a life-size picture of a naked woman in the toilet that "It was difficult to account for the existence of this ribald fantasy among such sober, austere people".)[8]

In the morning they decided to catch a train to San Sebastián.

Forced to retrace their steps to Alençon by bus, they abandoned cart and canoe at the *micheline* depot and left that evening for the border at Irún. Their train was being used to transport troops, and their third-class compartment was full of displaced first-class passengers, though the presence of the two unshaven foreigners in shorts – "we ... were already at the housebreaker stage, verging on the anchorite" – made no impact in comparison to another passenger, an epicene fop with manicured hands who held the compartment in silent horror, detailing his work as a venereal specialist. Norman and Eugene nicknamed him "the Countess". A *déformation professionnelle* had got him to the state where he never travelled without sterilised cup and knife, an antiseptic cloth for wiping any suspicious surface, and a medicated atomiser. On leaving the train at Bordeaux, Norman claimed, his final words to Norman and Eugene were "Well, good-bye, gentlemen. At all costs beware of Spanish women."

But the aborted canoeing trip's sour aftertaste condemned France, not Spain. The Bordeaux station breakfast was standardised, the Landes guilty of "unbearable monotony", the south perverted the rules of climate by getting colder the further they went. When a torn sheet of blue sky appeared over the Pyrenees and the sun came out at the frontier, it seemed to Norman "a gesture of almost propagandist partiality".[9] The propaganda had a credulous audience.

Once in Spain, however, Norman and Eugene experienced it with their habitual jovial scepticism and juvenile world-weariness. Beyond noticing the hammer and sickle painted on the station sign at Irún, under the words "VIVA ESPAÑA SOVIÉTICA!", Norman's observations were initially restricted to a touristic condescension. He spends several pages explaining how tiresome are the habits of Spanish hotel touts at San Sebastián and how far "the normal type" of Spanish woman falls short of her publicised legendary beauty. The laboured pomposity of these kinds of comment, which later he was appalled by and which were a main cause of his suppressing the book, doesn't wholly vitiate its readability: it is the pomposity of an intelligent observer rather than a stupid one, and founded on both some slight knowledge of Spanish culture and a wide (if thesaurus-dominated) English vocabulary. He quotes the sentimentalising writer Azorín (José Martínez Ruiz) in defence of his views, and with a swipe at bourgeois euphemism describes the stupendous busts of San Sebastián's women in the *paseo* as a "thoracic superfluity", "often detachable and assumed only for public occasions". Nor does he miss every deeper point about the city. San Sebastián, he says, is "remarkable for its bourgeois" in the same way as Zaragoza is remarkable for doughnuts, and its population appals him by the excesses of a caste system that reduces unmarried girls to feudal servitude and Basque servants to uniformed slavery. Quoting Sir Thomas More's protest that "The rich desire every means by which they may in the first place secure to themselves what they have amassed by wrong, and then take to their own use and profit, at the lowest possible price, the work and labour of the poor. And so soon as the rich decide on adopting these devices in the name of the Public, then they become law," he notes that the city's status quo rests on exactly that principle before pointing out, with some prescience, two facts about the opposition to that status quo: one, that it was widespread –

No edifice, however august, had escaped the indignity of bearing somewhere upon its imposing façade a roughly scrawled and indignant appeal, usually executed in tar or paint. "We ask for bread, they give us bullets," read an inscription on the walls of a police station. "Death to the Faith," was painted in huge red letters on a church door. "Create the Soviets!" demanded incongruously a notice that had been stencilled at eye level round the Doric columns of the bank

– and that it was also dissipated –

In the workers' districts where wall messages could be written in a sympathetic atmosphere and without exposing the writer to undue risk of arrest, the student was offered a valuable insight into the widely divergent tactics of the various schools of socialist thought. Only in the absolute essentials, neatly summarised by the classic quotation referred to, was a common platform to be found.[10]

He and Eugene spent two days in the city exploring its working-class areas – photographing the slogans and lurid election posters on the factory walls – observing the *paseo*, going to, and not being impressed by, the Basque Festival, most of whose events were athletic or reconditely to do with mountain crafts. He jokes about funny Basque names ("I think it should be mentioned that those who are addicted to the sport, habit or folk custom of wood-boring are known as Arri-Zulatzales . . . I propose to spare the reader further inflictions of this kind").

The two intended to stay the weekend to see some Basque dancing, but Spain had been disintegrating politically since the elections of November 1933 had left a vacuum of goodwill, the CEDA (the Catholic party) waiting in the wings, and the anarcho-syndicalists at the end of their patience. (In 1933 by no means all Anarchists were *pistoleros*, but between the derailing of the Barcelona–Seville express before Christmas, killing nineteen people, and the lengthy general strikes at Valencia and Zaragoza it was already hard to see peace breaking out, and through 1934, as the government repealed reforms and constitutional and separatist disputes fermented in the north, every grouping outside the bourgeois centre had begun to militarise.)

On 28 September, two days after Norman and Eugene arrived, a rumour circulating of cases of arms being brought ashore in Asturias for use by the socialists had galvanised the government to declare a state of alarm across the country. Norman felt that trouble should be avoided, but he distinguished between difficult personal trouble and exciting-to-write-about literary trouble and had no qualms at being a trouble tourist. It needed judgment, however, because "nothing is more difficult (as any traveller knows) than to establish a dilettante contact with it". He and Eugene reckoned that the epicentre of any upheaval would probably be Barcelona, but with Portugal as their destination, on the other side of Spain, they momentarily hedged their bets.

On Saturday morning, having disguised themselves as half-respectable travellers with suits and a new suitcase to replace their shorts and haversacks, they caught the bus for Pamplona, 130 kilometres to the south. The journey was remembered for the noisy vomiting of their fellow passengers, unaccustomed to bus travel. Their choice of hotel when they arrived in the city, the Hotel Montaña, might have been expected to produce an identical reaction. It charged 8½ pesetas a day full board; its meals of leftovers from the market, cooked in rancid oil, were overwhelming feats of falsification and camouflage ("The soup was pure water deflowered by garlic and superficially decorated with shining globules of black fat. Its surface reminded me of a distinguished Japanese 'New Angle' photographic composition entitled 'Petroleum and Pond'"). Its vermin were militant. He and Eugene lasted three days, then moved to a 14-peseta-a-day hotel in the plaza del Castillo run by a helpful Communist.

Pamplona showed them the beginnings of violence. They saw a group of youths beat up a municipal policeman, in retaliation for an incident at Lérida in which a Communist had been shot dead by an assault guard (*Guardia de Asalto*) for making fun of him. In Pamplona Norman and Eugene watched as another *Asalto* appeared, grabbed one of the youths, swung him round, and smashed his fist into his face. The attackers fled. This incident aside, Pamplona offered little diversion, and the travellers decided to spend a day walking outside the city as a trial for possible future movement. Observing people – French, Spaniards, men, more often women – Norman had not developed beyond a mocking, unforgiving eye: the owner of the Lion d'Or, the women with "rather stupid expressions" in the *paseo* and the "half-wit who advanced, slobbering with amazement" at their shorts at San Sebastían, the waitress at the Hotel Montaña ("Only the squatness of her stature spoilt the regal effect"), all elicited scorn.

Observing landscapes was different. Already they brought out what was best in his writing: visual exactness, a talent for economic metaphor, a sense of narrativising excitement: turning a description into a story, he could give the reader the feeling it was happening to them. It was his way of making the reader feel they were there. Possibly his privileging of landscape over humanity was to be expected. It had almost never been *people* who offered him liberty or harmony in his life, but *land*, unpopulated country, deserted horizons, empty sky, from the summit of Pen-lan and Gussie Bowles' woods to where he stood now on a Navarran plain. There were humans dotted across the land but their role was as elements of the scene; his interest in the workers in the fields lay in "their bent forms contrasting with unconscious symbolism with the erectness of the poplars that lined the paths". The paragraph prompted by the countryside outside Pamplona is also his statement on the singularity of Spain's landscapes, which was the predominant reason why he would return in future to that country more than any other. Spain was a country apart in Europe. Its physical scenes, "its surprising combinations of desert, forest and mountain, contain an element of the fantastic that is lacking in any other part of Europe".

I do not want to overstate the case. Part of the effects are obviously consequent upon the latitudes in which the country lies – though I have not found
anything to compare with Spain in Italy or the Balkans. But without implying
any disrespect to the straightforward immensity of the Alps or the Carpathians,
you have to go as far as the Great Atlas before you will find a sight so strongly
suggestive of hallucination or mirage as the snow-blanketed Sierras rising sheer
out of the cactus steppes. Only Spain can supply the profound and exciting
sense of personal incongruity which is engendered by finding oneself in a
boundless plain of billowing rock, from which all colour has been purged by
the sun, leaving a panorama empty of everything but whiteness of cloud and
rock and the blue of the sky. Against such terrestrial purity one is demoted to
the status of a stain.[11]

Whether he had actually seen Italy and the Balkans or not at this stage,
and whether it was partly inspired by his placing humanity's attractions a distant second to those of landscape, the felicity of that last
sentence is as great as any he wrote later.

He knew his birds too, identifying goldfinches and green singing
finches rising like an "anomalous yellow bloom" from an olive tree.
At a windowless barn that called itself a casino he and Eugene ate half
a loaf of bread washed down with jars of thin wine, and on the way
back in the dark they flagged down an ancient Morris Cowley whose
driver insisted on switching off his headlights to conserve power, leaving
them exposed to motorists who swooped down on them from both
directions. When they finally reached their hotel, they found a cable
from Ernestina, supposedly on a cargo boat to Istanbul, but instead
coming overland to Barcelona first. She suggested meeting them in
Zaragoza. (Ernestina is introduced in the text as "Eugene's sister", a
description that, like the convenient fiction of the cargo boat to the
Black Sea, allows the wife of the author of *Spanish Adventure* to appear
without his admitting that he is travelling with her.)

Norman and Eugene travelled to Zaragoza by bus, along ribbon
developments of cave dwellings, or more truly holes dug in the ground
by workers unable to afford houses. (The conditions in many country
districts were deteriorating rapidly in 1933 and 1934, with falling wages,
dismissals, and the slackening of safeguards for tenants. Landlords were
both aggressive and terrified. One group of unemployed *pueblo*
workmen, asked what their solution to the problem was, answered,
"Let them kill half of us."[12]) Every aspect of his journey seemed to be

bringing him into contact with depressing scenes of unsuccessful lives: at the Hotel Granadina where they put up, dry spittoons waited on its untrodden corridors, "a single-leafed and senescent palm" stood "on every third step of its monumental staircase", and its dining room choked with laid and empty tables held a single emaciated priest. The city too was mildly depressing, under the spell of vigilante offshoots of the Catholic Church that in advertisements and handbills invited residents to denounce any depravity in film or play. Zaragoza's *paseo* flourished correspondingly in a frigid and pointless way. The travellers were surprised to have thrust into their hands a flier advertising a cabaret in a shabby backstreet hall, where they watched an overweight "Miss Huelva or Almería 1933" perform in wispy clothing "a some-what overstated choreographic representation of sexual transports" before things began to improve. A *jota aragonesa* was danced with brisk grace, followed by the appearance of a Gypsy girl who, nowhere near five feet tall, still succeeded in overturning Norman's prejudices about short people and the authenticity of gypsy performers. With

her enormous eyes and fierce contemptuous expression, [she] represented so completely the Carmen of legend as to produce an intellectual crisis, calling once again for a revision of ideas on Spain. . . .

Travel is like that. The only certainty is that whatever the nature of one's preconceptions they are destined to dissolution. The frangibility of romantic illusions is a generally accepted fact, but the reverse is sometimes true. In the peregrinations of those who by long and patient self-discipline have acquired relative sophistication, Zenda will often assert itself.

Despite the re-emergent pomposity, Norman's appreciation was genuine. He felt himself lucky to have seen something so "astounding", to have witnessed true *cante jondo* at a time when both music and practitioners were under threat. The woman "whirled and leaped about in a tigerish Flamenco dance" to her partner's complex guitar patterns. Her perform-ance bore "little resemblance in its originality and animal vigour to the formal posturings of the average Flamenco dancer.

The audience yelled its appreciation. Abruptly, the gypsy stopped and stood thoughtfully snapping her fingers with a gesture of invocation. Suddenly, throwing back her head she emitted a low, quavering howl of the profoundest melancholy.

"*I felt death approach* . . ."[13]

While he and Eugene waited for Ernestina, Norman involved himself in what became a regular habit whenever he was in a port or a river town, of hanging around at the waterside. The appeal of quays and banks like those of the Ebro at Zaragoza was one of "a pleasant backstage atmosphere; an absence of *mise en scène*". As a contrast to the lifeless rectitude of the city centre, there was definitely interest for an observer, though the pleasantness was hard to marry up with the visible destitution of the city's sewer-rats scavenging life from the outflows and refuse heaps. Gypsy families were suffering from obvious starvation, and they counted fourteen drowned cats in a single short stretch of river. Crossing to the Ebro's far side and looking back to the city's distinguished silhouette, the outlines of the cathedral predominant, Norman seems to be expressing a subconscious political self-alignment. The poor shall inherit the rubbish.

They checked each day for messages from Ernestina at the Zaragoza post office's *poste restante*. The assault guards on duty were jumpy, scared of bombers – Norman claimed that he carried a parcel to see what their reaction would be and "This dislodged the whole posse from their pitch. We got the impression that an unrestrained sneeze would have been likely to bring about a tragedy." On Saturday morning they found Ernestina in person – haranguing the official in charge of the *poste restante* because he would not open early. The three's decision on where to go next was made rapidly: two days earlier, on 4 October in circumstances of acrimony and a number of political murders, the Catholic CEDA had withdrawn support for the government. The disliked rightist Alejandro Lerroux had been entrusted with forming a new cabinet, as he had been the year before. The Left parties had warned the President, Niceto Alcalá Zamora, that if any CEDA member was included in the new government, they would regard it as a declaration of war. Don Niceto had responded in a constitutionally correct way and instructed Lerroux to form a government including three minor members of CEDA. ("Correct perhaps," as Gerald Brenan writes, "but catastrophic in its results, when one remembers that all the disasters that have followed for Spain may be traced to this one unhappy decision."[14]) The following day, the 5th, a general strike was called across the country, and in Madrid socialist militants moved on the Ministry of the Interior, firing their weapons. In Barcelona Luis Companys, head of the *Generalidad de Cataluña*, proclaimed a "Catalan state". In Zaragoza the Lewis party joined the large crowds studying the hourly bulletins chalked up on noticeboards outside the newspaper offices. Seeking literary trouble, they decided to catch the express leaving for Barcelona next morning.

The Barcelona train did not appear. Transport timetables were casualties of the regional unreliability: the only train going anywhere was a stopping train to Madrid. Boarding it, and in relief at quitting the dull city, all three travellers leaned out of the window as the train pulled out and yelled ironically at the station staff the first line of the song "*Adíos, muchachos, compañeros de mi vida*".[15] The third-class part of the train filled with Spaniards who had heard that there were foreigners to be stared at. Ernestina was followed to the toilet by an awed entourage: one youth half-climbed out of the next window to catch a glimpse of her, and another, who had a master key, had to be kicked out. An hour short of Madrid, the train emptied and refilled, and Norman recorded the classic clash of the revolutionary worker, doomed by false hope, with the agent of reactionary authority.

"Tickets, please."
  "Tickets?"
  "Yes, tickets. Come along, please."
  "What for?"
  "What do you think, what for? Show me your tickets."
  "We haven't got any tickets."
  "Tickets have been abolished."
  "No need for tickets now, the revolution . . ."
  "Oh, it's the revolution, is it!" The guard was an enormously burly fellow. He combined as many of the physical attributes of a bull as is humanly possible.
. . .
  "Remember our interests are identical."
  "Where's your class-consciousness, comrade?"
  "Where's your solidarity with the proletariat?"
  "You're letting the bosses use you as a tool against your fellow workers."
  Deaf alike to criticism and appeal the guard was writing in his notebook.[16]

Threatened with the *carabineros* in the next carriage, the workers paid. The train arrived at the Madrid suburbs, and a youth in the corridor shouted, throwing himself down. Others followed. The atheistic Norman, thinking the train was about to crash, "envied the mental state of my lady neighbour, who, with her head in my lap, was trying to bribe the Virgin Mary". There was no crash, but in the momentary hush a single, small popping noise, like the sound of a tyre-burst. The sniper did not fire again. Risking a look, Norman saw, below the bridge they were passing over, two men in uniform carrying a third. At Madrid's Mediodía station a few minutes later, the platforms were deserted. Passengers scrambled down with their bags and families and ran, as the now constant popping sounds, regularly interrupted by explosions in the station's glass roof, kept up. Norman, Eugene and Ernestina took brief and unsuccessful shelter against a wall, then in the station buffet.

Norman wrote two versions of what happened next. In fact, he wrote two versions of the scene in the buffet, and of several other episodes related in *Spanish Adventure*: in his nineties, revisiting this first literary journey to Spain, he retold it in his last book, *The Tomb in Seville*, in which, coming full circle, he dramatised and altered it enough to remind readers that there is no immunity against the intrusion of the fictional process into non-fiction that deals with human events. It is not so much a question of the unreliable narrator as that of the innate unreliability of every human narrator (a phenomenon Norman himself became fascinated by after he saw Kurosawa's film *Rashomon* in 1952). The buffet scene in *Spanish Adventure*, for instance, has a terrified bartender refusing to sell even a glass of orangeade; in *The Tomb in Seville* a more phlegmatic barman shrugs, "Help yourself." In the later book Ernestina is probably absent more for literary reasons than emotional ones, and although Norman and his brother-in-law travel to Zaragoza in both accounts, in the later book instead of catching a bus they cover an arduous 175 kilometres on foot. Which version should we trust? Rather as with the early French chapters, the first book still seems ingenuous enough to be free of most of the shaping sophistication of fiction. But "seems" is as far as it is possible to go.

The Mediodía station of *Spanish Adventure* was defended by an ill-at-ease and jumpy platoon of conscripts. A foreign journalist, also from the Zaragoza train, asked their officer if it was safe to cross the street. He was advised to wait, and to keep his hands up when he crossed. After a couple of hours, when the shooting lessened, the Lewis party decided to make for a hotel directly opposite the station. The streets were deserted, and they didn't feel it was necessary to put their hands up. (Norman in any case couldn't, as he was carrying about 25 kilos of photographic equipment.) On the other side of the street they persuaded the hotelier to unbar the door and they took two balcony rooms overlooking the station, in case there was any more street fighting that Norman could photograph.

The manner of their leaving the Mediodía station of *A Tomb in Seville* is rather different. Norman and Eugene (without Ernestina) decide, as before, to make for the same hotel opposite the station: at which point

several of the people from our train demonstrated how this was to be done.[17]

This is the first in a string of alterations, by the end of which Norman and Eugene, with self-imposed English dignity, have refused to drop to the ground and crawl as the pedestrians they are accompanying have done, in the wake of a couple of hand grenades; upright, they have found themselves in the path and then the line of fire of an oncoming cavalry squadron, dropped instantly to their hands and knees, crawled with the rest and, reaching the far side, left behind one unlucky crosser dead from the cavalrymen's bullets. The curious (or perhaps not so) thing about the more highly coloured version of leaving the station is that Norman himself came to believe it; at least, it was the version he told later when he talked about the 1934 insurrection. If it were true, wouldn't he have included it first time around? It's impossible to know the answer, except in the light of something we do know, because most of us have experienced it: that the version of the story that lasts is the best told, not necessarily the true, version.

There was in any case little need to embellish the action in Madrid as it is related in *Spanish Adventure*. It was exciting enough without it. With fewer corpses but longer and more chaotic gunfights, and more political detail, than its successor, it offered both reader and writer a satisfying amount of literary trouble. In the evening, after dark, for instance Norman and Eugene, without Ernestina, went out for a walk in the working-class district of Atocha. They noticed that the trams were being kept running along the deserted streets, without passengers but with soldiers riding shotgun. Snipers were taking potshots, drawing wild fusillades of return fire from the police. They turned a corner and were confronted by a machine gun pointing "vaguely" at their stomachs. The "psychological inhibition" of their English dignity was shed immediately.

No man faced with the unenviable necessity of walking that night through the streets of Madrid, could have reached more enthusiastically for the sky than we did. There were not two pairs of arms in Spain maintained aloft with greater regard for geometrical parallelism.[18]

They returned through the back streets to their hotel, which had doubled the price of dinner and reduced its content to ham and biscuits, served by a waitress with an uncontrolled and peremptory conception of her revolutionary importance.

The firing continued over a long night. On Monday morning the sun beat down, and they decided to move to the city centre. On calle Atocha Madrileños lounged and chatted, the hills of uncollected refuse grew higher, and long bread queues snaked down the street. Convoys of army lorries raced through, doing their best to scatter all three. Norman approved archly of the weapons of the *Asalto* at the street corners, Mauser machine pistols "the designer of which has in my opinion combined functional efficiency with chastity of line in an altogether praiseworthy fashion".[19] Every Spaniard in a uniform was terrified and trigger-happy: the Bar Atocha where they stopped for a drink had been raked by machine-gun fire, so the owner said, just because someone had put a light on upstairs. They had a hard job finding another cheap hotel that wanted more guests, but eventually found a large, strictly run workers' hotel near the plaza Mayor whose owner took a lot of convincing that two bearded foreigners in the company of a woman who wore a hat were anywhere near respectable enough to be admitted.

The next week was, in several senses (politically, humanly, vocationally), a perfect foundation course in war experience and reporting. Madrid in October 1934 represented to Norman a free sample of what a possible writing future might be like. It was war on approval – "if after five days you aren't completely satisfied, you return home and you pay us nothing". He was completely satisfied. He saw his first street battle, heard his first machine gun, came under fire for the first time, saw his first man shot, sat up at night with poetry-reading Communists for the first time, and discovered that these were his kind of thing.

The insurrectionists' hopes were high at the beginning of the week, although in reality the rising in Madrid had already failed. Because of the strong garrisons at the exits to the city, an essential part of the plan had been to make sure the workers were supplied with plenty of weapons.

But the majority of the guns destined for Madrid had been in the shipment seized on the coast of Asturias in September, and never arrived. On the streets this fiasco was not yet generally known. (Norman seems to have been unaware of it.) Talk of the emergence of a "Red Army", if the various factions' leaders could agree on a strategy for co-operation, kept the city on its toes.

Monday afternoon passed without incident until, at five minutes to five, as the three were passing the Gobernación – police headquarters – in the puerta del Sol, the sound of a single shot set off, like one alarm clock setting off the rest, a cacophony of gunfire. (Whether it was the signal for an attack or just one shot blowing a powder keg of nerves, he doesn't say.) The chaos of people running for their lives in the crowded square – "How slowly and awkwardly the average human being runs for his life!" – was accompanied by the different sounds of weaponry, "loud melodramatic shots, that seemed harshly incongruous in those conventional precincts. They sounded in the air all round, seeming to have no definite point of origin. Machine-guns stamped an orderly pattern across the anarchic clamour of pistol and rifle reports. People were collapsing as they ran, doubling up and sprawling in the roadway. ... A closed motor car lurched with tyre squealing out of a side street. The inside back wheel bumped heavily on the kerb. We sensed rather than saw that a machine gun was being fired from it. An elderly man came running to meet us, stopped suddenly as if he had forgotten something, turned and bolted into a shop doorway where he fell on his knees."[20] They made it back to their top-floor room and threw open the window. Looking out, they saw an *Asalto* levelling his rifle up at them. They slammed the shutters.

That evening they sat down with the other hotel residents in the depleted hotel restaurant for another dinner of biscuits and met two Communists, an Andalucían lawyer and his Madrileño disciple who introduced themselves with the classic ill-fated pride of Civil War revolutionaries. "Good evening, I am Manuel Maltes. This is my friend, Esteban Iriarte. We are members of the Party of Lenin." While the residents waited nervously for a rumoured Communist air attack on the Gobernación, which was only two streets away, Manuel recited forceful poetry to Norman's party and Esteban wept. A worker wearing a bloodstained scarf at his neck came in and handed over two pocketfuls of bullets to a woman resident for safe keeping. A worry was that one of the residents would head up to the roof and use it as a base for sniping from – which it seemed had happened a few moments later when a guest ran into the dining room shouting that there was a sniper and that the *Asaltos* had come and had a searchlight trained on the hotel entrance. ". . . it is customary," the twenty-six-year-old Norman wrote, "to maintain a display of indifference and bravado even when staring down the barrels of rifles that are about to vomit death in one's direction. But there is no mistaking the flood of primitive and urgent sensations that assail one."[21] The sniper turned out to be a false alarm, though if the number of versions of a story is a supporting factor in its veracity the episode certainly took place. In *The Tomb in Seville* the supposed sniper is identified not by a hotel guest but by "a loud report seeming to come from the direction of the skylight"; the two *Asaltos* attracted by the noise drive away, "possibly believing themselves to be outnumbered". And in conversation sixty years later Norman remembered the occasion as a picnic on the roof with a group of insurrectionist sympathisers, one of whom got carried away and started firing into the street below; again the police, after hammering on the door, drove away.[22] Remembered or misremembered, the episode's intensity of emotion got it securely fixed in Norman's mind.

On subsequent days the three investigated a city regularly animated by gunfire and the crash of bursting hand grenades. A pendulum of *fiesta* spirit and scrambling panic swung back and forth in the city centre. To begin with, they spent most of their time in the cafés bordering the puerta del Sol, until the firing started in the late afternoon and they slunk back to their hotel and waited for it to subside. They were questioned by plainclothes police suspicious of their suits and ties: why were they staying in a proletarian hotel? They watched the double revolving beam of a powerful searchlight mounted on the Capitol cinema sweep the city's *azoteas* – flat, connected roofs that favoured the sniper – to reap its nightly harvest of revolutionaries. They got bolder and travelled out to the suburbs along straight, tree-bordered streets that eventually ran into the dirt of the Castilian plain. Norman's Contax camera was an occasional problem because of its telephoto lens's likeness to a gun barrel. One day they joined a crowd under surveillance by mounted *Asaltos* and out of politeness found themselves in conversation with some young men determined to demonstrate their fearlessness. At an alarm the crowd suddenly broke. "It's better not to move. . . . Only those who run get shot," they were told casually. At the other end of the emptied street a platoon of soldiers appeared with their rifles raised. The Spaniards tried to keep up their front. "One of them fumbled wildly for a time in an attempt to roll a cigarette, but in the end threw it away with a gesture of despair." This time the trio's social inhibitions saved them, compelling them to continue a pretence of conversation until the firing party eventually stood down.

By Friday the revolt had fully fizzled out in Madrid and Barcelona, though the Asturian miners had held the port of Gijón until 10 October and did not surrender Oviedo until the 17th. In the capital a sleek normality resumed, with its government propaganda on every radio set, its Te Deums in the churches, and its two nations (embodied for Norman by the patrons now returned to the smart cafés and the boot-blacks who prostrated themselves before them). Behind the scenes the police continued to arrest suspected protesters by the hundred. Manuel and Esteban, the two Communists, were expecting arrest, and to enjoy their remaining liberty suggested going out to dinner with Norman. (With their dignified fatalism and lack of strategy, the pair had more in common with the Spanish Anarchist movement, whose outstanding success was almost entirely due to the moral influence it exercised on the workers. "Whilst everywhere the workers' movement is bent on attaining comfort and security, the Spanish Anarchist lives for liberty, virtue and dignity."[23] Anarchists cared little for strategy because they believed that successful revolution would come "spontaneously as soon as the workers were morally prepared".[24] The Spanish character too played a part. It "is characteristic of Spaniards to be satisfied with gestures and with petty acts of defiance and courage and to neglect the real heart of the matter. The Arabs conquered the whole of Spain in two years. It took the Spaniards eight centuries to get rid of them."[25])

In the night the secret police came to their door and went away, and in the morning Esteban disappeared. Manuel decided it was time for him to go too. By Norman's account he was arrested shortly after leaving the hotel. (Norman had clearly taken to the two Communists – he shared their unconditional romanticism, they had eaten together and stayed up all night discussing Cervantes, Shakespeare and Wilde – but an emotional gap leaves his account of them incomplete. For the first time he is at a loss, writing about close relations with people.)

After a week of such excitement – a week, in effect, of perfect literary trouble – the rest of the stay in Madrid could not match up. On Sunday they went to the last bullfight in the old *plaza de toros*. Several gorings, including that of a well-known *rejoneador* (the horseman who at gala occasions in the season will fight the bull mounted on a horse bred for speed and dressage skill), left Norman bored, and he turned instead to analysing the sexual content of the small ads in the newspaper and the behaviour of an English couple sitting nearby who, intent on showing the correct enthusiasm, consistently waved their handkerchief at the wrong moments. Another excursion to Toledo, Cervantes' "glory of Spain, and light of her cities", brought out the now jaded traveller: at twenty-six, Norman wrote, he no longer expected what he had expected at eighteen, and Toledo's "well-fostered decrepitude" trodden by carloads of tourists and their attendant touts and beggars "did not disappoint me". In need of new stimulus, on the return journey he asked the bus driver to stop and covered the last 25 kilometres to Madrid on foot. He was in the kind of country he had admired so much in Navarra, and "I wanted an opportunity to analyse that sense of the fantastic which the Spanish landscape seldom fails to produce, and which was never to be felt more strongly than in these plains". The effect, he concluded, was partly due to the air's dryness "which leaves the remotest corners of the plains unsoftened by distance. In its turn this produces an almost eerie feeling of proximity with the very limits of vision. The rim of the horizon becomes almost tangible."[26] A perfect escapist's landscape, in other words; a perfect escapist aesthetic. The distant goal that the true Romantic is always reaching out for, so far only secretly yearned for in his or her mind, suddenly materialises within reach, thanks to a meteorological quirk. After the wan, irritable pages of bullfights and Toledo, Norman's description shows his desire to fix the place and the moment in his mind.

... there was the suppression of all irrelevant detail, a directness and an evenness of colouring, almost a stylisation of light and shade suggesting the miraculous realisation of a Metroland poster at its most improbable. The hollows and the hillocks and the lines of poplars arranged themselves in rhythmic patterns. The fields reeled away in all directions, forming immaculate designs in pale gold and silver. Summer had withered in a day and the sun glittered with chilly brilliance in the dark blue sky.

By turning through a complete circle one could observe almost every form of pastoral and agricultural industry. In one corner, the plains were being ploughed and sown. In another, grain was being winnowed, and in a vineyard they were gathering the grapes. ...[27]

I feel there is something emblematic too about this moment, looking on, or back, at the author looking at the panorama around him: something more significant for the source, and future, of his writing than his immersion in the failed Madrid insurrection. Halfway between Toledo and Madrid, in the middle of the plain of Castilla–La Mancha in autumn 1934, the twenty-six-year-old writer stands appreciatively alone in the kind of landscape he responds to more than he has to any other so far: as if, in that image, writer and subject, or the writer and the subject that will set off all the other subjects, are united for the first time with nothing between him, standing there gazing, and the curvature of the Earth.

Madrid a few hours later "looked like an avalanche of debris that had fallen on the edge of the plains from the slopes of the Sierra de Guadarrama". On the bridge of Toledo, after he passed an army roadblock, someone threw "a large, solid vegetable" at him. The spell was broken.

The bus they caught the following day to Salamanca opened his eyes to another landscape of "the most ostentatious splendour" as they crossed the rough Sierra de Guadarrama. Norman worried about the "tentacles" of the city and "the infections of civilisation" reaching out to the mountain wilderness. (As he predicted, the Sierra today is an area under intense pressure from tourism, mountain sports, and second homes.) He was impressed by Salamanca's buttery baroque, its prostitutes – it was market day – and the knots of tribal troglodytes who as hunter-gatherers ignorant of agriculture lived on lizards and birds and foraging for scraps at the market. Norman persuaded one of them to be photographed. The close-up of the man's face, the shadow of his hat brim masking eyes conscious of caste but unruffled, is the book's best photograph. Norman's technical interest in photography had made him a competent, often clever, photographer. He had taken the route, more productive in the 1930s than later, of thinking that if he took photographs it would improve the chances of his text being accepted. The pictures in *Spanish Adventure* have a period starkness to them – photographic art of the 1930s wrestled with the tension between its debt to the patterns and planes of modernism and its appetite for expressing warm humanity – but within their stylisation there is an occasional glimpse of a deep punctum of emotion. The photographer Don McCullin who worked with Norman (and regards him as responsible for teaching him how to travel) points out that Norman's photography was "governed by those kinds of publications of that day. You know, the sky always had to have a two times yellow filter."[28]

The rest of the journey to Portugal and on by boat to Morocco was more or less uneventful. Portugal left Norman cold literally and figuratively, its cabbages and vines failing to match the golden aridity of the Spanish plains. It was too lush, too well mannered, too drizzly: too much like England or, in the "cultural inanition" of its countryside, his native Wales. Norman wrung a joke out of the *azulejo* tableaux that politely advertised the attractions of towns they passed through – "We recognised the names of several health resorts euphemistically recommended in the guide books as . . . beneficial for those suffering from complaints of the loins. This is a pleasant idiosyncrasy of Portuguese advertising. They are always urging you to visit some place on the grounds that all the consumptives or syphilitics go there" – and the country took its revenge, putting him to bed for a week with an unspecified illness in Lisbon. A plan to stay in the Algarve for a while, fishing, sea-bathing, taking photographs and learning Portuguese, was cancelled by boredom and bad weather, but at Villa Real de San Antonio, where the party tried to cross back into Spain to catch a boat for north Africa from Cadiz, tedium turned to frustration. The ferry across the river had been suspended as a result of the Spanish state of alarm. Norman manages to make this Portugal's fault, not Spain's. Unfairly since, in a spirit of adventure, the Villa Real police chief was all for helping them to cross illegally. Villa Real had nothing to offer. "There is", Norman writes, "only one café in the town and if, after sitting in it for an hour or so, you yearn for fresh pleasures, you are at liberty to go and get your hair cut." Eventually, with the intervention of the British consul, a telegram to the governor of Huelva on the other side, and an enforced three-day wait, permits were issued and the three crossed. At Ayamonte on the far shore Norman's relief is palpable in his joyful comparison between the gentle apathy of the Portuguese he has left behind and the surly Spanish guards, the porters fighting over their luggage, "two blind old people quarrelling violently, and groping arduously for each other's faces to inflict punishment" and "a beggar whose leg had wasted away almost to the thinness of a finger".

Martial law in Andalucía did not slow them down this time, and after a night on the bus to Huelva they spent the next in a down-at-heel Seville, where, feeling entitled to some frivolity, they found it in a spectrum of diversions at a brothel-cum-cabaret, with the "obscenities of several entirely nude young ladies" at one end and the "virile Flamenco dances of an adipose middle-aged lady and her grey-haired, ascetic-looking partner" at the other. In the afternoon of the following day, 7 November, the train brought them to Cadiz, where by an immense stroke of luck there was a cargo boat leaving for Casablanca on the 8th. In the unruly way of ports, snipers had not been wholly suppressed in the city, and before they sailed they were again woken by gunfire and a couple of explosions.

What was Norman's motivation in going to Morocco? The itinerary of his first big (and literary) journey had been chaotic, its author conducting himself, from a geographical point of view, like a literate bull in southern Europe's china shop. But there was method to it, in the form of a substantial if indeterminate bet he had made with himself, its terms being that he had to get as far as he possibly could before he was forced back. His later journeys were without doubt better struc-tured, yet all journeys, with their forks in the road, their physical, geographical, linguistic, legal, military, political, health-, transport- and climate-related obstacles, their retarding dangers and pleasures, their wanton, unwanted, longed-for unpredictability, are subject to similar forces. Norman's desire to see north Africa may have been cognate with his liking for primitive, white-cube, Moorish Spain and his interest in places where Arabs were; possibly his desire was simple ambition; but there must have been a considerable part in it of sheer appetite, of going one, or two, or three steps further than he could easily have done. *Spanish Adventure*, in retrospect, would probably never have been as attractive a manuscript to a publisher if it had been neatly presented as a book about Spain. The element of day-dreaming, of irrelevance even, that enters into the book as he contemplates for no reason at all what lies *beyond* Spain reminds the reader of the pleasure of something approached with the absolute seriousness of a game, or with the gravity of a child marshalling every atom of enthusiasm. This characteristic of Norman's first journey, of going beyond, or too far, became progressively a self-fuelling secret of his later travelling and later books. Some critics have pointed out that his works of non-fiction often have unexpected endings. That is because, so long as he was not actually itching to finish a book in order to get up and go somewhere, he privately regarded his books of travels as one continuation.

In Casablanca the French came in for Norman's scorn again, though he admitted that the imperialism by stealth that had established French

Morocco as a colony was based on the same model deployed by all European powers. Beginning with the establishment of ports and areas of commercial influence, the developed nations inserted themselves into an undeveloped country's political equation until, as inevitably happened, some act of local resistance provoked them into direct action. Norman's comments on the political routine then adopted by the colonists are sarcastic and shrewd: "peaceful penetration" conventionally gave way to military intervention "for the beneficent purpose of straightening out the anarchy well-known to ravage the internal affairs of all but Christian nations". It should be mentioned that, fewer than three years later, he would be involved in a comparable effort at penetration of the kingdom of Yemen by the British Foreign Office, although one supposes he might be partially excused on the grounds that the British were attempting to stop the imperially ambitious Italians from doing the same, and that he was only present as a photographer.

In Casablanca the defining imperial moment had come at the building of a port railway through a graveyard in the summer of 1907. Offended tribespeople killed a number of French workers, and troops were landed to deal with the unrest. Bombardment, pacification, control, and the urbanising of the Arab population in a caste system headed by the French followed. Casablanca had boomed, with the indigenous population reduced in most cases to the manual rungs of labour and the most menial levels of service to their colonial superiors. "Arabs", Norman writes, "were to be seen everywhere performing with grace and dignity such tasks as bed-making, slop-emptying, and walking behind their French mistresses laden with the marketing bags",[29] although the Jewish population of the old town were in the saddest state, their ruined quarter more of an incubator of disease than a home to the close-knit, prolific families who lived by the hardest manual labour as cobblers, smiths and porters.

The three put up in a "small, disreputable-looking" hotel, run by a proprietor who suggested they would like to economise on the cost of their rooms by making them available when not in use to couples wanting to "drop in for a little private chat". Spaniards ran the café-restaurants and brothels they frequented, apparently on good terms with both Arabs and Jews. "There was a good proportion of Spaniards in Casablanca", he notes (one can take his "As in the case of all the other North African towns I have visited" with a dash of salt). But stimulated by his first intimacy with a true Arab world – albeit Arabised

Arab – as opposed to one of suburban fantasy, all of Norman's passion was for Arab Africa. Cosmopolitanism had led to most women of Casablanca discarding the veil, but there is a touch of disappointment in his familiar *épatons le bourgeois* tone when he adds, "It is said that the only place to see an Arab beauty dressed in the traditional finery is a brothel." In the kind of admiring paragraph that will be repeated, he generalises that

The Arabs, both male and female, are better-looking than the Europeans. On the whole, they have sensitive and intelligent faces. Their regular features contrast strongly with the colonial French and Spanish types.[30]

He enjoyed the chaos. He was happy to see that the model township built by the French on the heights behind Casablanca had been turned over to the Arabs, the consequence being that its open spaces had been instantly converted to cosy *bidonvilles*. Walking through the Sunday market (regarded, he notes approvingly, with indifference), he saw a gigantic Arab woman, a seller of charms against snake-bites, in a trance and naked to the waist applying snakes to her forehead for them to sink their fangs in – a far more convincing display than the son of spiritualists was used to – and he compared the assertion once heard at Speakers' Corner, that Muslims who brawled would, unlike Europeans, be gently separated by their fellows, with the reality of a fight in which the loser was saved from being cut to pieces in front of an appreciative audience only by a rainstorm materialising out of nowhere. They took cover in the old town as the rain fell solidly; for four hours they were the only customers at a café advertising Moorish dancing, watching a lonely orchestra accompany the reluctant contortions of girls in flimsy kimonos and French stays.

The lure of Arabism and constant rain are the competing themes of the Moroccan journey. The rain won narrowly. There was a chance of a dry route to the south if they crossed the Atlas via Marrakech. Norman was again excited by the Arabs he observed on the fast bus they took. "Their dignity was monumental. Their reserve, more than Anglo-Saxon", their cuffs and children spotless, they refrained from spitting or vomiting, and when they peed at the roadside did so with charming smiles. But the "great oasis of palms" with its red towers and disrupted ramparts beneath the Atlas's aerial snows let them down: although they saw more of the Arab world's systematised anarchy in and around the place Djemmaa El Fna than they had anywhere else – including hordes of homeless country Arabs lured to the town by economics and now unable to return to vanished oases – the rainy streets ran with torrents of mud and the dissident Berber village roads and the road across the Atlas to Taroudannt and the coast road to Agadir were cut in succession. Norman's party visited the souk El Ghemis, he probably smoked kif, and they caught the bus back to Casablanca. The rain had made miles of flooded plains; camels stood solitary in the waters. With heroic poise he describes the explorer's sense of anticlimax that so far "only the incidents of exceptional circumstances had saved our experiences from banality. Now we had come within an ace of cutting new ground. . . . Apart from the Foreign Legion and a few journalists, [the feudal communities of the Sous were] practically unvisited by Europeans. . . . But it might have been a month or two before the roads could be repaired, allowing us to go on. And we could not afford to wait."[31]

Back in Casablanca an exiled Russian artist attached himself to them as if summoned by the genie of disappointment, a failed portraitist by the name of Borissov[32] whose limpet-like attentions extended to inviting them to his apartment and performing for hours on end readings of his epic poems and plays. They humoured him because of Norman's desire to salvage some photography from the trip. Norman thought the man might help with providing models, but this failed: the Arab girls whose pictures Borissov painted went in fear of the camera's evil eye; one of the factors was their dread of appearing on postcards and suffering a progressive loss of their spirit with each image sold. The only place to photograph Arabs, Borissov said, was in the *quartier réservé*, the pragmatically organised official French red-light zone that called forth Norman's ambivalent admiration. The Bousbir or "Derb Bousbir" – in French "rue Prosper" – named after the M. Prosper whose development of the area had produced the first area of regulated prostitution in the country,[33] was a miniature walled city in which, as Norman writes, "Moorish architecture has been joined in Holy Matrimony with European drainage". It had an erotic cinema, fountains and decorative archways, shops, cafés, and a hospital where those working could be examined regularly and treated: "what was a stain and a reproach", Norman thought, "has become a tourist attraction, a curiosity worthy of visit with its coy paragraph in the official guide book". Borissov took them to the Café Tunisien which (as its name's coded otherness suggests) "specialised in unnatural vice". Norman was impressed by one of the hostesses, a Syrian homosexual named Quazim who had long, peroxided hair and a white-powdered chin to soften the inflammation of constant shaving.[34] When Quazim's turn came to dance he was

amazing. His serpentine contortions, the nicely synchronised clicks and snaps which proceeded from his various joints in time with the music, the expression of languishing lewdness stamped on his features, and, finally, the touch of burlesque he imparted to his performance, combined to put him miles in front of any female interpreter of similar dances that we ever saw.[35]

Photography in the Bousbir was no easier than in Borissov's studio from an artistic point of view. As soon as the lens was pointed at them, the Frenchified whores at the gateway were happy to flash and jiggle not just their busts but occasionally more at the photographer (or in Norman's throat-clearing phrase to "attempt more potent publicity by parading before us with skirts held aloft"). The women were invariably friendly and polite, especially to Ernestina when they found that she could belly-dance, but they were often scarred by disease and racially mixed, so less attractive to Norman than the "pure" Arabs. They, however, remained elusive, "tall, dignified and resplendently dressed", dropping their washing baskets and slipping back into their courtyards at first sight of the camera. These women kept their rooms and precincts spotlessly clean, even whitewashing the street itself once a day. This was in contrast to the Jewish quarter which seemed to overflow with disillusion and neglect (although Norman confounds the Mellah, Casablanca's main Jewish district, with the Bousbir's small zone of Jewish prostitution): an apparent source of horror to the Jewish elders was that their young men preferred the comfort of Arab prostitutes to that of the Jewish women. One unexpected factor in the stable existence of the Bousbir, Norman discovered, was the wide Arab acceptance of prostitution: besides its regulated brothels Casablanca possessed hundreds of unauthorised brothels, regularly raided, a police inspector told him, to prevent the worst excesses of exploitation and child prostitution; but even when a girl managed to escape prostitution as a child, she would probably be taken to a brothel by her husband as soon as money problems justified the decision. Almost every attractive Arab or Jewish woman, the inspector said, found her way into one sooner or later.

The passages of *Spanish Adventure* describing the Bousbir and Quazim and his fellow hostesses show Norman acquiring a fluency of reportage – slightly more fluent than the Madrid pages – that is never quite objective: his extensive curiosity and desire to say something interesting do not always match. There is too much of a desire to impress about his prose, and at the same time something startlingly successful in it when it works, when the observer demotes himself, to use his own word, to an object, a point of view speaking only through the developing rhythms and playful archness of language. The necessary subjectivity, in other words, is not properly harnessed, but it is beginning to be restrained in the forms of style; not as a first person singular, but as a voice singular. *Spanish Adventure* is a better book at the end than the beginning. But reading it one has the paradoxical impression that instead of knowing *more* about its author by the end of the book, one knows *less*: he is putting himself not into an ego to put himself forward, but into a style behind which to step backward. Like the Arabs he has identified with since he was fourteen and at last glimpsed in reality, he knows that he now seeks dignity – as monumental as is compatible with the low manual craft of writing – and elusiveness.

But the book is at an end. It was late November. They had run out of money. They sat on the bus to Tangier, Ernestina with the souvenir of an alleged peregrine on her wrist that was actually a kestrel, Eugene with a lump of kif that turned out to be as spurious as the peregrine, and Norman with "a heterogeneous mass of jottings and several spools of exposed film, most of which on development caused me to wonder why on earth I had ever taken those pictures". In Tangier they caught a boat to Algeciras, where they discovered that the Spanish state of alarm was still in force. Conditions had worsened. Incendiarists, desperate and starving, had devastated nearly a hundred Andalucian cork and olive estates. Edible goldfinches were fourpence a dozen. With most of the hotels closed, they went straight to Madrid: here, with the diversion of the police into political arrests leaving the city open to an epidemic of armed robbery, the newspaper *El Liberal* had nominated it "the Chicago of Europe". They caught an overnight express to Paris, steaming into the gare d'Orsay at eight the following morning, and were back in Bloomsbury that night. By 12 December "R G Lewis, Miniature Camera Specialist" – this time offering five assorted Leicas and other cameras for sale – was again advertising in the professional classifieds section of *Amateur Photographer*. A week later, and in subsequent issues, number 4, Gordon Street was included as "our London Studio", where any camera for sale could be viewed, in addition to the 5 Southbury Road address in Enfield. Norman was back at the photography racket. This time, somewhere among his cameras and lenses and ad copy, there was also "a heterogeneous mass of jottings".

I have rather furious reactions to business affairs. What I do remember enjoying about business was getting away from it.

Norman Lewis

I think that I was psychologically conditioned not to feel I had a free life in England. I'd gone through such unfree conditions as a child that I think I had to get out of England in order to be able to breathe: that's what it really amounts to. For example, I've been an asthmatic all my life but as soon as I go away, the very day I go away, I don't have asthma any more.

Norman Lewis

The fact of the matter was, having got to southern Arabia, I remember thinking that what I would really like to do would be to get out there and stay there, just drop all my responsibilities.

Norman Lewis

Do you know, Norman once said to me later on in life, "Where have you been lately?"

I said, "You wouldn't know it, Norman. I've been to a place called Suakin, where General Gordon landed."

And he said, "Oh yes," he said, "I did a book about that in 1935,"* and then I thought, You silly bugger. That was the year I was born. And I wished I hadn't opened my mouth.

Don McCullin

There might have been a slightly sad quality about my father. In my mother's case it would have been somewhat manic. She was a dreadful person to go out with because people were always staring at her, whistling at her. She was totally impervious. She was in a world of her own from that point of view.

Ito Lewis

* 1938.

7

ANYWHERE BUT HERE

"Diligence is the mother of good luck"

"Throw a lucky man in the sea, and he will
come up with a fish in his mouth"
Arabian proverbs

ON 15 May 1935 *Amateur Photographer* carried a full-page advert announcing that R G Lewis was opening a new London shop in "larger and more accessible premises" at 202 High Holborn. The announcement, written by Norman, offered, "a hundred yards from the Holborn Restaurant – a new shop devoted exclusively to the cult of the miniature camera". The particular style of personal, expert service to both professionals and nervous amateurs that he strove to communicate in the text ("we shall be delighted to offer an absolutely unbiased opinion, based on a long experience of the problems arising from miniature photography") would become an important element in his business success, along with his unusual articulacy – his publicity leant heavily towards the discursive – and his talent for browbeating customers with the utmost courtesy. With the opening of 202 High Holborn, he started the habit of writing a new half- or full-page advertisement every week, many with a strong narrative element or another new angle on selling small cameras. He also constantly adjusted the service R G Lewis offered, adding to the sales of Leicas, Contaxes and Zeiss Ikons with specially made and licensed accessories, lecture programmes, and testing and calibration services. In a 1946 advertisement he gave a romantic account of the premises he had moved into a decade earlier.

"Our Neck of the Woods" (Continued) – When, in 1935, we descended upon High Holborn, we settled down in a dreary, Victorian-romanesque building, chosen because the overheads were low. The only previous tenants of our premises over a period of some years had been rats of spectacular dimensions. The walls were lined with crumbling matchboarding, and as no self-respecting firm of decorators felt they could do much with the place, we ourselves, with our own hands, covered them with canvas and our staff painter produced murals thereon. As the artistic gentleman in question had previously executed only typical nightclub decors, these paintings are extremely unsuitable. However, we have grown accustomed to them and they do not worry us any longer.[1]

The change was sudden. The previous December he had been selling secondhand cameras out of his father's shop in Enfield and his second-floor room at the Corvajas'. Five months later, he was running a full-blown West End business, even if its muralled interior, bare, canvas-lined, without counters or showcases, sought the boho tone. The explanation lies in his father-in-law's willingness to provide a good deal of the capital (it is, although deplorably sensational, reasonable to describe R G Lewis as mafia-financed). But in taking on a shop, Norman had also committed himself to a stretch of strenuous work. Photography had plenty of consumer potential, but all the vices of retail. Wobbly trading conditions, tedious customers, less imaginative but more powerful competitors, could, if they didn't ruin him, all nail him to the job unreprieved for several years.

That was not all. Just over a fortnight before the new shop opened, on 27 April, Norman had also written to the socialist publisher, Victor Gollancz. In his letter he asked if he could submit the manuscript of "a travel book dealing with Spain, Portugal and Morocco".

It is possibly brought within your scope on account of the happy coincidence of my arrival in Spain ... with the outbreak of the October revolt, to my experiences in which, seven chapters are devoted.

The book is about sixty-five thousand words in length and illustrated by forty photographs (including representations of propaganda posters and street fighting). I can at least vouch for the quality of the photography, being concerned with it professionally. Several of the photographs have, in fact, already appeared in exhibitions.

If such a work is likely to interest you, I shall be delighted to submit the manuscript.

Yours faithfully,
Norman Lewis

Besides underplaying the book's length – the finished version is about 75,000 words – Norman obviously did not mention that it had only taken him five months to write and that for much of that time he had been setting up as a photographic retailer. Gollancz wrote back on 29 April to say they would be delighted to see it and again on 2 May to acknowledge its receipt. Norman submitted the manuscript with the title "The Spanish October", adding gravely that he was in touch with leaders of the Asturian revolt who had managed to flee to France and Russia and was preparing "the only complete and reasonably objective account so far" of the Oviedo commune, which could be added to the manuscript if required. Gollancz did not take him up either on his postscript or his title. They did accept the manuscript. Agreeing contractual terms less than a month later, with an advance of £25 due on publication, they fussed about the libel implications of Norman's sub-cultural photographs but were otherwise excited by the book. Norman Collins, Gollancz's young fellow director, felt that many photographs were "exquisitely good" and reported that

this is a very brilliant book, by someone who, in the real sense of the words, can write. And by this I mean that there are sentences on almost every page which Tomlinson, or Hudson, or Priestley, or Lynd, would have been glad to have achieved. To this, however, is added a kind of antiseptic quality which so entirely destroys sentiment that the book will be read with pleasure by precisely that public which in the ordinary way cares nothing for the Priestleys and the Tomlinsons – it is even possible that Tomlinson himself *might* dislike the book intensely.[2]

Apart from disapproving of Norman's manuscript reference to "wangling" a visit to the hospital in the Bousbir (cut from the finished book), Collins was enthusiastic about getting the book reviewed and eliciting quotes from more famous Hispanophiles and travellers of the day, including Hemingway, V S Pritchett, H V Morton, Peter Fleming, and Aldous Huxley. He felt they could sell between 1000 and 2000 copies (hardly different from today) at 15 shillings. Their early enthusiasm was justified: they quickly sold American rights to Henry Holt in New York.

Spanish Adventure was published in Britain in late September and mentioned in the "Some New Books" list in *The Times* of the 17th alongside Osbert Sitwell's *Penny Foolish*. It was reviewed with accuracy and condescension in the *Times Literary Supplement* of 26 September, the anonymous reviewer writing that

The reader will not find that Mr Lewis adds greatly to the common store of knowledge of the countries through which he passes, with the possible exception of their more sordid aspects. His method is essentially subjective, and his style is compounded of sharp observation, fine indignation and over-ponderous irony. ... This is emphatically not a book to be read by those of delicate susceptibilities, and it is to be hoped that in his next book Mr Lewis will shed the immaturities of style and outlook which are already less noticeable towards the end of the present volume.

One can understand Norman's decision after the Second World War, when, published by Jonathan Cape and enjoying buds of critical approval with his first two novels, *Samara* and *Within the Labyrinth*, he censored all mention of *Spanish Adventure* – there is little as shaming as one's juvenilia when one still has something to prove, and even in the language, "intersticed", "partook", "habiliments", this is a book pungent with juvenile desire (to flourish experience, make the most of every shock, show off ironic and rhetorical deftness, *perform*), but in longer focus his first book is far from shameful. It is better looked at as the statement of intent that first books are: the conclusion of a struggle – to be taken seriously enough to get into print – as much as the first act of a career. In Norman's case, as a spontaneous literary product out of nowhere (aka the suburbs, the desert perimeter), this was a reasonable achievement. To have been noticed, not entirely negatively, for the book's distinctive stylistic exactness and formal casualness, was another laurel. It must have had a reasonable trade success, because in 1948 Victor Gollancz would wrestle politely with his friend Jonathan Cape for the right to publish Norman's first novel, and it gained him some publicity. Shortly after its publication he was phoned by Ernest Wishart of Lawrence & Wishart, another radical publisher. He met Wishart, "a very sort of smooth, rather good-looking sort of left-wing gentleman"[3] (the Wisharts were a wealthy family of liberals), who asked him if he would care to go to China and report on Mao's Long March. Norman was pleased to be asked, but the project foundered on Wishart's patrician assumption that Norman would pay £200 towards his own expenses, a sum way beyond his means with the photography business just started.[4]

He also had his first brush with an angry reader who went to the Gollancz office "wanting to murder us and you"[5] for the jacket photograph of the cave-dweller in Salamanca which the Spanish reader said had been deliberately included to damage the reputation of Spain. Norman replied to Norman Collins that

I am staggered to learn that anyone could have drawn such erroneous conclusions from "Spanish Adventure". Among my fellows I am regarded as an ardent, even riotous, Hispanophile. At Christmas, after a year spent in the most arduous pursuit of surplus value, what did I do but rush off to Barcelona, spending half the days of grace in travelling to and fro.[6]

Quoting Norman's reply to the complaining Spaniard, Collins added that the book's author had concluded by saying that so great was his affection for Spain it had always been his ambition to settle there with his "Spanish-born" wife. Curiously, at this moment that was not far from the truth. With two possible livelihoods developing Norman was not about to abandon Britain for Spain. But Ernestina, first subdued, then antagonised by her experience of England (not to mention Wales), was militating. She told Norman she had given up the idea of "living anywhere in England" and was pushing for a move to Spain. Another factor in her feelings may have been that she had just found out that she was expecting a baby, and the wilder shores of hormonal tumult may have been calling her away from grey, convention-bound England as a poor place to bring up a child. Norman's own love of Spain did not drown out his murmuring genie of self-preservation, and his reaction that it "seemed attractive enough to me if only a way could be found of making a living there"[7] needs no reading between the lines. It was an utterly mad idea. Except that, as a pretext for a trip to Spain apparently to investigate the possibilities and simultaneously to revive his wife's mood, it was an excellent idea.

In early June he and Ernestina drove contemplatively (contemplating, I imagine, quite different things) through the unquiet peninsula as far as Seville. They stayed with friends of Ernestina's, the Estradas, in the calle Sierpes. The Estradas lived "in a tiny Moorish palace with an unimposing entrance next to a shoeshop", an element of bathos that resurfaces in The Tomb in Seville, Norman's 2003 remake of his 1934 journey, in which the search for the ancestral Corvaja palace ends at a shoeshop in the calle Sierpes. The contrast between the warm welcome they received from Juan Estrada and his wife, and the inhumanity of the Fascist circle they found themselves in as their guests, is probably embellished in Norman's remembered account, but his description of living conditions in Andalucía prior to the civil war is reasonably, and odiously, factual. The newspapers carried daily accounts of death from starvation, and at the restaurant the Estradas took them to a few miles out of town the evening they arrived, the tables were set with neat piles of half-pesetas for the diners to distribute to the ragged women and children who lurked outside the light (as soon as they approached too often, a waiter would whip them back). Estrada, a young landowner in an area of vast feudally run properties, explained calmly that, "the Reds" having stirred the villagers to discontent, it was time to deal with them: he and a posse of landowning friends intended to ride out shortly to settle matters in their own way. Another guest, a *rejoneador*, seems to have referred to the proposed manhunt as valuable practice.

Norman later characteristically understated his horror as a sort of personal incongruity. "It was an environment", he wrote, "in which Ernestina and I found ourselves out of our depths."[8] In his preference for evading conflict, he was still the tongue-tied victim of his Forty Hill oppressors. He didn't confront Estrada but, following the Lewis pattern, slipped away with Ernestina the following day. Outside Plasencia on the way to Salamanca a police roadblock diverted their car onto a dirt road across the medieval land of the Sierra de Gata to the tiny twelfth-century city of Ciudad Rodrigo. Here they were caught up overnight in the kind of situation Juan Estrada had talked about: a skirmish between impoverished Republicans and a Fascist band who had attacked their village. The villagers were as gaunt as any Norman had seen, but armed with hunting rifles had seen off their attackers, killing one. The wild-faced village schoolmaster in charge of the *milicianos* led him and Ernestina to a refuge in the *parador nacional* in the city, picking up a cook on the way. They heard shooting in the night. Next morning they were served a breakfast of wild birds' eggs fried with black mountain ham, and the schoolmaster, a true Anarchist of the moral school, returned, shaved and calm, to announce with pride that hostilities were at an end and that in future everything belonged to the people. Norman and his wife must consider themselves the people's guests. A week later, on the night of 12 July and just after they got back to Bloomsbury, Falangists in Madrid murdered a Socialist lieutenant of the *Asaltos* named Castillo and one of Castillo's colleagues shot dead Calvo Sotelo, the leader of the parliamentary opposition, in revenge. When civil war broke out six days later and Nationalists immediately occupied Salamanca province, the schoolmaster's hunting rifle and moral ammunition were almost certainly an inadequate defence.

A short break to Ostend was on offer to Norman and Ernestina when they got back. Ernesto and Maria had gone in early June, as they did every summer, to spend three months' gambling at the Kursaal and this time invited their daughter and son-in-law to join them. Possibly the Corvajas had decided to spoil the future mother of their grandchild and keep her close. By Norman's account the trip was an illuminating one, after he one night intercepted a phone call at the hotel from a man whose voice he recognised as that of the casino's head croupier; the inference was that the man was clearly on the fiddle with Ernesto. In his father-in-law's defence, no proof of the alleged scam appears in Norman's account, which has the air of a particular kind of vignette dusted with intrigue that Norman enjoyed telling when there was nothing else to say: they were the exercises of an unoccupied writer.

The summer and early autumn of 1936 radiate a curious sense of suspension. The photographic business seems to have been working well. (Even though Ernesto's money was involved, I assume that his son-in-law was supposed to make it profitable.) Norman had introduced a specialist "miniature only" processing service in the spring, he offered tuition in the use of miniature cameras and "welcome[d] the opportunity to pass constructive criticism on the results", and R G Lewis now boasted "the most complete stocks of new Leica apparatus in Great Britain". His wife was expecting an uncomplicated birth in December. There was no second book being worked on, unless one counts the booklets he was writing and publishing on subjects like "Miniature Enlargers and Dark Room Accessories". He and Ernestina went several times to Epping Forest (it seems to have been one of the few places outside London Ernestina liked) with her Moroccan kestrel: despite his published scorn about its commonness, he shared his wife's affection for the bird and took some Man Ray-like portraits of it nestling into Ernestina's neck, to the eyes-closed pleasure of its mistress.

Norman's mother broke the calm in late September. At sixty-nine his father had sold the pharmacy in Southbury Road and was spending all his time at home, waiting, he said, to be allowed to die in peace. Louisa asked Norman to come. When Norman arrived, he found a situation of Chekhovian terminus. Richard Lewis explained to his son that he had abandoned whatever Spiritualist certainty he had had, but he still preferred its doubtful promise of an afterlife to clinging on to an existence as an old man staring out of the window, as the cherry orchards of Forty Hill were felled to make way for the construction of expanding rows of new suburban houses. In any case it was, as he told Norman, too late. He had no pain, but the cancer was well advanced. He thought he might live to see the spring flowers – "the only thing that gave him any pleasure now". In the event he did not. Reluctantly on 10 October he submitted to an operation to remove tumours of his liver and gall bladder but died in Enfield War Memorial Hospital the same night.

The happier birth of Norman's and Ernestina's first child followed two months later, on 10 December. An indicative failure by his parents to agree on his name led to his being called Ito, short for the Spanish "Equisito" ("little X") that went on his birth certificate (though he eventually found himself with four and sometimes five names on official documents: Equis Ilar (Hilary) Rafael Norman). Despite the indecision around his name, Ito is a resplendently cheerful baby in Norman's copious snapshots of his son.

When not photographing him, his father was destined not to see very much of Ito until he was a teenager: a pattern that might have been foreseeable but all the same began suddenly. Ito was a few weeks old when his father first absented himself, in the kind of unplanned way that perhaps many shopkeepers long for. Not only keen weekend photographers walked through the door of 202 High Holborn: men (it was mainly men) for whom photography represented a specialist, strategic, even political, interest met Norman on his professional territory. Norman was discovering that he would periodically start shop conversations with customers that, as they progressed, went far beyond their technical photographic needs. He made friends this way, particularly among journalists in the 1940s and 1950s; in February 1937, when "Rex Stevens" came into his shop, he could hardly have made up the consequences. (It is a recurring paradox of Norman's story that he delighted in spicing reality with sinister/clandestine/conspiracy-drizzled episodes. Then stranger things happened.)

We don't know if Stevens was an amateur photographer who happened to talk to Norman and realised he could be the person he was looking for, or if he had read *Spanish Adventure* and intentionally pursued its author. We possibly know that Rex Stevens, whom Norman described as being from the Colonial Office,[9] was not his real name. There was no Rex Stevens in post at the Colonial Office in the late 1930s. Those involved in intelligence do not feature on establishment lists, or enjoy the "statement of services" published by the Foreign Office: "Stevens" could have operated (within the Foreign rather than the Home and Colonial Office) without being traceable but Stevens was probably still not his real name. One curious possibility emerges from the Foreign Office lists, where the career of a diplomat named Sir Ralph Stevenson, GCMG, is noted. Could Stevenson have been Stevens? Let's postulate that he could: there are strong structural connections. Lastly ambassador to Egypt in the frail and vain years leading up to Suez, Stevenson had become an Arabist in the 1920s. He was posted to Cairo as First Secretary in 1929. In 1933 he was brought back to London and on 1 January 1937 appointed Acting Counsellor, a post whose brief was loose and counter-hierarchical, in which he was free to advise on policy (in his case towards the Middle East) and to pursue overt and covert strategy. He was also, 1936–9, the first chairman of the new Joint Intelligence Committee. The British government had its hands full with Nazi Germany and its own procrastination; but a fraction of the Foreign Office's practical energy was channelled to rolling back the anxiety felt after Mussolini's seizure of Abyssinia in 1936. Search the National Archives at Kew, under "Aden" and "Yemen" in the date range January–December 1937; more than 50 per cent of the documents involve confrontations with, or annoyed reports on, Italian behaviour. "Rex Stevens" and his like were shadowing Italian intentions in Arabia wherever they found them in the name of British interest. Freya Stark, about to excavate Hadhramaut cities, summed up its kernel in her letter to Lord Halifax. The British belief that, if it could, Italy would violate the Rome understanding of 1927, which made it incumbent on both Italy and the United Kingdom not to impose sovereignty on Red Sea islands that were under neither Yemeni nor Saudi sovereignty, was widespread. Yemen itself was decisive because "the country is a sort of diplomatic vacuum"[10] for the British (the Italians were already doing well at buying influence) and because it derived "strategic importance from the possibility of the exploitation of its position in relation to our sea and air communications through the Red Sea".[11]

What did this have to do with Norman? Stevens or Stevenson had charge of a plan to penetrate Yemen using civilian observers to report and make contacts. (The one factor that argues against Stevenson-as-

Stevens is that in Norman's accounts Rex Stevens accompanied him, an unusual mission for a senior diplomat though maybe not for one with a sense of adventure.) In the course of a conversation about photography that extended to travel and foreign languages, including Arabic, Stevens asked Norman if he would be interested in travelling to Yemen and taking pictures. Norman's inevitable yes got him sent to a briefing that put the counter-case of the journey's dangers and discomforts, but he was not put off and met Stevens again to tell him he would be happy to accept the invitation. Stevens told him he must meet the other man who would be going, the Hungarian journalist Ladislas Farago. Farago, one of the world's opportunists who described himself as a roving correspondent for the *Sunday Chronicle*, had recommended himself by having written a first-hand, if highly coloured, account of his time in Abyssinia before the Italian invasion, *Abyssinia on the Eve*. The two met in Stevens' office. Though Norman later thought him "a great miser and bluffer. I found him flamboyant and unreliable",[12] his first impression was that the man was modest and possessed a reasonable sense of humour. An itinerary was confidently discussed. They would sail to Aden, Britain's Arabian entrepôt of gold, collect a letter from the governor for His Majesty Imam Yahya, and from Aden take the ten-day coastal journey by dhow to Hodeida. The journey contained several unknowns. Yemen was a closed country administered with ostentatiously severe Koranic justice. It had no electricity, no roads and not more than half a dozen doctors for three million people. The list of proscribed activities was long: no smoking, drinking or music-making, including singing or whistling or dancing, no wearing of gold or silk or contemplation of women or pointing at the full moon; almost the only foreigners admitted were fur- and coffee-merchants and arms dealers; least tolerated were journalists, academics and writers, who in the past had all turned out to be British spies. Photography was also illegal. To Norman's question about the objective of the expedition, Stevens' smiling response was that they would gain valuable information.

If 1936 had been a slightly slow year for Norman, 1937 was about to become an accelerating blur.

I find it hard to reconstruct precisely what happened between his departure for Arabia and return, for the reason that all three elements in the story – Stevens the spymaster, Lewis the photographer/writer, Farago the reporter in his exuberantly mendacious account *The Riddle of Arabia* – are infected into unreliability by their mission. From the moment when

Norman claims to have sailed with Farago on the SS *Llanstephan Castle*
and Farago to have sailed alone on the SS *Orford*, clarity is not fore-
most. Norman seems to have spent his time encountering Hemingway's
prose. "It was a small miserable ship [but] it actually had a ship's
library and this library contained a collection of short stories by
Hemingway and a collection by Somerset Maugham. ... I read them
both through two or three times, and at that time it struck me that I
enormously preferred Hemingway to Maugham."[13] He and Farago agree
on the name of the hotel they stayed at in Aden – the Marina – and
on the name of the British governor, Sir Bernard Reilly. But in their
contrasting accounts, for example, of a trip by taxi from Aden to Lahej
on the Yemeni border which each made separately, an interesting opposition immediately surfaces (Lewis: "Lahej came rapidly into sight,
surrounded by shining oases"[14] / Farago: "The sandy waste which lay
as a huge, desolate hyphen between Aden and Lahej is a branch of the
Rub al-Qhali, the Desert of the Flame, which Philby called the Empty
Quarter. ... Slowly I lost my time-sense"[15]). Their descriptions at Aden
of "the best-kept brothel in the Mediterranean" are, if not contradictory, at least reflective of what two observers, one a Romantic, the
other an opportunist, want to be true (Lewis: "It was ... ruled over
by a dazzling young lady of fourteen named 'Halva' (Sweetness), who
made no charge for her services for suitors who presented themselves
with an acceptable poem"[16] / Farago: "In Sheikh Othman I met a
Somali girl, the star of the district. She conducted a big house, had
three servants, more than £1000 in her bank account, and beautiful
jewelry. She even had a kind of business manager, a fellow named
Jacob, who took good care of her financial affairs. Her name was
Halowa and she was fourteen years old"[17]). Farago's tireless quest for
superiority of effect is well illustrated in his description of a "friend of
mine" and his beard.

Norman Lewis, an Englishman, whose pictures illustrate these pages, was
frequently a victim of anti-Italian feeling [in Aden]. With his Balbo beard [Italo
Balbo, minister of the Italian air force and governor-general of Libya] he gave
the appearance of a genuine Italian. In his presence our Arab friends were
always careful of their remarks; they were frightened into silence by the Balbo
beard. ... But sometimes Norman's little beard brought forth enthusiastic
demonstrations by the few pro-Italian Arabs. In the street his beard was sometimes greeted with the Roman salute. One day we were sitting on the terrace

of the Marina with an RAF officer, when the head boy of the Italian shipping line approached us and, encouraged by Norman's beard, shouted, "*Italiano force, Inglis makaki* – the Italians are strong, the English are monkeys!" This was too much for Norman, and he rebuffed the servant. The man, realizing his mistake, promptly changed his mind. "I beg your pardon, sir," he said, "I did not wish to offend you. But you see, I'm employed by an Italian firm, and the wops like it if we flatter them. Those macaroni eaters!"[18]

A complicated atmosphere of mistrust between Norman and Farago saturates the accounts they wrote later, Farago when he returned, Norman in his autobiography and other pieces. Though this was partly due to the climate and claims of espionage, it was chiefly Farago's fault, as Norman and he were supposed to be working together as writer and photographer (Farago never mentions Rex Stevens), but Farago kept every contact and activity secret from Norman – the visiting card he carried with him from London, for example, describing him as a representative of a Polish furrier named Klar – and refused to share any intelligence. A suspicion grew in Norman's mind that Farago was a double agent after he secretly watched him in close conversation with two Italian officers. When the chance came of smuggling himself into Yemen, Farago did not think twice about leaving Norman behind. For all the casual experience that Norman liked to radiate, he would have agreed that he was out of his depth with the older, manipulative Farago (to whom in the beginning he willingly deferred).

The result is that in the four versions of the expedition that came to be written, not one accords with the others. Farago's self-celebrating book is . . . a farrago, crumbling into a wasteland of anecdote; Norman's three versions, written between 1937 and 2001 – the text accompanying his photographs in the album *Sand and Sea in Arabia*, five pages in *Jackdaw Cake*, and a piece "A Voyage by Dhow" – are an assortment of storyteller's selections. (In which Norman too is not above fictionalising himself.) His last account, sixty-five years after the fact, contains the surprised discovery of the extent of Farago's infidelities.[19]

The one certainty of the journey was its profound effect. For more than two months Norman was plunged into "the dazzling simplicities of the Middle Ages",[20] returning to England stripped of dependence on modernity and in awe of the Arabic language and "the richness and subtlety of its vocabulary and the brilliant mathematics of its construction". (One might add its ornate and impregnable courtesies that Norman gradually adapted to his own use in encounters with strangers.) In two months he distanced himself so far from Bloomsbury, Forty Hill, fussy dignified inter-war England, that he came as close as he ever did to a point of no return.

Choosing between his accounts, the first – the text and photographs of *Sand and Sea in Arabia* – is most truthful about what he did and the effect it had on his sensibility, best seen in the sudden conversion of his writing style to a new and luscious sobriety. I think he saw that Arabia was no clever young man's theatre. Arabia fated him to involvement. Arabia silenced irony.

He spent seven weeks in Aden waiting for Sir Bernard Reilly's request for a permit to be answered by the king at Sana'a in order to be able to visit the Yemeni capital. He found something cruel about Aden's prosperity, its factories and cinemas, the "life of labour [that] replaces one of indigent leisure and reflection", the implied exploitation in opium and hashish being sold openly by licence in the town. He reports hearing a Yemen-born Arab say, "Better the exactions of an unjust sheikh than the benevolence of the stranger. Better the rocks of the Yemen than the gardens of Aden. Better a withered apple in my hand than a peach in the hand of a monkey." The city was full of Italians on leave, there for the mild debauchery of the brothels, and suffered the dulling effect of universal clandestine tittle-tattle. Norman gives the impression of being ill at ease in his clandestine role, part of the European colonial presence he had contemplated with scorn in Casablanca. Farago was at home in this atmosphere, but Norman needed to escape; he drove to Lahej, north of the city of Aden on the Yemeni border, and then to Ma'ala, the bay where most Indian Ocean dhows were built. In Lahej, all its colours muted by dust, he saw the sultan's Friday procession to the mosque, accompanied by drummers and a military band playing the European tune adopted as his anthem, and was invited to a party at which several guests arrived still cupped with cows' horns from visiting the barber to have their blood let. A guest offered to take him into the mountains on his camel-cart next morning, and two hours after daybreak he found himself unofficially across the border in forbidden Yemen. He found a climate that was astonishingly cool and temperate: the tracks he walked were profuse with aloe and tamarisk, date palms and bananas, jasmine and wild briars and even bluebells. He identified hoopoes, bulbuls and golden orioles. It was this atmosphere of lush virginity, as well as Yemen's mineral wealth and strategic position, that colonialists were desperate to exploit. For now the road to the coast carried Yemeni merchants to Aden and bedouin by day, and by night deserters and fugitives. Norman's oddest experience at Lahej was his meeting with El Hadhrami (literally "he of the Hadhramaut"), an outlaw wanted in Yemen for the murder of three soldiers of the imam. The photograph Norman took of him "waving his sword with obliging ferocity" shows a statuesque fighter in a kilt, disdainful of capture.

He returned to Aden, having found something for himself if not much for Stevens. He made a similar journey to the shipyard town of Ma'ala to watch square-rigged dhows being built "in a bay full of luminous shadows" beneath an extinct volcano and to photograph, with an organicist's enthusiasm, the details of their handbuilt construction "to much the same pattern as the Egyptian and Phoenician ships of three thousand years ago'.

Intervening centuries have brought the augur, various bladed shaping tools, and the steel saw to lighten the labour of construction, but modernity finds no place in the ship itself. Even in the building, difficulties are skirted in the traditional archaic fashion so that it is necessary to have recourse to no more than the minimum of modern technique.

Wooden plugs, for instance, always take the place of screws and, in the formation of angles, pieces of wood naturally possessing the tortuous shape required are sought, to avoid complicated joining or the hewing out of the desired shape from the solid wood.[21]

The dozen well-composed photographs that accompany the book's short but detailed text on dhow-building demonstrate his aesthetic attentiveness to the subject, repeatedly framing the labour of the carpenters with their two-man saws, the belts of stylised carving draped along gunwales, the chiaroscuro of equatorial light on wood. (The illustrations included in *Sand and Sea in Arabia* are better printed, and far better photographs, than most in *Spanish Adventure*.)

Finally, the permit to visit Hodeida, and then, if Imam Yahya remained willing, Sana'a, came through. His written accounts of the journey by dhow that followed bear a similar relation to each other as the stories he told in conversation and over dinner: the same elements are present, but no two versions are alike, the complication arising from the fact that – as in conversation – he enjoyed recycling his experiences into new narrative objects. *Sand and Sea in Arabia* offers the most plausible account, but still contains gaps and question marks. In its foreword he explains how his mission to Hodeida fell through for no apparent reason; in the text, the voyage by dhow is described not as part of his assignment for Stevens but as a way of salvaging something "on our way back to Europe", its itinerary taking him to Jeddah on the dhow and thence by steamer to Sudan. In *Jackdaw Cake* he supplies a reason for his failure to enter Yemen: that the Yemenis had apparently expected a cargo of arms, and the permission given to Norman's party had been intended for someone else. Even later, in "A Voyage by Dhow", his dhow is delayed for repairs at Kamaran island and he turns *back* to reach Hodeida on the steamer SS *Minho*. The differences are the usual results of the writer's licence to rebel against time's stony "And then". But add to their inconsistencies Farago's singlehanded, supposedly earlier entry into Hodeida from a Portuguese steamer, the SS *Ayamonte*, and Norman's confession that his voyage on the dhow "followed almost immediately upon a similar one, undertaken in a cargo steamer along the same coast",[22] and the questions multiply. Where did he go on the steamer? Did he perhaps after all go to Hodeida with Farago? Or somewhere else? Why, above all, given all the subjects he photographed, if he went to Hodeida, alone or with the Hungarian, or even if he only sat offshore, did he publish not one photograph of Hodeida?

Whatever the true sequence, the voyage that took place unrolled into a glorious dream. Dhows were still competitive for trade. Their tariffs were low and their exposure to weather, slowness and frequency of wreckage did not deter many merchants who did not want to pay steamship freight costs. They carried no lifeboats. "*Allah huwa al hafis*" ("God is the keeper").

Norman's dhow, a *sambuk* or small dhow of 80 tons "without colour or carving, but graceful of line", came from Makalla in the Hadhramaut. Her skipper, the *nakhoda*, was taking on fresh cargo at Ma'ala and repairing damage caused by scraping a reef, and agreed then to take them to Jeddah. While they negotiated, an invitation arrived to a wedding in a Hadhrami family settled in Aden. Being present, Norman's party were included. Before sunset the dancing began, ending hours later in a choreographed clash of swords and rifles loosed at the night sky. The next day came the main entertainment, a *khat* party for 200 male guests who, as the day wore on, carried on increasingly abstracted conversations or sang or laughed quietly. For Yemeni Arabs *khat* was a universal addiction, the one pleasure sanctioned by Imam Yahya, also reducing fatigue and intensifying concentration. Norman mourned its ultimate "reduction of the sexual virility of the race". The wedding feast on the third day, of "saffron coloured rice, mutton and goat's flesh, dismembered fowls, and many kinds of fruit", elicited reverence both for the food and his fellow Arab guests.

Their courtesy was of a very high order. Although I was known only to a few of them, none looked at me curiously or in any way let it be seen that they realized the presence of a stranger.[23]

At four in the afternoon the *nakhoda* gave orders to weigh anchor. The moment of departure breathed soul-stilling harmony into the end of the day.

The burnished breast of the harbour curved gently with some sinuous movement from the depths and, in places, a vagrant breeze frosted its surface with changing designs. Momentarily the great triangular sail filled with wind, and strained billowing at the mast. Then just as suddenly it drained out and hung down loosely. We moved so slowly that, looking at distant objects, we seemed to be stationary. Only a gentle straining of timbers assured us that we were under way, and in the water thin streams of iridescence spread out and curled into rings over the gently heaving wake, as the ship's sides disturbed the oiliness of the surface. Even the gull perched on the mast remained standing trance-like on one leg, and, as night drew close, only stirred to put its head under its wing.[24]

Exposure to air and sea, and to crew and passengers, were both sources of intense pleasure as the dhow drifted at infinitesimal speed along the coast of the Gulf of Aden. Hell was not other people, as it might have been on an uneven deck stale with "sacking and dried fish and bilge" whose only toilet arrangement was "the place of ease", a cut-out chair suspended by a derrick and ropes over the waves. At night the Hadhrami crew gathered in the bow and sang, while Norman and his fellow passengers defended themselves with blankets against the mosquitoes. The heat was stifling, the corners of packing cases made it hard to find sleeping space, and cooling off by jumping over the side was discouraged by the alarmed expressions of the crew. Aching and intolerably sticky bodies, unmoving for days at a time in windless waters, were the physical envelopes the passengers were doomed to;

but from the passing of the first cups of *kishr*, a decoction of coffee husks whose sharp pungency was preferred to coffee itself, a sense of fellowship developed among the thirty-odd passengers. All were devoutly religious, the actions of the Moslems directed by explicit Koranic precept – a fact that impressed the atheistic Norman as much as his own acceptance by them. Little division existed between passengers and crew. At the rare times when there was work to be done the dhow's male passengers joined in, and at meals everyone ate from a common plate. "We found ourselves part of a community in which the issues of life were suddenly simplified and the essential virtues became once again of supreme importance."[25] Norman photographed most members of the crew and passengers. His eye for facial portraits had improved: portraits like that of the young Kuwaiti steersman, a former trainer of falcons able to see landmarks invisible to the other passengers, or of the existentialist Sheikh Said, sickened by local wars into turning his back on his country, or of the Yemeni Jewish family on their way to Palestine, all faces suffused by their wearing of life and a handsome fatalism, are seventy years later one of the book's most memorable aspects.

On the third day they came near the straits of Bab al Mandeb. The coast looked unreal: the light and dry air produced an optical effect similar to the one he had noticed in Spain, and it lacked features of recognisable size. "In their place we saw outlines drawn across the sky like threads of gold, with shapes discerned by shadows of silver." They had left behind the milky billows of jellyfish shoals outside Aden and were sailing in a sea "lit up from below" by sunlight bouncing off sandbanks. As the dhow passed into the Red Sea at night, the doldrums were replaced by a stiff breeze. When two heavy beams of cargo had been discharged, the Yemeni slaves who had come to fetch the timber agreed to take a party ashore (in a later version, a pigeon-shooting party from which a member of the crew disappears).

Hodeida, when it was reached, was a poor anchorage. Taxes levied for years on passing ships for the harbour's improvement had disappeared into Imam Yahya's pocket or those of his officials, and vessels had to anchor a few hundred yards offshore. To Norman

Hodeida looked as desolate as a cluster of whitened bones. This impression was heightened by the broken-down hovels and the crumbling fort on the outskirts of the town.[26]

It would be bloodless to line up every contradiction in what Norman wrote about Arabia; but Hodeida's treatment is worth a pause. His first description has an immediacy that convinces. But it is as if, each time it was remembered, the light had changed. In *Jackdaw Cake* the port has been promoted to "a crystalline sparkle of dwellings on the dun Arabian shore", and in "A Voyage by Dhow", his last essay, it has become, Petersburg-like, a re-creation of a European model in the shape of the *ports de plaisance* of the French Midi, though the final result, "charming in a wan sort of way", reflects not the self-indulgence of Europe "but the inbred asceticism of Islam". He continues by reporting that "I had been cautiously taking my last photographs of the scene" when he notices the preparations for a public execution on the waterfront. The dark denouement, told in detail, is missing from his first account although present in his autobiography, with the embellishment of a torture – that of making a man drink water with his penis tied up, to extract an admission of guilt – that he first described in one of his Latin American novels of the 1950s.

What did Hodeida really look like to Norman? we may be nudged to wonder. The first version mostly, perhaps. But syncretically impossible to say. And how to explain the puzzle of one tightly cropped shot of four Yemeni slaves unloading bales of what looks like cloth as the only published photograph that supposedly relates to Hodeida?

The biographer must be aware that where the subject is a writer, such quarrels are poisoners. He or she knows that the writer does not lie in the way that others lie, for the basic reason that readers read partly for the pleasure they take in the *writer's* creation of verisimilitude. A writer's lie is more satisfying than reality's truth, should that be available anywhere. If things were the other way around, there would not be very much point in the writer writing (and less in biographers doing so). And in such cases the "intermediate truth" of the biographer, launched upon the vessel of their available facts, always risks spoiling the reader's pleasure. Facts can be as irritating as reality, or piety. As one of the characters in Kurosawa's *Rashomon* says, "Not another sermon! I don't mind a lie, not if it's interesting." To the conundrum of Norman's encounter with Hodeida, the biographer can, I think, only respond that this is a reasonable moment at which to offer what ultimately frames every view of another's life: the wisdom of uncertainty. He had his reasons.

The Red Sea breeze blew into a storm. The dhow's sail tore to shreds.

Drifting beam-on, the ship weathered the heavy seas until it reached
Kamaran island and a bay of healing glassiness. Repairs were needed,
and Norman used the stop to photograph the boys and men who fished
for pearls, an occupation he thought as hard as that of a farm labourer
in the most feudal parts of Europe. With some patriotism he declared
that "Under the new British administrator the worst abuses in the
Kamaran pearling industry [such as the punishment of setting a diver
adrift in a canoe without oars if he were found trading on his own
account] are being rectified".[27] His admiration for Captain Thompson,
the British administrator, was genuine, though "he and his charming
young wife were possibly the two loneliest people I had ever seen".[28]

It is very unlikely that Norman went on by dhow from Kamaran to
Jeddah, 800 kilometres to the north, though he describes the end of
his dhow voyage as being after his arrival in Jeddah, not before. Massawa
in Eritrea is 350 kilometres due west from Kamaran, but 800 kilometres due south from Jeddah. It would have been a terrific diversion for
the *nakhoda* to double back from there, even if Norman's "west" was
really south.) Wherever it happened, the farewell was charged. Some
of his Arab friends wept, and the *nakhoda*, as a gesture of parting
kindness, charged him 30 rupees instead of the agreed 45. "At dawn
we stood upon a rocky promontory and watched as the sail went up
and, faster than it had ever seemed to us to move before, the sambuk
sailed away into the West, towards Massawa."[29] Southern Arabia was
stamped on Norman's sensibility: the place where reality and the
authentic Romantic dream intersected was here. In the Arab world's
"dazzling simplicities" he had seen an alternative to the conventional
horrors of English social intercourse and heard, like others – Thesiger,
Philby, Lawrence – the Lilliputian threads breaking. With the difference of course that he wasn't Arab and didn't pretend to be. It would
be easy to say that Arabia confirmed him as a Romantic, and truer to
say that when he thought of getting out there and staying there,
"drop[ping] all my responsibilities",[30] the thought was a homage not
an intention: Arabia was not the possible end of his responsibilities,
but the beginning of his understanding and focusing his gift as a writer,
regardless of demands and obligations that existed elsewhere in his life.

The steamer Norman took brought him to an Arab city that came
as a surprise after the warrens he had known in north Africa, its street
plan studded with broad airy squares, a prosperous souk and magnificent houses. But Jeddah elicited fatigue. Most journeys are wired from

the beginning with the source of their end, a desire for an emotion or an electric current of recognition that this is what you came for, and when it connects the journey has served its purpose; to go further is to invite exhaustion, accident, dull prose. Norman already had his emblem of Arabia felix. One glorious dream was enough. With the dhow and its passengers gone, in his mind he was on his way home. Crossing the Red Sea by steamer to Port Sudan, he roused himself for a last excursion to the ghost town of Suakin. Appropriately, Norman summons up the vocabulary of reverie to include it in his mood.

We went to Suakin in a Ford saloon car over a rough desert track . . . we plunged into seas of mirage. Fifty yards away in every direction the earth crumbled and dissolved into waveless oceans of illusion. . . . We were very close to the sea, but could not tell where the mirage ended and the sea began. Sometimes a pink layer of cloud appeared in the sky on the seaward side. This represented the breakers on the shore, strangely immobilized by the process of change. Shapes of dhows floated above the pink cloud like white butterflies with motionless wings. Suakin appeared first like a row of dissolving pearls suspended in mid air.[31]

Suakin had been a centre of the east African slave trade: on its wealth a settlement more like an exclusive gated community than a town had grown up, an African Venice crowded with the dwellings of merchants whose taste for roof gardens and intricately carved cedar verandas was defended by brass cannons stationed at each entry. Deserted, its white ruins offered Norman, as he walked bare streets of crumbling four-storey houses and pushed open doors that fell from their hinges in an explosion of dust, a last Arabian dreamscape, a dying fall, a fantastic, echoing emptiness to carry back with him to the prosaic solidity of Gordon Street, and 202 High Holborn.

Before he reached London he had a chance encounter that briefly prolonged his contact with the Arab world. Arriving in southern Italy from Port Sudan, he caught a train to Rome and in the dining car was joined by a "breathless young Englishman". Oliver Myers was an Arabised archaeologist who was returning from a lengthy dig in the Egyptian desert. Norman recognised the true believer: Myers' fingers were cramped as he held his fork, more used to eating with his hand, and his high-spirited Arabic connoted the excited illiteracy of the *fellah*. They launched into an attempted conversation in Arabic that neither understood much of; reverting to English, they became friends. "Although it was years before I realised this had happened," Norman wrote at the beginning of his second volume of autobiography, "the direction of my life changed in 1937" with this meeting. He omitted to say how Oliver Myers had changed his life, but it seems reasonable to assume that with the cement of shared enthusiasms between the two men, one an eccentric authority, the other an experimentalist and dilettante, an important legitimising of Norman's changing arc of interests took place. Myers was going to England to promote a book about his work on burial-places at Armant in upper Egypt and happened to live near Gordon Street, in an apartment in Woburn Square. Introduced into the complicated household of the Corvajas, he met with approval for his regular gallantries, gifts and animation, and in the following months evolved into as close a male friend as the emotionally guarded Norman ever had.

It could not possibly have been better for me, that war. It wrenched me out of an impossible situation.

Norman Lewis

8

TO THE EDGE

"To sing before breakfast
is to weep before supper"
Welsh proverb

THE demands and obligations of England fell on him immediately on
his return. While he had been away Ernestina had been involved in an
unspecified accident that left her with a scarred upper lip. Norman
detected a moral scarring too. Rumours mentioned a suicide attempt.
He made efforts to shore up her failing satisfaction with English life:
the first was to accept a commission from her father Ernesto to act as
go-between in delicate negotiations with a senior Fascist figure who
lived in Milan and might support Ernesto's petition for his eventual
return to Italy. The journey suited him because he had also been discussing
with Arthur Baron the possibility of importing used Italian sports cars.
He travelled back to Italy, to Milan, in the middle of June. Ernesto's
potential sponsor, a fleshless count named Aldo Giordano, drove him
to lunch near the cathedral, giving him a tour d'horizon from the passenger
seat of his black Alfa Romeo of the triumphalism of Mussolini's Italy.
Dressed in the Fascist *squadrista*'s ill-borrowed formality of English
suiting and bowler hat, the count said he was interested in money: was
Ernesto rich? He himself was in import-export, he mentioned – giving
Norman a later opportunity for a typical Lewis sentence, whose end is
not to be guessed from its beginning – "trading in such diverse goods
and commodities as goat skins, ostrich feathers, bilingual talking dolls,
Hornby train sets, and camel flesh which, minced up with appropriate
herbs and served with pasta of various kinds, formed an important part
of the rations of the colonial troops". Norman mentioned his interest

in Italian cars, and Giordano replied that he might be able to help. Such was the sign that the conversation about Ernesto had gone well. A few days later Giordano delivered on his offer: on 20 June he took Norman and Ernestina to the Parco Sempione circuit for the Milan Grand Prix (won by Nuvolari that year in an Alfa Romeo), where he showed him a four-seater drophead Alfa Romeo competition car surrounded by a cluster of admirers. Norman took the opportunity to buy it "at an absurdly low price". He liked to say later that the car, a 1933 8C 2300, had won a 24-hour race at Le Mans. It could have done: Sommer and Nuvolari won in a factory car in 1933, and if Norman had acquired that car he would certainly have known. (The record of the 8C 2300 at Le Mans in the early 1930s was overwhelming. It won every race from 1931 to 1934 and in 1933 took the first three places.) His car did have the factory's long-wheelbase Le Mans competition body and the same race-winning supercharged 2.3-litre engine and might have been the Alfa, driven by Chinetti and Étancelin, that won as a private entry in 1934. Norman shipped the car back to England and collected it from the train a couple of weeks later. He kept it for twelve years before reluctantly selling it, and in addition to the pleasure he had from driving it its general effect was gratifying to the Romantic and self-publicist in him. In her photograph album Ernestina pasted a cutting from a London newspaper column that Norman sent to her in Guatemala in November 1940, in the middle of the Blitz:

In Passing

During a London daytime alert recently; the place was Ludgate Circus, the car, a spick-and-span "two-three" Alfa two-seater [sic] in that particularly flaming yet highly suitable Italian red. At that instant, somehow, it struck one more forcibly than it might have done at a more normal moment of an abnormal wartime world. "Whose?" one wondered at once, and "Whither?", the usual chain of recollections flashing briefly through the mind. It gave one a certain sense of pleasure to think that such a machine should still be able to amble along Fleet Street – a very normal-looking Fleet Street – on what happened to be a very beautiful November afternoon, more like spring than early winter. An Alfa, a red Alfa, at Ludgate Circus, after three months of all the German has tried to do to London.

The Alfa was also the cause of a curious friendship soon after collecting it off the train. He was trying its performance on the A120 up through Epping Forest and, satisfied ("The car accelerated easily up a slight gradient to about 110mph, with power clearly in hand"), he pulled in at a pub, the Wake Arms. Another car, of a grandiosity Norman had not seen, almost immediately pulled alongside: one of the most extravagant Mercedes ever built, a 500K convertible,[1] driven by a Cambridge undergraduate who turned out to be the heir to a Malayan rubber fortune, and who, once they had been introduced, was invited by Norman to try the Alfa. Coming back from the test drive, the young Chinese, Loke Wan Tho, immediately expressed his admiration for the car's spartan functionalism and noise in Woosterish terms ("Oh, absolutely! How absolutely!") and suggested a straight exchange. Norman realised slowly that he was talking to great wealth, the 500K being worth at least five times the value of the Alfa, but declined because he was interested in racing the Alfa. He kept in touch with Loke – their conversation over a drink disclosed their shared interest in birdwatching – and another opportunity for a swap came when the Mercedes had its rear sliced off by a train in Germany and Loke offered to have it rebuilt for Norman. But the war intervened.

Back in England in July, Norman began a course in Arabic at the School of Oriental Studies, got himself elected to membership of the Royal Photographic Society and decided to branch out into 16mm sound-on-film cine photography. His efforts to improve Ernestina's morale may have been partly successful. In September her submission of a bromide print entitled "'All-in' Wrestling" made it into the 1937 RPS annual exhibition. She had taken the picture at Blackfriars when she and Norman had accompanied Count Giordano and his beauty-queen wife to an evening of wrestling. The Giordanos had come to London by invitation soon after Norman's diplomatic intervention, to discuss future projects with Ernesto. Apart from the count's instant addiction to English wrestling (he and his wife went every evening of their stay: at one bout Giordano took off his shoe and threw it at a wrestler who displeased him), he made his presence felt by displaying an ability to boast for an entire evening and a taste for swinging. When the contessa put the partner-swapping proposal to Ernestina as, she said, a part of a normal Italian holiday experience, Ernestina's avant-garde views failed to stand up to the thought of carnality with the count. Ernesto and Maria however counted the meeting a success, and they left shortly afterwards for Rome and a reunion with the Sicily of his youth.

In September Norman and Ernestina also drove to a hill-climb event at Lewes in Sussex where his friend Arthur Baron, running for the first time the rebuilt Type 59 Bugatti he had bought from the Duke of Grafton's chauffeur, recorded FTD (fastest time of day). Norman was interested in the outcome because he and Baron had shared the purchase for around £200 of another Bugatti, the wrecked Type 51 that Mervyn White had crashed at Cork. This car had held a Brooklands lap record and, still bloodstained, been rolled into the Baron garage with the intention of Norman racing it the following season. "The excitement of racing, the enjoyment of it, captured me," he said later.[2] His first effort had had a pantomime drama to it, according to him, driving in another car of Baron's, a 1923 Brescia Bugatti to which Baron had bolted a supercharger and which they had hurriedly entered in a 100-mile race at Southport – "rather like rescuing an aged bullfighter from an old people's home, filling him with pep pills and putting him back into the ring". Beach spray covered his goggles and stopped him seeing where he was going; after driving in the sea for some time he moved up to find himself behind the race leader. The end "was proclaimed in a green flash that filled the sky, and then sweetly and in utter silence the car coasted to a stop. The bonnet was opened to reveal a great emptiness. Nothing remained of this car but a body, a chassis and four wheels. It was a stylish and definitive exit."[3] His excitement may also have been at finding another outlet for his escape reflex, into an activity in which he could empty his head of Ernestina or just of the constant negotiation of a life verging on the complicated, balancing R G Lewis business with writing ambitions, living with the Corvajas, and attempting to moderate the pendulum swings of Ernestina's disaffection.

He had always intended to offer a book about his Yemen journey. The proposal he came up with was formally unusual, an album that would have a photograph a page, each picture above a 150-word episode of text and arranged in a narrative series. In the summer he had selected the pictures and written the 20,000-word text. He submitted both to Victor Gollancz, who turned the book down. He then tried Routledge, who accepted it and scheduled it for publication in the spring of 1938.

Norman returned to the uneven routines of running R G Lewis and life at Gordon Street. Both were sources of ambivalence, even extravagant ambivalence. Business was very good. At the end of the year Norman exhibited a new range of Ampro 16mm cine projectors at the Royal Photographic Society Kinematograph Exhibition, and his weekly full-page advertisements in *Amateur Photographer* showed a healthy turnover of stock. He acquired a partner, a man named Harding, to inject capital and relieve him of excessive commitment to the company. Domestic life had reached a high plateau of complexity. The Corvajas' unchecked gregariousness had brought their household to saturation: Maria's brother Franco's family had moved in, Eugene and two artist friends had set up an atelier in the principal room, an Anglo-Indian schoolfriend of Ernestina's occupied one of the bedrooms with her elderly German lover, and another was taken by a former schoolmistress of Ernestina's. The house's Sicilianisation was reinforced by half a dozen pets ranging from a mongrel dog to a small, immobile owl. When Norman invited Oliver Myers to the house, Myers was charmed by the oasis of Mediterranean chaos it presented, though after the first occasion they tended at Norman's suggestion to alternate their dinners at the Corvajas' with drinking at the Fitzroy Tavern or eating at Myers' preferred Italian restaurant, Prada's on Euston Road.

Norman and Ernestina also diverted themselves with outings to Epping Forest with Ito, now one and walking, and race meetings. They followed the progress of Norman's and Baron's rebuilt Bugatti, the car being tried out by Baron as the more experienced driver. At the inaugural hill-climb event in the middle of May at Prescott near Cheltenham – hill-climbs were another motoring Arcadia of the 1930s, social, do-it-yourself confections of cars, picnics (and engine parts) scattered among the grass and orchards – the T51 won the 880-yard race against strong competition.

But Norman's situation in the spring of 1938 shared something with Britain's, as the nation found itself living, trivialised by aimlessness, in history's waiting-room. Something exhausted, and exhausting, was in the atmosphere: on the Continent in March the *Anschluss* expressly prohibited by the Treaty of Versailles came and went; in September German occupation of the Sudetenland snapped into place after Neville Chamberlain's rapturous reception at Heston aerodrome; in November news of the *Kristallnacht* pogrom was greeted with revulsion and inaction. Whatever the next stage was to be, it refused to start, and under the pressure of waiting, lives began to destabilise. At Gordon Street Eugene left for Spain to drive an ambulance for the doomed Republicans, Maria's alcoholic brother committed suicide by jumping from a hospital window, Ernesto's planned permanent return to Sicily was indefinitely postponed, and Ernestina's nervous tension and isolation, despite a course of psychoanalysis, worsened.

Nor had Norman's Yemen book been published. Production problems pushed the date back; printers and block-makers failed several times to produce results of high-enough quality. In frustration at the delays and wanting to try to restore his wife's equilibrium, in May Norman drove Ernestina to the Channel, caught a ferry, and started a motoring tour of central and eastern Europe that took them as far as the Bulgarian Black Sea coast. A small example of Norman's looseness with facts is in the car they drove: at different tellings it was a Buick, a Type 40 Bugatti, and a Ford V8. Perhaps it was the Ford, bought expressly for the journey, its tyres "worn down to their rims", and thrown away when they got back. In it they covered on a shoestring 6500 kilometres along roads that within sixteen months would carry, like the song of a million starlings, the squealing rumble of tracked German armour. Staying at roadside inns and with local people where no inn existed, they drove through annexed Austria and across the north Balkans into southern Transylvania, returning via Yugoslavia and Hungary. (Driving the same route sixty years later, with the occasional convenience of European motorways, I still took sixteen days.) On the return journey through Germany, Norman may have taken the opportunity of buying a large consignment of Leicas and smuggling them back to Britain in the Ford's spare wheel.

The gestation of his Yemen book in his absence ("Arab Dhow" was its working title) showed again the usefulness of 202 High Holborn as a meeting place. In the shop Norman had met an interesting photography-lover, a polymath in the Richard Burton mould: soldier, traveller, writer, translator with an interest in oriental erotica. "Egerton" (Norman always called him that), a lieutenant-colonel, had recognised that the clever dandyish proprietor of R G Lewis was not a run-of-the-mill camera salesman and the conversation had gone on from there. Colonel Egerton had suggested that Norman try Routledge with his book – he himself had a book with them[4] – and when "Arab Dhow" reached the production stage, he doubtless felt responsible. His camp, hectoring letters to T Murray Ragg, Routledge's managing editor, are probably the reason for the book receiving enough care to be published properly. "If I were Lewis, I think I should protest," he wrote to Ragg's secretary in June from Bricett Hall in Suffolk, to complain about the new proofs he had seen. "He is a photographer of standing. It is his business, and he cannot afford to have inferior reproductions made of his work which might give the impression that his work is not of the highest quality." And to Ragg himself the same day,

Heaven bless and preserve you! For I won't, unless something radical is done about this wretched book of Lewis's. I can't (as I have just told Miss Graham) tell the new pulls from the old except that the cream paper takes a bit of what life the others possessed, out of them.

As a lover of the firm of Routledge (sic!) I don't think their reputation (!) can allow them to produce a novel type of book, with first class originals in the way of pictures, in such an inferior manner. If photographic fans are to buy the book, which they might be expected to do in view of Lewis's position, they just won't unless it is better than this. (That's a good lucid sentence!) It would be far better to put another five shillings on the book and spend it on proper blocks, proper ink, proper paper, and proper printing!!!!!!!!!!!!!!!!!!!!!!!!!!!!!!!!

I guess I'll have to bring my weary bones up to Town and go into the matter again. A fat lot of anything but curses I get for it. Curses from myself to myself for spending time on it that I can't afford to spend; curses from G. R. and Sons for being a candid friend and not a bumsucker. . . .

Hell! said the Duchess.

Yours ever,

F Clement C Egerton[5]

Egerton's political tastes were errant – in 1943 he published an encomium to Salazar, the Portuguese dictator – but his friendship and scholarship were genuine. He encouraged Norman to write, and long after the war Norman used to send him things and ask for his editorial advice; he acknowledged him as one of the most entertaining men he knew. Egerton's erudition had its most lasting expression in his publication in 1939, as translator, of the Manchu literary masterpiece *The Golden Lotus* (*Chin P'ing Mei*) in four volumes. An enchanting soap of life and sexual intrigue in the Sung dynasty, considered so pornographic in the 1930s that Egerton veiled its most explicit passages in Latin, the book was familiar to Norman. In the early 1950s when he spent the evening with Gwen Merrington's eighteen-year-old daughter Julie he told her that the situation reminded him of *The Golden Lotus*, the author meeting the daughter of his past love.[6]

Back from the Continent in June, Norman distracted himself from the Routledge nuisance by taking the wheel of his Alfa at the Brighton Speed Trials on 2/3 July, coming, he claimed, second to last in his class. The Madeira Drive half-mile is shrunk on modern safety grounds to a quarter-mile, but in the inter-war years the speed trials were an annual climacteric of gaiety and risk-taking recklessness. Starting after break-fast, the weekend's programme had a class for every sort of car. Socially,

the meeting resembled a rave attended by every echelon of the motor
sport world, an all-day party against the howl of matched motors racing
axle to axle down the beachfront road's uneven surface.

Production controversy at Routledge was stoked by a new conflict
over the book's title. Norman had first suggested an Arabic title, "Es
Sambuk", Routledge had circulated information to booksellers about
a book called "By Arab Dhow Through The Red Sea". On 16 September
Norman rebelled.

Dear Mr Ragg,
    To say that I dislike your title would be an understatement, I detest it, I
loathe it, I execrate it and besides that I think that it is all wrong from many
points of view. In the first place it is too long. In the second place it is too
stodgy – it reminds me of all the mouldering and unread volumes in the
geographical sections of free libraries and the threepenny section of secondhand bookstalls.

He had also suggested "The Desert and the Sea", which Ragg had
rejected as "too vague and weak". He retaliated Shakespeareanly that
the book's title should be impressionistic, and that he had been here
before.

The same thing happened to me with my last book. Norman Collins of
Gollancz stuck out for a completely ridiculous title and much against my own
convictions I let him have his own way. I then had the mortification of reading
in a number of reviews that the commonplace title was the worst thing about
the book. One reviewer in particular said that it was only with the exercise
of his will power that he was able to bring himself to read a book with such
a title.
    If you won't have my title, let us think of another one, but as for "By Arab
Dhow – – –" etc. all I can say is, avaunt![7]

In early September he and Ernestina went to the RPS annual exhibition, in part to see another successful submission of Ernestina's, a
bromide print of "The Walls of Avila" taken on their 1936 Spanish
tour. On the 24th they drove to Brooklands to watch Baron race at
the heavily publicised Dunlop Jubilee Trophy meeting. The Weybridge
meeting should have been as gay as Brighton – entry fees were low
and the tyre company was offering a generous prize fund – but
Chamberlain's and Daladier's abandonment of the Sudetenland clouded

the day in crisis. The atmosphere was reinforced by the announcer requesting mid-afternoon that a naval officer thought to be at the track return to his ship immediately, and later announcing that a million Frenchmen had been called up.

1938's mood of depressed stasis produced "curious behavioural symptoms", as Norman wrote later.[8] Appeasement was a popular policy in Britain, but at the same time membership of rifle clubs doubled. R G Lewis took advantage of the rapid growth in numbers of Britain's amateur photographers, as people saw their cameras as indispensable to record a world many felt sure would disappear. The firm was becoming a sizeable success: Norman publicly acknowledged that it "makes us feel proud that we at '202' have, in just a few years, swung up the photographic ladder of miniaturism as if nothing could stop us".[9] He seems not immune to behavioural curiosity himself in the weekly run of full-page advertisements he wrote for *Amateur Photographer* through that autumn and winter. Composed with his usual ingenuity, topical and engrossingly readable by the standards of 1930s advertising, they slew in tone from the patriotic to the humorous. On 5 October, after Neville Chamberlain's return from Munich, he broke the advert into six boxes with connected headlines, so that the page read "WE FEEL PROUD / TO BELONG TO BRITAIN / AS WE SEE HER / CALMLY FACING CRISES / WITH HER ISLAND BROOD / UNSHAKEN AND READY", each piece of the headline unravelling cleverly from lines of jingoistic homily into promotion of R G Lewis or one of its products. Did he share the prevailing mood of relief that war had been avoided? The three striking aspects of Norman's output as a copy-writer are its quantity, extraordinary liveliness – he manages to be bumptiously witty and modest at the same time – and his use of it as a writing exercise. His text for that week's advertisement appeared to be catching the public mood, but he didn't, I think, care one way or the other about appeasement when he wrote that

CALMLY FACING CRISES

seems to have become second-nature to us all in the last few years; it's so strange that others mistake our calmness in trouble for what the States calls "dumb"-ness. In crises the Englishman, his Scottish, Irish and Welsh brothers usually have the wisdom to place complete confidence in their appointed leaders – a quality that makes for the strength of unity.

The miniaturist in trouble also turns to the leaders in the miniaturist world, which explains the unique place that "202" has in modern photographers' hearts.

We ourselves once felt the need for a service that would give good, unbiassed advice on photographic materials and apparatus. We decided that when we managed to fight our way up from a standing start we would still continue to give the same service when we were big as when we had only a few customers to help. Which explains why "Try 202 for Service" is a slogan famous all over the world.[10]

All he was interested in was selling cameras and accessories. His own programme for now was one of reverent egoism: he was as yet very far from ready to care about or help a country that had never helped him feel free. In fact he had taken a crash course in German earlier in the year, but that was not to understand the Germans' point of view; his only intention was to "increase my income by translating sensational and pugnacious articles from the German press for publication in English newspapers".[11] The concentrated entrepreneurial strain of his character that in the 1930s impelled his writing as much as his business activities can be seen as both a silent shout of revolt against what life in England, left to its own devices, intended to offer him, and as the subliminal engine of his insistence on managing his own life, with at times callous independence. On the surface his friendships, like his publicity, prove that he possessed a counterbalancing charm. A couple of weeks after his "island brood" advertisement, the boxes of his 19 October advert are all from fictitious departments of R G Lewis, the "'Oh, how mahvlus!' department" (on Leitz projectors), the "'Fan my brow!' department" (on something very technical about Exaktas), the "'Sink me, sir!' department" (on the high-end Tenax 1x1 format) and the "'You don't say!' department" ("'You don't meantersay a tiny negative like that produces an enlargement this size!' By gum, the Leica-man gets tired of it all, at times"). A week after that, his theme was popular songs. Even in his own advertising he seems to be setting himself a weekly parlour game, to take any theme and make it connect with cameras: the prize not a *John Bull* postal order this time, but ascending profits that would in an as yet unspecified way procure his freedom. "Hullabaloo-belay!" one box announces,

In which we are assured that "Me mother came back the very next day!" And for why? says you. You hardly need ask – it's obvious that Shallow Brown's darkroom was not equipped with an Optikotechna Ideal enlarger as was her husband's!

Seriously, though, these neat little outfits are amazingly efficient, and the Benar lens fitted is excellent. . . .[12]

In November the disputed Arabia book was eventually published. *Sand and Sea in Arabia* made the *News Chronicle*'s three-times-a-week books pages, C P Snow's magazine *Discovery*, and photographic magazines. The Christmas Eve issue of the *Times Literary Supplement* reviewed it with Freya Stark's album *Seen in the Hadhramaut*. The two photographers had been almost within shouting distance, one trying to find a story, the other to capture the harmony of a hardly known world (and control of its oil reserves). The *TLS* reviewer, the biographer Georgina Battiscombe, was breathless about Miss Stark's book ("It is hard to choose among such riches") and grudging about Norman's ("foiled in an attempt to enter the Yemen, [he] seems to have spent most of his time in or near Aden"). She nodded at the quality of his photography with queenly distance: "his photographs of Arab ships and seamen are remarkable both for the interest of their subject matter and for their pictorial beauty. Here the cluttered confusion of the dhow anchorage comes alive and baggala and sambuk sail again across the Red Sea with sails spread to catch the monsoon wind." Norman played his part in giving his book helpful publicity, playing a neatly twisted game of public bashfulness. "Modesty's a nuisance", announces one box of his 21 December page in *Amateur Photographer* (written by him as usual).

The Old Man has annoyed us lately. Time and again we have asked him to allow us to publish a note concerning his latest book – "Sand and Sea in Arabia" – but each time he has refused.

At last he has allowed us to do so, provided we do not enthuse about the book, as we confess we feel inclined to. Briefly, the book contains one hundred and twenty-three Leica pictures of very real interest and photographic excellence, each having a half-page description. We know how much work the Old Man put into making it, but "Sand and Sea in Arabia" more than repays his labours. To say that the book is excellent is to be very moderate in expression.

The Book, published by Routledge and obtainable at "202", costs 15s.

Norman's puff for himself is a witty microcosm of attitude. Its sense of something being forcefully propelled into prominence, its creator at the same time conducting a master class in self-deprecation, is also a metaphor for the future. The book itself, intermittently excellent, with its sharp change of style, is a snatched effort to establish himself as someone with something to say. He was making so much happen in his life in the 1930s, that overwhelmingly heuristic decade, that everything in it (apart from his ambition) was snatched, patched and without consistency. He had not decided yet what he was and whether he had more to say as writer, or as photographer. (He was shortly to be elected a Fellow of the Royal Photographic Society.) He had decided that whichever it turned out to be would be across the grain of his R G Lewis persona. Readers, he intended, were to notice the *seriousness* of his photographic and literary treatment of his subject in *Sand and Sea in Arabia*, whether that was colonial administration, the lives and work of dhow-builders, or the social conditions of pearl-fishers. Seriousness (this may seem a strange observation about a humorous Holborn copywriter who would in the future be an acknowledged virtuoso of the absurd) was the tone he found himself courting, the voice he found he liked, in the course of his failed spying expedition and his first journey where he had not, as previously, "travelled over well-worn trails". Spoken, his attitude was all comic self-deprecation. Unspoken, trenchantly, it was all about being listened to.

The sense of a life accelerating in lurches and not in great comfort, in contrast to the nation's stasis, gathers strength during that winter and spring. (By which I mean that the details of Norman's life in all of its strands – photographer, proprietor, writer, traveller, husband in an open marriage, live-in son-in-law – are beginning at the end of 1938 to radiate an impression to the observer of either crazily speeding up or imposing steadily greater demands. The faster they move together, the more demandingly they behave, the more irreconcilable they seem to be.) To the extent that Norman had created every one of the experimental conditions that had brought his life to this point, the experimentalist was in danger of being overrun by his own experiments. In fact he could hardly deny that, having created his life from scratch, the state it was in was entirely his own fault: *he* was responsible, nobody else, for his hasty marriage, his chaotic domesticity, his underlying conflict of business and artistic affairs. As manager of his own life he was at present not doing well. Ernestina's growing nervous problems were an added, and serious, destabilising factor. Was there competition there? Her cycles of laughter-obsession followed by drained inertia had intensified, and one psychoanalyst she saw had recommended her to reduce her involvement in life to thinking of it as a spectacle.

On the receiving end of such useless advice, Norman began to find his fought-for freedom constrained by the need to try new solutions to his wife's unhappiness. One, they decided, was for her to quit Gordon Street and her troubled relations with her father. In April 1939 Norman and she rented a small country house, Pine Cottage, at Iver Heath in Buckinghamshire. The dark brick house with leaded lights and a wild-flower garden and pond, owned by a never-seen aristocrat of lugubrious interior tastes, was surrounded by woods and fields and enjoyed by two-year-old Ito, who fed the fish in the ornamental pond and collected armfuls of daisies. Initially his mother shared his enthusiasm, and after a month again grew restless.

Possibly as a general antidote – even as a signal of his determination to master the forces of disorder – Norman had begun serious motor racing. In his autobiography he tidies up his racing career, writing that he competed, disastrously, only once at Brooklands in March 1939. On 11 March (not the 17th as he writes), before the move to Iver Heath, he entered his first race at a BARC[13] meeting at the Weybridge circuit, finally driving the Type 51 Bugatti he had bought with Baron. He would have been in no doubt that he was competing in one of Bugatti's quickest cars, one of forty made by the Molsheim factory, pale blue (much paler than the sky-blue referenced as Bugatti's blue today) with a white pigskin interior, supercharged to deliver 180 brake-horsepower at 5000 rpm. Five years earlier the car had lapped the circuit at nearly 130 mph. Norman did not come close to rivalling the feat. The pleasant weather broke into a torrent on Saturday morning and in the afternoon a "murk", as the announcer had it, hung over and hid parts of the mountain circuit including the Byfleet banking. Wet patches spread grease. Lighter cars suited the conditions and a 1½-litre Riley, first away, was never caught. Norman's inexperience with the T51's power output proved nearly fatal at the Members' Bridge turn. "N. Lewis, driving Baron's Bugatti, was noticeably wild," *The Autocar* reported drily. "He nearly disappeared over the top of the banking once, and eventually turned right round at the fork, a performance shortly repeated by R R C Walker with the Delahaye."[14]

Despite his claim that after that day he "never sat at the wheel of a Bugatti again", with creditable nerve he competed – and was again unplaced – at the Easter Monday meeting a month later. He dug himself into racing. Ernestina reclaimed the limelight by deciding again that her future was outside England. This time her Canaan was Cuba. A schoolfriend who had fled the civil war in Spain had written asking her excitedly to join her in Havana. Norman was patient and ambivalent: Batista's Cuba attracted the traveller, but the husband had little faith in any therapeutic outcome of indulging his wife. Her new fixation showed no sign of retreat; so he agreed and booked passages for the family for New York. He was entered to drive in the BARC International Meeting at Brooklands on Whit Monday, 29 May, and had hopes of a place in the Mountain Handicap event that afternoon. At practice the day before, something of the tension between the driver and the driver's wife was captured in several photographs of Ernestina taken by news photographers in search of a colour story. Under the headlines "Sombrero at Brooklands" and "Precautions at Brooklands" she is a glamorous presence in a checked dress, tailored coat, hoop earrings, a gaucho hat tied with a wide black ribbon under her chin and tight gloves. Competition again?

The racing, starting at 2 o'clock, was run in glorious sunshine with a cooling spring breeze. *The Autocar* called it "one of the best Bank Holiday meetings ever staged at Brooklands".[15] Close finishes made the tone of the day: in the second race Arthur Baron, scrapping with a driver named Parnell in a 5-litre BHW, edged him onto the grass on the last lap and took second place. Norman was entered in the number 7 Bugatti in the second Mountain Handicap at 4.35. He put in a more professional performance in the six-mile race than he usually admitted to, starting halfway down the field of ten, working his way up to third place in the second lap and staying there for two laps before he was pushed into fourth at the finish. He was consoled the following Saturday by chalking up a class win when he ran the T51 at the Shelsley Walsh hill climb in Worcestershire.[16] A photograph of Norman standing by his Bugatti at this hill-climb or another offers a spectacular meshing of subjects. The car is fitted as usual at hill climbs with double rear wheels for traction, making it look magnificently fit for purpose, the Balbo-bearded thirty-year-old driver is slouched next to it, in Oxford bags and white shoes.

Six weeks later, on 8 July 1939, he, Ernestina and Ito (John, Emily and Ivor Lewis on the passenger list) sailed from Southampton on the *Aquitania* for New York, third-class. Eighteen years earlier, in spring 1921, Scott and Zelda Fitzgerald had sailed the other way on the *Aquitania*, first-class, travelling to Europe for the first time. There are no comparisons to be made – Norman and Ernestina weren't a successful literary couple by any stretching of the category – except perhaps that the two marriages were, after their own fashion, already well on the way to being impossible, for similar pathological reasons of instability presenting as high spirits. And both couples may also, at one moment or another, have had the thought that there is nothing like a sea voyage for feeling one is leaving all one's problems behind.

PART TWO

BEING

A Life in Three Wars

Ernestina, the Axis, himself

The fact is that probably subconsciously, not knowing it, unintentionally, I fiddled myself into the Intelligence Corps in order to have a continuation of those adventures.

Norman Lewis

When the war started Oliver Myers told me to see somebody in the War Office and tell him I was an Arabic speaker. So I did that. And he sent me to someone else in Mayfair, and this man said, "Have you a sense of adventure?" I said yes. "And by the way, can you swim?" I said very badly. So he said, "Well, learn to swim." What they were proposing to do was to land a four-man submarine on the shore of North Africa with a radio transmitter. What I've only found out since is that five lots of people were sent on this exploit on this particular submarine, on five separate journeys, and they all drowned. The only reason I'm talking with you now is that at that point they decided to turn it in and not try again.

Norman Lewis

The Board has examined the above-named recruit
in accordance with instructions and placed him in Grade II.
Notes for information of recruiting staff only on posting recruit to corps[:]
Grade II = Fit for general service at home only,
or sedentary service abroad
– Army form E531, attestation of 10350775
Lewis, John Frederick Norman, Intelligence Corps;
Shrewsbury Medical Board, 10 October 1941

Army record

During the war, while waiting to be called for service, he had to cool his heels and with his marriage in the balance he and my sister Nance had an affair. I think she was very enamoured of his unique intelligence and personality. They visited me in Devon, she ostensibly to visit her two children, who were with my own. It didn't worry me a bit.

Gwen Merrington

9

FROM A WAR TO A WAR

"A lie runs till it's overtaken by the truth"
Cuban proverb

It is as the American historian Hayden White has written: whatever version of history we choose is unlikely to be on the sole grounds of accuracy. "The best grounds for choosing one perspective on history rather than another are ultimately aesthetic or moral rather than epistemological."[1] The Lewises' stay in New York was not long. That much can be worked out from the dates: arrival in New York on 14 or 15 July, likely arrival in Havana a good ten days before Britain declared war on Germany on 3 September (wherever Norman writes about his first view of Cuba, it is unclouded for several days by any looming or actual war); and they fitted in an excursion to the south. There are photographs, most from an album of Ernestina's, that run from a birthday party Ito attended on the *Aquitania* to the first views of Havana, a windy walk on the Malecon, Ito swimming with his father at Varadero or being buried in sand at the Jaimanitas Club. In the first New York photograph, taken by an unknown acquaintance, the couple stand on a sunny Fifth Avenue, both smiling, Ernestina in short lace gloves, high waisted skirt and white blouse, face shaded under the brim of her gaucho hat (now decorated with a posy of silk flowers), eyes gleaming with Latin vivacity. Norman is a step away from his wife, rather dressed down in a lightweight single-breasted suit, white shirt and spotted tie, hands in his pockets. His grin is directed at the sidewalk, as if thinking about something else entirely.

Apart from photographs, virtually no documentary evidence exists about what happened in the interlude en route for Cuba. (The only nugget of prose is a comment he relayed on the reception of his appearance, worked into the text for an R G Lewis advertisement of 2 August, referring to himself, as ever, in the third person. "We were hugely tickled at '202' recently when we heard of an incident in the Old Man's crowded hours in New York. ... Apparently he stepped out one morning on to Fifth Avenue, full of joydevivver, and had his peace of mind rudely shattered by a flagseller, who, after receiving his donation, remarked in a voice full of uncontrolled excitement to a friend twenty yards away: 'Say, aren't his little whiskers just cunning!'") So let us stay for a moment with the pictures. Pasted into Ernestina's album with her generally reliable captions, they throw up something unexpected. New York was in the grip of warm summer weather, probably more pleasant than the mugginess of today's Manhattan Augusts, with fewer cars, towers, air conditioning units and people to wring the oxygen out of the air. Norman and Ernestina did the rounds of the New York sights, smiling for the camera, with two-year-old Ito following their example in a sombrero. These are the pictures:

– a second Fifth Avenue photo taken the same day, angled from below, in which they stand in a deliberate line, Ernestina in front, then Norman, and the Indiana limestone-clad mass of the new Rockefeller tower racing up behind them

– a picture at the New York World's Fair, Norman looking frozen as he poses in a horse-drawn cab, its reins held by the same jovial unknown acquaintance

– a picture of Ito on a bench on a ferry to the Statue of Liberty

– several pictures of Ito sitting in the sun on rocks in Central Park

– and three photographs – the something unexpected – taken in desert country: all three of Ernestina or Norman posing with a car, a new Ford Mercury convertible, either perched on the seat-back of its bench seat or resting hands or elbows on the edge of the windscreen, like Bonnie Parker and Clyde Barrow. The Mercury's licence plate, 1C39-32, is embossed "New York World's Fair 1939". Ernestina, in a swimsuit and skirt, looks in-her-element happy, Norman, in an unbuttoned short-sleeved shirt and felt hat pushed back on his head, a bit sweaty. They are on a long dirt road with dusty scrub and palms on either side, a range of hills in the background and no other cars or people visible: a wilderness. The pictures are captioned "Mexico 1939".

Mexico? Were they really in Mexico? How? Did they win a trip at the Fair? We cannot know. But if we are to be entertained by the meanings that we put on the past, in the process we will also, as with all entertainment, set up an attempt to distil meaning. At first I assumed

"Mexico" had to be New Mexico, far enough by anyone's standards from New York; Mexico was just too far for a side trip. The car came from New York, and they probably returned it there. In an effort to shrink their mileage to something even more reasonable, I briefly felt they might have left the car at New Orleans or another southern port, but I don't think Grace Line ran sailings out of New Orleans or anywhere else on the Gulf of Mexico to Havana in the late 1930s.

And that was where I left it, until I came across a single spoken sentence of Norman's in an interview recorded fifty years later by the American writer Pico Iyer. Iyer had sent me the original cassette. In it he asked Norman for his view of the USA.

"I've been there several times," Norman answered, "and I've done some quite biggish trips. I drove from New York to Mexico City and to Puebla and back, many years ago."[2]

There is little reason to doubt his words or timing. They fit the photographic evidence well. So he and Ernestina – and Ito? – did drive as far as Mexico, and the attempt to distil meaning now has to take a more protean tone in relating a story not of a longish, self indulgent but perfectly sensible tour of 4000 kilometres or so to New Mexico, but of a monumental gamble of 9000 kilometres that took them through more than 20 degrees of latitude *and back again* in probably less than three weeks. Why? What spell were they trying to weave? The biographer's try at meaning is this: tiring of New York, twisting and turning in each other's company while they waited for their booked Grace Line sailing, they burst out of the city heading south, propelled by a nervous explosion of Norman's escape reflex and Ernestina's manic appetite for experience. If so, the drive sharply illustrates the dimensions of Norman's compulsion to get away, and how unrestrainable at any given moment it could be (he had an appetite for driving enormous distances for those days, but would have had to cover an average 500 kilometres a day). It also fits the lineage of his and Ernestina's experimental, not to say convulsive, approach to life and to escape. "I don't like it here" was always a password to action and motion with them.

It was an oddly pointless journey too – unless the point was that sitting side by side in a Mercury convertible and covering an immense distance together was one of the few remaining pleasures they shared.

So great was the general American reluctance to get involved in the coming European war that on the sailing to Havana the Lewises were regularly lectured, as they had been in New York, on the foolishness of British belligerence. Steaming into Havana harbour, international political discussion ceased. Cuba, as the storyteller remembers in two versions of his arrival, was "a different planet".

A norther, lifting the sea, had thrown a great curtain of spindrift over the city's façade, over the bay's curve of lean houses, granite-grey, pink, coral, pistachio as their owners had painted them in the colour of whichever political party they supported.[3]

[Havana] abounded with pleasure of the kind that London could not supply. It was an anarchy of colour, for rather than jettison unfinished cans of paint, people splashed what was left on the nearest wall.[4]

Whatever discrepancies surface in accounts written forty-five and fifty-seven years later – in *Jackdaw Cake* the friends of Ernestina's whom the Lewises stay with are the Castaños, fascists from Santander who have fled the Republican town and are planning their return, in *The World The World* they are the Molas, Republican sympathisers facing years of exile – Norman's reaction to Cuba remained passionately appreciative. "It was fabulous, outstandingly good. The music was extraordinary, because everyone in Cuba is a musician. There were flutes and guitars wherever you went. And the girls! Because the sugar plantation owners were so rich, they could always buy the best-looking slaves off the boats. So they all have these terrific genes."[5] On his first day in Havana, he claimed, hearing the noise of a sub-machine gun in the Parque Central he saw three men sprawled in pools of blood, murdered for demanding more than the offered dollar for their vote in an imminent election; in Cuba one became habitually immune to such "violences and tragic scenes . . . just as, by the coarsening of habit, a humane man may eventually come to tolerate the spectacle of a bull-fight". The antithesis of violence was that

There was a leisure not to be found elsewhere, with twenty-five men enthroned in a row to have their shoes polished for the third or fourth time that day. At nine every morning a religious procession formed to study the numbers of the lottery tickets on offer as soon as they were put up on the stand. In Havana it was normal, as we ourselves found, to be stopped in the street by absolute strangers wishing to communicate their thoughts on anything that happened to have caught their attention. The mulatta girls of Havana were seen to flaunt the biggest posteriors and the narrowest waists in the world.

Havana exposed the newcomer to an overpowering vivacity, the street overflowing with beautiful bronze bodies, dressed as if part of the overflow of a carnival taking place round the next corner.[6]

Thus life in Havana went on; a city always dressed for carnival in which the rich feasted in sedentary fashion and the poor danced and starved to music.[7]

Europe's political reckoning was converted to celebration in Havana like everything else, as a ten-year slump in Cuba's sugar market – the consequence of manipulative American quotas – looked like ending. The city's sugar brokers toasted Chamberlain's failure, Hitler's megalomania, and the instinctive human imperative to stockpile commodities in times of threat. Into a city "awash with money" and daily news of record sugar prices, the Lewises were rapidly assimilated on the strength of Ernestina's animation and talent for party-going. In Havana, for the first time, she had discovered a way of life whose exuberance matched hers and Cubans who liked having her around for any number of reasons. She

was the centre of attraction at parties given not only by Spanish expatriates, but by native patrician families, *gachupines* (wearers of spurs) who felt themselves a cut above Cuban colonists, most of whom had a dash of negro blood. At such gatherings she sparkled, being a lively conversationalist, better-read than anyone else in the room, and fresh with tidings from Europe, in the direction of which the eyes of all Cubans of the upper class were turned with yearning.[8]

Throughout August, a sequence of privileged entrées made their landing as soft as any amateur expatriates could hope for. At the outset Norman was stimulated by the top-down insights into Cuban life, but membership of the Jaimanitas Club with its "perfect beach", a drizzle of invitations to hospitality at estates across the island, and the loan of a Cadillac in which to accept them, steadily abraded rather than stroked his sensibility. (In England he had still been insisting to Gwen Varnals that he was a Communist Party member.) Nor had the situation he had been in before leaving England evolved to any practical degree. His problems, chiefly his relationship with Ernestina, had boarded the *Aquitania* with him and kept themselves close. Though his scepticism about a positive outcome for Ernestina in Cuba had been confounded, he was, I'm certain, beginning to realise that her happiness was of as little use to him as her unhappiness had been. She *was* happy. In Cuba her moods were at last built on a solid apparatus of enthusiasm: she was truly enjoying herself, not clinging to a pendulum's bob. But to stay happy she would have to stay in Cuba. And despite Norman's pleasure in the island's tropical confection of music, architecture, colour, leisure, melodrama and beautiful girls – was it like being slightly drunk all the time? – when it was suggested that they might stay (a scheme Ernestina enthusiastically advocated was to buy a vacant colonial house and convert it to a hotel) he interrogated his feelings and felt the approach of boredom's hangover. Such a round-up of the arguments emphasises one side of Cuba's temperament, of course. The country's political outlook, allowing for the pleasure-seeking that came naturally to Cubans, was less superficial than might be imagined. Fulgencio Batista, whom Norman cautiously approved of, on his way to becoming president and already the real leader of the country, had been on the side of radical liberal change since the mid-1930s. When he finally ran for president in 1940, he would do so with the support of the Cuban Communist Party and, elected, initiate a substantial social reform programme. It was just that, as with Ernestina's earlier plan of settling in Spain in 1936, the idea of staying in Cuba was dynamically all wrong. It would satisfy the search for a new country to live in – if a new country was what was being looked for. But it could not satisfy an escape reflex whose fundamental act was, self-evidently, to get away – to enact a pathology of escape that had been acquired in Norman's childhood and could best be managed, with the least psychical wear and tear, by returning each time to the starting point. (In order, after a suitable interval, to escape all over again.) If Norman had ever moved to Cuba, to Spain or anywhere else, he would have had to run away again after a short time: a nomadic and chaotic version of existence that, as an escapist who was simultaneously interested in stability and had a certain ambition about managing his life, he would have rejected, consciously or unconsciously.

One of the entrées he was offered during August was a presentation at Batista's villa, "The Palace". He was ready to be impressed, having heard that Batista, handsome and witty, was generally unpretentious and ready to be amused by attacks on his character. But in what would become the first of several missed appointments with dictators in his career, the timing went wrong and he arrived too early: the face of the president-to-be, appearing around a door, "was concealed by the band-ages soaked in lemon juice he often wore when relaxing, in the vain hope of reducing the swarthiness of his skin. Through this covering protruded a substantial cigar. He gave a flip of the hand and slipped back out of sight, and I withdrew."[9]

At the end of August he and Ernestina drove to the gracious old town of Santiago at the other end of the island and stayed at a sugar estate near Bayamó, where they were entertained by a planter who showed them a glass case containing the collection his great-grand-father had made of the ears he had cut from insubordinate slaves: the planter blamed their insurrectionary spirit on the tantalising closeness of the Sierra Maestra, where runaways took refuge in the thick woods believing they would be safe, and from where they were always fetched out by dogs. Not all planters had been as cruel as his great-grandfather, their host said, but with the cane-cutting several months away Norman noticed no wages were being paid: ragged black workers were mooching about killing time and, he discovered, living on handouts. A drum thud-ding regularly in the background elicited a claim by the planter that he and his fellow estate-owners had been enslaved in turn by their workers' voodoo cults (to Norman this seemed, if nothing else, an unbalanced defence). Returning via the coast, Norman wanted to do some birdwatching and drove to the town of Nuevitas, known for the many species of birds that nested on a broad cay offshore. Instead he and Ernestina found themselves in the path of a hurricane. "As it struck, the cay appeared to put up a crest of white water from one end to another, and we looked up to see thousands of sea-birds flying before the hurricane, like grey ash from a conflagration blown across the sky. As the shacks clustered on the headland caught the first lash of the wind, walls and thatches were snatched away. The next gust pelted us with airborne debris of all kinds, rocked the car on its springs and cracked a window."[10] They retreated to Camagüey, where they heard that the German army had overrun Poland's borders. By the time they reached Havana next day, Britain had declared war.

The news, if anything, intensified the rhythms of pleasure in the Cuban capital. "Secretly . . . nothing could have caused more joy to the small percentage of Cubans who in reality owned the country than the news that war had finally been declared."[11] Within two weeks Roosevelt had suspended sugar quotas. Planters and brokers sold their surpluses at the utmost leisure, stroking the rising market upwards.

Americans descended in speculative clouds to grab their cut and, while they were about it, exploit the expanded service industry available to the newly fortuned: waiters ready to wade into the sea to serve a cocktail, laundresses who, smelling of cotton and soap, were offered straight from the laundry to hotel guests. A climate of competitive excess swept the city, creating a vortex of gaiety – most of Havana *was* slightly drunk all the time now – that sucked in new tides of tourists to fuel the gaudy spree. Norman's own hangover, well established, made him practically invulnerable to the city's extravagant allure. Again he was retreating from becoming a social casualty, later describing himself credibly as "not overendowed" with patriotic fervour but feeling that he had put himself in the wrong place to make the most of life. "I had placed myself in a position where great experiences might be missed."

His decision was confirmed by reading a biography of Cervantes (possibly Mariano Tomás's 1933 *Vida y Desventuras de Miguel de Cervantes*) and concluding that it would be better to have his misfortunes (wounded at the battle of Lepanto in 1571, then taken captive and enslaved for five years to a Greek renegade at Algiers) than to vegetate in providential luxury. Another factor counted. Ernestina remained happy in Cuba and could be abandoned with dignity. She and Ito would be safer there, staying with friends, than in England. They agreed that she would return "in the spring". Sailings to New York were full, and at first Norman could not get a passage. Eventually, some time in October, he sailed out of Havana harbour and, in New York, booked the first passage he could get to England. Someone took his photograph standing on a gangway in front of the ship he sailed on, the SS *President Harding*, before it left New York on 25 October. In the picture he is leaning against the wire rail, a smile of cheerful good fortune on his face. Who could blame him? He was alone and at liberty. Ernestina and Ito were well looked after. Equally significantly, he and his wife would be several thousand miles apart for the foreseeable future. This time he was leaving (most of) his problems behind; Europe's war was already being good to him.

After the war he went back to Cuba several times during the 1950s and 1960s. Impatient with the life of its basking upper class, he felt passionate about the country. It is worth a moment's acknowledgment that it was Ernestina who offered Norman Cuba, as she had offered him Sicily and would, after the war, give him a reason for getting to know Guatemala, a country that fascinated him throughout his life.

Out of incompatibility and pain, frustration and annoyance (eventually he reached the point where he simply could not stand his first wife) came some of the longest-lasting of his literary interests.

Disembarking at Southampton, he announced his return in his R G Lewis advertisement on 15 November. "THE WANDERER RETURNS. When taking a trunk call a few days ago we were pleasantly surprised to hear, in response to our own 'Good afternoon, R G Lewis,' the Old Man's familiar accents as he greeted us with 'Hallo, Lewis speaking.' He had just landed safely after crossing the Western Ocean safely in a freighter [sic], but was bewailing the confiscation of some striking shots he had made on the passage. In spite of the loss, however, and though minus beard, he seems to be plus several sound schemes. . . ."[12]

In the first days back in England he was surprised to find a nation hanging around, waiting for something to happen. He was taken aback – as many people were – by how slowly mobilisation was going. He was thirty-one, and the call-up was not to be extended further than the younger 23–7 age range in January. He spent December reorganising business at 202 High Holborn, partly a question of accessing US material supplies that were superior to the limited stock from UK firms, visiting his mother, and keeping out of the cold weather. London had passed through its first fears of overwhelming air attack, replacing them with a sense of anticlimax mildly spiced by stern talk, blacked-out streets and full restaurants for those who could afford to ignore rationing. Norman made some sense of what was happening militarily after meeting Oliver Myers, also back in London from Egypt, who told him the War Office were urgently looking for linguists, in particular Arabic speakers. He attended a first interview with an "elderly and bookish lieutenant. He gave me a simple English sentence to translate, and I did what I could. 'Where did you learn your Arabic?' he asked, and I told him that I had picked it up in the Aden bazaar. 'Yes,' he said, with a sort of gentle disdain, 'so I would have thought. And would you be prepared to tackle the considerable task of making it work for north Africa?' I said I would."[13] The academic lieutenant told him he might have months to wait before he was called up, a prediction that turned out to be accurate.

In the new year he returned to the School of Oriental Studies (a course to improve his Arabic was followed by another, six-month course in Russian). Early 1940 was freezing, with persistent snowfalls and ice – it was one of the coldest Januarys on record – weather that added to the sluggish tension of the phoney war. Norman stayed with either his mother or the Corvajas and waited. Ernestina's letters from Cuba, where she was living at the Hotel Presidente, gave no indication of when she was planning to come back. Not until all hell broke loose in the Low Countries in early May did the national mood of anti-climax give way, but still Norman did not hear from the War Office again until the summer, after the collapse of France, when he was called to interview at an office in a Mayfair flat. In his account of the occasion he establishes a tone to the atmosphere of his military service, one part speculative improvisation, three parts incisive vagueness, that rarely varies. It is a tone that anyone who has read Evelyn Waugh's *Sword of Honour* suite, with its driven slide from satire into disillusion, will be familiar with. At this point Norman too was at the earliest satirical stage.

This time, although I was bursting with new vocabulary and had conquered the ten forms of the common Arabic verbs, there was no linguistic test. Instead the captain examined my face with interest, commented with satisfaction on the aquiline nose and dark eyes, and asked if I'd ever done any amateur theatricals. "We might want to dress you up a bit," he said.

The upshot of this meeting was that I agreed to be enrolled in the Intelligence Corps, with deferred embodiment. It was a safeguard, he explained, as my age-group grew near to being called up. "We'd like to keep you on ice," he said. For how long might that be? I asked, and he replied, "I wish I had the faintest idea."[14]

While he again waited, he appeared on Eugene Corvaja's behalf at his tribunal after Ernestina's brother, back from Spain, registered as a conscientious objector. Directed into the fire service, a job that during the nightly bombing of the London Blitz was as dangerous as front-line service, Eugene imperturbably carried out his duties. Norman also did his best to keep R G Lewis going under wartime regulations. Security measures restricted the taking of photographs out of doors, and shortages of film, paper and chemicals all reduced trade. The sale of new Leicas was banned. (It was not publicly known until 1999 that Ernst Leitz, whose company made the Leica at Wetzlar, had deliberately apprenticed young Jews in the 1930s and arranged for many of his Jewish employees to emigrate and work in his and other optical businesses in the USA.[15]) Norman exhibited a print entitled "Dhow"

at the RPS annual exhibition in Knightsbridge in September and kept
his shops ticking over.

On the evening of the exhibition's opening, 7 September, he was
having dinner with Oliver Myers at Prada's when the first of the great
raids of the Blitz began. With bombs falling on the London docks and
everywhere in the city, they watched through a peephole in the blackout
"while a fiery glow enlivened with golden sparks rose over the roof-
tops across the road". Norman's memory may have dressed the evening
in reckless rapture – his account was written fifty-six years later – but
his picture is pleasantly credible of Prada himself joining them at the
window and, believing his restaurant doomed, offering to sell them any
bottle from his celebrated cellar for £1. Their choice was meritorious.
"We chose a Madeira in a long narrow bottle that he swore was from
1822 and an 1878 Château Yquem, drank them slowly and awaited
with fatalism the decisions of destiny. When we staggered out it was
to discover a new beauty revealed by fire in the normally dismal surroundings of Euston Road."[16]

Over the next fifteen months, from autumn 1940 to the end of 1941,
Norman's own "deferred embodiment" status added to the latitude he
had as a self-employed businessman. There is no knowing how he felt
about having the role of a privileged civilian, whether he was impatient to be more than "a spectator of world-shaking events" (his own
summary of his impulse to get out of Cuba), or not. But it is a fact
that while waiting for embodiment he was *allowed* to be almost anywhere
he wanted. His contribution to the war effort not yet made, he was
exempt from criticism. He was able, for example, to go regularly to
Devon and visit Gwen, who had evacuated herself to a house in the
village of Atherington outside Barnstaple. She was looking after her
own children, a friend's children and her sister Nancy's, whom she had
taken with her, and she ran the house like a boarding school. "I had
a teacher installed, and the children, and we ran a little school, grew
our own vegetables." Nancy (the sister Gwen had stayed with in East
Africa) was separated from her husband and had been supposed to
share in the running of the house with Gwen. "Instead of that she had
this affair. I never resented it, so it just shows how I didn't want what
she was having."[17] What Nancy was having was a relationship with
Norman that had started in Enfield when Norman had gone back there
after Cuba: a relationship made rather more intense by the fact that
Nancy had gone to live with Norman at his mother's house at Carterhatch

Lane. "His mother wouldn't have been at all pleased," Gwen says. Louisa was still "very resistant to Norman having anything to do with females, especially in our society, our area. They had separate rooms, and it was probably passed off as her 'being helpful', but his mother must have known what was going on."

One of Norman's ways of being helpful in his turn was to bring Nancy down to Devon to visit her two children. "We'd go out together," Gwen says. "I remember going to the Umberleigh pub, which meant we walked down three miles [from] Atherington, to the Rising Sun. [Norman] immediately recognised that a part of it went back to Saxon times" and took pictures of the inscriptions on the timbers. "We'd float back up those hills on two or three pennyworth of rough cider. I can see us standing over the Taw, watching the trout jumping." Gwen's own marriage was cracking around her ears at the time. "But somehow it was an incredibly fulfilling time. Even that didn't make me want to weaken."[18] She still didn't fancy Norman physically, but felt one couldn't say that to a man, so the situation wasn't without sexual tension. Norman's affair with her sister did not much restrict his renewed attempts to conquer her. More than sixty years later Gwen remembered that in the house at Atherington "He *still* tried to get into my bed."[19] According to Gwen, her sister, three years older than Norman, dark-eyed and ripely attractive, had been attracted by his brains "to such an extent that she'd let the rest happen", even to the point of falling in love with him. Nancy needed the affair badly, Gwen feels, because she had had a bad experience of married life. As a partial consequence she built their relationship to be more than it was: "she was always building things beyond their horizons".

Aware that Norman was still drawn to Gwen, Nancy worried that whenever her sister came up to Enfield, "I would be distracting him while he was having this affair".

Lewis certainly took every ounce of sexual pleasure out of the affair that he could. But my sister was demonish in her behaviour too. . . . I think she was fascinated by him, and she let him do what he wanted. But he was tender with her too.[20]

Norman had "always been attracted somewhat" to her sister. For him, though the affair went on for more than a year its companionship was time-limited: it fell somewhere between healthy human hypocrisy about sex and that being what you did – taking the pleasure that was to be had – when there was a war and each day things could change for ever.

Those visits were lively and enjoyable. Although I always felt [Nancy] knew how much I meant to him, I don't think she knew that he had tried to join me in my bed. It was on one of those visits that he informed us that the male possessed a much larger brain than the female, whereupon I knocked him off the five-bar gate on which we were perched. It was in return for this hospitality that he suggested that on my next visit to London he would take us to a nightclub.[21]

The nightclub excursion a few weeks later fell into the same pleasure-taking category. Norman, fully earning his "son of Satan" badge in Gwen's version of the evening, continued to have a different idea from hers of what constituted the greatest pleasure. "I . . . found myself in a most awful scene. I wasn't that type. This is what intrigued him really. I think he always thought he could find some flaw, and I wasn't going to let him." At the Soho nightclub they went to Gwen was paired with an Indian friend of Norman's, a young, entirely correct maharajah whom he may have known through Alexander Hagen. Gwen felt she and the maharajah were both out of place, while Norman and Nancy were very congruous. "I was amazed at Lewis's and Nance's gyrations on the dance floor, so abandoned and extreme, *everything* that I'd not seen before. . . . My sister was doing the most incredible dances. Lewis was loving it. Things I'd never seen people do before. How could she?" It was, she insisted, more than exotic dancing. "A little bit beyond that. I've never seen anything even in modern times quite like that." (One of Norman's children later described his dancing as chiefly elaborate hand movements, a mixture of tango and Thai, that they found very amusing. His love of sexual sensuality had been evident already in his appreciation of the "serpentine contortions" of the Syrian homosexual, Quazim, in the Bousbir in 1934, whose lewdness sounds close to a description of Norman himself.)

Things got more serious when Norman spiked her drink. "Someone came across to our table and suggested, a true blue type of Englishman, that I shouldn't be there. The next day I had such a high feeling I know someone had put something in my drink. [I'm sure it was] Norman. He was dangerous chemistry. I never felt so naked in my life, I had to go back to friends." Eventually she asked the maharajah to take her out and stayed the night at his apartment, "sat on the bed talking. . . . I'd got no money with me, having thought I was going to be wafted home, for a fare. So I had to ask him for the fare in the morning and then go to my friends."²²

Gwen's long-standing relationship with Norman – since before they were ten – makes this occasion a bit less exploitative than it sounds. Norman knew Gwen was resistant to his charm, though she admitted he had charm. She returned it by flirting, which is a kind of devilry too. Both knew each other's devilish side. If he spiked her drink or got her drunk he may have thought (unjustifiably of course) that if only he could get her to relax her "I wasn't that type" primness, she would accept his overtures. The rejected are a determined lot. And he may not have been entirely wrong. Gwen was aware that she had fearful inhibitions about relationships, perhaps as a result of losing her father so young, which left her with "the ultimate in fear, the absolute fear of a contrasting ecstasy".²³ That may be why she never really blamed Norman for his sexual determination in her direction.

In London and other British cities the war still felt close. Bombs fell on Enfield, one, which did not explode, close to the house at Carterhatch Lane. Bill Nicholls remembered "the rattle of machine-gun fire and the swirling winding vapour trails . . . occasionally the sudden shock and roar of warplanes sweeping over at roof-top height".²⁴ In the last thousand-bomber raid on London, on 10 May 1941, number 4 Gordon Street was in the line of the blast of a 1000-pound bomb that flattened the other side of the street and reduced the Corvajas' house, with its gilded doors and frolicking *putti*, to a shell. Eugene was able to make it barely habitable again for his parents, and Ernesto and Maria Corvaja predictably continued to camp in it until the end of the war. Norman had evacuated the business out of London to Shrewsbury in January, managing a new branch of R G Lewis at 38 Castle Street that now carried most of the limited stock, waiting for his call-up papers. Gwen remembers him writing to her that he was attempting to write to relieve his utter boredom. "He said he'd got cotton wool streaming from his ears because he couldn't concentrate with the noise and he'd gone to an inn and he was writing me from the inn, and he said he'd just heard one old codger say to another, 'Cheer up, us'll soon have the cuckoo to sing to we'."²⁵

Living at the Golden Cross Hotel, he was getting regular letters from

Ernestina in Guatemala City, where she had moved with Ito in mid-
1940. In the only letter that has survived from that year, dated 25
November 1941, it is clear that she had been trying for several months
to get back to England on the Pan-American clipper service. It was
almost impossible to get seats, and Ito posed a problem.

My very dearest Norman . . .
Since my last cable [Pan-American] now tell me that it is not possible to guarantee any reservations, all mail having priority. An average of five passengers
travel on the clipper (usually accommodates 14 passengers) and the rest consists
of mail, moreover I have to obtain a permission from England to enter in view
of the fact that I am bringing a child. Perhaps you could investigate this. The
legation here also tell me that I cannot enter England without permission.[26]

Reactions in the Americas to the disruptions of the war could also be
comical: Ernestina had been told by a friend, a Major Peltzer, in some
indignation that he had had to wait two months in New York for a
reservation on the clipper, and because he wanted to be in England for
his son's wedding he had, in desperation, gone eventually on a convoy
that took seven weeks. But the tone of Ernestina's letter is that of a wife
and mother keeping busy, feeling isolated, missing her husband. She
writes to entertain him – in the United States (reported approvingly in
Guatemala) they are trying to revive the fashion for hand kissing ("results
proved practically 100% in favour") – and to assure him she is not being
lazy. "When I go to the States, I am going to try to place my photographs. It is very difficult to do anything from here." She consoles him
for his varicose veins and compliments him on his new efforts to teach
himself Portuguese. Most of all she misses him, signing herself with
"Millions of love and kisses from your loving, doting and adoring wife",
imagining him finding a job in Brazil with his Portuguese and showing
her frustration that the situation conspires to keep them apart. To
encourage her, he has apparently mentioned the possibility of doing business in America and being able to see her and Ito that way. "What I
cannot understand," she writes with powerless annoyance, "is if you
were able to guarantee a business of ¼ million sterling why on earth
they don't send you to the States?" A possible answer lay in his having
no intention of acting on the possibility. Here were two married people,
the writer of a conventionally loving, anxious, frustrated wartime letter,
a letter fit for a future exhibition of "Letters Home", and its recipient;

with as much distance between their readings of what separated them as there was distance between them.

By November Norman had in any case finally been called for war service. He was examined by a medical board at Shrewsbury on 10 October and on the 25th enlisted at ARO 55 Centre, Shrewsbury. He was judged grade II at his medical board because of his asthma ("Fit for general service at home only, or sedentary service abroad", both instructions ignored in the event), and approved for appointment to the Intelligence Corps, with a further deferral "to await instructions from War Office". Under "Specialist Qualifications" his tracer card listed "Languages: Spanish, Italian, Arabic, French, German". After just short of two years' wait, 10350775 Private Lewis, John Frederick Norman, was in the Army.

He had to wait another two months before reporting for any kind of training. He finally arrived at the Royal Irish Fusiliers depot at Omagh on 29 January. For three months in a Northern Irish winter he experienced, with other Intelligence Corps trainees undergoing basic infantry training, the overwhelming civilian impression of army life as conjoined absurdity and farce. The endless marching, saluting, naming of rifle parts, and cutting of lawns with a dinner knife were interrupted when he was admitted to hospital with an asthma attack. Transferred to the Queen Alexandra Military Hospital at Watford for ten days in April, he was discharged on 1 May 1942 and posted later that month to the Intelligence Corps depot at Winchester with a cautionary note about his condition. If he expected to learn about intelligence work at Winchester he was disabused. His routine made him suspect that the Intelligence Corps might have been a short straw, including no mention of intelligence but a lengthy and numbing repeat course of parade drill under the orders of Grenadier Guards NCOs, whose pride in their skill at the flamboyant arcana of ceremonial marching was very great. He managed to avoid some of this strenuously boring activity by hospitalising himself again, more dramatically. On arrival at Winchester he was ordered to attend a three-week motorcycling course. He could already handle a motorcycle, but the Army applied its own standards.

Squad after squad of trainees, mounted on ancient and often defective machines, were taken to the top of a steep grassy hill on the city's outskirts down which they hurtled, brakes disconnected, into a field at the bottom where the ambulance awaited.[27]

His account of the instructors' suicidal methods seems to gleam with satirical polish, until one reads similar accounts by other trainees. A Captain D M Jacobs described how at Winchester "we had military training. ... We were also trained in how to cope with gas attacks[,] unarmed combat, physical training and driving motorbikes. [The] driving lasted three weeks, not just on roads but in fields, up hills, through a forest and even along a narrow and small stream. In my section of twelve men only three of us succeeded in [passing]."[28] The hill climb, on an abused Norton, BSA or Matchless, was experienced by another intelligence trainee named Hopper. "Another thing we were taught at Winchester was how to ride a bike up a high, steep, grassy hill (St Catherine's Hill), and, near the top, to lie the bike down on its side, then move the bike around so that it pointed down the hill, remount and ride the bike down the hill. If this sounds easy, it was not. There were one or two broken bones on every course."[29] The hazards of the course were tolerated at senior level, and training was acknowledged as "frequently lethal" by the Advanced Training Company commander, Sedgwick-Rough.[30] Whether Norman's brakes had been disconnected for training purposes, so that he should stop by braking the engine, or were poorly maintained, his skills did not preserve him. He crashed, broke several ribs, and was stretchered to Winchester Hospital.

Ernesto, who as his official next of kin had been informed of the accident, was at his bedside the following morning. By a feat of extraordinary determination, he had found a taxi driver as soon as he heard the news and persuaded the man, by paying him an outrageous fare, to get him through the shattered London streets and closed roads to Winchester. He had managed the trip in three hours. Norman later wrote that it was in Winchester Hospital that he realised that Ernesto's apparently "conventional and meaningless" response to the news that Norman had married his daughter – "I give you my blood" – was anything but.

By the end of June his ribs had knitted together enough for him to return to No. 2 (Training) Company. These first two hospitalisations would not be his last. The entries on his Army service and casualty form continue through the war with regular "X list" postings (hospital admissions) arising from various causes: malaria, another motorcycle accident. One such admission would, in the wartime fashion, have personal consequences and result in post-war repercussions for everyone involved.

In July and August 1942 all he had to bear was the remainder of his basic training. Towards the end of August events at last acquired momentum. (Bogged down, in common with the overall military situation, almost everywhere until mid-1942. But in August the British Eighth Army, thwarted in north Africa by Rommel and defeatism, at last got a new commander, General Montgomery. Assuming command two days earlier than authorised, and ordering all contingency plans for retreat to be destroyed, Montgomery by his breaking of the Axis line would let Churchill announce with justice less than three months later that "it is, perhaps, the end of the beginning".)

In the last week of August Norman's company got seven days' leave. Leave was followed by two weeks' training at the War Intelligence Centre at Matlock in Derbyshire, where they were taught misogynistically that security was threatened by "the Three Ugly Sisters: espionage, sabotage and propaganda". Matlock was twice distinguished, for being the place where the word "intelligence" was at last mentioned to trainees, and for its corresponding atmosphere of suspicion. "If you had a haircut every two days at Matlock you came under scrutiny, if you had a haircut every three days then you were definitely suspect. Most soldiers at Matlock had their hair cut every day."[31] Throughout his service in the Corps Norman believed that it operated on the footing of a set of well-prepared prejudices based on this distrust: the smartness of a soldier's education was one, eye colour another. As he fell the wrong side of every prejudice, he did not expect to shine. One member of his section remembers that "he felt a bit about class distinction, he hadn't been to a public school and all that".[32] In his autobiography a tone of comic abridgement hangs over his description of the selection process at Matlock, though there is little doubt about the correctness of his analysis:

the only instruction we received was in lecturing "other ranks" on security. "It's a good thing to get off on the right foot and put them at their ease," the officer said. "You'll find it helps to address them as 'you fuckers'." He called me in at the end of the course. "I've given you a commendation," he said, "but it won't make a scrap of difference. There's a dozen things wrong with you, including the colour of your eyes. You have to have blue eyes to get a commission. You'll go into the dustbin with the rest of them." By the dustbin he meant the Field Security personnel, and he was right, I did.[33]

On 10 September he was promoted to lance-corporal and posted to his first Field Security section, 91 FSS, though he remained attached to 3 Company at Winchester, hanging around for ten days until something could be found for him to do. "Superior shit house art at Winchester," he wrote in a red notebook he kept. "Very high artistic quality of the nudes." On the 23rd he was finally attached to 118 Home Port Security Section at Ellesmere Port (a temporary attachment: he wasn't posted), and caught the train to Liverpool.

Field Security sections – FSS – were a brainchild of the Second World War. They functioned within a curious sphere, half envied, half distrusted, virtually autonomous. The official intention was that as sub-units of the Intelligence Corps they should contribute to both theatre intelligence and security. At the blunt end of their activities they were, as their other early name suggests – "PSS" or Port Security sections – detailed to guard wartime ports against sabotage and looting and to inspect vessels and aircraft using harbours and airfields; at the sharper end, FSS members were "first in, last out", their task to secure key buildings and arrest enemy stay-behinds, or spread disinformation for Axis troops. In between they officially operated as information gatherers, route finders, security for conferences, liaison, interrogators; they organised house searches, improvised prisons, rounded up suspects, and in the second stage of post-occupation security made contact with resistance organisations, screened refugees, imposed curfews, intercepted Axis agents, watched brothels, vetted war brides, sometimes prostitutes, and attempted the, as in Italy, insoluble problems of controlling black markets and mafia allegiances.

Recognised by their battledress's green flash, they operated in practice in a fine bubble of liberty that made Field Security work abroad to be savoured. As NCOs with a reasonable level of intelligence and specialist expertise they lived with the suspicion of officers who saw them as too clever by half and in need of constant oversight. In the conventional structure of a section, a dozen NCOs were kept in line by a regular sergeant-major, officered by a Field Security Officer who, by virtue of a good (private) school and eyes of the right colour, usually combined with some reliable sporting ability, had passed through the mesh of snobbery. Section members learnt to ignore the restraints and the odium of being clever, and to take pleasure in the fact that "Nobody really quite understood what we were doing", as one section member remembered, "– we enjoyed a certain mystique and even senior officers were chary of challenging our activities."[34] "Notes on Field Security, MEF [Middle East Force]" was one army document probably among many written to shed light on what was a slightly irritating mystery to the rest of the Army: "These notes have been drawn up by FS Headquarters, MEF, in response to the requests of General Staff officers and others for information as to what Field Security Sections are, where they are and what they do." The suspicion that attached to their activities was in spite of the fact that they were not secret police vis-à-vis Allied troops but were there to "neutralise" the activities of "strangers and civilians in the theatre of war".[35] But they could be authorised to wear plain clothes on duty, and their curious status with its archetypal contradiction – at liberty and distrusted – was backed up by the extraordinary accessory of the "spot card". This laissez-passer had a black spot on the cover, a photograph and description of the holder, and in English and other languages a genie's grant of a declaration. "The holder of this card is engaged in SECURITY duties, in the performance of which he is authorized to be in any place, at any time, and in any dress. All authorities subject to Military Law are enjoined to give him every assistance in their power, and others are requested to extend him all facilities for carrying out his duties".

At Ellesmere Port in October 1942 Norman none the less got thin pleasure from patrolling the docks and stealing cobs from quayside depots for his coal-obsessed sergeant-major. Housed in a Nissen hut, he no doubt started to construct attitudes while observing his fellow NCOs and their duties: one was to search every vessel that docked, but even their senior NCO, a local man, saw "that this was a task to occupy a thousand men. 'Forget it, lads,' he said, 'there's nowt we can do.'" This man, whom Norman named Fitch, spent his days in bed at home, his evenings wrapped around a glass of porter at the pub, and his passion on gleaming pyramids of coal that he constructed in his back garden. The bones of Norman's perspective on the value of field intelligence lie buried in Sergeant-Major Fitch's garden. "For centuries the meaning of the word 'intelligence' had been changing, slowly assuming overtones of intellectuality it never originally possessed. Even the Army had fallen into the error of upgrading the mundane task of gathering information, suspected now of breeding a kind of sinister power."[36]

The heir of a gross inflation, he felt, more than the descendant of Joshua at Jericho, he spent a tedious October at Ellesmere Port. He was unconscious of the exceptional good fortune that service in the Intelligence Corps was about to bring his way. One deadly fact about Corps life during the war is rarely mentioned: of the 295 FS sections constituted in the British Army, eighty-one never left the United Kingdom, but remained, stunned with boredom, at ports and airfields from Avonmouth to Stranraer, Tilbury to Poole. Other sections went abroad for brief periods. As part of 91 FSS Norman was about to find himself in the first of a sequence of postings that would keep him out of England for more than two and a half years. And not only that: with the expansion of the Corps as rapid as that of the rest of the Army – 180 new members flowed in and out of Winchester every fortnight – organisation was a euphemism for logistics chaos. A fluent Japanese speaker could find himself in Iceland, a Farsi expert in the Nigerian bush. Norman, as an Arabic, French and Italian speaker, spent the war entirely in countries whose languages he spoke and whose cultures he found interesting. His good fortune, in another sense, did not cease there. Even more significantly for his soul – in the sense of the soul as the body's greatest motive – his service overseas interrupted and fused his life, homerically, in two halves. It completed his escape from Enfield, from dingy rooms and mediocrity, from reliance on commerce, from Ernestina, and in north Africa, Italy, Austria and the Persian Gulf supplied continuous situations in which to reinvent himself. With the demands it imposed to render tragedy and absurdity simultaneously, the war was central to his development as an observer and stylist and confirmed him in the kind of writer he would become. And in the course of the confirmation, something else surfaced.

"The war was something fantastic. I hate cruelty of any kind, I am a passionate person, but every minute of the war, all the time I was abroad, [was] absolutely paradise."

Those were his words more than fifty years later. The intense pleasure of his war years became the banner and device of his post-war adventures: the reality that he was always seeking to re-create. In the exhausted domestic peace of mid-1945, all his problems, literary and personal, would begin to reduce to one problem: how to retain the happiness of war.

And all you know, security
Is mortal's chiefest enemy.
(Hecate, *Macbeth*)

Notebook

We did a certain amount of security work, mainly listening to the
Arabs complaining about the French and the French complaining
about the Arabs. And they thought we were something like the
Gestapo or something, so we could do things, and the local brothel-
keeper became very friendly with us because he thought we could
protect him, and he even gave a dinner for us, for our section. We
were the only section in Philippeville. So that was quite amusing. I
think the only thing was he was offering us virgins, very expensive
normally. Otherwise I think we had quite a good dinner.

Derek Wise

The FS personnel who went to Tripoli with seized lire which they
converted into £1000 and sent home. The FS personnel in Sicily who
released notorious criminals under the belief that they were political
prisoners. Morgan's story about the 2 British soldiers who deserted
in a jeep & lived in a gourbi 100 miles south of Batna, marrying into
the tribe. Story of the deserter with pass printed with "No.1 Section
Field Security Police" – chap who took a fortnight's leave to England
by American plane.

Notebook

She was a Queen Alexandra nurse and he was some dashing Army
bloke. She used to say that, and then my brother, teasing her, used
to say, "Ah Hessie Bessie, le bossa nova se fout à Tanger."

Karen Holman

In the Army they issued books to take away, and one was of French verse. Can you imagine squaddies being issued with that? Did I ever show it to you? Actually, this was an edition for the forces with French verse, much of it very early French verse too, but I brought the Herodotus which was quite a thick thing and what I used to do if I had to carry various bags, I used to tear bits of it, tear it in pieces, and stick it around in various bags so that if some of it was lost I would have other bits.

Norman Lewis

10

NORTH AFRICA

*"The different sorts of madness
are innumerable"*
Arabian proverb

THE gloomy trick played on Norman at Ellesmere Port was briefer than its horrors seemed. By the end of October he was back at Winchester drawing kit for service overseas; at that depot and another the elements of 91 FSS assembled in early November with all of the army's cool randomness of social and existential experiment. Another section member was Derek Wise, a young, recently qualified lawyer, who remembers that at thirty-four Norman was one of the oldest members and amusingly critical of authority. The section was told that there was to be an invasion, but not where, and sent on embarkation leave. Norman went back to London to sort out the running of R G Lewis in his absence and to say goodbye to his mother, Nancy, and Ernesto and Maria Corvaja. He had dinner with Colonel Egerton and invited Derek Wise, who lived in Kensington, to join them. "We had dinner in London with a friend of Norman's who was a colonel, I think it was in Lisle Street. And this chap said, 'I don't think it's any secret, you'll be going to north Africa,' and of course that's what it was."[1] On 15 November Norman endured Ellesmere Port again, going aboard the 21,000-ton *Maloja*, a P & O liner converted to an armed merchant cruiser, to join the convoy assembled there in support of Operation "Torch". The main landings on the north African coast had taken place on 8 November. Norman's convoy eventually sailed on the 26th, and the wide swing out into the Atlantic to evade German U-boats was uncomfortable, the men (as opposed to officers) crammed in their hundreds into hangar-like compartments below decks, in bunks and on the floor, the ship rolling heavily through a November Atlantic swell. "The occupants of [the bunks] were forced to vomit over those beneath, and by the first night . . . the floor had become a lake of vomit, sluicing round islands of retching, groaning men and, whenever the ship gave a great slow roll to one side, pouring down to spill over the bedding of those placed at the edge of the hold." The rough seas did not let up, and the puking parabola of Allied ships was eight days in the Atlantic before passing, to the relief of 15,000 men, through the Straits of Gibraltar. On the *Maloja* a few men struck up "Tomorrow Is Another Day" and the rest joined in.

> *Though skies above are grey,*
> *You know they won't stay that way,*
> *A shoulder to cry on,*
> *Something to rely on,*
> *Tomorrow is another day*

Norman was carrying a tiny red oilcloth notebook with him. In it he noted coolly "Straights of Gib. 'Tomorrow Is Another Day' sung as a hymn. The Welsh would have sung 'Rock of Ages'". (He asserted that they did in *Jackdaw Cake*.) With the convoy thinning out on 5 December first at Algiers, then Bougie (Bejaïa) along the coast a few hours later, Norman's ship was left alone on the final leg, escorted by a single corvette that, as the *Maloja* hugged close to the shore, turned on and depth-charged a U-boat that had been sniffing about it. Remembered much later, the sudden, joyous sharpness Norman adds to the soldiers' apprehension is persuasive: the troops' eyes were "fixed longingly on a rapturous pre-Raphaelite landscape, spring-like in winter, of fields sloping up to green hills through the deep, mossy shade of oaks. Among them glistened small white domes that marked the tombs of saints."[2] With that landscape in their thoughts, many slept on deck that night – the 6th – as a precaution (if a torpedo struck, they could try to swim ashore).

"My first impressions of Africa at war," Norman writes in *Jackdaw Cake*, "are conveyed perhaps more vividly by a diary kept at that time than by resorting to memory." He did not keep a diary: not one nearly as relaxed as the pages included in his autobiography, at any rate. As his editor in the early 1980s, I look back at the original typescript of

Jackdaw Cake and see my diligent alteration of his past-tense narration into a diary-suitable present. The contemporary record he kept was all in the tiny red notebook. The landing at Bône (Annaba) next morning was noted briefly, "Bône. 'Ville coquette.' 7th December at dawn", followed by a holy trinity of impressions for a soldier just ashore. "Tobacco factory. Free wine. Mandarines." The notebook is a jumble of pages of addresses, scribbled words, terse summaries of his movements, scraps of poems and plays, precious "overheards" and quick practice at conveying what he saw around him. One note perceives an interesting contrast between officers and men – "men bow legged, officers knock kneed" – another evokes "the porcelain like quality of FSOs" (Field Security Officers).

If his diary was invented, it none the less played to the strength of his memory. Derek Wise, who spent several months in Algeria and Tunisia with him before being repatriated with a broken leg, was convinced by Norman's account of their existence. "What I remember of him most [is that] he was always taking notes and taking photos, because he was a photographer. He was very intelligent and he had a way of getting on with people."[3] Interested in the photographer's view, tending to a mental processing of the world in terms of surfaces, especially in terms of their possibilities for irony (the revealer of what the surface tries to hide), Norman's later descriptions are those of a witness who can forget the elements of a scene and still, years later, throw them effortlessly onto his mental retina. It was an ability nurtured by photographic and literary training. It was also an ability nurtured in years of exclusion, when, as a child, looking on was an activity that possessed all the intensity of trying to solve a mystery just by staring at it.

Straight after the Bône entry, his red notebook records "9th Dec. Leave for Philippeville." His autobiography's "diary" contains a page of picture-perfect images, of Bône "disfigured by several columns of black smoke" after a Stuka raid, of the lengthy disembarkation of more than 2000 men under the menace of imminently returning bombers, of a visit to the *épicière* who refuses payment for her wine and a hazardous night spent under the tobacco factory's glass roof (in fact the section spent two nights there). It does not say that it was Norman who went "off with another chap, Ted Kingham I think it was, and [found] some Algerian wine to keep us cheerful, and so we survived".[4]

On the morning of 9 December, hung over, 91 FSS collected its motorbikes and left Bône on a 100-kilometre drive to Philippeville where, as part of First Army, it was to take over port and other security. Several members, still drunk, crashed en route without serious injury. Stopping for lunch at Jemmapes, as soon as the section arrived in Philippeville it was ordered to the *mairie* where the FSO, after summoning the mayor and other local officials, introduced himself and the section in Latin. "God knows what he was doing in the section," Derek Wise remembers. "Extraordinary idea. He was a classical scholar, thinking that they'd understand Latin." Introduced to Captain Mahler at Winchester, Norman had summed up his FSO as having "at first glance" everything the Corps demanded. (Mahler became Captain Merrylees in *Jackdaw Cake*, for reasons that become clear.) Though not a regular soldier but a schoolmaster, he was tall, fair-haired and with eyes of an intense blue, he had read languages at Cambridge, and at his Corps interview the fact that his linguistic proficiency was in Old Norse and he could not muster conversational French had probably been overlooked in favour of the fact that he had also been a rowing Blue. Norman also noticed that Mahler, though relaxed and charming, had a smile and frown that he applied randomly to the moment and had also alluded, Shakespeareanly ("Each man in his life plays many parts, and now it seems we're soldiers. Ah well"), to the unreality of army life. This awkward officer was not helped by having as his senior NCO a tall, not very intelligent regular named Lev whose manner "seemed to contain both ingratiation and menace" and whose handling of the captain reminded Norman "of a snake-charmer at work". Aggressively down to earth, Lev (Sergeant-Major Leopold in *Jackdaw Cake*) had received the section for their preliminary chat in his quarters while in the middle of shaving off his pubic hair.

He spoke something, maybe it was Russian, maybe French, [so] they put him in Field Security. You see, the idea was that we were all rather amateurs and not real soldiers, so we had to have a sergeant-major who had been a real soldier, otherwise there would have been no discipline. . . . [But] they were a bit haphazard, anybody who spoke languages that they thought reasonable, they put them in Field Security. It wasn't always a very sensible thing to do.[5]

But in overview Philippeville (Skikda) wasn't generally a sensible place. Founded by French colonists in 1838 on the ruins of an ancient Phoenician city, surrounded by orange, lime and lemon groves and with the agreeably choreographed squares and palms of a Mediterranean port, it combined an unreliable colonial prosperity with a volatile soul. A dozen years after Norman was posted there, in 1955, a Front de Libération Nationale (FLN) attack on French civilians and suspected collaborators became a watershed in Algeria's war of independence. FLN fighters and their supporters killed 123 people, including some old women and babes in arms; the French, led by paratroopers, in retaliation killed 12,000 Arabs, and the bloodletting of Philippeville became the signal for all-out war. In 1942 the town was a mess of factions, of pro-Vichy and pro-de Gaulle French, and anti-French Arabs (with good reason, after a century of intellectual suppression). All believed that the British presence could aid their interests. At the *mairie* Mahler's speech, translated into French by Ted Kingham, passed off as English cultural colour and was cheered, more wine was poured, and the section (including two unconscious with drink) shown to its headquarters. A sizeable nineteenth-century French colonial house, the Villa Portelli, on the corniche road behind Philippeville had been found for the section, its FSO with driver and batman, and its transport of bikes and the captain's jeep. The men had to look after themselves and ate in the house, taking it in turns to do the cooking. "Norman was a good cook, put lots of garlic in everything." Derek Wise's impression was that the section was more or less killing time,

pretending to do security work, because there wasn't much to do. This was about December '42 and there was a quite good beach not far from Philippeville and occasionally you'd go there and have a swim, because it was still pretty warm weather in December. It was a bit of a phoney war for us, a little like a holiday in the middle of the war, because it was a pleasant place and we had good food and wine there, which in England you weren't getting. Unless there was something specific which our officer wanted us to do, we more or less did things on our own, trying to get bits of information to put in a report and justify our existence. We had this extraordinary pass ... saying that we could sort of go anywhere at any time in any dress. I remember there was a bar reserved for officers and we could go there, they didn't know what we were doing. [So] one had to give our captain something to pass on and I don't think anybody much at HQ read about what we were up to. I mean, in a war you get an awful lot of wastage from people doing nothing. The waste of manpower is enormous because you're there "in case", and then the "in case" doesn't happen.[6]

But idleness is diverse in content. When Captain Mahler and Sergeant-Major Lev allocated duties, Norman's ability in Arabic made his perspective on Philippeville more involving than his fellow section members'. Others liaised with the French, or were "sentenced to the boring sinecure of patrolling the port" or maintaining vehicles and ration supplies. Norman, "given the task of studying and reporting upon the Arab attitude towards the Allied cause", was able to dream himself into a job, conceiving an intelligence panorama out of what absorbed his attention.

This vague but highly educational assignment took me on motorcycle jaunts into remote villages in the Petite Kabylie and the foothills of the Monts de Constantine, where I found the Arabs endlessly hospitable within the possibilities of their diffi-cult circumstances, although lukewarm towards our war effort. The illiterate 99 per cent favoured Hitler because he was believed to be an orthodox Muslim, who under the name of *Haj el Jema* – the Friday Pilgrim – had made the pilgrimage to Mecca. The educated handful would have welcomed anyone prepared to rescue them from their servitude to the French.[7]

He negotiated where he could the lines of hatred between French and Arabs and the complex zones of score-settling between the knot of pro-Free French and the pro-Vichy majority. The unfraternal squabbles of the French produced the chief dramas and initial confusion. Few members of 91 FSS had any idea of what Vichy or its government signified before they got to Algeria: it was generally only remembered that at Ellesmere Port there were orders to arrest de Gaulle if he ever tried to leave the country. The squabbles of the Algerian French were also just that: what the section had to get used to in its first days in Philippeville was the unfamiliar rapid scene-shifting of an occupied and distantly loyal popu-lation, whose interests were massively personal and minutely political. Before the British arrived the default stance was logically pro-Vichy; the minute First Army landed the same logic sent de Gaulle's popu-larity rocketing.

Norman's wide-ranging analysis of the French in Algeria was written with some decades' more experience than he had in 1942, but grips by its evidence of what he must have seen daily.

The friendly, expansive Algerian French appeared as wholly pleasure-loving opportunists, supporters at the bottom of neither Pétain nor de Gaulle, concerned with neither a collaborationist France nor an independent one. There was no intellectual life, nothing of the spirit to be discovered in Philippeville. No one picked up a book, listened to music, read poetry, or found entertainment in anything but the most mediocre Western films. The Algerians ate too much rich food, drank too much, slept too much, indulged in too much sex. Chronic complaints of the liver and stomach plagued them. They suffered from gout, hypertension, giddiness and worn-out hearts, and their life expectancy was in the neighbourhood of fifty-five years. It was the good life carried almost to its fatal conclusion. The preferred drink, for example, of Philippeville was *anisette* made instantly by dissolving a chemical supplied by any pharmacist [anethole] in pure alcohol. . . . In the first weeks of our presence cases were reported of citizens going into a bar and drinking *anisette* until they died.

The full-blooded climate and the way of life took their toll of the character of all Frenchmen who had been born or settled in Algeria. They lost control of their passions, were prone to a kind of hysteria which drove them into mutually antagonistic feuding groups. Nowadays they were pro-Vichy, or pro-de Gaulle, taking furious sides in causes which were only old quarrels under a new name. The Algerians had become irrational. This was a country where ripe fruit hung for the picking on every tree and if a man wanted a woman there was always an unpaid Arab girl around about the house to be pulled into a quiet corner. The Algerian had come to expect the instant satisfaction of his slightest desire. With all this, and perhaps inseparable from it – because in this interminable underground civil war every man was on the look-out for an ally – went a tremendous drive towards *camaraderie*. There was no more generous and firmer friend than the Algerian. He was willing to give, as well as take, on a scale no metropolitan Frenchman would have understood. There was something infectious in the atmosphere of this country, leading to a loss of nordic restraint. Likes and dislikes tended to become coloured with love and hatred. I wondered how long it took to turn a man into an Algerian, always ready to hug someone or reach for a gun.[8]

Michel Fortuna was an Algerian of the persecuted pro-Free French minority that Norman, and the section, had dealings with. This small, wiry and melancholy brothel-keeper, under sentence of death on the arrival of the British and released by one of 91 FSS's liaison NCOs minutes before the executioner from Algiers turned up with his portable guillotine, requested the honour of organising a dinner for his saviours. His crime had been to get his retaliation in first, killing the man who had taken out a contract on him. The dinner Fortuna[9] gave, attended by the whole section in the presence of town officials and their wives, a visiting Academician, and local businessmen, radiated a showy mix of convenient allegiance, embarrassing sentiment (Englishmen in the

1940s were unused to being kissed on both cheeks and addressed as "*mon copain*"), and *La Grande Bouffe*-level gluttony. The appeal of Fortuna's insistent invitation to the section to regard his house – next to the brothel itself, where needy British soldiery waited in good order – as its own declined faintly under the onslaught of *anisette*, garlic-drenched wild boar, local red wine and unsophisticated accompaniments that included, in Norman's words, the wife of the town council's *chef de cabinet* offering to show the youngest section member her private parts ("*Veux-tu voir ma belle craquette?*"). Deplorably, virgins were also on offer, according to Derek Wise.

Or were they? Like a candidate for a maths exam, the biographer needs periodically to show his working. Here, then, are two surviving accounts of the dinner, or *a* dinner: one written forty years after the event, one remembered sixty years later. And they contradict as much as they corroborate. Friends, Lewis and Wise both evoke a dinner with "Fortuna" or "the brothel-keeper" which all – or most of – the section attended, though in Wise's remembrance, "I'm not all that sure that everybody wanted to come, I think some were a bit shocked at the idea. They thought it was rather a shameful thing." But the occurrence of a dinner is a point they agree on. In tabular form their unagreed points are more numerous:

Lewis	Wise
Date	
11 or 12 December (3 days after arrival)	"Midway" through their five-month stint
Other guests	
Fortuna's wife Mme Renée, "several officials", a visiting Academician, local shopkeepers	"We were just with the man who owned it and a few girls. There weren't any local people there"
Quality	
"Vast and interminable"	"We had a good dinner, with girls"
Other interest	
"*Veux-tu voir ma belle craquette?*"	"He was offering us virgins, very expensive normally"

Do the contradictions matter? Possibly they do; but not just in the self-cancelling way one might think. Rather, I think they function as emphasis, since two versions that seem to threaten each other's claim to be the truth enshrine also at least one other thing which we know to be true: that there is infinite variety to eye-witness testimonies. Norman's own enthusiasm for Kurosawa's *Rashomon*, when he saw it at the Mayfair Curzon cinema ten years later, was partly based on the film's potent explication of the impact of subjectivity on recollection (in the film a murder is retold by four witnesses in four mutually contradictory ways), and, to take the argument a step further, on the film's implied belief in the subjectivity of all history. A stage further still, and what matters (to invoke Professor Dening) is the *performance*, "not another sermon". Not another deadly assembly of facts. Not when an event is impatient to be transformed into a *meaning* – which is its chief value to us as humans. Not when the narrating that is the point of living is itself a lived experience, essentially mythopoetic, presenting the past (as Dening writes) with the double meaning of the word "presents", both making a *now* of it and delivering it in some dramatic display.[10] Not when a double meaning can be increased to a treble meaning, for aren't narrations a form of gift, one of the forms of the generosity that connects us?[11]

Norman's account of the dinner at Fortuna's, subjective, transformed, expressly composed, a little fabricated, nevertheless provides meaning: even provides meaning *because of* its distortion. (Generalisation and metaphor, for example, are both sorts of distortions.) When Norman writes of the town's citizens – Fortuna's guests – as "like Brueghel's feasting peasantry in modern dress", occasion and guests become symbols of a truth about the tortuous self-indulgence of Philippeville life with the author providing an articulated meaning, not a mute mass of facts. (Thus the question usually posed about modern dramatisations of "real" events is always the wrong one. The important question is not "Is it true – good – or invented – bad?" but "What quality of meaning does it offer?")

Michel Fortuna likewise is a likeably corrupt Virgil, guiding the reader through the meaning of the circles of wartime colonial purgatory. His role is also one of narration, as all informers' is – though he may initially have been under a misapprehension. "They got mixed up with us and the military police, you see," Derek Wise remembers. "It wasn't our job to close brothels unless they were a security interest, but the military police might have. [People like Fortuna] didn't realise that, they just wanted to get on the right side of us, that was all." But when "nine-tenths" of the information collected by Intelligence Corps sections was rubbish, the factual revelations Fortuna was able to provide were unusually valuable – and if Norman's claim that 91 FSS did not know that Fortuna and his wife ran the brothel until several days after the dinner is true, there was hardly a question of passing up his information when it did.

Norman's first encounter with Arabs ran true to Field Security type. A signal from GHQ requested an urgent interview with a non-existent leader in a place that could not be found on any map: eventually the man and his village, their names correctly spelt, were identified as being in another section's territory. Informed, the GHQ Intelligence major at Algiers replied that he had no idea that another section existed. Captain Bouchard, head of the Philippeville gendarmerie, warned Norman against involvement, the subject being a notorious trouble-maker, although Bouchard like others was known to judge Arabs in general as "*une race infecte*" and mockingly garbled their names. On 15 December Norman rode his Norton out to Bou Zerqa, the chief's village, across mountains hardly penetrated by the French and unreached by Allied forces, into "an entranced landscape from the dawn of history, pristine and empty of humanity, massed with cork oaks, with deer and wild goats scrambling on the mountain sides and eagles swinging like pendulums in the sky". At the chief's "castle", a squalid abandoned filling station, a conference and lunch of *meshwi* patrolled by flies provided the information that, despite his disappointment at discovering the British to be on the wrong side, the chief was willing to send a hundred horsemen to stiffen their numbers. On the point of leaving and having promised to pass on his offer to his general, Norman was offered the usual courtesy of a barely pubescent girl to take with him, which he declined, citing the lack of proper transport.

A complication of Norman's dealings with Philippeville's Arabs was the French disdain for them, universal and intense. So horribly treated were the Algerian Arabs that a sympathy for the underdog was hardly necessary. One of Norman's most useful contacts was a taxi driver called Hadef, "a handsome, generous and irresponsible man" who had a reputation as a dangerous intellectual because of his reading of *Reader's Digest*, a unique activity among proletarian Arabs. Hadef helped Norman to solve the mystery of disappearing stores from the base supplies depot. The depot "was an irresistible magnet to a people many of whom had

been slowly starving to death"; but Hadef pointed out that the fence
who distributed the supplies after they had been smuggled out was one
of the *colons*. This represented a problem because French premises
could not be searched without a warrant, and, as soon as one was
applied for, the colon in question would be tipped off. To make some
show of enforcement, some young Arab boys between the ages of ten
and fourteen were rounded up. Before questioning them, one of
Bouchard's gendarmes opened proceedings, as the gendarmes always
did, by jumping on their bare toes with his boots. Norman got the
boys, with crushed and bleeding feet, taken to hospital, widening the
breach between himself and Captain Bouchard. A handful of Arabs
had made it into the middle class, and he made friends with most of
these; the rest lived in conditions "inconceivable to Europeans. Most
of the males observed on our arrival wore garments made from sacks."
A consequence of the Allied landings was to explode the old power
equation of wealthy colons and a surplus of Arab labour. Offered by
the Allies nine or ten times what the French paid, and reasonably
treated, Arab workers abandoned the colons' farms in their hundreds
and descended on the coast. It is certain that this unintentionally offered
taste of justice from Allied quartermasters helped to light the popular
fuse for Algerian independence and deepened the bitterness of the
conflict, "for," in Norman's words, "Algerians as [the colons] were,
and subject to the passionate irrationality of this land, they saw in this
[situation] nothing but an attack on themselves".

Relations with the French, especially the section's informers, offered
it a number of lessons about applied intelligence-gathering. Immersion
in the drains of Algerian loyalties carried the price of implication. While
Allied Forces HQ in Algiers complimented Mahler on his section's efficiency, the alliance with Fortuna produced hostility from Captain
Bouchard who (despite Fortuna's stock with most of the town officials)
dismissed him as a gangster. Unmoved, Mahler and Lev refused
Bouchard's request to requisition Fortuna's car and hand it to the
gendarmes (whose only reliable transport was three bicycles) and instead
gave Fortuna a windscreen notice announcing him to be on essential
duties for the Allies. He was able as a result to impose his commercial
control on the small towns and villages within a 50-kilometre radius
of Philippeville – and with Lev's acquiescence get any who resisted put
on the section blacklist. "We only knew half of what was going on,
but apart from that we did not greatly care," Norman noted. "Let the

Algerians settle their differences in their own way, was the general verdict."

When the theft of petrol, one of the section's biggest problems, threatened to get out of hand, one episode illuminated Fortuna's opportunism, in his arranging for the section to pursue one of his personal rivals in a raid of force excessive in any other context. Most of the colons, secluded like chieftains on their farms, trafficked stolen petrol. Under Fortuna's direction, a few days before Christmas most of the section left on the armed raid. But they raided the wrong house; losing the element of surprise (a boy would have been sent immediately across the fields to alert the suspect), they knocked on the suspect's door to find him waiting with a tray of champagne. Fortuna, or possibly another enemy, did not give up: kidnapped, the man, a White Russian settler, was soon afterwards drugged and dumped staggering around the Philippeville port, his abductors phoning the guards and telling them a spy had just been put ashore. He was seen and shot.

Axis air raids against Allied convoys in port and off the Algerian coast had continued since the landings in November. Philippeville was an important resupply port and at the turn of the year, as First Army consolidated its position, raids intensified, regularly timed to take place after the arrival of a convoy. Typically, on 7 January a thirteen-ship convoy bound for Philippeville was attacked by Stuka dive-bombers and a flight of Savoia torpedo-bombers. The SS *William Wirt*, a Liberty ship carrying 16,000 cases of aviation fuel, counter-attacked, a Norwegian freighter was set on fire, and the British SS *Benalbanach* was torpedoed, exploded and sank with a cargo of ammunition, stores and vehicles, and the loss of 410 out of 430 men. Norman described one week of nightly attacks as "a classic, oversimplified vision of war, not devoid of its savage poetry". The Villa Portelli was close to the raiders' target area. Half a dozen planes, circling in the dusk "with premeditation", would then begin their bombing run.

We would listen to the howl of the accelerating engines, interrupted by that of the high-pitched and penetrating scream of the approaching bomb. At this point the gunners operating the two anti-aircraft guns at the bottom of our garden would give up and jump for their slit trenches, although the pageant of fire and flame was kept going by many other guns placed round the harbour.

The glass fell away in an icicle shower from our windows and all that we saw through it had been balefully transfigured. Hundreds of guns were pumping

thousands of shells into the sky, which opened up to spew fiery lava over ten
ships sitting in a carmine lake.

The shards and chips of the scene projected onto Norman's remembering retina, pictorial and human, are transcribed with reconstructive
brilliance.

We heard the walls crack, and the villa shift and settle, breathed layered smoke
and felt the concussion of the bombs in our eardrums and the soles of our
feet. Our two worst cases of uncontrollable apprehension were clasped together
under the table in the foetal position of twins in the womb, but even Sergeant-
Major Leopold [Lev], our man of steel, seemed influenced by these happenings,
revealing suddenly his Sephardic origins in an urgent outburst of *cante flamenco*.
The FSO, after declaiming a passage from Ovid, bounded up to the roof, where
he stood – as he admitted later, in a state of disbelief – while the shrapnel
from anti-aircraft bursts tinkled around him.[12]

The section's life in Philippeville remained undemanding outside
these disturbances. Internal incidents had to be dealt with: 311 Section
had to be consulted at AFHQ as to whether it was possible to put on
a charge an American soldier who had bought an Arab girl for 2000
francs. But Derek Wise started a more conventional affair with a French
girlfriend, and in the general vacation atmosphere he, Norman and Ted
Kingham established a routine away from the Villa Portelli that embraced
women's company. "We rented a little flat, three of us. We didn't have
much furniture, I remember we had a mattress on the floor."[13]
Throughout the day, on the square near the port the Café du Commerce
and Café de la Marine were meeting places of 91 FSS personnel, including
Sergeant-Major Lev, so influenced by the frontier-town atmosphere that
he had taken to wearing two guns. A drawback to the tone of relax-
ation watered by illegal *anisette* was the pointless buzz of whispered
secrets from informers: futile as most of the section did not speak
French but tolerated for the greater good of the holiday atmosphere
and spectacles like the passing parade of the Senegalese battalion,
always led in exquisite drill by trumpeters whose instruments at the
end of a verse "would be flung high into the air, turning smoothly as
they fell, splashed by the sun with a row of brass stars, then deftly
caught, pressed to the rich indigo lips in readiness for the next perfectly
synchronized spurt of martial music". Determined denouncers went

further and carried their horrific treacheries as far as the section office, but were rarely listened to as the wealthier colons who were always their accused were untouchable.

A particular sort of military frustration, however, was endemic for called-up men like Norman, whose level of intelligence was greater than that of their senior NCOs. Responsibility for decisions lay with the regulars; often, through educational shortcomings, the wrong decision was made, the wrong button pressed, the wrong calculation performed. If 91 FSS was not exactly a pride of lions led by donkeys, it was the straggling tail of an incompetent comet. A corollary was that Norman found many of the situations that engaged him to be purely and simply outside any military remit. On 7 January an Arab Sûreté agent named Bou Alem showed him the stinking *oubliette* of a Philippeville prison where several Arab village leaders had been dumped to freeze to death in the dark among their own ordure. "I told him I was horrified and disgusted, as I was." But the Allies had an agreement with the French not to interfere in French affairs, and he could do nothing. Afterwards he avoided Bou Alem, but, cornered in the office several days later, agreed to meet the Sûreté agent in private to hear serious news. Bou Alem's message, that the French had decided to break the relations between the British and their Arab workers by inducing British troops to take bloody reprisals for the looting of Allied supply depots – the one chronic cause of friction between Allies and Arabs – was again one that Norman could do nothing about. Nobody would listen to him, he told Bou Alem. Bou Alem replied that the looting could be stopped (and the attack called off) if the local saint, Sidi Omar Abbas, could be persuaded to intervene. Reporting his meeting to Captain Mahler on a day when Lev was absent, Norman was astonished to find that the erratic FSO agreed with Bou Alem and, having made a public display of blood lust the day before, was "apparently eager to find some way of holding the commandos at bay". On 15 January Norman rode out on his Norton to locate Sidi Omar; their eventual meeting, on one side the angular British Army corporal, on the other the elderly but agile and humorous anchorite, would set a pattern for Norman's future contacts with the country Arabs.

On these expeditions I always took a packet of tea, and sometimes, about midday, spotting an Arab hut on a mountain-side, I would climb up to it, and if a male came out to meet me, show him my provisions and suggest we might share them. The offer was always accepted with enthusiasm. Quite often on these occasions an egg or two would be produced to complete the meal. And in this way – two ... men trying to make themselves heard, and understand each other above the vociferous singing of nightingales – a pleasant and indulgent hour would be passed.[14]

On this occasion the saint, sole occupant of a shrine at the summit of a mountain of scree outside the town, bounded down to meet him in a dishevelled turban and "a tattered but splendidly laundered" djellaba. Over a bowl of fly-encrusted black honey he listened to Norman's attempt at Algerian Arabic "attentively with the slightly wincing expression of one who hears great music being played badly". Eventually suggesting that they speak French ("I made a vow only to speak the language of my people, but God is very understanding"), Sidi Omar agreed to speak to the Arabs at the depot, assuring Norman there would be no more trouble from them. There would be plenty from the French, he added, but they would soon be gone. The French had been God's lesson, he said, to cure the Arabs of drinking wine and of soft habits such as seeing their wives' faces before marriage and wearing silk; but their time was up.

The visit by Sidi Omar to the supply depot produced the required effect. A curious subsequent event related in Norman's autobiography was that when he was called to receive Captain Mahler's congratulations, his FSO informed him with "one of his broad and crinkling smiles ... accepted by us now as heralding momentous news" that he was to refer to Mahler henceforth not as Mahler but as Captain FitzClarence. The implication is a bit hard on Mahler, as, although there seems little doubt that he was at the early stage of a breakdown and the motive Norman implies for his change of name is a plausible paranoia, Norman may have been exercising literary licence. His red notebook records a more prosaic weakness: "Mahler: Capt. FitzClarence for brothel crawling purposes".

An unwanted and more serious consequence to Norman's success in stopping the looting of the supply depot was that the *provocateurs* among the French, thwarted of their bloodletting, made the saint's prophecy of trouble start to come true within a month. At the same time the rift between Arabs and French was beginning to infect the British: in the space of one week, *anisette*-drinking British soldiers tore the veils off, and otherwise assaulted, several young Arab women, another group of drunken squaddies entered a mosque with their boots on and poured a jug of beer over the protesting imam, and an Arab child was killed by a British jeep in a hit-and-run accident. Norman felt that "we are beginning to copy the attitudes of the French who are out to persuade us that Arabs don't matter". In his notebook he recorded the unofficial advice of "reversing [your] lorry over a knocked down wog to avoid hospital fees". The gangster elements among the French had embarked on a campaign of escalating intimidation: in one incident the house of Norman's friend Mohammed Kobtan, Philippeville's one successful Arab merchant, had had its windows smashed. After talking to other Arab friends – a doctor named Kessous, an official named Meksen, and the taxi driver Hadef – Norman broached the idea of an Anglo-Arab friendship club to his sergeant-major. Couching it as "the possibility of dining at the house of a rich Arab", he found Lev enthusiastic. In the event, two weeks later the lunch was cancelled, Mahler having accepted then made an excuse, he and "half the section" instead being entertained at Fortuna's the same day. Around the same time Hadef's taxi was raked by machine-gun fire as he passed Fortuna's farm. Norman was beginning to understand that however amiable a gangster the brothel-keeper was, it was he and his kind, posing as zealous resistants, their windscreen stickers saluted by the MPs at Army checkpoints, that the section was keeping in business, to the Arabs' fatal disadvantage.

In the last week of February Norman was called to Allied Forces HQ at Algiers. An American soldier described the Britishers' baggy, schoolboyish impact on AFHQ. "It was the first time I saw British soldiers. . . . In the AFHQ offices there was an Englishman to counterbalance every American. Thus the streets of Algiers clomped with British hobnails. The British wore shorts till 1800 hours. Through the leafy heat their legs bobbed like brown pistons."[15] Norman was interviewed by one of them, a cheerfully patrician Intelligence major, who promised him at last "something useful to do". Conducted in the tone of pithy vagueness Norman was used to, the meeting came to nothing. All that happened was that on the last day of February he was ordered forward to deliver some documents to a frontline FS section at Mejez el Bab and, getting drunk with them on Tunisian wine and listening to a German offensive thumping away to the south, witnessed the depressing atmosphere of Allied forces convinced of the enemy's fighting superiority. (The US II Corps had just been routed by a much smaller Panzer force at Kasserine Pass.)

Back in Philippeville in early March he initiated an attempt to roll back Fortuna's influence, after learning via Bou Alem that every man in the *milice populaire* under Fortuna's command had done time. Something of the guilty pleasure of associating with crooks clings to his account of the meeting with Fortuna. Norman was fully aware of his depravity. "Unfortunately – hard as it is to admit it to oneself – he is likeable. . . . We have all dragged him from under the guillotine, and this salvation has given him a kind of emotional claim on us." Fortuna instantly agreed with him about cleaning up the activities of his *milice* members, then led him into a cellar to show him something he thought would interest him. The "something" was several panels of Roman mosaics. Stopping in front of one, of Roman girls dancing to a lyre, he offered to pack it up for Norman as a gift.

March, and the arrival of spring, was spent in military stagnation. Captain Mahler, more or less bedridden with deepening mental disturbance, had ceded the running of the section to Sergeant-Major Lev, who, having obtained the authority he coveted, found it a chimera. The section was losing its grip. After a quarter of a year in Philippeville, it had discovered something worse than not very much happening: that virtually nothing could be made to happen. Norman had lost sight of his Arab friends, who had retreated in disillusion at the British inability to check the excesses of the French. Bou Alem tried to impress on him the inevitability of French reprisals against the Arabs as soon as the British withdrew. Norman, "with a feeling of cowardice and shame", explained that "no one who had the slightest power or influence in our Army could possibly care less".

He spent a probably slightly melancholy March and early April in which, left to himself during the day, his chief pleasure became the circuits of exploration that he made on his Norton through the Algerian spring landscape, riding for hours down empty roads with no sign of human habitation. However far from Enfield, in every category, these escapades must have had something of Forty Hill about them. Like his solitary roaming over the Bowles estate, they were immersions in a lushly natural, and unpopulated, hinterland whose flora and fauna he recognised and could give himself the pleasure of naming; they also represented a gentle exercising of his escape reflex, itself an affirmation of his identity always at the edge of the group, where it had been

located since Gwen Nicholls first noticed him in the Freehold, outside
whatever activity was going on, looking in, never joining.

Rural Algeria impressed him visually as something neither European
nor African, that he had never seen before.

The outstanding feature of this landscape was its splendid oak forests, with
glades stretched to infinity between the stands of majestic trees. . . . I rode
as quietly as I could along the empty roads, coasting softly in neutral with
the engine switched off down the long, winding, slopes, and in this way
frequently took the animals by surprise: a brace of elegant foxes and – I
could hardly believe it – a single jackal, traipsing dutifully like a well-trained
dog through the buttercups. Deer were everywhere, wild boars frequently
spotted at the edge of woods, and once I saw a sow chased through an open
glade by her litter of sportive piglets. The best of the birds were of the
flashing sub-tropical variety, such as bee-eaters, rollers or orioles, displayed
like bright toys or Christmas-tree ornaments against the rich but sedate
foliage of the oaks.[16]

With his packet of tea in the pocket of his battledress jacket to be
offered to any solitary Arab he might come across, he had what he
needed for brief but complete evasion from Army life – and notably
from its steep descent into unreality as soon as there is nothing for
its soldiers to do.

On 9 April, a Friday, the alleviated stasis of his existence suddenly
ended. "Norman liked riding motorbikes. He was a bit reckless on
motorbikes," Derek Wise remembers. "In hospital" is the record in
Norman's notebook. The motorcycle accident[17] was severe enough to
keep him in the 100th General Hospital at Philippeville for nearly three
weeks. He had suffered a fractured skull (in the accident's aftermath,
the medics who attended him reported, he had told them to bind up
his head and he would keep going) and stoved in his ribs again.
Conditions in Allied hospitals in north Africa were not luridly bad, but
shortages of soap and "army form blank" (toilet paper) and surfeits
of heat, flies, and dysenteric amoebae made hospitalisation less desirable than it was sometimes imagined. (The flies' habit of laying their

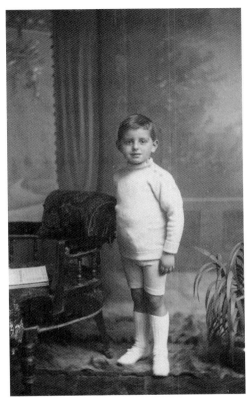

"Self, washed and polished for the occasion"

David Warren Lewis, tea tycoon. With Norman's grandmother and father

The Lewises of Forty Hill: Richard, Monty, Norman and Louisa

Aunts Polly (standing) and Annie

343 Carterhatch Lane

Life after Forty Hill: the Beacon of Light Spiritualist church

Forty Hall

On the roof of 343 Carterhatch Lane

First vehicle

The Arab of Enfield:
self-portrait with
headdress, dagger
and handguns

At 17 with Louisa and one of Sir
Henry Bowles' maidenly "visiters",
possibly Miss Phoebe Tupperton

At 19 with unknown
Welsh attendants

First motorcycle, a Reading-Standard

The dust roads and orchards
of Forty Hill

Family, and Carmarthen relations

Gwen Nicholls in British East Africa,
holding off another suitor

Levantine swell, Nice, March 1930

Studio subject, by his friend Alex Hagen

In Paris with Ernestina, 1933

Driver: Bugatti dual-cowl Type 30

Driver: Bugatti Type 40

Driver: road-race FWD Alvis

Tea with mother

Hotel breakfast, late 1930s

Ernestina and her Moroccan kestrel by Norman, Epping Forest, 1936

Norman by Ernestina

Writer: dustjacket of his first book, *Spanish Adventure*

Businessman: advertisement from *Amateur Photographer*, 19 October 1938

Spy: "The sambuk was a small one without colour or carving, but graceful of line.... The negro waved his arm irritably and shouted in Arabic that it was improper to photograph him undressed"

Suakin, "a habitation of dragons and a court for owls", 1937

Milan Grand Prix, 1937

London garage, 1937

Iver Heath, spring 1939

Ernesto Corvaja with grandson Ito

Father and son at Pine Cottage

eggs under wounded men's plaster casts was an interesting bonus, the larvae aiding recovery by nibbling at the putrefaction of a soldier's wounds, so long as he could tolerate the sensation of maggots wriggling inside the plaster.)

The 100th General Hospital was staffed by, among others, nurses from Queen Alexandra's Imperial Military Nursing Service. One of the QAIMNS nurses who looked after Norman was a sister whom Derek Wise subsequently met. "Fairly tall, blonde, very attractive. She was pretty senior, and I think very efficient." When Wise himself broke his leg in Tunisia a few months later, after an unpleasant few days in a field hospital he was moved back to the 100th General. "And the first thing I did was ask for Hester. She was very kind and came and made sure that I had enough cigarettes and chocolate and things and told them all to look after me."[18]

Norman's seduction of Hester Reid was a considerable achievement. She was not tall, as Wise says, but petite and bonny, a lively Scot with white-blonde hair and a fair highlands complexion. She had come from the granite of Deeside, the youngest of twelve, a local village girl made good; not highly educated but at thirty-four, a year younger than Norman, with skilled sister's hands and a strong, friendly look about her. Charming, practical, with playful animation in her pale blue eyes that disguised a manipulativeness behind them, she was the perfect spritzer in the downbeat canteen of wartime. Perhaps she was unlucky. The war had broken out just when she might have thought of finding herself a husband and starting a family. But she was much pursued at the 100th General, and most of the time she probably did not feel unlucky.

Norman had few advantages. Unwell and unsteady for most of his time in hospital, he was also an NCO, and in the Army – to forestall exactly such fraternisation – nurses had officer rank. He made a note in his red notebook, among the scribbled dates and overheard remarks of other soldiers ("'Tea's me life's blood'", "'I bin divorced once.' 'The hell you been. Where was you born?'") that shows he was aware of the gulf, referring to one officer as of the type that subscribed to "droits de seigneur over hospital sisters". But he was seldom indecisive where women were concerned. "She was a good-looking girl," her son Gareth remembers, "blonde and vivacious and all the rest of it, and her spin was that he chased her around north Africa."[19] There are grounds for believing that by the time Norman was discharged from hospital at the end of the month he had secured Hester's complicity, and grounds too for believing in his emotional authenticity. In short, he had, if not fallen in love, found a good masculine reason for living. On a page in his notebook is a series of dates written in pencil, annotated in blue-black with the letter "H":

(TUESDAY 4th May (H.), 1 JUNE, 29 June)
(SUNDAY (H.) 4th JULY) left for TUNIS and Sousse Monday morning
(25th July (H.), 24th Aug)

Glued into the red notebook too is the only photograph he kept of Hester: a black and white contact print he took of a handsome, laughing woman against a desert background, scrub and low dunes: a nursing sister in her Army skirt and blouse with a sultry head of mussed blonde hair, laughing complicitly, at something Norman had said, or at nothing, from pleasure. Norman possessed without doubt the knack of entertaining women: even those who, like Gwen Nicholls, might not accept his physical advances remembered the quality of his intelligence and humour and something unusual, controlled and memorable, "charm as Keats would have used it", as Raymond Chandler once said of Scott Fitzgerald. From his point of view, in an unstable era the simple novelty and novel simplicity of the blonde, practical Scot must have seemed valuable holdings, despite the reservation that he and Hester did not share much of an outlook. He convinced both of them of his feelings, which experience suggests is generally enough, certainly in time of war. Hester's daughter Karen says

I was trying to square how they were with each other, thinking how could she have possibly thought ... what would she do with a complex man like this when she'd had very little formal education, she hadn't read, and she was not of an intellectual bent? And then I came across letters that he'd written to Auntie Docie [Hester's older sister Joan], plighting his troth, saying, "Look after her, how much I love her, blah blah blah," and I thought to myself, Well yes that would have convinced me too, if somebody had written to say [that]. Words and phrases of endearment and responsibility and all the kind of stuff Dad shied away from all his life were in those letters.[20]

To this atmosphere of emotional and sexual heat was added the sudden opportunity for action. In the second half of April, everything involved with Hester found itself abruptly rolled up into the wider fate of the Allied attack on two fronts, east and west, against the Axis. In late March General Montgomery's Operation Pugilist had broken Axis defences on the Mareth line; by mid-April the Germans and Italians, outmanned and outgeneralled, were being fatally squeezed. Tunis would fall in two weeks, Norman was told on a hospital visit by Sergeant-Major Lev, his face "a vaguely sinister angel from an El Greco background afloat somewhere above me", and 91 FSS would follow immediately behind the infantry advance. It was up to him to get fit or find himself off the section, Lev told him. With the co-operation of the duty medical officer, Norman wrote, agreeing to alter his injury records from a fracture to concussion, his recovery took place rapidly after Lev's visit. Discharged from hospital on 28 April, a Wednesday, he returned to Philippeville for a few days, still suffering from loss of balance. The following Tuesday when the rest of the section left for Tunis he stayed behind but instead of resting saw Hester again that day. British troops entered Tunis on Friday and by Monday Norman was well enough to follow. The day before he left, Hadef the taxi driver threw a picnic for him, driving out with his family to a secluded part of the cork forest where his wife and sister-in-law could take off their *jalabib* and veils. The women held hands with Norman and danced tentatively to the songs of Abdel Wahab played on Hadef's portable gramophone while Hadef poured *anisette*. It was a moment of innocent contact, and the last Norman would see of Hadef.

He wrote later that he set off alone on a motorcycle for Tunis, handicapped by having to ride with one hand because of his fractured ribs. His notebook records more company.

Left Ph'ville for Tunis with rear party 10th May. Stayed [with] section [at] Souk Ahras, 2nd night with unit at Thibor [Téboursouk]. Arrived 12th May.

He remembers riding in a chill dawn on the 12th at Béja, 60 kilometres from Tunis, and being used as target practice by German troop lorries which "had either been disarmed and directed to the rear, or were actually trying to escape". Driving straight at him, one lorry forced him off the road, "this possibly being my nearest escape from death in the war".[21] Riding on through Mejez el Bab, where he had got drunk with the frontline section in February, he saw the battlefield, "numerous shattered or burnt-out tanks" and in the villages "rows of bloodstained stretchers stood against the wall to dry in the

sun, recurrent accents of bright colour in an otherwise drab and desolate landscape".

The city of Tunis, on the eve of the final surrender on 13 May of
more than 275,000 Axis troops, was pure bacchanal. He saw "thousands of unconscious British soldiers – I counted over fifty lying on
the steps of a single church – a Goyaesque muddle of bodies, and
bottles, and wine vomit". He was astonished to see Germans freely
looking on, and more surprised to be elbowed away from the first
bar counter where he tried to buy a beer by the Germans who had
taken it over. He found the section's quarters, a more luxurious villa
than the Portelli at Philippeville, in a quiet suburb. It had previously
been a Gestapo residence and was still a little incongruous slice of
Bavaria, full of beer *Steine*, carved pipes and mechanical wall-clocks,
and cupboards containing preserves, prophylactics and feathered hats.
Derek Wise remembers that "The Germans had much nicer shirts
than we did, so we had these lovely silk khaki shirts that were left
behind."[22] The section benefited from Lev's glee at finding himself in
such sumptuousness and were allowed – unusually for other ranks –
to occupy the villa's beds. The only ominous note was sounded by
Captain Mahler informing his men of another imminent change of
name, and that he was imposing an 11 p.m. curfew which he would
enforce with his pistol.

Remembered in *Jackdaw Cake,* Tunis in the drunken grip of British
victory was a Hogarthian chaos of incautious euphoria, observed with
distant disdain by hundreds of still-at-liberty Germans. Norman had
a conversation with a German who assured him that the Afrika Korps
was not defeated, merely adjusting, and met an FS member he had
last seen at Mejez el Bab, who swore gloomily that Tunis had only
been won by superior numbers and that when 300 Germans had
advanced, tired of waiting, on Mejez, 3500 Allied troops "pissed off
as fast as we could". After only a few days in the city, 91 FSS fell foul
of the Army backlash against the celebrations. Significantly composed
of heavy drinkers, the section found its surroundings of luxury termin-
ated abruptly when it was identified on two counts of unreliability –
its FSO's increasingly obvious signs of instability and its NCOs' drunken
state and unregimental (brown shoes, unblancoed webbing) appearance during a search operation at German security headquarters – and
redeployed.

In Derek Wise's eyes the port of La Goulette, a bombed and empty backwater 10 kilometres across Lake Tunis, was "a nice place on the sea, a sort of peninsula if I remember. We were very lucky," but Norman, more restless, felt a "terrific tedium". The port's only distraction was its waterfront café-bar where the section was served indulgently by the three Jewish daughters of the owner, all "beautiful, though extremely fat, with wonderful complexions of the palest gold and enormous soulful eyes". The soft epicentre of desire that these young women embodied in the desert of the section's existence rippled outwards into a predictable episode of matchmaking, manifested in a voluptuous cabaret arranged by their mother of sticky sweets and belly-dancing; but no marriages followed and the section was back to killing time. Norman was occasionally saved by getting back to Philippeville to see Hester. The rest of the time he and the section played poker and waited for the daily sightings of spies, reported every evening after sunset as soon as any local resident saw an unfamiliar light. To inject activity into their collapsing unit, Sergeant-Major Lev and Captain Mahler first vied with each other for the most futile demand that could be made of the section, and subsequently for the title of who was most speedily deteriorating mentally. Mahler's appetite for pointless reports led to Norman being detailed to count the traffic on the La Goulette–Tunis road, while Lev induced the men to drill by offering local leave with free transportation thrown in, permitting him free play with his war cry, "Roll on the day, when the Good Lord shall say, Heaven and Earth, close order, march!"[23] He simultaneously demonstrated his mood of readiness by keeping a loaded sub-machine gun in arm's reach. His hair-trigger temper wrapped up one evening's socialising with the local MPs when he threw their sergeant-major off the roof of the section's villa.

Lev's borderline sanity seemed to restore Captain Mahler to a state of balance briefly – "deploying his always alarming smile, he issued his orders" – and so it went on, one waxing as the other waned. At the beginning of June Norman got away to Philippeville, though his notebook records a small mystery. He rode his Norton along the marvellous coast road via Tabarka and "slept [in a] field [at] Ain Mokra", arriving at Philippeville at "7.15 J. Monday 7th June" before reporting at the 100th General Hospital at 10 a.m. "J." reappears in a trip to Bougie later that month with Ted Kingham: when they arrived at Philippeville late on the night of the 26th because they had had "Trouble near Bône", they reported straight away and Norman went to "Clean up at J. & place Marquet". Initials found in notebooks are one of the biographer's drugs; in this case the biographer's craving is unsatisfied.

Back in La Goulette, the meaninglessness of the section's tasks increased. Norman was ordered to count all the houses along the peninsula from the port to the other side of Carthage, and his FSO had decided to arrange a series of inspirational lectures to neighbouring units, together with readings, on the Norse sagas. Lev refused to report Captain Mahler, knowing the army's usual treatment of such messengers. Morale was also being undermined by ruptures in the Army postal service. Norman himself had not heard from Ernestina for several months. When he did, she blamed the censor for leaving "not a single comprehensible sentence" from him. "I know you're out there somewhere, that's all. The rest is silence," she wrote distantly and regretfully. She admitted that life in Guatemala had anaesthetised her spirit.

I'm afraid it has to be faced. I've given in. This is like a bullfight. I'm there for no other reason than that the others are, half-asleep, up in the *tendidos*. We go to the fiestas and throw confetti at each other, and the men get on their horses and pull cockerels' heads off. Remember when I told you about the first one I went to. You were disgusted, and so was I. Now I'm beginning to stop thinking, nothing has much effect. ... Perhaps I see myself for the first time, and realise I'm a very ordinary sort of person. Just like a lizard, lying in the sun.[24]

There were perhaps times during spring of 1943 when Norman's own experience, of the army's jangling notes of anonymity, routine, stagnation and madness, made him wonder what *he* was doing, and when the diapason of adventure would finally sound. It might have been in La Goulette that he wrote out in his notebook feelingly the second half of Macbeth's "She should have died hereafter" speech. Life in 91 FSS can rarely have resembled a walking shadow more; counting cars and houses for an FSO whose smiles contained the authentic suggestion of lunacy can rarely have seemed more like a tale told by an idiot, signifying nothing. Yet consider: a curious aspect of routine is that it can offer not only the situation to be broken out of, but the mental space too in which the breakout may be prepared. Norman was, I think, making the best of the curious freedom of Army routine, in which physical needs are catered for in exchange for submission to orders: despite the dusty tedium of his posting, and the indifferent farce that section life had turned into, almost every day in north Africa, he had found, provided a new surprise to the receptive observer. In the accumulation of those days, he was beginning to see from both human and literary perspectives the formal connection between the sad lyricism of experience and the revealing comic detail, between tragedy and futility and their offspring, absurdity. Consider, too, these last of routine's virtues: that it can remind the beleaguered individual of how long real improvements can take, and of their unexpected ways of showing themselves.

A week after his return from Philippeville an unusually alert and well-dressed customer ordered midday tea at Le Chat Qui Rit, the waterfront café-bar where the Jewish girls waited. He greeted Norman in Arabic and with "a routine insincere compliment" began a conversation. First it was La Goulette's lack of interest, then the common factor of the British and Tunisian royal families, then the hopelessness of the French. "Arabs frequently sought to curry favour with us by remarks of this kind, as if purporting to be aware of hidden tensions in the relationship between the two nations." The dark-suited Tunisian came inexorably to the point. He represented the Bey of Tunis, who wished Norman to speak to his brother, the vice-Bey or Bey du Camp. "I think for your country it would be interesting." Norman offered to pass the request to Lev. The man insisted it should be Norman himself who visited the vice-Bey at his palace, underlining the personal nature of the meeting by implying that Norman's name was known to him.

The Tunisian was Jean-Claude Mélia, counsellor to the Bey. When Norman reported the meeting to Lev, his senior NCO was enthusiastic, though for what reasons Norman was uncertain. Norman met Mélia later that day and a visit was arranged for the following day. Norman remembered that Mélia drove him to the Bey's palace at Kassar Saïd "among the orange orchards five miles out of Tunis", though Derek Wise recalls that it was another dramatic motorcycle ride. "I remember I was on his pillion, and it was quite a hair-raising experience." The audience in a rose arbour in the gardens of the palace, Norman reported to Lev later, was "like a film set". The Bey du Camp, "a man in early middle-age" carrying a white, silken-haired cat and "saturated with patrician Arab restraint", welcomed him and told him in aristocratically lucid Arabic that Tunisia was in the process of cutting its ties with France "which, legally, had no longer any claim upon a protectorate which it had failed to protect".

"The amusing thing", Wise says, "was that he thought that we had more or less a direct line to Churchill."[25]

The Bey sat with his back to the opening of the bower on a scape of lawns and flowering trees, and beyond the janissary in his braided gilet and tasselled cap, with his scimitar resting on his shoulder, a capering juggler, brought to entertain us, played on a pipe held in one hand and threw balls into the air and caught them with the other.

The Bey said, "We are not prepared to surrender our country to socialism. Instead, we wish to become part of the British Empire."[26]

Norman wrote afterwards that he had been tempted to think there was a directing hand in the choice of him as messenger, that some impenetrable rationality of the Corps had led him through "the long odyssey of stultification" from Omagh and Ellesmere Port to the Bey's palace garden. His credulity had not lasted. Instead he began to feel that he was being set up as a patsy, by a GHQ that did not want to risk high-level contact that might lead to recrimination between allies. That the vice-Bey himself had his country's future seriously in mind was beyond question. He also knew the date of the Sicilian landings (still secret at the time) and was in close touch with fellow Sicilian separatists who planned, he said, to re-create the Kingdom of the Two Sicilies and request protectorate status from the British.

Norman's account of the days after the meeting – he had agreed to meet the Bey again in a week – is charged with the faint paranoia of association. His weekly report, playing down the meeting on Lev's advice, went in to his FSO next morning, as every Wednesday. That afternoon Mahler ordered his office cleared, and his uniform pressed and equipment polished. On Thursday he paraded the section unexpectedly. "There was anger in his expression but also a kind of bewilderment, and when his lips moved as we stood facing each and he seemed about to speak, I half-expected him to ask the question, 'Who are you? Do I know you?'" Afterwards Mahler drove to GHQ to deliver his report to the G2 in person. On his return, and the next day, he seemed "not only calm but unusually cheerful". On Friday evening[27] Norman saw Mélia – "*un señor muy grande*", one of the Jewish sisters whispered – at Le Chat Qui Rit and told him to be patient until Tuesday. Later that evening, if Norman's nicely timed version of events is to be believed, he saw Lev beckoning to him from the door:

his sergeant-major had come to tell him, with the unusual solicitude senior NCOs kept for bad news, that he had been posted.

After asking for details, Norman asked Lev if he was going to do anything about the Bey.

"Fuck the Bey, and fuck the Empire," Leopold said. "The report went in, and that's the end of it, so far as I am concerned. What more do you expect me to do?"

His posting was to 47 FSS: a port security section to which his friend Ted Kingham had also been posted. Both men left for Algiers the next morning, Saturday 26 June, Norman surprised to find himself quitting with a wrench of regret the empty, bleached port that he had disparaged. He felt he had not admitted its quality as a refuge, as a place passed by, "in which to go to earth while the spirit renewed itself", that "pacified the thoughts and replaced the noxious habit of action with a taste for introspection". In La Goulette people lived unselfconsciously together, whatever their ethnicity and religion. "The Jews played their bandurrias at Arab weddings, and the Arabs sat down to eat at the tables of Jews." He felt his new posting as a banishment (though his claim to have been depressed at the prospect of involvement in the Sicilian landings has something of a performance to it: a man admits to frailty most readily when he knows the strength of his taste for action). He picked on the figure of the mosque's electrician to incarnate the port's diffident charm.

No one here, except for the Jewesses in making their music, did anything well, and this man's inefficiency never failed to enchant me. . . . The fishermen, still at the quayside, who seldom caught a fish by day, let alone by night, turned to watch the performance. A dozen or so lights came on, then, in a shower of sparks and a wisp of smoke, went out again. . . . Through faults in the system I had never known the affirmation of the Muslim faith to be given in its entirety, but at least hitherto it had got as far as "There is no God, but God". This time it spluttered into silence after the atheistic declaration, "There is no God –". Beliefs were held lightly in La Goulette and fanaticism unknown. Everyone, including the electrician, laughed.[28]

He travelled 800 kilometres from Tunis to join the section in Algiers, where it had landed, then moved back with it in stages along the coast to Bougie and finally to Sousse, 120 kilometres from where he had started. (On the way back Norman succeeded in arranging a complicated date with Hester, leaving the returning convoy at Constantine on 3 July, a Saturday, to spend Sunday with her. Something happened to make him underline the day in his notebook, and he did not leave for Tunis and Sousse until "8.30 a.m. Monday 5th".) At Sousse 47 FSS was attached to GHQ, 15th Army Group (the British Eighth Army and US Seventh Army its main constituents), awaiting the invasion of Sicily. Its FSO was Major Hume Boggis-Rolfe, a genial, liberal officer who had been at Trinity, Cambridge with Philby, Blunt and Burgess.

Norman however did not make Sicily. Malaria was endemic in north Africa, and he spent most of July in field hospitals with a serious attack. Recovering, he saw Hester on the 27th and was discharged on the 30th. With little to occupy him, he drove up the coast to revisit 91 FSS at La Goulette. He found the section without Captain Mahler, who the previous week had called another surprise morning parade. Marching into his office, the men had found him dressed only in a burnished Sam Browne and his boots. Holding his pistol, Mahler announced that he intended to shoot one of them and then himself. A lurid climax to the episode was averted by Lev having already made a phone call, and when a medical officer arrived with an armed infantryman in tow Mahler was talked into dressing and going with them.

A day or so afterwards, Norman received an urgent letter from his Arab doctor friend, Kessous, in Philippeville. Kessous wrote that there had been a massacre of Arabs in the town by the Senegalese battalion, and warned of worse to come. Norman could do nothing, but wanting to find out what had happened, on 5 August he secured a few days' leave. At Dr Kessous' house he learned that the Senegalese had gone to the armoury, found it "mysteriously unlocked", and shot or bayoneted "every Arab they could find". Norman felt that Kessous, beneath his furious indignation, regarded the death of a hundred or so Arab workers as regrettable but also a valuable political fuse for the cataclysm that had to come. He visited Madame Hadef next, who had bad news. The Arab cab drivers, Hadef among them, had been cut off by the Senegalese as they tried to drive out of town on the corniche road, chased from their cars to the cliff edge, bayoneted and thrown off. The funerals of the victims, she said, had provoked an unprecedented demonstration by their women who, flouting strict Algerian Moslem custom, had gone into the streets in their hundreds. "The first time since the beginning of the world," she told him, "Moslem women have followed a funeral. [They were] tearing [their] cheeks with [their] fingernails."[29] Norman had himself driven out to Fortuna's farm, where he told the brothel-keeper that a friend of his had been killed; when Fortuna expressed regret, saying that he could have fixed him up with a pass, he felt he had proof that Fortuna's *milice populaire* had guided the hand of the Senegalese. Since the Allies' arrival at the end of 1942 the French had been determined to have their revenge on the Arabs for breaking out of near-slavery and earning a reasonable daily wage, and now they had had it. Norman wrote later with feeling and some justification that in the "huge final tragedy" of the Philippeville massacre of 20 August 1955 in which 12,000 Arabs were killed, and the inevitably ensuing civil war, "our section ... succouring through ignorance and gullibility such gangsters as Fortuna, played its tiny part".[30]

With this episode the wearying slowdown of life ended. Shuttling back and forth to Sousse, he was next sent briefly to 4 Bn General Reinforcement Training Depot to await posting. On 15 August he left Philippeville again, arriving to be hospitalised again two days later at Hussein Dey in the suburbs of Algiers. This time he was declared fully fit and, after being briefly attached to 311 FSS, the headquarters section based in rue Charras, joined his new section at no.1 Transit camp on the 27th. Two days later, on the 29th, he left Algiers for the last time to cover the 300 kilometres to Mostaganem. He was leaving Hester behind, but no great deal of sentiment could be apportioned to separation: such partings were painful but another of the inscrutable routines of wartime. He carried his contact print of her in his notebook and looked forward to seeing her again. One curious question mark hung over the relationship: a chance meeting Norman had had with Arthur Baron, commissioned as a captain in the REME and serving with Montgomery in north Africa. Norman had an opportunity to introduce Hester to Baron, and afterwards he asked his opinion. "This is a wartime thing. Don't do it," Baron is supposed to have replied.[31]

"1st SEP. LEFT MOSTAGANEM FOR ORAN," Norman wrote in his notebook, "same day boarded 'Duchess of Bedford'". The *Duchess of Bedford* was lucky, known as "the most bombed ship still afloat".

Between 1939 and 1945 she sank one U-boat, crippled another, was bombed and fired on dozens of times, and rammed an iceberg without serious damage.

The next two entries were a few days later.

5th SEP Convoy sailed from Mers el Kebir
8th Sep 6.30 p.m. due off Salerno tomorrow at 'H' hours (3 p.m.) when Italy packs in.[32]

With a curiosity at least equal to his first visit, one supposes, he was about to set foot in Italy again.

While Cambyses was carrying on this war in Egypt, the Lacedaemonians likewise sent a force to Samos against Polycrates, the son of Aeaces, who had by insurrection made himself master of the island. At the outset he divided the state into three parts, and shared the kingdom with his brothers, Pantagnotus and Syloson; but later, having killed the former and banished the latter, who was the younger of the two, he held the whole island. Hereupon he made a contract of friendship with Amasis the Egyptian king, sending him gifts, and receiving from him others in return. In a little while his power so greatly increased, that the fame of it went abroad throughout Ionia and the rest of Greece. Wherever he turned his arms, success waited on him. . . .

The exceeding good fortune of Polycrates did not escape the notice of Amasis, who was much disturbed thereat. When therefore his successes continued increasing, Amasis wrote him the following letter, and sent it to Samos. 'Amasis to Polycrates thus sayeth: It is a pleasure to hear of a friend and ally prospering, but thy exceeding prosperity does not cause me joy, forasmuch as I know that the gods are envious. My wish for myself, and for those whom I love is, to be now successful, and now to meet with a check; thus passing through life and alternate good and ill, rather than with perpetual good fortune. For never yet did I hear tell of anyone succeeding in all his undertakings, who did not meet with calamity at last, and come to utter ruin. Now, therefore, give ear to my words, and meet thy good luck in this way: bethink thee which of all thy treasures thou valuest most and can least bear to part with; take it, whatsoever it be, and throw it away, so that it may be sure never to come any more into the sight of man. . . .'

When Polycrates read this letter, and perceived that the advice of Amasis was good, he considered carefully with himself which of the treasures that he had in store it would grieve him most to lose. After much thought he made up his mind that it was a signet-ring, which he was wont to wear, an emerald set in gold . . . and, manning a fifty-oared galley, he went on board, and bade his sailors put out into the open sea. When he was now a long way from the land, he took the ring from his finger, and, in the sight of all those who were on board, flung it into the deep. This done, he returned home, and gave vent to his sorrow.

Now it happened five or six days afterwards that a fisherman caught a fish so large and beautiful that he thought it well deserved to be made a present of to the king, So he took it with him to the gate of the palace, and said that he wanted to see Polycrates. Then Polycrates allowed him to come in, and the fisherman gave him the fish. . . . Meanwhile the servants, on cutting open the fish, found the signet of their master in its belly. No sooner did they see it than they seized upon it, and, hastening to Polycrates with great joy, restored it to him, and told him in what way it had been found. The king, who saw something providential in the matter, forthwith wrote a letter to Amasis, telling him all that had happened. . . .

When Amasis had read the letter of Polycrates, he perceived that it does not belong to man to save his fellow-man from the fate which is in store for him; likewise he felt certain that Polycrates would end ill, as he prospered in everything, even finding what he had thrown away. So he sent a herald to Samos, and dissolved the contract of friendship. This he did, that when the great and heavy misfortune came, he might escape the grief which he would have felt if the sufferer had been his bond-friend.

Herodotus, *The Histories*, folded in Norman Lewis's notebook

Re the Comitato di Liberazione – CSM's remark: "Is there no Conservative party in Italy?"

Girl selling her honour at entrance to Naples.

CSM Drakeley's exploits in selling used tea (dried) to the natives.

OSS looting at Lauro's.

O's cutting pictures out of frames at Princess's palace.

Dashwood offered ½ million for release of Signorini.

Motor car racket conducted by officers. Selling requisitioned cars & saying they have been stolen.

That finely balanced trick of fortune that makes sometimes a Guy Fawkes, sometimes a saint, sometimes a Lenin, sometimes a Lambert Simnel.

Propaganda – get there fastest with the biggest lie.

Lecture by A force [officer] who tells us only to apply for help to the poor and humble "as they have nothing to lose".

Notebook

11

NAPLES '43

"A war leaves three armies:
an army of mourners, an army of cripples
and an army of thieves"
German proverb[1]

IN October 1943 the British public saw on film some of the results of
the Allies' campaign in Italy. In a Ministry of Supply film produced by
Warworks News they saw the high-level bombing of the port of Naples.
The newsreel was entitled "Italy 'Gets It' from North Africa" and its
footage voiced with the parting words, "Good work, America!" A British
Movietone News newsreel, "The Battle for Naples", played scenes of
rousing celebrations as Allied troops entered the city, with the smartly
trimmed voice of Leslie Mitchell assuring viewers that "General Clark
and the 5th Army had arrived" and that the Allies' intention to drive
the Germans from Italy raged unabated. "The main body of the German
forces withdrew in good order, but the Allies are hot on their heels."

Only Roy Boulting's film *Naples Is a Battlefield* put the scene differently, dwelling silently on roofless and skeletised buildings and on a port
that had been bombed into a ruin, its roadstead choked with fat hulls
of drowned ships, its berths marked by twisted cranes clawing at the
sky. By 1 October, when the US Fifth Army entered the city in triumph,
Naples had no fresh water or electricity and food was almost impossible
to find. With water being taken from the sewers, a million and a half
people faced plague and starvation. The city's ordeal had been going on
for ten months. First bombed on 4 December the previous year in a raid
that had left 400 dead, it had been regularly attacked thereafter, and in
the carpet-bombing that had taken place through August and September

to weaken the German occupation, thousands of civilians had been killed. One raid alone, on 4 August, had killed 700. A difference of degree exists between the fate of Naples and that of the firebombed cities of Germany; but only of degree. Norman's notebook records the truth on his entry into the city, that "the last glimpse of the streets is the Movietone man photographing corpses".

For all his time spent in the obnoxious colonial shadows of the north African campaign, Norman was unprepared for the descent into the Dark Ages that Naples turned out to be. No other experience of the war made as deep an impression on him as the first days he spent in the devastated city. More spectator than combatant in the landings at Salerno, he nevertheless witnessed first hand the controlled anarchy of a land offensive. Following Fifth Army west for a month, he expected to find himself doing something like serious counter-intelligence work in a correspondingly chaotic but static mode. Occupied, or liberated, Naples would be a more ruptured and battered version of Tunis or Algiers. He did not expect to be confronted with entropy, bedlam, implosion, an enclosed labyrinth teeming with a million and a half citizens at the limits of restraint and endurance.

The weeks after landing on 9 September were disordered enough. *Naples '44*, the account he published in 1978 of his thirteen months in the city and the template of the invented diary technique he used in his autobiography, is a narrative everywhere scored and coloured by its detached and sensitive remaking, a book that offers its reader intense pleasures of immediacy and volume, of synthesised closeness and shaped chaos, of privileged information and a penetrating gaze cloaked in modest reflection, of judgment that is never rash or arrogant but always firm-minded, all in a sharply realised human sphere: pleasures that would not, in literary terms, have been available at the time. A Naples diary exists from January 1944 onwards: he wrote it in the found, or confiscated, barely begun address book of an educated, possibly dead Neapolitan. It is more detailed and discursive than the red notebook. But for his first months in Italy the hurried notes in his red notebook and his official "Military Police and War Department Constabulary" report book are all we have (and he had in the writing) to go on. More than three decades after the event, he used one-line entries to irrigate seeds of memory that, once germinated, could in his intentional hands be arranged into high display. Waiting on board ship off the coast of Italy again in his mind in the 1970s, he could summon, for instance, a precise incident that symbolised the randomness of fortune in war: the incident became an opening paragraph of perfect appropriateness, told with more spartan clarity than he can have felt at the time, in which 312 FSS, as the only British unit on board the Fifth Army troopship, was "cold-shouldered and left to our own devices" by the Americans, with the exception of "some poker-playing sergeants, probably Mississippi ferry-boat gamblers in civilian life, who remove[d] my poker winnings accumulated in the past year in a half-hour's play".[2]

If *Naples '44* is more a portrait of creative recollection, consciously and subtly nuanced, than of events, his notebooks tell the jumbled version that he experienced, ordered by the unrolling hours. On 9 September he waited the whole day to be landed, and finally went ashore at Paestum that evening. It was 8.30. His section was without its FSO, Captain Cartwright, still in hospital in Oran after a car smash. The section had no orders and the men, ten sergeants and a sergeant-major, pushed their motorbikes off the landing craft past the neatly laid out corpses of men killed earlier in the day and scrambled them into the wood at the top of the beach. To defend themselves they had "a Webley pistol and five rounds of ammunition apiece. Most of us had never fired a gun." The immiscible contrast of war and rural peace came suddenly to them as they emerged from the wood and saw Paestum's three temples glowing pink in the last rays of evening sun. The scene was "of unearthly enchantment . . . an illumination, one of the great experiences of life". More than forty years later he recalled "the shock, the aesthetic shock".[3]

Sleeping in the undergrowth that night, Norman woke to hear movement and German voices that moved away, and slept again. "The walls of Paestum serve as usual as air raid shelters," he scribbled, but a clear-cut enemy was hardly in evidence in the next days. The earliest entries of both notebook and published account replace the German hazard with that of a raw, jumpy and aggressive American ground force whose state of nerves regularly constituted, as it did the following day, "a much greater threat than the FW190 which paid us a visit about once an hour".

Armed hill-billies were constantly jumping out from behind a hedge to point their rifles at us and scream a demand for an answer to a password that nobody had bothered to give us.[4]

He and his section, Norman felt, were seasoned in small but important ways and had mentally adapted to "a relative loss of security, and minor dangers". In the notebook he "note[d] how one sleeps through our howitzer bombardment from next field but is awakened by the faint whine of an 88 shell from the other side".

With the proper superiority of a soldier with nearly a year's field service he judged the American HQ troops unadapted, having been shipped straight out "from the eternal peace of places like Kansas and Wisconsin". There continued to be no orders and, isolated from an indifferent HQ, Norman felt further isolated as the newcomer within the section. Two days into the landings, on 11 September, panicky American gunners were still committing the act now known by the excusing oxymoron of "friendly fire" – "3rd Spitfire brought down by US ack-ack", he wrote[5] – and Fifth Army HQ was moving east in an unreal calm to Albanella Stazione south of the Sele river, where he was fascinated by "Blue grasshoppers in the olive grove" and incredulous to hear from Americans of 45th Division that their officers had ordered them to take no prisoners and to beat to death with their rifle butts any Germans who tried to surrender.

On the 12th the war arrived suddenly. There was a gas alarm. "Situation 'liquid'," he wrote. "HQ stated to be moving back from Ricciardo's [Casa Ricciardo at Casa Barone]." American tanks rolled forward. "Tank battle about 3½ miles away." Very soon the tanks were back, driven erratically and reduced in number. "45th div. lose 7 out of 17 – officers scram."[6]

The battle for the beachhead lasted through the 13th and 14th, with tanks from 16th Panzer Division being shelled from offshore and American officers continuing to pull out and abandon their men who, without command, were unnerved and began shooting each other. Four 312 FSS members were quixotically ordered by their sergeant-major, Dashwood, to try to get through to Salerno to locate their FSO and some orders.

On the 15th one of the sergeants returned. Amazingly he had found Captain Cartwright, who ordered the section to make its way to Salerno by any possible means. A command car was found but the next day, Norman noted,

decision reversed owing to lack of space in jeep. Later hear officer in charge arranging for transport of wine in same vehicle.[7]

On the 17th, still kicking his heels at Fifth Army HQ, he went sight-seeing as far as the villages of Capaccio, where he saw his first dead German and took pictures, and Ogliastro Cilento. This incongruous life of leisure went on, giving the curious reporter time to observe. On the 18th, on a circumspect excursion to the Salerno road, he saw shelled German tanks and a puddle of human fat under one burnt-out wreck "quilted with brilliant flies of all descriptions and colours". He stayed in Giungano, a hill village founded when the Saracens had threatened Paestum, and had his first quiet night.

On the 20th he finally began moving up to Salerno by jeep through the "shambles" of Battipaglia. General Mark Clark's wild tactics had brought in heavy bombers and made a Guernica of it. There was looting at "Castello Castelluccia where CSM [Dashwood] manifested embarrassment at perquisitioning" by officers. In Salerno Norman found that Fifth Army were "Still shelling [German] mortars in mountains behind"[8] whose bombs were falling close to security headquarters. He also witnessed the episode he later described as the "most revolting episode I have seen since joining the forces", of an Allied interrogating officer repeatedly beating an Italian civilian around the head with a chair, then soliciting his murder. Unnamed in *Naples '44*, the officer was a Cambridge-educated Australian named Jack Horsfall.[9] In January 1945 Captain Horsfall was mentioned in dispatches for his work in interrogating Italian prisoners. The performance between the officer and a private standing by, overheard by Norman – "Horsefall [sic] to Hampshire pvt. 'Would you like to shoot this man?' 'I don't mind if I do sir' (spitting on his hands)"[10] – may have been purely theatrical, intended to break the prisoner's defences, but Norman felt he had seen a failed interrogation and an icy act of barbarism, which the Italian detainee, "his face a mask of blood, suffered with stoicism".

On the 23rd Captain Cartwright ordered half the section, including Norman, back to Paestum, as it was still officially attached to Clark's erratic headquarters. On the return journey Norman spoke to an American paratrooper of 509th Airborne who confirmed another disaster of the chaotic campaign. The paratroopers' objective on the night of the 13th had been the Avellino bridge and tunnel: instead many of the Americans' planes had dropped them off target "in the middle of [a] car pool and about 15,000 G[erman] troops. 116 back so far out of 600."[11]

At Paestum there was nothing to do, except drift into something like the kind of absurd refinements practised by the Sybarites who founded it. In the middle of an invasion and a theatre of war the section sunned itself, studied the temples, read poetry, practised its Italian and, when bored, strolled to the beach to catch an instant or two of the aerial ballet of Allied naval guns retaliating against the last of the FW190s. Probably fortunately, Norman – unlike Polycrates – met with mishap and on the 28th was removed from this place of content and admitted to the 16th Evacuation Hospital with a re-infection of malaria, where five days later the tent he lay in blew down in a storm and flood that carried away his kit (but spared his camera and notebook). Discharged on 5 October, in a borrowed US private's uniform and without clear orders, he decided to make for Naples, which Fifth Army had entered four days before.

"In early October, 1943," John Horne Burns wrote in his episode-masterpiece *The Gallery*, "Naples was a city of chaos,

of movement with no purpose, of charnel smells, of rain, of army truck head-lights coming out of the mist like eyes without lids. The shoe was on the other foot now: the Germans had taken over bombing the town as soon as they'd vacated the premises in favor of the Fifth Army. After the sun set through the fall rains, the few who dared go abroad stumbled their way over sidewalks in a close dreadful blackness. There wasn't a light, except from the truck convoys. Corpses were let lie where they fell, creasing and bloating from the rain. Living Neapolitans stripped the clothing from them: the living needed the cloth. The city's sewage had all backed up in a spasm of vomiting, like stomachs nauseated with war. What stench didn't renege from the bay wafted through the ruptured mains in the streets. There were red whispers of typhus, and prayers that it was true that the Americans had a new disinfectant. And in the daytime the poor sun squeaking through the rains showed a spectacle more ghoulish than you imagined by darkness.[12]

"Girl selling her honour at entrance to Naples," Norman noted,[13] a note he expanded in *Naples '44* to describe the reality of Neapolitan wives and mothers offering themselves for sex in the town hall of Torre del Greco on the outskirts for the price of a tin of army rations. His descriptions of his entry into Naples, and of the city itself, match Burns's in *The Gallery*, though he writes with a more dispassionate impartiality of the city's residents "stood in their doorways, faces the colour of pumice, to wave mechanically to the victors",[14] of the city's smell of charred wood and burst drains and its landslides of rubble, and of the starvation that drove people to walk miles out of town to strip the roadsides of dandelions. In his official notebook he noted that "The Americans made the V sign but the Italians didn't know whether this represented victory or spaghetti at 2 o'clock".[15]

Glutted by the palaces and churches of the Kingdom of Two Sicilies, Naples had been the last continental stop on the summer Grand Tour. Now honoured as the first city on the Allies' tour of European liberation, its magnificence was hard to perceive among the vileness and contagion they had inflicted on it. Norman's section was lucky: 312 FSS found itself installed in a discreet but outstandingly located and decorated palazzo, the Satriano at 287 riviera di Chiaia, on the elegant sash of Naples' seafront. Chiaia – the district behind the seafront and piazza Vittoria, which the security headquarters on the principal floor overlooked – became his village: the place where he lived, in a boarding house on via Giuseppe Martucci, worked, and drank, at the tiny Bar Vittoria facing the sea, a dusty place specialising in *marsala all'uovo*. Chiaia's first virtue that he remembered was – as elsewhere in the city – its domestic life, lived openly on the street from morning onwards. In the via Calabritto, running down the side of his office, he saw how "Quite early, a family living in the house opposite carried out a table and stood it in the street.

This was briskly covered with a green cloth with tassels. Chairs were placed around it at an exact distance apart and on it were stood several framed photographs, a vase of artificial flowers, a small cage containing a goldfinch, and several ornate little glasses which were polished from time to time as the day passed by to remove the dust. Round this table the family lived in what was in fact a room without walls; a mother, grandfather and grandmother, a girl in her late teens, and two dynamic boys, who constantly came and went. Here the mother attended to the girl's hair, washed the boys' faces, served something from a steaming pot at mid-day, sewed and did the family washing in the afternoon. There were a number of other such tables along the street, and constant social migrations took place as neighbours paid each other visits.[16]

In *Naples '44* he returns repeatedly to the city's quality of determined routine in its deserts of bomb damage. It is present in the dignified person of Vincenzo Lattarullo (he doesn't write very good Italian and spells the name "Vincente"), the emaciated lawyer he befriended, of his friends the Gemellis, of Lo Scalzo, the one incorruptible police marshal he met, and of many of the young women he had to vet for their genuineness as war brides. Many of these women were, or clearly had been, prostitutes, and Norman's comprehending attitude caused him eventually to fall out with his FSO. His friend Sergio Viggiani remembers that in the 1970s when they went to Naples together, "He [Norman] said, 'You know, some of these girls were prostitutes by necessity, they had to be, there was nothing else they could do, so when I used to do the assessments, I used to write that the best, the most faithful wives are ex-prostitutes. Somehow their morality is detached from their business activity.'"[17]

At the start of his Naples duties he was less reflective. He was overwhelmed by the matter of being one of only four sergeants dealing with, on top of the usual vetting procedures and security alarms, the energetic denunciations and residual Fascist activity of the entire city. (Within days of arriving two thirds of 312 FSS had been detailed to work outside Naples. Only he and three others, Parkinson, Evans and Durham, remained.) The section had inherited the archives of the Questura – the central police office – and the Fascist contact files from the German consulate. A massive sifting had to be carried out against a background torrent of arriving informers, good and bad, useful and malicious. On his first day, 8 October, he visited the suburb of Ponticelli, the Socialist headquarters at Torre Annunziata – a place he would often visit – met a Dr Reale, and at 6 p.m. was at the palazzo Schlitzer. Within two days the first neatly entered names of subjects for investigation in his report book gave way to hasty scribbles: "HERRMETER, Giovanni, born DOBBIACO – 1887, automatically Italian 1919 – never visited Germany." His fellow sergeants he found hard-working, the section ethos more bureaucratic than before. In 312 FSS civilian clothes were not worn nor spot passes issued. "Military Police and War Department Constabulary" notebooks had to be carried at all times, their daily notes to be condensed as a log submitted to the FSO and discussed at each morning's formal parade.

Captain Cartwright was not always welcomely different from Norman's previous officers. "Cartwright's rudeness, 'Get out' to parachutist," he noted, and he identified a verbal habit of the officer's that he disliked. "FSO orders [the] sgt-major not to use the word please in his instructions to us . . . Cartwright's insistence on 'it is requested that' to avoid the courtesy of the word 'please'."[18] If an officer failed to show signs of paranoia, was rudeness the next fault with which to belabour him? One wonders whether all Norman's officers were predestined to crack in the heat of his caste-conscious gaze.

Early security problems among the Allies' own troops in and around
Naples were chiefly about looting. Casualties included the paintings
and porcelain of the palazzo della Principessa and everything moveable in the opulent residence of the mayor of Naples, Achille Lauro,
then in custody. Looting was generally the preserve of officers, Norman
noticed, sometimes with the collusion of the Navy as getaway drivers.
Army units were also an annoyance by their habit of inciting false
alarms and wild goose chases. A kind of totalitarianism was enshrined
in the regulations imposed by AMGOT, the Allied military government, which behaved, quite incorrectly, as a conquering power. The
Neapolitans had liberated themselves and, in the Four Days of
Naples,[19] driven the Germans from the city before General Clark
entered it in triumph, but under AMGOT they were subject to relentless supervision, with ruthless and vindictively applied penalties.
Everything they did that deviated from narrow norms, however innocent, was loaded with suspicion. Mail and phone lines were tapped.
The absurdity of officious intervention was enshrined in one telephone intercept transcript received at the palazzo Satriano headed
"Illegal use of telescope": the intercepted conversation between two
lovers contained the sentence, whispered by the woman, "I can't see
you today because my husband will be here, but I'll admire you, as
ever, through love's telescope."[20]

An inevitable participant in the imposition of control, Norman made
links with the population, as he had in north Africa, among the stream
of informers arriving daily at the palazzo Satriano. He understood
better how to judge and befriend the more useful ones, and the best
gave him a wide spectrum of observation. If he or she was of any use,
"informer" was rapidly elevated to "informant", then "contact". Most
came from the professional classes, Norman noticed, and every one
was loyal to only one master, "like a duckling newly freed from its
shell and in need of fostering". In mid-October he made the acquaintance of the lawyer Lattarullo, who would become one of his most
highly valued sources. Struck by Lattarullo's shabbiness and whispered
ardour for justice, his sympathy was roused when he realised the man
was starving.

Lattarullo was a collector's item, and Norman particularly cherished
the idea of his other profession, as a *zio di Roma*. Naples is a city of
theatre, a permanent stage. Whether as the result of centuries of playing
the role of the defeated to the strings of Norman, Angevin, Habsburg

and Bourbon kings who have occupied its royal residences, or whether from a pure love of drama – *recitare* – its citizens are natural performers. In their speech there is an inventive drama in the delivery of Neapolitan dialect that outstrips the natural expansiveness of other Italians,[21] and as a result of their willingness to put a joyful front on reality or drama-tise it somehow, Neapolitans have probably never felt themselves to be truly defeated. A traditional expression of the city's desire for display among citizens of restricted income was in the figure of the *zio di Roma*, the "uncle from Rome" who, dressed in tailored morning suit and conducting himself with patrician reserve, was hired to appear at funerals to dignify the corpse's send-off. The starving lawyer had been one of these. No "uncle" ever came from the capital, the part being played by an educated professional supplementing his scant income (the city was surfeited with *avvocati* and *dottori*) who would offer himself for such occasions of theatre, speaking on his arrival about his journey down on the Rome express or showing up in a heavily borrowed Alfa-Romeo with a Roman plate.

October was busy in the city. On the 7th a delayed-action charge set by the Germans blew up the main Post Office, killing a hundred people, including women, children and members of an 82nd Airborne unit. A stream of (false) alarms about mined buildings, including the section's palazzo, followed. A report was received that a squad of SS was concealed in the San Gennaro catacombs: Italian police, a unit of US counter-intelligence, and 312 FSS raided the tunnels and found nothing apart from, as Norman wrote, a "civilian challenged by [a] sentry, with his trousers down".[22] On the 20th sporadic but destruc-tive German air raids began. Three days later the population was ordered out of the city to the heights of the Vomero, after more rumours that the Germans had set thousands of mines to detonate when the switch was thrown to restore the electrical grid. Awaiting the cataclysm, Norman looked down and appreciated the city's splendour, cleaned by distance of the war's damage, and realised how oriental it looked. "Nothing moved but a distant floating confetti of doves."[23] No explosion disrupted the majestic silence, and next day Norman was sent to Poggioreale prison to interrogate the seventeen-year-old German who had surren-dered in order to spread the rumour among his captors. Knowing that military opinion was tending to the view that the boy was a spy who in the usual course of things would be shot, Norman reported instead that he was mentally unbalanced.

The section's workload continued to be heavy. Occasionally off duty, Norman began to acquire a taste for the city's improvised existence, in which as far as possible neither the war nor politics, shortages, or the rumours of typhus were mentioned. One of his first acts was to go to Casella's bookstore and buy "an excellent print" of the temples at Paestum, animated by "a splendid collection of buffaloes". He bought paintings from Ciro Gallo's functioning gallery in via Chiatamone, and was invited to dinners at which from somewhere food – sometimes German – and good wine were conjured. (General Clark had benefited handsomely from the city's culinary ingenuity: it was universally believed that, ordered to produce a celebratory banquet, Neapolitan chefs had fished out and cooked the contents of the city's aquarium, the dinner's centrepiece a boiled baby manatee in garlic sauce.)

Gaining insights into the city's social organisation, Norman found that its hierarchical structure and sexual attitudes embraced extremes, possessing an aristocracy pauperised to a level lower than its working class by being unable, for reasons of social pride, to work, and a gamut of sexual practice that ran from obligatory conjugal visits at midday to the thriving business of hymenal restoration for brides. He became familiar with the smiling corruption of the police, the Army's impotent struggle to control the most successful mafia black market of all time, and the regional appetite for scheming and vendetta.

A lingering quality of *Naples '44* is its sense of a city conveyed without mediation or reservation: a city liberated but under siege: possibly, as the Italian novelist Curzio Malaparte judged it, the most wretched city in war-torn Europe. One of the strongest appeals of the city remains its quality of paradigm, its Naples-ness or *napoletanità*, that offers both definitiveness and elusiveness in its account of humanity's struggle: "its perverse complexity robes itself in naturalness, as an eternal dispensation . . . it is the almost perfect replica in miniature of the conflicts that gash the Universe", as the writer Maria Vittoria Vittori has it.[24] Naples may not be a permanent stage then: it is, instead, a permanent actor, its citizens its accessories. This ambiguous quality is one that *Naples '44* seems to recognise: in Norman's hands nothing is left out of the microcosm, from the tyrannical ineptness of its Allied authorities and its typhus epidemic (long considered a humiliating taboo) to the passing glimpses of *scugnizzi* masturbating happily in a fountain or of a dinner of notables, including a director of the Banco di Roma, whose high-light in the midst of famine conditions is a spaghetti-eating contest.

Resonant by its accumulation of detail, free of mystique despite being the account of an outsider, his reconstituted diary attains to the status of a kind of documentary symphony – a composition more than the sum of its incidents and tones, closer to a rhythm that might be that of the city itself: a city of paradigmatically determined character. "*Si vedrà chi ha più pazienza, la guerra o Napoli*," as Malaparte writes in his novel *Kaputt*. "Let's see who has more patience, the war or Naples."

Given the city's "chunk of myth",[25] and the distance in time at which Norman was writing, it is unsurprising that not all the episodes he records ring factually true. A sparse, elaborately presented lunch that Lattarullo invited him to, for instance, framed an invitation to Norman by a friend of Lattarullo's, a *cavaliere* Visco, to take up a commission at the end of his present commitments in a separatist army being planned by a group dedicated to restoring the Kingdom of the Two Sicilies. The secessionists' justification was that with the collapse of fascism there was bound to be a leftward swing in Italian politics (to be avoided at all costs). The drawback to the story is that in Norman's notes Lattarullo's name is mentioned with the words "Socialist Party" in parenthesis and an *avvocato* Visco is reckoned to be of "no party" and the "best contact for vetting lists [of civilian workers] once a week".[26] Even if (another) Visco was a separatist, the encounter bears too strong a resemblance to Norman's previous separatist meeting in the Arabian gardens of the exquisite vice-Bey of Tunis. The story without doubt reflects a slice of Neapolitan feeling at the time, and reflects too Norman's powers of invention in the face of his scant notes for his first three months in the city.

Another thread of *Naples '44* that owes more to the future novelist than to the witnessing sergeant is the chronicle of Captain Frazer and Lola. Met at a dinner, the woman Lola appeared at security headquarters with a request. Would Norman negotiate with her lover, a British captain who spoke no Italian? Frazer, a captain in the Royal Army Service Corps with sexually attractive access to unlimited quantities of bread and other necessities, turned out to be inexperienced in erotic matters, though a dandy in his dress. Lola's main concern, according to Norman, was that her neighbours were starting to talk because the captain never called on her during the day; Frazer was told by Norman that he would have to match the keenness of Neapolitan couples for lunchtime sex if he wished to be taken seriously. Frazer's own concerns, voiced later in private, were, firstly, that he had found his lover's bottom minutely scarred with hundreds of pinpricks, and secondly that he suspected her of carrying on an affair with a senior Neapolitan bank official. He was also made nervous, he told Norman, both by her claim that her late husband had made love to her every night, continuing until she had had at least six orgasms, and by her habit of watching her bedside clock while he, Frazer, made love to her. Norman advised him to drink *marsala all'uovo* like the locals "and to wear a medal of San Rocco, patron of *coitus reservatus*". For the other items he reassured him that Lola's buttocks probably bore no more than the evidence of the usual fortifying injections dispensed in Naples pharmacies to keep her sexual powers up to scratch, and asked him if he was really prepared for the expense of keeping Lola to himself, at around £10 a week, on a captain's pay. Through most of *Naples '44* the comic stages of Lola's and Captain Frazer's relationship counterpoint the city's own burdens of existence. In reality, fractions of their intimacy, doomed to inconclusion, were happening to soldiers in every Allied unit in the city – Neapolitan women took sexual attachment seriously, which did not mean they had no intention of enjoying it, only that hunger was their overriding concern – and, as a literary object, the shaping of those myriad fractions into a single story has an enjoyable credibility and a useful moral to offer. Who exactly is liberating whom? As a factual history, however, Frazer and Lola are unsupported by any notes or names in Norman's Naples notebooks.

Another story related to the sexual attitudes of Neapolitans probably is true. A man mentioned as "Prince A" and already known to Norman as an enthusiastic informant from the riviera di Chiaia area, appeared one day at security headquarters with his sister to enquire whether Norman could arrange for her, as a way of earning enough to support them both, to enter an army brothel. "We explained that there was no such institution in the British Army. 'A pity,' the prince said. 'Ah, well, Luisa, I suppose if it can't be, it can't be.' They thanked us with polite calm, and departed."[27] My own Naples informants, who included a duke and a marquis, assured me that no "Prince A" had existed in riviera di Chiaia, but agreed it was completely possible that an ordinary Neapolitan of the ruined middle classes, seeking advantage with the occupiers, should set up as a destitute nobleman. More theatre.

One matter Norman did note was a week of depression. "12th–18th Dec. Cafard."[28] Why he should experience depression at this moment is as hard to say as it is of anyone at any time. He was tired after three months of Naples' misery and frustrated by the army authorities he represented, but he was also busy, involved, out of England. He was lonely after not seeing Hester for five months; but was up and doing. He felt tension between his situation and the Neapolitans' and hated making arrests; the impossibility of making any positive impact was getting to him – everywhere people looked to him to put things right and he couldn't – but he had made genuine friendships. He felt, again, outside the group, isolated from his section's *esprit de corps*; but the warmth of his contacts with Neapolitans compensated. And so on. The causes of depression make a bad guessing game – coached as we all are in glib histories of disorder to be snap psychotherapists, couch clinicians; better perhaps to describe its context and, as in life, be ready as a reader to sit it out with him.

One incident, though, does stand out. Thirty-odd years later he recalled sitting in an unheated restaurant near piazza Victoria with Vincente Lattarullo and seeing six orphaned girls "between the ages of nine and twelve" appearing in the doorway. They wore hideous black institutional dresses and were crying. As they groped their way between the tables, he saw that they were blind. The other diners paid no attention. The experience, he wrote, changed his outlook. The intensity of the memory – expressed in *Naples '44* in language of unprecedented emotional vehemence – perhaps indicates that the tragedy and despair he had been thrust into in Naples had not only touched him, but triggered something below the threshold of his conscious emotional apparatus.

I expected the indifferent diners to push back their plates, to get up and hold out their arms, but nobody moved. Forkfuls of food were thrust into open mouths, the rattle of conversation continued, nobody saw the tears. . . . Until now I had clung to the comforting belief that human beings eventually come to terms with pain and sorrow. Now I understood I was wrong, and like Paul I suffered a conversion – but to pessimism. These little girls, any one of whom could be my daughter, came into the restaurant weeping, and they were weeping when they were led away. I knew that, condemned to everlasting darkness, hunger and loss, they would weep on incessantly. They would never recover from their pain, and I would never recover from the memory of it.[29]

What experience, one wonders, could have given him his initial optimism that people come to terms with pain and sorrow? We might, I think, suppose with some justification that it was paradoxically his own, accumulated in his own childhood; and that his way of "coming to terms" with his sorrow had been to shut it away. Now the sight of these half-dozen orphaned, famished, blind children stumbling through an unconcerned restaurant had opened the container he kept it in. Since Sigmund Freud wrote his essay "Mourning and Melancholia", the belief has existed that depression can be seen as eventually adaptive. In Norman's case that might perhaps mean an eventual realisation that he needed to feel his sorrow and pain, not shut it away, before he could feel more fully human. Generally, however, the process of adaptation takes rather longer than it does to describe it, and, before depression leads the subject to alter his or her patterns of feeling, it often roughly expresses the contrary, a flat denial of the call to change.

Perhaps, and perhaps, and perhaps. To my mind, the most helpful part of trying to understand Norman's predicament is the opportunity it offers to recall that sympathy is our mechanism for never being able to know the objective truth about another life (and not just because such truth doesn't exist). What *can* be said for certain is that two weeks before Christmas 1943 something – his word for it was the distancing French term *cafard* – happened that had not happened before (or not been written down), and – I'll say it since we know the future – would happen again.

Naples was in the throes of the "plague".

Curzio Malaparte, *The Skin*

Without water the Neapolitans could not wash their clothes or their bodies. As they became progressively more dirty they became better and better hosts for body lice which carry typhus fever. In the crowded slums of the half-homeless city these typhus-carrying lice crawled from one person to another spreading the infection as they went.

Life magazine

There was an epidemic of typhus in Naples last week – not the mild kind that lurks in some US rats and mice, but the European epidemic typhus that kills 20 out of 100 victims and held up the Austrian attack on Serbia in World War I.

Time magazine

But Malaparte's opening operates a narrative double bluff: this is a metaphorical plague, which would have given the book its title, if Camus had not got in first. The plague is the false relationship between the Neapolitans and the Allied forces, who present themselves as benevolent liberators and see the Neapolitans as defeated and contemptible enemies.

John Gatt-Rutter

... with our Hollywood ethics and our radio network reasoning we didn't take the trouble to think out that the war was supposed to be against fascism – not against every man, woman, and child in Italy. ...

I remember the crimes we committed against the Italians, as I watched them in Naples. In the broadest sense we promised the Italians security and democracy if they came over to our side. All we actually did was to knock the hell out of their system and give them nothing to put in its place.

John Horne Burns, *The Gallery*

12

NAPLES '44

"This is the world. Some sail. Some sink"
Neapolitan proverb

Two US Navy sailors stand on a precarious Naples balcony. One photographs the other, who has an arm curled around each of two young women and a rueful, half-ashamed, half-greedy got-lucky look on his face as each hand squeezes a breast. Pulled in towards him, the women's expressions are more timid, their smiles more forced. Among the innumerable photographs of the Naples occupation this one seems to stand out: the tension in the three subjects' faces expresses not debauch or corruption – brothels licensed and unlicensed were everywhere, and the euphemism *casa de tolleranza* suggests acceptance of an army's needs – but a particular relation between power and repugnance. Neapolitans had been forced into hunger and squalor by the wasting of their city, and the Allied forces did not let them forget their situation of inferiority. The outburst by Colonel Jack Hamilton, one of the fictional US officers in Malaparte's *The Skin*, as his uniform is rumpled by the press of the crowd on via Toledo – "This bastard people! ... This bastard, dirty people" – is a signature of their occupiers' attitude towards them.[1] The shame of the sailor in the photograph is, in part, the shame of hatred, of having descended to the Neapolitan level.

The relationship between occupied and occupiers was institutionalised in the typhus outbreak that winter, when the number of cases increased from 55 in the month of November to 41 in the first nine days of December. Wide areas of the city were made out of bounds to troops and delousing with shakers and pump dusters of the new "miracle dust", DDT, mixed with talcum powder began on the 16th. "Contact delousing" was liberally interpreted by the medical teams; altogether 1,300,000 people, almost the entire population, were dusted. Afterwards, according to the Naples historian Sergio Lambiase, Neapolitans remained humiliated enough by the disease and by the authoritarian application of US disinfectant measures to censor the epidemic from public consciousness for many years.[2] Malaparte went further, writing that Neapolitans believed the Allies, who mysteriously remained immune, had introduced both the typhus and its cure – which, though not in the way he meant it, was certainly true, as they had wasted the city and created the conditions for infection.

In the diary Norman started on New Year's Day – an outcome of his *cafard* as he mobilised good intentions into keeping a regular record?[3] – the first entry notes another sign of pestilence that the authorities laid at the Neapolitans' door, quoting a circular letter informing all units that prostitution and the soliciting of troops in Naples in particular had reached a pitch greater than had ever been witnessed in Italy before, and that the encouragement of prostitution was part of a formulated plan of pro-Axis elements in the population to spread sexually transmitted disease among Allied troops and obtain information from them.[4] The circular ignored the fact that it was a criminal offence in Italian law to pass on syphilis and that, with a far lower incidence of sexually transmitted disease in the German-occupied north because of strict surveillance by the Germans of their brothels, the reintroduction of venereal bacteria in southern Italy had largely coincided with the arrival of Fifth Army. The circular was followed by messages printed in Italian and English in army newspapers for troops to cut out and show to any Italian approaching them: messages that would have been insulting without the reference to the recipient's sister.

ATTENTION! I have no interest in your syphilitic friends, much less your sister.

The allied troops are not in Italy to admire Vesuvius or to catch diseases. No! We are here to win the war and to make Italy free once again. Why don't you help?[5]

Not offensive in every case, the linguistic traffic of the occupation was lasting and demonstrative. In Napoli dialect the word "*sichinenza*" from "secondhand" still means "of little or no value", "*sciuscià*" is still used for "shoeshine". The popular song "Tammurriata nera", about the birth of a black baby to a Neapolitan mother and the efforts

of Neapolitans to assimilate this disturbing phenomenon, is familiar to
Italians, voicing both the shock of the wartime irruption of ethnic diversity into Naples' homogeneous ethnicity (many Allied troops were black
Americans, north Africans, Indians) and the willingness of Neapolitans
to excuse so much by the occult power of the eye: "all a girl needs [to
be impregnated] is a look".

At the beginning of January Norman's duties were added to when
he was also put in charge of security in several towns north of the city.
His diary for January provides a compact biopsy of his workload and
of the organism of greater Naples under occupation.

Jan 2   Went to Succivo and Sant'Arpino to investigate case of CALLISTI
imprisoned as a result of vendetta with CC RR [Carabinieri Reali] Maresciallo
ALTAMURA arising out of the reprisals taken by G[ermans] – 24 shot – at Orta
di Atella, following CALLISTI's guerrilla activities.[6]

The entry lets in a crack of light on a complicated story. The massacre
at Orta di Atella would be source material after the war for his second
novel *Within the Labyrinth*; paradoxically it is part-fictionalised in
Naples '44, at least to the extent that in the book his visit takes place
in December and all the names are changed (Callisti becomes Giovanni
Albano, Altamura becomes Marshal Benvenuto, Orta di Atella becomes
Torrito). Investigation of the case – the capture by Callisti's partisans
of two Germans, the assumption by the SS that they had been killed,
the hurried massacre of reprisal at the crossroads – was made more
complex by its location in the bandit- and vendetta-ridden *zona di
Camorra* and Norman's suspicion that the situation was being manipulated by the thuggish marshal to avoid blame. He returned there in
the afternoon two days later.

Jan 4   Unsuccessful *perquisizione* [search] of ROSSI, Pasquale at Portici. Succivo
and S. Arpino afternoon.
    Parky [Sgt Parkinson] complains that his prospective m[other]-in-law objects
to his professional association with German women.

Another pressing concern was an outbreak of cable-cutting on the
Ponticelli road, classed as sabotage by the authorities but mostly carried
out for the value of the copper. At Poggioreale prison he interviewed
a suspect whose case was a perfect example of the misapplication of

Allied justice, with large-scale criminals using every resource to beat the rap and minor suspects having to take it.

Jan 5   PRIORE Antonio aged 80 [arrested] for taking wire to bind faggots. Half insane, deaf, didn't know what was happening. Had been in prison for 2 months, trial having been postponed by mistake on 4 previous occasions: no transport available from prison. Held at disposition of CIC [Counter-Intelligence Corps] etc. Remanded on our request to a superior court owing to gravity of offence.

(The request for remand was Norman's roundabout effort to prevent the old man being lost for good in the freezing prison.) Duties that after three months in the city might have seemed challengingly mundane now evoke a Fellini-like storyboard of fantasy, invention, and irrational inversion of justice.

Jan 6   Commenced work in the case of Prof[essore] dott[ore] Forte,[7] midget gynaecologist, said to require a step ladder to mount his gynaecological couch. Suspected of being central collecting agent [for] messages to Rome.

Jan 7   More wire-cutting [on the] Ponticelli road. Parky's story of the black marketeer sentenced to a year. [Wrote a] letter smuggled out of Poggio Reale for 100L. explaining system to his wife. Wife goes to brothel and pays 4000L. to a prostitute there who goes to the American captain involved and impersonates her. As a result of the ensuing seduction husband is released next day after doing a month.

Shops full of the most sugary sweets, *torrone*, marzipan – all from black market. But no bread.

Citizens being disinfected in the streets against typhus. No vaccine, little medicine.

Jan 8   Lattarullo reports case of American officer demanding 100,000 lire not to requisition [a] car. Finally accepted photo outfit said to be worth 40,000.

His entry that day also included a warning to himself, "Note: gradual onset of enthusiasm for security. Hope mania for sleuthing will disappear rapidly after the war." Some stories made his enthusiasm excusable,

Jan 11   The leader of the women's *fascio* [Fascist party] who had highly original though transitory affairs with very young boys who she took on horseback rides and subsequently paid 50L, and three days later he heard a bizarre sequel to the circular about VD.

Jan 14   Story of the pro[stitute]s enlisted for A force and S force, trained for the job and then turned loose on the streets when the idea was dropped.

Twenty attractive but infected prostitutes had been induced to sign on for a plan of infiltration that involved their being sent into German-occupied Italy to infect as many German troops as possible; a plan that had ended when the women rebelled at the thought of economic and medical stringency in the north and of being separated from their pimps. A-Force, incredibly, had ended the plan by turning the women loose again without treatment into Naples itself.

Further incompetence materialised three days before the planned Anzio landings.

Jan 19   35 maps of operational significance left in warehouse in Torre Annunziata. Civilians taking them away to make a fire – about 500 had previously been strewn about on the floor of the warehouse in question.

The rest of January was full of similar investigations: a deserter claiming to be a member of 3 FSS had to be questioned, a mass arrest of letter-passers took place in piazza Dante (it was a spying offence to send or take messages to German-occupied territory), and the chief of the transport office at the Municipio was investigated for taking bribes and losing (i.e. selling) requisitioned cars. On 22 January the Anzio landings took place more or less unopposed despite the security breach (though bombardment of the bridgehead by long-range guns and Luftwaffe bombers two days later sowed heavy casualties in a tightly packed landing force). On the 27th Norman went with his friend Gennaro to a "private dance" where the "Baronessa Marino asks for some louse powder on the occasion of our next visit". By early February he had given up hope of seeing justice done in the AMGOT[8]-administered courts, after he attended the trial of the Arcari brothers,[9] arrested as agents for letter-passing.

Feb 4   Arcari family tried at Castello Capuano. Farcical situation in which the procurator had not familiarised himself with the case, did not know which of the persons concerned had been brought to trial and had lost the translations of the letters.

Bed with malaria afternoon.

Raising himself for the Arcari brothers' sentencing next day, he noted with disgust "Alberto 2 months, Giovanni 3 months". On the 6th, bedridden with a temperature of 102, he was admitted to 92nd General Hospital, not eating for two and a half days and developing jaundice, but, left to the sudden freedom of his mind's fever-provoked wanderings, dreaming the "first portentous dream for many years. Riding on the back of an enormous shaggy ox of which I was slightly afraid, through the scenes of my childhood. Special attention was paid to the church. A religious atmosphere seems frequently to be present in such childhood reminiscent dreams."

A group of Polish soldiers he had become friends with visited him, spreading anti-bacterial alarm among hospital staff. "Arrival of Poles bearing lofty feathers in their headgear. Consternation amounting almost to panic on the part of Hospital staff. Major directs that beds in the vicinity be disinfested [sic]."[10]

The episode became a perfect archetype of the reordering (or fictional) process that events underwent when Norman came to write Naples '44. The narrator of the published version went down with malaria on 7 June, not 6 February as in his diary (which also notes that from 4–11 June he was actually on leave); and the Poles who triggered the disinfection alarm were stripped out of the story. All that remained was their offending feathers, worn in Naples '44 by two of the procession of Norman's more literarily useful but invented or embellished Neapolitan visitors – Lattarullo, his friend Del Giudice, the trusted marshal Lo Scalzo, "Donna Maria Fidora, the ex-python wrestler from Caivano", "a sincere but saturnine-looking member of the Camorra of Afragola", and Lola and her friend Susanna "in slave-jewellery" and, crucially, spicing panic with disapproval, "feathered head-dresses".[11]

He was out of hospital on 20 February: its legacy two filthy French poems that he copied in his diary and a new clarity and motivation, he felt, "a general heightening of the enthusiasms" (given the poems, he presumably included sexual enthusiasm) – "coupled with a new found more objective view of things in general. Effect of malaria, or rest?" He returned to duty to take part in the counter-attack on the black market. It was believed that by the end of February the contents of one Allied ship in three docking at the port of Naples were vanishing. Of extraordinary significance in the criminality of the whole Bay of Naples area was Vito Genovese, who had fled the USA after his employer, Charles "Lucky" Luciano, was arrested in 1936 for his takeover of

New York's brothels. Genovese had succeeded in attaching himself to Mussolini's coat-tails, then, when Mussolini fell, to the Allied military government in Sicily, where he had become a pillar of the Sicilian-American mafia revival, at first employed as interpreter to the US military governor of Sicily, Lieutenant-Colonel Charles Poletti, and rapidly a major stock-holder in the Sicilian black market. In February 1944, when Poletti was moved to Naples as Regional Commissioner for Naples, Salerno, Benevento and Avellino, Genovese followed him. With the kind of irony for which war is not quite worthwhile, Poletti's transfer was intended to speed the clean-up of known Fascists in southern Italy. As an ex-governor of New York and an Italian-American with the common touch, he was profiled in *Time* on 1 May 1944.

It did not take long for Lieut. Colonel Poletti to put war-shocked Naples on the way toward recovery. Now the city gets regular street washings. Over the radio the Regional Commissioner appeals to Italian patriotism to help stamp out black markets. He has granted labor unions collective bargaining, encouraged a manufacturers' association. In Naples he has installed veteran anti-Fascist administrators.

At the same time as Poletti was repainting his *prefettura* and seeing all callers, Genovese and his network of Italian patriots were unable to resist smuggling shipload after shipload of Allied supplies from the docks. In his rise to becoming the controlling force in most rackets within 100 kilometres of Naples, he was aided by the many Italian-Americans who officered the AMGOT administration and closed ranks immediately one of them was threatened, citing the revivalist dictum that Naples' racketeers and pimps were disseminating prosperity city-wide by "giving work". Thus did Genovese's control, and the entire black market, become institutions of the occupation. (Wanted on charges in New York, Genovese was eventually identified, not by Poletti but by Army investigators, and returned to the USA in 1945 where, since the main witnesses for the prosecution had been killed before he arrived, he was – need one go on? – acquitted on all charges.)

In February and March Norman witnessed plenty of results of the supposed drive against the mafia-controlled rackets. These included open movement of Allied goods, and turf wars that broke out between competing gangs. "Riot at Resina [Ercolano] between *contrabandisti* of R[esina] and T[orre] A[nnunziata]. 1 dead, 1 wounded. Other *contra-*

bandisti arrested are making an agreement with the CC RR of Resina to pay 15,000 lire each for their release. Another load was stopped by the CC RR who let it go for 30,000."[12] At the opposite end of the spectrum, on 20 March, a Monday, he observed a snap check at a Royal Engineers depot. "13 arrested. One for possession of about 2 feet of string!"[13] One consequence of the situation, as far as Neapolitans were concerned, was an intensification of doubts about their occupiers' effectiveness.

General impression that things are going badly and that the Germans will return: "If you can't drive them away in the winter they will drive you away in the spring." The attitude of the population is completely changed.[14]

It had been another full week. The previous Tuesday a bad air raid in Chiaia and the port area of Santa Lucia had sent bombs into two squares behind the section's palazzo. "The Germans murder only the poor in these indiscriminate raids, just as we did," he wrote later. He recalled the infants, many apparently unmarked, dug from the rubble and laid out next to each other in the street with brand new dolls placed in their arms to accompany them to the next life.[15] On Thursday something new happened. Using an admirably tantalising notation, he wrote "16th. S. +". "S" was a Polish dancer he had befriended, one of the city's many displaced entertainers. On Friday he moved to a new boarding house at 48 via Giuseppe Martucci, behind the riviera di Chiaia. On Sunday Vesuvius exploded. As he heard a Neapolitan say, "*Ci mancava anche questo*" ("That's all we needed"). In the last great eruption of the century, by day the towering ash cloud swelled to a shape like Pliny's pine tree at Pompeii; by night, "fiery symbols were scrawled across the water of the bay, and periodically the crater discharged mines of serpents into a sky which was the deepest of blood reds and pulsating everywhere with lightning reflections".[16]

By Wednesday the eruption's violence, and people's fear, had increased. Showers of small volcanic stones were falling, and Norman was ordered to San Sebastiano al Vesuvio to assess the threat at close quarters. Underneath the grey cloud, "like some colossal pulsating brain", on a tongue of land surrounded by the lava fields of 1872, it seemed impossible that the people of San Sebastian could ignore the statistical certainty of destruction, yet, with its houses' backs to the volcano and its windows turned to Naples, "civic permanency" in the town was "a matter of

religious faith". In the town the lava, having covered half the houses
– his photographer's eye saw chimneys like a "Field full of pisspots
with Vesuvius in the background" – was flowing in leisured force down
the main street, taking buildings with it in slow motion. Hundreds of
people knelt in prayer, a line of young men brandished crosses within
a few metres of the lava, and a statue of San Gennaro shipped from
Naples as a last resort (carved arms outstretched, the saint had halted
the lava in 1855 as it threatened to engulf the city) stood by. Half the
town was salvaged when the lava slowed that afternoon and stopped,
though San Sebastiano was of less importance to the Allies than the
eighty-eight B-25 bombers from four US squadrons that vanished under
the ash at Vesuvius aerodrome.

For the rest of March his diary fell into reflection and, of the subjects
noted – mortality ("The Italian cemetery in which no single occupant
has died a natural death"), ruin (for all who shunned the black market),
and sex – he dwelt longest on the Italian manners of love. Analytically
he noted the widespread generality of the visits to the pharmacy that
in *Naples '44* he attributed to Frazer's lover Lola.

One contributing cause of Italians' natural decadence [is] possibly the exac-
tion of mutual sexual servitude. The Italians take pains over their reproductive
activities. Italian bourgeoise [sic] women with their buttocks covered with innumerable punctures of *iniezioni recostituenti*.

He was amused by "Crawford's [another sergeant's] girl who had a
cake made for him with a heart in it and blood flowing out" and by
the

Italian *mantenuta* [kept woman] who rather respects a *strozzamento* [throt-
tling] as a rather complementary evidence of passion but would in no
circumstances tolerate a *schiaffegiamento* [slapping], regarded as unbearably
vulgar.

He noted drily that the best known *ruffiana*, or madam, of his street
happened to be the wife of an attaché to the King of Italy's legation
to Brazil, and that "Venereal casualties now considerably exceed battle
casualties" in southern Italy.

He was also thinking of writing a novel. In his diary he wrote that
the Neapolitans' slang for Fifth Army was "L'Armata di boiterelle"

with a note: "always refer to it in novel as this". (He misheard this expression. The phrase was probably "*l'armata delle buattelle*", "the army of canned food".) But his diary remained mostly the instrument of his record of extraordinary times, alongside a tentative chronicle of – an interesting tandem – his depression and the coded scheme of his amours.

On 18 April he recorded another set of initials "HL. +", the "L" to distinguish whoever it was from Hester, a note that by robust coincidence was followed five days later – was he startled? – by the sudden arrival in Naples of Hester herself. Sudden in any case from the biographer's perspective, without mention of her in his Italian diaries so far. What were their feelings? Their nine months apart, tenuously connected by letters, must have recalibrated their short intimacy to a level of wary warmth. War's citizens, they had got used to living at distant ends of its republic. In Naples Norman had started to feel himself more than a posted soldier, if less than an assimilated Neapolitan. The ten days from the day of Hester's arrival were an "intensive period", he wrote. "HL" does not reappear, but "S", the Polish dancer, was still evident. On Monday 24th, the day after Hester arrived, a bomb fell at the top of Norman's street in another raid. On Tuesday he wrote with enigmatic satisfaction "As expected (developments)". During the week he took care of Hester's practical wants. She needed some dressmaking, and he found her a tailor. He bought her a bracelet. On Thursday he enjoyed the distraction of being sent out to search the property of Prince Pignatelli, arrested for spying. In the prince's bordello-baroque apartment in the extravagant villa Pignatelli in huge shaded grounds on the seafront (now a museum) he found the prince's "pornographic literature and ½ million lire". On Saturday there was a "Visit to tea by H.". Four days later, in the tone of a man enjoying seeing two women compete for his affection – or of an observer slightly decoupled from his emotions – he crammed the whole period into "H. and S. with H. in ascendant".

Hester was posted a few days later to Cancello Field Hospital outside Naples, the situation calmed, and he did not see her for a fortnight. The day after she left, another German raid on Chiaia forced him out of via Martucci into a hotel further from the port. The heady, even operatic intensity of his single way of life had not quite erased Ernestina. He noted the arrival of her letters – one in April had taken more than three months to reach him and the next did not arrive until mid-June

– but nothing of their contents. Not just his spirit but his actuality, all the performance of his life, in the Army, in Naples, in and out of uniform and incident, in and out of lust if not love, were at practically unbridgeable distances from his wife and son. After four and a half years Ernestina had been promoted to a formal figure who provoked his mild curiosity, the curiosity of someone diarising a problem that they occasionally remember will have to be dealt with.

The problems that faced him in the city with the coming of spring remained both chronic and acute in kind. Little had improved. The ordinary sympathy he felt for some cases increased his workload. On 3 May he again visited an Italian prisoner of war, a corporal named Polgrava, intending to get him out of the prison hospital and released because he was "Dying with tuberculosis. These secondary and less publicised manifestations of the horrors of war [are] far more terrible than its direct and obvious effects." In pure numbers, 312 FSS's throughput of work was impressive. There are around 2000 names in the five Army report books Norman kept his notes in while he was in Naples: civilians to be vetted for employment, suspects investigated for Fascist and/or Nazi connections, others processed if believed to be criminal or a security risk, women interviewed for marriage to service personnel, contacts to be supported, helped, sometimes befriended. Not all the names are Neapolitans'. The list of those to be investigated included Allied deserters, including a British soldier who had deserted from the Italian front in the previous war; Montenegrin and other Balkan nationalists; a boatload of French returning from Argentina who claimed to be FFL;[17] and his friend Norah Gemelli, met in the course of his reluctant arrest of one of her female neighbours, who had an Irish mother, spoke perfect English, and liked to discuss James Joyce's novels.

The daily tasks facing the section were no less diverse, from deserters attacking shops and cases of rape to repeated requests by one faction of socialists to close down the activities of another. Every solution had to be put through the correct channels. "The farce of 'channels'", he wrote on 20 June. "Vetting handed straight to [a] unit would take 2 days. Instead [it goes] from formation to formation until it finally reaches us (with insufficient details) several weeks later."[18] The ever-present problem remained the rackets. By May he was noting that "all photo shops black market" and that several categories of items in short supply to Army units were available openly in shops in via Roma. According to *Naples '44* large-scale thefts of medicines and particu-

larly penicillin were also taking place, peddled by Genovese's lieu-
tenants of whom one, Vittorio Fortuna, gives a model reaction to his
arrest by Norman for handling the drug: "This will do you no good.
Who are you? I was dining with a certain colonel last night [i.e.
Poletti]. If you are tired of life in Naples, I can have you sent away."[19]
Since the rackets overlooked nothing profitable (scuttling in the wake
of Rome's liberators that month went a thousand Mezzogiorno racketeers seeking teats for babies' bottles and house-nails that would sell
at 100 times cost price), penicillin undoubtedly figured on their shopping list. It's also fair to note that the two Normans, author and diarist
related to each other in something of the fashion of Shakespeare and
Holinshed, disagree on the precisions of the theft. No reference to
Fortuna's arrest, or the arrest of anyone like him, or to his incarcer-
ation and his slipping through Norman's fingers appears in his report
books. Like Lola and Captain Frazer, he is almost certainly another
finely actualised dramatisation.

Occasionally Norman got away. In early June he had a week's leave,
and on the 24th he swapped a bottle of whisky for a day's use of a
CIC jeep from the Americans upstairs to drive to Sorrento. He took
with him one of the 4000 unemployed lawyers of Naples, Lattarullo's
friend Del Giudice, who eventually confessed that the reason he had
come was to collect some of the fluid miraculously secreted by the
bones of St Andrew in the crypt of the cathedral at Amalfi on this day.
Two weeks later he had the chance to go to Pozzuoli with a CIC agent,
an occasion on which he was disappointed by the pleasant insignificance of Lago Averno, the reed-edged pool of water believed to have
been the entrance to the underworld, but saw the cliff cavern of the
Cumaean Sibyl which he later said had "made a greater impact on my
imagination than any other place in the world"[20] with "its hundred
entrances, and as many issues, whence sound in many voices the oracles
of the prophetess".[21]

Standing there at the mouth of this tremendous chambered corridor cut deep
into the rock, it was entirely possible to believe this. Down through the openings in the cliffs, their faces pitted with innumerable caves and sanctuaries, lay
the ruins of the most ancient of the Greek colonies in Italy. Here the spell
remained, and here the sense of the grandeur of the past was overwhelming.
Cumae would have been worth a journey of any length.[22]

Naples seemed, as it always did on his return, extraordinary, "the only Eastern city where there is no residential European quarter", as he quoted the Italian writer Edoardo Scarfoglio – a reference as much to the city's population density as to its definitive contrasts of luxury and poverty. Twenty per cent of the city, 300,000 Neapolitans, still lived in the *bassi* that would have been cellars in a north European city, surviving on the cheapest possible diet of offal from the abattoirs, fish heads, and edible roots dug from the roadsides – and yet there was an impossible display to even these dark, semi-submerged rooms.

In Italian squalid one[-]room habitations the furniture tends to be subordinated to a splendid bed. The walls are hung with cheap reproductions of degenerate Byzantine art, the most pretentious example being illuminated with an extremely low power electric lamp in the form of a candle.[23]

The *bassi* were the home of the unlicensed brothels, the *case de tolleranza*. Marsala and greasy glasses were placed on the table later to be cleared and used as a stage for erotic display, with or without gramophone. These were also the places to which most street prostitutes brought their customers. Other tenants, old and infirm, turned to the wall in their bunks. What could be said for the arrangement was that the going rate, much higher in Naples than Rome, would contribute to starkly improving the family's diet and that it was, in Norman's words, "arranged with as much civility as possible".

On 12 August he was abruptly posted out of the city to the town of Benevento, 75 kilometres north-east of Naples, to fill the gap left by two departing security sections. The town was another casualty of General Clark's panicky bombing, and the Allies had added to the damage done by his Flying Fortresses in stationing in it a Canadian section, 9 Canadian FSS, whose sergeant-major had preposterously carried, and used, a whip.

As a result of the town's smashed drains and a water supply turned on for one hour in twenty-four, rumours of a typhoid outbreak were circulating on Norman's arrival. It was an omen. Benevento evolved by smooth stages into a comic-horror episode that lasted eight weeks. Initially alone in charge of 50,000 inhabitants, Norman was forced into alliance with the town's omnipotent marshal to secure, among other things, a car, a Bianchi running on stolen Dunlop tyres. His office was in the bombed police station, from where, half marooned and guarded by a half-crazy porter naked under his army greatcoat, he was cautioned by his predecessor to make sure all favours were paid for according to a list of customary gifts. After several futile days he was joined by another half-section manned by more luxuriously equipped, gun-slinging Canadians, but as his regular duties were made more feasible he and the Canadians were simultaneously drawn into the pursuit of a band of Italians and American deserters who were taking control of the roads around the town. In early September, as the typhoid outbreak was augmented by smallpox, two cars were shot up on the Naples road and Norman returned to fetch a Beretta to improve his weapon-readiness. Events in Benevento provoked a reaction. "Depression", he noted on 8 September. He managed to get a few days away, and was in Ischia on the 12th and at Rome on the 16th, but returned to find that his comrade Bernard Durham had been shot and wounded, not seriously, probably by the same bandits near Avellino. A night roadblock mounted against them was semi-successful, though inevitably the vast majority of goods confiscated vanished once in the marshal's hands, and Norman's reputation in Benevento sank in its aftermath, the result of a series of his actions designed – like the arrest of a farmer for harbouring one of the bandits – to demonstrate honesty but locally interpreted as overturning the balance of nature. He was hurt by the people of Benevento shunning him, but they were in any case, he thought, "thoroughly sick and tired of us". The situation seems, in retrospect, a vivid prototype of a now so-familiar misapplication of values.

A year ago we liberated them from the Fascist Monster, and they still sit doing their best to smile politely at us, as hungry as ever, more disease-ridden than ever before, in the ruins of their beautiful city where law and order have ceased to exist. And what is the prize that is to be eventually won? The rebirth of democracy. The glorious prospect of being able one day to choose their rulers from a list of powerful men, most of whose corruptions are generally known and accepted with weary resignation. The days of Benito Mussolini must seem like a lost paradise compared with this.[24]

In his diary he added notes on his own condition. "Notes on depression: acquisitive sense declines as does feeling for dress. Increase in masochistic inclination accompanied by conviction that all creative impulse is dead & that the future holds no promise." This time he was rescued. Recalled to Naples, he wrote, "6 Oct. Return NAPLES. Morale high."[25]

His return lasted two and a half weeks. Work at riviera di Chiaia had accumulated while he was away and his 312 FSS comrades had been debilitated by sickness, he thought from overwork. The pattern of working fifteen-hour days, in which he shared, had its source in the section's enthusiasm for security, "the fascination of this legalized eaves-dropping on humanity", that he had noted in himself back in January, as much as in oppressive military conditions. He participated, found time to see Hester again. He collected the curiosities of army life, espe-cially of caste and language, noting the "butler-like impassiveness" of Intelligence section NCOs in their relations with their FSOs and the "Stilted speech of OR [other ranks] to officers – 'Do you *wish* to see the sgt, sir?'" He thought about stories he might write. "In Florence a block of flats changed hands each night, certain chosen female resi-dents being possessed alternately by Germans and by British. Expand this theme." He came across a nurse in a prison hospital whose actions became an episode in his published account. "Nurse in the POW compound whose day off depended on the timely death of a German." Three Germans in fact, two of whom had already died. The last of the three had been appallingly wounded, and while he was alive she was supposed to stay on duty. He would die some time after six o'clock, she told Norman – the time she would take the drip out of his vein – because her boyfriend was picking her up. "He'd be dead by morning anyway." Beneath this note in his notebook is another by Plautus (which he may have got from Montaigne). Women were on his mind. "*Mulier bene olet quae non olet*", he wrote ("She smells good who smells not at all").

The section's work was not just the result of its obsession with secu-rity. On 8 October Norman, Sergeant Parkinson and another NCO were up before dawn to take up guard duty at Harold Macmillan's house on the outskirts of Naples, where Winston Churchill and Anthony Eden had arrived at 7 a.m. for a conference on their way to Moscow for talks with Stalin (Macmillan was then Minister Resident in the Mediterranean and effectively political adviser to Field-Marshal Alexander). Then, on 17 October, a sudden end to his Naples adven-ture was announced. "Bought a picture [of] Santa Caterina from Antichità for 10,000L. [£18 at 1944 prices]. Cable to E[rnestina]." The urgency was because he needed to tell her he had been posted, for "as long as necessary". He had six days' warning of the move to Taranto for embarcation on the 23rd, slightly more than the twenty-four hours of *Naples '44*.

A possible reason for the posting might have been an undercurrent of conflict with his FSO, Cartwright. His return to Naples had been overshadowed by a divergence of views with Captain Cartwright about his leniency to the Italian women whose files came to the section for marriage vetting. In his absence at Benevento the GOC, No.3 district, had issued a circular stating the general's concern at the increasing number of applications for marriage with civilians and his intention to discourage such marriages by every means possible, on the grounds that almost all would turn out unhappily. Prompted by the general's disapproval, Cartwright had decided to audit Norman's marriage-vetting reports. In a sad last episode of *Naples '44* Norman is sent to vet one Liana Pagano, a "cheerful, fresh-faced (no make-up)" 22-year-old living in two respectable whitewashed rooms in the Vomero with her four-year-old son. Norman's favourable impression is reinforced by the local police *commissario*, who calls Signora Pagano "as good as bread", and he concludes that her marriage should be allowed. Cartwright then sends Norman's comrade Robert Parkinson to vet the woman again. Parkinson, "that investigatory tiger", immune to the "moment of poetry" of the young woman and her sparkling-eyed son, the bare white walls around them, "gloriously sculpted and dimpled by light", writes a new report. "When the FSO called me in and read out the two reports no one would have believed that they could have had to do with the same girl." It's a touching, Chekhovian-toned story with a slight inconsistency. Parkinson is described rather differently in Norman's diary: "Feb. 11 – Parkinson pulled down to Cpl on account of his inability to maintain discipline, acquire a soldierly bearing and take an interest in the men's welfare." And Parkinson himself had an Italian fiancée, or had had back in January. To be unwilling to extend to others a chance of happiness that he had had himself would seem to be particularly heartless.

There was still little time before Norman left, and the pace of work did not slacken. Returning from Moscow through Cairo, Churchill paused at Naples again on 21 October to meet Alexander and other Allied commanders (one of Alexander's pressing requests was for more beer for British troops, saying that the Americans got four bottles a week, the British one if they were lucky), and Norman was again on guard duty. He, like the remaining depleted 312 FSS members, was suffering from sleep deprivation and at one point began hallucinating, calculating that the only way to get some sleep was for Churchill to die. The delirious conversation developed with one of the guards making a mock bullet-spraying gesture and saying, "What would happen if we bumped all this lot off?" and briefly three British soldiers plotted to kill their prime minister in order to be able to sleep.

Norman's quitting of Naples was a sorrowful moment. It removed him from a place where, over thirteen months and despite moments of illness and depression, he had enjoyed participating as much as observing. It also removed him from a city that in its Italianness and uniqueness, lightness and suffering – the atmosphere of half sunny, positive pole of humanity, half *basso* of the soul, that gave it its *napoletanità* – had liberated him as much as he had liberated it. On reflection, liberated him much more: exposing him to its incidents and secrets, to some of the deepest currents and trickeries that kept it alive, to the teeming backstage of its permanent theatre, it had drawn parts of his own psychic makeup into the light of day. Just one unlikely example: his first occurrence of depression, or first admission to it. Would it be too psychoanalytical to say that Naples had unlocked some emotional openness and initiated a therapeutic process possibly as valuable as that of many consulting rooms? Certainly too early to say.

"23 Oct. Embarked Reina del Pacifico. Troops & 3rd class families." The ship in Taranto harbour was bound for Egypt with 3000 prisoners of war on board. The prisoners were Soviet central Asians, Uzbeks, Kyrgyz, Kazakhs and Tajiks plus a handful of Russians, ordered to be repatriated to the Soviet Union after fighting for the Germans. At the official level the repatriation was a simple execution of a British–Soviet agreement. But AFHQ orders, in deliberate disregard of their own consequences, bore no relation to the events that unfolded and made Norman's part in them one of the most distasteful duties of his army career.

Assigned to the Soviets as an interpreter, he found that just before his arrival they had been put on board the troopship with difficulty – meaning force – having previously been inspected by a delegation of Red Army officers. Until the inspection they had had no idea that they were to be sent back. Having fought under duress for the Germans in Italy and deserted at the first opportunity to Italian partisans, they had been promised, they said, Allied status by the commanders of the British forces that had rounded them up. The realisation of their repatriation – they knew the reality of what awaited them in the USSR, since surrender was a criminal act subject to the death penalty – had provoked panic and several suicides. On board, still in filthy German uniforms, many were singing an endless Kalmuk death chant.

Between Taranto and Port Said Norman, mediating between the prisoners and the infantry company guarding them, could do little beyond assuring the men's Russian commander that the British promise of Allied status would be kept. He elicited some facts: the men had become members of a pressed force, 162nd Turkoman Division, after being taken prisoner by the Germans in the Soviets' improvised two million-man sprint to defend Stalingrad. Once prisoners, the alternative to fighting for the Germans was a miserable death by starvation and unrestrained brutality. In one eastern prison camp 8000 men were reduced to 3000, Jews murdered immediately (and circumcised Muslims with them, though as Soviet Jews were not necessarily circumcised the selection was semi-random), others killed under a regime so violent it finished off all but the most resistant. Cannibalism of the dead and dying had been routine.

The four-day Mediterranean crossing was hot and tense; branded by their camp experiences, the Soviets were divided below deck, and a mullah among them was whispering mutiny. On the 28th the *Reina del Pacifico* finally tied up at Port Said. Norman was back on the continent he had left fourteen months before. "Unmistakable smell of Africa. Dried earth and decaying vegetation. In the town charcoal braziers, incense and, of course, shit. Beer-selling cafés out of bounds to other ranks."[26]

A three-day wait followed before the prisoners were transshipped to the heavy cruiser HMS *Devonshire* in preparation for the journey that would take them around the Arabian Sea and up the Gulf to Khorramshahr, an uneasy crossroads between the western armies and their Soviet allies. Two more interpreters came on board, both fluent Russian speakers. Norman felt under strain, superfluous and annoyed. His efforts to secure permission from the Movement Control officer to return to Naples met with failure. His Intelligence Corps spot pass was dismissed and he was told to get back to the ship. "A typical Army

fuckup", he retaliated in his diary. Despite the arrival of new interpreters, GHQ Cairo had interpreted his orders "as meaning that am
obliged to carry on to Persia although of no use on voyage".[27] While
he was trying to sort out the fuckup, however, things improved. British
uniforms arrived, and with them an instant surge in the Soviets' morale
and a willingness to submit to their officers' discipline. Their senior
lieutenant, a Muscovite named Golik, took control, the mutinous mullah
backed down temporarily, and the men were further distracted by the
cornucopia of mostly (to them) useless kit issued with the uniforms –
mess tins, water bottles, toothbrushes, combs – which they adapted to
produce "a variety of miniature musical instruments: strange antique-
looking fiddles, lutes, pipes and rebecks. Soon the bowels of the ship
quivered with the wild skirl of oriental music."[28]

One of the interpreters, a sergeant of Bulgarian Jewish descent
named Manahem, told Norman more stories of the treatment of the
Soviet prisoners, some of whom had been fed by the Germans on
rotting horse carcasses and forced to crawl to their food under machine-
gun fire. One man told him he had eaten the calf of another who
was dying. On 2 November the *Devonshire* sailed. Norman's respect
for the Soviet Asians increased as the ship slid south over the Red
Sea's hot glitter. In the Russians he saw a reversion to early modern
masculinity, "tattooed" as they were "with female circus performers,
pouncing eagles, women's heads wearing hats of a generation ago &
sword-transfixed hearts with names in Cyrillic"; but the Asians,
"smooth skinned and hairless of limb as young girls, however lined
their faces",[29] were immune to modernity. They gave a concert with
improvised instruments.

The art of the nomads had grown up without the aid of stage props, and
depended on mime and masquerade, plus a dash of shamanistic witchery; it
lifted the mind clear from unacceptable reality to glowing new worlds of the
imagination. Costumes were procured by magical adaptations of camouflage
netting and gas capes. Supreme theatrical art had transformed a man who had
tasted human flesh into a tender princess, stripping the petals from a lily while
a suitor quavered a love song; we heard the neighing of the horses and the
thundering hooves of a Mongol horde on their way to sack the town. Whatever
these men had suffered in the camps, nothing had been able to take their art
away.[30]

In his diary he commemorated the "delicacy and grace of the Asiatic dancers in comparison with the merry and boisterous European Russian dancers".

On 8 November the *Devonshire* paused offshore at Aden to take on fuel. Norman overheard that an officer named Myers was in charge of port defences. He and Myers snatched a meeting on deck, one reminded of the other's imperturbable otherness: finding leisure among his wartime duties to conduct research into Arabian jinns, and recounting to Norman "the man who was 13 years in a cave with the jinns & the man who is still with them", the Calculus-like Myers had also startled his Army colleagues by sowing his paperwork with biblical quotations. "'How long, O Lord, how long?' etc. when requesting through channels that the delivery of his launch be expedited."[31]

Fear of the prisoners staging an attempt to get ashore cut the stop short. In the week taken by the *Devonshire* to steam on from Aden to Khorramshahr, more about the German treatment of the Soviets came to light. At Salsk in the Rostov *oblast*, some of the men had been kept in a prison camp "for 7 days without food & then bread was offered to those who would betray communists, officers & Jews. Two or three did so ... the Jews were buried alive by their own comrades (who were forced to do this)." Some of them, Norman added, "were anti-semites and boasted about it".[32] At sea he spent as much time as he could talking to the men, transcribing their Symbolist-like poetry and songs. Scraps found their way into his diary and report book: an Uzbek song,

> You found my handkerchief at another factory,
> please, my beauty, give it back to me
> That aeroplane flying in the sky is landing,
> write a letter, we'll send it to the motherland

which annoyed the Armenians because it was too inconsequential, and a line of poetry, or a proverb,

> The river flows, and man lies down to sleep and dies

that would have made some sort of epitaph for the homecoming men. On the 15th Khorramshahr was reached and the men were handed over in the drizzle of the port shunting yards to a Red Army infantry detachment and a train of pygmy livestock cars. The prisoners, disembarked and mustered in their British uniforms, clung to the belief that their Allied status would mitigate their fate – and one wonders how much Norman realised at the time what exactly was in the process of happening. His diary is silent, mentioning instead in detail the "severely utilitarian, crude black-engraved silver jewelry, wristlets and belts with painted traditional Persian motifs" on sale around the port. In the four accounts he published later, the first after a gap of more than forty years, the finely described atmosphere of bleak inevitability on the dockside is the same, but the confirmation that most of the prisoners would be shot different in each. Before the 1970s, in fact, nothing was known publicly about the British government's forced repatriation policy, set in train not at Yalta in February 1945 (which merely ratified existing British policy), but by Anthony Eden in Moscow in October 1944 when, bargaining hard at Churchill's side over British percentage interests in the nations of central and southern Europe, he offered his Soviet counterpart Molotov the loss leader of the unconditional return of all Soviet prisoners of war. By 1985, when Norman's first account was published, several books had appeared on the shocking consequences of the repatriations, so it seems likely that Norman may only have acknowledged in retrospect the truth of his Soviet prisoners' fate. At the time, who knows what he thought? – but his view of what was likely to happen to the men may have lain somewhere between their own evidently strong fears, which he witnessed at close hand, and a sense of yet another wartime tragedy that he did not particularly want to think about.

He spent the next two or three days trailing back south to Abadan, forgetting about the prisoners, trying to interest himself in Persian art, transferring to the *Duchess of Bedford* again (the ship he had arrived at Salerno on), and escaping into intellectual pursuit to the limits of possibility on a British troopship. He wondered about the geographic origins of Christian artistic expression, and noted that "the religious ages were ages of creation and destruction, the non religious ages of passionless restoration and conservation". On the 21st the *Duchess of Bedford* sailed from Abadan, carrying a number of aloof British civilians and Persian Jewish refugees "wearing bracelets and earrings of golden sovereigns". In a day the climate was transformed from cool drizzle to tropical heat again. He spoke with the Jews, noting the mixture of homily and confidentiality in their speech. "Always with the truth," one man said with comic sententiousness, "with clean face and clean hands you might get something. If you want to speak with me in the correct English language I shall tell you what I mean."[33]

His mood improved. He tried to analyse the depression that he had suffered since his transfer to Benevento and now felt he was coming out of. Three months before, he had been sick of the war. Now he felt that "on no account is the occupation of Germany to be missed". His ambition for another book had also expanded. (His choice of possible subject within his narrower ability when miserable is very interesting: a book about England, from the point of view of strangers.)

Compare the present period of high personal renascence with the peak reached just before starting the voyage when the limit of self expression was envisaged as the book on foreigners' impressions of England.

How long can this pitch be maintained? Was the period of depression due to the body or the mind? Can a determined fortitude withstand a new depression having its basis in an infirmity of the former? In fact is the act of making resolutions of any value at all?

The resolution, formed in humility and almost with diffidence is to be calmer, to show more fortitude and to be less troubled with the petty things of life.[34]

Arriving back in Cairo on 1 December and based at 152 Transit Camp, El Abbassia, for a few days he spent time checking the market for cameras, visiting an exhibition by a painter of the Armenian diaspora, Puzant Godjamanian, and trying and failing to find books on Egyptian culture and folklore. He did find the "railway station classics" of Cairo – Marie Stopes' *Enduring Passion*, *Lady Chatterley's Lover*, *The Well of Loneliness*, the wild Australian William Willis's inspiredly salacious *White Slaves in a Piccadilly Flat* – and Sirmali's gallery, whose display of sixteenth-and seventeenth-century Russian, Greek and Armenian icons for sale fascinated him, though he did not buy. On the 6th he embarked on the SS *Cape Town Castle*, the "usual sausage & liver troopship", and two days later sailed from Port Said with 2500 troops on board. "Seating capacity in recreation room approx. 60. No library." But he found somewhere to sit and to come back to his resolutions. "To consider the passage 'Time hath, my lord, a wallet at his back'. To remember the consolations of reading. Discipline & will power." Ulysses' "Time hath" speech[35] is an interesting choice for a man focused on himself, torn between himself and the world around him. It's a recognition, a willingness of the heart to detach itself from the ego, so that to endure becomes more important than to nurse his lyric self, and that to achieve anything "honourable", in Shakespearean terms – in his own case in aesthetic terms – will be at the cost of long labour. Depression, in the space of that one diary entry, is becoming the beginning of a conversion.

On the 12th he was back at Taranto. Seeing Italy, he made a part-confession that he hadn't understood the plight of the prisoners on the *Devonshire*.

For the first time [I] appreciate what Europe must have seemed like to the miserable Asiatics. Grass, olive trees. Soft sunlight. The terrific impact of the sunlight on stern resolve. Life never felt more charming.

Three days later he had found his way to Naples, where the city immediately re-exerted its microcosmic power. There was trickery – "Find attempt made to reduce my rank in absence to U/L/C [unpaid lance-corporal]" – within and without; the Catholic Church; and the everlasting bartering to survive in the form of

The rather refined woman in the Swiss watch shop who asked what my religion was and on receiving the answer none said she would pray for me, if I would get her some louse powder.[36]

You can recommend that to anybody who writes. The only fundamental thing is to take notes. You've got to take notes. Stop what you're doing and take notes. Go to the lavatory and take notes there. Because you will never catch that exact impression in retrospect.

Norman Lewis

The street vendor of Naples whose cry is like a few bars taken from a Shostakovich symphony.

In the 42nd Armoured Div. section 5 members including FSO went mad, the clerk's lunacy taking the spectacular form of conducting a phone conversation on his head.

Capt. Hornby, 50 Div. section, poisoned by his driver batman.

Although this is spring it corresponds with the late autumn of the Italian campaign. There is a seasonal cycle in all human enterprises.

The awful facility with which the prison turnkey puts the key in the lock.

At S. Giorgio, the one-armed bandit who nobody dared disarm until he inflicted with his revolver a flesh wound on a British officer's dog.

Yorks & Lancs at Judenberg. Volunteers were asked for to take part in execution squad as it was intended to shoot 3 members of the Cossack division for every one that escaped. 8 + 1 sgt were wanted but only one man volunteered.

Hitler disappeared in the Celtic tradition of Arthur and Owen Glendower.

Notebooks

13

NAPLES '45

"Sex makes you lose your head"
Neapolitan proverb

PATTERNS exist to most writers' notes, as to most things people say, and in looking at the patterns one sees, sometimes, identifying signs of pre-occupations or coming distress. In Norman's notes one sees both. In Naples in the first months of 1945 his mood did not stabilise, for all his resolutions. He was able to see Hester from time to time ("5th Jan H+"), but in March she was posted, leaving on the 9th on the hospital ship *Oranje*. His duties had resumed, despite drawn-out rumours of a posting as liaison with Soviet troops on the eastern front. In his diary he was as sarcastic as ever about the Allied administration and continued making notes, drawing vignettes and collecting curiosities, like the woman rack-eteer in a *basso* in the Vergine district who had 4 million lire in gold and precious stones concealed in her furniture. "She was visited by a bishop, his chaplain and majordomo, the former suffering from a sudden attack of illness. The woman stayed respectfully outside while [they] cleared out the house."[1] But the sarcasm and curiosity are wearing flat: the tone is mechanical, of weariness and saturation with Naples' predicament. This was not Naples' fault but the war's. Life had coarsened. Allied rule had normalised daily excesses. The equations of the occupation economy had institutionalised the equation of power and contempt.

A month after coming back to the city, he wrote in his diary of the "Albergo Vittoria at Sorrento. [A] rest hotel for American personnel. 12 pro[stitute]s laid on. They got 1000L. a night. One left the job with 90,000L. after working 3 months." This decadence was harmless by comparison with the urban situation. One of Naples' most pressing problems was its epidemic of venereal disease. To work, prostitutes needed a health certificate that had to be regularly renewed. Security headquarters had long suspected corruption. In January Norman noted "The system at the Pace hospital by which prostitutes were issued with a health certificate on payment of 5–10 *milla* lire to the *direttore* by their pimps. Dr Capece said that through bribery about 3 infected prostitutes per day were released from the Pace. He estimated that these would be responsible for 15,000 fresh cases annually." (His informer, a hospital consultant, was not above lucrative activity himself. His specialisation was hymenal reconstruction, at 10,000L. a time. "Prof. Capece sewed his secretary up with sutures of a fine, dissolving & invisible type. Took her husband 3 nights to affront this reconstituted virginity.")[2] The military police dealt crudely with the crisis by conducting blanket roundups of women in bars, cafés and dance halls, regardless of their reasons for being there. Norman's presence was expected at the roundups and examinations that followed, where the level of what would now be called violence against women was shocking. A Psychological Warfare Bureau bulletin of 26 April 1945 added to the casual misogyny by claiming that there were now 40,000 prostitutes in Naples, equalling 10 per cent of Neapolitan womanhood. This was a mass examination at the Pace Hospital recalled in *Naples '44*.

The operation moved at the pace of a bull-fight. The first six women, some of them sobbing and protesting, were led forward, ordered to remove their knickers, pull up their skirts, and settle themselves in the chairs in which their legs, were grotesquely raised and separated ... the majority looked like young housewives, some with their shopping-bags on their arms ... Parkinson, Placella [Capece] and I walked dutifully past the exposed pudenda, nodding our satisfaction at the work, waited while another row of victims, knickers in hand, faces streaming with tears, took their places, then returned. ... An ugly and most depressing experience.[3]

Norman's focus on the occupation's sexual corruption and cruelty in early 1945 – he writes about little else – points to something more than itself. Though not in the front line he was feeling, I would guess, a form of combat fatigue that expressed itself in despair at an absence of improvement in living conditions under Allied control so abject that they had actually been reversed for many. By the same token his focus points to a revival of his depression. He had a week's leave in Sorrento

and saw Hester at the end of February, and after her departure on 9
March his mood curiously eased, but then returned for the rest of
March and April, always with an "extra dose . . . after seeing pro[stitute]s
passing the visit" at the Pace. The dirty dehumanising routines of occupation had abraded only his private reflexes, but those severely. He
made the effort to record "neurotic notes" about his condition:

Inability to sit through a film dealing with family life or to read sensitive short
stories by women authors, to listen to sentimental tunes.

Inability to read any of the *New Yorker*'s psychological short stories dealing
with frustrated human relationships. Phobia about anything English noticeable when attempting to read *Lilliput*.[4]

Family life. Relationships. Englishness. In short, he was unable to face
the things he had successfully suppressed his feelings about since he was
ten. Each time the depression lifted, it came back. They were false dawns
in the mess of Naples days. On 2 May he wrote that "After 7½ weeks
this depression suddenly appeared to collapse in the early evening, next
morning still there but less strong". Four days later he recorded "violent
oscillations of moods & intentions within every ½ hour. Recollections of
only neurotic phases in the past." With that devious benevolence that
belongs to the psyche, his black dog went on running him up against
feelings he had wanted boxed up, making him face distress he had locked
away. Naples and its predicament were the catalyst. He cared about the
city, felt his friends' distress and those more intellectual distresses: injustice, cruelty, violence, inequity, contempt. He had had a more complete
relationship with Naples than anywhere else he had lived.[5] Its distress
and his intimacy with it were strong enough to invoke in him for the first
time his own anguish. Naples, of course, was not the cause of his depression. Graham Greene's well-known citation of Æ's poem "Germinal"
condenses Norman's own case well.

> In ancient shadows and twilights
> Where childhood had strayed,
> The world's great sorrows were born
> And its heroes were made.
> In the lost boyhood of Judas
> Christ was betrayed.

In early May the anticipated German surrender finally separated him from city, and catalyst. On the 11th, three days after VE-Day, he was posted to a new section, 96 FSS, and sent on a secret course at Intelligence Corps headquarters at Castellammare di Stabia. "19th May. Depression lasted over 2 months but has been slackening since news of posting."

He later wrote that the course was about effecting a security plan to encircle Germany behind radar-controlled fences – a typical high-concept Intelligence *scherzo* – but in fact it mostly concerned the protocol of meeting the advancing Red Army and the task of containing high-ranking Nazi absconders streaming through southern Austria. At the Corps depot the quartermaster, "taciturn and sly as an old pike", issued him with a 15-cwt truck that had been driven to death. "Nothing works. In its 406 it is described as 'unfit for detail'." In this tragic vehicle he left Castellammare, and Naples, on 23 May for Venice. He was accompanied by another sergeant, a Hellenicist PhD from Aberystwyth named Hopper for whom the Intelligence Corps had played Hera to his Dionysus, cursing him to wander the Earth. Sent to Nova Scotia by mistake in 1943, Hopper had journeyed south in search of the British Army until he reached New Orleans, where a lone British captain had suggested he make for Jamaica or, if he didn't like it there, Trinidad. In Trinidad, hearing of a shortage of NCOs in British Guiana, he had moved on again. By the time he arrived back in Europe, en route for Athens, the war was almost over.

Averaging a remarkable 250 kilometres a day, the two sergeants drove north through the Italian springtime via Rome, Iesi, Ravenna and Treviso to Palmanova near the Slovenian border. Here nearly 500 had died in the battle for the town. Norman noted the "Elegance of young female communists at the funeral procession of 4 exhumed comrades". The task of 96 FSS was to operate along the Austrian–Italian/Yugoslavian border in an effort to secure it, and to hold and interrogate suspected Nazis. Doubling back to report to Venice on 7 June, Norman was hit by the "worst depression . . . on 8th–18th" on his return to Palmanova and the beginning of duties. Fatigue was part of it. He felt "most normal after a period of deep sleep". His duties were also disturbing, and he had ceased to be able to treat them as a purely practical activity. He saw an Italian partisan who had been beaten with hammers by the Germans, bitten by dogs, shot and then had a knife twisted in the wound. He found a photograph in the possession of a spy, a doctor shot by the British, inscribed with the words

"*Si je te perds je suis perdue*";[6] the words were the man's mistress's, who had given him away under interrogation because she was jealous of another girl. In his tiredness his frustrations shadowed his existence. He was hanging on to his idea of a relationship with Hester but hadn't seen her for three months. During the ten days of depression he conducted a hectic correspondence with her that brought in her older sister, Joan.

9th, letter to H.
11th . . . letter.
13th, Tel[egram] to H. Letter Joan.
14th, letter to H . . . & tel[egram] to Joan.
16th, letter Hester. Very despairing.[7]

Joan Reid was suspicious, as elder sisters are, of her younger sister's choice of lover. He did his best to appease her. A scrap of a draft letter to Joan is scribbled in one of his report books, written in language indicating that, like many soldiers who went without sex for long intervals and found themselves at a cool distance from the emotional and sexual heat of their wives and girlfriends, he was ready to say whatever was necessary to regain access to Hester's heart, and knickers. That his language now sounds quixotically old-fashioned is probably evidence that men and women have learnt to be more open sexually and emotionally: within the social customs of the 1940s, where dishonesty or marriage or both were often required for sex to be forthcoming, its chivalry was normal.

Joan, I assure you from the bottom of my heart that I am ready to give all I have to the poor, and work as a labourer for the rest of my life. . . .[8]

In his note of the next move by his detachment, across the frontier into Austria on 29 June, there is no doubt that women were on his mind. "Left Palmanova for Klagenfurt. All women plain and uninterested. Some wearing large squeaking shoes. Ugly false peasant clothes with mannish jackets." He described the Austrians he saw as "goitrous". But he also found reason to quote (hopefully?) Hesiod: "High summer, when men are their weakest and women their most wanton."[9]

Initially his detachment's role in southern Austria was the same as in Italy: to arrest wanted Nazis, and attempt to maintain security on the frontier. He wrote in his autobiography that "Those we rounded up for investigation proved nothing but small fry",[10] but he was belittling the section's activities. Patrolling a porous border – "Owing to the nature of the country, frontier control has never even pretended to exercise any considerable effect on pedestrian traffic" – and following through from the work of other sections, Norman's section was not supposed to grandstand but make efforts to consolidate frontier control. (A task that 96 FSS stayed on to perform in this part of Austria until 1947.) "The most outstanding Nazis had been disposed of by either 31 or 97 FS Sections", a section report notes, adding with a suggestion of smugness that "it was found that other, and perhaps more interesting, material had congregated locally to await the British entry into Graz".[11] The section carried out its work during a hot alpine July perfectly creditably.

From Klagenfurt in Carinthia Norman arrived at Köflach the next day. Here, in the plump wooded gradients of western Styria, the section was based for most of the month before moving a couple of kilometres up the road to Voitsberg. The section had a warm reception from the Austrians. In May Styria had been occupied by the Soviets and Köflach/Voitsberg had been in the Russian sector before being turned over to the British. The civilian population had lived "in fear and hatred" of the Red Army, which had "stripped [Voitsberg] bare"; the British, by contrast, they addressed "in a conciliatory and flattering way".[12] Norman reacted with unusual cynicism. "One gains as a leading impression from this war a sense of the essential traitorous character and aptitude for sycophancy of most human beings [observed in] the fawning way in which all conquered peoples fall over each other in their eagerness to lick the boots of their conquerors."[13]

Red Army troops were still in the area, operating with little restraint from their officers. In facing them, as he did on one occasion, Norman perhaps proved that the Austrians' eagerness for the British was not pure fawning. At Köflach he was billeted above a pharmacy run by a young, pretty, blonde pharmacist. Soldiers came one evening, Soviets with sub-machine guns, hammering on the door. Norman answered it with his pistol drawn. "There is a woman here." Norman answered in Russian, "You're soldiers, I'm a soldier. Can't I have a woman?"[14] On another occasion he was less successful. Driving out to arrest an Austrian woman who was a suspected Nazi, he had information that she was to be found at the local lido. He arrived with two other sergeants to find an attractive woman lying in her swimsuit on a chaise longue at the poolside, surrounded by four or five Soviet officers. Norman's arresting party, armed with unreliable Sten guns and no more formidable in appearance than FS NCOs usually were, showed their Intelligence i.d. and Norman informed the woman he had come to arrest her. The Soviet officers stood. One strode to the pool's diving boards and climbed to the 3-metre board, at the tip of which he executed a perfect handstand and backflip. Swimming to the side, he pulled himself from the water and said, "She's my woman." Norman remembered later, "These men were massive. I thought better of what I had come to do, and we left."[15]

In Austria he had problems with another section member, a Sergeant Colthart. "The first day we were in Köflach C******* took me aside and said gently, 'I don't like you.' As he said this he was wearing a one-sided smile. This smile had been one-sided for some time and had been getting worse."[16] But his own situation was equally ill-suited to a soldier on edge with fatigue and frustration. Activity was chaotic. His report book lists several times a need for "more Corps instructions" and more copies of blacklists, and contains lists of names with a query as to whether they fall into an arrestable category. A number of substantial Nazi figures remained to be taken in, including the local *Kreisleiter* and a senior SD officer who had taken refuge in a hunting lodge at the Gaberl saddle, above Köflach. But generally soldiers viewed the wider denazification process sceptically. Another member of 96 FSS wrote that "Denazification is by its very definition an impossibly large task for an occupying force to set itself. The spirit of nazism . . . has entered into the life and being of Austria so deeply that no matter how great the efforts by the occupying force, some of it will still remain."[17] Another FS sergeant in Carinthia (also named Hopper) dismissed it as "a lot of nonsense. . . . The policy assumed that there was a crust of Nazis over a large pudding of anti-Nazis, or non-Nazis, but that was not really the case. Nearly all the Austrians had been Nazis. Willing or not, they had to be."[18]

For part of the month Norman was billeted outside Köflach in the village of Engelsdorf near Friesach. Between Engelsdorf and Köflach the hills were alive with minor Sicherheitsdienst and Gestapo personnel waiting, often co-operatively, to be winkled out. Many Nazis who were interrogated considered eradication of the Third Reich inevitable and offered all collaboration, including the names of fellow SS members, to FS interrogators. One account by Norman of an owlish SS colonel he interrogated – another composite creation out of the many Nazis he interviewed – describes a short, inoffensive, bourgeois, unmarried German, devoted to his mother and to the white rat he had carried through the Russian campaign.[19] Denazification may have been futile as triage, but was perhaps useful to the extent that it made flesh the concept of the banality of evil.

Norman came across one detainee who introduced a train of thought that he would come back to, about the physical detachment advisable when large-scale killing is proposed.

Fischkeller the driver batman to the Graz SD Abschnitt, although robust and unimaginative, announced himself to be unnerved after the completion of about 25 executions in Untersteiermark. . . . The killer par ex[cellence] regards his work more or less mathematically & is usually repelled by crude detail. Hence tendency for intellectual planners of mass extermination to pass the final arrangements over to the secular [sic] arm.

Thus cultured Panzer and Luftwaffe generals exterminated life as a normal man crushes an anthill out of existence but would prob[ably] have been unable to equal Fischkeller as close quarters killers.[20]

Towards the end of July, on the 22nd, Norman suddenly returned to Voitsberg. In June he had applied for compassionate leave to see his mother, and it had been granted. (In the draft of a letter to Dr White, Louisa's doctor in Enfield, asking for confirmation of her physical and mental state, he mentions her deterioration after being injured in a flying bomb raid the previous autumn. To her frailty of body was added a confusion of mind that imagined him already on his way home, and the father of another child.)

At Voitsberg he packed, made his farewells, and transferred to Villach, the army's transit camp in southern Austria and the drains of the occupation, its population of poverty-stricken Austrian civilians and cashed-up, leave-happy soldiery frothing muddily in rackets of cigarettes, drink and prostitution. He left Villach on 26 July for Innsbrück and reached Ulm the day after, where he noticed the cathedral frescoes' "typical gothic taste for the horrific" and the pictures of "blonde, ruddy Christs. Female saints are nourished Bavarian peasants." His first view of a smashed Germany struck him, as it did many, by its incongruities. "A wake of French rose perfume follows a hausfrau through the ruins."[21] On the 29th he left Ulm for Mainz (30th), Sedan (31st) and Calais, arriving back in England at Folkestone on 3 August.

He had seven weeks' leave and was still on the strength of Central
Mediterranean Force. But his war suddenly, and possibly with feelings
of disbelief, was over. The process of adjustment was difficult for almost
every serviceman and -woman returning home; there is no doubt that
re-entry into peacetime England jarred in Norman's mind. Britain and
the British had suffered harsh years of conflict, yet, uninvaded, most
British values and prejudices had come through, so far, without a scratch.
His return snapped slumbering antipathies awake.

Sense of shock in picking up first *Times* and reading through the insane normality
of the Personal columns commencing with the smug and typical passage from
HABAKKUK II, 4. "The Just shall live by his Faith."

His plans were not fixed, nor, almost certainly, his feelings. His mother
was a priority, a more or less practical problem. So was the photography business. But he had also come back to the bigger deferred
problems of Ernestina and Ito, and the question of a future with Hester
and whether that was desirable. The unsteady landscape of his emotions,
not particularly adequate to supporting important sentimental decisions, was in no way stabilised by finding himself back in a country
whose impact on his reflexes, after nearly three years away, was wholly
negative. In a sense, two far less visible questions than what he was
going to do about Ernestina and Hester were the more essential ones.
What place could he bear to live in? And what man would he be there?

PART THREE

NARRATING

A Structuring in a Storm of Alterations

Demobilisation and disentanglement,
furious evasion and literary objects

I spent thirty years among the hard, clear realities of England, and then I went back to Wales and spent three seasons in search of the cloud cuckoo land of my youth.

Unpublished typescript

The time that she met him to the time that I was born, that's a kind of blank. All I know is that she used that expression, that he chased her around north Africa. Knowing my mother as I obviously knew her, and knowing Dad, I think they were probably not a good match. Then there was the whole mystery that surrounds our suddenly arriving in the Highlands in my aunt's four-bedroomed house. It's like a relay race, it's like a really slow baton change, as he moved away from one woman on to the other, it was like running them in parallel, but this one was getting left behind. And he never said anything about it.

Gareth Lewis

I said to him, "Norman, why did you rent these flats?" He said, "I don't know." The only one that he'd lived in was Orchard Street . . . by the time I met him he didn't have the Chelsea Cloisters one and he didn't have the Farm Street one, but he'd had them I think concurrently, those two.

Lesley Lewis

14

"KEEP MOVING"

"This caravan is lame until doomsday"
Persian proverb

So many thought when they came back from Italy, north Africa, France, Palestine, Burma, Greece, Germany, that they would return to being a bank manager in Dulwich, a patent clerk in Chancery Lane, a brewery salesman in Cheshire *for the time being*. The controlled irresponsibility of service life made thousands of serving men and women vow not to be caught permanently in the torpor of peace. Yet the mass who elected to pick up – for now – the threads of their pre-war lives found themselves unable for the same few reasons (insecurity, the savage winter of 1947, individual inertia), as "for now" crept past a credible interpretation, to give up familiarity as the price of continuing their adventure. In that single respect Norman's childhood was providential, having pushed him, years before the war, into improvisation as a necessity.

Yet however improvisable his future might be, it could not materialise very much faster than anyone else's. Shortages, restrictions, controls on everything from eggs to the profit a company was allowed to make slowed England down. Norman's pre-prepared antipathy and restlessness, and the frenetic pace of his last two years' activity, rendered his re-insertion into English life as painful as it was for others, if not more so. There were matters to be got out of the way; things urgently to do – to look after his mother, settle the question of Ernestina, bring Hester into his life. He needed for financial reasons to re-establish R G Lewis. On 19 December his weekly advertisement in *Amateur Photographer* indicated progress.

THE ROAD BACK (By R.G.L.)

Advertising, which used to amuse us so much in the good old days, became during the war, of bitter necessity, just an extra job to be piled on to an already overworked member of staff.

Now, as we travel the Road Back, it is our ambition to be able to modify our late highly utilitarian style. Anyway, here goes with one of those "personal messages" which we photographic advertisers used to indulge in from time to time.

Our first view of "202" after 3 years of broadening the mind by involuntary foreign travel put us in mind of a passage from a certain Shakespearian sonnet, which we probably misquote, "bare ruined choirs where late the sweet birds sang." However, a process of sweeping and garnishing has been taking place; the bomb-blasted windows have been repaired and filled with interesting things, and best of all the majority of the old staff will be back in the New Year. As most of these will have done what amounts to five years of intensive practical photography with the forces, the old-time protracted discussions with our customers on obscure photographic topics, which were so much a feature of the old "202" atmosphere, should shortly be resumed on an even more rabid scale.

Among all the other matters lay his private and most urgent priority, *to publish a new book*. A few years later, still at the start of his "real" career, he gave a clear if mildly earnest version of the urgency of his need to write. "I began to write *seriously* after the war, when I felt myself sufficiently endowed with the raw material of experience to commence my literary apprenticeship. The desire to write arose from my reverence for books, which were my refuge and ultimate salvation from a drab and apparently hopeless youth."[1]

There was too, as there always is, the question of the exact nature of the future improvisation: how to balance his life between business, a more settled relationship with Hester, and his escape reflex; what book to write. We generally want to control our lives because we know that some futures are better than others; but the future we imagine for ourselves is generally fundamentally different from the future it actually turns out to be.

On long leave from the Army in August 1945, Norman's state of mind was volatile. What he later called the "paradise" of his war experience was an overall memory that had edited out his depressions. He could remember them if he wanted to, but he *wanted* to remember the war for something else, for its "endless variety and excitement".

Memory's benevolence is to overwrite the negative phases of an active period, especially one that becomes – as the war had for him – an indicator: he didn't want war itself in future, but he wanted what it had shown him, its stimulants, activity, bouts of emergency, surprises, extemporisation. He may have wondered whether going on pursuing its variety and excitement might not drag in new depressions, but it did not stop him: that variety and excitement was what he wanted to try to re-create.

He might have analysed his depressions to the point of realising that they had a therapeutic aspect, or understood that he had placed himself in the middle of a redistribution of personal priorities whose consequences were unforeseeable – I'm inclined to think he didn't get that far – but he certainly knew that he needed to pursue *his* expectations to the exclusion of anything anyone else might be imagining for him. If he was ever to have a future close to the implied future his imagination presented him with, as writer and man of (some kind of) action, then he had to be the implied central character of his imagining.

None of it happened for six months. On 20 September he was struck off the strength of Central Mediterranean Force and had his leave extended. Three months later, on 22 December, he was relegated to the Reserve with another sixteen weeks of leave, and on 16 April 1946 his release was finally "converted into an indefinite release on compassionate grounds" with a note, "Military conduct Very Good". He dealt with the things that required his attention. R G Lewis was returning to strength. By March he had closed down half of the Shrewsbury operation, which had grown to a showroom and offices by the war's end, and made 202 High Holborn the main showroom and mail order centre again. His mother was frail – she worried continually about unimportant things like her son's wine collection, destroyed in the flying-bomb raid – but she stabilised after his return. He stayed at first at Gordon Street, a few blocks from Holborn, where he and Eugene (Ernesto and Maria had evacuated themselves to a cottage in Kent) camped in the basement, the only habitable floor, among stacks of secondhand motor tyres that were Eugene's current line of business. Negotiations with Hester's elder sister Joan ended in her reluctant agreement that Hester should join Norman in London. In a bombed capital whose accommodation market was stamped by scarcity and spivs making fortunes in key money, he was clever enough to pick up a flat for them both between Knightsbridge and Kensington, near the Albert Hall.

But his existence in 1946 was drawn out like a phoney peace until he could get to Guatemala to see Ernestina. After Easter, without having settled one situation, he found it supplemented by another: Hester was pregnant. What he felt about her news can only be an intelligent guess (not even a coded note went into his diary). He can't have been wholly taken aback. In March she had turned thirty-seven; intending to have children, she would not be doing herself a favour by waiting. For his part, having decided that she should succeed Ernestina, he must have imagined the possibility of becoming a father again. Why is there a temptation to speculate not on how long their relationship might last, but how soon it would end?

It fell, of course, into a notorious category. Arthur Baron, who had witnessed the wartime romance that started it, had told him not to do it. Hester, he felt, was not lively enough for Norman. At least part of the answer lies in Norman's facility for attracting women. He had unconventional and saturnine looks, was awkward and intense in his attention, and would not have attracted most women by his looks and manner. But he had a knack for entertaining women, for making them feel they were the focus of his cleverness and humour, and they – and he – enjoyed him doing it. (Gwen Nicholls and her sister Nancy are not the only ones to testify to that aspect of his character.) So Hester was entertained. But if the entertaining performance also happens to be a display element of sexual pursuit, then when the entertainer/pursuer has captured his audience he expects to be entertained in turn. Once Norman's pleasure in the catching of Hester and its successful emotional and sexual outcome was past, he was not a harsh judge – there is plenty of evidence that he did not discard Hester easily or dislike her. He enjoyed women's company. But he was a complex and a demanding audience.

No evidence of disaffection exists in the second half of 1946. In Knightsbridge he and Hester lived glamorously by comparison with British living conditions generally. (Before 1950 a quarter of Britain's homes had no toilet of their own, nearly half had no bathroom.) R G Lewis flourished (it had trebled its number of phone lines by June) and in September he opened a new bespoke shop in Bond Street, Lewis Newcombe Ltd, in partnership with the writer on 35mm photography, H S Newcombe. The same month he showed three prints at the Royal Photographic Society annual exhibition, down the road at the Science Museum. The couple saw friends – Oliver Myers was one whom Norman saw often "in a rumpled jacket and black hat", and on one occasion he drove to Stonehenge to help in an inevitably unsuccessful Myers experiment in thought transmission. He had reunions with several section members, including Derek Wise of 91 FSS at Philippeville. "He came to pick me up, I was living in Kensington and he turned up with this enormous red Ferrari [sic].[2] We went to his flat where he was living with Hester, a rather nice flat. . . . He [had become] rather different, bourgeois, because she was very much feet-on-the-ground."[3]

Eventually Norman managed to book a passage to New York for November (not mid-April, as he wrote later). Ernestina's response to his news that he expected to be able to reach her in Guatemala within a few weeks was "rapid and enthusiastic", but he could discover in her letter "no evidence of joy".[4] It was a mutual feeling. In early November he crossed the Atlantic by Cunarder. He was planning to reach Guatemala via Mexico, and to gather material for a book that was so far dim in outline. A smart traveller was in evidence in his packing list of "shoes, shoe trees, lounge suit, dinner suit, shaving lotion, bottle [of] brandy, haircut",[5] though his bag was half-empty: his stay in Manhattan was part planned as a plunge into the gorgeous abundance of goods in American stores out of range of Attlee's restrictions.

In New York he shopped at Abercrombie & Fitch, Brooks Brothers and Macy's, looked at jewellery on Fifth Avenue and hats on Broadway, descended on the New York Leitz headquarters and other equipment suppliers, and gathered anything he could find on Guatemala and Mayan civilisation. He made a note to himself to write to the New York publishers, Knopf, and may have suggested the book project to them. From New York he flew to Merida, taking rolls of photographs, and on to Guatemala City into a reunion of strangers.

He found Ernestina living comfortably with a Guatemalan diplomat, Rafael Aparicio, and was, I think, relieved. Ito, whom he had left when the boy was three, was nearly ten. In Guatemala City, for its Indian poor the cruellest metropolis in Latin America, Ito had grown up living the life of a street kid – his mother being less than conventionally maternal – and he remembers that meeting his father "was all a bit of a strain for me because my father was the typical gringo. He had short trousers which weren't all that short, they came down just to the top of his knees, and sometimes I'd say, 'Why don't you put some long trousers on? You look ridiculous,' I used to tell him. 'Put some long trousers on, please.'"

Ito's unease can stand for the discomfort of the whole visit. Norman played with all the sense of honour he could muster the part of the returning husband, but with less than zero desire to revive his marriage. With the reluctance of pride, Ernestina had accepted by degrees the events she had allowed to happen and the country she had drifted to. She had no intention of returning to England, although she was more emotionally involved with her first husband than he was with her and she remained more hurt by their split. Both were preparing to admit that their ties had broken, less perhaps in the atmosphere of "deadly consideration" Norman described in his autobiography than with the dull shock of contact with reality, an impact that would take time to get used to.

To Norman Guatemala was a further shock. He was unprepared for its extreme, often unearthly beauty, "[lying] under the shadow of thirty-two volcanoes, its towns rattled constantly by earthquakes, like dice in a box, its villages peopled by a race who never smile". Its Indian population's resistance to centuries of enslavement had given it a particularly visceral vitality; the oscillation, and relationship, between beauty and violence fascinated him. In 1946, as a democratic state briefly under President Juan José Arévalo, it took root in his imagination even as his wife was being purged from his thoughts. In his 1957 novel *The Volcanoes Above Us*, his hero David Williams expresses the briefest summary of his creator's feelings. "For anyone who has lived in Guatemala, other countries, by contrast, are lacking in savour."

A starting point for research into the country was the National Museum. Ernestina, working there part-time, introduced him to the curatorial staff. He met Janos de Szecsy and his wife, Hungarian refugee friends of Ernestina's living in hope-filled poverty, who were knowledgeable about the endlessly varied symbolic figures woven into Indian clothes, particularly the women's *huipiles* (thick blouses).[6] Trips were organised through the de Szecsys and a group of American women anthropologists Ernestina also knew and had travelled with. In the weeks he was there he, she and Ito visited Chichicastenango, Quetzaltenango and Totonecapan. Almost exactly forty years later, in "The Shaman of Chichicastenango", Norman offered a version of his first visit to the town: a time-slip between the dignified Indians who walked its streets wearing shirts woven with symbols and sixteenth-century Spanish hats, and a gold-rush atmosphere of contemporary drunkenness and movie-going at a fleapit cinema, invariably showing some instalment of the old B-movie series *Crime Does Not Pay*. The cinema could only operate when two policemen were available to control the audience. Among it there were always a few for whom this was a first-time experience, and they were prone to violent intervention, in the belief that what they were viewing was an episode from real life. Whenever the policemen were called away to deal with some emergency the cinema closed until their return.[7]

Norman had already noticed the Indian servants at the house where Ernestina was living with Aparicio's mother Doña Elvira, young women supplied by a Christian mission, and in Chichicastenango he encountered an American evangelist, a Mr Fernley, scourge of local Indian ceremonies and enterprising dealer in the most traditional examples of *huipiles* – except that wherever one of the classic woven designs featured an unacceptable representation, such as horses copulating (meaning creativity and fertility), he destroyed it. Fernley sowed a seed of loathing.

On one trip Norman flirted with buying a coffee finca in the isolated north-west. He was disabused on discovering the fragility of land ownership, but was as impressed by the Indians' resistance as he was by many of their responses to their conquest. In pressing their claim to land they thought belonged to them they showed subtlety and determination, simply creeping in and crippling the coffee-tree roots one or two trees at a time until the non-Indian owner gave up in despair. Ito remembers that "we went to offbeat places, villages where maybe the last European they'd seen was probably fifty years before. We went to places that no one really ever went to and he was able to get some really good photographs." His father's dress style continued to bother. "I didn't know whether to walk in front of him or a little bit behind him just so that people wouldn't connect us. On the other hand I thought he was going to be assaulted, so I used to take secretly a knife which I kept hidden. We used to go to the cantinas which were full of drunken Indian *macheteros*, they had long machetes to cut sugar cane with, and they were so sharp. [But] nobody ever did anything to him, he had a kind of a sense of diplomacy, he was very careful, very diplomatic, there would be nothing they could actually get hold of to feel aggressive about."[8]

As part of his visit he had arranged a family holiday in Jamaica. The Lewises flew by DC3 to Kingston and put up at the Myrtlebank Hotel (in whose dining room Errol Flynn, among others, held court). Ito was surprised again.

He had this beautiful suitcase, and the smell of that when he opened it. This was a real foreigner, I couldn't imagine anything more foreign. We went into our room and he unzipped it and the first thing I saw was a set of shoe-shining brushes. I couldn't believe it. It would take him five minutes, he'd be very, very thorough and he'd put them aside and they'd be gleaming. And of course in Latin countries you never shine your shoes, you always get someone else to shine them for you. He was so meticulous, so soigné. I saw not one pair but about five pairs of shorts and one pair of long trousers ... I thought to myself, Maybe if I just throw the shorts away.

They moved on to Montego Bay. Father and son breakfasted on the balcony outside their room, hummingbirds at their shoulders. Out swimming, Ito was stung by a man-o'-war and came ashore crying with pain. Norman told him, "You must stop crying or your mother will think I've smacked you." Father and son went fishing, and Norman caught blackwater fever.

We were all being bitten alive. My father in a matter of thirty-six hours was very, very ill. It came out when he went to pee, and the pee was black.

The death rate today from blackwater fever, a complication of malaria, is lower than from cerebral malaria, but free haemoglobin in the urine initiates kidney failure (and causes the raven-black discolouration). It was "like pissing Guinness," Norman noted later. "It even has a head."[9] There is no doubt he came close to dying; he was rushed to hospital in Montego Bay and treated with quinine and intravenous fluid for several days.

The book on Guatemala would not be written – its scope got too large, it became a blizzard of facts – but Norman came back to London in late December with material and a literary alibi. Convalescent but buoyant, he spent Christmas with a heavily pregnant Hester and visiting his mother. Three weeks later, on 17 January 1947, Hester had their daughter at Bearsted Memorial Hospital at Hampton Court. The late stages of the pregnancy and the birth may not have been very comfortable. Mistrust dating from some time during the pregnancy was a part of the story Hester rehearsed to herself and her daughter, Karen, in the years afterwards. Karen remembers "Mum telling me in one of her rants that when Dad came to visit her in hospital when I was born, she looked out of the window and saw him with a blonde in a sports car".[10] It's a cast-off lover's entitlement to overwrite the affair with contumely; whatever the actual status of Norman's passenger, something was wrong. Karen feels her mother "was skating on thin ice even then".

At the time his daughter was born, the business aspects of Norman's life were also stretching him. He was dealing with a constant flow of new products: an adapter for plate cameras to use 35mm film, new projectors, and a clever Contax-to-Leica lens adapter. On the night of 20 November, when he was in Guatemala, 202 High Holborn had been the victim of a smash-and-grab in which the thieves had got away with most of the Leicas in the shop, causing stock problems, and he had had an exhibition of his pictures to organise at the Shrewsbury branch for mid-January.

He was also newly occupied with a novel, a book he thought might produce quicker results than the Guatemala project. Notes start appearing in his notebook in January, reminders to collect his French dictionary from Enfield and buy a copy of the Koran, sentences as they occurred to him. "The Senegalese's muscles glinted with the sheen of iron or polished ebony." The book had a working title, "Filfila". It was based on his experiences in Algeria and during February and March competed for his attention, as did Hester, whose life with a baby was additionally complicated by the sudden onset of the ferocious late winter. Six days after Karen's birth, in the worst winter weather in memory, mean day temperatures fell below 0°C and stayed there for nine weeks. The sea froze off Margate, icebergs appeared at Great Yarmouth. People went hungry, stole coal, and froze to death. By 1 March "power supplies across the country had almost broken down. Over 2,000,000 people were thrown out of work; people worked in offices by candlelight; fires and traffic lights went out; lifts stopped; the national newspapers were cut to four pages. . . . No one was allowed to cook on an electric stove from 9 am to 12 pm and from 2 pm to 4 pm."[11]

"I wish I were anywhere but in this goddamned country" was a sentiment spoken everywhere, "where there is nothing but queues and restrictions and forms and shortages and no food and cold. Flu and the fuel crisis is the last straw."[12] Britain was paralysed streets, shabbiness and sheer exhaustion. When the level snow lying at least 60 centimetres deep everywhere for nearly two months melted, Britain's burst pipes gushed. At Teddington Lock the Thames recorded its second highest stream-flow. At Maidenhead in Berkshire it was almost a kilometre and a half wide.

Norman seems not to have paid much attention. His concerns were different: office space, advertising for a secretary, petrol coupons, new fittings for the shop, a flow of new accessories and new cameras; a planned escape across the Channel ("Book Channel passage as soon as car bought") that did not happen. He nodded at the crisis, quoting Keats' "I am certain of nothing" at the head of R G Lewis's advert in *Amateur Photographer* of 5 March: appropriately because the advert should have gone in on 19 February but the winter weather closed the magazine for two weeks. But the uncertainty didn't bother him. It was a good time to buy cars, and he thought about buying a Healey and another Alfa, and bought a Lancia (he still had the Alfa 8C and a prim baby Fiat that did 50 miles to the gallon). He had started spending evenings after the shop closed drinking at the York Minster, then a lazy, uncongested French-run pub that functioned as one of the informal clubs of Soho. (In his diary he called it Berlemont's after the proprietor, Gaston Berlemont. Others knew it as the French House.) Some of those he drank with were a heterogeneous group of marginal bohemians he had been introduced to by a customer at 202, Malcolm Dunbar. Norman warmed to Dunbar especially, a photographer who had fought and been wounded several times in Spain and ended up as the 15th Brigade's chief of staff at the battle of the Ebro. A man of courage and sensitivity, Dunbar was aristocratic, intelligent, cleverly read, addicted to Mozart, gently homosexual with few if any boyfriends, and a private income. (He was cursed by his solitude and killed himself in 1963. Twenty years after his death Norman memorialised their friendship by choosing Dunbar's favourite Mozart piece, the clarinet concerto in A major, as one of his *Desert Island Discs*.)

Some of Norman's activity was tending slowly to his ambitions. A lot of it was a busy dead end. The Guatemala book did not progress. Apart from the unending and overwhelming fall of facts he found a peculiar problem, in that he wasn't able to talk about Guatemalan history without flamboyantly attacking Spanish Catholicism each time.

By May his business ventures were tying down his time. For all his restless spending of energy and his evenings at the French House, London and England were responding with ungenerous amounts of progress and excitement. Gwen Nicholls, now Varnals, who had lunch with him whenever she came to London, remembers his growing distraction – and his concealing of his gloom. "After the war I think he really came close to a breakdown. I think it was a time of reckoning after the experience of war. ...[13] Of course one hasn't said how much we enjoyed laughing together, you couldn't be with him without cracking your sides over certain things."[14]

He took his problems to a doctor who, he said, advised him as he had advised others "to keep moving, revert as far as possible to the health-giving occupations the army had provided, be on the alert – ready to spring into action both by day and night".[15] This pointless regime and the surreal picture it evokes, of thousands of suburban Britons padding around their front rooms taut as piano wire, had a grain of sense: he needed continuous, explicit challenge, physical and mental. He chose rock-climbing as the most plausible suggestion, partly because he could combine it with birdwatching, and, taking the opportunity to give his mother a change of scene, drove her to Carmarthen while he and Hester looked for a cottage to rent on the Pembrokeshire coast. His plan for himself, Hester and Karen to spend half their time in Wales, half in London, was part romance – the romance of the impossible return – part escape, part new beginning. It seemed promising, with the spring of 1947 turning steadily warmer, but the reality was more difficult.

In the beautiful places where I wanted to live the countryside is as sparsely populated as the Balkan mountains, and accommodation hard to come by. I spent a month in what had been described as a flat, over the post office in a village appropriately named Noland. The flat was reached by ladder from the ground floor. Sanitation was on a level, say, with that prevailing in the Atlas mountains.[16]

The mild overuse of comparisons – and the fact that there is no such place as Noland (the village was Neyland) – don't diminish its melancholy. After a month living with a postmistress for company who sang Welsh hymns, "stopping her carolling only to weep with loneliness",[17] he and Hester finally found a cottage in Little Haven, a fishing village in a spartan cove. Shuttling to London for business and meetings with friends – Loke Wan Tho, the Singaporean owner of the gaudy 500K Mercedes, appeared at his suite at the Dorchester in late June – he came back to enough calm to be able to start writing. He had an impression of progress on the novel and managed to spend most of the settled perfection of the summer working on the book. He took a week off when Derek Wise visited. "We didn't do very much, had some very good fishing."[18] Loke also visited, dragging cases of sensitive camera equipment with him: a passionate birdwatcher and photographer doomed to a rich man's kismet of steering a business empire. He and Norman sailed to Skomer, a few miles offshore, for a few days to photograph wrens and study the habits of the Skomer shearwaters before Loke had to go back to Singapore. The two men had a sensitive friendship, and Norman's liking was partly a sympathy for Loke's imprisonment in the "empty rituals" of business that he himself was in the process of evading. His description of the stark escapism of Little Haven omits his writing and the glorious weather.

Littlehaven offered a majestic seascape but little else. At night huge docile rats patrolled its few yards of water front, hardly bothering to avoid the residents who crept out to empty their sewage into the sea. Exceptional tides accompanied by a wind blowing in from the sea swept the water a foot deep into the cottage's downstairs rooms. The worst hazard in Littlehaven, however, was a corvée imposed by the village's unwritten law on those whose cottages overlooked the beach. These were supposed, on observing any boat coming in at low tide, to rush out and to help its crew drag it up the shingle. I spent about five months in Littlehaven, and by the end of that time had developed a set of extraordinary muscles quite useless for any purpose beyond dragging boats up beaches. I was permanently in a state of semi-starvation as a grocer-cum-butcher from Haverfordwest, about 12 miles away, only delivered once a week, and as is always the case in such seaside places, fish was never to be had unless one caught it oneself.[19]

Asceticism is a particular form of hedonism, a pursuit of harmony in the barest minimum. Norman's portrait of life on the Welsh shore wraps its author in a recluse's cloak of bleak minimalism that was belied by his pleasure that summer. A telltale sentence written about an unnamed character in a later diary indicates the extent of his pleasure.

Somehow or other he never seemed to extract the full glory from life's brief golden moments. (The summer at L. Haven)[20]

His description also excluded another event at the end of the summer. In September Hester told him she was pregnant again.

A reflection on where his and Hester's ease at producing children might end probably crossed his mind, although a respectable result from his summer's writing might have eased anxieties he had (even if writers are rarely as satisfied with their work as non-writers). The positive answer he received in December from Jonathan Cape to his request to submit a novel with "a contemporary Algerian theme" might also have helped distract him from worries that the prams in the hall would stop him establishing himself.[21]

His efforts to get published after a nine-year break were not as haphazard as he later implied. He hadn't tried "Filfila" on Routledge and had it rejected, as he self-deprecatingly writes in his autobiography. He remembered perfectly well the mess they had made of his Arabian album, and instead found himself caught in an exchange of letters between publishers when Routledge found that he had submitted a novel to Cape and tried, unsuccessfully, to enforce their option.

After he had read the typescript Jonathan Cape's reader, Daniel George, wrote to invite Norman to the offices to discuss some editorial changes. Before the appointment was kept, George contacted him again. Norman's account was that "Jonathan himself passed [George's] desk, picked the book up because he had nothing to read and took it to lunch. When he returned Daniel was back. Jonathan handed it over and said 'we'll publish this.'"[22]

Norman's relations with the firm of Jonathan Cape, whom he stayed with until 1961, remained for a long time tinged by his surprise at that first acceptance, though in 1948 Cape was far from its peak of prestige. In the twenty-seven years since its founding it had published a catalogue of world-class writers, from Doughty to Joyce and T E Lawrence to Hemingway, but the war had made life hard for publishers. In the late 1940s a shrunken Cape lacked editorial originality. Michael Howard, the gentle, browbeaten son of G Wren Howard, Jonathan Cape's original partner, and eventually Norman's editor, did his best to update the flat list, but until 1960 Cape chiefly existed on its past glory.

By secret aspiration, Norman felt he deserved to be of that company. With the sense of suburban inferiority he reverted to under pressure, he felt he was an imposter. What levelled the balance slightly were his relations with Jonathan Cape himself, who had risen from the humblest start as a delivery boy at the Piccadilly bookshop, Hatchards, to become a bizarre fusion of autocrat, publishing genius and courteous bore. Whenever he and Norman lunched, Jonathan reserved the bulk of his enthusiasm for a protracted account of his most recent holiday at Eastbourne. The publisher's Georgian offices between Bloomsbury and Soho, where he held lunches for authors, were known as "Heartburn House" in tribute to the reliably charred Irish stew cooked by Cape's ill-tempered chef, but Norman, sympathetic to his publisher's self-made trajectory, relaxed in Jonathan's company. Cape for his part was willing to play a long game with his authors. "Filfila", which became *Samara*, was not intended to sell in thousands; he had simply enjoyed it. When Norman asked Daniel George why, George told him it was because it was "about abroad. He never goes anywhere except New York on business."[23] (Daniel George was one of the most human figures at Cape. Silver haired, rubicund, a smoker, he wore bow-ties and looked like a sedentary elder brother of Yves Montand. He once wrote a disguised epitaph of himself in Cape's readers' magazine, *Now & Then*: "Here lies the body of Timothy Hillier, / Who died a victim of haemophilia:/ He was a publisher's reader – / Poor bleeder.")

Mirroring his publisher, Norman too went (almost) nowhere in 1948. His business judgment about the small-camera market went on paying off. In January he opened a new branch of R G Lewis at 125 Strand, near the Savoy Hotel, with more and more space at 202 being taken up with the company's cine projection business (the following year a dedicated cine projecting room was built on the first floor of 202 for customers to be able to watch their films and slides under ideal conditions). Less than six months later, R G Lewis's turnover was matching that of a firm called Wallace Heaton which had the King's warrant. Heaton's and Lewis's had competing weekly double page advertisements on consecutive spreads of *Amateur Photographer*, though Norman's low copywriting style, with its knockabout headlines – "Dick Barton, where were you?" the week 202 was burgled – and its literary habits was more entertaining. No one else quoted Shakespeare, Swift, William Cowper and Milton in a single advert.

A GOOD DEED IN A NAUGHTY WORLD shines brightly, said Portia, but she should have likened it not to a little candle but to the Aldis Miniature Projector, which shineth brightly in the home of many a contented miniaturist. ... "FEW ARE QUALIFIED TO SHINE in company", wrote Swift, "but it is in most men's power to be agreeable." Had he been writing of 35mm projectors, he would not have been far wrong. ... THE LIE THAT FLATTERS was abhorred the most by William Cowper, but the Modulo, performing the same service in portraiture, is universally acclaimed by photographers. ... THE BRIGHT COUNTENANCE OF TRUTH is beheld in the quiet and still air of delightful studies, according to Milton, but according to modern miniaturists it is seen in the prints yielded by coated objectives.[24]

R G Lewis differed at the physical level too. When readers attracted by his adverts came to 202 they saw no counters or showcases. They talked to the staff on the shop floor, and the staff advised as specialists. It was a gift of an intensely private Norman to be able to create, through both advertising and personal contact, unusually loyal *business* relationships with his customers, appealing to them, involving them, always emphasising his service to "our many keen photographic friends". He consistently promised "the best prices in the United Kingdom for apparatus in really fine condition" and "sane and sensible dealing" all the time. "Be wise," he advised his readers, excruciatingly, "and R G Lewisize your photography." They did.

On 24 May 1948 Norman's second son, Gareth, was born at Hampstead General Hospital on Haverstock Hill. After Gareth was born his parents' relationship fell apart.

They had been no closer during the second pregnancy than the first, and Hester suddenly realised the enormity of what was happening. She was thirty-nine years old, an unmarried mother of two (though she had changed her surname by deed poll to Lewis), living with a man whose attention she could not keep. It was clear to Norman, now at forty the father of two small children (and one eleven-year-old) and still a long way from possessing the future he had imagined, that he didn't want to go on with the relationship. It was a crucial moment, another sudden and ruthless rupture with the past that would drive Norman onwards to another self-conversion and all its consequences. For Hester its emotional impact was awful. About a year later, in Scotland, Karen remembers – it is her first memory – being "cuddled with a desperation in bed by my mother" still feeling the uncontrolled anguish of her separation, "weeping and crying in the room in Breen Cottage, the room on the left-hand side as you go up which is historically her room, and saying over and over again, 'Oh God, help me, oh please help me, oh my God help me.'" Norman and Hester did not part definitively, but in a curious finesse he manoeuvred her and the children to Scotland, back to the house where she had been born. It was an admission that the relationship had been, as Baron had implied it would be, an utter disaster. Norman suffered some sorrow and remorse at the split, by his later behaviour showing considerable willingness to be Karen's and Gareth's father and keep up the idea of a family, but he did not carry its heavier emotional or practical burdens because he, unlike Hester, was able without loss of love or liberty to walk away from it.

But –

The reader is owed urgent scrutiny of that paragraph. As biographer, I believe that what I've written *may* be an accurate reflection of what happened after Gareth was born. Although some of it may have happened before he was born (and he himself obviously bears no responsibility for his parents' separation) it seems likely, if not probable, that the arrival of a new baby, the presence of two very small children with all their demands and call to involvement, were what finally lamed this caravan. Absence of documentation and witnesses makes it impossible to know in an unqualified, let alone factual, way. Apart from the date and place of Gareth's birth, the sentences of Karen's (from an interview with her, recorded in her sitting room overlooking the Tamar estuary fifty-seven years later), and the gross facts – Norman and Hester had two children after the war, didn't stay together – the how, and when, and why, of what happened at their separation is an invented guess.[25] (Norman never referred to Hester in anything he wrote, or spoke about her outside his immediate family. His published version of his life, in contrast to its materialising of both Ernestina and his later partner Lesley, dematerialised her.)

And there is one other thing. The vacuum of consultable records, letters and verbal testimony is only the physical, that is to say apparent, reason for not knowing more. It is not hard to suspect that the underlying reason is something more metaphysical, a mutual deliberateness obscurely composed of pain and shame, hers and his, that lies somewhere between not wanting to remember and not wanting to be reminded. Which is only human. So that all that the biographer has to hand are the threads of the situation, to be picked up with a knocking heart at the next capsule of facts, the next fresh isolate of circumstances. Everything begins again. Which is also only human.

Norman spent part of that summer in Wales, though "After Little
Haven there was worse to come. The road was always downhill. I
listened to the beautiful voices of my Welsh neighbours – always, it
seemed, on the threshold of song – through the cracked walls of remote
farmhouses. It was a life of leaking roofs, lamplight, boiled rainwater,
and the mewing desolation of the curlew calling over the marsh."[26] He
made no mention of whether "worse" included sharing living space
with Hester. He started work on a new novel, again based on his war
experience, this time with the treacherous web of loyalties around Naples
as its subject. In late September he escaped across the Channel, reporting
himself in an *Amateur Photographer* advert of 13 October as "on safari
in darkest Europe at the moment". In London he initiated an enigmatic reorganisation of living arrangements, renting, as well as the
Knightsbridge flat, another in Farm Street in Mayfair and one in
Chelsea Cloisters. One explanation is that for a few months Hester
and the children carried on living near the Albert Hall while he lived,
difficult to find, nearby. That would mirror the situation that followed
for the next fifteen years, because this was an unconventional separation, one in which until the early 1960s Norman and Hester both kept
up a pretence, for the children's and social forms' sake, that they were,
even if remotely, man and wife.

By January 1949 Norman had persuaded Hester to move back to
Scotland with the children, to her sister Joan's house at Banchory near
Aberdeen. He destroyed his will and sent money, showing in his diary
note that he suspected Hester read his diary: the note reads "ДЕНГИ
[*dyengi*, 'money' in Russian] sent to H".[27]

Breen Cottage at Banchory was a granite house in a granite village
on Deeside, "a lovely house" in Gareth's words that overlooked the
railway station. Norman made plans to visit but on the evening of 19
February went down with malaria for four days. He did not get to
Scotland for another month, part of the delay involving a crucial move
of his own. He had freed himself from Hester partly to lock down his
ambition – it is impossible to read the next two months another way
– and he needed time to organise. His intention was to take himself
off alone on a driving tour through France to the Camargue and along
the Mediterranean coast as far as southern Italy. This road trip was to
be a return to himself, a release, a ducking away from all pressures, a
laboratory in which he would write and take pictures as he went, closely
observing his mood and what he saw around him, making notes for

his novel; surviving alone. He intended it to be, in that bluff Conradian phrase that connotes both harmony with, and disclosure of, the self, "a strictly professional feeling",[28] with only his senses and reactions for company; nothing and nobody else.

His trip to Banchory was, rather heartlessly, to double as a tryout. After spending three days with Hester and the children he drove north to do some birdwatching. The day he left, Sunday 20 March, he was excited enough at the thought of a new stage beginning to write "FIRST DAY" in his appointments diary. He drove to Dingwall and had lunch in Brora, relishing the air of the Cromarty Firth thick with seabirds, seeing scaups and an albino oystercatcher before cutting across the Caithness moorland to Melvich and Bettyhill on Scotland's northernmost coast, the "most attractive spot" of the journey.

He covered 1900 kilometres in four days and high spirits, getting back to London on the 24th. The next week was spent crossing things off a long list: organising R G Lewis stock, collecting private papers from Gordon Street, assembling petrol coupons and items for the Lancia's toolkit, visiting Anderson & Sheppard's at Savile Row where he had taken to having his suits made. He called his mother at the nursing home she had moved to in Enfield and dealt with his solicitor, Hilbery, over the future sale of the no longer necessary Carterhatch Lane house.

On 29 March he "Crossed Channel. Very cold, misty. Worse still at Calais." In Calais he booked in to the Hôtel du Littoral. But he had not left England yet: two other British guests were at the hotel, and his antipathy level shot up. He made a note in his diary about one of the guests, who looked like the monocled ventriloquist's dummy, Charlie McCarthy, and shared his character, "at about 40 going through the agonies of a difficult adolescence – avenges himself on mankind by taking an immense time in the lavatory. The only place where he feels safe."[29]

He took a brown notebook with him too, to fill out his diary notes with the casual events of a crowded journey. It begins with a reader's list from things he was reading at the time – two pages of collected word-currants that might be delicious enough to enrich his buns of prose if he got the chance:

a vesper mood
an air of apostolic detachment
mystagogue
mephitic waters

syncretism
tilth
eld
anfractuosity
untamed telluric forces
vermiform
perlustration
qualified praise
elucubration
cerulean
hyperborean gloom
rebarbative
caul

And the last word before the journey started. "Euphoria."

We are all capable of positive good or evil, he cried, but most of us are just negative, we want to be allowed to live and die in peace. In the name of this huge good natured majority all sorts of things are done. The woman who through her desperation killed her baby – are you personally responsible for hounding her down – condemning her to death? Do you know what took place in the condemned cell – in the death chamber? You are as much the prey of a democracy as we of a dictatorship.

She typified – symbolized – the pleasures of the flesh. Smiling. Silent. Acquiescent. One day goaded by some mood he asked her, "But have you a soul?" and to this she only smiled in reply.

He was eating fast now and with every mouthful his rage increased. He stuffed his mouth with potatoes. "Who does she think she is?" He munched vigorously as if crushing her pretensions between his teeth. A forkful of young asparagus. "My god that bitch." The asparagus stuck in his teeth and made him feel all the worse.

1949 notebook

15

JUST GOING

"You go up the mountain to get rid of your problems and people say:
What a happy man! He has gone to his summer place to rest"
Azerbaijani proverb

The route chosen was unfortunate. The road to Paris, Calais, St Omer, Péronne,
Senlis, included maximum of pavé stretches. Distance about 200 miles, ca.
120 were through heavy rain-loaded mist. Cold. Weather became fair outside
Paris.

N7 followed through Nevers and Moulins after which N9 becoming extremely
windy. Uninteresting and desolate after CLERMONT-FERRAND (NOT recommended).
Stayed at Grand Hotel. Tout compris – 500frs. A barrack of a place with
fragile lift and bare echoing plank floors. Commercial neighbour carries on a
telephone conversation about markets, every word of which is clear.

An attractive gorge before ST FLOUR & then desolation to Mende (lunch p[rix]
fixe vin compris 228 frs against average price of 1000 fr for a meal).[1]

So far, so unpromising. Continuing south, Norman judged the Cévennes
desolate too, winter bare, cold and windy despite the "spectacular"
gorges of the Jonte, and he saw no spring green until Lodève. "All this
route is disapproved of," he wrote *ex cathedra*.

But his pocket diary contains a surprise. He liked to keep track in
it of hotels, menus and prices, the distance covered, how much fuel the
car used. On Friday 1 April, the day he had lunch in Saint-Flour, he
notes starting at ten a.m. and covering 275 miles (442 kilometres) on
8 gallons of petrol to Béziers, where he stayed at the Hôtel de la Gare
(room and supper 1200 francs). On the 2nd he used another 4 gallons

of petrol and made "150 miles to Saintes-Maries-de-la-Mer. Sunny in afternoon." Then the flow of details breaks.

"No depression. Very bright today."[2]

So another part of the journey's experiment comes to light. By setting out on the drive – and by avoiding the phrase "clearing the decks" we can get closer to the idea of construction rather than waste disposal – he was looking for a way ahead, a *Lebensstil* that might encapsulate the extremes he was feeling. Clinically, his feeling euphoria and depression in succession was perfectly rational, a clinical pendulum of cyclothymia. The depression was probably brought on by the messy panorama of England and Hester, post-war boredom and unsettled ambition; all he now had to do was find out how it could exercise some therapeutic pressure on him. In his imagination there was no uncertainty about what he was looking for – a way that incorporated a life of writing – but his performances henceforth had to be not to himself, or to a woman, but to the outside world. It was on this journey that he had to stop playing the lyric poet – hopeful and narcissistic – and start to play the writer-in-the-world, who would turn his narcissism inside out and care only about the writer's instrument, of a way of seeing the world in words that could compel readers to share it.

There is a little mystery to his diary notes about his mood. Every time an entry touches on his mood or spirits, a code is ascribed, "SXX" at Clermont-Ferrand, "SX" (less depressed?) at Saintes-Maries-de-la-Mer two days later. Later the code "No SR" is associated with a good mood. Nothing explains the letters. Whatever he meant precisely stays beyond the biographer's reach (and the biographer salutes his outwitting).

On the way to Saintes-Maries on 2 April he stopped at Agde – a "magnificent line of cobalt boats drawn up along weathered facades of riverside houses. . . . The boats are those made familiar by Van Gogh. They exactly reproduce the shape of those made to amuse children, to be floated in ditches from sheets of paper." He was starting to find colours, surfaces and warmth to ease the gnawings of depression, enthusing at the murals at the "wonderful Café du Sport" and Agde's "many WCs and urinals, the older of the latter being ornamented by a tasteful frieze in the ironwork". The plane trees on its promenade, the names of "charming hat box like villas, Son por Son, Bamboula, Syrène", the landscape "enhanced by advertisements in which even Texaco have cooperated by the use of exactly [the] right colours" all pleased him. Sète, the next stop, was a less pleasing version of Agde that carried the "scar of modernismus", its boats "the colour of robins' breasts ... seen coquettishly through a gossamer of drying nets". But its "frank industrialism" was to be preferred to Palavas which was "one of those 'nice little places'" where he felt the stifling approach of bourgeois habits. He struck back. "It abounds with professional wives and mothers in slacks showing pinched and sagging posteriors." Improving his mood, Le Grau du Roi later that afternoon was "enchanting", as was the road to Aigues Mortes "fished by winch contraptions at every 100 metres".

Finally at the fishing village of Saintes-Maries he found a hotel that satisfied all his criteria. "An almost snobbish avoidance of AA-starred hotels is counselled," he told himself. Instead the Hôtel de la Plage had "considerable dignity of architecture" and offered a display of waders, flamingoes and avocets, so abundant that it confused him. "The flamingoes were at first overlooked – taken to be a sandbank in the Etang." He was impressed by the hotel's "fragrance of decades of good cooking [and] cavernous passages and stairway ... you dine en famille in a riotous still-life of trachomous mirrors, artificial flowers, plates in racks, a baby's high chair, signed pictures of cowboys, sick radio sets, armoires loaded with litre flasks and upturned glasses of all varieties". The houses in the village were left unlocked at night and the bags bulging with snails hung "at each door to absorb the dew" were unmolested.[3]

His close descriptions of Camargue towns, landscape, wildlife, the post-war atmosphere – and his aversion to bourgeois life – continue. The French Army was everywhere there was a river. Many towns had a barracks feel. On Sunday he zigzagged to one, Le Salin de Giraud, then up to Arles ("On Sunday evening groups of young men wander for considerable distances along the road, playing bowls with silver balls") and down to Martigues. He enjoyed the impermanent moment. "The lady in charge of the level crossing gates spends her spare time fishing in the nearest ditch." He noted an effect fetishised by twentieth-century metropolitans. "The pleasant bleaching of woodwork left without paint produces an effect much sought after by modern furniture producers." He had no depression that day but was a "Bit moody in evening. Probably tired. SX." Martigues, he wrote, "smacks strangely of the Orient". Dining on bouillabaisse and an entrecôte at the Hôtel Pascal (run by an Algerian called Isaac who had "not very good Algerian carpets in all his rooms"), he extended an imaginative hand to its atmosphere.

One sensed in the *chambres* of monsieur Ishak a ghostly emanence of love's despairs. The faint fragrance of Chanel 5 left by an endless succession of clandestine beauties from Marseilles. The repinings of clandestine lovers between repasts in which figured the *loups*, the *homards*, the *soles* of monsieur Ishak (*prix selon grandeur*).

The rough sentences are interesting. More concise and more suggestive than his pre-war writing, they have several tokens of his later style: musicality, the ironic intervention of reality, a compassion for the ridiculous, the absence of an author. The last two are more or less new, a result of the war's effects on him, its imposition of the need to describe comedy and horror together.

After Martigues began the Côte d'Azur and the first proper fine weather. He lunched at Le Luc with a French party, two Americans ("the girl of the type voted second most likely to succeed"), a Swiss and an Englishman, then drove through the Esterel to the coast. He was "much fluttered by the beach at Cannes";[4] his photographer's eye also noted the change from cool colours to the "incredibly rich dull red, relieved with yellow" of the arcaded houses that framed the port at Villefranche. "Here, then, red seems to be the *decent* colour, just as blue further westwards and brown or bottle green in England". Stopping at San Remo that night, his spirits reasonable ("Fairly evenly SX"), he found himself in mixed, even grotesque company including "two of the most incredible English spinsters ever seen" and an English motor racing party that included "a plump pink girl" who warded off the local wolf repeatedly. His descriptions of the seducer's approach and of other people – a widow dripping with jewels, a sluttish woman, another solitary diner – hover transitionally between observation and fictional exercise, but one reflection evokes the wry memory of a romantic egotist who once, with a rake's suit and fair years to waste, ran after a jeweller's daughter.

That which you lose goes from you slowly. So slowly that it is unnoticed. It is only when you lean out of a window at night and breathe in a certain perfume of flowers of 20 years back that you realise with a choking shock, how much has gone away.[5]

The next day, Tuesday the 5th, he reached Viareggio where it was raining and cold, but had "No SR. Good spirits." On Wednesday morning the unbeliever went out of curiosity to an early funeral service, finding that "when the priest commences the office ... the tears fill his eyes. He begins to mumble the half remembered words in English: I believe etc. Sternly rebuking himself with the other half of his mind." Not the theatre but the words caught him out, twice: "Lovely words in Latin quoted on the gate of the cemetery: *Credo quod redemptor meus vivit et in novissimo die de terre surrecturus sum, Et in carne mea videbo Deum salvatorem meum.* These words [are] equally beautiful in any language." The sun came out and he pushed on south like Gatsby, "fenders spread like wings", another 320 kilometres down the coast to Santa Marinella, his spirits holding though he noted that "Sunshine is like alcohol. It aggravates moods in any direction."

The pages of his notebook began to surrender to longer, more frequent extracts from a fictional imagination, little of it connecting but unfolding some similar themes: encounters with legal authority, relations between men, women's sexual indifference or independence, their deafness to male needs for love (both sexual and emotional). The rhetoric of the last two categories conveys not so much the authentic atmosphere of misogyny as an undertone of masculine helplessness, of not being heard.

A. carried on the internal argument with his wife. "– But it's clearly understood. . . ."

"No," said his wife in that uncompromising manner with which she was unfailingly armed in their imaginary disputes, "nothing's understood, nothing of the kind." She wouldn't let him finish a sentence. Not even in his imagination.[6]

Is it too inevitable to point out that anyone with such a partner, or such a belief, has no alternative to getting rid of them or it, if they want their own mind ever – in Fitzgerald's phrase about the moment of Gatsby's doom – to romp again like the mind of God? The quarrel between A and his wife may be the truest outline we have of Norman's and Hester's relationship and its failure, from where he was standing. It may not. But a preoccupation with such failure probably underlies another scrap of story in the notebook that has plenty of wish fulfilment about it. A German who kills his lover is driven by his conscience, or his ego, to attempt to confess his crime to various other young women he meets, "for", as his thought processes significantly conclude,

to create consternation as a villain is better than to evoke no interest as a law abiding citizen. None of the girls to whom he tries to confess are in the slightest degree moved except one[,] the sweetest and the one he knows to be the most virtuous, who wishes she had been there to see it."[7]

On 7 April he swung another 400 kilometres south to Positano in "Good spirits slightly down on [the] way to Sorrento. No SR." Workers were sowing in the hot fields in rows of six abreast, but he was "Immediately struck with the extreme filth of Naples and the surrounding villages". Its post-war peace had become the peace of stagnation. "Washing fluttering like rags from every facade, paint scaling off everywhere. Everything a dirty dull yellow." He did not stop. After seeing bats flighting in bright sunlight on the Sorrento peninsula, there wasn't a lot to do except regret that the "fantastically typical" Pensione Roma was full and enjoy the San Pietro white wine, "best Italian wine on the trip".

The next day he went on to Salerno, halted by pleasure at the operatic tableau of a tiny fishing hamlet after Praiano where the voices of the fishermen "passionately descended half an octave in semitones" as they echoed in the inlet, and then doubled back to Amalfi for the night, disapproving of the hotel's overrunning by Americans and Swiss in bow-ties, taking a diarist's revenge by satirising their dinner conversation.

Early on the 9th, a Saturday, he left to navigate across the ankle of Italy. Reaching Manfredonia in the afternoon brought him to the trip's vaguely publicised goal. He had felt there might be an article in the Gargano peninsula north and east of the town and had sought books about the area before he left, and on the way. (He found none.) Manfredonia heralded the peninsula's isolated, disregarded, quasimedieval identity: unsophisticated, poor, and fundamentally Catholic ("Long live the missionaries. Down with blasphemy" replaced the political slogans on Italian walls elsewhere), the town's apparent ambition was to be cheaper and more virtuous than any other. He stuffed his notebook with notes. "In the morning street vendors pass below the window crying their wares in the voices of demented flamenco singers. . . . the owner of the [shop] says *al piacere vostro* when asked how much. In the shallows men armed with tridents are prodding among the rocks for *frutti di mare*."

In the article he wrote about Gargano when he got back to England are several future marks of his interest: the preference for material simplicity, the pleasure in human idiosyncrasy, the belief that the characters of places and people are preserved by the negative cultural verities, in Gargano's case "the absence of exploitable wealth, bad communications, the poverty of the soil, Bourbon misrule, and the malarial mosquito".[8] Many travellers' preferences, with few exceptions, are antinomic of course: Norman's preference for material simplicity in other people's lives did not disturb his personal desire for Lancias, Leicas and Anderson & Sheppard suits. The eventual distinction between him and most travellers was not so much his loyalty to travel (which was more or less a reflex) and its ambiguities as his loyalty to language. He immersed himself as deeply as he needed for his prime purpose, of description, disclosure, verbal discovery and composition. And in Gargano he found, delightedly, the raw material for his purpose in its forests, unusual architecture, and ancient (often Greek in origin) customs. The Catholic lived next the pagan.

Emblem of fertility: a horizontal phallus about 24 feet long drawn on a wall. Repeated along the wall and tolerably well drawn.

PESCHICI is the weirdest town I have ever seen. It grows like a parasite. . . . Large proportion of all houses are caves carved out of the limestone rock and the front of these or round the doors are often as in Africa or Spain painted white. NOT A SINGLE WOMAN SEEN IN THE STREETS. A fox's skin hanging from a pole.[9]

Gargano had a town, Monte Sant'Angelo, that had become the centre of European angel worship; it had a habit of medieval nicknames and of the evil eye, and a gravity of demeanour unparalleled in the south. Through Mattinata, Vesti, Peschici, Rodi and Cagnano, in a hundred miles he went back 100 years: to go to Gargano was to "learn what it was to be a traveller in the Mediterranean in the early nineteenth century . . . and the only difficulty that is likely to arise will be in discovering some way of making repayment for the kindness you will receive; for bad communications are often linked with old-fashioned traditions of hospitality".[10]

On Monday when he left he felt "All day a strong inclination to turn back and revisit the Gargano area. Stopped car several times."[11] He also planned to incorporate dramatic events there into the novel featuring A, the unheard husband; but he continued north, leaving the dull Adriatic coast behind for Rieti, Cattolica and Milan, where he was rooked at the Hotel Seviglia and suffered "SRX probably through slight boredom with scenery".

Back over the border, he gave a lift to a girl with "hair of imperial purple and lipstick smeared teeth". He was freshly irritated by the Swiss "everywhere" with their "helmets and porous driving gloves". "The meek shall inherit the earth", he drily noted. From Aix he accelerated, driving fast up through the Rhône and Burgundy to Paris, arriving on the 19th.

Two days later he was back at Banchory, with "SRXX".

He had been away for just over three weeks, driven much more than 6000 kilometres, and crowded sixty pages of a notebook with his tiny spidery script. The road trip had been a lightning conductor, and down it had flowed an enormous bolt of restlessness and purpose. A Spinozan restlessness, a classic ontological desire to be somewhere he wasn't, whose most practical outcome was that it permanently loosened, and on his own terms for the first time, his ties to the static, suburban, mortgaged proprieties he had grown up with.

This was probably more the nature of what he constructed than anything else. The journey had completed an alteration begun by manoeuvring Hester to a distance and laying down some parameters for his own existence, and it would not be unfair to say that the *most real* Norman Lewis came alive (in the sense of passive emotions becoming active) on the drive to the Camargue and Italy in 1949. He could now feel and act *at last* as if he were a writer; not a possible or would-be or potential writer, but a writer and nothing but – a feeling that also meant he had agreed to live with the risks of being a writer and doing as he liked, mainly solitude and artistic failure. In the comparative terms biographers are fond of using in giving the process of a life its shadings and emphases, calibrating backwards the muddle of a life lived forwards, the 1949 Italian experiment was a watershed. That does not make of it a glorious culmination, more a squeak of transition: a shaky template that would quickly lose its fascination and indicative power if it wasn't followed up.

The world of ex-partners and commerce hates to let its actors go, as much as does the world of white-bread conformity. He had dependants on two continents, a business with the hungry exigencies of growth, a good publisher but negligible book income. Assertion of literary freedom in such crowded circumstances is, like anywhere else, always possible, but only by kicking the circumstances aside with rough, repeated energy.

On some like train of thought, Norman set out. He was initially not helped by Cape's publication of his first novel on 25 April, as soon as he returned. *Samara* had already been reviewed in the previous week's *TLS* by Alan Ross alongside a novel by a new American novelist, Norman Mailer. Ross wrote as if he was unsure what to feel about *The Naked and the Dead*, a novel whose descriptions of men in combat would alter the popular view of warfare, except that it was formless and that "in spite of the feeling of conviction Mr Mailer's writing generates, the book grows increasingly unreadable". The author of *Samara* still suffered by proximity, his "anaemic" study of Arab-French conflict unfavourably compared with "Mr Mailer's full-blooded American vitality".

Credited with "a sense of place", Norman was criticised for lacking "that necessary compulsion, that passion which writing at full stretch always exudes". What Ross was perhaps neglecting, at a period in which the USA was perpetually held up as a cultural ideal, was that the two novels showed the difference between American and British reactions to armed conflict, one buoyed, sometimes overwhelmed by its own confidence, the other able to be fatally tethered by its own caution. Thus Edward Langland, the British officer in charge of an army supply dump allegedly looted by Arabs, acts too late to warn local people that the French will use the looting as a pretext for a massacre.

Samara puts useful questions about the limits of civilised prudence and the can-do standards that throw it into relief. An Arab plays a trick on an American soldier, pretending to sell him his wife, "a negress". When she doesn't come back, he complains to the soldier's commanding officer. The officer's reply is to ask where he can get a black woman for himself. This is the stuff of Norman's experience of the wartime world; as is his joke about Arab victimisation and American literalism. An Arab leader tells a US army doctor, "'There are three diseases we suffer from here. . . . Liberty, Equality and Fraternity.' 'Well, thank God they're not contagious,' the commandant said."

What Norman wanted to do in *Samara* was to give the strange flavour of reality, not use it to shed light on his characters. He could not help – a more self-indulgent impulse – giving the flavour of what had been marvellous about the war for Langland / Lewis at the same time. "He saw [again] the Kasbah with its cracked walls and the snaggle-toothed jaw of a bombed sea-front; and the streets with shell-hollow buildings, with gaping, pitted window-frames, into which hair-cutting booths had been built; and he saw the earth, golden-carpeted with fruit, in the bombed orange-grove. . . . And he smelled the blind-walled lanes through the vegetable gardens that held in the earthy fragrance of the night, and the scent of over-ripe melons, and the sharp, exhausted fragrance of dust and earth . . ." and so on, through the yellow dogs barking out of boredom and the songs sung at weddings while shells thumped, to the skewered kebabs sold with contempt by Arabs to unbelievers.

Samara is a more existential novel – in the sense of how an honourable man can fall short by misreading reality – than Ross gives it credit for, and Norman was a better writer, as Ross implied fifty years later in a memoir, recalling *Naples '44*: "*Naples '44* is a wonderful book and I have learned much from it, not only about the Italians but about the calm, unsensational ordering of material. The writing of prose, in fact."[12]

At lunch at Heartburn House, Jonathan Cape asked Norman what his plans were. He mentioned the Guatemala book and wrote later that Cape "pretended not to have heard" then advised him, "Always write a book about Nelson. Never write a book about South America."[13] Norman was in any case already well advanced on a second novel in the same wartime vein as *Samara*. Despite his rejection of Latin America Jonathan agreed guardedly that there might be room for a book about abroad and speculatively suggested that Norman might think about a journey to, and book about, Indo-China.

And his recent road trip had galvanised Norman's escape reflex. It inaugurated a demotion of his English life and a period of escalating disappearances that lasted for the next five years: travelling so intense that he sometimes appeared to be pursuing subjects and places as if they would disappear (as some did), and was always planning two or three departures ahead.

A fortnight after getting back from the Continent, he was watching peregrines and shelducks on the Taf estuary, and a week later was at the Grand Hotel at Lerwick on Shetland, having stopped the night at Banchory and caught the ferry from Aberdeen. At Ness he saw "20–30 pairs Great skuas" and an Arctic skua. He was, deplorably, collecting eggs, though on Bressay the next day, walking for four hours, he found the nests more scattered and got "only one". Malcolm Borthwick, a birdwatching friend from the 1960s, remembers his seriousness about birds.

Not only did he know all his bird calls, his knowledge of birds was a side he didn't show people unless he knew they understood. He always kept binoculars in the bathroom upstairs and he used to phone me, once he phoned up and said very excitedly, in that dry voice of his, "You'll never guess what I've seen in the garden this morning when I was on the loo: a Golden oriole in a flock of starlings." And the thing is that the Golden oriole is a distant part of the starling family, so knowing Norman I never doubted for a minute that it was a Golden oriole.[14]

Ten days later, on 29 May, he was back at Laugharne watching young shelducks and on the 31st kites at Cilycwm. London claimed some attention – the sale of 343 Carterhatch Lane was still going through, his mother was to be visited, a part-time secretary had to be advertised for, the Alfa needed to be readied for sale, and he was in pursuit of new friendship, in a note to himself written in Cyrillic script to prevent Hester reading it. "Regent Introduction Bureau. Stanhope Bureau. 121 Western Rd Brighton." But he was in Shetland again on 13 June, where a north wind froze him, and two days later walked 25 kilometres and counted 50 pairs of Great skuas, though "most of eggs probably taken", and later on Bressay saw Arctic and Little terns and Eider ducks. Curiously, next to the times of the Bressay–Lerwick ferries in his diary, he wrote in Cyrillic "Robertson, Beach View Cafe, Brae".

Travelling back to London on the sleeper, he met Daniel George at Cape on 23 June to deliver a first draft of his new novel. A week later he had lunch with Michael Howard, his editor. Howard liked the novel and wanted to publish it the following spring. Norman also sent an advert for the Alfa to *The Times*. A beautiful car, often the substitute choice of a man in search of something that has nothing to do with cars, will become dispensable when the thing it is a substitute for is found. Though he immensely regretted his 8C Le Mans winner, owned for twelve years, he had less impulse to play to impress. The advertisement went in on 1 July. Four days later the car sold.

On his weekends in Wales in May he had looked for another place where he could take refuge in the summer, as he had done the two previous years. Whether he and Hester had agreed that they would spend summers together as a family as compensation for her exile is unknown, but she and the children were a part of the summer's plans. He had seen an improbable advertisement in the *Western Mail* for a castle to let, "comfortably furnished. All modern conveniences", its only snag being that it was cut off by the tide twice a day. More factually, it was a disused fort on a whale-backed rock, St Catherine's Island, just offshore at the town of Tenby.

Tenby was new to me. As principal town of that enclave in Pembrokeshire known as "Little England Beyond Wales", it was gay and un-Welsh. . . . There were streets that started as staid Georgian terraces and took on frivolity with every few steps in the sea's direction, until, overlooking the tide, walls became crenellated and balconies roofed with tartar cupolas. Tenby, with its enceinte of fine medieval walls, was scented with brine and make-belief.[15]

Temperamentally St Catherine's Fort faces Tenby's saucy flaunting with prohibitionist dourness. Functionally it is a lavishly specified memorial to British suspicion, built from 400-millimetre granite blocks in the late 1860s against the soberly considered threat of a French invasion. Ordered by a usually cool-headed Lord Palmerston whose senses, this time, had deserted him, it was to be one of five defensive forts on the Pembroke coast. As sometimes happens with government capital projects, it was politically and practically obsolete at completion and, accumulating shocking cost overruns, was sold shortly afterwards for a holiday home for next to nothing.

Norman's accounts of his stay differ (none includes Hester),[16] but he certainly hid away in the fort's main hall and / or one of the turret rooms for three or four stretches during the summer while he worked on various things: an article about Gargano, some short stories, his Guatemala research, some descriptive essays about England that he didn't go on with. His lease started on 21 July, and a problem presented itself immediately with Hester breaking her ankle on one of the granite steps. He needed a housekeeper but had difficulty persuading anyone to keep house because of the fort's inaccessibility and the local belief that a ghost roamed its empty rooms. Eventually he engaged a Mrs Rhys and her daughter Eiluned and

with the arrival of the Rhyses I took off time to explore our surroundings, to climb and descend crepuscular winding staircases, open locked doors, and pass through them into the cold, fungus-scented darkness within. The castle's ground floor comprised the great hall, and six living rooms. There were three rather dismal cells in each turret, all lit by windows that had once been gun embrasures. Beneath the ground floor extended a huge single chamber, which had probably once been a barrack room, and was now stocked with thousands of pairs of antlers. A final flight of stone steps led down to a fetid and dangerous pit known as the powder-magazine.[17]

Living at the fort imposed some hardship: balanced meals were rare with food shops often closed at low tide and Mrs Rhys's dietary interdictions – as a lay preacher and "high priestess of an obscure sect called The Sons of Gideon" she apparently refused to touch eggs; the tides varied with the onshore winds and returning from London Norman sometimes had to wade or wait till the tide ebbed; and over time the island exerted a "subtle claustrophobia". (The garrison posted to the fort when it was first built had demonstrated this effect by deciding one morning, in its cooped-up boredom, to be entertained by "conducting a brief point-blank bombardment upon the town it was supposed to defend". Cannon balls turned up in seafront gardens years later.) But there were compensations in the privacy and Parnassian silence, and in being able to work outdoors in fine weather "on a small plateau overlooking the mainland . . . among the flowers and the strangely tame seagulls". He wrote, read Evelyn Waugh and Graham Greene (*Journey Without Maps*), wondered if *Love in a Cold Climate* was worth reading, and worked his way through a pile of old travel books about the Far East. He wrote in longhand, with a curious quirk: on rereading a page he had written he would cut out any sentence or passage he disliked with scissors, then glue the two halves together or add a blank sheet to the original. (The technique may have been developed when he was writing copy for R G Lewis, adding the newest changes or commercial *jeu d'esprit* to the original copy without having to write the whole thing out again.) It was an efficient way of producing a draft for the typist, occasionally resulting in a "page" that was more than a metre long and stiff with glue and multiple sheets of paper. It was a habit he maintained for the rest of his life.

When he wasn't working he went birdwatching along the Pembroke coast. He visited the bardic colony at Penglas where the chief bard, Caraddawg, and his wife Branwen confessed that the "constant shortage of drinking money was the main drawback to the poet's vocation". He did not have to suffer that indignity with R G Lewis turning over successfully in London. In late August he came back to London to visit his mother, whose health was wavering, and to take Hester and the children home on the sleeper to Banchory. He shuttled to Tenby for shorter periods in September. Finally the fort's claustrophobia, worsening with the first autumn storms and the alleged return of a ghost that scared Mrs Rhys and her daughter into new employment, made him abandon it in early October, his shopping lists of the summer, "frying pan, tea pot, matches, torch, Calor gas, gas mantles, blankets, garlic salami, eggs, wine, glue", succeeded by new urban needs, "*New Statesman*, haircut, pernod glasses, jug, shoes, hair oil, gramophone and records".

The return from Tenby was the start of an annual routine: one that combined mild depression at being back with an outbreak of organisational and social energy. Many of the places Norman travelled to from 1950 onwards were best visited in the dry season, a fact that suited a Christmas- and winter-hating Welshman perfectly. He spent October and November dealing with commercial business – the R G Lewis branches now counted around twenty-five staff, including the recently returned Herbert Currey as manager of 202, and the newly built cine projection room was about to open – and reading about south-east Asia. He was also busy, most days at any time after five thirty, drinking with Derek Wise, Malcolm Dunbar, his Bugatti partner Arthur Baron, and others from Berlemont's like Frank Allen. He could afford to. R G Lewis was making him mildly rich. Crokie Allen, Frank Allen's wife, remembers that "When I first met Norman he had rolls of notes coming out of his pocket." He kept occasional contact with acquaintances at the Foreign Office, the successors of "Rex Stevens",

connections that survived actively for most of his working life. He went
to Banchory, trying to maintain for Karen and Gareth the performance
of the father who was there but not there, and did the same for Ito in
Guatemala, jogging himself in his diary ("B[irth]D[ay] present for I.")
to keep in touch. He rang his mother and visited her at the Claremont
Nursing Home at Enfield. But he was in a frame of mind to enjoy
himself. His diary reverts to the buying of liquor and records. A musician whose records he hunted down was the Cuban pianist and
bandleader Armando Oréfiche, whose pathos-filled but essentially
untragic stamp of love songs and rumbas, including the enigmatic
"Almendra", the cheerfully syncopated "Paracalo", "La Conga Se Va",
and "Rumba Blanca", and the Cuban answer to Gershwin's "I Got
Rhythm", "Conga de la Martinica", met his mood. Despite being
bound to London with winter coming down, energy and pleasure had
the edge over depression. His second novel was to be published in
spring, the *New Statesman and Nation* had accepted two stories, and
Jonathan Cape had commissioned the book about Indo-China, leaving
him a task he liked well – reading books of research and accounts by
long-dead writers – and a couple of problems. Currency restrictions
were still repressive. With Cape's influence he was able to get his travel
allowance doubled to £200, and he bought a gold watch to sell if necessary. And despite his preparations, the question of research remained
hanging. To help solicit the aid of the French colonial authorities he
was introduced to Peter Fleming at *The Times*, another Cape author,
who agreed to underwrite his journalistic credentials; but no one in
London knew what was happening on the ground. All information was
from before the war and Japanese takeover, ten years out of date. All
that was sure was that when the French had tried to reclaim their
empire in 1945 a nationalist rebellion led by Ho Chi Minh had punc-
tually started, provoking a new colonial war that was still going on.

Before he left for Indo-China his first published short story, "The
Señores", appeared in the 7 January issue of the *New Statesman and
Nation*. Its assets were its ease with its Spanish background and its
post-war moral ironies – a British businessman, sent to Spain to appoint
a Spanish agent, inspects a dozen companies under two headings, "organ-
isation" and "morality". He is wined and dined by two men from a
Catalan firm who fix him up with a tart. He doesn't sleep with her.
When asked, he explains that the experience was too cold-blooded.
The next evening the men set him up with a seamstress instead, an

"honest" girl who earns 10 pesetas a day. He spends several nights with her, becoming fond of her "in a well-regulated way", not paying her because his interpreter tells him she would be insulted. When he breaks the news to her that he is leaving, she weeps. At the station she comes to see him off, giving him a parting gift of a small framed photograph of herself and a box of chocolates, before saying goodbye with deep unhappiness.

The story's interest is partly a reversal of his Italian preoccupations of a year before: it is the young woman, not the man, who is treated with indifference. But its chief interest is its working-out of cultural exploitation. The first agreeable experience the businessman has in Spain is that a tailor in Barcelona can run him up a tussore suit in three days for "five hundred pesetas – a fiver. He was enchanted." Afterwards, in his encounter with the young seamstress – a classic "native" and "stranger" encounter – he doesn't really treat the girl as human, but as another of Spain's economic benefits. His materialism ensures that she never exists as a human being. In fact neither woman nor country signify themselves as subjects; they are instead objects of exotic, agreeably cheap consumption. Accidentally – though in the deep narrative of a writer's interests there are probably few accidents – the story sheds some light too on his work's capital theme. To see cultures as subjects not objects would provide the intention, motive and tone to all his future writing about travel. Writing that would also point in prophecy at the antithesis of that theme, that it was all too easy, as in "The Señores", for cultures to be seen as objects – which would become the guiding axiom of the first fifty years of the history of Spanish tourism.

Look, you have to imagine you're travelling in a carriage in an ordinary train. There are two types, and right at the extreme of the range there's Chatwin: it would be the most beautiful man in Greek mythology who had suddenly arrived in your train. Now that's one kind of travel writer, Apollo in your carriage or whoever the most beautiful Greek god would be, and of course he would be homosexual.

Now also you hadn't noticed, but in the corner is this dark-haired, thin man who hardly said a thing, and you instinctively liked him. It was obvious that he seemed to be working-class but he also seemed to have some quite extraordinary depth of wisdom, and a look of self-mockery, mockery of the world – everything that women want.

Nobody would ever have said this about Chatwin, but if you're a heterosexual you'll find that every woman says to you, "I want a man who has a great sense of humour." Why? What does that tell you? A man with a great sense of humour is an alpha male. Why is he an alpha male? Because you cannot produce jokes or treat life as a joke or self-mockery unless you're full of confidence. It can't be done if you suffer from anxiety, if you're a junior male.

Norman as it were came out of nowhere, created himself full of mockery, humour. You'd never notice him in the corner of your carriage, but there was your great travel writer. That was the man that I admired the most. They're both dead so I can say whatever I like.

At the time Norman was writing, Chatwin was the other pole. I first heard about him talking to Fenton and Jon Swain. It was the foreign correspondents, people who'd been shot at in Vietnam, and who was their hero? Well I'd never heard of him. It was Norman Lewis and *A Dragon Apparent*, he was their master. And perhaps they'd read him in the Eland Books reissue, but I don't think so, I think there were still these books as it were passed around in the hotels that the journalists stayed in. They preserved the memory of Norman Lewis.

Redmond O'Hanlon

People used to say at the end of the Vietnam war that Graham Greene's novel *The Quiet American* had foreseen everything that would follow. But Lewis was there before Greene and you wonder whether Greene had read Lewis's book and thought, This place sounds interesting.

James Fenton

16

A NARRATIVE EMPIRE

"The greatest honour any human being can possibly hope for is to return to his village with the degree of doctor of letters awarded at the triennial competitions at Hue. After that it is not a bad thing to come back as marshal of the empire, having won a great victory over the enemy"
Vietnamese proverb

LET us not suffocate in the long tunnel of chronology, and resume, if we can, Norman's two months in south-east Asia in a collection of scenes. After a rapid visit to the Musée de l'Homme, where he found that it knew no more than anyone else of the recent situation in Indo-China, he left Paris on the afternoon of 25 January 1950 bound for Saigon. The Air France DC4's first stop was Tunis that night. It stopped at Cairo for breakfast, flew on to Al-Mukharram in Syria and landed at Karachi at 10.30 in the evening, where Norman was struck by the Pakistanis' new delight in concrete – his wardrobe had concrete shelves – and gleeful to discover they had "produced a china tea service which is an exact faithful copy of bakelite".[1] The French passengers "with a fierce nostalgia for Saigon" shook their heads dolefully at the stew, cabbage and chips that was put in front of them. Thirty-six hours later, as he wrote in *A Dragon Apparent*, "On the morning of the fourth day,

the dawn light daubed our faces as we came down the skies of Cochin-China. The passengers were squirming in their seats, not sleeping and not waking, and the air-hostess's trained smile came stiffly. With engines throttled back the plane dropped from sur-Alpine heights in a tremorless glide, settling in the new morning air of the plains like a dragonfly on the surface of a calm lake. As the first rays of the sun burst through the magenta mists that lay along the horizon, the empty sketching of the child's painting book open beneath us received a wash of green. Now lines were lightly ruled across it. A yellow pencilling of roads and blue of canals.[2]

The book is not the journey; but the description has precision as well as musical magic. Today still, by a geoclimatic influence, Ho Chi Minh City is approached across an unusually wide horizon, the city of ten million below you like an expanding drift of colourful smashed crockery, a columnar heart of fresh skyscrapers at its centre. Above it, the air still seems like a bath of clear vapour in which the plane, bouncing in its currents, rests briefly before landing. Several of Norman's fellow passengers were French military. In his diary he noted "The easy going good fellowship of those ... whose lives are devoted to violence as opposed to the unfulfilled expressions of those who follow peaceful professions".[3] In the finished book one was a Foreign Legion colonel, who noticed from the window a cloud of smoke from *"une opération"*. In the figure of this officer (whether he existed or not) Norman established a tone and offered the first observation that, by its acuteness, seems not just to describe the present but foresee the future.

Somehow, as he spoke, [the colonel] seemed linked psychically to what was going on below. Authority flowed back into the travel-weary figure. With the accession of this priestly essence he dominated the rest of the passengers.

Beneath our eyes violence was being done, but we were as detached from it almost as from history. Space, like time, anaesthetizes the imagination. One could understand what an aid to untroubled killing the bombing plane must be.

It was a highly symbolical introduction to South-East Asia.[4]

The observation picked up a memory from his time interrogating SS suspects in Austria, when, questioning the driver/batman in the Graz SD who was disturbed after completing more than twenty executions, he had speculated that physical detachment was advisable where large-scale killing was planned. Its tone is important, not just because the scene is entertaining as well as sinister. We feel the shameful excitement of war at a safe distance, and quite suddenly we know what it's like – the remote chaos in the rice fields, the mind of the man of action, the turn the future is bound to take – just as, within a few pages, we will get to know the Sunday diversions among the silk-gowned Vietnamese girls in Saigon's Jardins Botaniques, "utterly immaculate and addicted to swan-like movements", and the melancholy of rural French administrators bickering over the latest parcel of Sartre sent by the Club Français du Livre. And always overlaying the book's ironies – the proximity of civilisation/violence, the horror/excitement of war, the French colonial integration of *égalité*/exploitation – its tone, using photographically exact and prosodically expressed detail, conveys an impression that the reader is not reading *about* an experience but is apparently both inside and outside it, experiencing it *and* observing it – as, generally, we are in life.

About that exactness: Norman travelled to Indo-China four years before the defining calamity for the French at Dien Bien Phu, when they left the territory free for the Americans' more protracted disaster. Afterwards he was often called a lucky writer, in the respectful sense: skirmishes, spectacles, wars seemed to find him, he seemed to have the right-place-right-time knack. But that wasn't the case. Rather than something occult, alchemical, his ability was to see (as he had after first discussing the subject of Indo-China with Cape) where things were happening, to hear where history's orchestra was tuning up, and then, *once there*, to observe as closely as almost anybody could what would be likely to happen next. He rejected the idea that he had special powers. "In Indo-China I could see it coming. . . . Anybody could have seen it coming. The Americans should have seen it coming."[5] He did not mention the United States in his finished book (it would have been strange if he had); but to read *A Dragon Apparent* is to identify every element of their future downfall in Vietnam.

He was ten days in Saigon. It was "a French town in a hot country. . . . Its inspiration has been purely commercial and it is therefore without folly, fervour or much ostentation", but he investigated it with curiosity. On his first day he noted with a political leniency that later vanished, the "Delightful spectacle of French soldiers with elegant Chinese girlfriends in white silk draped alongside them, legs up Chinese fashion on a park bench". He gravitated to the waterfront of the Saigon River, two or three degrees cooler than the streets, where he was fascinated by the frieze of fishing, washing, "dicing, chatting, sleeping", the pigs brought ashore to be exercised, the partly hatched eggs and bottles of brilliantly coloured lemonade set out for the dock-workers' evening meal; and where he saw no Europeans. He was struck by the Annamite beauties in their *aodai* costume who "On Sunday morning . . . go on their bicycles to the Jardins Botaniques [in] impeccably pressed white silk pyjamas, sometimes with a narrow fringe of lace at the bottom [and] have themselves photographed. . . . Sometimes they caress the snout of a dragon. . . ."[6]

Saigon's state of normality was artificial. Next to the betel-nut sellers were brick watchtowers, and on the approaches to the city were

Vietnamese villagers "who spend all their time digging trenches for one side or the other". Soon Ho Chi Minh would go to Moscow; China was already providing sheltered rear bases and heavy weaponry to the Viet Minh. Holding much of rural Vietnam, they were readying themselves to push on French-occupied areas.

Norman arranged the first leg of his journey, a 300-kilometre bus ride outside the city to Dalat in the central highlands, with a Monsieur Ferry at the Office of Information and Propaganda. From Dalat he would be passed northwards to Ban Méthuot (Buôn Mê Thuôt), after which, he was told, he might be able to cross over to Laos but would be out of range of help from Saigon.

He had a week to wait, and while he waited Ferry offered him an official visit to Tây Ninh where the French High Commissioner, Monsieur Pignon, was to pay his respects to the Pope of the local Cao-Daïst religion. It was his first experience of how the French travelled.

There were about 20 cars, 3 armoured cars and one or more trucks with foreign legionnaires, mostly Algerians. At Trang Bang we entered the region "under control" of the Caodaïst army, but towers were still visible at kilometre intervals and the villages were stockaded. Mortar fire could be heard in Trang Bang and the convoi [sic] still moved where possible at 65 mph with armed soldiers facing away from the road.[7]

Cao-Daïsm, a soup of rituals whose believers were humoured by the French because the Pope's private army was anti-Viet Minh, was made for Norman's pen with its pompous obeisances, Disney styling, and eclectic parade of saints – Sun Yat Sen, Victor Hugo, Joan of Arc among them. His notebook dwells on the interminable champagne and biscuits and he wonders "At what stage in a religion does taste develop?" In *A Dragon Apparent*, his memory summons eleven pages of narrative so well tuned they are only a wavelength from absurdity, and he concludes ironically with the news that a Cao-Daïst force is fighting the French to the south of Saigon just as M Pignon's visit is taking place.

Notes, published account, and later autobiography (he wrote again about south-east Asia in *The World The World*): there is a familiar mismatch at Tây Ninh between the contents of Norman's notebook and his subsequent printed accounts.[8] But the book is not the journey. Must it be? As an object it is always something different: a printed collection of chapters; a written outline of events transformed by memory, forgetting and selection; a literary object; a composed artefact. Yet the two objects are connected, one an account of the other, so how great may the mismatch be allowed to be?

Two events in the first thirty pages of *A Dragon Apparent* are interesting in this respect. In the first, shortly after arriving in Saigon, Norman steps out of his hotel, the Hôtel Continental on rue Catinat (Dong Khoi Street today).

There was a rapid, silently-swirling traffic in the streets of bicycle rickshaws mixed up with cycles; a bus, sweeping out of a side-street into the main torrent, caught a cyclist, knocked him off and crushed his machine. Both the bus driver and the cyclist were Chinese or Vietnamese, and the bus driver, jumping down from his seat, rushed over to congratulate the cyclist on his lucky escape. Both men were delighted, and the cyclist departed, carrying the wreckage of his machine and still grinning broadly. No other incidents of my travels in Indo-China showed up more clearly the fundamental difference of attitude towards life and fortune of the East and West.[9]

This event happened – it is also in Norman's notebook – but not for nearly two months: it was one of the last things Norman saw in Saigon before he left at the end of March.

On the second occasion, on Monday 30 January, after meeting Ferry, he returns to his hotel room "at about seven-thirty, switched on the enormous ceiling fan and went to open the window". As he opens it, there is a thump of blast from an explosion caused by a grenade thrown at a café across the square. His description of the bombing's victims is memorable, detailed, with a streak of extended realism: the two men who "got up from a table, arms about one another's shoulders and reeled away like drunkards who have decided to call it a night", the waiters who "snatched the seemingly wine-stained cloths off the tables". The explosion "caused fifteen casualties – a Saigon record to date". Except that it also did not happen. Such explosions did occur often, and one in a restaurant in Cholon that he heard about when he was back in Saigon three weeks later did cause, according to his notebook, fifteen casualties, but he was not there. On that Monday his notebook only records that he went out for the evening "With George Herman, Robertson of the *Christian Science Monitor*, Ferry and Bollo to the Florence and the Bodega". (He was not impressed by either their Chinese rumba band or their pseudo-Spanish floor show.)

An event that didn't happen when he said it did; another that did not happen, though was the kind of event that did. Should either be included according to the usual definitions of "authenticity" or "integrity"?

I would argue that the question is unimportant. To clarify: it may be helpful, if a truism, to point out that the *journey* happened to Norman but the *book* didn't (except in the highly restricted sense of the several months he spent writing it when he came back). A book "happens" to its reader; it doesn't "happen" at all until somebody does read it. Why linger on these distinctions? Because there is an observation about writing – any writing in which a literary process is at work – that is not routinely made: namely, that because the book can't happen to the writer (he or she has to *make* it in order for the reader to *experience* it), as a curious consolation, in return for *not* having the experience of the book, more constructed, more composed, more artistically pleasing than the physical experience that gave rise to it, the writer is allowed freedom, an aesthetic territory that is his or hers alone. A territory where he or she is free to choose; order; adapt; omit; invert; shuffle; reverse; borrow; modify; intensify; extend; poeticise; theatricalise; normalise; sharpen; blunt; extend; telescope; magnify; minimise; steal; invent the experience he or she did not have. It is a territory that contains all the writer's selfishness, all his or her sovereign, organising, superhuman impulses, and all the writer's generosity, all his or her desire to please, provide meaning, present the most transforming experience. It is the writer's narrative empire.

The biographer can indicate the mismatches, but hardly for the sake of listing the discrepancies. Why would he or she bother to do that, unless the mission was to undermine? The reason for showing the differences can only be aesthetic. Why? Because that is the only truth that matters. It sounds a wild claim. But the proof is that Norman's notebook and diaries of the journey could be published instead. No one would read them (unless, possibly, published after the book as an interesting source). A lie is not believed not because it isn't the truth, but because it isn't aesthetic, because in its performance it doesn't supply meaning. A writer smuggles art, not bombs, into reality and lets the reader feel the (aesthetic) explosion of meaning, which succeeds when the reader cannot distinguish the fine line between the "actual" and the "composed".

As the critic Harold Bloom recently wrote of Don Quixote's talent for fabrication, "I do not believe the knight can be said to tell lies, except in the Nietzschean sense of lying against time and time's grim 'It was'."[10]

A last point: Norman did not invent such episodes to fill a gap, make events more dramatic than they were, himself more heroic. He was placing them, as episodes, in a composition; not self-consciously, but something like the way a composer composes, instinctively, sifting, turning over, hearing, playing back. They may have borrowed, in Milan Kundera's memorable phrase, "the beauty of a sudden density of life" that is by convention the property of novels, but the process by which they came to life was one of felt aesthetic necessity. Placed like notes, like a phrase or a theme, they are the emblems of the writer's freedom: far from being irresponsible, delinquent, impure elements of the truth, they are *indispensable* to his truthfulness.

On his return from Tây Ninh Norman did the rounds of the restaurants and nightclubs of Cholon, noting their folded iron grilles and stockaded defences, and the following Monday, 6 February, boarded the convoy to Dalat. It was a twelve-hour journey. He wanted to be able to feel that this, at last, was the real journey, but as so often it was as muddled as the preliminaries. Planes moved continuously over the slow train of vehicles, guarded ineffectually by two armoured cars. The bus was cramped, beggars surrounded it at stops, and the Moï people whose cultural singularity he had been told about appeared wearing borrowed battledress jackets with bare buttocks. After Kilometre 113 the Viet Minh had cut ditches across the road and the convoy was reinforced, but no attack took place.

Dalat was wrapped in pine forest at 1500 metres "like an Alpes Méditerranées resort out of season, but a distant coughing of tigers comes up through the pines at night".[11] He located his contact, Madame Schneider, after a comic contretemps of mispronunciation and was invited to dinner, during which his next move suddenly materialised.

A lieutenant of gendarmerie was leaving for Ban Méthuot before dawn the next morning. Norman's brief night in the Grand Hôtel was mutually ill-tempered.

The fool at this hotel asked: Vous voulez prendre le petit déjeuner demain matin? – Est-ce que c'est possible à cette heure? – Non, c'est trop tôt.[12]

The lieutenant's Citroën collected him at 5 a.m. Fortune works paradoxically for writers: after turning off the main road at dawn, the way was a fresh jungle *piste*. By the afternoon the "lieutenant who is so worried about his n.c.o.'s [overcautious] driving and whether the brakes are overheating" had decided to take the wheel. Within minutes he had overturned and wrecked the Citroën on a hilly bend. Norman's later approving portrait of Lieutenant Suéry as "the only Frenchman I ever saw a Vietnamese treat with affectionate respect" was also a sign of gratitude: the non-fatal car crash and interesting "lost" situation the lieutenant provided gave him perfect prose capital.

The lieutenant, with a gashed brow, had come off worst from the crash. All three walked to a *poste de garde* manned by Moïs a couple of kilometres away.

When asked at the poste de garde if they have any rifles (apropos tigers) the gardes proudly say that they have one each. English ones. But they have no bullets. The corporal, when he thinks of a new hazard, such as the Viet Minh, Japanese deserters, or the lorry being crashed into if we sleep in it, interjects: "Oh malheureux."[13]

The three had to sleep in the Moïs' hut, which creaked and swayed all night. In the morning, leaving the corporal behind, Norman and the lieutenant walked 13 kilometres to Dak Song. Norman managed impressive quantities of notes on his forest surroundings and on the bird song that accompanied them "taken from Spanish popular music, madrigals, symphonies". "A brief calamitous sound" broke in "of [a] panther – tiger? – at close quarters with no climbable trees", but fortunately the animal did not show itself. They were in M'nong territory, "*une région très mystérieuse*," the lieutenant said, which had only submitted to the French in 1939, since when a dozen French administrators had disappeared, murdered for enigmatic offences against the local people.

At Dak Song he was lucky again, finding a delayed convoy that ground on to Ban Méthuot "in the dark and a fog of red dust". (Another placing: in *A Dragon Apparent* this convoy had been attacked on the way to Dak Song; in his notebook it was "3 weeks ago the convoy to Ban Méthuot attacked with loss of 7 military vehicles – 1 civil[ian], a captain captured – or 8 military".)

On arrival he was welcomed by the *chef de cabinet*, Doustin, a cheerfully imperturbable diplomat who gave him categorical news.

M Doustin laughs loudly at the idea of going by road to Paksé – the state of security [is] unknown & anyway no one has been up the track for a year or two. The word *pirates* is used.

M Doustin states that 8 days ago the Viet [Minh] killed the males (16) in a Rhadé village near Plekeu [Pleiku] for giving information. Killed as cattle are with blows of the *coupe-coupe* on the neck & lance stabs in the chest.

He has disinterred one "traitor" buried alive.[14]

Next morning, meeting Doustin again, Norman was told that in the absence of any means of getting out of Ban Méthuot he, Doustin, had put on an interesting journey for him into Moï country. The unwelcome implication of a guided tour was mitigated by the thought of anthropological adventure. Before leaving, Doustin suggested, Norman should see Bernard Jouin, a doctor in the town who had lived for years with the Moïs and published several books.

Everything the white-haired, illuminated Jouin told him over several hours whetted Norman's interest. The Moïs, known, as natives routinely are, by the strangers' word for them (Moï = Vietnamese for "savages"), are a mountain-living Malayo-Polynesian group. Today probably a fifth of the million who existed in the 1950s are left. Western contact began the winnowing, importing disease and slavery, Lyndon Johnson's bombing campaign continued it. The Moïs have a hold on the narrative of *A Dragon Apparent* because they were the first emblem of the "sublime humanity, supreme humanity" that Norman was always looking for;[15] a search he summed up at the other end of his career in his declaration that he was looking for the people who had always been there, and belonged to the places where they lived. The Moïs, like the Indians of the jungles of the Amazon and Orinoco he encountered later, became a part of his antinomic belief system, the part that believed in his own escape reflex (constant de-adherence) *and* in the grace of harmonious cultures and of those who belong to them (constant adherence).

The Moïs, for example, refused to work for wages and had a block-buster tribal memory: Moï sagas, handed down through generations with an interdict against changing a single word, possessed words for, and descriptions of, the megatherium and mammoth. Moï rites were solemn, innumerable, complex, all requiring lavish ritual consumption of their filtered sour-mash rice wine: a conviviality extended to their dogs, pigs and hens as well as visitors (who were supervised to ensure they consumed a minimum of three cow's horns). Moïs had no concept of right and wrong. Every act was ticketed with a yes or no, moral condemnation was meaningless. A good end to life was by illness in old age; medicine was refused as it amounted to robbing the sufferer of a chance of a good death. The greatest Moï crimes were the theft of water or rice. For that the thief could not stay in the village. The beginning of the Moïs' end came with the planters – whose pressing of labour brought disease and prevented the performance of their rites – and with the timber companies who did not so much offend against the spirits as cut down the trees that contained them. Preserved in stability since prehistory, the Moïs' spiritual world started to vanish at the whine of a chainsaw. Their physical world had been disappearing since the first colons came in 1860 to force them to harvest the Frenchman's rubber, indigo, tobacco, tea and coffee.

The four-day journey with a young administrator, Ribo, and his colleague Cacot, an inspector of schools, impressed Norman by its atmosphere of existential gloom. At their post the Frenchmen were addicted to their bookclub parcels of Sartre and Aymé; in the field they hunted obsessively to stave off pessimism. In several M'nong and Rhadé villages progress had encroached. Norman was impressed by the univer-sality of drunkenness and by the scale and formal order of the 50-metre communal longhouses, but a curious power struggle was taking place between missionaries and colonial administrators. Its battleground was the female torso: one side preached modesty and issued calico blouses, the other insisted on cultural preservation. "The village elders screamed with indignation at the girls' slowness in taking off their blouses", Norman noted, though he also suspected Ribo and Cacot of demon-strating "the usual European fetishism over the mammary regions". Finally, at one Rhadé village it was clear that men were being forced to sign work contracts for a local plantation. Visiting the plantation, an estate of the Compagnie des Hauts Plateaux Indochinois, suppliers to Michelin, on the way back Norman witnessed another reason for

Ribo's dejection after his interview with the director: without labour, a plantation would fold, and if all its local workers had been forced into work contracts – as all but three had here – no administrator, however fair-minded, could pursue such an injustice. Not when plantations were what colonies were for.

Back in Ban Méthuot, Doustin knocked on Norman's door to offer him a promising lift to Pleiku with a visiting French deputy named Dufour. Pleiku was 200 kilometres to the north. The convoy left at 3 a.m. Dufour, armed with a new five-shot repeater, shot at everything in sight. But Pleiku, when Norman arrived, was a shabby frontier town of "improbable villas among the pines", where everyone went out armed and the Bar des Coloniaux sold whisky made in Bordeaux.

Planters only a few kilometres from town were beginning to be kidnapped and killed, and the Viet Minh had recently occupied much of the zone. The possibility of going on from Pleiku to cross the border into Laos was nil, and after three days he made it gratefully back to Ban Méthuot. The town was in the grip of Tet and no one moved in the streets. His notebook filled up with "impossible to go past Bo Kheo because of pirates", "plane full tomorrow & Wednesday", "convoy Thursday, maybe". The only person travelling, strangely, appeared to be the puppet head of state, former emperor Bao Dai, generally more visible in the restaurants of Paris, who arrived the following day, Sunday 19th, and chafing with boredom Norman was thankful to be offered on Monday the only way out: a return to Dalat with two French officials who had been given permission to use the emperor's private hunting *piste*. He was back in "the Margate atmosphere" of Dalat that evening.

How much he hated being forced back to the resort is clear from his insults. "Within 20 miles of Dalat the countryside suddenly loses its character. Begins to look like Hampstead Heath. . . . This is like the outskirts of Bayonne out of season or a drab little resort in an unfashionable corner of Switzerland."[16] Next morning he heard that there were no Air France seats to Saigon until 1 March. Frustration elicited action. He wangled an "*ordre de mission*" from someone, booked an Air France flight for Thursday, then succeeded in getting bumped onto that day's Cosara flight.[17] Back in Saigon, he enjoyed the city's integral weirdness, the man fishing through a manhole on the Cholon road, the Annamite babies smacking their mothers, the restaurants with their grenade-protected *emplacements discrets*, the room he shared at the

Continental with "a gentleman whose luggage curiously bears an address in the town.

"The mystery is solved when he turns up at midnight, with a fille."[18] The man was Gautam Chautala, Reuters' correspondent in Saigon. The two briefly became friends, and Norman later shared the flight back to Paris, via Calcutta, with him.

He needed a Viet Minh point of view about Indo-China and made approaches. A semi-official attempt, through the editor of a recently closed-down nationalist newspaper, is noted in *A Dragon Apparent*. His notebook records, more briefly, an accidental meeting with a Madame Phuoc, a go-between. "She was attractive and unusually tall for a Vietnamese," Norman told a later girlfriend, Lesley, who believed he had a fling with her.[19] In his published account he met Mme Phuoc at the Paradis, a Cholon nightclub in his preferred part of town, away from the European quarter. How much contact followed with the nation-alist revolutionaries is unclear.

He had, in any case, an intuitive feeling for the justice of their demand for full independence. He knew self-determination did not come without a fight. He saw that their situation, fobbed off by the French, with nominal concessions and a *deuxième bureau* operating at the end of every corridor, had little future without armed struggle. He achieved more contact with the revolutionaries later; he used to say that when his partner in the photographic business, Harding – a nit-picking pest of a man – died, he had discovered in Harding's office cupboard at High Holborn a years-old letter sent from Vietnam. The letter had been hoarded unopened by Harding because of his passion for foreign stamps. Opening it, Norman claimed, he had found it contained an invitation to him from a senior Viet Minh official to become a spokesman and head of propaganda.

Two days after coming back to Saigon he found a *moyen de fortune* – a car agent's Land Rover – that would take him to Phnom Penh. He had a long weekend to wait, and the French authorities obliged by taking him on the standard foreign correspondents' tour of occupied Cochin-China. His impression was one of political fragility plus mili-tary uncertainty and jumpiness: on a trip upriver from Tanan on 25 February in a heavily armed landing craft he was aware of the "matelots exchang[ing] nervous smiles" and the commandant drinking quantities of gut-rotting coffee. The terrain had been secured but the Viet Minh were only dormant, allowing schismatic Cao-Daïsts to soak up French

resources. Although half the land in the zone was owned by big proprietors, they found it impossible to collect rents from their Annamite
farmers: the excuse was "too late, I gave it to the Viet [Minh]". Efforts
to enforce payment were met by kidnapping and arson attacks.[20]

On Monday 27 February he set out for Phnom Penh in the Land
Rover belonging to Valas, his acquaintance. The road was terrible; the
car rushed past known danger spots to avoid supposedly "isolated"
cases of piracy. The landscape suddenly changed. "Immediately on
crossing [the] frontier forests disappear and give place to a prairie of
short grass with coconut palms growing." The reality of Cambodia, a
place whose name had always tinkled in his mind with soft percussive
music, subdued him. "The neat Annamite has gone and now [there is]
the drab skirt, sarong and turban. The loose, dreary weeds of India."[21]
Reaching Phnom Penh the same afternoon he found vicious mosquitoes that stung through his trousers, and at the Royal Hotel picking
at stewed meats he thought longingly of Saigon's *écrevisses frites*.

Phnom Penh was tawdry and insubstantial. Pagodas were starting
to bore him. Phnom Penh's were shoddy, and at the museum the Buddhist
and Brahmanist art was "intolerable", the Buddhas convertible into
Sivas, he noted, simply by adding extra arms. The town's one node of
activity was its Chinese casino, opened six months before and already,
as a result of the Cambodian mania for gambling, sucking the country's
money out to Hong Kong. (After a few days he noticed that even in
the *dancings* there was a gambling annexe "where the taxi girls lose
their earnings every evening before leaving".) The Chinese had overwhelmed and stifled Cambodian culture with their synthetic glitter.
Valas, his car-agent friend and colonial magnate (who had flown from
Saigon to avoid the uncomfortable drive), gave him his cynical summary
of the Asian populations. All Vietnamese loyal to Ho Chi Minh were
"*de la poussière*", the Japanese were "*un peuple sans espoir*", and the
Cambodians, at the bottom of the pile, had "one object in view, to fill
their pockets and get out to Paris".[22]

Norman's priority was to arrange the next stage of the journey, to
Laos. The news was poor. The road was under attack by Issarak nationalists, river traffic was in a slump. Again it was a matter of waiting.
Fatigue was creeping up on him. He picked up the alternative attractions of Phnom Penh reluctantly: Madame Shum's opium den ("a tedious
process") and a *dancing* where the demure star's vaginal ornaments
tinkled as she sat down with him and Valas; meetings with General

des Essars, commander of French troops in Cambodia, and with the
Cambodian Prime Minister Yem Sambaur, and an interview with
Cambodia's ruler, King Norodom. Des Essars he found to be a realistic soldier, unmoved by French political optimism. Yem Sambaur
produced a smiling procès-verbal on the best way to convert a villager
to Communism – burn down his house and kill one or more members
of his family – and pointed out that "the Asiatic" found the transition
less difficult anyhow. "[The] prospect does not alarm us. There are
times when one feels that perhaps it would be even better to be a little
poorer, if at the same time one could be a little freer."[23] The King
echoed his prime minister with all the vehemence allowed of an impeccably suited Buddhist semi-divine. The French lagged behind the times,
he said, and could hardly boast of having brought civilisation to
Cambodia. So were Cambodia's portents resumed by Norman: an
inevitable, probably bloody arrival of Communism, unhindered by the
gentle sorrow of its king.

No overland way of reaching Laos materialised. On 3 March he
decided to accept a military transport to Siem Reap, the nearest town
to the thousand temples of Angkor and an area temporarily calm after
the local Issarak commander, Dap Chhuon, had been bought off with
a governorship. Happier in the country than in the city, he found that
as he neared Angkor tourism cast its exploitative spell, raising prices
and dressing the girls who strolled out of roadside hovels with suspicious smartness and smiles of welcome, but when he arrived he was
compelled by its magnificence into listing the memorable elements of
what he saw.

The negligent elegance of the displaced block of masonry, of the half obliterated carving, of the faceless lion. The steps lead down to a lake – an immense
artificial lake, its rectangularity softened by subsidence of banks and encroach-
ment of trees. The lotuses spread a blanket on the surface. There are huge
kingfishers and a thousand ducks that warble like a collection of finches.
Buffaloes wade in up to their necks. The Khmers would have been delighted
by the spectacle of tall trees sprouting from their temples' supports in a
symmetrical arrangement of roots. The water is the colour of milk chocolate.
The spread of roots across a flagged approach is infinitely ornamental.[24]

The ruins of Angkor were more impressive than the city in its heyday,
time and vandalism having "done much to mute that excessive symmetry,

that all-pervading symbolism, that repetitiousness that I find so irritating in far-Eastern art . . . it is an aesthetic advantage that the majority
of [the seven-headed serpents] have been broken and are missing".[25]
Other signs of wilting Cambodian culture – the closed theatre in Siem
Reap replaced by a Chinese casino, the demotion of the gods of the
Khmer empire into tree spirits to frighten babies with – joined his other
disappointments with the country. Among a busload of Siamese tourists
he met a young American woman from Des Moines, Iowa. Her style
of tourism was earnestly programmatic. "Say, have you seen Indra on
a three-headed elephant?" she called in the ruins. She had been tasked
by the *Des Moines Register*, she told him, with a surreally improbable
mission: finding other Des Moines citizens in the Far East and writing
up their stories. She had found one so far. Norman paused in admiration for an ambition more quixotic than his.

In Saigon he had booked a seat on a flight to Laos on 9 March in
case no land route was possible. The day approached. On 6 March, a
Monday, he boarded a Chinese bus at 4 a.m. for Phnom Penh, another
stifling ride crushed between the driver and the panels of the bus, then,
with the rumour of bandits ahead, ordered among the luggage as the
most vulnerable passenger. A sole polite *pirate* at a ferry crossing,
extracting a protection fee that was nothing more than an unofficial
toll, was all that transpired. On Wednesday he was back in Saigon. On
Thursday he arrived on an Air France flight at Vientiane.

"In most journeyings there stands out the memory of days of discouragement; when the enthusiasm flags under the strain of petty physical
discomforts. The introduction to Laos was spent in such a period. This
was the earthly paradise that all the French had promised; the country
that was one vast Tahiti, causing all the French who had been stationed
there to affect ever after a vaguely dissolute manner." He spent eleven
days in Laos but felt he had spent longer: he was spent himself, dented
by the journey: by uncertainty, discomfort, climate, repeated early starts.
"If one could have only visited [Vientiane] for a weekend, straight from
England, impressions fresh."[26] The attractions of the capital were rapidly
exhausted. At the end of the dry season, huge leaves falling like heavy
parchment, you only had to brush a water pot for clouds of mosquitoes
to be released. Dust was everywhere, and mist wrapped the sun in a swel-
tering veil. "The charm of Vientiane lies in the life and customs of the
people", he wrote generously (a virtue of *A Dragon Apparent* is the
constructive note, a kind of compassion for tedium, that he unfailingly

gives to places, especially cities, where he did not enjoy himself. He had felt the same at the repetitiousness of Angkor). "Unless one is an amateur of pagoda architecture there is little else to be seen [at Vientiane]." He found a bizarre highlight for Europeans in the night-time spectacle, lit by flares, of the slaughterhouse at work, but his main preoccupation was getting out and onwards to Luang Prabang, the royal capital and spiritual centre of the country. At the weekend he fell with relief on the prospect of a convoy to Xien Khouang, from where an official named Chantereau (Dupont in the finished text) would leave the convoy and continue to Luang Prabang in his Jeep.

The two-day journey was slow, the convoy dribbling through a fog of red dust, with rumours of Viet Minh or Khmer Issarak dressed in new American uniforms on the road ahead holding up progress: after ten hours he and Chantereau had covered 130 kilometres. At Veng Viang his companion, wildly impatient, sneaked away from the convoy, took Norman to bathe in the river, and then on to spend the night with a company of army engineers at Muong Kassy. Here there was proof of Viet Minh activity: when darkness fell the villagers hid in the forest. After an evening of wistful barrack gossip about Laotian women (whose sexual spontaneity led them to make love with any European immediately if left alone with them) and an asthmatic night in a military straw hut, they pushed on again to a digression promised by Chantereau. On the way up the Frenchman had tried to buy every animal he saw – dogs, a parakeet in a village restaurant – as a present for his Laotian wife. Now he wanted to visit a Meo village to buy one of their fine white dogs. The Meo (today known as Hmong: "Meo" was, as habitually, an insult, in this case a Chinese word meaning "barbarian") were hill people of Mongolian ethnicity, hunters, silversmiths and animal breeders dressed in the embroidered and silver-ornamented finery of nomads. Norman and Chantereau were received at a semi-derelict village with rich offerings of sugar cane, bananas and maize alcohol. To Chantereau's ebullient request to buy a dog, the headman apologised diplomatically that they were all in the poppy fields with their owners. Norman may have underestimated the Meos' nomadism that led them to value, like those they descended from, only what they could carry, and he was perplexed that they should be "the most elegantly dressed and the worst housed people" he had seen.

Arriving at Luang Prabang on 16 March after a long descent through a hazy smoking landscape of bamboos, he was invited to stay at a small mansion belonging to the regional *conseiller*, Monsieur Leveau. Luang Prabang, at the junction of the Mekong and Nam Khan rivers, saturated by royal and Buddhist tradition, parcelled out its atmosphere in sedative gusts of tranquillity. Other calmants were superfluous. After dinner with Chantereau, "The evening was rounded off by a routine visit to the local opium den, which, probably by design, was as decrepit and sinister as a waxworks exhibit. We stayed only a few minutes in this green-lit, melodramatic establishment. . . . One had to make some show of going to the devil."[27]

Despite his host Leveau's diffidently offered but splendid hospitality and the royal capital's immaterial serenity, its streets barely ruffled by clouds of monks in saffron robes, its temples enveloped in the invisible compelling of Buddhist spirituality; despite the town's "infallible sense of colour, the blending of gold, turquoise and greys", the sweetness of the Laotians he met, and Chantereau's amusing company, Norman felt his energy suddenly declining and a horror of finding himself stuck there. No pirogues made the journey south; the weekly DC3 to Vientiane was booked weeks ahead. He walked up Mount Phousi, the sacred hill in the middle of the town, and needed a pre-lunch siesta. Visiting a Chinese doctor, he was diagnosed with a chronic imbalance of yin and yang and acupuncture was administered. He felt briefly better and went back to filling his notebook – interviewing Leveau about another tribal people, the Khas, distant relations to the Moïs – but began to write sarcastic asides. "Even watches go slow in Laos." After three days Leveau told him that a military plane busy with a droppage in the north might stop on its way back through to Vientiane. On Sunday afternoon, only four days after he had arrived, he took off from Luang Prabang on an elderly French army Junkers whose pilot had no time to clear the mountains before nightfall but decided instead to fly straight down the gorges of the Mekong, navigating by sight and trying to avoid the river's fatal downdraughts. The flight was a perfect antidote to the glorious draining peace of Luang Prabang. The following day, 20 March, he caught an Air France flight from Vientiane back to Saigon.

Four days later he met Mme Phuoc again and photographed her. What contact she offered him with the Viet Minh is unclear, but she had a woman's and a nationalist's pride. "I suppose you'll show my photo to your friends and say: that's an *indigène* I know," she told Norman. "I detest that word. *Tous les hommes sont pareils*."[28] Norman began to make clear distinctions between the conduct of the French and the supposed liberty of the Vietnamese. "The *poulet* used to be attached by the legs," one informant described the Vietnamese condition to him. "It has been freed but put in a cage." A Viet boy who came top in an exam was the subordinate of a French boy who came out bottom, and was paid a third of his salary. The French had handed over control of the Sûreté to the Vietnamese, but kept their own Sûreté and removed all the files. The *cercle sportif* – this was possibly one of the greatest French blunders – did not admit Vietnamese.

Although his notebook contains an appointment with Nguyen Binh, the general in command of the southern Viet Minh armies, it makes no mention of the arranged excursion into Viet Minh territory and the attack on the watchtowers in the *plaine des joncs* outside Saigon that ends *A Dragon Apparent*. It is a long, detailed account and wholly plausible, from Norman's own self-confessed enthusiasm for an attack to his criticism of the Viet Minh commander's use of his weaponry and the scale of the returned fire from a French 25-pounder. Such confrontations were in any case more or less staged, in the tradition of Vietnamese warfare, its archetype so opposed to the French and later even more the American method: the one grounded in personal contact and theatrical chivalries (soldiers carrying lanterns at night so the enemy could see them), the other originating in the contempt of preferring to kill an enemy without seeing him ("One could understand what an aid to untroubled killing the bombing plane must be"). By its place in the narrative the episode also leads back to what Norman had most admired in the Vietnamese, to their "essential pacifism and civilization" that ranked the achievement of a doctorate of letters above elevation to the rank of marshal of the empire.

By the time he boarded his flight to Paris he had not written that observation, or the rest of his memorably chiding summary –

I wondered whether it had all been worth it – the brief shotgun marriage with the West, now to be so relentlessly broken off. Had there been, after all, some mysterious historical necessity for all the bloodshed, the years of scorn, the servitude, the contempt? Could some ultimately fructifying process have been at work? And would the free nations of Indo-China, in their coming renascence, have gained in the long run by the enforced rupture with the old, unchanging way of life, now to be replaced, one presumed, by a materialist philosophy and the all-eclipsing ideal of the raised standard of living?

These were questions, since there is no yard-stick for felicity, to which no final answer could ever be given. And even a partial answer would have to be left to an observer of the next generation.[29]

But in his notes on his notebook's last page, taken down in a conversation with an unnamed Viet Minh interlocutor, listing in detail the independentists' principles of free education, universal suffrage, abolition of head taxes, the right of wounded soldiers and widows to land, the confiscation of collaborationist products, free healthcare, the obligatory working of land, and equality of wages and food for soldiers and officers, his sympathies were clear.

To step out of chronology: Norman spent the rest of 1950 writing *A Dragon Apparent*. It fell naturally into the category of travel when it was published in July 1951, and was acknowledged as a travel book with a difference. In the writing he found a way of fusing his egotistical (escape, adventure) and literary (language, scenes) loyalties into a tone that could bear something more than both. Travel books, as Paul Fussell has elegantly written in *Abroad: British Literary Travelling Between the Wars*, are displaced romances of the quest and courtly (Fussell calls it pastoral) kind. The 1930s, the decade Fussell discusses, had been the great decade of the travel book as interior quest; Samuel Hynes' book *The Auden Generation: Literature and Politics in England in the 1930s* is not the only text to have noticed that the journey was "the most insistent of 'thirties metaphors". Its products, by writers as different as D H Lawrence and Robert Byron, Graham Greene and Peter Fleming, framed their general self-reflexiveness in tones that veered from Wodehousian comedy to Arcadian elegy, via periodic reportage and occasional (in Greene's case almost continuous) weariness and disappointment. Travel, in their books, was testing, adventurous, mysterious, lightly allegorical, and an unadmitted metaphor that represented all their desire to get away from Orwell's "deep, deep sleep of England": a personal Romantic vehicle, disguised by its tone, for those who could afford it.

A Dragon Apparent stands in unusual opposition to those books. With its ironic narrative of colonialism – particularly the French kind, but standing for colonialism universally – with its accuracy about the way things had gone in south-east Asia and the way they would go, with its long (not always congenial) immersions in traditional societies' efforts to retain identity, and by *its* tone – the reader at the centre, writer at the periphery – it revealed the existential significance of travel; and not as a personal matter but as a category of action. It did so through the way of seeing that Norman had developed, starting in the 1930s but rejecting the decade's (and his own) solipsism and refined by his experience at war: a mongrel combination of news, anecdote, essay, prophecy, philosophy, and comic bathos: and through the priority he gave to composition. Neither of these is just a technical skill; they are part of his originality of style. His aesthetic placings are a part of his tone. (As are all his other selections and orderings, his constructive slant on hardships and tedium, his vivid indefatigable descriptions, and so on.) He worked at his style. In his notebooks this translates into copious, occasionally repetitive effort, to enrich a description, to ironise more subtly, to extinguish musical falsehood from his sentences. And as an adapter of the real, not its copyist, he thought about what his book was *for*. In Saigon he came across a popular scientific magazine that had devoted an impressive edition to the Moïs. "There is one tremendous and all obliterating piece of information omitted from all these researches, a fact [the systematic exploitation of the Moïs by the colonists] which can be read in a travel book but never in a magazine which sets out to offend no one. In this perhaps lies the chief value of travel books at their best: they give information that can rarely be obtained elsewhere."[30]

Apart from that kind of knowledge, of historical and anthropological situations, his tone includes another, even more important to his revelation of what travel means. In a post-war world of forced travel – refugees, displaced persons, homeless – and multiplying bureaucracy that are both still with us, A Dragon Apparent presents the voluntary journey as a freedom, an escape from both, with responsibilities. One is the responsibility to understand where the journey is ultimately going: a sort of continuous self-examination. The other is an equally continuous effort: to understand the meaning of what is seen and heard. The destination (the metaphysical one, not the one on the ticket) is to gain the kind of knowledge that goes into the "soul" of a human situation, that grasps its human content. That is the final objective of its author's narrative empire, a territory that he conquered first in A Dragon Apparent: that it leads us to understand the soul of the places he saw, and so the soul of travel, in the shape of a meeting between the resolute de-adherent and the admirable adherent and the dialectic between the two.

Those are the outsider's words, the train of thought of critic and biographer. We have an idea of what Norman thought his book's point was, what it was for. It would be interesting to know how he felt about the other things, composition, the line between actual and composed, "truth" and "fiction", tone.

And in 1950, or more likely late 1949, in a comic letting-off of steam over six pages of his diary before he went to Vietnam, he gives a very good idea. He probably wrote it after a meeting with one of the editors at Cape, or Kingsley Martin at the *New Statesman*: it was an appeal to have his Welshness forgotten *and* to be understood and sympathised with for his awful Welsh childhood, and, in a period apparently of sexual privation, a heartfelt lament for his imagined lost attractiveness.

The editor said to me, what about writing something about Wales? You write about Africa, Italy, Arabia and Spain. But you don't write about your own country. Are you a Welshman or aren't you?

I'm always having this question asked me. The answer is yes, more or less, with reservations. But I couldn't get down to more stories about Dai bach . . . and so on. Anyway, all the critics say us Welsh writers are too parochial. I've been frustrated in 4 countries, why should I get down to writing how I was frustrated in the Pentrepoeth school in Carmarthen town and all the rest of it? Nothing doing. I'll tell you what I'll do. I'll give you a few excerpts from my terrible childhood and there's plenty more where that came from. The story is about how I got kissed. It's a fragment of autobiography, and how much of it is fiction and how much of it isn't I couldn't tell you. Leave anything to my imagination and nobody could recognise the facts after a few years. Anyway what's the use of being a Welshman otherwise?

At all events here goes with the excerpt for my autobiography, real or imaginary or a mixture of both, I don't know.

Up to the age of about 9 – after this I became dolichocephalic. . . .

I'm not a liar, countrymen, but my imagination sometimes takes control. Let it go a few years and I'm never sure myself what happened. I'm noted for it in London, they say bloody Welshman (like in Carmarthen, it was always cockney). Let me break a secret to you. Let me paint you a portrait of myself

in a few strokes of a jaundiced pen. Now I'm 41, haggard looking, melancholic look as if my thoughts are far away – and they are, I imagine things
and when I go into a hospital for a dose of malaria they give me a free ex
ray for my lungs [and] I'm afraid of my shadow. This, fellow countrymen, is
my situation. . . . I groan in my sleep.

It's all of 25 years since a Welsh woman offered to kiss me and it isn't likely
to happen again. You know you read about these tough shrewd French peasants, well my relations were like that. They probably buried their money in
the garden. I've been kissed all over Carmarthenshire and in . . . districts of
Pembroke and Brecon. To qualify as a kisser a woman always had to have a
beard.

That, countrymen, is my predicament.

My grandfather was a tea merchant in Kings Street and of him I'll only say
that he never rose above his environment. I have his blood in my veins so I really
can't let myself go. I will just say that he never rose above his environment.

Don't believe this if you don't want to, but the woman who came towards
me had a full grown beard and moustache. Countrymen, for a paltry reward
I was pursued all over the southern part of our country. Don't I deserve better
of you all?

I look like a minor character in an El Greco picture, sketched in not by the
master himself but by one of his pupils, if he had any.

Bear with me, countrymen.

Countrymen, don't call me a liar. Don't say my imagination runs away with
me. All I've said so far may have been a bit strained, but this woman had a
beard like Nebuchadnezzar. She should have put ribbons in it.

Countrymen, what I want to say is [that] though this is the kind of thing
that makes an exile of a man, aren't I entitled to get some of my own back
in this kissing business?

. . . . Countrymen, we have the most beautiful women in the world. That's
all I can say for our country. But why have I only kissed the bearded ones?
. . .

Nobody can tell me that these things don't exist. Nobody can say that these
women were a figment of my imagination, I tell you. Could our own Welsh
tongue describe better than the English the agonies I suffered? I don't know.
My tariff was one penny. But there were certain cases where more was asked.
There were women who put down their pigs to kiss me and then picked them
up again. They used to start mumbling together, my aunts, using their broken
Welsh. I knew what was coming – "Mrs Morfanwy Williams says for a little
kiss. . . ."

All right, I used to say. You know the fee.[31]

Lunch at the Union Club, Rangoon. The centre of the table decorated with alternate HP and Lea & Perrin's Worcester sauce (probably in my honour). Clear soup. Duck and roast. Great chatter about mutual acquaintances "up at Oxford".

The English dislike for mixing with foreigners. Probably due to the inhibition of small talk: they cannot talk about people they both know.

Local English is partly archaic and biblical ("stricken with divers sicknesses") and partly slang – "the dickens of a row", "to clear off" – sinister booths selling tripes are referred to as "tuck shops".

It has taken 5 hours to do 43 miles with the mad girl singing "You are my sunshine", hymns, "Swing low sweet chariot", "Happy birthday to you", and "I put my money on a coal black mare, doodah, doodah." She is being exiled to this remote place for giving cause for scandal in Lashio.

The butler with his testimonial – "a dear old fellow, one of those old fashioned Burmese servants that are so fast disappearing". His yelping interrogation. "E oi?" ("Eggs boiled?") "A' oi?" ("Boiled water.") "Fi 'e." ("Fried eggs.")

Asiatic speech: sometimes a passage of almost Johnsonian graveness and rotundity – or a sentence dealing with the scarcity of some radio part may carry the distant rumble of Sir Thomas Browne. They like to refer to others by mystic letters showing that they are officials of any kind, in the spirit of "of course you know he's the cousin of the seventh earl":

"Yesterday I encountered at the residence of one friend of mine the ADPW [Assistant Director of Permanent Ways]."

"That's funny, I also took food with the DIW [Deputy Inspector of Waggons]. After saluting him, I broached the matter without delay."

"And what response did he vouchsafe?"

"He told me to get the hell. . . . Indeed he chucked me out."

"These buggers are all the same."

Burma notebook

THE LAND OF THE BRAIN-FEVER BIRD

"Memory slips, letters remain"
Welsh proverb

WHAT Evelyn Waugh called "the turgid, indefinite feelings of home-coming" aptly describe Norman's return. At his arrival there was upheaval. His mother died quite suddenly on 5 April of cerebral arteriosclerosis at the age of eighty-five. He knew that Louisa had treated him perversely, that she had been over-protective and authoritarian when he was a child, and a snob and the greatest of wilful eccentrics as he grew up, but he was also aware that by the creation of her little world of herself-and-Norman she had reinforced his self-confidence. Perhaps it was with love and something of his compassion for the absurd that he mourned her.

While he was away his writing career had evolved. The *New Statesman and Nation* had published another story, "Socialism and Don Erminio", and three weeks before he came back his second novel, *Within the Labyrinth*, had come out. The novelist Anthony Powell reviewed it kindly but unlavishly in the *Times Literary Supplement*, as his aloof recourse to double negatives shows.

Within the Labyrinth owes a good deal to *South Wind* in its handling of the Italian scene; but this does not mean that its author lacks gift for describing characters and surroundings. The narrative is entertaining and at times exciting, though never achieving some basic quality that might have made it even more successful. . . . However, *Within the Labyrinth* is by no means without interest.[1]

The review does not say what the missing "basic quality" might have been. Possibly Powell felt that Norman's portrait of Manning, a Field Security sergeant posted to administer a filthily corrupt town in the Naples hinterland, did not rise to the rough, complex vectors of tragedy. If so, he was right. Norman's use of his own background and feelings from the grim weeks he had spent posted at Benevento (Malevento in the novel) in August and September 1944 was too close an identification to allow for any ironic space: the novel's tone is at the level of the novelist seeking to justify or excuse Manning's actions. Norman had not got away from his own deeply negative memory of those two months, and was really pleading for sympathy for the predicament he had found himself in. Powell puts his finger on it when he talks about "the suggestion of self-pity" in Manning. At an artistic level the novel was not a success.

Norman spent the spring in a further reshuffling of his life – all such reorderings were interim – dealing with his mother's estate, moving into the flat in Farm Street and starting on the south-east Asia book. The threads of his London existence, Scottish family visits, and Welsh escapes nestled down restlessly with each other. Alternating trips to Banchory with two birdwatching and egg-collecting fugues to Skomer and Cilycwm, he spent April and most of May in London assembling his notes and, at the end of the day, drinking with Malcolm Dunbar, Frank Allen and others at Berlemont's. He condemned a fashion for greasing up to the pub's owner, scorning "The way French-speaking beginners . . . jerk & hunch their shoulders and shake & wave their palms when they try to talk French to Gaston".[2] He had adequate female company. On the sleeper on one of his visits to Scotland he had met a young actress called Dorothy – Dottie – who lived in digs in Upper Montagu Street, parallel to Baker Street. A girlfriend describes her as "sweet, very pretty" and her relation with Norman as "not a very deep-rooted thing . . . he'd just come back [from a journey] and he'd ring her up".

He was also seeing, in a less simple way, the Latino-Welsh poet Lynette Roberts whom he had met at Laugharne. They shared a love of the area around Llanstephan, where Roberts had got married to "the best sort of crank" according to his best man Dylan Thomas, the poet Keidrych Rhys: a selfish Welsh flamboyant who dressed in good tweeds and spoke Welsh with the accent of the public schools. Rhys and Roberts had divorced in 1949 and she and her two children had moved to a caravan in the churchyard at Laugharne. (Roberts could have been a much more celebrated poet. Her work was championed by T S Eliot, Edith Sitwell and Wyndham Lewis, but her best poetry, forged from an existence in rural Wales overwhelmed by penury, marital horrors and bleak mother-hood, was the fruit of conditions not even a poet should endure.) Norman liked her and sympathised with her; they met at Berlemont's when she managed to get to London, and he maintained his loyalty until at least the late 1950s, when the address of her caravan slips from his diary. His not fancying her did not stop her attempting some bizarre seductions, including sending him her knickers in the post.

Gwen Nicholls, his childhood friend, had also divorced and had remarried that year; she was now Gwen Merrington. Norman had not given up the ritual of teasing and chasing, and still had a childhood reflex that Gwen was his property. Gwen enjoyed the rehearsal of their relationship every time she came to London, including her refusal. "I can remember him getting me back to his flat to see some things on one occasion and having a real old tussle with him physically. He was *always* hoping." After she remarried, she remembers, Norman went through a period of calling her on the phone and giving her coded messages for her husband that she didn't understand for years (she didn't pass the messages on either). "It only occurred to me recently [what he meant]. I was so pure-minded and innocent. He told me to tell my husband to keep away from the keyhole. I thought, whatever does he mean?"[3] Without a single stabilising sexual influence, he did not restrict his quests for conquest, even on the grounds of taste. On one occasion at Banchory, his daughter Karen recalls, his interest miscarried wildly.

Mum and Dad went horse-riding when I was three, in Banchory, can you imagine? And Dad fancied Bobbie Dunns who was the owner of the horse-riding place. Bobbie Dunns, blonde Bobbie Dunns. I don't know how I know this because I was only three, but Bobbie Duns once said, "Hold out your hand, Norman" in the dark, and he did, and she put a frog on it. I don't know whether she knew he was phobic and did that, or whether he became phobic from that.

He went to Banchory as close to once a month as he could manage, never for longer than four or five days because, Karen remembers, it was like "welcoming the godhead back [and] I don't know how long people would have been able to sustain that".[4]

Although it was brilliant and the weekends were brilliant because everybody was on their best behaviour, it was a very artificial sort of situation. What he didn't see was what happened before he arrived and what happened after he left, all the distress and the anguish [and] the general sort of hype, you know, Mum always putting him down and saying, "The bastard, I'm sure he's got loads of women."[5]

Breen Cottage was austere. "We only had coal fires in the house," Norman's son Gareth remembers. His father "paid the heating bill and the lights",[6] and gave Hester a weekly amount to cover family house-keeping. There was no fridge or washing machine. In winter it was north-east-Scotland cold. Karen says, "I remember sometimes you'd have a glass of water at your bedside, and it'd be frozen in the glass." The cottage was sizeable: Karen remembers its layout as a result of running from her mother's anger and frustration, which fell more on her than Gareth. "There was a bedroom off the kitchen where Docie slept and then there was another bedroom off a passage where my grandmother slept. So when I was going to get smacked I used to run in and hide and my grandmother, bedridden with arthritis, would say, 'Leave the child, Hest, don't smack the bairn.'"[7]

From June to August Norman worked on the south-east Asia book, at the beginning of September going to Paris for a long weekend for research and to visit the Geuthner & Maisonneuve bookshop, oriental specialists in rue Vavin. He also saw his mentor Colonel Egerton. He had lunch with another friend from the 1930s, Oliver Myers, in London the day after he got back. He generally worked at friendships, partly because he was often away and partly out of insecurity, keeping regularly in touch with anyone he liked and making certain he phoned or wrote if he had not heard from them for a month or so.

Familiar signs of restlessness began to show in the autumn. He found the Farm Street flat too small to live and work in and started looking for another, in Bloomsbury or north of Oxford Street. Among the mundane claims on his time – the staff ("Offer Webb more holiday" in his diary) and stock at R G Lewis both needing attention – he chased new literary stimulation that he found at book auctions at Sotheby's and in eclectic reading lists:

BOOKS
The Age of Scandal
The New China (Turnstile Press)
Louis Couperus, *The Hidden Force*
Multatuli (Dutch author)

Robin Fedden, *Crusader Castles*
Publications on the Caribbean
André ~~Maurois~~ Malraux, *La Voie Royale*
Verga, *The House by the Medlar Tree*

His curiosity was both pure and applied: a new subject would have to excite him as much as Indo-China had, and soon. An auction catalogue entry he marked was perfect Norman, as disciple of the peculiar: "Fleschen, Florian von der. *Wunderbarliche, seltzame, abenthewrliche Schiffahrten und Reysen.*[8] A rare book on Peru. The author speaks of islands containing rivers of wine and mountains of cheese and butter, of others with rivers of beer and milk, and of Tetsap where partridges and hares fall from the clouds."

By November he was rewriting and talking to Michael Howard about his next book. He was close to moving into a new flat in Orchard Street, across the road from Selfridges, but before he did he had to drive to Spain to test a new underwater camera housing he had had designed for the Leica, the Lewis Photo-Marine. For the journey he slipped a new car into the equation: a '49 drophead straight-eight Buick with a power hood and high bullnosed bonnet, in red, that flouted English canons of restraint and, not content, added to its swank with an unremoved *Corps Diplomatique* plate. Its registration number was KLO 10, and Norman could not resist pretending that it had belonged to Joe Kennedy ("Kennedy London 10") when Kennedy had been US ambassador – though the car was ten years too young. He left on 27 November, driving south and stopping at Chartres, Brive, Narbonne and Gerona. In the four days he spent swimming and testing between Castellón de la Plana and Valencia, the idea may have taken root of coming back to Spain the following summer: on 8 December, going north again through Barcelona, he reminded himself to get the "Papers advertising houses Mallorca".

Back in London on the 15th, he had decided what he wanted to write next – where he wanted to go next – and after he had lunch with Michael Howard on the 20th to celebrate Cape's acceptance of his south-east Asia manuscript, he started planning for Burma. Christmas was spent at Banchory. January, to his relief, was taken up with lists. He had already had lunch with the Burmese ambassador, U Ohn, who had given him a letter of recommendation. He applied for his £200 spending money and bought another gold watch; made plans to sell his Lancia and cleared the Farm Street flat, bought his tropical shirts from Lillywhites, medicine (including a wide range of anti-malarials – he had had an unpleasant attack after Christmas, "high fever, straining, intestinal pains, great thirst, characteristic looseness – coffee grounds") and brilliantine; had visiting cards printed and – a rite of departure – a haircut, and told his partner Harding "to take [a] shop in Oxford St if one offers". On the afternoon of 4 February 1951 he got on a BOAC Argonaut at London Airport, bound for Rangoon.

After stopping to refuel at Rome at 9 p.m. ("very cold"), a coincidence lay in store at Beirut, the aircraft's second stop: a coincidence that was instrumental in convincing Norman for the rest of his life that he personally attracted such baroque accidents of chance. Before leaving, he had asked for proofs of the south-east Asia book to be sent to him at the Corvajas' at 4 Gordon Street (theirs was his home, despite Ernestina's continued absence, whenever he was between addresses). When the proofs failed to appear he rang up Cape and was told the parcel had been sent in error to 4 Gordon Square – an address recently vacated, as if the gods of comic opera were directing, by another Norman Lewis. There was more: at Beirut Oliver Myers, working in Lebanon, met Norman off the plane, telling him a small party was planned for him at the British Embassy. When Norman arrived, one of the first guests he was introduced to was the other Norman Lewis, also on his way east. It was "a surprise from which I have never wholly recovered".

"Leave anything to my imagination and nobody could recognise the facts after a few years" – Norman's account of this postmodern vista in The World The World has a beautiful symmetry. We aren't surprised that the actuality is more mundane. The "other" Norman N. Lewis was living at 4 Gordon Square, in spring 1946, where he once received a royalty cheque intended for Norman. In 1951, living and working in the hills above Beirut as a teacher of diplomats, he was invited by "a friend" – Oliver Myers? – to meet "the other" at a party. But actuality also has loose ends: Norman N. Lewis was also an author, but was not the Norman Lewis – a third NL – who was author of the updated Roget's Thesaurus that Norman often used, nor of another book entitled Instant Word Power. The other odd aspect to the story is that Norman N. Lewis, though an admirer of Norman's writing, does not remember meeting Norman in Beirut despite going to the party.[9]

In the evening of the 6th Norman's flight went on via Cairo to Rangoon. On the last leg of the journey he sat next to a Canadian official from Ottawa on loan to the Burmese government to help take a census. Nathan Keyfitz remembers that "As the plane flew along Norman regaled me with an endless series of stories. He liked talking, and I liked listening. . . . We got off and headed for the Strand Hotel where, since there were few choices in Rangoon, we were both lodged."[10] Arriving at 3 a.m. he and Norman slept late and had their first meal in the "economic atmosphere of England". There were "grilled kippers on [the] menu [and] no scope for luxury spending". Norman noticed that the English "flock in quickly at 12.30, eat dutifully and with promptitude and are finished by one". Amid the incessantly tinkling piano, the diplomatic pudding and "violence of the British cultural injection . . . like an ancient odour of cooking vegetables in a boarding house" Norman found himself in a country of splintered divisions. Three years after getting independence, the republic faced a profligate array of opposition that included Red Flag and White Flag Communists, two versions of Aung San's People's Voluntary Organisation, regional and ethnic rebels (western Arakanese Muslims, eastern Karens), and Kuomintang exiles. Outside Rangoon and Mandalay security and facilities were nominal. Forty years later Norman remembered that "the element of rough travel was so strong in the case of the journeys to Indo-China and to Burma, particularly to Burma, that that to some extent took a little of the gilt off the gingerbread. Sometimes it was exceedingly uncomfortable, and very often very boring."[11]

Rangoon showed off Burma's problems in microcosm. In its rectilinear streets and Victorian massiveness it was sprawling, filthy, encrusted with poverty, and an unharmonious map of unmixed Indians, Chinese and Burmese; its authorities could not control its squalor or its annual epidemics, or the insurgents who sometimes cut off its water. Norman was cautious: within a day of his arrival he realised he might have come several thousand miles and found himself without a subject. Rapidly starting to grab at the sort of shallow judgments exemplified by his verdict that the state of the nation was proved by its bookshops – no books about Burma but a flotsam of hard-boiled sex novels – and that the Shwedagon Pagoda was the city's only bolthole from the "undigested Westernism" of mass public callisthenics and the products of Hollywood and Detroit, he realised he would have to find a story, soon. He took his letter of introduction to the Secretary of the Ministry of Information, U Thant (to be the first non-Western secretary of the United Nations ten years later), and, as no one had asked him before,

U Thant agreed to his travelling to Moulmein and Mergui, further
south, by boat in a few days. Other ports were out of bounds. Further
enquiries with an official of Burmah Oil supplied the news that a trip
to Mandalay might be a possibility, if he didn't mind sleeping on deck
and being mortared.

He was forced to be in Rangoon a week before getting away, visiting
pwès in the suburbs – open-air festivals of puppets and drama – and
the city's prison, run on Buddhist principles, where the "I[nspector]
G[eneral] aims at producing eventually a prison without walls. Head
warders are called housemasters and do not have the psychopathic
expressions of screws *de carrière*. Of the wooden bars IG cheerfully
admits that they are very easily cut through."[12]

On the 16th he found the SS *Matang*, 1463 tons, in Rangoon
harbour. He gave a kind account of her in his notebook, recording
"tactful seating for tiffin and dinner" and passengers "lured to their
meal by a melodious gong, indistinguishable from that on the *Queen
Elizabeth*", but later exploiting a comic opportunity recast her as the
Menam, a bubble of British colonial absurdity, "a little enclave of
diehard Englishry" where the allocation of places in the dining room
was made on a strict basis of colour and race. He found himself
among the Anglo-Burmese.

The next day the *Matang* approached Moulmein, "a town of baroque
flavour and charm, an essence of Portugal strained through an Indian
mesh". In *Golden Earth*, the book written on his return, he mentions
the readability of the descriptions of early Victorian missionaries such
as the American Baptist, the Revd Howard Malcolm, who toured the
Baptist missions of the Far East in the 1830s. Their accounts

are full of exact information about the geology, the natural history, products,
commerce and customs of the people ... they are scandalized by everything
they see; but the main thing is that, whether they disapprove or not, they write
it all down. With all their arrogant fanaticism, their stupid condemnation of
all they do not understand, how much more one can learn about the country
from them than from so many modern collections of impressions, with their
amused tolerance, their tepid, well-mannered sympathy.[13]

Over and over his own descriptions are offered with another sort of
exactness, in the sort of language we would use to describe a painting,
precise and prosodic: a language that has decisively shifted its category

in fifty years, from romance to pathos, as so many of his scenes are now only available in old paintings and photographs.

The morning was lustrous. We were about half a mile off shore, approaching Moulmein. . . . There was a narrow coastal plain, with oxen feeding in the grass down by the many creeks that intersected it. Gondola-like sampans were moored at the mouths of inlets, their double sterns painted in red, white and orange geometrical shapes. . . . An occasional tall tree among the luminous serration of water palms by the shore was silhouetted against a soft, water-colour smear of hills. From each hill's summit protruded the white nipple of a pagoda. . . .

   We passed a headland tipped with sand, on which egrets swarmed like white maggots. A junk reeled by in the glassy billows; a black, raffish silhouette, with delicately tapering bows, and a tiered poop with the passengers in their coloured silks crowding to the balustrade.[14]

Descriptions of course are not photographs or paintings, when the writer's contract with the journey is to transform it into metaphor. Here is part of Norman's pre-metaphor description from his notebook. And this has a touching element too: something quixotic again stirs in his note (" '*Be quiet*, Sancho, for although they seem to be watermills, they are not") as, in his effort *not* to see, he clings to romance.

Pass a headland and a factory and try not to see it. In any case sheds are raised on pylons and roofs are so ragged it might be a large mature shrub.[15]

   He had become friendly on board with a "most delightful" elderly Burman, U Tun Win, whose family took him under their care for the day he was in Moulmein. He was the only Briton who left the ship. "None of the sahibs went ashore at Moulmein", he noted. "Until now I thought Orwell's account exaggerated."[16] He spent the morning at a young Buddhist's novitiate party, a friend of U Tun Win's family, and in the afternoon squeezed into U Tun Win's son's Jeep, one of seven passengers, "the oriental minimum", for a drive to the pagoda at Mudon, the sort of journey strenuously unadvised by the police because of the risk of ambush. The country was "green and ethereal" and smelt not of flowers but spice. There was "charcoal burning and tobacco" in the villages. He joined in the visiting of relations "in the way of honest country people, by sitting down, smiling and waiting a little, and then going away" and back in town had dinner with U

Tun Win and his cat, who fought decorously over the most succulent parts of the fish.[17]

The ship's next stop was Mergui from where Norman was supposed to fly back to Rangoon, but no seat had been booked and he was stranded. Mergui from a distance was a run-down South Seas arcadia: at close range it exhaled the foulest smell of drying fish and harboured lawless bands of tumorous pariah dogs. At a restaurant run by an amiable Chinese he was offered two tables pushed together as a bed, but at the last minute was able to sleep on the delayed *Matang*, still loading rubber, and the next day to get a cancellation on the Rangoon flight. The price of comfort was interrogation after dinner by the expatriates on board. Did he intend to write a book after a visit of a couple of months? They huffed with offence.

Without having suffered with them the long, boring years of expatriation, it was an impertinence to have an opinion. And yet when questioned they would often boastfully display their ignorance, their contempt and their distaste for everything about the country. . . . [And] on close examination, of what did their memories consist? Of the insubstantial scandal of the southern jungles and coasts, which is no more than that of the suburbs, grown a little garish and fantastic in a lush climate

he contemned in return.[18]

In Rangoon prospects for travel had got bleaker. Norman found that even Mandalay was now on the list of places subject to a vicious official circle of stamps and permits from government offices, designed to weaken and eventually break the traveller's will. The sheer difficulty of leaving Rangoon almost made him give up. "On the point of packing up and going home", he presented himself directly at the War Office. A Major Maung Maung, who found his account of his predicament amusing, told him to apply through the British Embassy and that he would grant a permit for the Shan States, later cheerfully keeping his promise and having ten copies typed out for him. Permits were one restriction: another he was reminded of the following day, when he crossed the river with Nathan Keyfitz to look at the former Portuguese outpost of Syriam (Thanlyin), was the smiling handcuff of the conducted tour "from which it was impossible to break free. When we said we wanted to walk back to [the] ferry, the Township officer, finally convinced and trying to conceal his surprise, has the lorry follow us while the three of us walk gravely ahead."[19]

On 27 February he flew to Mandalay. The leitmotif of disappointment continued.

Mandalay. The room overlooking *The Desert Hawk* and various booths. Inevitable sobbing Chinese crooner and "My melancholy baby" from film trailer. . . . Toilet is performed in front of a not very interested public on a rude exposed platform on top of outside steps, out of the only decent pot seen in Burma. Probably very ancient. Filthy, chipped, unnoticed & beautiful. While I am squatting there a man comes up and asks casually if I want to go to the film.[20]

The tonality of the name "which beckoned to the imagination" was gone: this was Mandalay's "bitter, withered reality". Night in the city, in a lovely trope of understatement, "called for special qualities of endurance". After visiting the Arakan pagoda and the leper asylum of St John, where the disease's many slow stages somehow seemed to him to echo the city's death by tedium, he slightly lost track of time. By "about 1 March" when he travelled out to the village of Taungbyon, deep in PVO territory, with a military escort to view the pagoda of Anawrahta, he was desperate to leave Mandalay though he had not been there more than two full days. His onward itinerary to Myitkyina, Lashio and Taunggyi by air, road and river, elaborately laid out in his War Office permit, immediately fell apart. As he searched for a lorry to get him at least as far as Lashio a pariah dog added to his vexations, shadowing him and "in a rather detached and experimental manner" biting him on the calf. He washed the wound in Fire-Tank Brand Mandalay Whisky and wrote later that he "offer[ed] as a testimonial the fact that I suffered no ill effects".[21]

With the feeling that his Burmese journey was turning into the story of its obstructions, he accepted with relief a lift from the British Consul that would take him thirty miles along the Lashio road, to the consulate at Maymyo. Maymyo was touched with the uncompromising stiffness of British outposts: he found it austere, sporting and faintly dull – archetypally insular – though the bazaar next morning (possibly as a result of his having slept deeply, in freshly laundered sheets) he found "wonderfully lively". From it a lorry was at last going to Lashio. It left without him. With the consul's driver's help he caught it up, arriving after a switchback ride through nondescript hill towns and tunnels of forest at Lashio as the sun set. Invited to stay with the father of the young man, Tin Maung, he had met on the trip, he stayed awake for several hours awaiting the return of the tarantula or scorpion that had scurried across the corner of his vision as he was falling asleep.

At an interview the next day, 5 March, with the Special Commissioner, a civil servant who also happened to be a Shan prince, a *sawbwa*, he had a change of fortune: if Norman was willing to put himself under his protection, the sawbwa told him, and to travel north to Hsenwi, Nam Hkam and Bhamó instead of south to Taunggyi with the army, he would get the chance to go some way along the Chinese frontier. It was a chance not only to go as far as he could go, but also to see the most interesting of the northern Shan towns.

Lashio became the most pleasing stop so far: Norman was able to talk to Tin Maung's father, U Thein Zan, to water the old man's garden, bathe regularly and start to distinguish the character in Burmese faces. He enjoyed the family's relaxed routine and relationships, the way they called lunch "breakfast", the sight of Tin Maung's mother "pad[ding] about chain smoking cigars", the son relentlessly scolding his father that it was time to "die, old man" because of his losses at gambling. Norman repaid their hospitality by inviting the family out to dinner, alarming them at one Chinese restaurant with the smell of opium and the giggling of "unserious" Chinese-Shan ladies drifting through the lattice from the next booth.

From Lashio onwards, the journey was easier. He was able to leave for Hsenwi on the post-wagon, an exhausted and decayed Dodge. This was Kachin territory, though in Shan State, inhabited by Shans and Kachins and several smaller groups: he was struck that the Palaung people he saw (a Shan minority) possessed beautiful woven and lacquered baskets that were identical to Moï baskets he had seen in Vietnam. The Palaung were of Mongol origin, the Moïs Malayo-Polynesian: the similarity, he thought, had been overlooked because ethnology in the 1950s relied on linguistic classification. He was undoubtedly right to suggest that its categories be broadened to include legends, laws, ceremonies, and craft and weaving designs in its comparison of ethnic variations.

At Hsenwi, a cluster of huts on a bare plateau, the local sawbwa sent him on with a letter commending him to future officials. Twenty miles further on, at Kutkai, the post-wagon broke down beyond repair.

Seng, a Kachin boy, invited Norman to go by bullock cart to the house of his brother-in-law to wait for new transport. On a hilltop, the house of the brother-in-law – a Kachin headman, a minor warlord

– dominated the surrounding country. Mandalay rum and beer were drunk as an apéritif to a copious dinner of curries, rice and three kinds of river weed. The problem of Chinese bandit bands from Yunnan was discussed. These raiders caused regular trouble for Kachins and Palaungs, and in *Golden Earth* Norman wrote of joining Seng and his brother-in-law's men on horseback in a raid against the Chinese the following day. This was an adventure there cannot have been time for – he was in Nam Hkam by the 8th – but it gave him the chance to describe the jungle borderlands, the wretched conditions of a Palaung village and the irritable cross-border atmosphere. He discreetly took no credit in the fictional pursuit – bestowing on himself an attack of malaria that "cushioned the edges of sensation" and kept him on the edge of the narrative.

In the morning the headman's soldiers flagged down a Jeep, and with two Chinese merchants he went on to Mu Sé, short of the border, where he was welcomed by the hospitality or protective custody – he was not sure which – of an anxious local policeman. Next morning he walked casually but purposefully to the border, where the frontier police arrested him properly.

In another example of ambiguous kindness he was held at the police post until transport for Nam Hkam could be found. The lorry ride that followed was "an excruciating journey of 19 miles, wedged in [the] front of [the] lorry with old Shan lady struggling for non-existent inches in an endeavour to stop burning her legs on the engine". The scenery was beautiful, "terraced paddy fields coming down [the] mountains like ceremonial stairways and lapping the plains in waves".[22]

Nam Hkam, between immaterial Burma and purposeful China, had the tidal splendour of a great frontier interchange. Norman was a guest of the *amat*, the senior administrator, a weighty position in a town with the reputation of having the biggest bazaar between Calcutta and Shanghai. Breakfast was served at Nam Hkam as breakfast, not lunch, because of the market's early opening hours. Norman went out for a dawn walk to fortify himself for "The relentless arrival of the breakfast to be tackled on the disturbed stomach of the night".[23] Afterwards the bazaar, first glimpsed in the discomfort of a selection of too-early curries, still delighted him: every five days swelling the town's population by 6000, it was a convivial reunion of tribes: Shans, Kachins, Palaungs, Lishaws, bands of Yunnanese he could not identify, white-turbaned women. He was interested in the signs of the West's approach to trade taking root via the East's passion for alchemy and horoscopes – all Western cosmetics and proprietary medicines were highly saleable – and in how the sequel would take place in the habitual way, of increasing local people's purchasing power with aid. "The consumption of branded laxatives, stomach powders and cough cures would then be colossal." The bazaar sold everything from crude Burmese toys to the finest Chinese china, and two-thirds of it was already given over to Colgate toothpaste, Vaseline and Horlicks.

The appeal of the people remained. The market remained neutral, he was told, whatever wars and feuds occurred. In his notebook the utopian atmosphere made itself fully felt.

"A spirited ballet of girls with tall waggling Cossack hats and pigtails like black hawsers run giggling and flouncing from the camera. It is all an extravagant crowd scene from a lavish production of *Prince Igor*. Here was the Tatar camp. Trailing robes, panels and sashes." The traders bought and sold from an hour after dawn until the afternoon, when the flasks of country spirit came out and polite tipsy groups patrolled the streets until sunset. "Slowly a blue twilight settles on the town. The mountains recede in haze. The colour drains from the scaled curving roofs of the marketplace. The last pack ponies are led briskly away. The lorry drivers climb into their cabins to sleep."[24]

On 10 March he came down from Nam Hkam to Bhamo, torpid and scrappy by the Irrawaddy, on his way back to Rangoon. Waiting for the river-steamer to turn up, he hired a jeep to see the jungle west of the town and Myitkyina, the flimsy, Indian-influenced state capital. Urgency had been lifted from his shoulders after several weeks' wondering whether he would ever manage to get deep enough into the country to see it, and he sat in a tea-shop on the main street and drank tea, reflecting on the complex attraction of travelling and its slow, insinuating impact.

Rapturous happiness can only be set in a chiaroscuro of joy and anguish. The pleasure of travelling is a subtle satisfaction – from it is distilled a happiness of nostalgic recollection which matures like good spirit.[25]

Memory made its own decisions about what to preserve. As it had done for him in north Africa and Naples, it would benevolently overwrite the negative aspects of travelling in favour of its stimulants, improvisation and "subtle satisfaction". Interestingly, he identified happiness not as something of now, but a part of memory, with movement as its raw material – something like what Pascal meant when he famously wrote that "Nothing is so insufferable to man as to be completely at rest, without passions, without business, without diversion, without study." Writing of course deepens the moveable theme of memory – a written-down memory is not exactly the same as what was remembered, and memories change and reorder themselves over time (not to mention being influenced by what is written down about them) – and presumably it did not occur to Norman what we now know to be neurologically true about memory, that writing things down, taking notes, is also a form of *not* remembering. The brain surrenders memories remembered by the hand; so the act of writing offers a counterpoint to memory as well as an account of it. Taking notes – recording what will be forgotten – and making the brain forget, writing can restore the pleasure of the ephemeral that otherwise fades instantly in ephemera's ever-spreading twilight.

Two kinds of ephemera were constantly part of the satisfaction of Norman's travelling as he defined it, and of his notes. The flora for one: around Bhamo it becomes more various and mysterious than in the mountains, the forest is scented, and "Each tree stands out in its own pool of shade projected from the sun overhead. [They] are of all shapes and of all degrees of luminosity and colour. . . . You could count the trees as easily as you could in an early 19th century painting. . . . Road carpeted [with] red edible flowers." Birdlife was another. The road is full of it: "Bee eaters with their elegant flight – a few wingstrokes and then a pause to show the most streamlined of avian shapes. [Also] wagtails, hoopoes, doves, rollers and a heron with a yellowish neck." Later,

Over the Irrawaddy an Indian kingfisher hangs motionless in the air, long beak pointing down like a hornet's sting, then it drops like a stone on some unseen insect a hundred feet below.

Leaving Bhamo on the *Pauktan*, a steel river-steamer of 106 tons, next day he recorded his admiration for the astonishing agility of another kingfisher he watched from the deck.

The extraordinary faculty of the pied kingfisher to hit the surface of the water while travelling at full speed and allow itself to be bounced back, at the same time reversing its direction of flight, thus saving time on the tightest of turns.[26]

The steamer was full. "The number of passengers is fantastic." It had an escort of fifty soldiers, carrying embroidered pillows to sleep on, plus another twenty to guard some Chinese internees and dacoits being transported south. Upriver from Thapeitkyin the next morning there was an alert – the *Pauktan*'s sister ship, passing on her way upstream, signalled that she had been fired on – during which Norman noted the "impressive Noël Coward deportment" of the monks on board who walked the deck with serene indifference as defences of rifles and Bren guns were set up. A few minutes after the soldiers were stood down a machine gun started up from the shore. No one was hit, which he attributed to the insurgents' desire not to kill but to tie down Burmese Army troops in perpetual escort duties.

Three days after leaving Bhamo, early on 16 March, he caught the Rangoon express at Mandalay. It was a sun-parched, mosquito-ridden journey south on a line under regular attack. The "up" train reported that three bridges had been blown below Yamethin, and after spending the night there he continued by lorry to Pyinmana, a desolate, surreal stronghold of government troops that included an occult fairground overrun by *nat-ka-daws* or prophetesses. He accepted an offered bath at the railway staff flats, crushed all the cockroaches and mosquitoes he could find in his new train compartment – to the grief-stricken horror of one of his travelling companions, the Wincarnis-drinking, born-again Buddhist Mr Pereira – and after another night of thirst, waiting at the platform for the train to go, arrived back in Rangoon on the 19th. Booking into the Strand Hotel, he went to bed for a week: he had progressively lost weight on the journey and somewhere along the line, probably around Hsenwi, had had another attack of malaria. On the 23rd, Good Friday, he roused himself to visit the annual pagoda festival at the Shwedagon. This embraced, incongruously, the gorgeousness of the great stupa banked with flowers and the greyness of an adjacent government-sponsored industrial exhibition, which was rescued from monotony by its Anti-Corruption Pavilion, in which a self-critical campaign by the authorities showed in luridly Dantean terms the story of the rise and fall of a crooked employee, to riches and then plummeting, via a tour of hell, back to earth to glimpse his wife spending his ill-gotten gains with another man.

His own journey, rough as it had been, had been a success – he had seen more and travelled much further north than he had thought possible – but in a sense it was such experiences, some comedy or other briskly dotty stimulus snatched from the jaws of anti-climax, that had stamped it. That, plus his own childlike enthusiasm, with something of fixation about it, which he reflected on in the last pages of his Burma notebook.

My advantage as a travel-writer [is] that I can suffer a childhood nostalgia over impressions first received in middle age (the Brain-fever bird).

Kipling's "dam' Brain-fever bird", the Common hawk-cuckoo, *Hierococcyx varius*, not particularly gaudy and looking like a cross between a hawk and a pigeon, had first got under his skin when he crossed the river to Syriam. F W Styan, the Victorian author of *On the Birds of the Lower Yangtse*, describes its three-note call, "who-are-you?", as "uttered first moderately loud in rather a low key; after a few seconds it is repeated louder and higher; again a pause and another call, and so in a crescendo scale until it ends in a piercing scream, after which the bird is silent for some minutes. . . . It is very difficult to locate the bird in thick cover, each call sounding as if the bird were approaching."

Norman had heard the Brain-fever bird all spring, the countryside echoing incessantly to its call through long moonlit evenings. "Certainly it would aggravate cerebral malaria," he wrote. Yet only the British know it for its aggravation: in India it is one of the two favourite birds of Sanskrit poets, who hear its call more lyrically, as *pee kahaan* – "where is my beloved?" or *paos ala* – "summer is coming". It took Queen Victoria's testy colonial servants to find a bird so irritating that it annoyed them to the edge of madness (perhaps because unlike the country they colonised, the Brain-fever bird was untamable and uncullable).

Norman, as he left Rangoon after Easter, felt nostalgic for the sound of its three repeated notes in his memory's landscape. Brain-fever is not a bad British description for his intense, very un-British enthusiasm.

The air of the Pyrenees blew down on us limpid with nightingales.
                                        Diary, 22 August 1951

Gorse smells of apricots. Evening fields. The brown meadows burned
with dim fire. The pink clouds lay piled up on the horizon against a
deep purplish sky. The fields were combed by the plough and barred
with tree shadows.
    The sun splashed on the hoar-frost dazzle of the fields.
    Trees wept their leaves.
    The falsetto mooing of a cow.
    Purple clouds leaned over the horizon.
    The fields newly combed by buffalo ploughs crept to the horizon.
                                        Diary, 1952

Histories that contain no lies are too dreary for perusal.
                            Anatole France quoted in 1952 notebook

A WORLD OF INTENTIONS

"Who makes baskets makes some ugly and some beautiful"
Sicilian proverb

THE 1950s were a good time to be a writer in Britain. Change and the redistribution of priorities and wealth were everywhere in political, economic and cultural spheres, yet the vantage point that individual thought and creativity stands on was peculiarly solid. Living was cheap and improving materially faster than its cost, and the territory under scrutiny, as limited, mercifully, as the British state's bureaucracy, was equally balanced between domestic and foreign worlds. At the start of the decade the extent of social armament and inhibitions, the means by which British society remained nostalgically retrospective (in class, privilege, cultural attitudes to everything from sex to women's rights), was still wide, but in the 1950s social permanences that had been bricked in until the war turned out not so resistant to erosion after all, and the many-accented voices of the suburbs and provinces, the not-public-schooled, not-country-housed, were no longer bricked out. Ignoring the Cold War, which people tried to, it was a secure decade, even a decade of opportunity. Artistic freedom was in the air, if not around every slum corner. People read books. Parts of the 1950s were already beginning to look like the 1960s.

It was an even better time to be a writer with money in his pocket. In April 1951 Norman moved into the new flat in Orchard Street, opposite Selfridges department store, started to plan a summer in Majorca, and before that a trip to the United States and Canada. One piece of shocking news was waiting on his return. His father-in-law, Ernesto Corvaja, had had a fatal heart attack while Norman was in

Burma. This was at least as much a blow as his mother's death, in some respects more so. The bond between him and Ernesto had deepened in the twenty years they had known each other, despite Ernestina's mysterious continued absence (which her father never referred to). It had evolved into a reciprocal surrogate father-and-son relationship. To Norman Ernesto had been a role model of generous stoicism, a Romantic throwback, and he loved him. After Ernesto's death he talked about him throughout his life; he wrote about him, real or imaginary, often. One of his last scraps of writing, a handwritten sketch describing a return to England written shortly before he died, mentions repeatedly a need to speak to Ernesto.

He arrived in New York on 30 April, "Too warm for tweeds." He had a visit to make to his new publisher, Scribner's, who had bought US rights to *A Dragon Apparent*. He had photographic suppliers to see and a Buick agent for parts for the car, which needed rehooding, and he wanted to meet Harold Isaacs, a China journalist and one-time Trotskyist who had covered Indo-China after the war and warned the US State Department not to back Bao Dai. His plan was then to go on to Buffalo and cross into Canada to see his son Ito, who was at boarding school just across the border.

The level of note-taking and description in his diary indicates that he also thought of using the trip as background, for a novel or at least an article. "Perfection of skyscrapers spread like a series of fangs in wings of cars", he wrote, and made notes on slang, drive-in banks "with inhuman voice issuing from speaker", Americans' habit of weighing themselves, their habit of not talking in restaurants ("During the meal one sentence was exchanged. His wife said, 'This ice cream is kinda cold', and he said, 'It's cold all right'"), their unfamiliar jaunty commercialism ("*Dialogues* of Plato are shown on a bookstall with opinions of well known writers printed on jacket" next to "How to survive an atomic bomb"). Unusually he tracked his own feelings too, revealing a hardly seen intensity.

Setting out on this US trip, I could not envisage anything but boredom. But it is just like the "change" of childhood, full of keen, intangible joys, of rejuvenation and brain clearing. The impact of spring is agonising. Why do I forget these delights so soon? Now each day ahead seems precious. I look forward to such experiences as Buffalo and long to explore Long Island and the waterways around N Y City. In winter, then, there is a kind of sluggishness invades the spirit, a hibernation of sensation. Spring is compressed into the one month of May.

On the trip to Buffalo he noted that "as you went away from NY the cars got shorter and darker, they glistened less and began to develop a grape-like bloom on their roofs". He saw pass the "turbans, hatboxes and pumpkins of an oil refinery", but came back emotionally and devotionally to the spring.

A white carved-jewel house in spring feathered trees, the plush avenues of brilliance in the meadow bearing their hectic rashes of yellow flowers. The latent bushes with spring light pouring through their sunken branches lowered to screen . . . gables of white frame hotels [that] glistening weave woody patterns over cars parked in the village. Slag heaps sprout delicately their green; a long aluminium ribbed train passes gleaming softly. A notice on it says "Athens" and a black man in a cook's hat sticks a rubber face out of a window. Black hooded nuns holding breviaries sit withdrawn, forming with bloodless lips at peace the words 'Ave Maria'. The trainman has a face of decades formed professional reserve and severity. His jaw has lengthened from a habit of aggressive thought. Spare jowled and spectacled. A wide river with white spent rushes and fierce green ones submerging their bases. Blossom gushes from black branches.[1]

He did not think much of Buffalo, or Niagara. He stayed at Flommerfelts Indian Village Cabins at Chippawa, a collection of "imitation birch-panelled log cabins in cement" that sold "Indian souvenirs (pathetic)", and spent two days crossing over to visit Ito, in his second year at Ridley College, St Catharine's, Ontario. Under Ernestina's casual guardianship Ito had spent his time on the streets and had had no schooling.

My father sent me a bicycle, which was the pride and joy of my life, [and] my days were cycling, swimming and exploring. I had no education whatsoever, nobody taught me to read, write or anything. My best friends were the boot-blacks, and a lot of these kids were being killed in Guatemala, so-called street kids. . . . My mother must have realised that it was going to end badly, one day she was going to get back and I wasn't going to be there, I was going to be dead somewhere. So she said, "Right, I've got to get you out of this country."[2]

After eighteen months at a private school in Guatemala City run by an eccentric elderly Englishwoman – "She looked at me and she said, 'I can always tell a little rotter when I look at one'" – he had been bundled out to Canada. The Ridley College regime was severe but an English master named Higgs (who had read Norman's writing) had taken Ito under his wing, coaching him in English each day so that he would get through the first year's teaching. In his second year, after his father's visit, he finished by winning the school public-speaking competition.

Norman got back to New York City on 5 May, from where he went out to Great Neck and met Isaacs, visiting Scribner's again before he flew back to London on the 9th.

Three days later he was at Banchory with Hester and his other children, and "absolute winter on moors". A week after that he was at Llanstephan in pouring rain with his aunt Margaret and the "white orchid not fully out" but the banks "full of primroses, ladies' smocks, stitchworts, birdsfoot trefoil, bluebells [and] marsh marigold".[3] Six days later he was on Orkney for a birdwatching trip that was cold, wet and abortive. Spring was always his season for birdwatching, partly because it was the season for eggs; but he didn't want to settle. Peace was like the lips of the nuns on the train to Buffalo, bloodless. He had set himself the difficult balance of getting away each summer to write, and of keeping to his responsibility as a father. The children were growing, Karen was four, Gareth three; by taking Hester and the children to the Mediterranean each year he could give them a holiday and, in theory, keep a quantum of acceptance between Hester and himself about their limited relationship. The summer holidays that started in 1951 were perhaps the oddest sequel to their affair, partly because, as they continued into the early 1960s, they were its most stable and durable one.

On 20 June he, Hester, Karen and Gareth left for Spain in the Buick. (The arrangements may have had a sting to them. But this was glamour. Who in the 1950s could afford to travel like this?) "First day 150 miles, nearly to Meaux. Second day 315 miles to Uzerche. [Third day,] 240 miles to Ax les Thermes mostly through pouring rain. A town stiff with bad hotels."[4] It rained like Wales as they crossed the Pyrenees. At Barcelona they caught a ferry to Palma, the Edwardian-era *Plus Ultra* which amused Norman with its scrollwork and lamps suspended from the bills of swans and affected German tourists, while "In the third class food is shared with ancient grace". But something unsatisfactory, the island's smartness or its affectation, meant that within a fortnight they were back on the mainland looking for somewhere else. Talking to a hotel manager on the main road south, which still sweeps away from the coast between Perpignan and Barcelona and particularly from the blunt, rubbly promontory that pushes out into the sea on the border's Spanish side, Norman was directed to an isolated fishing village at the end of a pitted track. After a collapsed bridge, where the car had to be left, he found Tossa de Mar backed against a semi-circle of low cliffs, a web of tight-cornered streets and haphazard houses. It was

what a gifted child with paintbox and chalks and a fresh vision of childhood would make of such a fishing village; a gap in the cliffs with a line-up of almost windowless houses, coloured washing on flat roofs, a scattering of black goats, a church tower with a stork's nest, yellow boats pulled up on the beach, and pairs of women in bright frocks mending nets.[5]

In Tossa he stumbled on paradise regained. He felt that the village had reached one of the best forms of development, in a seclusion and self-sufficiency that were close to medieval – though he typically viewed the fundamental sense of belonging of the fishermen of Tossa through the prism of the hatefulness of modern English class consciousness. The fishermen's way of life was the utter reverse of class, a kind of idyllic socialism he could sign up to.

This was a little self-sufficient group, a microcosm of humanity, in which everyone has his role, his task, he does a certain amount of work or a certain amount of production a day. There is no class of any kind, except at a later period when the richer fishermen changed their boats . . . and also there were no real state medical services, there was extremely severe rationing, and no crime, one policeman that nobody spoke to, no lawyer, so you see, here were people living in a state of extreme [happiness], they all knew each other by their first names only . . . and it was just a place where everybody was busily occupied and happily occupied all the time, supremely happy, that was all.[6]

His scepticism led him to approach Tossa's bounty with caution at first. The later description of "one policeman that nobody spoke to" jars with a diary note that in the village "Everyone wants to be a Civil Guard. They are badly paid but can throw their weight about. Sell their rations of brown bread & go to the baker & buy white at 1 or 2 p[esetas] a kilo. Right price 7."[7] The *civiles* also controlled the black markets in government-gathered olive oil and sugar. Tossa was not fully the foxhole he described it as, either. His diary of 19 August scorns the incursion of another "English car with" – was there *no* hiding place from the suburbs? – "chained spare wheel and toilet roll in back". But he liked it enough to stay at the village *fonda*, carry on writing his first draft of the Burma book and, when he had to fly back to London at the end of July for R G Lewis business, to return till the end of August.

He was in Tossa when Cape published his south-east Asia book, *A Dragon Apparent*, on 19 July. It turned out to be an unexpected alternative success, selling 18,000 copies before Christmas with book club sales of another 16,500. Its ironic notations of colonial neurosis balanced against its vivid, enquiring, modestly passionate accounts, full of pleasure, of indigenous people (allowing him implicitly to denounce their oppressors), were a heady contrast to the domestic introspection of the era. The book's kaleidoscope, plus its sheer informedness, offered an effective antidote to the flag-fluttering self-consciousness of the Festival of Britain. Its author had shed his dandyish pleasure in language as a tool of promotion, replacing it by a series of essays in understatement, which he had learned could be powerful in itself *and* a subterfuge that allowed him to magnify events while seeming to do the opposite. *A Dragon Apparent* was composed in language that knew how to be both subtle, almost invisibly humorous, and direct – alive to the bold absurdities of life and to its innate melancholy. "The book sold in tens of thousands to an eager public", his editor Michael Howard wrote. "Little had been written yet about the situation in [south-east Asia]. It was the highlight of Cape's spring season in 1951."[8]

Reviewers praised the book, when what reviewers said mattered. To the *Daily Mail* reviewer "the great charm of the work is its literary vividness. Nothing he describes is dull." Peter Fleming in the *Spectator* called it "A brilliant report on a period of violent transition in a strange land . . . a very good book indeed". The *Economist* felt it "should take its place in the permanent literature of the Far East". Only the *Times Literary Supplement* sounded an opposing note. Its reviewer, Barrington Gates, a consultant to the Ministry of Aviation, conceded that it was "very penetrating" and complained that "for all its throng of sharp-set portraits and its evocative natural descriptions, his book wears a somewhat excluded, lonely air . . . chillier, and not so wise . . . a disappointment". The mandarin's disaffinity for the rebel surfaces from his distaste for Norman's critical perspective on French colonial authority – an outlook that might have been a part of the book's appeal to readers

– although unconsciously his verdict on the book's "excluded, lonely" atmosphere reverberates all the way back to the childhood lanes of pre-war Forty Hill.

In London in September Norman got on with the Burma book, assembling the dozens of descriptions, cameos and vignettes that fill his diaries as well as his notebook. His initial idea of a single book on the Far East, later followed up with a second book, had turned into something more conceptual. Writing to Michael Howard from Mallorca on 28 June in response to Howard's request for something to say since Norman would not be in London for his publication, Norman had put down his intention in a tortuous but revealing way.

Ultimately I shall try to become a good novelist. The furtherance of this ambition has been only temporarily postponed owing to an overwhelming desire to see and describe the countries of the Far East before it is too late. I am convinced that these countries are about to enter upon a long period of seclusion and that when – probably not in our generation – they emerge they will be utterly transformed. The short series of works, probably three, on which I am embarking may then constitute something approaching a modest epilogue to the accounts provided by the traders and adventurers who visited the Far East when European influence was at its height.[9]

Well, yes. Writers like to make broad statements of ambitious intent, especially to their publishers. What is strange about Norman's is that he begins by confessing his intention to be something completely different: "a good novelist". *That* is what he really wants to do, that is where he has sensed his real ambition and self-respect to lie; and yet, as soon as the words are out of his mouth, he wants to smudge them, take them back, cover them up with an arching project for a trilogy of Far Eastern non-fiction – because he lacks quite enough confidence to stand by that first intention. This was a struggle in him that continued acutely through the 1950s, and chronically beyond the decade. In 1986, when his novel *The March of the Long Shadows* was submitted to his publisher, his editor, as I had then been for three years and three of his books, suggested that, given the manuscript's discursive, plotless character and his better sales as a non-fiction writer, he might consider publishing it as non-fiction. He reacted sharply – and I feel as ashamed of bruising his feelings as of my pragmatism – instructing his agent immediately to seek another publisher for the book.

Despite his feelings of unconfidence, in late 1951 he was impatient to write fiction. One of the consequences of being merely a witness, as he was in his non-fiction, is perhaps a sense of helplessness, an ultimate uninvolvement, that the novelist overcomes by godlike involvement. In winter 1951 Norman went back to trying to finish stories and filling his diaries with fictional scraps. He was remarkably busy. Always in the background were the demands of business (where he kept it as much as he could): lunches with Kodak, dinners at the White Tower or the Étoile with suppliers and partners, adjustments to stock and strategy, the opening of new shops. Before he sold R G Lewis in the 1970s, the business had expanded to run branches in Shrewsbury, Worcester, Bristol, Cambridge, Southampton and Aldershot as well as the London shops at High Holborn and Strand.

He was also making domestic changes, redecorating his flat in Orchard Street. His friend Malcolm Dunbar had talent as an interior decorator and offered to help him furnish and decorate the flat, on the top floor up a tatty staircase past the offices of the theatrical impresario Dmitri Spount. Dunbar's taste was informed. Beyond the grey theatrical offices, a door opened onto an expanse of deep red stairwell striped with balsa and at the top of the stairs an enormous wall-hanging from Heal's. It was a flat to make an impact. The kitchen was ignored, but the dining room and sitting room had polished wood floors and plain Wilton carpets; the dining room had a wall of bookcases, the minimalist sitting room displayed some of Norman's pictures around a grand, fossilised marble fireplace, a splay-legged sofa and easy chairs its only furniture. The bedroom was the culmination, with a deep pink ceiling and elaborate, wall-width, heavy black and dull gold curtains. In a city whose smog and greyness still oppressed, the flat was a place of splendour. He enjoyed living in it – but it never made up for the summer in Spain and having to return to English winter. "People can get used to living in dark cellars and igloos. It is inadvisable to fix one's scale of happiness on too high a level," he had to remind himself.[10]

Discussions with Cape in the autumn led to agreement that he should return to Asia, this time on an extended Indian Ocean tour, finishing in the South China Sea at north Vietnam and Hanoi. He found himself

faintly unwilling, but eased his reluctance after he had an invitation
via Oliver Myers to meet representatives of the Borneo Company in
Thailand – one of the networks of British trading power in the Far
East – who were looking for a writer for a commissioned history. On
5 January he left London for Bombay. The "usual emotional climati-
sation took place as soon as taking off. Felt no need to stay night at
Rome. Would have preferred to carry on to Beirut." Impatiently he
flew by stages to Karachi, then to Bombay where on the 10th he
boarded the SS *Ratnagiri*, bound for Goa. The coaster was "a small
curry smelling boat". A woman, "voluptuous and gratifying"; first-
class passengers wearing "corduroy and [carrying] riding whips"; and
a socialist-minded Goan merchant who confused democracy "for fascism
or tyranny", caught his attention. Descriptively however he was waiting
for the oxblood-painted Hotel Central at Goa, with its "decorative
white balcony moulded in relief" and its green roof-tiles, and the beach

painted in pastel reds and pinks on the edge of the sea. Scarves of mist wind
through the palms and the recoil of the waters has left arcs of coconuts. Boats
with lateen sails are always about to be launched or are just coming in. . . .[11]

He liked the Conradian view down the beach road of thin, elegant
calèches drawn by tiny ponies, while behind them dhows from the
Persian Gulf sailed slowly into the harbour, but culturally he found
Goa "more westernised-Americanised than provincial Spain or Italy".
The Hotel Central was "so called to disguise its inaccessibility" but he
preferred it to the Imperial. "It lives on memories and hope. The Goans
probably haven't noticed the decline they have lived with, the picturesque assimilation with the palms and red earth; the shrubs that have
seeded themselves among the fine old roof-tiles." At the Imperial "you
get Heinz baked beans on your breakfast eggs".[12]

Catching the train east to Bangalore on the 16th, he plunged back
into "Englishry": the women wearing stockinette dresses, the men,
incredibly, in tweeds and flannels, the "ecclesiastical hush in the
dining room only broken by the faint chinking contact of eating uten-
sils with plates. . . . The sight of all the English is particularly depressing
after the unearthly elegance of the starving peasantry of India." He
went on via Madras to Pondicherry on the Coromandel Coast, where
he found the colour and scene of the streets "like a museum the way
they tire the brain". Visiting the Sri Aurobindo ashram, he tried to

assemble its activity – the working, studying, tennis, boxing, praying – into a practicable philosophy, but after talking to the ashram's spokesman, Norman Dowsett, whom he found gentle and honest, it seemed to him that Dowsett had made "the usual mistake" of mixing up reasonable Vedantic philosophy and miracle-working. More tartly he noted that the main difference between the ashram's cult and primitive Christianity "is that the latter said give what thou hast to *the poor* and come follow me".[13]

Crossing to Ceylon, he stayed the night at Colombo, travelling up the next day to Anuradhapura. A perceptible onset of fatigue, of mechanical reactions to impressions, colours his notes on its pagodas and its monkeys; only the "hideous vivacity in the local ponds, snails, ugly fish, frantic frogs and turtles with mouths like the necks of bottles" animates them. The setting of the temple complex at Mihintale a few kilometres away was "sublime" but he was distracted and then made distraught by the hunting of the "painfully beautiful" birds – green pigeons, bee-eaters, herons – which with unpleasant skill a local hunter brought down, some of them three with a single shot. The people here, he felt, were Buddhists in name, no more. (He didn't equate the killing with his own egg-collecting.) His horror lasted through the next day at Habarane then Sigiriya in repeated admiration for "the authentic glitter and panache of real jungle birds. ... The Ceylon jungle-fowls have a yellow patch on comb and wonderful purple-blue feathers on rump." He turned back to Colombo with relief, meeting on the way to Kandy a corrupt Vedda,[14] an old charlatan with a heavy betel habit who pandered to Europeans and mercenary Ceylonese, who seemed to him "more venal even than the Indians because ... they come more into contact with tourists". Increasing boredom made him interested in the scurrilous aspects of Ceylonese life. He noted that "the smart set go on pilgrimages to Rome and are 'county', which means they practise lesbianism and homosexuality" and that the "local murderer (of wife) [is] to be let go because he is [the] best cricketer in Ceylon. He f[uck]'d his wife before strangling her. This fascinates the local women."[15] One has the feeling he was daydreaming, his recording mind away off from the journey: apart from these wicked asides, his descriptive notes, usually so worked-at and vivid, got increasingly dutiful, and the occurrence of passages in his notebook boxed off for possible later use in a novel became more frequent.

Finally, on 31 January, he flew from Colombo to Singapore. He sent a message to the office of his birdwatching friend, Loke Wan Tho, and found himself becalmed – embalmed – at Raffles Hotel waiting for an answer. Loke's appearance had the usual surprise elements, Norman said later. He had resigned himself to English dinner in the garden at Raffles and

had just committed myself to [savoury meat loaf] when everyone seated in the vicinity was suddenly distracted from whatever they were doing as five white Cadillacs, moving so silently that only the scrunch of their tyres on the gravel could be heard, crept up the drive to form a line outside the hotel's entrance.[16]

Loke was on his way to his sister's themed birthday ("black tie, white Cadillac") and insisted Norman come. Loke's enthusiasm redeemed the awful mix of modern teetotal Seventh-Day Adventist atmosphere and a playlist that included "Bluebells of Scotland" and "The foggy, foggy dew".[17] Norman was glad in retrospect that he went; Loke, ever the tragic obedient son chained to the duties of business, drove him from the party to the airport as the sun came up.

Hong Kong; Macao; Saigon; Hanoi. The cities came with their dipping junks, Portuguese balconies and cognac advertisements, and went. His interest revived at Hanoi with the faint but familiar smell of warfare. At Saigon – where he arrived the day after another writer, Graham Greene, left flying in the opposite direction – he got permission to visit the north from the ever courteous French Information and Propaganda office. In early 1952 the French were struggling again. In January the courageous General de Lattre de Tassigny, their military and political commander and seen as the only officer who could "save" Indo-China, had died of cancer in Paris; meanwhile in the north French Union forces had underestimated Viet Minh resilience, and de Lattre's victories of 1951 were slipping away. The battle of Hoa Binh, his offensive attempt to draw the Viet Minh down from the mountains and interdict their supply route from the coast, had been continuing inconclusively since November.

Norman continued to admire the Viet Minh for their ingenuity and doggedness. Their camouflage was "extraordinary. Even when an area is surrounded and the troops move in, nothing is ever found", and when they attacked a French post they would carry on digging assault trenches under French fire until they were killed or the work was finished. "Many hundreds are often lost in this way." They almost never lost *matériel*, attaching cords to their machine guns so that when a gunner was killed his gun could be pulled back.

At Hanoi, staying at the *camp de la presse*, Norman was invited down the Hoa Binh road south-west of the city to visit a French defence post. When he reached the post at Ao Trac, the war was visibly harsher. At the small officers' mess, pastis and lunch with Algerian wine were served while French 155-millimetre howitzers on the edge of the camp, and then tanks further down the valley, fired on Viet Minh positions that were trying to sink a nearby river ferry. He felt something last-ditch in the air.

At Ao Trac a soldier who looked as if he wept perpetually takes our particulars. . . . After the Premier left the other day [the Viet Minh] mortared the camp, killing 4 and wounding 6, from the low jungled hills on which the clouds are pressing down. . . . The [French Union] Vietnamese infantry clamber up the road laden down with grenades like merchants carrying fruit. . . . On the way down we stopped and a sgt-major said the road was quite clear. "Had a bit of a do half an hour ago in the woods and two fellows caught a packet." He is rubicund and nonchalant. There is a man in the ambulance with both legs blown off.[18]

There was a rush to get to the coast at Haiphong by six, to Le Relais for dinner and the slatternly, peeling Hôtel du Commerce and its hostesses. Norman's accompanying lieutenant, "at once affable in a suburban saloon-bar manner and haunted", assured him, "It is very gay at Haiphong. *Nous avons beaucoup de parties.*"

The next day he was taken along the coast and shown Appowan island. Two years later these defences would be so much military debris. Not even an American offer in spring 1954 of tactical nuclear bombs to turn the tide at Dien Bien Phu would save France's glory in Indo-China.[19] The premonition was in Norman's mind as "the thin broken strains of Melancholy Baby", drifting across from the Commerce, were disrupted by the almost continuous thunder of guns.

"The atmosphere", he wrote in his notebook, "is truly Brussels on the eve of Waterloo."[20]

Hanoi, Saigon, Bangkok. He left Hanoi on 25 February, the day the gamble for Hoa Binh was lost with the French completion of their withdrawal. He did not reach the Borneo Company's headquarters at Chiang Mai for another ten days, after an attack of malaria sent him to bed at Bangkok. When he did, on 6 March, there was no book for him to discuss; another writer, Compton Mackenzie, had been approached. Chiang Mai, Bangkok, Songkhla: the Borneo Company's managers showed him lavish hospitality, and the trip fizzled out, maybe of necessity (he had been on the move for three months almost without a break), in convalescence and recreation. He got back to London on 30 March, a warm spring evening. As an idea, a journey that would form the basis of a summary of Asia before the fall, the trip had been a failure. It was not surprising: as a project it had a whiff of opportunism about it, and surveys always lose in passion what they gain in suavety. But it was a failure that would have interesting consequences.

The pattern of Norman's life was not quiet when he got back; his escape reflex steered him. He had not made a quiet life, of course. Between the beginning of April and the end of June he travelled to Banchory five times to see the children, on the sleeper or in the Buick. Two weeks after his return from Asia, he took Dottie to Dorset for Easter. In his judgment on Weymouth his fictional characters struggle to break free from reality (and melancholy).

We sit in the silence of Bank Holiday breakfast in a commercial hotel among drooping daffodils and clock mechanisms. Outside: thrush songs over slate roofs, broken clouds and the snuffle of early departure of old cars. Guests wait inside the cave-like openings of bedroom doors, waiting to rush out as they hear the lavatory flush. . . . A wonderful Victorian clock-tower in cobalt. Devenish pubs. An old lady comes out of [a] general shop and polishes a thin brass strip across floor in entrance. The girl with pointed breasts mooning at holiday time. Tall and hunched with unconscious humility; the harridan muscles sketched in her face in the position in which they will develop. The new mistress in the Sunday morning snack-bar with morning curled hair and fat hand-bag, fresh from the secret back streets bed.[21]

Another four weekends that warm spring were spent birdwatching at Brancaster and Blakeney Point in Norfolk and on the Suffolk coast. "Bungay–Lowestoft [is] full of moats. *This* is the writing of history. Bell Hotel, Walberswick. Southwold, pretty & Georgian Southwold House Hotel overlooking sea (& 6 cannons)." The desire to get away was so strong it included buying a faster car. The Buick was family transportation. He wanted something quick that would be only his (and probably Hester would not know about). He considered buying a Jaguar, cancelled the order, and bought a baby-beautiful white Porsche 356 instead, one of the first two to be imported, proving that, with almost every car in London black or dark blue, and British, he had not purged himself of automotive gluttony or exhibitionism.

At the end of June he had to garage the Porsche for the summer; on the 27th in the Buick in a heat wave he and Hester, Karen and Gareth left on the four-day drive to Tossa, this time via the Loire and Aquitaine. By the time they reached the coast the heat was "terrific". After two nights in a hotel, on the last day of Tossa's *fiesta mayor* and its ceremony of nine dances, or gallops, along the main street, they moved to Gracia's, one of the bare white houses squeezed into the protective crescent of cliffs. With the children playing under their mother's eye he spent his time working his way gradually into the company of the fishermen. He didn't ignore the children completely. Karen remembers that

[We] spent a lot of time on the beach in Tossa while Dad and the local fishermen went out on their frolics of adventure. Dad could have bought the whole of the fish market for a fiver in those days, but he loved the hunter-gatherer adventure thing. A lot of time on the beach, a lot up around the castle. I remember Dad pretending he was a ghost in the castle and I was saying to him, "It was you, Dad, wasn't it, it really was you?" and he wouldn't admit to the fact it was him or not and I was always [left] with that little bit of doubt.

In fact it was Norman's belief that Hester did not always look after Karen that produced the first public instance of side-taking. "There were people that Mum and Dad must have known that were going out in a sailing boat," Karen says,

and they said, "Do the kids want to go?" and I think Mum kept Gareth because she thought it might be too dangerous, but I was allowed to go and it capsized, and I was trapped under the sail. [There were] people throwing lifejackets, lifebelts to us from the point, and once I got out from underneath the sail and got hold of one. . . . And Dad was furious with Mum that she'd allowed me out on the boat without a lifejacket, but she'd kept Gareth. He was really, really angry with her.[22]

Nothing happened to change his mind about the idealness of Tossa. However incomplete his view (he never spent a winter there), the village spontaneously became one of the very few places where he felt he belonged. It was a feeling founded on two things: his veneration for the fishermen, and his own primitive sense of being alive. Beneath his love of cars and planes lay a paradoxical pastoralism; or perhaps it would be fairer to view him as a transitional Romantic, beguiled *both* by speed and slowness, mechanisation and nature. His pastoralism was not soft-centred in an idealising way so much as the product of being compelled to stand outside a situation in order to observe it. He shared Lévi-Strauss's "rustic conviction" about modernity: he believed in "the purity of water and air, the charms of nature, the diversity of animals and plants"; believed that we are stripping ourselves of the values that we once cherished, that by brutalising indigenous cultures we are brutalising ourselves. The fishermen of Tossa were symbols of both natural values and human values.

The fisherman's life was one of constant adventure. "If he leaves the sea at all," Norman wrote later in the 1950s, "he is driven from it by failure, not tempted from it by success."[23] Philosophically, the lives of fishermen provide an outstanding motif – the capital motif – of Norman's writing, a motif that counterpoints the temptations of cash with the non-economic benefits of adventure and connection, of belonging. A fisherman could go out in the morning and with luck return home in the evening; could have his adventure and still belong to the company of his fellow fishermen and to his community. Belonging, immersion, self-dissolution, coming home: they are the components of the great Romantic quest, of which Norman himself is among the most ironic exponents, his books full of the quest, his search always bent that way but conducted, undeviatingly, by the arch non-belonger.

If the fishermen's happiness lay in the balance of their relationship with the sea, their freedom was expressed in activity not acquisition.

Another thing was this, you'd see a man, he'd done the fishing with a long line and lots of hooks on it, and then I'd see him in the evening, I would be living next door and I would say, "Francisco, what are you doing this evening?"

He'd say, "I'm going fishing."

I'd say, "Look," I'd say, "man, you've been fishing eight hours."

"No," he'd say, "I'm exceedingly enthusiastic because I'm going fishing tonight with a torch in the deep pools and that's very fascinating." You see, they would vary their forms of specialisation, there'd be a specialist in everything but they'd make this little change and keep themselves interested.

And then of course whenever there was the big fishing, once or twice a year they would catch a fantastic catch, either tunny or sardines, and then they had a system. They would go immediately and buy their wives and children new clothes and bits of jewellery. Now two miles away there was the peasant community, which never spent anything. They knew exactly what the return of the earth would be every year, they could calculate absolutely [that] a certain area of earth would produce a certain amount of produce, and they were very penny-pinching, they always lived within the narrowness of their sphere of semi-prosperity.

The fishermen, it was always an adventure every time they went out. Mostly the catch would be poor but you never knew when you'd get a great windfall and on those days you'd come back with the boat sagging, so you'd have a great time, everyone went home radiantly happy. They were all gamblers, the fishermen were gamblers. The peasants never gambled.[24]

Norman's son Ito spent the following summer of 1953 in Tossa. He remembers his father's delight in the fishermen's sense of life as a gamble.

My father was infatuated with Spanish fishermen, totally infatuated because in the Spanish fisherman was a kind of reunion of all that is best in humanity. The first thing he liked: they were gamblers. Why? They had to gamble on the weather. In the morning they'd go out in the boat but they didn't know really whether it was going to blow hard. They had an idea but it was always a gamble. They were very poor swimmers or not-at-all swimmers so they were taking another gamble – if they ditched they were going to drown. Taking a gamble as to where they were going to find the fish: they may find the fish or they may not find the fish.

Everything was a gamble for them, and he thought this was an extraordinary thing. It's a nowness, you know, every day is now. It's not like the peasant, he knows his potatoes are going to come out, whatever he sowed the season before it's going to come out at the right time. . . .

And what astonished him was that when they came back to the port and they had these catches, you'd get these old widow women and they'd come along and just stand there, they wouldn't do anything but the fishermen would automatically come and bring them fish. They were too proud to ask, far too proud to ask, but the fishermen didn't have to have anybody ask them.

My father spent hours and hours and hours talking to them. They used to have these little sayings, and some of the sayings are quite spectacular. He would repeat them again and again to us. "Don't you think this is wonderful?" he would say. Eventually a fisherman used to take us out, long distances into really faraway places, and this guy used to be with us all day while we fished and my father would be in conversation with him for hours. This guy used to be totally drained by the time [we got back] . . . the information my father used to get, he was [still] like an Intelligence officer. He had notebooks all over the place which he could never utilise because there was so much material.[25]

When he was not fishing – in the pools or diving with a speargun from the boat of Narciso, another fisherman he often went out with – he was writing. Unconfident though he was as a writer of fiction, an impulse to lie more expressly had been his refuge in Asia when the journey was getting him down, and as soon as he got back he started filling the first of three pocket diaries with paragraphs of a novel written in no particular order, to be pieced together later. Some of these paragraphs turned into other stories; the *New Statesman* published one, "The Adopted Son", an allegory of imperial misunderstanding in Indo-China, on 12 July.

He carried on noting in Tossa until the end of August, stimulated by the daily predictable routine of Mediterranean sun and activity at his doorstep. When he fished from the boat he and Narciso sometimes went far, to inlets and caves that sucked at the glittering blue swell. On 24 July they made a "Trip to Llansá. Puerto de la Selva. Cadaques. Caught 2lb grebia. Puerto de la Selva wide and blue with background of bare mountains." A month later, on 27 August, he burst his eardrum diving.

He flew back to London to see a doctor and to deal with business, as he had the year before. Though he was careless about the occasion, he was also in time for the publication of his Burma book, *Golden Earth*, on 1 September. The reviewers were as complimentary as they had been about *A Dragon Apparent*. Though the travelling had been more scrappy and difficult than in Indo-China, its sting in the finished book was drawn by Norman's readiness to mock his own suffering, and his view of the richly social and spiritual Burmese may have been pastoralist and Romantic, but it was also, as his Rangoon friend Nathan Keyfitz says, sound social science.

Norman saw the romance going out of the world, that we are the last generation to be able to see strange cultures in their unspoiled condition. The world is modernizing, Americanizing, the enchantment squeezed out. That is good sociology; Max Weber spoke of the disenchantment of the world in his own day. Like the alienation that marks the modern workman as contrasted with the old-style craftsman, it is the price we pay for high productivity.[26]

"If only science could find some way of increasing his production," Norman had written about the Burmese peasant, "he might eventually become a consumer of shirts with non-shrinkable collars, ball-point pens, and electric shavers." His Weberian attitude to progress was more about conformity's annihilation of adventure than a dislike of ball-point pens, adventure that *The Times* applauded in "a continuous vivid record of an experience which is not static but dynamic". The *Manchester Guardian* went further. "It is hard to remember any better travel book published during the last twenty years ... the author combines delicate description with unobtrusive scholarship and robust but subtle humour."

In the *Times Literary Supplement* Barrington Gates again issued the one sceptical note, this time that "It is difficult to isolate the peculiar dryness of his writing ... its failure to bring real warmth and depth to any of the human figures who decorate his journey", but his grudging review again touches a nerve. Ever since his account of the two saintly Communists, Manuel and Esteban, whom he had made friends and stayed up all night with in Madrid in October 1934, Norman's writing had shown that one emotional gap in writing about – or writing about *having* – close relations with people. But even Gates submitted (almost) with pleasure to "the light lash of Mr Lewis's irony" and "the beauty of the land and its frequent reflection in Mr Lewis's close-packed prose"; and surrendered his review's conclusion, as he had done with *A Dragon Apparent*, to a paragraph extract of that prose.

Norman, Hester and the children finally drove home from three and a half months in Tossa in mid-October, via Béziers and Avignon and Burgundy this time, getting back to London on the evening of the 19th. Norman's novel had begun turning into manuscript pages. His pocket diaries revert to London appointments and the precious oddities of seen and overheard England (class is an abiding category – "Can a family develop through wealth, a long, aristocratic face, in 2 generations?" he asked, and noticed a curious habit of the 1950s, that "Women who were not schooled into a good accent try to remedy this with a strange drawl – sometimes nasal." At Dunwich in Suffolk, birdwatching, "the best view of the day was of sheets of slate-grey water soaked with the greens of unfamiliar water-weeds, a background of white and yellow reeds", to which he immediately added how "Birdy women use school-girl slang – 'Come on chaps. Good egg. I'm pushing off. All in a tizzy'."[27])

With more work to do on the novel, he also had plans for his autumn social revival, with a difference now that the Orchard Street flat was redecorated. The first party was a late celebration of *Golden Earth*'s publication at the end of October. His drinking friends from Berlemont's and their friends and wives and girlfriends were invited. Dottie was asked to bring girlfriends and came with an Australian friend who shared digs with her in her warren in Upper Montagu Street. It was a successful party, and a cautious blueprint for what would become frequent and increasingly relaxed evenings that combined convivial global company, heavy alcohol consumption and lawless behaviour. After wine, Norman's favourite party trick was to open the connecting door between dining room and sitting room and invite guests to fire his silenced Beretta rifle through it, across the Heal's furniture, at a target on the far wall (from time to time he offered his underwater spear gun). The flat was on the top floor, and above it was a flat roof edged by a low parapet, where he barbecued and sometimes took the record player for guests to mambo outside.

The boyhood spirit that drove him to ride his bike along the capstones of Maidens Bridge lived on. Dottie's Australian friend remembers "seeing him walk all around this parapet. Very drunk. Death imminent if he'd fallen." The first time she met Norman, in October 1952, was in the Orchard Street bathroom where they did no more than chat, she remembers, "over a bath of ice, because he didn't have anything newfangled like a refrigerator. So he went down and got loads of ice and put it in his bath. That was my introduction." She was more fascinated by the flat's extraordinary look than by its occupant. "Coming up the stairs, on one side there was a closed-in balustrade and in front of that were metal window-boxes, filled usually with very vivid cinerarias. So you had this wonderful display of colour, tremendous impact. It was fabulous. It used to wow everybody."[28]

Lesley Burley was twenty-two. She had left school in Sydney at sixteen, and with a young woman's prerogative steered a string of jobs – Elizabeth Arden salesgirl, fashion photographer's assistant, front of house for the Orient Line – into providing what she wanted: excitement, travel, London. (Her mother had been brought to England by her mother, and been presented at Court, and encouraged her daughter to go.) Lesley had come over on an Orient liner from Australia in 1950, switched to a better job at Qantas, realised that Britain's state-run airline, BOAC, had more routes to travel and a 90 per cent discount for staff who had worked there for a year, and moved again to work at Airways Terminal at Buckingham Palace Road. When she met Norman she was slim and voluptuous, a soft blonde, not easily scared, and twenty-two years younger than him. She was naturally friendly. A BOAC colleague, Peggy Milton, remembers her unusual kindness. "I was not very experienced and I was in quite a panic about something and there was this new girl and I said hello to her. She said something to me which I was so unused to hearing I had to ask her three times what she'd said. And what she said was, 'May I help you, my dear?' Nobody ever said that."[29]

"I think Norman fell for me," Lesley remembers. "I had a boyfriend at the same time which was a very on and off thing, so Norman was in a sense held at a distance a bit. I probably didn't pay very well! But I didn't feel so badly because he had his own commitments." Lesley's friend Dottie was one. "He must have rung me up and asked me out, and of course it was a slightly tricky situation because of Dorothy." The trickiness was resolved, up to a point, when Lesley introduced Dottie to a Canadian whom she later married, though as late as 1958 Dottie sent Norman a publicity still from a film she was appearing in, signed "Thought you might be interested to see it" and, defensively, "You can tear it up if you like. Once again / Love Dottie".

The other manifest trickinesses of a new relationship were then free to start appearing. "From the very start Norman adored me and that was maintained," Lesley says. "And because I was badly educated of course I was fascinated by Norman because he was the whole time educating me. And he led from my perspective, of course, a very exotic existence. I suppose with my background subconsciously [he was] a father figure." She also didn't care, as an ambitious English twenty-two-year-old probably would have, about the question of class. Norman did not tell her he was an actual father. "Not straight away, no. I can always remember a funny dinner at Orchard Street – I think it was Alan Pote [a doctor friend from Berlemont's] who almost let the cat out of the bag. And then of course finally he had to tell me about it all."

He spoiled her with dinners and flowers, "the usual role", and didn't strike her as old at forty-four. "No, Norman always looked very young for his age." He tried to carry her off by boyish enthusiasm, and because she was not thinking about the future she almost let him. Simultaneously she was experiencing the exquisite distress of having two men fight for her. "This on and off boyfriend wanted me to live [with him]. He was a journalist, and Norman kept on, he was very much, 'Please, please don't have anything more to do with this man. Please come. . . .'"

She did not come. But she did not *not* come either.

Norman guessed he had a pursuit on his hands; Lesley would make him work for her attention. But her forthrightness and sexiness stirred him, and going after her was not a burden or a charge. He was fit for challenges, and older, more patient, not so over-demanding as he had tended to be. He balanced one pursuit with another. His time was regularly taken up that winter with writing hard to finish his novel. As the rest of the year had been, life was still not rectilinear. But if 1952 had been anything it had been an inaugural year of the prizes of self-pleasing: of what he had aimed to do since his adolescence, what he had settled seriously to do since 1949, what writers always do when they can afford to. Say yes only to the things and persons they want to say yes to, and no to everyone and everything else. Do only the work they want. Live how, and where, they want, without fear of retribution from the gas or drinks bill.

In answer to the questions that had faced him seven years earlier, at the end of the war, he had not fully found a place he could bear to live in, though the combination of Orchard Street and Tossa came close. He had begun to discover what man he would be. He had, also, avoided having to write a book about Asia he did not want to write; had begun to be recognised; had emptied his literary intentions into the effort to "become a good novelist". And he had met a young Australian woman who had not said no definitively. He had the satisfaction of holding at once, for the first time in his life, several positions worth consolidating.

The house was not really home to him but a covering to protect him from the mosquitoes and the rain. He had enormously extended the normal human feeling of cosy familiarity with an immediate environment, which was what the word home usually meant. It had become inseparable from an infinitely complex network of keen sensation, an awareness of many things: for example, of the roaring flight of hornbills in the dawn sky, the ethereal sunless elegance of the misted landscape, the muscles of the bamboo thickets cracking in the deep afternoon silence, the laced-over sky a freezing blue-green in the early night hours, the pagoda by the moat with the moon's image shivering under the gong-strokes, the night sound of pheasants flapping their wings in the underbrush with the noise of a carpet being lightly beaten. This feeling about home included a grateful acceptance of the strangeness of his surroundings, a quality which he tended like a rare and delicate plant, never seeking to squander his curiosity by an excess of brutal investigation. There was a peach-like bloom in innocent illusion, a rich glaze for a connoisseur of the subjective. These were some of the things that Crane had brought close to him, that had become the comfortable background of his life and of his beloved work.

A Single Pilgrim

TO THE WICKET GATE

"I rest more when I work"
Ibizan proverb

"I did it mine own self to gratifie."[1] Norman's motive for writing "Death and Rebirth", which would lose its awful title and be published as *A Single Pilgrim*, was close to John Bunyan's, though less ingenuous. His third novel was a long-nursed ambition finally coming into the light of day, a very conscious, very assiduous attempt to raise his status. A part of his self-gratification was to prove something: neither of the novels he had so far published had been greeted with the praise his books about Asia had had, and he privately and badly wanted to be viewed not as a writer of travel books but as a novelist. (In wanting this he was slipping into a peculiar English trap of privileging a form – the novel – as the yardstick of literary genius rather than a quality of writing: a slip that in retrospect deserves large sympathy, the same trap eventually destining him for decades to the description "great travel writer", with its scent of condescension and oxymoron.)

He handed the manuscript to Daniel George on 17 February 1953. Writing to Wren Howard, one of the Cape directors, the same day, he communicated his ambitions and, unintentionally, how prickly he felt, telling Howard his new novel had "taken more than twice as long as any other book, and my feeling is that it is the best thing I have done" and demanding explicit commercial reassurance.

What I feel is that, although a book may be regarded as publishable, it can have no chance of success if its publisher remains unexcited. Therefore, although my tremendous enthusiasm for Jonathan Cape's is in no way abated, I should like to have your permission, in the event of your not feeling *enthusiastic*, to offer this particular book – into which I have really put a heartrending amount of work – to another publisher.[2]

The new novel's setting was taken from his three years' experience in south-east Asia, its intention to unite a picture of what was politically and morally "rotten" in the remnants of British imperialism with a picture of one imperialist's deep emotional inadequacy. An empire, he wanted to say, was a machine for producing economic wealth that could only be run with destitute emotions. The novel's descriptive background is as luxuriant as its plot is simple (with a significant twist). John Crane, manager of a timber company in Laotian Thailand, faces awkward choices when his company's application for renewal of its logging permit is refused: personal decisions of the domestic life (what to do about his loveless relationship with his wife Charlotte in England) and the professional (what to do about the sudden end of a career wedded to company service).

Before the permit runs out, however, other developments occur: coexistence with the local opium smugglers is disrupted by a spate of murders, and one of Crane's men, Richards, disappears after falling in love with a Viet Minh girl from French Laos across the border.

Crane is capable, likeable, and weak, with a half gone-native affinity for the harmony of his surroundings. He gives others the benefit of the doubt not from kindness, but from an unwillingness to engage with them. Historically, his understanding is fatally complacent: it mirrors the company's own flaw, its self-satisfied belief that few things truly change and that if there is a problem, "Things are sure to straighten themselves out in a day or two."

Both tendencies cause Crane to underestimate a reticent new arrival, James Confelt, a rice expert who turns out to be nothing of the kind. An "Apollyon in modern dress", Confelt turns out to be responsible for contracting the murders and disruption. Confelt, considering that "humanity in its highest form is tied up with mathematics", considers himself a political realist; his agenda is simply to prepare the area for US jets, using "the newest type of napalm bomb", to fire the jungle and, having achieved a scorched-earth cordon and the deaths of perhaps 100,000 villagers, block Viet Minh expansion across the border.

Characteristically, Norman's mindset allowed him to write a novel that was a homage to Bunyan despite harbouring almost every sort of objection to what Bunyan's religiosity represented. His, Norman's, pilgrim's progress is not up to the Light but down to the dark: one of the most affecting scenes in the novel occurs when Crane, discussing *Hamlet* with a Viet Minh lieutenant, is led down to the river to be shot. But Crane's path is also strewn with revelations. When Apollyon appears in Bunyan's allegory he is the "foul fiend" who assaults Christian on his way through the Valley of Humiliation. Confelt does not attack Crane personally, but Crane's fate is the result of the application of Confelt's values: murdered because a report he writes about Confelt's activities gets into Viet Minh hands and he is caught in the resulting quickening of the Communist advance.

Not even the CIA now denies that the Apollyon from Princeton "with a crew-cut, and gilded with the eternal youthfulness of the Far West" had his place in the catastrophe of Indo-China that followed French withdrawal. But in 1952 it was early to be writing about the true activities of members of US aid missions. Confelt, as a self-confessed part of "a private army" – "If things come off, the regulars can move in; if not, well – nobody ever heard of us, and no harm is done" – belongs to the same club as Alden Pyle, Graham Greene's quiet American. Greene's given inspiration for Pyle came from an American attached to an economic aid mission, whom he met before he quit Saigon in March 1952[3] – but *The Quiet American* was published two years after *A Single Pilgrim*. Was Alden Pyle partly inspired by James Confelt? Maybe not. A "third force" is not explicit in Norman's novel. But Confelt and his strategy of co-opting, in his case the tribal opium smugglers, resemble Pyle and his strategy like tragic variations. One fictional quiet American was – sure as shootin' – up and doing well before Greene disclosed another's activity.

A Single Pilgrim is not always successful: its lush ornaments of description slow down the narrative, its side-taking subordinates and spoils its art. Despite the energy expended, the whole is downbeat: it reads like a book written by a writer fighting his way out of low-level depression. A kind of Ford Madox Ford-like inevitability, a built-in "saddest story" tone, is hard on the reader (unless a "saddest story" is what he or she is looking for). To make another comparison with his contemporary, *A Single Pilgrim* reads as if it's Norman's *A Burnt-Out Case* – Graham Greene's most consistently negative novel, about the architect Querry who takes refuge in a leper colony after losing both vocation and faith. Querry and Crane, philosophical cousins, the one without faith, the other exposed to the emptiness of his vocation, his "beloved work", both die. It may be an odd coincidence that both novels were written at a time when their authors were seeking emotional attachment, Greene before he became fully involved with his long-time companion Yvonne Cloetta, Norman before he was fully involved with Lesley.

Yet Norman's characters have still a marvellous opacity of ordinary life and contrariness of ordinary character – Crane's two juniors, Gilroy and Richards, sceptical and idealistic, live in delightfully pointless antagonism – that the novel doesn't as a rule disclose to us. And his plot has a congenial day-to-day randomness that still provides most of the necessary thematic underpinning. *A Single Pilgrim* is, at one level, a very British novel – if we allow for the fact that the British novels that voiced the wider world disruptions and their impact between 1920 and 1960 (the ascendancy of fascism, decolonisation, the domination of politics by global economics) had their feet planted in a moral universe that was not British at all. It was Joseph Conrad who delineated the mess that ensues when people use "right" causes to guide their actions (in his novels *Lord Jim*, *Under Western Eyes* and *The Secret Agent*), and who first asked, in a twentieth-century, post-revolutionary context (the bulk of his work was written before 1917 but his ideas tend to hold the key to events, not the other way around), What is worth fighting for? Where does life's value lie? Conrad's British descendants have tended to be interested in those questions in contexts such as the fragility of history (Eric Ambler) or the unpleasant odour of human worldliness (Greene). Norman was interested in the loss of belief and above all – as we might expect – in its endgame. What happens to the misfit, who is, after all, a kind of pilgrim seeking a place? Near the end of *A Single Pilgrim* John Crane, on his way downriver to buy logs from a company in French Laos, sees "with the clairvoyance of despair" the hollowness of his values.

The firm to which he had bound himself so blindly, so uncritically – because he had never found a worthier object for his allegiance – would eventually come crashing down. Even if it survived the present crisis, a greater would arise to destroy it, because there was something at its heart that was rotten; something in the very nature of it was out of harmony with the epoch. Crane prided himself on freedom from political beliefs, but he could no longer blind himself to the fatal weaknesses in the colossus to which he had dedicated his life's labour.[4]

The answer of what he could bind himself to was that whatever is worth fighting for, it is very explicitly not a shadowy institution, and not an empire.

The post-war displacement that was felt by Britain as an imperial power was not, personally, a new feeling to Norman. It matched his long-nursed deep feelings of displacement. But he had already been through the long process of finding ways for himself of managing his traumas and exclusion, of successfully sublimating in the act of writing his deficit of belonging. He was, in a specific personal sense, ahead of his country. It was what made the 1950s his time.

Finishing *A Single Pilgrim* disrupted his routine. He did not get his winter escape until early March. The project this time was a tour of the widest (and vaguest) definition of the old Levant that would also take in Phoenician settlements and Crusader and Saracen sites of the eastern Mediterranean and Middle East; and it was fruitless. From Beirut and Sidon at the end of the first week of March he travelled to Cyprus, Paestum, Cetraro, Reggio di Calabria, Naples and Turkey, and was back by the beginning of April. Something had not fitted, at all. His notebook, usually packed, was thin. The emotional upheaval of writing, and anxiety about getting right, the recent novel still inhabited him. Rewrites of Crane's story take up more than twice as many pages. And the Turkish part of the trip had been "an unqualified disaster", he told Michael Howard,

owing to the weather (snow), which I was told (as usual) was the worst within living memory. I got very tired indeed of sitting in sad little cafes eating three kinds of sour cream, looking moodily at Coca-Cola advertisements, and listening to the remorseless patter of the rain.[5]

Cape had reassured him of their enthusiasm for his novel, however, and he had signed an agreement with them waiving the suggested advance, and removing their option clause. "I prefer not to sign an option clause for another book. . . . I certainly would not like to have to make a change, and would far prefer to remain with Cape's for the rest of my literary career, which should be good," he added accurately, "with reasonable luck, for another twenty books or so."[6] And the best sort of pleasure awaited: Lesley had agreed to spend a long weekend in Rome with him. The tickets were booked – £5 return – with her BOAC staff discount. Norman reciprocated. They went on to Naples and stayed at the Excelsior at the tip of Santa Lucia, overlooking Zì Teresa's, where the waiters' chirping of Neapolitan songs on the water-front was a fine fusion of art and soliciting. (About Zì Teresa's wartime practices Norman later had this to say: "At Zì Teresa's, a large lobster is said to cost up to the equivalent of a pound. . . . There is no need to pay these extravagant prices. All one has to do to have the restau-rateur instantly and smilingly knock off half the charge is to ask him to sign the bill.")[7]

Lesley was almost beguiled. By her agreement, their relationship had developed to the point of his pursuit being accepted but not surren-dered to. He had given her a lacquered box from Burma, and inside it a little carved jade cat diving for a fish. In Italy, the fish found the cat easy to be with. "Norman loved to talk. Off he'd go and of course I was spellbound by it all. It was fascinating to me to hear all this. I mean, living with him in that way I was forever learning."[8]

In London Norman kept up the pace of seduction, throwing parties at Orchard Street that Lesley and her friends were invited to. Peggy Milton, her colleague at BOAC, was one. "She was on shift and I despatched Norman in his Porsche with an old friend of his, Alan Pote, a doctor, and he scooped up Peggy." Peggy Milton remembers her first sight of Norman. "Lesley just rang me up, I was at work, and there was a party at Orchard Street and she said, 'Norman will come and collect you.' This was in the evening . . . and another girl who was working with me was invited as well, and so we waited outside Airways Terminal and suddenly this very glamorous sports car zoomed up."[9]

Another girl who experienced Norman's glamour was Julie Varnals, Gwen Merrington's eighteen-year-old daughter, whose mother had suggested she phone him in London. "He arranged to meet me in his white Porsche by Chelsea Town Hall. . . . He explained that white was a good colour as it didn't need so much cleaning but I got the feeling he liked cutting a dash. We went to his very posh flat where he plied me with gin [and] talked endlessly about all his travels." She was impressed by the red staircase with its sweep of traveller's objects up one side, puppets, silks and vases; and that he kept taking calls "from diplomats and princes while I was there". On the way back he told her the meeting reminded him of *The Golden Lotus*, the author meeting the daughter of his past love.

Julie Varnals met Norman once more, when she went with Gwen to Orchard Street that August. Norman was briefly back from Tossa. Gwen wanted to ask him if he could offer her son some kind of employment at R G Lewis between his leaving school and going to St Martin's School of Art. "He had said not to fail to get in touch if there was any way in which he could be of help." But Norman's answer was peremptory. "He responded by saying that he was of the strong opinion that young men should solve their own problems, as he had done. I felt affronted, knowing that he had not coped unaided until he was in his late teens, and as an only child had been cushioned. I'd not travelled from Devon to be told how the young should cope with hardship." She cut the conversation short and walked out on him with Julie. Norman went after them. "I could see his head as we walked in the crowd down Oxford Street and realised he was trying to catch up with us but couldn't." He sent a telegram to Forty Hill that night where Gwen was staying with her mother, but she didn't phone him. "I didn't have to, because when I got to Paddington Station [next morning to go back to Devon] he was there. And that's how Lewis was, all my young days. He was always there."[10] It was the last time. He told her he hadn't meant to be unhelpful; she replied that it had been her fault for taking him at his word. They corresponded later but never met again.

There were dinners too, for eight or ten at a time, that Lesley helped with. "Selfridges being handy, it was no problem to get food. In fact I never had a shopping list, I'd just run down the stairs." These were not so riotous as the drinks parties, apart from the flat's being used as a shooting gallery after dinner, and the heavy drinking, and the dancing on the roof, and guests passing out.

"I remember Frank Allen being there one night, and Peggy. We all drank wine [and] we might have had an after-dinner, because Norman at that stage liked that Spanish liqueur, Anis del Mono, so we might have had those and that would really kill you. I always remember Frank lying out on this bed in the dining room and then in the end we had to put Peggy round the other way and lay her out.

"There was talk of taking Frank home, and he said, 'Darling I am a mulberry, and mulberries do not travel well.'"[11]

Frank Allen often drank with Norman at Berlemont's. As the chief pharmacist at Whipps Cross Hospital in east London, he has important form in Norman's 1950s. Norman's thirst for activity and stimulation, his ever-restlessness, and his need for ordinary endurance to keep on keeping his plates spinning – Hester and the children, Ito and R G Lewis – while maintaining space for his own private, inner and literary lives, invites the artful question. The answer was Benzedrine. Allen was his supplier, along with sleeping pills to manage the drug's effects. In the 1950s and early 1960s, the long decade of the upper – is that why those years now look celluloid bright, asparkle with an innocent vitality? – Norman had casual, unlimited access to its drug of choice. Jack Kerouac reputedly wrote *On the Road*, his single-spaced 36-metre "scroll", on Benzedrine; Anthony Eden, the British prime minister, mishandled Suez on Benzedrine; in June 1957 an American public health expert told a conference that a drug such as Benzedrine might have allowed athletes to run the mile in under four minutes. My father, an entirely sober person, took Benzedrine before a demanding Civil Service interview. Norman took it whenever: driving long distances, at parties, rarely when working.

"When I think of it," Lesley says, "one was so lucky to have escaped." She drove the twisting, crash-barrier-less coast road from Positano to Amalfi with Norman one afternoon in the 1950s. "I remember going round there with Norman, and he was under the influence of the Benzedrine to keep him awake because we'd always have wine with lunch and then he would feel sleepy. All I can say is, thank God there were few cars on the road. Can you imagine doing the Amalfi drive with Norman on Benzedrine after a boozy lunch?"[12]

In other ways also Norman found, on Lesley's side, an unusually accepting temperament. She lacked Ernestina's competitiveness, and unlike Hester was emotionally undemanding by circumstance – she stuck with her on-off journalist boyfriend for several years – and by nature. She was uncommitted and relaxed. An example: in early June, as Norman was organising to leave for the summer at Tossa, another element of his baroquely peopled life surfaced. A year after his visit to see Ito at Ridley College, Ernestina had put a stop to his improving education by taking him out of Ridley and sending him to spend the next school year at Port-au-Prince, Haiti, where Rafael Aparicio was

Guatemalan ambassador. His visit and the subsequent Haiti situation together had persuaded Norman he should take more responsibility for his son's welfare. After struggling for a year at Port-au-Prince Ito was in need of scholastic rescue, and Norman asked Ernestina to send him to England. Ernestina agreed, though she later felt it was a mistake that she had been swayed into because "as soon as Ito saw [your letter's] contents his face became suffused with such joy that we really did not have the heart to keep him".[13] Norman did not tell Lesley. Instead he timed Ito's arrival for just before his departure for Spain, collected Hester and the children from the overnight train with their "untidy parcels" – "We used to carry our toys or things to amuse ourselves in the local butcher's brown paper bag"[14] – put them and their half-brother in the Buick, and drove to Dover and the ferry. In October when they got back to London Ito got the bed in the dining room at Orchard Street, and Lesley first met him with his father and Arthur Baron at the Motor Show at Earls Court. At their meeting Norman resorted to a typically implausible subterfuge, Lesley recalls. "I was palmed off as Arthur's girlfriend at first because Norman didn't like to present me as the girlfriend . . . of course it was nonsense. Norman would dream up this nonsense and then it couldn't possibly be carried through."[15]

Coming to London, Ito's life was transformed. He owed a good deal of his happiness to his father's girlfriend's kindness. "I arrived in London with a slightly Canadian accent and was made to feel immediately at home by Lesley," Ito remembers. "[She] was an extremely warm and welcoming person, and they had a flat just opposite Selfridges. Both of them loved cheese, and there was a great thing of just nipping down and getting some cheese from Selfridges, Camembert, Brie or whatever. I sometimes ran the errand for them. To me this was a kind of magical time. [My father] put me in a little tutorial school in Holland Park where as you can imagine, with my school background I had to start from zero again. . . . My father was extremely easy to live with as well. Both of them were. And for me it was magical. That's the only word for it."[16]

PART FOUR

LOVING

A Reclamation in Two Decades

1950s, 1960s

In the matter of classification you might, for example, say that there were some countries that washed into the sea and others that did not. You could literally sit down on a boulder and hear the Spanish earth trickle and pour in sudden gushes down the hillsides. The movement of life down to the sea was effected in other and less obvious ways. For example in the spring countless millions of caterpillars moved down the hillsides, consuming the leaves as they went, always going in one direction, and they too died and returned to dust and were washed away with the torrents.

Tossa 1953 notebook

Story of Rosita: Her mother at the age of sixteen fell in love with an officer in Madrid. She followed him to Ibiza and when abandoned entered the brothel. At seventeen she gave birth to Rosita who was blind and paralytic with syphilis. The brothel keeper contacted Pepa Boix and offered her 300 pesetas a month to keep the child. She paid for two months then left Ibiza. For the sake of the child Pepa went to Santa Eulalia and her father left trawling and bought a small boat-house. The child is more loved by all the family than their own children. She has been taken to Barcelona by Pepa, and Pepa's father takes her on his shoulders to the cinema once a week.

Ibiza 1957 notebook

Each ruin is claimed by a convolvulus with deep blue flowers which look like a painted decoration that has escaped from the red stone surfaces. In the heat of the afternoon their flowers close and wither and they are revived by the night's dews.

The sounds are those of waterwheels turned by blindfolded donkeys – an old fashioned slow ticking clock, the twittering of finches in the pines. Sometimes the donkey is beaten into a trot and then the ticking speeds up.

At 7 pm the village water cart comes through the street. It is a 1000 litre wine barrel with a bunch of fresh vegetation stuffed into the bung hole.

Santa Eulalia notebook

20

SPANISH EARTH

"Where an illusion dies,
there always a hope is born"
Spanish proverb

WHETHER as a novelist or a writer of non-fiction, Norman was over-whelmed by the siren of Spain during the 1950s. It even overwhelmed his dilemma. A part of him wanted to be there when he was not there. "On his return to London from Spain," Ito says, "he would have what can only be called depressive episodes, which he would fix with, for example, obsessive cinema-going."[1] The far peregrinations of the decade – Vietnam and Laos, Burma and India, Mexico, Guatemala, Algeria, equatorial Africa, Cuba – pale beside the peculiar radiance of Tossa and later Ibiza where he stretched the summer from June to October each year. Despite the Franco tyranny, "In this relatively incorruptible country, where merely by leaving the main road you could, and still can, plunge immediately into Europe's prehistoric past, I spent – divided over a number of visits – a total of about three years, and I still go there to get away *from the insipidity of modern times whenever I can*", he wrote in 1959 (my italics).[2] Spain was his emblem, his supreme objective correlative for happiness, his sublime. Even when he wasn't there, the knowledge that Spain *was*, that it existed, impacted on his writing. Its hard, unshadowed, emphatic surfaces drove him deeper into the writer's precious dialogue between landscape and interior life (the two novels he wrote there are undoubtedly two of his most involved and achieved), while "modern times", that included his own self-pleasing, Porsche-driving, self-made times in London, were by comparison a curtain of tawdry givens, so much cheap lace drawn across sensations that mattered, whose aliveness was unmediated. In Spain you might, doubting, say everything was amplified, overstated, every point romantically stretched; or you might concede that in Spain life's connections, between fishermen and land and sea, between friends and enemies, poverty and virtue, between individuals and the earth they stood on and the air they breathed, and their water and wine and living and dying, are quintessentially direct.

The truth is that even the amplifications are natural, to a willing eye. "The sun in Tossa was so intense in midsummer," Norman noted, "that it seemed to exaggerate everything about the place. Splashed over the highlights of people's faces, it made them animated caricatures of what they really were, their smiles and scowls became immense grimaces of joy and discontent."[3] And in Tossa the sense of belonging, the intimation of humanity, the pre-modern relationship with the world he was always looking for, were all rolled up in the fishermen he lived with every day. They communicated their sense of adventure; they vouchsafed by their every small action and enthusiasm – listening for a tunny shoal, lightly wounding one dolphin to make a pod leave the grounds, recounting their day in Castilian blank verse at its end – a sense of a life lived opportunely and well; and so an answer that he was continually seeking. "Can it be that the satisfactory life needs hazards and uncertainties such as those of the fisherman? – and that the worst thing about industrialisation is that it tames work and removes the spice of risk, windfall and disappointment?"[4]

A reader of his much later book about Tossa, *Voices of the Old Sea*, wrote to him in 1996 to identify with his view of Spain. In the late 1940s the writer had saved some money by teaching English in Madrid and used it to travel the country by train.

At that time even the poorest Spaniard seemed to regard himself as an ambassador for his country and I was forever being bought drinks, or even meals, by Quixotic, ragged individuals. The haphazard nature of the train journeys of those days still lives on in my mind – the boys clinging to the outside of the moving carriages selling *gaseosa* and, in Andalucia, the itinerant farm workers with naked children, and often without tickets, who were obliged to throw themselves on the mercy of the ticket collectors.

My own trip ended up in Ibiza, long before there was a tourist in sight. There my landlord was an aristocrat who owned many run-down *tierras* on the island, who spent most of his days clad in a dressing gown in a vast, dark-

ened room, emerging only in the evening to tend his flowers. Rumour had it
that the Republicans had come to shoot him at the start of the Civil War, but
his mother had persuaded them that he was so sickly that he would soon die,
anyway, and they went away.[5]

In summer 1953 Norman was not sure whether Spain would make
a novelist of him or a non-fiction writer. In the long run it did both;
but uncertainty rises from the pages of his Tossa notebooks. In the
beginning he intended to write a non-fiction account ("End the first
chapter with tourist's comfortable declaration just after he arrives: 'I
get the impression that nothing ever happens here'").[6] Later, the notebooks are full of notes headed "Novel", but their subject and style
belie it. Little sense of plot, or characters, emerges from them. It is
more as if he is walking through the haunting glitter and the confusion of boats, figures and nets in a state of hypnotised fixation, picking
up hot pebbles of fascination wherever he goes, without asking what
they might be for. He does not need to. He is in a state of riches, like
a small child: what these baubles and stimuli will turn into, he will
find out. He has the world, and time.

On 26 July he wrote from the Casa Palomé at Tossa to Jonathan
Cape that "The present book is going on well. I have so far resisted
the provocations of an ardent and constant sun".[7] We can assume this
to be the usual temporising of writer to publisher. Norman had published
a book every year since 1949: now he wouldn't (after *A Single Pilgrim*
in November) publish another until 1955.

The first hint of a plot comes in his second Tossa notebook, with
mention of "the falangista whose fish no one would buy". This
became the key to the novel he eventually did write about the fisherman Sebastian Costa, *The Day of the Fox*, but to begin with he
was entirely taken up by background: landscape, attitudes, language,
nuances (and recipes). The liberality of the villages, for example, varied.
"Lloret southwards is avaricious, Tossa northwards generous. Only
2 or 3 from Tossa have ever migrated – and then for marriage – to
Lloret, but many to San Feliu. At Tossa the people don't have to buy
fish when good catches come in. Everyone goes to the boat where
there is a distribution."

He was scooping up everything he could, alerted to its coming disappearance by his fine nose for change and two recent crises in the villagers'
lives. The sardine shoals had not come, having been late the previous

year. "On 19th Sept", he had written in 1952, "the boats go out for sardines, but the light of the quarter moon is too strong." Six days later, on "25th Sept, first boat-loads of sardines and anchovies were caught. A boat of 8 men caught as much as 2–300 duros worth [1000–1500 pesetas])", but the following year

The departure of the sardines [has] thoroughly upset the balance of nature. The numerous cats for instance, who fed exclusively on fish and who, until this crisis, had led passive, tranquil, beachcombing lives, now plunged into the struggle for existence. Becoming lean, muscular and ferocious they soon killed off all the pigeons which had previously only been obliged to keep away from the cliffs where the peregrines lay in wait for them in order to keep alive. The falcons, driven by their hunger, were also obliged to change their habits and took to dashing themselves against the wire netting (committing suicide) of chicken pens. People began to eat acorns on which the pigs had previously lived.[8]

The other crisis, deepening the first by affecting the wider economy, was the sudden death in the hinterland of the cork-oak forest that produced cork for the manufacture of champagne corks.

This year a pest has stripped the leaves from all the cork oaks, so that the landscape was silvery and transparent, the trunks of the oaks writhing and gesticulating among the spiny fragrant shrubs. You could see the hoopoes dipping and fluttering through them right across the valley and there was no foliage to muffle the harsh laughter of woodpeckers and the snapping of dogs in distant farmyards and the bleating horns of the old taxis. . . . The totally leafless cork oaks have given the landscape a fragile delicacy. They go in smoking swathes of brown and lavender across the hills.[9]

Foreigners from the north were coming to holiday on the coast in bigger numbers, alleviating the poverty caused by these crises, but Norman could only feel that the village's adaptation to tourism constituted a further disaster. Tossa would not turn into the concrete slum of tourist-silos that Lloret to the south had become by the 1970s when I, for a university vacation, worked there as a guide; but its shift to the slick rewards of supplying boat-rides for foreigners dressed in their "strange uniforms of pleasure" and gigolo services for sex-deprived northern females undermined the fishermen's collectivity and the village's cohesion.

Norman scrambled to record what he felt would disappear, and what he might not voluntarily see again: the fishermen's continual hunt for fish, the daily, nightly, weekly changes in the sea, "the thumping pulse of the fishing-boats at the end of the glazed lanes of water in the heat-mist, lemon boats with a green stripe painted round their middles and their bottoms painted purple"; the men's refusal to wear leather or go to church, and the convention of leaving the poor a few moments to snatch handfuls of sand-eels from boxes in the market after they were sold; the twenty couples in the village unable to marry because the only houses available were let to tourists who paid more for three months than a Spanish couple could in a year; "the backwash of the sun into the pale shadows", the pressure of hunger that turned fishermen into smugglers and male prostitutes, and the weird behaviour of the foreigners, immersed but seeing nothing. "There were a hundred painters perpetually stationed at all the accepted viewpoints. All the pictures were identical, insipid – the agony had escaped them. It was just like the tourists who said, 'Nothing ever happens here.'"[10]

He pumped his fishermen friends – Sebastian, Narciso, Francisco, Jaime – for information, fished with them the length of the coast from Lloret to Salions and the rocks past Sa Futadera, at the entrance to Giverola and the far end of Las Encinas up to San Feliu. He took Ito spearfishing in the main bay, and his son caught a 3-kilo *mero* – a grouper – to the shock of the villagers who hadn't seen such a fish close in for five or six years. The fishermen accepted Norman because he spoke Spanish, he made it clear in his deferential way that he wanted to learn, and he tutored them in mental arithmetic. He wrote later of his first invitation to join the crew of a fishing boat, when his neighbour Francisco said to him with a sweeping gesture of mastery over a stiffening swell, "Let us confront the sea together," that he "could think of no honour and no prospect that had ever delighted me more".

One of the most regular figures in his notebook was not a fisherman. A local aristocrat, Don Federico, became, under the same name in *The Day of the Fox* and as Don Alberto in *Voices of the Old Sea*, his enduring representative of Spanish idiosyncrasy and Romanticism in a rotten, factual world: an emaciated, free-thinking Cervantean reactionary who possessed – how it must have endeared him to Norman! – a banned copy of Montaigne and like a revised Quixote "a two-stroke motorcycle on which he sits like a black praying mantis with a huge celluloid visor attached to a peaked cap, which comes halfway down his neck". Don Federico's Spain was becoming, he said, as class-ridden and greedy as it had been in the sixteenth century. He told Norman that, "Here there are some of us who resent the present and distrust the future. I am one." He grew bushes around his garden to cut out "the steady vulgarisation of the view", leaving only the flat village roofs where he could train his binoculars on the maids hanging out the washing, and the beach with its "crouching crone-like figures at work repairing the nets". His day began with

a *merienda* at 10.30 at an elaborately set table in his garden. Sometimes he stands up and looks over his wall at the incredibly dressed foreigners walking up the path below. His *merienda* is light with a little red wine. His problem is to stimulate a palate ravaged with spices. Everything is a little *fade*. Everything except the view, which never failed to attract.[11]

In Don Federico Norman had stumbled upon a character of Lampedusa-like richness and somnolence. Except that Don Federico possessed no earthly existence.

Do not say that I am robbing you of your illusions. Even if the fictional "Don F" of Norman's notebooks became, as the valedictory grandee Don Alberto, one of the most memorable figures of all Norman's non-fiction, his lack of factuality hardly diminishes his impact. The writer pits his private, composed world against reality because he believes *he* is right. As long as *we* believe that an elderly Spanish nobleman can say, "Here there are some of us who resent the present and distrust the future," we can agree that he is right. Don Alberto, *c'est nous.*

"Don F" was intended at first as part of a mixed factual/fictional account of a Catalan fishing village during and after the Civil War, wrestling with political repression and modernity. A film crew's arrival was part of the story (Ava Gardner had filmed *Pandora and the Flying Dutchman* there in 1950, swimming naked in Tossa's main bay in front of a village instructed not to watch). But the project's scope was too baggy, compacting instead into the novel of the *falangista* excluded from the fishermen's community – a familiar Lewis theme.

How, incidentally, do we know that "Don F" is not a man with a birth certificate? Because Norman's notes are all about placing him, not reporting him. He did not, for instance, tell Norman that, "Here there are some of us who resent the present and distrust the future. I am one". Norman noted instead, "Don F. says at one stage, 'Here there

are some of us [etc etc]'". Sometimes his two-stroke motorcycle with
sit-up-and-beg handlebars is a Vespa scooter. The writer delineates; puts
on flesh and gestures, and ends up describing a character as real as
himself.

Summer 1953 was long, the longest he had spent in Spain, as he worked
out what to do with his knowledge of Tossa, and about his need for
peace and quiet. As developers and their attendant scene-shifters began
moving in everywhere along the coast, his village's dismantling by
tourism threatened to leave him without a refuge to work: without a
sea to cast his imagination on. He took advice from a local schoolmaster and others, and the following year, in June 1954, the Buick
passed the turning for Tossa on the Barcelona road without stopping.
It halted overnight at the city 80 kilometres further south. Next day it
was hoisted by crane into the hold of the *Ciudad de Ceuta* ferry – the
only car on board – which arrived the following morning shortly after
dawn, trailing its "thin smoking wake in the crisp sparkle of the sea"
and easing into the harbour at Ibiza town.

His first impression of Ibiza was of a pellucid tranquillity, glassy
water across a bay as wide as a gulf, a steep fortified outline and a
heaven of blue air. Karen says, "I still remember when you'd come
round the end of the island and then you swung round and in and
then this magnificent gleaming city rose ahead above you, absolutely
fabulous."[12] Flat, whitewashed façades hung before the docks like a
painted cloth along calle Garijo, which shook itself awake as the
steamer came alongside. In the 1930s Albert Camus had remarked on
the harbour's social centrality. "In Ibiza I sat every day in the cafés
that dot the harbour. Towards five in the evening, the young people
would stroll back and forth along the full length of the mole; this is
where marriages and the whole of life are arranged. One cannot help
thinking there is a certain grandeur in beginning one's life this way,
with the whole world looking on."[13]

At nine in the morning the Lewises disembarked and ate *tapas* while
they waited for the Buick to be unloaded, watching the livestock and
the fighting bulls come off first. Norman asked for "a cognac", Ito
remembers, "and then they gave you a little plate of olives, and they

gave you a plate of almonds and a plate of something else and charged
you less than a peseta for it".[14]

That year Norman rented a house in the old town below the cathedral, at 11 calle de Sant Ciriac, with cool, shuttered rooms, a courtyard
with a well, and a citrus tree. The Buick was parked the next level down,
the street too narrow for it to pass any higher. A few metres further up
were the cathedral and the episcopal palace from where, as the real
power on the island, the bishop waged war on the influence of foreigners.
The town was beginning to face the prospect of change with the arrival
of northern Europeans and Americans attracted by the island's cheapness, antiquity and infallible summer. In the country the bishop's flock
remained loyal. In 1954 in Santa Eulalia del Rio, a village up the eastern
shore, an American woman was stoned by the villagers for wearing
trousers. Living so close to the doctrinal epicentre roused Norman's irre-
ligious instincts. As white-gowned processions passed under their window,
his daughter Karen remembers, "He'd say, 'Tell them, "Up your pipe."'
So I'd lean out, this cherubic little girl, as instructed, and translate literally into Spanish and say '*Arriba con tu cigarillo!*' which meant 'Up with
your cigarette!', losing all its evil connotations."[15]

He had sought a place where he could bear to spend the summers.
He had found it: from his window that year he could see a dock full
of lateen-sailed fishing boats, and salt being loaded for Brazil, or charcoal for the mainland, on chipped schooners the colour of mustard;
across the bay apricots dried on the flats, tended by girls in soft straw
hats, and inland flocks of goats blocked the roads on their way back
from being blessed by the priest. Girls and women throughout the
island wore their hair in a single thick plait, tied with a bow whose
colour indicated its owner's status: pink for a girl without a particular
suitor, red for one affianced, pale yellow for a wife, black for mourning.
One called Lupita, twentyish and responding to Norman's attention,
let herself be photographed. Mountainous, forested, self-sufficient, its
almond and olive groves cultivated to a cycle of biblical memory and
flinty pride, as private as an island could be (he would not get as close
to Ibiza's fishermen as he had to Tossa's), Ibiza "stupefied" Norman,
Ito says. "He used to say to me, 'I am a perpetually mildly sad person',
but in Ibiza he was euphoric.'

In Ibiza there was the kind of junction of all my father's fondest dreams,
conscious, subconscious and unconscious desires and drives, where everything

came right. It was in the middle of the Mediterranean, it was steeped in antiquity. You went to the main town, Ibiza town, everything is at a different angle,
no straight lines. The streets are narrow, they wind. The place is a trip. And
the people are courteous beyond imagination. They're courteous with an old-
age, antique courteousness that you don't see anywhere else in the world. I
was so privileged to have made the discovery of Ibiza with my father. It was
an incredible piece of luck, because this was an extraordinary thing, to come
on this just at that particular time.

My father said to me that this went above and beyond his Army career.
He said, "I never knew I could be so happy." He was in a state of continuous
euphoria.[16]

That summer Norman worked on in Ibiza town, continuing the novel
about the *falangista* he had begun in Tossa the year before; fished with
Ito and filled negative wallets with underwater photographs; and looked
for a house outside the town for the following year. After excursions
into the country that convinced him he was closer to Africa than Spain
– "All the shapes in this landscape were different; even the air itself
carried a dry, spiced scent" – he came back to the coast and, with the
help of an Ibizan painter he had been introduced to, Antonio Ribas,
found a half-ruined seaside mansion a couple of kilometres north of
Santa Eulalia del Rio. The journey alone excited him. Fifty years later
you can still see why. I drove across the island with Ito: the earth is
purple-red, and every older house has a Carthaginian Cubist line and
solidity. "My father was in a state of complete delirious shock by the
time we got to Santa Eulalia," Ito recalls. "He wasn't getting his breath
back, his eyes were popping out of his head, and he was lost for words."

The Casa Ses Estaques was a flat-roofed cube of two storeys at the
sea's edge, private and protected behind a lush perimeter of Aleppo
pines. Norman confessed a few years later that it

was the house I had always been vainly looking for, a stark and splendidly
isolated villa, on the verge of ruin, with an encroaching sea among the rocks
under its windows. I paid instantly, and without question, the extortionate
price of 3000 pesetas (about £23) demanded for a season's tenancy. . . .

The Casa Ses Estaques (House of the Mooring-posts) happened also to be
the port of Santa Eulalia – or at least, its garden was. Its original owner had
been allowed to build in this superb position among the pines on a headland
commanding all the breezes, only by providing in the rear of the premises, as
a quid pro quo, several small well-built shacks in which the fishermen stored

their tackle. . . . When the windows were first opened – they opened inwards – a number of nestlings which had been hatched in the space between the glass and the exterior shutters flew in and perched on the pictures.[17]

Though the house lacked basic amenities (the toilet was an installation overhanging the rocks, every bed was broken, the only lighting was from oil lamps), and was not quite the harbourmaster's mansion he made it out to be – Ses Estaques inlet was a shallow, glassy curl north of the harbour – his description happily lingered in the notation of fairytales. The villa was remote and full of the most elaborate furniture; its previous tenant had been a fading Turkish princess whose "beautiful seventeen-year-old daughter" had fallen in love with a young fisherman. "The civil guard were called up to intervene, but in Spain a romance is never abandoned as hopeless on the mere grounds of an extreme disparity in the social position of the parties involved, and eventually, notwithstanding the mother's wrath, the marriage took place. The couple are now in the process of living happily ever after – their first child has already arrived – on a fisherman's average income of 25 pesetas (or about 4s.) a day."[18] The house also offered him the advantage of being able to study the fishermen who came and went past his door, "a sober and softly-spoken breed – quite unlike the boisterous hearties of the Catalan coast".

Norman spent three seasons – 1955, 1956 and 1957 – with Hester, Ito, Karen and Gareth at the House of the Mooring-posts. Local gossip spread his name: each June word passed around that the Buick, which the Ibizans called "Don Coche de Ses Estaques", was back on the island, and Eulalians remember his buying quantities of wine in carafes and olives and tomatoes from them but shunning the town's expatriate community, preferring its fishermen. These were a small, closed group, and his contacts were not easy. Ibizans, heirs from the time of the Phoenicians to waves of invasion and pillaging, were suspicious of foreignness. Fishing was on a smaller scale than on the Costa Brava, carried out mostly by men fishing alone. The cycle of windfalls and dearths, the communal tunny- and sardine-fishing Norman had known at Tossa, were far less evident; in this cradle of reticence life carried on, mostly, at a more even pace until in the late 1950s modern fleets from Barcelona and Valencia began to invade the Ibicencan fishing grounds. In reality, the speculators and promoters of the tourist industry were not alone responsible for destroying the island's labour market and traditional way of life (as they did for most of coastal Spain); also answerable were the bosses of the radar- and sonar-equipped trawler operations.

Two blemishes existed on the perfection of the Casa Ses Estaques. The journeys to Spain had become more tense as the children got older. Karen was philosophical. "He used to get Benzedrine, speed, you know, to keep him going. And if he started to slow down we'd say, 'Take a benny, Dad, take a benny', and he'd take a benny and on we'd go." But she remembers him as a diabolical driver "because he never used his rear-view mirror and asked us always to look behind for him". Driving on the right, he would ask Hester in the front (who didn't drive) to look out when he wanted to overtake. "He would pull out and because she had no judgment of car speed or distance she would say, 'Oh it's all right now, Norman.' Out he'd pull and [seeing] something bearing down on us, say, 'Christ, do you want to get us killed?'" Hauling a speedboat complicated the journey, and their father's regular outbursts of botanical enthusiasm made the children more impatient. "It used to be a nightmare, because obviously going up the Pyrenees there's lots of flora and it was really interesting for him. All we wanted was to get over the bloody Pyrenees, get into Spain."[19] At Barcelona the pressure eased: a highlight was staying at the Hotel Oriente in calle Escudieres overlooking the red-light area, where Norman played up the suspense.

I remember the pleading with Dad. "Please can we have a room with a window and please can we not have an interior room?" which was excruciatingly hot. So there'd be all this joke of pleading with him, "Please", and he'd come in and we'd say, "Did you get a room, Dad?" "Yes", and he'd look sorry and I'd say, "What kind of room did you get?" "Sorry, it's a terrible room." "Ohh!" Disappointment, shock, horror. "No, no, no, it's one with a window." Oh, joy, joy. And the window would overlook the hairdresser where the prostitutes would go to get their hair done to ply their trade that evening. And if the Sixth Fleet was in, which it sometimes was, you'd see them negotiating, being picked up, you'd hear the banging in the rooms because they used the hotel as a knocking shop. It was wonderful for somebody to come from the north-east of Scotland to this [life] on the street. Everybody would go to bed and I'd stay at the window until three and four in the morning, watching it all happening.[20]

The ferry was a less dear memory. The Spanish, poor sailors, would begin throwing up before it left port, and the segregation of the sexes in the *generales* – the big general sleeping areas – upset Gareth, still dependent on his mother. Ito remembers too that Gareth was demanding about eating on the journeys south, and that in restaurants his father would insist that Hester and Gareth eat at a separate table "because my father could only take Gareth's crying and complaining for about two minutes. He had a tendency to be slightly harsh where Gareth was concerned."[21] Gareth remembers the unpleasantness about food as being the result of his father's cowardice. "We'd stay in hotels where the food was good, but when it came to eating the more exotic things, I or Karen would be charged with eating them, just to make sure they were not. . . . He wouldn't do that himself, he'd watch you do it and try a piece of yours." But he admits that a line grew between him and his sister that mirrored the line between his parents. Hester had no special affection for her daughter, whereas "I was loved to death by my mother, spoilt to death, lazy. I had no discipline because I was indulged and of course Dad was never there."[22] Ito remembers that "Karen was sunny, charming, easy, enthusiastic. Hester was perfectly maternal but treated her with condescension, calling her 'wee wifie'."[23]

The difficulty of maintaining family appearances was harder to live with. The massive unadmitted rent in Norman's and Hester's emotional unity was medicated with alcohol when they were together, though Ito's inclusion in the family group helped. "Hester treated me as something of an honoured guest," he says. "There were long periods of silence between [the two of] them. At those times Hester could speak to me and my father could speak to me."[24] During the days at Ses Estaques Norman was determinedly, as at Tossa, in pursuit of his own interests of writing and fishing. (The first year, he also filmed a ten-minute home movie of scenes from across the island, remarkable for its underwater photography and for the fact that, though Karen, Gareth and Ito are present, all that is visible of Hester – if it is her – is feet and ankles as she sits on the rocks.) He developed friendships with the painter Ribas and Juan Ripoll, an Ibizan farmer in his thirties who had lost his farm and wife through gambling and lived in a shack on the shore. Past sunset, when Karen and Gareth were drifting to sleep and Ito left them alone, Norman and Hester sat under the twisted pines, a hurricane lamp hissing near them, drinking wine, then Anis del Mono, and began by laughing but regularly ended by arguing. Norman eased the strain with his rhythm of returning to London to look after R G Lewis (and see Lesley, whom Hester didn't know about).

Excluded from fishing with the Ses Estaques men by their shy prohibitions (it was certain ill fortune for a foreigner to touch their nets), Norman went out with a combination of Ribas, Ripoll, Ito and later Gareth, often as the Ses Estaques men came home to the sound of "conch shells in the morning. Even the cats run for the door at the sweet, melancholy hunting horn of the sea."[25] Ito remembers fishing the blue sea, shredded white by the limestone cliffs, all along the coast as far as Portinatx. (At Portinatx he speared a huge *mero*, and when the virgin bay fell to developers in the 1960s the underwater photograph Norman took of him bringing up the catch hung in one of its hotels for two decades.) At the time his father was passionate about spearfishing, and

we used to – at his age – spend five or six hours a day diving. He was always enthusiastic, he was exhilarating company. So there would be him and me in the middle of the sea somewhere, diving down to 50, 60, 70, 80 feet – his ear would stop him going down [more than 50 feet]. But he was always there . . . he used to say, "Listen, don't go into any caves because I can't get you out, I can't get down that deep." And I'd go into a cave and then I'd come up again and he'd say, "I thought you'd drowned." By this time we were fit people, who could hold our breath for three and a half, four minutes.

There weren't *any* people diving in those days. So the whole territory was virgin. We used to go out and catch these boatloads of fish, really boatloads which we then had to eat and give away. We were having fish five times a day. Remember he wasn't a young man any more. We were swimming for hours on end every day. It was an amazing effort on his part.[26]

With the two Ibizans he used the excursions, as he had at Tossa, to quench his curiosity for history and custom. Afterwards "There would be very little in a landscape that he would not be able to describe or that he would not be able to give, in terms of structure, some historical fact on".[27] The existence of Carthaginian tombs in the woods, and the tall, grey, fiendishly smiling ghosts they sheltered, delighted him; the discovery of a cave-shrine to the Phoenician goddess Tanit near Cala San Vicente, provoked an instant pilgrimage. An ardent connoisseur of nuances of fact and surface, he was not really a contemplator of human depth, and so – a reason why he wrote little about England – poor at sociological analysis. In Ibiza he hung on the words of Ribas, whose insight into the delicate social mechanisms of the island was copious. "He was always saying, 'Antonio, do you mind if I just write this down?'"[28] It was Ribas who offered him the few careful notations about Franco that went into his notebook. "Ribas' analogy of Fr[ancoists] and a fire brigade. They came and put the fire out but after it was out they refused to leave. They make what use of the house they like, sleep in your bed with your wife. You wait outside and knock at the door and ask humbly if they'll be leaving one day. (By the way, in this case it was the fire brigade who started the fire.)"[29]

While he worked and fished, Hester fitted her life around her children. Pepa Boix, a widow, cooked for the family. "She was a woman of about fifty-five, very angelic, and she worked with a kind of fanaticism for me."[30] She offered Hester company, although Hester didn't speak Spanish and it was Norman, not Hester, who was looking over Pepa's shoulder to see what she was cooking and writing the recipes down. Hester endured the isolation out of a mixture of passivity and readiness to sacrifice herself to the pleasure of her children. "She was not a woman that was strong on making any efforts," Karen remembers. "Her favourite phrase as she got older was 'I cannae be bothered'. I used to say, 'Well, what are you still doing here, Mum, why don't you get a divorce?' 'Oh, you don't understand, you don't understand.' She couldn't tell me."[31]

But it is easy to reduce Hester to invisibility. In "Assassination in Ibiza", in his collection *The Changing Sky*, Norman describes how he cut free an Ibicencan hound whose owner, a local farmer, was keeping it hungry. But "it was Mum that cut it free, and we fed it so it stayed with us. For all [her faults] she was a generous woman, I don't think Dad was as generous as Mum was, and she had an immense capacity for kindness which Dad could sustain for just a certain length of time, and then it would go."[32]

In August 1957, to mark the last summer of Ses Estaques, Norman showed what generosity he was capable of by throwing a party for Pepa and her family. The price of land was rising, and the house had been sold to be demolished that autumn and replaced by a hotel (now the Hotel Catalonia Ses Estaques). On 15 August, the feast of the Assumption of the Virgin, a procession of guests and fiesta seekers passed through the garden by the sea. Watching Pepa's children, Norman felt that in one generation "the young people had moved forward a thousand years or so, even though they were still not quite modern Europeans". After collecting limpets for their midday paella, the boys disappeared to watch a football match while the girls read Spanish

versions of Mills & Boon novelettes. Seeing some French women illegally sunbathing in bikinis, they shed their dresses and sat defiantly in
their petticoats. Later one of the fishermen took his wife out in his
boat, normally "definitely taboo"; but the man's wife knew that he
had been taking out parties from the nearby hotel and demanded the
same treatment. Another fisherman, according to Norman, who like
others had been approached by an unattached stranger, asked him if
it was a fact that foreign women usually suffered from syphilis?

The "golden day" was a turning point.

Just outside the fine ruin of the archway entrance to what was left of the
garden, a family of peasants were gathered round their cart. They lived in a
fortified farmhouse in the mountains in the centre of the island, which sheltered several families and was in reality a hamlet in its own right. At this time
they were relaxing over a late meal of goat's flesh and beans. One of the men
had invoked the holiday spirit by blackening his face and dressing up like a
woman, and the other, sitting apart, was playing a wistful improvisation on
his flute. The sister had left them. She had been studying the French women,
and the Ibizan girls, and she had pinned back her skirt from the waist so that
it fell behind in a series of dressy folds, to show an orange silk petticoat, and
was gleefully dabbling with her toes in the edge of the tide.

The men spoke Castilian, and one of them told me that it had taken them
half the morning to get down to Santa Eulalia, which, because of the difficulty of the journey, they only visited once a year – on this day. But next year,
he said, things would be a lot better. The roads were going to be made up,
and the piles of flints were already there, awaiting the steamroller. With a
good surface on the roads they could cover the distance in half the time, which
meant they would be able to come more often. They all agreed with me that
Santa Eulalia was a very wonderful place.[33]

The following year, with the house Norman "had always vainly
looked for" gone, he found a new place to stay with Hester and the
children a couple of kilometres further up the shore. Summers continued
at the Casa Sansón at La Caleta, a collection of adobe huts next to a
silver beach of shale and sand. Even though both parents continued to
put a united face on their circumstances for the children's sake, deception, both of the children and each other, and self-deception increasingly
directed their actions. The situation was stable but untenable; yet the
crisis did not come for several years. Until it did, Hester's and Norman's
days and nights were spent separately, and Anis del Mono increasingly

turned their evenings into a zone of hazardous catharsis. The children anxiously accepted. Karen, who was showing ability as a linguist, stepped in when the drinking scared her.

The only thing they did together and really seemed to enjoy was [to] get blind drunk at night on Anis del Mono, the pair of them, and I used to be so disturbed by their obvious change in behaviour I used to take the bottle off them and hide it. They [would be] outside under a tree, hitting the bottle and talking and laughing inappropriately and uproariously at nothing, whereas up to that time it would be the show going on and all that malarkey. [Later] he used to love to say how I came out of the mud hut and told them to "yield the bottle". I was very young at the time but I could see that that was a dangerous situation, because it could have burst the bubble. So "yield the bottle". He liked it if you used flowery language in a desperate situation.[34]

Lesley was a revolution in his life, and I don't think there was ever anybody else whom he felt close to as he felt close to her.

London became a place where artists or writers or would-be writers wanted to live shortly after the war. All sorts of people began to live in places that they didn't know existed, good places as it turned out, and I guess Norman would agree that that was what he did. He had a very useful shop, perhaps the best shop in London if you wanted to buy photographic equipment. He was an extraordinarily interesting person and very very unEnglish in the sense that he really had been brought up in unorthodox ways. He had his line in a very clear way and he stuck to it. It was not an obvious one.

Lesley took him a little bit by storm, and he wasn't accustomed to being taken by storm. I remember thinking to myself, Good, that's very good, Norman needs someone who's going to be like that.

Basil Davidson

Offhand, I could not think of a single Latin American dictator whose fate it had been to die quietly in bed in the land in which he had been born. They came to power to make, or to keep, their country safe for foreign investments, and in the course of doing this they usually managed to turn it into something like a private farm.

The Volcanoes Above Us

"Please close the window," General Velez said. "The noise oppresses me. What do their banners say?"

I read: "Fatherland or Death. We will fight to the last drop of blood against foreign aggressors."

"And they will," the general said. "And they will if necessary. Alas, haven't I seen it all before."

"Two Generals"

SEVERAL REVOLUTIONS

"In the hotel of decisions the guests sleep well"
Persian proverb

SINCE their first meeting in October 1952, and against his usual rack-
eting background of writing, business and repeated absence, Norman
had pursued Lesley Burley, the twentysomething BOAC employee. His
appointment diaries for the mid-1950s contain repeated "LM"s
(Maureen is Lesley's first name) and "LB"s. The relationship had developed but still not to the point he wanted. A year after their first meeting
Lesley was beginning to stay at Orchard Street and, after meeting Ito
and though only seven years older than he was, willingly became a
substitute mother to Norman's son. She knew about Hester, Karen and
Gareth; they did not meet; she remembers going once to Ibiza in the
1950s "with Norman dodging into every doorway, afraid he might be
seen by people who knew him and Hester".[1]

Despite her involvements, she stayed very cool. There was something about her of Kathleen Moore, the object of Monroe Stahr's
woken-up tenderness in *The Last Tycoon*: thirsty for liveable life, wary,
"irresolute herself . . . but there was a fierce self-respect that would
only let her go so far". Norman's relationship with her became a
compound of these complications, of his impermanence and her irres-
olution. His own attitude to love was detached to the point of mockery.
I remember his poker-faced reply when I once asked him what he felt
about it. "I see it as more or less a biological addiction."[2] He reserved
his most wary, self-defensive irony for it: by his manner and utterances,
it was at best a sort of sloppy mess that other people allowed themselves to get into, at worst an uncontrolled self-delusion and mythomania.

As early as *Spanish Adventure*, he referred with supercilious scorn to the "biological attraction" that preceded the rigid rhythm of Hispanic wooing. In *A Single Pilgrim*, the novel he was writing when he met Lesley, he describes John Crane during the time he was in love with his wife as living "in a concentrated kernel of ecstasy and despair, oblivious of the world around him".

Yet an irrefutable tremolo reverberated through his moves to turn friendship with Lesley into serious courtship. In London the dinners, more than the parties, continued at Orchard Street. He took her out often to good restaurants, Mon Plaisir, L'Étoile, Quo Vadis, the White Tower; she remembers going regularly to Gaston Berlemont's minute first-floor dining room.

There were two old waiters there, one was Italian and one was French, and the French one was an alcoholic and the Italian was a little guy. The food was very simple, nice. Once rabbit was on the menu and I said to the alcoholic, "What do you think of the rabbit?" And he looked and he said, "Ze rabbit is ze most syphilitic of all animals." So I thought, Well I won't have the rabbit. The Italian one used to swear at the customers in Italian, because everybody used to like to go up there and show off their French.[3]

They travelled together to Italy and Spain, to Morocco, the Canaries; journeys that became more relaxed, less intended to impress. In Italy they found themselves at a village in Calabria for the night where, at the only place to stay, "the old crone had her skirts looped over the brazier to keep warm, and it was very primitive, grey army blankets, hospital type beds, you know those old iron beds. Norman just said, 'In this situation, will we have tyres on the car in the morning?'"[4] They went to north Africa with Ito, on their way to test the Photo-Marine underwater camera in the Canaries. At Rabat they were introduced to an artist who offered them dope cakes. "It was the first and only time we tasted marijuana. Norman and Ito became more and more silent, while I became more and more talkative."[5] At Rabat airport, as Lesley struggled, post-dope cakes, with the weight of the diving leads hidden in her hand luggage, her difficulty in handling her bag aroused the suspicion of a customs officer, but she and Norman got away with paying excess baggage charges. At Tenerife Norman enquired about a good place to dive; a local doctor with a barrel chest rampant with hair took them to a beach where he pointed across the water to a far distant islet. It would be a long swim. The doctor, at a peak of fitness, was preparing to go, and Lesley remembers Norman saying, "I'm going to have to do it, aren't I?" A small boy suddenly came running breathlessly, saying, "Doctor, you must come, your mother's desperately ill." The doctor, excusing himself, rushed away. "Norman said to me, 'What a lucky man I always am.'" (After testing the camera housing Norman suggested Lesley accompany him to Cornwall for publicity pictures, where she could pose with basking sharks. He assured her basking sharks "eat nothing but plankton". She knew perfectly well how a basking shark's skin could wipe off a human epidermis if it basked too close, and declined.)

And despite the uncertainty between them, their circumstances fitted. Reluctant to concede it because it did not fit his idea that he should have Lesley to himself, it suited Norman that she didn't make heavy demands on him. She was not jealous the way Ernestina and Hester had been; there were no scenes, she recognised his commitments, and she never asked for pertinent details of his relationship and absences with Hester or any others. She was simply not ready and not sure, not wanting to commit to her journalist boyfriend any more than to Norman; and Norman may have sensed, before she did, that the round of attraction could only be resolved by an eventual emotional calibration of relative commitments and pleasure, when she was ready to make it.

He was more patient than he had been, and for at least two years after they met the young Australian surrendered only to the enchantments of her experiences; often, but far from exclusively, with Norman.

"We had long conversations. Although Norman was a very funny man and would say things that were so cleverly put together and they could be very funny, he wasn't a sort of jokey man, so I wouldn't have said we laughed a lot. But we used to have, particularly with a bottle of wine between us, long long discussions on all sorts of things."

But she was not constant.

"No. But you see my attitude was, he isn't either in that respect."[6]

A good thumbnail of Norman's temperament and velocity in the 1950s (with a single error) is recorded in a letter the *New Yorker* writer S J Perelman wrote in December 1953. When younger as blithe a traveller as he was a humorist, Perelman had written enthusiastically to Norman after reading *A Dragon Apparent*. They met in London, similarly gifted but not rivals, rapidly liked each other, and had dinner together three times that month.

He is forty-five [Perelman wrote to his wife Laura], a product of Cambridge (I think; the British are frequently reticent about admitting this sort of thing), Welsh by derivation ... feverish black eyes, hair, and mustache, pallid face. ... He was at one time a professional motorcycle racer. ... He has a weird kind of flat in a very commercial district of London, with some marvellous Burmese paintings. ... He drives a German car called a Porsche at a nervewracking rate around London and I thought my hour had come the last night I was there when he picked me up at the theater and we drove to Soho for supper. In short, he's a wack, extremely good company (and very funny, as his books suggest), and a man I know you'd take to.[7]

In another letter to a girlfriend, Leila Hadley, Perelman enlarged on the context of meeting Norman, name-dropping a "partial list" of who else he'd seen in London, "Alan Moorehead, Angus Wilson, Eric Ambler, [T S] Eliot, C Day Lewis, John Hayward, H B Ellis, Ronald Searle, Richard Burton (the actor), my friend Sir Leigh Aston of the V & A Museum, and several others. ... The best times I had, however, were with Norman Lewis."[8]

The "nervewracking rate" applied to the rest of Norman's life. Ito, installed at Orchard Street in winter 1953, felt the force of his energy.

I had the most extraordinary education. He took me round all the art galleries and gave me the complete lecture tour. I think there was an element of pretension to it, though he knew his stuff. I mean he liked Stravinsky because he thought you should like Stravinsky, but then he actually did get to like Stravinsky.[9]

Norman's experiments with food, fishing and hunting were included in Ito's education. At one occasion at Orchard Street, barbecuing on the roof in the rain in an Anderson & Sheppard suit under an umbrella, to the wonderment of the Selfridges seamstresses opposite, Norman had cooked his signature London dish, grilled prawns in chocolate sauce. Ito recalls his father asking Malcolm Dunbar with his usual solicitude, "Is there anything else you want, Malcolm?" and receiving Dunbar's drawl in reply, "Possibly a dry crust."[10] On another occasion Arthur Baron described the prawn dish as odd, to which Norman, nettled, boasted that if he thought that was odd, he, Norman, had eaten plenty of things that were odder and that it was possible to eat anything if you turned your mind to it. A few days later a shoebox arrived in the post. Inside it Norman found the corpse of a grey squirrel that Baron had shot in Surrey. The implication was clear, and after Lesley refused to have anything to do with preparing the squirrel Norman cajoled Ito to do it. The stink was so bad Ito put on his diving mask before he went into the kitchen.

[I] skinned it and gutted it. And the smell was unbelievable. It was very very smelly indeed and it was appallingly awful, dreadful. Maybe we had under-cooked it. We had to eat it in [Baron's] absence. My father in an honourable way said, "Yes, we ate it and it wasn't good." The understatement of the century.[11]

Ito remembers that "We used to do weird things in the flat." When father and son became heavily involved in spearfishing, Norman acquired a new speargun and brought it to Orchard Street.

My father was saying, "These are really powerful weapons", and he actually put the spear into the gun and somehow he pressed the trigger and this bloody thing was [propelled by] compressed air – as you know they travel in the water so fast you can hardly see them, but in the air it's just horrendous. This thing went straight through the sitting-room wall. If anybody had been there they would have been impaled.[12]

Ito accompanied his father to Banchory, where one of Norman's entertainments was to take his son poaching on the queen's estate (something he also later did with Karen and Gareth). Once

we had a .22 calibre rifle in the boot and we got a couple of partridges and two or three pheasants. [Then] you could be a paedophile, you could be a serial killer, you could be almost anything and get away with a reprimand, but if they got you for poaching they'd have your testicles and cut your throat. Here we were, two quite dark guys, and we had a couple of Scottish policemen with sweet accents come up and enquire politely what it was we found so interesting about a bare landscape, and I think my father said, "Well, you know, we're English tourists. Is this the way you look after your tourists? What would happen to the Scottish economy without any English tourists?" The more things he said, the more uptight these two policemen got, until

finally my father lost [his temper], and went very cold and very sort of sarcastic
and for a matter of a couple of minutes just ripped both of them to shreds
verbally, and they had to let us go.

All they had to do was to go back to the boot and we would have been
incarcerated.[13]

Norman was able to build a better bond with his son now in his
adolescence than he would have done when Ito was a child. He could
be a father, without the deep impatience that accompanied his restlessness coming between them. He saw that Ito was ready to learn and
possessed his own energy; he was unusually sensitive, for him, to the
fact that Ito, as an adolescent in a situation of considerable strangeness, was unstable.

I was extremely moody and introspective. He did say, "Look Ito, you're ideal
in all sorts of ways, you're terrific, but can I make a point?" I said, "Yes
please." "Just a suggestion," and it took about five minutes before he got to
it, skirting around. "You're a little bit inclined to be morose." I thought to
myself, Jesus Christ, if he says so, it's true. But this was the only time . . . and
what he was trying to do was to give me a bit of advice, because his idea in
life was you always have to be cheerful, relatively cheerful . . . so he had a
very positive attitude towards life.[14]

The tables were also decisively turned on his criticism of his father's
fashion sense. Lesley remembers that there was always Latin American
music being played at the flat and that Ito, at seventeen, with an adolescent's idea of cosmopolitanism was often to be found dancing around
the sitting room in beret, and shorts.

As part of his cultural education, father and son went weekly to the
Curzon cinema together to introduce Ito to French film. Somewhere
among the works of Carné, Renoir and Clouzot they saw a Japanese
film that had impressed Norman on its release in 1952. Akira Kurosawa's
Rashomon, the story of the samurai Kanazawa-no-Takehiro's murder
and the rape of his wife Masago, told by four different witnesses and
then retold during a storm by a priest and a woodcutter to a cynical
countryman, delighted him. It also seemed to synthesise a part of his
predicament as a writer, struggling between the jealous god of truth
and the impossibility of objectivity. He saw it several times. "*Rashomon*
was the one film he always kept referring back to." It articulated his
instinct that reality was subjective, an act of composition, of rendition

and of creation, and that the only ascertainable truths are the ones that
we improvise for ourselves. However objective a writer is impelled to
be, Norman felt, he or she will never escape his or her subjectivity –
which laid a duty on the writer or artist to cultivate their own form
of physical observance, of being *in* the world, as part of the instrument of their truth-telling. He, aided by the asperities of childhood,
had learned to descend soundlessly on his world like a softly beating
shadow, ready to vanish at a second's notice, a wraith whose two defensive weapons were his invisibility at rest and, when in action, a courteous,
fascinated inquisitiveness. He had first offered himself as a witness
before he was ten, standing always on the edge of the games in the
Forty Hill Freehold, nearly two decades before he set himself up as a
published writer, and he was more experienced as a witness than as
any other kind of human being. It's logical that both his first books,
and best books, were witness statements. But a witness statement, as
he knew, is, fundamentally, the *story* of an *act* of witness.

His literary intentions continued to be trained on recognition as a
novelist. Between 1953 and 1960 he published four novels and a single
book of non-fiction – a collection of articles he subtitled "Travels of
a novelist" – despite, in the same period, travelling to and in almost
every case writing journalism about Belize, Guatemala (twice), Mexico,
Italy, Cuba (at least twice), the Dominican Republic, Haiti, Panama,
Liberia, Ghana, Senegal, Mali, Algeria and, of course, Spain. Although
he contemplated a non-fiction book about Africa, nothing came of it;
it seemed that the only way he felt a country now deserved a book to
itself was as the setting for a novel, and that the traveller's life only
became significant when it found a pattern in fiction.

The rationale he offered in 1957 was that he felt he might have
written more travel books if he hadn't started with south-east Asia: his
later journeys through Latin America and Africa had turned out "tame
and flat by comparison", and what most interested him now were the
decade's many revolutionary movements and their transforming impact,
which he could explore better in novels.[15] I'm not sure we should buy
this, except possibly as a well-mannered way of explaining that to be
a passive witness was no longer enough in terms of added value (which

might, in turn, explain why beginning in the 1970s he produced a second wave of non-fiction writing about the experiences of thirty years before, having grasped the appreciation in his own value as a witness to irrecoverable events and places). Lesley, who later typed his manuscripts, judged that his ambition as a novelist was simply the result of "the Welsh Calvinist in him: the more difficult he felt something was, the more he had to do it".[16]

In November 1953 the first of the novels, *A Single Pilgrim*, was published. Cape, under pressure from its author, advertised it widely and it sold well. *The Times* called it "effective" in its characterisation, observing that its descriptions had "an attractive air of authenticity" though curiously condemning the story's dark climax for its "touch of nightmare".[17] Alan Ross, reviewing Norman again, felt his style was "not quite, for all its exotic natural images, individual or distinctive enough; possibly . . . in trying to impart too much topical information, his novels do not contain enough of the true yeast of fiction", but called it "on all but the highest level a singularly satisfying book".[18] Norman was generally pleased, and "staggered" to get a review from the Catholic weekly *The Tablet* which gave him a long, closely observed and positive notice and called the novel "moving and charming".[19]

He was already working on his next novel, about the *falangista* fisherman, and because the usually well-organised mechanism of his winter cycle failed and he did not make his usual expedition in early 1954, he was able to get on with it. He had planned a journey to China, started planning it nine months before, but his first application for entry to the People's Republic had gone astray, and despite efforts that autumn by himself and Cape, who re-sent copies of *A Dragon Apparent* to two sympathetic Chinese ambassadors, nothing came of it.

Novels took longer than travel books. The plot of the new book, as summed up in one of his Tossa notebooks, is economic and timely. "Distinction unsought is thrust upon Sebastian in [the] Spanish Civil War. He has been unwillingly conscripted in Fascist troops. Regarded as an enthusiastic fascist by [the] village who isolate him. Flattered by police, he boasts of deeds done by accident. He is ready to do anything to be accepted."

A tragedy of the ordinary man, erected on Sebastian's abject longing for acceptance, pours forth in Norman's descriptions of Sebastian's fishing, his boat swinging "gently in polished hammocks of water", and of his "beginnings of a slight intoxication from the effect of the approval" of the local police lieutenant. Norman's aficionado's understanding of the sea, and of everything that moves and drives the fishing community from which Sebastian is excluded, provides the tragedy with a potent background of practical life. (He knows it is of capital importance to the fishermen, for example, that in ostracising Sebastian they are deadly polite, for "He was somehow or other unlucky. They wouldn't take the risk of him bringing them bad catches. 'Good day, Sebastian. Blowing up from the west – eh?' No staring, no nudging, no sly remarks. Always very polite.") Condemned to fish alone, Sebastian decides to "emigrate" up the coast, and catches a monster grouper which will put him in funds to do so (maybe with enough too to entice his girlfriend Elena back: she has left him for a future in Barcelona). But the fish market closes ranks against him, and the great fish is eaten by the village cats. Half-mad, Sebastian goes to Barcelona, finds Elena has been tricked into prostitution, and murders her pimp.

The Day of the Fox is a novel with a steady gaze, without rehearsed responses: despite reviewers' comparisons, and its subject, nothing very much connects it to Hemingway's *The Old Man and the Sea*. It sold well, culminating in a 155,000-copy book club printing. It is the kind of novel that made the critic G S Fraser feel that "The 1950s . . . have been a period particularly rich in novels which, without being wildly [in other words formally] ambitious, hold one's attention by their general economy, intelligence, and obviously accurate portrayal of some cross-section of contemporary life".[20]

Yet it throws up curiosities, and questions. One is that Norman chose to extract, from the fishing village where he spent some of the best summers of his life, a story of a single persecuted fisherman. If one substituted "Forty Hill" for "fishing village" and "schoolboy" for "fisherman", how close might that be to an account of his childhood? Two, despite the story's political maturity, its subplots and relationships are left unassimilated, in particular that of an interesting Anarchist named Molina, returned to scout a place for a *guerrilla* landing party and existing in the throes of a dying idealism. Most surprisingly, although Norman concludes the story open-endedly, and satisfyingly, the novel as a whole has a slightly unsatisfying, rough quality all the way through. This was, I'm sure, the result of his publisher's failure to edit him: Norman was a novelist of sufficient ability that if his publisher chose to be careless, readers did not instantly notice, and only over several books can it be seen that some of his work is less finished than it might have been. Jonathan Cape, uninspired and understaffed in the 1950s, did choose to be careless. (As his editor later, it occurs to me that if I'd been his editor then I would not have been the agent of his producing more perfect novels – but I might have suggested he be less impatient with their structure, suggested he not turn his characters into such explicit symbols nor depend so heavily on context: in the alchemical process of a novel's narrative shaping, a process in which the writer advances often blind and by feel, it is not good for him or her to know too much.) Michael Howard or Daniel George could – should – have said to their author, early and gently, "If you really hope to be a good novelist, Norman, you've got to pay more attention to mood"; there is no evidence that they or anybody else at Cape did. Instead, with their rival William Heinemann publishing Graham Greene – the most successful English novelist of the 1950s – Cape hoped and thought that in Norman Lewis they had their answer to Greene. If Jonathan had been a less commercial and more literary opportunist, editorial standards at Bedford Square would have been higher. Instead, Cape let Norman down.

Norman had shelved his project on Mayan civilisation conceived on his first visit to Guatemala nine years before, but his friend Janos de Szecsy, the Hungarian historian, had revived the subject in his mind, sending him a letter detailing what had been happening in the country since the CIA's overthrow of (elected) President Arbenz Guzmán and his replacement in July 1954 by the debonair fascist Castillo Armas, an officer who looked like a baby-faced Hispanic Hitler. In 1953 de Szecsy had been appointed director of a short-lived institute whose aim was to rescue and protect Guatemala's popular (Indian) arts. As soon as Castillo Armas came to power, the institute had been closed and de Szecsy had become a marked man. Norman, he urged, should come and write less about history and more about what was happening in the country now.

Not quite as hurriedly as he claimed – he dates his journey as summer 1954[21] – in early February 1955 Norman left for Central America, having arranged with Lesley that he would meet her in New York on the return journey. He landed at Belize on 5 February.

"The airport at Belize was negatively satisfying", he wrote with the pleasure of purging the West from his system; unlike New Orleans where he had changed planes, "There were no machines selling anything, playing anything, or changing money."[22] In his notebook he added that "A nurse with a fine bottom takes [your] temperature and then helps to carry [your] luggage through to customs, where it is ignored by an officer with the silent aloofness of a voodoo priest".[23] He spent a pleasing week at the Fort George Hotel tasting "the rich, homely, slightly dotty savour of British Honduras", including its inability to serve a double scotch (two singles always arrived), and wires crossed so often that room service might deliver the most surreal item, "a raw potato on a silver tray", for instance. It was really too pleasing. Halfway through the week he spent the day fishing on the Turneffe islands off the coast and felt overwhelmed. Like the "clean, fresh, fragrant" landscape full of pied kingfishers, yellow shrikes, pelicans and macaws he had seen when he arrived, the first impression of Turneffe was that "this was the kingdom of heaven. After a few hours the spirit grew gradually sick as if liverish with beauty."[24]

He flew on to Guatemala City on the 12th. A country where in places only seven children out of every hundred were legitimate was more his kind of territory: within twenty-four hours of arriving he was making notes not for the Mayan culture book but a novel. Three days later he was looking for background at Puerto Barrios on the Caribbean, an important, slummy banana port "mysteriously full of Americans in Maya jackets, reporter caps" who turned out to be tourism specialists. It was a place of painted cabins, cantinas, wheezing jukeboxes and "cowboy types" who stood on one leg on the verandas staring into space. United Fruit's writ ran large, with its own worker district, free buses and compulsory inoculation. Turning his back, Norman flew west, meeting de Szecsy a couple of days later. His notebook filled with his conversations with the historian; he noted the extreme stoicism of the Indians "carrying huge burdens and when they have unloaded their goods they load themselves with stones. ... They never laugh when they are amused but only at the sight of blood or death." He and de Szecsy drove to Quetzaltenango and Chichicastenango, where, on the steps of the sixteenth-century church of Santo Tomás, they saw lit fires tended by Indians conducting Mayan rituals with incense and flowers.

Dozens of candles flickered the length of the church's stone nave, among red petals strewn to represent the living, white to represent the dead (as they still do: to walk as far as the smoke-blackened altar is to walk through a fluttering field of light). Norman was impressed by the appropriation of Catholic dogma and by the Indians' remaking of relations with the afterlife into an ongoing candleside conversation with their dead.

On 21 February he reached Huehuetenango, a frontier outpost supine under its varnish of dust and aguardiente at the foot of the Sierra de los Cuchumatanes. Remote in its valley just south of the Mexican border and Chiapas, governed by its own law and custom, and seething behind its sheen of immobility – fifty years later, staying at the Hotel Zaculeu where he stayed and sensing the town's simmering wastedness, it still feels that way – Huehue is a background too good to be exhausted on a single story. That may be why Norman gave two accounts of his days there. In his autobiography it is where he met Lazlo Papas, or Janos de Szecsy, under house arrest and seeking an exit visa,[25] but in "A Quiet Evening in Huehuetenango", written for the *New Yorker*,[26] he gives a more boisterous version in which, seeking a quiet drink, he and his driver find themselves matching glass for glass a group of aguardiente-drinking bandits. Addicted to a song called "Mortal Sin", the *macheteros* could not operate the cantina's jukebox. Norman obliged several times. There was no getting away. "The most important thing taught after religion is good manners," his driver tells him. "I do not think we should risk offending these men by showing a desire to leave before they do." A providential earthquake, cutting the power and silencing the jukebox, gave him a chance to escape.

"A Quiet Evening" is a textbook example of elements of actuality – his flirtatious but deadly urbane driver, Indians who wore the codpieces of Alvarado's troops, the man who rode into town bringing the rockets for the next day's fiesta "like an Englishman dressed up for a fancy dress ball ... enormous spurs, Mex[ican] saddle etc",[27] the cantina called "I Await Thee on Thy Return", the "wonderful scene when Guatemalan farmer with old Dad and son (who waits respectfully outside until invited in) comes up and respectfully asks if we could find him a marimba on the Wurlitzer"[28] – that he recomposes with a subjective richness and texture and a comic-lyrical acceptance of life into the effect most worth producing for a writer: an imaginative reader.

(A postscript: wherever he did meet his friend de Szecsy, and whenever they actually parted company, Norman never saw the Hungarian again. In his case, the tragedy of life kept pace with invention: marked by fate de Szecsy, talented and owed much by Guatemalans for his historical and archaeological work, was killed in May the following year in a plane crash in the Sierra de las Minas.)

By 3 March Norman was back at Belize, moving north to Chetumal and Merida on the Yucatán peninsula. The "good manners", *urbanidad*, of Huehuetenango were as present in Mexico and "higher than at Belize". He indulged in contrarian theorising. "Perhaps this is where D H Lawrence and all the rest fall down on Mexico. The first class public school educated Englishman is a bit of a Mexican in his manners, the dour, blunt, forthright, plain, honest businessmen and government officials fall short."[29] He didn't spend long either in Mexico or Cuba where he flew next, although the short stop at Havana had sufficient impact to plant the seed of several returns to the island. These were the bitchy, fading years of Fulgencio Batista: Norman saw the swagger of his policemen, the gentle café concerts in the Parque Central ousted by American coin-in-the-slot t.v.s, detected the atmosphere of decadence that would give rise to the typical periodical Cuban eruption. The historian Eric Hobsbawm remembers the intellectual impact of Castro's revolution, how "After the triumph of Fidel Castro, and even more after the defeat of the US attempt to overthrow him at the Bay of Pigs in 1961, there was not an intellectual in Europe or the USA who was not under the spell of Latin America. . . ."[30] Norman was those intellectuals' precursor by at least half a decade – and wise enough not to write from their position of bubbling idealism. He understood, for instance, that Batista had not been a monster, judging him deliberately and with good evidence in 1957 "the most capable and progressive president Cuba has ever had".[31] His only errors, in Norman's view, had been to alienate the middle classes and to stay in power too long.

From Havana Norman flew to New York to meet Lesley. In the midst of seeing Manhattan and the Perelmans they had lunch at the Algonquin Hotel, arranged by Sid Perelman, with William Shawn, editor and caliph of the *New Yorker*. Stories of the contrast between Shawn's cryptic, aloof authority and his appearance are legion. Lesley remembers "a little grey Alfred Hitchcock, a little round man, extremely nervous. Norman, thank God, saved the day by launching into one of his things, telling stories all through lunch."[32] After staying with friends in Baltimore, they came back to England separately. Lesley had taken a cheap BOAC flight and was returning by ship; Norman flew. It was a short separation that came with significant consequences.

In London Norman wrote several pieces, including two for the *New Yorker*; one the Huehuetenango piece, which the magazine published as fiction, the other "A Letter from Belize". On 4 July *The Day of the Fox*, his Spanish novel, was published. Cape had budgeted £200 for advertising and spent more than £400: it was advertised twenty-eight times, in all the main English and Scottish newspapers and magazines from *Encounter* to the *Spectator*. The appetite for novels that narrated "abroad" to a British readership was great in the 1950s for plenty of reasons (currency restrictions; the expense of travel and concomitant interest in exotic backgrounds; a curiosity for interpretations of distant places that was as yet unmediated by post-colonial theory and the saturation of newspaper travel pages). The reviews Norman took with him to Ibiza were good: *The Times* called the novel "written with distinction and economy and of more than transient value",[33] the *Times Literary Supplement* decided that "There is much that is very good in *The Day of the Fox*", though Arthur Calder-Marshall noticed the failed fusion of the stories of Sebastian and the Anarchist, Molina.[34]

In Ibiza, at the house of "the Catalano" – the "always looked for" Casa Ses Estaques – for the first time, he worked on the beginnings of a new novel, going on with it that autumn on his return. He was on his own in London, up to a point. When Lesley was not there, other companions materialise, referred to by initials and phone numbers in his diaries. One is "N"; another, "K", was his secretary – Katherine – who had a long crush on him. Ito was doing his National Service in the Marines. Lesley herself was out of the country. On the transatlantic crossing that spring, alone and sharing some of Norman's restlessness, she had met two architects who were opening an office in Algiers. By the time the ship docked, she had accepted a suggestion that she come and work for them. "They were going off to Algiers," she recalls, "and I thought, Well that will be fun." It wasn't fun. Thirsty for experience, she had made a wrong move. What she was unaware of until she landed in Algeria two months later was that the "public order operation", begun by the French the previous November, to contain the independentist FLN was evolving into a war. In August 1955 the FLN carried out its attack on Philippeville. The massacre in reprisal by the French Army and *pieds noirs* radicalised the Algerian population, and support for the FLN in urban areas rocketed.

In Algiers that autumn Lesley was cold – it was an unusually bad autumn and winter – and increasingly tense and scared. Hearing that she had decided to move to north Africa, Norman had not done as he had with Gwen, laying siege and pleading with her, even though, as Lesley recalls, "Norman was never sure about me in the early stages". He had been unusually patient; but now he decided that her fugue and predicament required intervention. In January 1956 he flew to Algiers. "Norman came out and got me and said, 'Come on, I'm bringing you home. It's not a good place to be.'"[35] His rescue, an act of friendship and at another level of chivalry, altered their relationship. Norman rose in the unconscious stakes in Lesley's mind; she began to make the instinctive calculation of his (and her) commitment that would lead her to shift her affections decisively away from her Australian boyfriend and towards Norman. The journalist and Africanist Basil Davidson, who had met Norman at 202 High Holborn at the beginning of the decade and become a friend, says that in going after Lesley Norman was also rescuing himself. "He was I think pretty lost for a time because his private life was a complicated life, but then Lesley arrived and everything became obvious and very interesting and very pleasant. I think she explained him. And she made him very happy, there's no doubt about that, and happiness is important in this world."[36]

The next three years saw that happiness and becoming-obviousness coming into being; and simultaneously, if more gradually, a change in Norman's view of his work. In 1956 and 1957 the intention of "becoming a good novelist" still impelled him. By the end of the decade his ambition had all but abandoned him, leaving him satisfied, up to a point, with what he had achieved but exhausted at the prospect of continuing to try to reach the heights of recognition that he had aimed at for ten years. Each new novel seemed to him an improvement; but the books were taking longer and more energy, and the growth of the reward in terms of audience, renown and sales was not matching the effort.

Working intensely on his new novel set in Guatemala, he had not yet reached that point. The line of his life continued to pay out rapidly, with many spring weekends spent in Scotland (and a spring visit, possibly his last, to Lynette Roberts' caravan, currently parked at Bells Wood, Bayford in Hertfordshire. "Season very delayed. Trees only just coming into leaf. First cuckoo").[37] Gareth remembers the attractions and repulsions of the Scottish weekends.

He loved walking in the hills, so he'd take us on holidays to the west coast. We went to Oban, we went to the island of Mull, we went to Tobermory, up to Inverness, right over the very top, Caithness, and right down the other side because there were botanical gardens on the north-west coast.

We'd have these dreadful Sunday lunches and he'd insist on taking us to some ghastly dour Scottish hotel to have Sunday lunch, and I'd hate it, and I don't think he even liked it much either, but he got some kind of perverse enjoyment out of taking us there.[38]

R G Lewis was also turning over at a high pitch. "Britain's Scientifically Minded Camera Firm", as the sign claimed over the Holborn window, continued to earn its scientific reputation. It had an engineering firm, Sands Hunter at Croydon Airport, making a widening range of Leica adapters (many still used), and its own chemists developing and manufacturing chemicals such as Ergol, a high-speed, high-temperature developer for black-and-white film. In Bond Street alone, Lewis Newcombe Ltd made a profit of nearly £34,000 in the 1956 tax year. Norman's relative wealth and business ability made Basil Davidson feel that his relations with people – both real and the fictional characters he created – sometimes suffered as a result.

He was better off than I was, better off than most of us were, because he had a very good source of income. The shop was very successful. He was a very good businessman, he understood all that backwards. And that's really the point at which he lost interest in other people: if they couldn't follow how sensible it was to do this kind of thing or that kind of thing, he lost interest in them. His standards were very exacting and I think that some of his books, some of his novels, suffered from that because he couldn't see the point of arguing the case very often.[39]

After a shorter than usual two months in Ibiza, at Ses Estaques again at 800 pesetas a month, he was back in England in early September, and by December had the manuscript of the Guatemala novel ready for the typist. *The Volcanoes Above Us* is the first-person narrative of David Williams, a soldier of fortune dispossessed of his coffee finca after one of Guatemala's epileptic reversals of power, and his confrontation with a bland US monopoly intent on "guiding" the country's Indians to civilisation. The company's "ideal conditions" are, as Williams quietly clarifies, the moral equivalent of the slavery imposed by the conquering apocalypse of Alvarado. In the wake of capitalist pacification, inevitably, come the tourist planeloads, and the Indians meanwhile, with few resources but admirably – and as they always have done – rise up. In literary terms, the novel's almost-success is so striking that its two blemishes are thrown into deep relief: one, that David's lover Greta never comes fully alive because the reader never quite believes David's weakness for her (although he captures well the fashionable acting-out of neurosis that was de rigueur for young women in the 1950s); two, that the book is again feebly edited. Despite the growing confidence and instinct of his fiction writing, Norman was capable of writing plodding scenes – the confrontation with the US company's manager Elliot at the fiesta organised for the tourists, the reflective what-to-do-about-Greta? scene, and a number of others – that could have been cleaned up. They were not. There are also lunatic type-setting/proof-reading errors: on the last page "lucidity" is rendered as "ucidity". (Does that sum up the publisher's not-quite-lucidity about their author?)

As an allegory of civilisation and progress, however, wrapped in a satisfying existential adventure, the novel's portrait of the amoralities and stupidities of corporations and its thoroughgoing assault on the tourist industry still read as inspiring contributions.

We rode in a jingling, creaking horse-cab to the Alameda Gardens, listened to the blaring music, bought lottery tickets, choosing the good, balanced numbers admired by real connoisseurs, had ourselves photographed together by a hooded photographer against a backcloth of skyscrapers and spaceships, went on to the Indian Village and watched the sad, industrious Mixtecs sneezing over their labour. Guadaloupe was illuminated this day, under its dark, transparent sky supported lightly at the four corners by the domes of churches, and the summer pigeons twinkled like showers of metal parings overhead.

It was also a little unreal, as if the presence of the tourists with their big bones, their confidence, their pink flesh and their earth-inheriting voices had turned the town into a series of stage-sets into which other human beings were introduced only so far as they were necessary to enhance the sentimental background – dozing theatrically at their market stalls, kneeling theatrically on the steps of the church, propped theatrically drunk against a wall in the shade of their big hats. Elliot had called all this forth from the void of his imagination to satisfy the craving for unreality of these real and solid people. At that moment I was in no mood to dispute the universal need for illusion. The tourists sought and found it at its lowest level. The rest of us got it from such things as religion, opera-going and, of course, love – and the religious man, the happy tourist and the lover were all united by a single blessing: their capacity for suspending belief.[40]

He delivered *The Volcanoes Above Us* to Jonathan Cape, he claimed later, with a note saying "Here's the book you wanted about Nelson."[41]

Handing over the typescript, he was ready for a winter escape that he had been planning for a year. His friend Basil Davidson, a frequent visitor to Orchard Street with his wife Marion by the mid-1950s, was implicated. Norman had been commissioned by the *New Yorker* to write about Ghana's independence celebrations in March 1957. Davidson, then a leader writer on the *Daily Mirror*, was travelling for his paper, and the two left on 28 February for Accra. "He was a good companion," Davidson says. "He was a very unusual person in that he was very private but he was also very determined and knew his way around very well. He was secret in many ways and completely indifferent to whatever anybody might think about him. I've met a few writers in my time and they tend to be show-offs if they get a chance, and he didn't ever, he wasn't ever like that."[42]

Ghana on the eve of independence was another British possession that allowed Norman to indulge his pastime of detecting what it was that their colonial subjects had eventually grown tired of. Travelling thousands of miles from the country of his birth, he seems to have used this game as a way of keeping his negative view of Englishness alive, and close. His investigation was carried out, he wrote, "in the full prior knowledge that the findings . . . will [always] be the same". In this case the bedrock objections, his Ghanaian companion Joseph told him,

amounted to the fact that the Englishman had never learned to stop complete strangers in the street, shake hands with them warmly, and ask them where they were going, and why . . . the Englishman had learned to become a better mixer than his French neighbour [but] there remained a trace of that aloofness . . . which makes it so difficult for him to be loved as well as respected. Here, as in India and in Burma, the European clubs preserved their exclusiveness to the last ditch. The Englishman was received socially by the educated African without any reserve whatever, but the African's civility was not fully returned, and there was an offensive flavour of patronage in this lack of reciprocity.[43]

Non-admission to the colonists' clubs, which he had first written about after being in Vietnam, was the thin end of the wedge of anti-colonial feeling. We might feel that that observation discloses as much about Norman's own sense of exclusion.

His account of the country also shows his skill at creating maximum impact by underplaying, creating a permanently contemporary, irony-bespattered anarchy by use of an almost Victorian reticence of rhetoric, from the first sentence.

The important thing to bear in mind when visiting what was once the Gold Coast and is now Ghana is that the advice liberally proffered by the old Gold Coast hands in retirement will be designed to perpetuate a nostalgic legend.

In other words, ignore everything you're told. He describes the crowds, the men in togas, the women in Edwardian-style dresses originally introduced by missionaries and now "transformed by the barbaric gaiety of the material from which they are confected", and goes on, "The designs with which these cottons are printed demand some comment." It is difficult to say why that is so clever: partly because the sentence is itself a Victorian or Edwardian construction. It is also an example of how able Norman was at the substructural level of style: the transitions from one sentence to the next. Instead of catching the dresses' "barbaric gaiety", then moving on to justify the observation by the detail of their designs, a surreptitious imprisoned comedy is maintained in the implied question, "Why do I need to write about these designs anyway?" and its answer, "Well, because frankly they were *so* bloody bizarre."

The African trip could not be faulted for range. After Accra and Cape Coast he and Davidson parted, and he travelled over the next six weeks to Liberia (Monrovia, Robertsfield, Clay, Gbarnga, Goodrich) and then north to Senegal and Guinea (Dakar, Tambacounda, Simenti, Sambailo, Youkounkoun, Djirun, Labé, Mamou, Conakry) and east to Mali (Bamako, Mopti, Djenné, Bandiagara, Sangah and Goundam), finishing with a nod to convention – less of a convention in 1957 than now – at Timbuktu. On the *piste* to the fabled desert city he noted the bird life, the sky studded with great bustards, hornbills and doves, but when he arrived he found its architecture discordant, half washed away, and the town, stinking of bats, blanketed in "a dreadful dusty exhausted whiteness everywhere". Jaundice and typhoid were endemic.[44] His reaction to Timbuktu does not quite stand for his response to Africa as a whole, but nothing about west Africa, despite his identification with the colonised and his admiration for the Africans' "extreme and innate sociability", exhilarated him. His notebooks point to an intention to enlarge his journalism into a full-length account, but no book would be written. In a conversation thirty years later he described the mismatch between himself and Africa, a continent that (apart from its Mediterranean littoral) never got under his skin.

I spent three months in west Africa at the time when I wrote about Liberia and Ghana, though I couldn't achieve any fondness for it. I attribute that largely to the sensation I have that it really hasn't a history. And I like the element of historical interest to be included in my investigations. I enjoy writing about the history.[45]

One could take issue with his equation of (European) linear history with Africa's historicity, but the lack of historical curiosities to write about left a void. Africa in its age-old, non-linear state was, for Norman, a sponge porous with a million narrative absences. He could go some way towards rendering it, acknowledging that Monrovia "taught me the beauty and the interest of corrugated iron as a building material", but couldn't compose it except in fragments of high irony, like the portrait he wrote on his return for the *New Yorker* of the Liberian President Tubman, who was adulated to the tune of "Jesus Bids Us Shine" and "performs the considerable feat of leading a parliamentary democracy in which no official opposition is permitted to exist". That incapacity to narrate Africa may have been Norman's fault, though it is hard to think of a non Africa-born white writer who has allowed black Africa to challenge his identity or not used black Africa as, at best, theatre or borrowed finery. The other continent available to the white man and woman, the Africa of the heart embraced by Graham Greene, Isak Dinesen and Ernest Hemingway, is not a concept Norman's emotion-shy genius would easily have subscribed to.

In England at the end of April, he made a rapid turn-round and left again on 9 May for Spain on a long-arranged trip with his racing friend Arthur Baron. Acute to the arrival of the new season as he was every year, he saw that, as they drove fast south (Baron had stayed a furious driver), the late English spring had been left behind by Tours, with "lilac wisteria and horse chestnut in bloom . . . the town penetrated by the ripping exhaust note of Vespas always with girls on pillion". After "520 miles" (837 kilometres) on the second day they were already at Salamanca. Heading for Jerez de la Frontera for Norman to visit the marshlands at the mouth of the Guadalquivir where camels still grazed, they were delayed by the absence of the estate's owner and waited at Sanlúcar. It was the annual *feria* and he and Baron went to a bullfight, an afternoon written about in an essay, "The Bullfight Revisited", with a curiously sharp tone of both comprehension and distaste. In the essay, unexpectedly describing himself as "lacking natural passion for the art of tauromachy", he attends with an aficionado's eye to the spectacle, rules and embedded trickery of the *corrida*, and to the brutal ritual of dispatching a particularly dangerous bull (rumoured among the crowd to have been fought before). The essay is almost unique in his writing for its negative tone, though the reader learns a good deal about the finer details of the bullfight on the way, and in a rather clearer-eyed style than Hemingway's standard work of *afición*, *Death in the Afternoon*. Commenting drily on Hemingway's sentimentally anthropomorphic thinking, for instance, that "an exceptionally good bull . . . noble, frank, simple, brave", keeps its mouth shut even when full of blood, "for reasons of self-respect, we are left to suppose", Norman exposes the never-spoken sporting fallacy, as an almost throwaway *coup de grâce* remarking that

No one in a Spanish audience has any affection for the one bull in a thousand that possesses that extra grain of intelligence. The ideal bull is a character like the British Grenadier, or the Chinese warrior of the last century, who is supposed to have carried a lamp when attacking at night, to give the enemy a sporting chance.[46]

In London, transformation. On her return from Algeria Lesley had gone, reflectively, to share a flat with her Australian journalist boyfriend at Golders Green, but Norman's regularly renewed petition to her to finish with him was finally answered. "Fond and all as I was of [the boyfriend], it was a reverse thing, I was more interested in him than he was in me, and he didn't want to settle down, that was for sure, so then I thought, No, this is silly. . . . In those days sensible was about the last thing I was," she says, "[but] eventually I thought, You're right, yes, you're right."[47] She moved out of the Golders Green flat and into Orchard Street. Forty years later when Norman related Lesley's and his decision to live together, his standing avoidance of personal feelings made it impossible for him to express its substantial emotional aspect, leaving the reader with probably the most austerely spurious explanation anyone has ever given for setting up home with someone.

It was about this time that I learned through my solicitor that I had long since been divorced according to Mexican law and that my ex-wife had forthwith taken a husband. I therefore married Lesley, an old friend who had been helping me to organise my books.[48]

In fact, although Lesley Burley changed her name by deed poll to Lewis, she and Norman did not get married for another twenty years.

Sharing the Orchard Street flat, almost immediately she and Norman both found it less appealing, for practical more than emotional reasons. Across the street Selfridges had started a rebuilding programme, using heavy demolition equipment and pile-drivers for an expansion of their food department. The construction work from early morning onwards was deafening; each time a steel pile was struck, their own building bounced a millimetre. In concert with the rebuilding, the whole district north of Oxford Street was shedding its cheapness and nonconformist possibilities, becoming neither a reasonable place to live and write books nor a place to contemplate a settled future. In the interests of finding both, in early summer they rented a house outside the city at Wendens Ambo in Essex, where Lesley could live while Norman was in Ibiza and from where, when Norman returned every few weeks, they could explore the countryside for a suitable house to buy.

On 4 October Cape published *The Volcanoes Above Us*. The critical response was by far the widest and most approving he had had. V S Pritchett called Norman "one of our very few capable experts in the novel of the exotic and revolutionary setting",[49] Philip Oakes recommended the novel's "Violence made meaningful; characters and country sharply seen."[50] The fullest coverage was in the *Sunday Times* two days after publication, where Cyril Connolly, who rarely reviewed fiction, gave Norman a solus review and unprecedented acclaim. Under the title "Machine-Gun v. Marimba" Connolly described *The Volcanoes Above Us* as "a novel which cannot fail to give immediate pleasure from the first page to the last" and, comparing Norman to Koestler, Malraux or B Traven, though "on a less philosophical and more sensible, happy, British basis, comic rather than tragic", he called him "witty, crisp and master of his material; he might have lived in Central America all his life and been born to the music of the marimba; he is also a genuine novelist with a sense of drama and place. I am afraid," Connolly concluded, "*The Volcanoes Above Us* would make an excellent film."[51] His one criticism was that as a creator of characters Norman was "perhaps, still rather a lightweight", but he willingly conceded that the combination of sociology and excitement was near faultless; he understood the subtlety of Norman's achievement in constructing Winthrop Elliot, the American company's manager, as "like a certain type of oil man or copper or tobacco man . . . almost a democrat, and almost an intellectual" so long as the company's interests came first, and he endorsed the novel's introduction of tourism as the new, destructive force. "The tourists of our time are an implacable, a ferocious phenomenon who recognise no authority but their light-meters, who require local colour for their colour film and folk-lore in action for their cine-camera . . . sometimes they procure the release of Barabbas." Connolly admitted that he had been wrong to think that Norman had shown in previous books a schoolboy fascination with cruelty and torture. He may have had in mind the scene in which David Williams watches as a platoon of his men, ambushed by government soldiers on the far side of a river, have their legs slashed from under them by machete blows.

Our men now formed a small, tight circle facing inwards, and the enemy officer had placed one of his own men behind each one of ours. . . . As they struck, the Patriots cried out in agonized surprise. Some of their utterances seemed very absurd, such as *no quiero esto*, which means, "I don't want this to happen." Of course they didn't want it to happen. The Indians appeared to be accepting their fate with their usual submissiveness, and the men with the machetes continued to slash at them, both Patriot and Indian with quick, short strokes, so that sometimes they struck three or four times at a man's legs, almost before he had time to fall. It was as if they were trimming bunches of bananas, and you could hear the dry chop of the machetes all the time. . . .

At that moment I vomited.[52]

"Mr Lewis is drawn to these scenes", Connolly allows, not from
voyeurism but "because he is so horrified that they can happen, because
they are an aspect of the problem of pain." The absolute insignificance
of individual suffering in a world filled with pain – "an expanding
universe of affliction" as Williams calls it – cannot diminish its reality.

Maurice Richardson agreed in the *New Statesman* that "humanists
are advised that there is unlikely to be much hope south of Mexico
City." Richardson, a long forgotten master of English surrealism (author
of the marginal masterpiece *The Exploits of Engelbrecht*) was a rare
dissenting critic who noticed a difficulty in processing emotions out of
events that left Norman unable to go further than swinging between
moods.

There is discordance between the satirical and the tragic mood; but the writing,
and especially the descriptions of action, is so sharp and economical that it
carries you all the way with it, so that only when you have finished do you
start asking yourself why an unusually good book was not better still.[53]

Though the era of the literary adventure novel is gone, more or less
surrendered to the realisms of the next forty years, *The Volcanoes
Above Us* still crystallises important, salvageable aspects of Norman's
fictional enterprise. (It was also one of his most successful novels, a
Book Society choice for October 1957 and, in its Russian edition, a
novel with a two-million copy sale.) In August 1957, when *The Day
of the Fox* was being issued in a bookclub edition, Norman had given
an interview in which he had summarised not just the theme of his
Spanish novel (and his Guatemala novel), but, in a phrase of prescience
about the way the world was going, his capital theme as a novelist. "I
am especially interested in people who form resistance movements to
the slow, paralysing drift towards a uniform world-civilisation, which
is so rapidly spreading its insipidity to every corner of the earth."[54]
"Globalisation", had that plump, foolish justification then been coined,
could hardly have been closer to his lips.

Adventure stories though his novels of the 1950s and 1960s might
be classed as – romances of lost and broken utopias – they can also
be read to effect as studies of attitudes to human value, of attempts to
recover the human worth in pre-civilised societies and to understand
the direction of this present by the light of that past. We might argue
about where exactly on the intersecting lines of aesthetics and ethics

the novel, as a form, ought to lie, but I cannot, just now, think of another twentieth-century novelist whose dramatisations of the dragon of Western economic progress were so determined, prophetic, or sociologically mature.

One of those sent a copy of the novel at the author's request was another of Cape's authors, Ian Fleming. Norman and Fleming had met at a Cape party (Norman dates the meeting to "shortly after the publication of *Casino Royale*", Fleming's first novel, but he probably meant *From Russia With Love*, published in April 1957), and partly out of mutual recognition – the awareness of being a misfit ran high in both – they became friends. "I found myself in an almost separate room, though there might have been two or three other people strolling around, looking very miserable. [Ian] introduced himself and he said, 'You know why we're here in this room?' And I said, 'No, tell me.' 'It's because we're both extremely unpopular authors; they put all the second-rate people in this room.'"[55] Fleming, a man of chilled charm who had the curious trait of liking others to fear him, sent Michael Howard a note that *The Volcanoes Above Us* was "one of the best novels I've read for years" and that it showed "a fascinating mind and startling powers of description and simile". To Norman he responded remarkably shrewdly, seeing formally where the novel fell short and where it stood up. "How very kind of you to have sent me a copy of this year's best-seller. . . . If I have a criticism it is that the hero and heroine are almost too shadowy. You seem to shy away from delving too deeply into your principal characters. . . . But . . . I am every time arrested by your genius for intellectual photography in prose."[56] Fleming promised to send a copy to Somerset Maugham "with whom I was staying last weekend" but Maugham's reaction isn't recorded.

Bright swathes of Norman's life, some of its most adventurous episodes, are told (and told again) with that carnival splendour of his in published books of travel, autobiography, essays and pieces that have no counterpart in the seventy-odd notebooks I was given as his biographer. To know what happened, simple cross-referencing can sometimes settle contradictory details. He can't have been in Burma in early 1952 (*The World The World*) because *Golden Earth* was published less than six months later, etcetera, etcetera. But to attempt to re-create the life – rather than just précis the work – that will not always do. A case in point occurs at the end of 1957 when Norman went, at length, into Central America and the Caribbean. Lacking notebooks, there are published sources not always consonant with each other, mainly his politically revealing and considerably invented Chapter Eight in *The World The World*, four pieces in his collection *The Changing Sky* and two in *A View of the World*, that point to (a) a remarkable sequence of encounters and adventures and (b) a packed schedule even by Norman's standards. Can we know what actually happened?

By educated guess and a weighing of likelihoods it may have gone something like this. In autumn 1957 Norman met Ian Fleming, a former commander in British naval intelligence. Fleming, finding that Norman spoke good Spanish, invited him to lunch at the White Tower shortly afterwards, then back to his office at the *Sunday Times*. In the "understood" manner of British post-war intelligence, Fleming's position as foreign editor (he preferred "foreign manager") blended with his role in gathering intelligence for the Caribbean area. Together he and Norman assembled an itinerary that would result in an important intelligence trawl for Fleming and an adventurous journey for Norman, providing material for a series of articles Fleming would publish in the *Sunday Times*.

Fleming was particularly interested in Cuba. The Foreign Office was not, he felt, getting acute enough reports from its ambassador Stanley Fordham, and he was currently having to rely on information from Edward Scott, a New Zealander, editor of the *Havana Post* and one-quarter allegedly of the character of James Bond. He needed more. Fleming, i.e. British intelligence, wanted to know what was going on with the young revolutionary, Fidel Castro, and what were his rebel band's chances of success. Scott was not close enough to the ground, and Fleming disbelieved his dismissal of Castro as a nuisance who would soon be dealt with by the Cuban air force aided by the US. Lastly, Fleming wanted Norman to meet Ernest Hemingway, partly for intelligence reasons and partly on account of Fleming's own extreme admiration for him. Hemingway was then residing, as the world's most celebrated living author, a short distance from Havana.

Norman flew first to Guatemala in early December to report on the assassination of President Castillo Armas, who, once in office, had become less and less of a dictator despite his Führerish moustache.

Castillo Armas' murder, and various associated killings, gave Norman an opportunity to study at close hand the murky linkages of Central American political assassination.[57] From Guatemala City he flew to Havana on 15 December, coincidentally booking into the same hotel, the Sevilla Biltmore on the Prado, where Graham Greene was staying with the actress Anita Björk and writing *Our Man in Havana*. "I never spoke to him," he said decades later,[58] though he was aware of Greene's presence in the corner of the "ghastly American blue-lit bar".[59] (Greene in turn described the bar's drinkers, Norman among them, as "crouched in silence and shadow like parachutists gloomily waiting the signal to leap."[60]) He met Fleming's contact Edward Scott as soon as he arrived, though Scott was preoccupied by having just challenged Hemingway to a duel after an incident at a British embassy party when, to lighten the atmosphere, Hemingway's companion Ava Gardner had taken off her knickers and saluted the other guests with them.

Norman's visit continued in this absurdist-satirical vein. The short, fat Scott, a screwer of callipygian black Cuban women whom he liked to have wandering his apartment naked, turned out to be a poor shot when he took Norman to his private shooting range, and also told him that Hemingway spent all his time drunk at Sloppy Joe's and had no interest in the Cuban revolution. With Scott's help, however, and that of the *New York Times* correspondent Ruby Hart Phillips, Norman was able to interview a wide range of Cubans who could tell him (and Fleming) what was happening: bishops, disaffected army officers, senior politicians, students and members of the Cuban business elite, without whose support Batista's regime would definitely fail. He saw the bodies of murdered students in the city morgue, and one evening soon after he arrived machine guns opened up wildly on the roof of the presidential palace, felling a man standing on a balcony opposite. He travelled the length of the country to Santiago, not only the city closest to Castro's refuge in the Sierra Maestra but also the capital of the sugar economy where he found that workers unemployed for seven months of the year after the sugar harvest finished, were ready for any revolutionary activity that would feed them. He talked to cane-cutters and estate owners and tried to make contact with the rebels. On the recommendation of someone in Havana, or more likely because he enjoyed talking to fortune tellers, he visited Tia Margarita, Santiago's most famous clairvoyant, who told him that the war would be over in a year, "which, give a few days, it was". (In an odd counterpoint to his rejection of his mother's spiritualist mission he was prone to consulting fortune tellers wherever he found them hanging on, especially in the Americas. They might be quacks, he felt, but they at least showed people how to put up with life.) At night, from the roof of his hotel on the plaza Cespedes, he heard gunfire and saw delayed-action devices of paraffin-soaked rags wrapped around candles flickering in the cane fields, waiting to ignite; but his arrangements to travel beyond Manzanillo, the nearest point to approach the mountains, failed. He was stopped and searched, he said, eight times on the way, and at Manzanillo "it was only too clear by the sandbag parapets and the manned strongpoints, that the army was ready for anything . . . as soon as I took out my camera a rifle was levelled at me".[61]

One fact emerged clearly from his information-gathering. "Castro's revolt, so far from being a proletarian revolution, knew nothing of Marxism and took little interest in the industrial workers. This was the middle class in action, and the hundred or so sons of good families who had taken to the mountains were not only not Communists, but they were at daggers drawn with them." With Castro receiving funding from many of the sugar magnates it was a moment for intelligent handling by Cuba's chief ally, the USA. Instead Washington assumed that any movement opposing a right-wing government must be acting on Moscow's orders. "What little the majority of Castro's followers knew of Communism in December 1957," Norman wrote, "they distrusted or disliked. Three years later, largely through the success of the economic boycott organised by the United States, they had been herded into the Communist fold."[62]

There remained the meeting with Hemingway. Its serious political content would be negligible, Norman suspected, after what Scott had told him (and what he had also heard from Sid Perelman, who had recently met Hemingway in Africa and found him interested solely in the availability of young women). Despite his expectations and his reservations about Hemingway's writing, Norman was nevertheless slightly in awe of the encounter. He was driven to La Vigia, Hemingway's finca at San Francisco de Paula outside Havana, ringed by a high fence. Dropped a short distance from the house, he felt the force of the Hemingway legend, a part of which still elicited admiration:

it was Hemingway who had the courage and the vision to come out in support of the Spanish republican government when it was under attack not only by

Spanish rebels but by troops sent to Spain by Mussolini and by Hitler's Luftwaffe.
. . . He had pleaded with the English who had invented "non intervention" to
realise that their turn would be next. . . . Now, as I walked up to the door,
the driver at my heels, the great moment had come.[63]

Politically and in every other sense, the meeting was a disastrous
disappointment. Hemingway received him in a bedroom, in pyjamas,
mumbling, and lumberingly offered him a drink. He poured himself a
full tumbler of neat Dubonnet and gulped half of it down. To Norman's
cautious questions – about his next book, where Castro's rebellion
might end – he answered suspiciously, angrily, finally evasively. He
finished his drink and poured himself another. There was "exhaustion
and emptiness in his face: the corners of his mouth were dragged down
by what might have been despair, and his eyes gave the impression that
he was trying to weep". Later Norman connected the stumbling, depleted
figure in front of him with one of Hemingway's own characters, the
revolutionary figurehead Massart from *For Whom the Bell Tolls*; as
the chief commissar of the International Brigade, an aged ideologue
who only believes in betrayals. Shocked by the transformation of a
writer who in his imagination had remained "boisterous and vigorous
– a moving spirit in the never-ending fiesta of life", Norman wrote in
his notebook that he was "amazed that this man who must have seen
so many people defeated by age, power and success and have written
so convincingly about them should have fallen into the trap set by life".
Hemingway showed him the letter he had written to the *Havana Post*
declining Scott's challenge "in the belief that he owed it to his readers
not to jeopardise his life", a response Norman privately recoiled from.
When Norman asked him how he saw the present unrest ending, his
refusal to comment again signified to Norman how far he had fallen.
"My answer to that," Hemingway told him, "is I live here."

Norman's account of the meeting probably contains little exaggeration. Hemingway and his wife Mary had been in bed with influenza
shortly before Norman's arrival, which may excuse his appearance in
pyjamas, but Hemingway's steepening downward path into alcoholic
schizophrenia that finished with his suicide in 1961 had been under
way for several years. On Norman the encounter had a profound effect.
Ambitiously courting literary recognition, socially he withdrew into
shyness at the slightest provocation. Hospitable and flamboyant among
a small circle of friends whom he trusted at Berlemont's and Orchard

Street, among strangers he married a suburban boy's foundation of inferiority to a writer's scorn for the general stupidity of polite society. He forced himself to enjoy cocktail parties, generally left early. He was nervous of celebrity well before he met Hemingway in Cuba. The meeting transformed doubt into a profound precept. For the rest of his life he retold the encounter as one of his key stories, referring to it as "an experience which was to change my outlook on life, not instantly but slowly over a period of time".[64] In his autobiography he quotes a letter he wrote to Ian Fleming directly after the meeting. Although he almost certainly didn't write the letter at the time but composed it for his memoir – he communicated with Fleming mostly by phone and cable – it conveys to the reader with as much finality as he felt the erasure of illusions that the moment represented.

There was something biblical about the meeting with Hemingway, like having the old sermon on the vanities shoved down your throat in the middle of whatever you happen to be doing with your life in the workaday world. They give funny names to the buses in this town and there's one that runs past the hotel that says "We just ran short of greatness", which just about sums him up, although perhaps understating the case. This man has had about everything any man can ever have wanted, and to meet him was a shattering experience of the kind likely to sabotage ambition – which may or may not be a good thing. You wanted to know his opinion on the possible outcome of what is happening here. The answer unfortunately is that he no longer cares to hold opinions, because his life has lost its taste. He told me nothing, but he taught me more even than I wanted to know.[65]

From Cuba Norman travelled on to the Dominican Republic and Haiti. He had a nose for political sickness as well as revolutionary upsurge. Both places were small playing big, and put him in front of canvases of interesting historical bizarreness. In both he extracted, as in Guatemala, the kernel of the country's mess from a crucial recent event. The vanishing the previous year of Dr Jesus de Galíndez, a Dominican dissident academic, in broad daylight at a Manhattan subway station, and an ensuing surreal US murder inquiry during which every witness died or was assumed murdered by President Trujillo's henchmen, gave him the opportunity to execute literary judgment on the Trujillo dictatorship in his most impassively ironic style (mentioning Trujillo's largesse to his bloated family clan, he writes that "Never can there have been such a family man since Pope Alexander VI"). In Haiti his absurdist description of the spectacle of 25 May 1957, with "badly armed, badly trained men making a botch of murdering each other" in Port-au-Prince's Champ de Mars, allowed him to go deeply into Haiti's accentuation of the Caribbean's ills, in particular the colour conflict. The subsequent articles he wrote have little to do with travel writing. They are instead investigative essays, rhetorically disciplined, tending towards Swiftian grotesque but with a more deadpan humour, that mark the beginning of a non-fiction method in which the author's personal role, hardly pronounced before, is reduced to the thinnest thread. The rest is two parts present, as acerbically pared reportage, one part past (succinct historical analysis), and a last part of timeless irony, in which the entrenchment of folly in human affairs is ubiquitous. He deeply enjoyed writing about history; this was another way of doing it. The result is a style he would use to lasting impact in his two main non-fiction works of the 1960s, his historical investigation of the Sicilian mafia, *The Honoured Society*, and his 1969 *Sunday Times* article "Genocide", about the extermination of Brazil's Indians.[66]

He was becoming adept at moving between journalism and books, writing for the *Sunday Times* and *New Yorker* between writing novels. His novelist's instinct was at full stretch in his reporting. (In the 1950s, print media, not entirely infected by breathless magazine culture, also allowed journalists the same potentialities as writers.) Norman was becoming expert at the factual background while bringing to bear the persuasion of his richly textured, ironised and understeered style, infinitely sober, lushly humorous, in a nuanced political view that, because he was an autodidact outsider, was profoundly personal in its humanity. A paradox of the 1950s is that, alongside all the possibilities of serious journalism, for most Western newspaper and magazine readers the decade centred around the Cold War and its rebarbative polarities that in Britain thoroughly infected everyday thought. Basil Davidson, working at the *Daily Mirror*, recalls the Cold War as "an endless disaster because it turned serious conversation into subjects which were not serious at all: are you for the Americans or not? And the only way in which you could handle it was to sail through it as though it didn't matter, as though it wasn't there. Of course this was an impossible situation for most people. If you worked for the *Daily Telegraph* for instance, you can't imagine what the *Telegraph* was like in those days. Really dreadful, really dreadful." Norman made light of the Cold War – the phrase almost never makes it into his writing – and disparaged its institutional lunacy, seeking instead to understand piece by piece a few of its component parts (the revolutionary movements of Latin America, or US policy in the Caribbean). The result, Davidson says, was that

It was wonderful to find somebody who knew more about the things that interested me than I did, and he did. I mean that he understood the transatlantic situation, he understood what was happening in Cuba, he understood what might be happening, how you could possibly explain Guevara and other[s] without falling into some ridiculous attitude of unlimited admiration. And then of course he lived, from an ordinary intellectual middle class point of view, in a very unusual way. They couldn't follow him. They didn't care what had happened in the Caribbean forty years ago, they didn't care whether or not it had been wise to follow the attitude of the British government towards Cuba, for instance.

I don't think we ever had serious talks about writing. [We had] serious talks about how you would react to this and this . . . the big subject must have been how we were going to get out of the mess we were in, not we personally but the country. The Cold War was a disaster for all of us, including the Americans, perhaps more for the Americans who didn't understand what was happening to them. It was no good talking about it because if you said it was a disaster, the answer would be, "Are you a Communist?" It happened that I wasn't a Communist [but] I could see quite clearly that this was going to be a disaster unless some good stroke of fortune would come and stop the wheels of history from turning, and they did do that.

One of the reasons I became attached to Norman, and vice versa I think, was that . . . he regarded the Cold War as a ridiculous, absurd invasion of our privacy which the British government and others here took seriously. You couldn't take it seriously, not if you had your head screwed on. If those crazy Americans want to take that line, that's their affair. Don't expect us to follow. The Cold War brought us together . . . one of the reasons we found each other congenial [was] because we both ignored it or pretended it wasn't there, with the way it had of reducing all conversation to the idiotic binary of "Are you pro-American or anti-American?" It was a mad time. It killed off interesting thoughts, interesting people, interesting ideas and introduced this dreadful thing of "Are you for or are you against?" That is to say, are you for whatever policies Washington happened to be advancing? And if you were not, why were you not?[67]

Norman came back from the Caribbean satisfied. His sponsor was more than satisfied with the results of his intelligence-gathering. Fleming published the first of his articles, "Haiti – the Caribbean Africa", in the *Sunday Times* on 16 February. He and Norman tried to arrange to meet but kept missing each other. In March Norman flew to Algeria where as part of his sequence of novels with revolutionary settings he wanted to set a new book; an idea that had germinated after his 1956 flight to Algiers to rescue Lesley. On 17 March Fleming wrote

Dear Norman, Please contact and have lunch as soon as you get back, as I am off again the first week of April.

    I thought the articles were <u>splendid</u>, but we will talk of those when we meet.[68]

    The Caribbean journey signalled a change in Norman's routine. For the next two years he did not (if only by his own standards) travel as much or for long. The consolidation of his life with Lesley needed more of his presence in England, and in spring 1958 he and Lesley moved out of Orchard Street again to stay with Frank Allen and his wife Crokie in a flat in their ramshackle Georgian house at Leytonstone. At Whipps Cross Road they were on the right side of London to look again for a house. Their search the previous summer had produced no result, partly because of Norman's height: all the village houses they had seen in Suffolk and Essex had had dangerously low door lintels. Another benefit of staying at the Allens' was that, when Norman did travel, Lesley had Crokie Allen's company. They were already friends and the year before had gone to the Edinburgh Festival together to see Crokie's son Mark act with his schoolfriend Derek Jacobi in *Hamlet*. At Edinburgh Lesley, curious about Norman's other life, had suggested she and Crokie take a train along Deeside. Inevitably, as soon as they got off the train at Banchory they saw Hester and Karen in the distance. Crokie Allen told Lesley to get straight back on the train, which she did.

    For the rest of 1958, apart from his commitments to R G Lewis and in Scotland and Ibiza as usual for the summer (the first at the new beach house at La Caleta), Norman devoted himself to beginning his Algerian novel, assembling the pieces that would make up a collection Cape would publish the following June, and to Lesley's and his domestic situation. At the end of June they celebrated his fiftieth birthday, he bought them a new car, a Ford Zephyr convertible (the Buick was sent north to be garaged at Banchory), and they again rented the house at Wendens Ambo for the summer months and again failed to find somewhere to buy. In late September when they returned to the Allens', Ito (who had been at a summer school in Guatemala) began an anthropology degree at the London School of Economics, moving to share a flat in Chelsea.

In November Norman had a letter from Tran Van Dinh, a Vietnamese friend at the consulate-general at Rangoon, encouraging him to return – "The situation in this part of the world is becoming more interesting and might be inspiring to you. There are volcanoes here not only above us but below us"[69] – but he kept his feet on British ground until Castro's complete victory in Cuba in January 1959, and likely later, aside from his usual rejection of England at Christmas when he, Lesley and Ito flew to Barcelona for New Year. They had a hedonistic few days. Lesley remembers "we had to be poured onto the plane" home.[70]

He later organised together, with a little hindsight, his impressions of Castro's new Havana: the civic solicitude and courtesy deployed by Castro's warriors to persuade sceptics of their good intentions, the very gradual fading of the capital's fiesta mood and takeover by a Communist Calvinism, combined with the undisturbed business of paid-for sex provided by many of the city's 6000 laundresses (such were apparently several of the liaisons JFK enjoyed when he quietly weekended on the island), the new government's snowballing enthusiasm for nationalisation and its justice for war criminals, most of whom were small fry too poor or uninfluential to flee the country in the chaos of defeat, and so on. Many of these impressions could not have been had in early 1959 – it was simply too early – and are either misremembered or another finesse of his timetable, belonging to a later visit in April 1960. He may not even have visited Cuba that January, as his autobiography had it. In April he published two full-page essays in the *Sunday Times* on Castro's revolution, but both were based on his Caribbean journey of sixteen months earlier.[71]

The reason he was probably not in Cuba that January was that he and Lesley had at last found a possible house. On 24 January, staying with friends,[72] they had looked at a former parsonage for sale at the nearby village of Finchingfield, where the downland meets the edge of the mute Essex plain. "The Parsonage House" had been on the market for months, its remoteness and uncared-for look putting most buyers off. To Norman its isolation was an immediate virtue. Finchingfield was served by one bus a day and a railway line (stopping a dozen kilometres away) that ran some of the filthiest and least punctual trains this side of the Balkans: it conformed to his belief that the preservation of the way of life of the places where he travelled most happily was generally abetted by abusive governments, malaria and poor communications.

The house's other virtues he underplayed. The Parsonage House may have looked ragged, its roof ready to slide earthwards, but it had originally been a medieval hall-house and was now a spreading gabled and pargeted building with an outbreak of high chimneys and a falling-down barn at the side. Most of its ceilings and lintels could accommodate his height, and it appealed to the pastoralist in him with its sweep of overgrown garden and stream at the garden's end, and to the historian: a local builder pointed out to him what looked like thirteenth-century bricks. It also hooked the Romantic. Inspecting its rooms, he looked out of a window and saw a Green woodpecker feeding on the lawn: the only bird in England that can be mistaken for a parrot escaped from its aviary, bright green and yellow with a bright red head. He clapped his hands decisively. "We'll take it, this is the place we're going to have."[73]

The following Friday, 30 January, the vendor accepted £4250 for the house. This was reduced to £4000 a couple of days later due to the "land being less than described", but Norman, careful with money, was not done. A survey reported the presence of a rare species of beetle in the house's oak frame that would be impossible to remove. The beetles later became a favourite way of introducing the house to visitors. The builder, called to advise, had "scraped and tapped ... then examined the powdery detritus. ... 'They're still there,' he said, 'but why bother? Whatever you do this house will outlast you and a few generations of your descendants.' He held a nail against the wood and struck at it with a heavy hammer, the nail bent but left no more than a mark on the beam."[74] Norman held the immovable beetle over the negotiations for a month until, on 4 March, the beaten seller slashed the price. On the 23rd Norman and Lesley completed the purchase for £3250, moving in a few days later.

Why was it another house, the House of the Mooring-Posts on Ibiza, that was "always looked for" but allowed to slip through his fingers (and at 40 pesetas a square metre he could have bought it three times over), while the Parsonage was where he chose to live for the next forty-four years? One reason is that at Ses Estaques Norman anchored his mobile imagination too well in reality. After years of pursuing his quest Ses Estaques *was* freedom, liberty of action, doing as he pleased. The escape reflex had found its destination. The Romantic had attained his goal: Ses Estaques' walls and its glittering shore, its ruined arch and shushing scoop of bay, were the walls and shore and archway and bay of his lost domain.

But to keep one's lost domain, having found it, is not victory but defeat. The escaper's destination is merely a place whence he or she can escape again, very soon (in Norman's case, England each time). The secret is not to find the lost domain but to *not* find it, and keep on searching. Otherwise what hitherto has always pulled you on – in Norman's own formulation of his childhood "the idea that the farther I was from home the better it would be" – becomes "home", the converse of the quest, and you stop caring to be pulled on. So Norman willingly saw Ses Estaques slip through his fingers and chose instead the best place for him to live: a place to put up with the world comfortably until his reflex got to work on him again.

The Parsonage also provided him with an increasing measure of comfort and calm, adding to the stabilising process that Lesley had started. It was only after moving to Finchingfield that he found any kind of comfortable routine, writing, when he was there, in the mornings from around nine-thirty until one, and after lunch going for a walk around the village with his notebook or spending hours in the garden. (Not as good a gardener as he sometimes made out, he admitted to the "purely snobbish foible" of collecting esoteric and often impossible species that were cared for with extravagant precautions before they died, but he became a lover of lilies, stuffing the conservatory with them, and a member of the Royal Horticultural Society's Lily Group. Later he also took to ordering, and reading, plant catalogues in secret, away from his family's mockery.) When working on a book he wrote seven days a week, though almost never in the afternoon. In his quiet suburban rasp that never completely lost the Enfield "oi", he once described this unwinding typically self-deprecatingly but with a rhetoric of archaism, humility and comic double negative that (typically) vaporised the self-deprecation. "If I can muster up the energy, I sort of go over it and correct bits of [what I've written], but all the main work goes on in the morning. At the end of that time I can take on any sort of average job but, insofar as it is not impertinent to talk about creative powers, I have none."[75]

The Changing Sky, his first non-fiction book for seven years, was published a few weeks after the move to Finchingfield. In an epigraph, a poem by Horace that also supplied the title, he showed he had understood at least part of his escape reflex.

> They change their sky, not their soul, who run
> across the sea . . .
> . . . when o'er the world we range
> 'Tis but our climate, not our mind we change.
> What active inactivity is this,
> To go in ships and cars to search for bliss!
> No; what you seek, at Ulubrae you'll find,
> If to the quest you bring a balanced mind.[76]

The mostly previously published pieces covered experiences dating back to his time at Philippeville in 1943 up to the latest of his Spanish and Cuban journeys. To forestall any slippage of his reputation, he subtitled the collection "Travels of a novelist". The book's reviewers tended to take the pieces themselves rather than his self-definition at face value, but praised it abundantly. Norman was, accidentally, right to want to set himself apart at the time: a travel-writing boom, its bubble of mediocrity looming, was evident on literary editors' desks. "The sun surely never sets", the *Times* reviewer wrote, "on a figure with notebook and indelible pencil jotting down impressions for a travel book." The writer's worst fault, either knowing or innocent, was to be over-eager to impress. "Mr Norman Lewis in *The Changing Sky* is one of the knowing ones. . . . It says much for his good manners and skill that he does not put us against him. Instead he leaves us quite free of an inferiority complex and admiring him for having compressed into these always entertaining and sophisticated sketches material that a duller man would have hoarded for half a dozen books."[77] (The point about Norman's good manners: it's an important one, the *urbanidad* of a writer contributing as much as that of a Guatemalan *machetero*, and as much as his skill or talent or any other description of competence, to time's refinement of his reputation.)

Despite the subject matter Alan Ross, writing in the *Times Literary Supplement*, went back – again – to his favourite topic, Norman's shortcomings as a novelist, though he finally admitted "how good he is as a reporter, how unobtrusive, yet inquisitive and alert". His "somewhat sweaty route . . . sets Mr Lewis apart from our guzzling European

sybarites, our conventional culture-mongers, our slaves of boredom.
He is to be envied and congratulated."[78] V S Pritchett, an admirer of
Norman's novels, wrote in the *New Statesman*

He knows what he wants to see. He can put down the essence of a place; he
is piquant, enterprising and concentrated. He is also embarrassed. That is excellent: the world has become an embarrassing place ... he really goes in deep
like a sharp polished knife. I have never travelled in my armchair so fast, variously and well.[79]

The book sold very reasonably for a collection, more than 4000
copies in hardback by the end of the year, and today it seems less,
rather than more, like a collection of pieces struggling with a freight
of out-of-date political information. Its vanished topicality allows it to
be read without excessive effort as a series of very reliable parables on
twentieth-century progress, power, prosperity, democracy, religion,
romance, hubris and similar false gods and cockinesses.

Norman was pleased by the reviews but I don't think they were his
central concern. His new novel was progressing slowly, and he was
becoming frustrated by how long it took him to write fiction. This is
an almost certain surmise, given the time it took him – two years – to
get his Algerian novel finished to his and Cape's satisfaction, and the
crisis that came after it. That summer followed the usual pattern. He
drove Hester, Ito, Karen, Gareth to La Caleta in the Ford convertible
and flew back every few weeks to see Lesley and look after the business, which, still expanding, had needed and had his attention in the
past two years. Simultaneously he was starting to tire of its demands
in tandem with a waning interest in his own photography. As well as
the R G Lewis branches around the country, and Lewis Newcombe,
he had opened a new colour-processing lab in the West End; but *The
Changing Sky* had been his last book routinely to include his own
photographic work and in 1959 his membership of the RPS lapsed.
Like Baudelaire and Ruskin, his passion had come down on the side
of words' more modellable truth.

He worked on his novel, dropped its title, "The Avengers", after
Michael Howard wrote to him at Santa Eulalia rejecting it, and drove
back to England in September with an unfinished manuscript. At
Finchingfield he found that Ito, or rather Ito's mother, had a problem
for him. Ito had decided to give up the LSE after one year, about which

Norman was philosophical but Ernestina so much less so that in a long letter she took several swipes at her ex-husband, calling him "stingy and thoughtless. . . . You and I both know that you are well fixed as they say", and accusing him from every angle, from his failure to give Ito an allowance to his alleged refusal to respond fully to him emotionally, of taking insufficient care of their son. "Although a fine writer, you can be at times insensitive to the point of callousness," she wrote.[80] To read Ernestina's letters now is, I think, to see a nervous mother attempting to balance anxiety with reasonableness and not fully succeeding, rather than a rancorous ex-wife.

In one of your letters you said that you thought your son might very well need to turn to his father someday and I scoffed. Well Norman, I believe that Ito needs you and your advice very badly now. I have no reason for wishing to increase his love for you, but it would be bad for him not to like you. I don't know what your personal rapport is but it must be good since he always speaks well of you, and on the rare occasion I make disparaging remarks, you should see with what alacrity he rises to your defence. . . . It would have been awful if he had been bitter when he became enmeshed in your strange life. . . . Please try to understand. Will you write and tell me how you left him. I am so terribly worried.
Friends?
Ernestina[81]

Norman was annoyed enough to wait four months before replying. When he did, his letter, setting out to reassure, contained an interesting domestic application of the belief put forward in his Diogenes-like foreword to *The Changing Sky*, that places and people are destroyed by the "flaccid and joyless prosperity" of the modern world. "Firstly this phenomenon [of dropping out] is a very common one in our times," he wrote to Ernestina.

Young people soon become dissatisfied with the affluent society, which although it guarantees every one a fair degree of comfort, or rather let's say security, whatever sort of effort one is prepared to put into one's life, is in the very nature of things basically unexciting. At a low level you have enormous numbers of Teddy Boys, Blue Boys, beats and layabouts of all descriptions filling the streets of industrial towns at night – just mooching. Higher up the scale you have students who get fed up with their courses. In great numbers. . . . Should he decide to give up the present line and come back to try something else, whatever it is, scholastically or otherwise he can always rely on me, and I'm sure that he knows this.[82]

More troublesome than his ex-wife was his novel. He finally finished it in late October, a couple of weeks before the Cape Christmas party ("I thought your party was magnificent", he wrote to Jonathan. "Twenty-four hours later I am still in its torpid aftermath! It was a memorable evening").[83] Cape were satisfied enough with the novel to agree to an increase in his royalties – he had never taken an advance from them, preferring to negotiate a favourable royalty deal – but in mid-December he was still "Doing a fair amount of rewriting"[84] and discussing the title. On 19 December the interim "On a New Frontier" was finally dropped for the more gripping *Darkness Visible* (it would have been hard to find a title less gripping).

Aside from literary frustration, the move to Finchingfield had begun to work a beneficent spell. In September, on his return from Spain, Lesley had become pregnant. As a result he arranged to spend Christmas at Banchory early that year, though he held back from telling Hester why (it was by far his most successful concealment that Hester still did not know Lesley existed), and travelled north for the last weekend of November. His visits continued regularly, though they were, increasingly obviously, for the children's sake. Gareth, sent to Lathallan boarding school at the age of eight, remembers the annual expedition to liberate a Christmas tree.

There was a kind of adventure thing with Dad . . . there's Christmas trees as far as the eye can see in Scotland and they're cheap to buy, but we had to go and hack one down from the Forestry Commission because it was an adventure. With an axe. That was fun. He used the expression that he "deputised" people to do his dastardly deeds. He actually used that word – we were deputised. He was the sheriff so we were the deputies, so we would go and do the dangerous stuff.[85]

Karen remembers hunting for ceps in the forests, and going with her father on what he called "think walks, where he'd take out his little scrappy notebook and his pen and go into the country and I would walk with him". Her father, in memory, dressed in a long black wool coat with deep poacher's pockets that served for many uses.

You know how he loved plants? He would take me to Crathies Castle, which was the local fine garden place, and he would carry a trowel in his pocket and he would pay me 50 shillings to dig up the plant of his choice. I didn't mind doing it but when it came to doing naughty things he was a little bit cowardly and I think the fear gave him the frisson of excitement. With this great long black coat always, lurking behind a wall somewhere, he was meant to be the lookout while I did the digging. He thought if a child was caught doing it it would just be looked on as naughtiness, whereas a man of repute caught digging up this stuff. . . . It never entered my head to ask him which garden this was for, or where he was taking it, because it obviously wasn't for our garden.

I never remember my mother going, never. It must have been a bit demoralising to Mum to think that he had more fun with his daughter, or he had more in common with his daughter.

I still remember [his long coat] being hung up where it was. And to my shame, because I thought my mother was badly done by, I used to pinch the change out of the pockets. That's how I knew how deep the pockets were.

Her father also used Banchory as a base for finding furniture for the Parsonage at better prices than in London.

Auntie Docie was very good at spotting antiques, and he would get her to go round and buy [them], and they too would be shipped away and nobody would say to themselves, "Oh, well if they're not coming to this home, where are they going?" I think he said, "It's for a friend."[86]

Whether or not he flew to Cuba in late December, as one collection of journalism has it – nearly certainly he misremembered the date as he would have had hardly more than a week (or he may have wanted it thought that he was away) – the first documented Caribbean return took place three months later. On 25 April 1960, again through Ian Fleming at MI6's instigation, he flew to New York.

This time he went on to Washington before continuing to Havana and finally to Panama. He was away for nearly three weeks, his mission more sensitive by a wide margin than before. At a time when there was no official contact between the USA and Cuba, his briefing for the second visit, as he disclosed in a private letter much later, was to visit Washington and discuss the impasse with members of the State Department (meetings that indicate a high level of cooperation between MI6 and the CIA on the Cuba question).

It seems somewhat fantastic that, despite Cuba having signed its first aid agreements with the Soviet Union a month earlier, in March 1960, the people Norman saw at State "insisted that the US had accepted that the Cuban revolution was purely nationalist, with no desire to provoke conflict elsewhere, and that the US's sole concern was to obtain fair treatment for dispossessed nationals. I was to present this viewpoint to the Cubans in the hope that discussions could begin."[87] In Havana a few days later he saw Enrique Oltuski, the young Minister of Communications, "who was both conciliatory and receptive to the point of enthusiasm".

Oltuski promised to arrange a subsequent meeting with Che Guevara and possibly Castro but a few days later telephoned Norman to say the meeting would have to be postponed "owing to unexpected developments that had arisen". Norman later found out that these "developments" took the form of information the Cuban government had received about preparations for the Bay of Pigs invasion. The USA, inevitably, was playing a double game. The Cubans' information at least proved the admirable quality of their intelligence gathering, acquiring it within six weeks of Eisenhower's first agreement to the CIA's invasion proposal on 17 March and nearly a year before the abortive invasion took place. By asking Norman to act as its intermediary the State Department had set him up as a patsy. The experience probably did little to alter his views of US foreign policy or of CIA activity, but any negative statements he made about either subsequently at least bore a stamp of personal exposure.

He spent the rest of his Cuban stay seeing as much as he could of the consequences of Castro's accession, in particular the trials of alleged war criminals. (In the course of attending the trials he agreed to interview Castro's executioner, a prolix, self-justifying American named Marks, and afterwards effectively ventriloquised Marks's wheedling tone in a monologue for the *New Statesman*.) At the end of his 1957 trip he had felt that Castro, if he gained power, might well outlast Batista. This time on his return he told Fleming that he saw nothing to change his view – possibly repeating his last-minute "Author's Note" to *The Changing Sky* that "Cuba with Castro in control remains Cuba". He bumped into Hemingway again in a bar a couple of months before the author, his disintegration accelerating, left Cuba for the last time. "I saw him get this crayfish and chew it so he crunched up the shell. All his blood would run down his chin. Ridiculous."[88] "Quite secretly" he also found a Cuban girlfriend. "Unfortunately it was an extremely short time," he told Pico Iyer thirty years later. "I made the acquaintance of this marvellous, marvellous girl," he added, briefly lapsing into questionable social philosophy. "As you probably know, the Cubans paid more than any other slave buyers. That is why the Cubans are such handsome people. The [plantation owners] only bought the most handsome men and women, at 50 per cent over the market rate."[89]

Another meeting was with two of the last surviving soldiers from Cuba's war of independence against Spain, the elderly generals Loynaz and García Velez, In his autobiography he describes Loynaz and García Velez: they are in their nineties, and García Velez, former ambassador to Britain and converted pacifist, lives in a re-creation of a Victorian London apartment surrounded by aspidistras. He also possesses an album which he shows to Norman, inherited from his relative, the Venezuelan revolutionary Francisco de Miranda, and containing fifty-one snippings of the pubic hair of his female conquests. All "much of a muchness", Velez admits, apart from one "little ragged tuft" identified only by the signature "K".

"Catherine," Loynaz murmured reverently.
Velez nodded. "The Great Queen."[90]

The album is a delightful one-time eccentricity, composed years after the event (Catherine the Great's imperial wisp does not make it into a *New Statesman* article, "Two Generals", that Norman published in July 1960). But for all their questionable accessories, the generals provide Norman with the opportunity for a striking analysis of Castro's revolt. Nothing to do with Marxism, Velez tells him. It happened because the Americans snapped up all the decent land and the Cuban middle class was left without prospects. Fidel had started out as a lawyer, but his few clients were too poor to pay; the "present bother" was sparked by nothing more than an increase in bus fares. Therein lay the trigger of the Cuban revolution: "University drop-outs who refused to walk".[91]

He flew on to Panama City for the presidential election, which unhelpfully had placed the country, and all travel, under an interdict. In intelligence terms Panama was a washout; he could not see anybody and wasn't there for long enough. In desperation visiting a tourist agent, so he later claimed, for the first time in his life, to try to see something, he signed up for a tour to visit the country of the indigenous

Choco Indians. The account he wrote later of the journey, "High Adventure with the Chocos of Panama (six hours required)", contains little politics but is instead a farcical subversion of the usual travel article, taking aim in every direction at the expectations and corruptions of the tourist industry – which may be why it stayed unpublished for twenty-five years. The Chocos, no longer remarkable, were a shrunken, decaying group who had learned the market value of being photographed naked (four dollars), and the real high adventure was the journey back downriver in a hellish rainstorm. "When the rain started in real earnest, it seemed to close in on us until we were in a prison-cell of water. . . . Dominguín's canoe, only a few yards ahead, had vanished. . . . I found it helped to hold a hand over my nostrils to avoid breathing water."[92] He floundered to the bank after his canoe sank beneath him in the swollen rapids, to the sound of his impassive Indian guides finally laughing.

He was back in London in mid-May, a few days before the publication of *Darkness Visible*. Although he claimed later to have forgotten he had written it,[93] he had accumulated more nervous hopes about his new novel than before. After five novels he now badly wanted to produce the breakthrough of recognition that had tantalisingly, despite growing sales and the acclaim he had had for *The Volcanoes Above Us*, stayed outside his reach. He had impressed on Cape the need to do more with the book, and *Vogue* had bought an extract to coincide with publication. The novel is noticeably better edited and presented than its predecessors, with a consciously modernist jacket design by Denis Piper and a thoughtful jacket blurb written by Norman that attempted to position him in 1960 as a figure justifiably viewed as not only in the Greene and Ambler category but also the newer Braine, Sillitoe and Burgess category of younger novelists associated with social confrontation.

But that was part of the problem. The attempt to occupy both camps clarifies how much the territory of the English novel was redefining itself, coming home from adventure and abroad to "the marvellous world of the ordinary".[94] The experiential thriller, the genre novel turned to high literary ends that had been set in motion by Greene and Ambler (it was a form defined by motion, travel, elsewhere), was giving way to the first of the late twentieth century's realisms: the urban realism of working- and suburban-class life as it existed in post-war Britain. Norman had stayed decisively interested in the wider world at a time when, in literary terms, the world had adopted local-vernacular, manual-industrial, social-reformist interests. Yet *Darkness Visible* is one of Norman's best constructed novels, its story of a group of European and American oilmen attempting to exploit a valuable oilfield during Algeria's long-running civil war a persuasive fictional anatomisation of a "clash of cultures". It is a text that in some magnificent descriptions of rural Algeria, of the ambiguities and menaces of Arab-French cohabitation, and of Arab customary life and its fatalistic aftermath in the face of catastrophe elucidates as closely as a Western atheist ever might the foundation and attractions of Muslim life. This is a passage about the Arabs' attachment to water.

Water, I thought. A good supply of water – that was all an Arab really asked for in the way of living conveniences. They were connoisseurs and lovers of water. They treated it with respect, almost with veneration, and the uncivilized ones from the mountains still apologized to the great benign spirit that inhabited it when they washed their private parts before prayers. When an Arab came into money he would put a fountain in his house and have water running where he could see it.[95]

Steve Lavers, the mildly cynical oilman at the centre of the narrative, has (like Norman himself) attractive observational and analytical powers. He has the sympathy, you feel, to turn the oilfield and even the story around when, inevitably, the murders of European settlers – the local brothel-keeper, his French wife and a guest – are used as an excuse for reprisals against the Arabs, but he is led into collusion with the oil company's interests. In the novel's concerns about the sincere affront to Islam caused by Western practice, about the West's uncomprehending imposition of its civilisation on the Arab world, and about the "black blood" of modernity – oil – it is a prescient, even astonishingly prescient, analysis not just of the Algerian war but of a capital conflict of the next fifty years. As Lavers' Muslim friend Kobtan tells him, the West does not understand, or want to understand, that Western notions of progress do not resonate in a Muslim culture.

Kobtan smiled. "As a Muslim I am compelled to accept that even the assassins who burned our town yesterday were no more than tools in the hand of God. The peace Colonel Latour [the novel's French peace-broker] gave us has been taken away. His experiment has failed. Why? We do not know, but can it not be that all those things that Colonel Latour would have given us are not necessarily the things that God intended us to have? If Colonel Latour had succeeded, our sons would have been educated with yours to think like yours, our daughters would have received the kind of emancipation your daughters receive. We should have had what you see as progress and what you call democracy. But, Mr Lavers, cannot you possibly understand that these ideals are not those of Islam, and that we believe that by the sincere practice of our religion we can reach human perfection by a different road from yours?"[96]

Lavers' view of the Arabs is ethical, if simplistic. In his contempt for the fashionable support for their plight, expressed to his assistant, an echo can also be detected, I think, of Norman's own contempt for the fashions of the contemporary West (including the fashionable themes of contemporary British novelists?).

"I like the Arabs, too. In so far as they're victims of the present situation I'm on their side. Why, has the fashion for commitment come back again?"

"I don't know about the fashion. Most of us manage to have some sort of viewpoint these days, though."

"It's all fashion," I said. "The herd instinct dressed up. Viewpoints, and isms, and moral crusades, and adolescent anger, and salvation through copulation. It's only the herd being together. The howling of blue-arsed baboons in the forest."

"Does anything really affect you, Steve?"[97]

And there lies the other half of the problem. Nothing really does affect Lavers, not even the conscious delusion of love he feels for his girlfriend Helen. The relationship, despite Norman's felicitous description – "For a moment her weightless arms were around my neck" – never quite comes alive; and so their developing affair, and his eventual betrayal by her, does not affect the reader. Nor does the novel's conclusion, which seems more or less arithmetical. There is a curious, Baptist-like trait to Norman's novels that seems to indicate a belief of his that only diligent choreography of his plots and extended descriptive passages offer good value to the reader (novels have few prerequisites, and neither feature is one). *Darkness Visible* demonstrates that belief fully, yet despite the author's evident interest in his reader's needs and the richness and authenticity of his physical situations and characters' backgrounds, the reader is left to fluctuating degrees thirsting, emotionally unsatisfied.

The novel's reception hardly met Norman's ambitions for it. The tone was set by a short, uncommitted notice in *The Times*. "*Darkness Visible* is a thriller in the modern political vein but owing much to Buchan, set in Algeria. Mr Lewis writes with gusto, and all the descriptive gifts of a good newspaper correspondent."[98]

With hindsight it is easy to say that if Norman had more fully constructed his own agenda, made clearer the common identity of his novels as a fictional sequence reflecting on, as Cyril Connolly had it, "the meaning of civilisation and progress", he could have established himself as a more fully individual voice, and imposed his own view of his novelistic technique as expressed in the jacket blurb for *Darkness Visible*. "His method", he wrote (about himself), "is the opposite of the school of Somerset Maugham in that, although deeply concerned with the secret motives of the human heart, he is aware, by personal observation, of the social, racial and political background of his characters."

But the question hanging hugely in the air in that statement can only lead us straight back to where we were: to our own impression of what it was that stopped Norman from becoming the complete novelist he so ambitioned to be in the 1950s. Which is that, without much room for doubt, he remained a hostage to the shell he had cast around himself at Forty Hill. Choosing not to deal then with emotions that might have overwhelmed him but to survive instead, fifty years later he was still unable to go very far into himself, and so could not imagine himself fully into the human interiors of his characters.

Whatever he himself felt, in August that year he came to the same general conclusion, that he was not, at least temporarily, a novelist. He had already started a novel set in Ibiza when *Darkness Visible* was published, and he took it with him to La Caleta for the summer. From there on 12 August he wrote to Michael Howard at Cape

I have stopped work on the novel, or at least paused – as they say on the Stock Exchange – for reflection. The fact is, I am dissatisfied with my progress as a novelist, and am beginning to wonder if I am not wasting rather a lot of my life grinding out books for which there is not a very large potential readership.[99]

His reaction at the setback was not to renew the depressions of the past. After the melancholy of his war's end and return to peace, he had reclaimed enough enjoyment of life during the 1950s not to be destabilised again. From his operating base at Orchard Street he had made the most of his post-war business winnings, and with them the most of the 1950s' unconfinedness, its limited bureaucracy and loosening structures, its lack of crowds and cars and advertising, its sense of an unoppressed, airy physical world, breathable and meditable, always reachable; had succeeded in fact in summoning and enjoying a decade of such discreet, self-pleasing freedom and glamour (in retrospect there is no other word) it compels the conclusion that for himself he made the 1960s happen ten years early. At such a moment – as he might have observed himself in his murmured drill-sergeant's rasp – it was a not inconsiderable irony that one of the strengths he had got from his childhood's emotional deficit, his really strikingly successful ability to direct his own life, did not allow him to pause for long on the discouragement but started him thinking about a new direction.

Yet a sinew of stubbornness remained. If there is one theme that plays through Norman's writing life after 1960 and the maturity of the books to come, it is that of his perceived failure as a novelist and his need – or that of the Welsh Calvinist in him – to keep returning to try to crack the problem.

The president has a niece – in her early thirties – who has decided to separate Rafael and me, because he is much too nice for an old hag like me, and would be much better off married to her – she sees herself as an ambassador's wife. As a start she sent me a venomous little note informing me that he had a Mexican mistress, which I know is not true, and even if it were, I would not care anyway. Seeing that this did not work, she got going on some really fancy scurrilous stuff.

Ernestina Aparicio

I still remember the embarrassment, so does my brother. She would always be saying snide remarks, "Oh but of course you love children, don't you Normie?" And always digging and making references. It's dreadfully embarrassing to children, it's horrendously embarrassing to teenagers which we were at that time.

She could have had other men. There were men who given half the chance would have plighted their troth or paid suit to her or asked her out or do whatever you did that was socially acceptable in those days when courting a lady of an age whose husband has gone, or who hasn't even got one. But I don't know whether she'd have looked upon that as an admission of defeat. I remember what she used to say a lot to me. "Look at all the sacrifices I've made for you." As if staying in Banchory and not following Norman was an excuse to remain negative about life.

Karen Holman

It cannot be claimed that in the years following the publication of Norman Lewis's book the mafia has been defeated, or even held in check. Indeed some economists forecast that in Sicily the mafia economy will, in the end, expel the normal one, as it extends its empire even further into business, banking, and drugs.

Marcello Cimino

22

SECRET STATES

"It's impossible to hold two watermelons in one hand"
Azerbaijani proverb

IN spring and summer 1960 the alterations to Norman's life were intended to move towards the matters a biographer can record with pleasure and with a trace of regret at their absence of drama: the deep satisfactions of life with Lesley, a third sequence of fatherhood, establishment at Finchingfield, a reconsideration of his writing. But Norman's "strange life", as Ernestina accurately had it (the only thing she omitted was how big a part of its strangeness she was), fought back hard against a too well-organised course of things, and the fifteen months from March 1960 to May 1961 offered more beginnings and ends, and more disorder in between, than Norman might have thought he was entitled to. All his "wives" were involved, plus his publisher and, in a hardly necessary embellishment, another of the spectral figures who peopled his thirty-year association with Britain's intelligence services.

His letter to Ernestina drew an instant response on 8 March. She told Norman he had reassured her about Ito and "what a comfort it was to receive your letter, and I am happy that I was wrong in thinking that a dingy soul shambled behind your bright exterior". But the bulk of her 3000-word reply was an urgent plea for help in another area. Few things were ever not urgent with Ernestina. This time she and Rafael were in serious trouble. A niece of President Ydígoras Fuentes, a schoolteacher and "silly little bitch [who] also practises black magic", was attempting to force Ernestina and Rafael to divorce in order that she could marry Rafael. Having failed to persuade Ernestina that Rafael had a mistress, she threatened to denounce Ernestina as a Communist if she did not comply. As an example of how damaging such an accusation could be in Guatemala, Ernestina confessed to Norman that "when I knew that you were coming to Guatemala, I could have put you through some humiliating and harassing traces [sic] just *por molestar*. . . . The Allens told me that you were here, described the various trips you took, and never did I say anything against you, I just did not go out in the daytime not to bump into you."[1]

She begged Norman to obtain in London whatever documentary evidence he could to prove she had never been a member of the Communist Party but before she had his reply she wrote again, motivated by the horrors of her present situation into regretting her wilful escapes of the 1930s. "I should never have run away years ago from the truth and reality, and the squalor of Gordon Sq."[2] Norman was somehow able to reassure her that nothing damaging could be fished up in England, and on 18 April her confidence was restored enough to think of "preparing some batteries against the St Trinian's horror". She also offered Norman a warning about "how undermining skeletons in closets can be", telling him "For heaven's sake don't reveal any to your children – I really mean this".[3] That was all, for now. It was just the beginning.

He had a small trauma of his own to deal with. On 23 June Lesley gave birth to a healthy girl. Norman had arranged to be away, on a short trip to Cuba. Happening to be out of the country when your partner was giving birth was not felt to be particularly callous in the 1960s, but Norman's express preference for being so far away when his children were born is extreme, and oddly symbolic. There seems to be in it a correlation between the (dangerous) proximity of intense emotion and the urgency of escape, with flight planned for the precise moment when his emotions would be most fully involved. Though he welcomed being a father again, Lesley's giving birth was in one sense – the messy, emotional one – intolerable to him. One result of his absence was that their daughter got a Cuban name, Sarita (which first became "Squeaker", then Kiki). Sarita's birth, like Ernestina's muddle in Guatemala, was fated to have a powerful sequel.

On his return from Havana there was not much time to spend with Lesley or the baby; he was due in Ibiza in July. That may have been why he made particular arrangements for Lesley to write to him, giving her several envelopes with his Santa Eulalia address.

On 2 July "Two Generals" was published in the *New Statesman*. Three days later, before he left for Spain, taking his notebooks and the manuscript of the new (about to be put aside) novel, he had an interesting offer from a person he evidently knew.

25 STONEHILLS COURT
COLLEGE ROAD
DULWICH SE21
TELEPHONE GIPSY HILL 7717

4th July, 1960

My Dear Lewis,

I have been reminded by my secretary that you asked me to return to you the enclosed copy of your article which, rather belatedly, I am herewith doing.

The main purpose of this note, however, is to ask you in general terms whether you would be interested in making another trip to these parts, in particular Venezuela, during the next month or two. I was thinking of your having a look around Caracas for say 3/4 weeks apart from other excursions in the area. Do you think the S[unday] T[imes] would be sufficiently interested to engage themselves financially? If not, we for our part might be, and you and I could put our heads together on that score. If you are interested perhaps we could meet in town sometime convenient to you and discuss it further. Please keep it to yourself however meanwhile.

I will give you a ring in the next day or two at your town number.

Tim Frenken
(L A FRENKEN)[4]

This insight into Norman's relations with British intelligence (evidence, if any doubt remains, that he had relations) discloses his usefulness as a Latin American expert. "Tim" Frenken's role in the traditionally casual approach (the deniable Dulwich address, the undisclosed "we") is not clear. From 1940, possibly before, Frenken had been part of Claude Dansey's "Z" organisation, a network of business contacts channelling secret intelligence on Nazi intentions in Europe back to London. "Z" was so clandestine that no one at SIS headquarters except Sir Hugh Sinclair, the organisation's head, was aware of it; Frenken had been the "Z" agent at the all-important Basel, Switzerland border crossing. An educated guess is that like Ian Fleming, he continued to have a close advisory status after wartime service.

There are good reasons for the British government being interested in Venezuela in 1960. The CIA was producing anxious digests at the rate of one a month detailing Venezuela's volatile and, to the agency, ambivalent relations with Cuba (Venezuela hosted at the time more US investment capital than any other Latin American nation). It's hardly astonishing that SIS, in the person of Frenken, should seek out Norman to have "a look around Caracas" and try to bring light to bear on the CIA's confusion. Norman replied by return that it was probably too far for the *Sunday Times*, but "I should certainly be interested myself". Frenken wrote again, promising to "talk turkey" in a week's time, but nothing came of the discussion before Norman left for Ibiza.

The Ibizan summer of 1960 was different. It was inevitable, if only in retrospect. Stability and durability had been purchased at a high rate, and the artifices and secret-keeping of Norman's and Hester's domestic setup were wound unbearably tight after ten years of deception practised for various people's sakes (not just the children's). The holiday began without incident. Norman enjoyed Karen's and Gareth's company, Karen's particularly. In the last couple of years, with her growing taller and pre-pubescent, he had extended the range of his mischief making.

We would be walking in Barcelona and in those days of course you weren't allowed to make any passes at women, everything was very chaperoned. And I was blonde and quite, I suppose, curvy and we'd be walking together and Dad would suddenly drop away so I'd be walking on my own and a bloke would be coming towards me and I'd think, I know what's going to happen. So the bloke would start saying what he'd like to do and how many times and when and where, and then Mum would rush up and shout at him, "*Cerdos!*", which means "pigs". He used to find this endlessly amusing.[5]

How the crisis came about after they reached the island is not wholly clear. Hester's frustrations, like her suspicions, were running high. Given the opportunity to look upon more than Norman was telling her, she took it. "She was a mixture," Karen remembers, "a very sociable person, friendly and outgoing. But there was also another side to her. She was cunning."[6] As for the specific events of that August day, the surviving observers give eye-witness accounts that characterise it – outside its qualities of drama and violence – as a model *Rashomon* moment: accounts so conflicting that they mostly reflect the non-existence of a single truth.

To go first with the facts: at La Caleta one day, in Norman's absence, Hester walked to the *correos* in Santa Eulalia, up on the second street next door to the butcher. She collected the mail and noticed that one of the letters was addressed to Norman, in his own handwriting. She opened it and read it. The letter was from Lesley at Finchingfield. It told Norman her news and described how she was getting on with the new baby Sarita, "Squeaker".

After eight years the secret of Lesley's existence was out. And not just Lesley's but that of the daughter she and Norman had had.

When Norman arrived back at La Caleta, the row ignited. It was, both children (thirteen and twelve at the time) agree, an argument with all the explosive proportions of marital betrayal. It raged for hours, dying down for a time, flaring up again. But the children's accounts diverge in their details from the start. In Karen's version Norman was off the island on business and Hester (who for years when she was in a bad mood had accused him of having "another woman" but never had concrete proof) had to wait several days to confront him; the confrontation, when it happened, started in the morning when he arrived back off the ferry. By Gareth's account, the confrontation happened in the evening of the same day Hester read the letter.

The children's stories of the confrontation and quarrel itself are equally at odds. Karen remembers telling her mother that Gareth must not know the contents of the letter. She also firmly recalls that as the shouting went on, a handgun was brought out. She remembers "it was a small brown" gun and that her father "was always carrying guns". "A gun was brought out. I thought somebody was going to kill someone, one of them was going to kill the other. I'm not quite sure which way round it was, although you think to yourself, did you actually feel at the end of the day relief that this whole thing had come out now?"[7]

Gareth's version reveals a different scenario: that he knew everything, the letter, the row, the threats, and that when the shouting began to get out of hand his mother came to him and he fetched his own gun, an air rifle. "I think my father was getting very heated and eventually my mother rushed into the house and was crying and grabbed me and said, 'He's going to attack me or kill me', or something like that. So I got out of the house with her, grabbed the air rifle and we rushed off into the night together. Into the bushes, they had these quite short bushes with little pellets on them that we used to stick in the air rifle and shoot at each other. Dad wasn't coming after us. . . . "[8]

Karen believes it was not her brother and mother who rushed into the woods, but Norman and Hester, to take their argument elsewhere, out of earshot of the other beach houses. A point the children agree on is that eventually, though not for several angry hours, the argument finally died down not to be resuscitated – as if after exposure to air a hidden, long festering sore had finally burst. And for several years afterwards, the Ibiza summers continued. "Curiously enough, we still went on having these summer holidays," Gareth recalls. Karen remembers that afterwards it was not quite the same, that Hester "would never miss an opportunity to say [to my father], 'But of course you like little babies, don't you, you like children, don't you?' And Gareth and I used to cringe,"[9] and sometimes in later years Karen came home with her father alone. "Family" arrangements persisted between Norman and Hester for the children's sake until both were eighteen. But it was a permanent end to their parents' complicit pretence of a semi-detached marriage, and to the strangely durable sequel of their wartime affair. As Karen felt among her other reactions, it was a relief.

Discontents often come accompanied. Norman's frustration with his progress as a novelist in 1960 was attended by frustration with his publishers. He did not universalise Cape's liability but felt they could have done better for him: better dustjackets, more advertising, more subsidiary rights sales, more sales in bookshops; more recognition. On 17 December "Fidel's Artist", about the executioner Herman Marks, appeared in the *New Statesman*. A week earlier, Norman had stubbornly written to Michael Howard suggesting – with robust business sense – that the imminence of large-scale civil war in Algeria was an opportunity for additional advertising of *Darkness Visible*. Howard, ever gentle, responded and sent Norman a case of sherry as a Christmas present, for which Norman thanked him coolly early in the new year.

Both he and his publishers were unsettled: Cape with the death of Jonathan Cape in February 1960 – Norman was one of the few

authors who was invited to his funeral – to which they had reacted
by appointing an energetic 26-year-old, Tom Maschler, as managing
editor. Norman met Maschler the following spring and instantly disliked
him. He also felt that Maschler didn't like his kind of writing and
may have been annoyed at the suggestion that the extremely young
editor could teach him anything: "it is just possible", Maschler wrote
to him after their meeting, "that I may be able to make a helpful
suggestion or two and certainly nothing could be lost" by reading his
new work in progress.[10] Michael Howard wanted Norman to stay
with Cape and wrote two weeks later, urging him to accept an immediate £500 advance for the new book, but Norman in the same cool
language replied that he would rather postpone "until the book is
somewhat nearer completion". "The book" was the Ibiza novel he
had set aside. Nothing had come of his exchange with Tim Frenken
and he had stayed at Finchingfield that winter, apart from visits to
Banchory, and picked it up again. (Although it was more than twenty
years before Norman actually went to Venezuela, in 1983, and no
evidence of further contact with SIS exists, Norman had a high level
of welcome from British embassies and unusually close co-operation
with them when he travelled.)

At the point of reconsidering his career, with time and space (and
partner) to do so, in March 1961 Norman heard from Ernestina again.
Her tone was unusually calm. "What follows in this letter," she wrote,
"will be a demonstration that even in a backwash like Guatemala there
can be as much excitement as in any front line or Malaparte's Naples."

Since August the previous year, she said, Rafael had been increasingly worried and miserable. His mood had deteriorated, and after
making a will leaving half his estate to Ito, he had slashed his wrists.
When he recovered (Ernestina had found him in time), he had told her
after lengthy probing and pleading that the woman named Soledad,
the president's niece, was pregnant and he was the father. During
Ernestina's convalescence from an operation when she had been unable
to commit to sexual activity, he had drifted into an affair.

He wanted to end the affair, he told Ernestina. Boosted by her
forgiveness, he had informed the niece he had no intention of divorcing
his wife; the niece had retaliated by denouncing him as a Communist,
his and Ernestina's house had been surrounded by "over a hundred
troops all armed with machine guns" and he had been summoned to
the Casa Crema, the president's palace. "Besides Rafael's version," she

wrote, not entirely untouched by the situation's farcical dimension, to Norman, "I have that of a friend – [a] palace secretary who was in the anteroom.

Pres[ident].	Mr A[paricio], have you seen my niece?
Raf[ael].	Yes.
Pres.	What are you going to do about it?
Raf.	If the child is mine, after a blood test, recognize it.
Pres.	You will go next week with my niece to Mexico and marry her there – in my position I cannot afford a scandal.
Raf.	But Mr Pres[ident] I would remind you that I am already married – both civilly and by the church. (This last is not true, but he thought it might serve as a deterrent – it did not.)
Pres.	That does not matter – you can get a divorce in Mexico. By the way, how is your wife going to take this, I understand she has quite a temper.
Raf.	Yes, she has a temper, but only when provoked, and I don't know that that is a crime.
Pres.	Go and get your picture taken tomorrow and bring it to me, and I shall have your passport ready for you to leave as soon as possible with Solita. You may go.

When Rafael came home with the outcome of this interview – we had just moved into the house and [were] making preparations for a house warming and wedding anniversary [–] he again threatened to commit suicide rather than marry that *cabrona* (his words). Boy, was that a night.[11]

The Aparicios' situation had thereafter gone further to pot. Wise to the possibility of Rafael's taking Soledad to Mexico and dumping her there, the president then decreed that Ernestina had three days to leave the country and that Rafael must sue her for desertion. Ernestina's lawyer visited the president (after packing a bag and warning his wife to be prepared for the worst); but Ydígoras Fuentes simply repeated that if his client and her husband did not wish to comply, "any day Mr A[paricio] could be found *muertito en el camino*". Ernestina had therefore agreed to divorce Rafael, and the day following their divorce on 7 December Rafael had married Soledad who, a month later, gave birth to a baby girl pronounced, by a presidential doctor choosing his words with caution, to be "premature". All that was left for Ernestina to do was rent her house and leave for Mexico City, hoping that Rafael would be able to disembarrass himself eventually and follow her.

(Ernestina's letter ended here, but it was not the end of the story.

Six months later, in September 1961, she wrote again, the last of her letters in Norman's possession. Ydígoras Fuentes, that "crazy bastard" of a president, was about to name Rafael ambassador to Spain, and she was planning to follow him and Soledad to Madrid, still hoping that he and she would be able to rid themselves one day of the president's niece. Could Norman provide her with a power of attorney with which to buy a house in another name? He did, and Ernestina left Mexico City for Madrid, though there her meetings with Rafael dwindled to encounters at cocktail parties as he displayed an emotional paralysis that he increasingly medicated with alcohol. When his posting ended and he returned to Guatemala, Ernestina stayed on at Madrid, working as an occasional journalist and promoter of young Spanish painters until she died from a fall from a hospital trolley when being treated for leukemia in the mid-1980s. To her last, Ernestina never lost her pleasure at being the focus of attention, or shocking people. "Towards the end [of her leukemia] she was having almost daily transfusions," Ito says, "and she was blue from so much iron inside her. She was active right to the last day. She used to say, 'Ito, I love going out for walks, and seeing people in the street back away from me.'")[12]

Against the distant tumult of his ex-wife's life – a tumult that for all his willingness to help and residue of admiration for her emotional clarity and zest, he remained relieved to be shot of – Norman's existence was gradually reconfiguring. He was researching a new book, looking for a new publisher, calmly combining activities in his habitual unplanned way, travelling speculatively. In September 1961 he travelled to Cuba again and interviewed the commander of the Cuban air force, Enrique Carreras, who with three planes barely airworthy had helped destroy the US-based invasion force at the Bay of Pigs that April.[13]

While he was away Lesley, pursuing concerns of her own, dropped her daughter with the Allens and on 17 September went up to London to be part of the Committee of 100's civil disobedience campaign against nuclear weapons in Trafalgar Square. 1314 were arrested that day. She was not among them, but a young teacher and writer from New Zealand found himself getting ready to link arms with her.

It was raining. There were a lot of people and we were all determined to be arrested. There was a rather attractive woman next to me. She had a copy of the *Sunday Times* and we looked at each other because the monitors suddenly said to everybody, "Sit down", because the police were arriving and we were to sit down and link arms so that we would be harder to arrest. And she said, "Would you like to share my *Sunday Times*?" and we got talking. She said, "Oh you're a writer. I'm married to a writer."[14]

James McNeish had been recording folk music in east and west Europe and had spent several months in Sicily. Lesley felt that he and Norman might have something to talk about, and when Norman got back from Havana she phoned McNeish and invited him to the Parsonage for lunch.

In December Norman and Lesley flew to Tunisia on holiday with Kiki (Sarita), a trip with a double purpose, part family rest, part work. They stayed at Tunis for a couple of days first before going down to Hammamet. They saw the ruins at Carthage, where Norman indulged in a moment of archaeological casuistry. "Norman went back to pick up, or put closer to the edge of the site, a sun sculpture. His view was that he would be helping to preserve it. He didn't return for several hours, and when he did he said he had spent all the time going round and round the site, which at night was wire-fenced and drenched in searchlights. That was another failed collection of his."[15] But his main objective was to try to see for himself the most recent consequences of the Algerian war.

I had to wait in my room one day when Norman met his contact in the hotel. Norman's code name I remember was "Bismuth". He went up with the FLN over the border. It was just one night but Norman saw enough, he had a lot explained to him in one night. The things the French were doing were terrible.[16]

Through the Red Crescent they were also taken to see the refugee camps along the border. Though she saw her situation against that of the refugees, it was not an ideal holiday for Lesley, left behind when Norman went over the border and again when he flew home alone "because [he] felt he had to fly back to Scotland for Christmas".

The question of who his new publisher might be was solved when Bob Knittel, Jonathan Cape's former American partner who had moved to William Collins, suggested that Norman also move to Collins. On 29 March 1962 Collins published the novel he had refused to Cape, *The Tenth Year of the Ship*. Set on an Ibiza-like island, Vedra, and a further variation on the meaning of civilisation, the novel is many-charactered, many-fragmented with an absorbing and slightly distracting factuality whose source, again, lies in the greater relative importance its author attaches to the soul of the island than to the souls and destinies of his characters. There is no protagonist apart from Don Flavio Tur, virtual lord of a utopia who has watched mistrustfully the deepening of its harbour to allow a regular ferry service to operate and whose realm, after ten years of regular traffic with the mainland, is on the brink of being swept away by imported speculation. But Don Flavio Tur is tied down by pessimism, while it is the others, Tur's daughter Basilia, the English artist Beckett she randily craves, Tur's venal son-in-law Valentin, the idealistic English girl Laura, the chief of police, the governor, the fisherman Toniet, who are the agitators in multiple concurrent subplots, each a stone in Norman's overarching theme.

I'm at the end of my tether, Tur thought, and really not too soon. . . . The three defeated trawlers would be replaced by an invincible score. Tur's peasants, enticed away by La Palomita and leaving the lands deserted, would discover a new kind of servitude, disguised as freedom. Their bondage would not be to a master of flesh and blood, who could be to some extent manipulated, or even moved by compassion, but to a brass-gutted Moloch known as the shareholder; voracious, pitiless and – above all – stone deaf. Capitalism had arrived, and the only way to survive was to join forces with it as Valentin had done.[17]

Tur's defeatist conspiracy against progress, Laura's search for the quick fix, Beckett's mean affair with Basilia, Valentin's mercenary manoeuvring, the peasants' fight to mechanise and slip Tur's shackles, and the fishermen's ordeal against the superiority of the foreign trawlers, are woven in a mesh of economic interrelation over which Tur presides but never rules in the way that Lampedusa's Don Fabrizio Corbèra rules over the irreversible diminuendo of princely Salina splendour (despite the similarity of the name of Don Flavio's estate, the Salina of Sagral).

The Tenth Year of the Ship is a constantly entertaining novel on the level of events even if, in formal terms, it is a piece of unfulfilled artistry. Most interesting about it in terms of Norman's work as a whole is how repeatedly, and with insight, it attends to questions – of change, exploitation, interference, forces exterior to ourselves – that waited another fifty years to become common currency. It is not a dynasty's diminuendo he is writing about, but a system's; if his novel seeks an ethical pole more than an aesthetic, what it offers in compensation is his depth of understanding of how Vedran society works, his premonition of what the new Vedra represents, his making of a symbol of the way the West will go. Norman's commercialised future is not the surrealist, bureaucratised universe of Kafka; but is capital's inexorable, blindly impersonal reshaping of people's lives any different? Growing numbers of citizens today will freely count mass mobility, applied materialism and the vanishing of social capital among modernity's plagues. In Norman's novel, a passage commenting Laura's idealism – "The facts were that for years she had been engaged in the search for the short cut, the key she knew must exist, the successor to salvation through prayer" – might in a moment of uncharity be repeated today about gap-year backpackers or home-in-the-sun retirees remortgaging bull-market house values.

If there was anything spurious in a person's character, Vedra could be relied upon to bring it out. One had only to remember the annual quota of fake suicides among the members of the foreign colony – the overdoses of barbiturates and the wrist-slashing, which were the histrionics of bored, hemmed-in, and also demoralized people. They were emotional cannibals who fed on each others' tensions, and [Laura] had certainly provided a juicy bone for them to pick over this time.[18]

The question of Norman's new publisher had been answered. A long standing problem remained. "I don't think there was any editing done [at Collins]," Lesley says. "I think the books just came in and Bob read them and he thought they were fine so they were published."[19] It did not seem to matter on this occasion. The *Times* reviewer found no fault with the novel, reviewing Norman's island with Aldous Huxley's *Island* and placing it a good deal higher. "Nothing is more signal about Mr Norman Lewis's achievement than his ability to keep several plot lines moving at the same time," and his characters had the "right tumbledown air of unmade beds to reinforce the atmosphere of squalor, colour and discomfort which constitute Vedra".[20]

So Norman had not given up being a novelist, and was still working occasionally as a journalist; later that year, shortly before the Cuban missile crisis, he wrote a sharp, almost clairvoyant piece, "The six thousand generals of Haiti", for the *Sunday Times* about the Caribbean and US foreign policy. A refinement of self, and of literary means, was taking place. As a novelist only – an exacting experiment he had stuck with for the best part of a decade – he may have understood that he had been over-demanding, pursuing a quotient of recognition he couldn't attain. From the early 1960s, living in the confidence of his relationship with Lesley and of a nascent conviction that what he had begun to achieve in the totality of his writing so far might not, after all, be utterly nugatory, he felt intuitive enough (and possibly, since his transforming encounter with Hemingway, less loaded with ambition) to write what he felt like writing – which did not for a moment rule out the periodic whisperings of his psyche to conquer the territory of the novelist.

Whether so or not, his next book was a new genre. Neither travel-composition nor novel, it aimed to extend his journalism deeper into history, argument, serious study. The least *Rashomon*-like of all his work in its effort to avoid subjectivity, it was the first of his "retro-spective" books: stories whose literary interest suggested itself to him years after he had had the experience that gave rise to it. His interest in the subject – the Sicilian mafia – was self-evident. He had lived in Sicily-in-Bloomsbury for most of his twenties, greeted Ernesto Corvaja's Sicilian emissaries in his absence in the blaze of the Gordon Street lights, admired the implacable mask of Sicilian stoicism, assimilated Ernesto's Sicilian advice – "Before you speak, think, then if necessary remain silent" – and associated it all with the pull of the then unknown, mysterious south: "it was inevitable that a kind of obsession with the enigma of the Mafia grew upon me". It was his friend Sid Perelman who, on a visit to Finchingfield with his wife Laura in the winter of 1960, encouraged him to put his interest together with the material. The *New Yorker* might well be persuaded, he told Norman, to publish some substantial part of a book. (Perelman's visit to Essex was his last for a decade. The newly occupied Parsonage, with its bare floors and icy rooms, was to his Manhattan soul of a level of barbarism on a par with the Stone Age.)

Norman began to research that winter and continued through the following year, finishing *The Tenth Year of the Ship* at the same time. Lesley's meeting with James McNeish was providential. When they met at lunch McNeish was charmed, though he didn't find what he expected – "I remember thinking, What an odd man to be a novelist ... the Penge accent, it wasn't Penge but it struck one as the Penge whine [and yet] I think immediately he was able to establish a quality of intimacy. Slightly elder statesman, but with a small 's'."[21] Norman was planning to complete his research in Palermo and western Sicily and had invaluable help from McNeish. Among those McNeish introduced Norman to was Marcello Cimino, a journalist on the left-wing *L'Ora* newspaper, a warm Sicilian from Palermo, tirelessly obliging.

Marcello spoke beautiful Italian and, as I recall, cultured English. [He] was one of the few Sicilians writing about the mafia without fear or favour at the time. I used to marvel at his temerity. Norman wrote to me at one point – I was living in the mountains – about a key episode in mafia killings ... it was a series of articles in *L'Ora* that Marcello had written. Marcello bundled them up and sent them to Norman. The relationship developed from there.

In Palermo Cimino gave Norman access to the newspaper's archives and toured the island with him, interviewing, observing, interpreting what Norman saw. Cimino became Norman's touchstone in Sicily, and his admiration was shared by McNeish.

Of all the Sicilian journalists that I met, with perhaps one exception, he was the one who got closest to the mafia. He was the one who wasn't assassinated. ... He had amassed apparently such a tremendous fund of knowledge about them but was in his own right something of a scholar [and] they had a sort of sneaking respect for him.[22]

If Cimino was able to write in his epilogue to the 1984 reissue of the book that Norman eventually wrote, *The Honoured Society*, that "To read it again today one finds little there to alter or correct", it was very substantially the result of his guidance. He and his wife Giuliana, also a journalist, and sister-in-law, Gabriella Saladino, shared an eighteenth-century palazzo on via Maqueda; he and Giuliana on the fourth floor, Gabriella on the second where she worked as a theatre designer. Gabriella's atelier is the palazzo's former ballroom: its frescoes are unrestored, the netting under the ceiling to catch falling plaster has been there since 1943, when Allied bombardment shook the city. "When Norman came in here," Gabriella says, "he just sighed and said, 'Ah. Art and decay.'"[23] In the next thirty years Norman counted Cimino, Giuliana and Gabriella very high on his list of friends; Marcello he referred to simply as "a hero".

By early 1963 the new book was in progress – he made a further trip to Sicily to complete the research that spring – though he had one fright after the lunch with McNeish, who in the meantime had gone to work with Danilo Dolci's social-activist organisation and recalls that "Norman wrote to me after I'd been living [in Sicily] and he said, 'What are you doing there?' I wrote back, 'I'm doing a biography of Danilo Dolci,' and he wrote back, 'I was worried stiff that you were writing a book about the mafia'." Norman had met Dolci at Partinico west of Palermo, where Dolci had his centre, and years later remembered Dolci's revelation of the beauty of western Sicily. "He took me up to the house-top [where] behind us Sicily imitated the Sahara, with its bony, sun-eroded landscape and its spectral peaks. Ahead the civilization of antiquity had filled this place with a brilliant filigree of gardens. I wrote in my notes 'no place in the world reeks more strongly of a remote past than this. Any house that is more than a hovel is the ghost of a Roman villa.'"[24] McNeish readily acknowledged that Norman was the person to write the book. "I had been living in Sicily on and off for about three years, I'd never seen a body, or not that I recall. On Norman's first trip in pursuit of the mafia he stays somewhere near Corleone in a hotel, comes out in the morning at six o'clock to relieve himself or whatever, and trips over a body in the street, a peasant shot by the mafia. He used to tell this story himself and say how lucky he was . . . there was always an element of luck, but he knew when to go and the right time."[25] (Whether the story actually happened, however, is impossible to say.)

The book took shape against the shape of life. In September 1962 Gareth, having failed common entrance (admitting that "I had no discipline because I was indulged"), left Lathallan and started at "another bleak school [at Carlisle]. . . . Dad came to one rugby game when I was scrum half for the school, and he was perplexed why the ball went over the bars and not through the bars. He hadn't grasped rugby or pretended not to because it was funny." Karen, educated at the austere but outstanding village school, was finding that she and her father had languages in common.

Most people were quite timid around Dad, because they thought, Oh what an intellectual, what a great intellect. But I in my small way had crept along quite nicely and could read German in the old-fashioned script . . . he and I would do lots of things, "Tell me the German for this" – he remembered till [his last illness] the German for "twig" which was "*Zweig*". He remembered me coming up with that because I beat him on [it].

After he helped with her homework, they went out on "think walks" with the dogs and often finished up reciting poetry in unison. Despite Lorca's being his favourite poet, it was four lines of Campoamor's that were his favourite poem.

"En este mundo traidor", he used to love that.[26] And he used to do "The king sat in Dunfermline toon"[27] – we used to go through all the [languages] –

> The king sat in Dunfermline toon,
> Drinking the blude red wine,
> "Ah waur will I find a skeely skipper
> Tae sail this ship o' mine."
> It's up then spak an eldery knicht
> Sat by the King's richt knee,

this was the Scottish accent thing you see,

> "O Sir Patrick Spens is the skeeliest skipper
> That sailed upon the sea"

and he used to love all that, he used to really, really enjoy that. And we used to do the French ones,

> J'aime le son du cor, le soir au fond des bois,
> Soit qu'il chante les pleurs de la biche aux abois
> Ou l'adieu du chasseur, que l'écho faible accueille
> Et que le vent du nord porte de feuille en feuille

– I can see him now –

> porte de feuille en feuille.[28]

We'd whisper that together. And Lorca's "Córdoba" –

> Córdoba.
> Lejana y sola.
> Jaca negra, luna grande. . . .[29]

There was a menace in that one, because there was Cordoba distant and lonely and there was this man with olives in his saddlebags and a lovely black horse and he said, "Although I know the road, I'll never arrive in Cordoba." There was a menace about that and he loved that.[30]

In late autumn 1962 Lesley became pregnant again. She was content with life at the Parsonage, but the house and village were no substitute for London when Norman was travelling. "He was always going away to Scotland, and then the travelling, and the summer holidays, so there were long periods when he was off the scene. I didn't like being in that big house by myself, but I put up with it." She had had a young writer, Jennifer Lash (the future Jini Fiennes), staying with her au pair, Ito and Crokie Allen came down and kept her company or she would go to the Allens'. Norman's absences continued to give her the right to dispose of her time as she wanted, she thought. He did not always agree. "Norman was not tolerant of [the vagaries of my life], I think, but I was tolerant of his."[31]

Meeting Sid Perelman in London in June 1963, where Perelman was disgustedly writing a flavourless script for the CBS television travelogue *Elizabeth Taylor's London*, Norman showed him several chapters of *The Honoured Society*. Perelman offered to take them to William Shawn on his return and did so, phoning Norman several days later and telling him to get to New York as soon as he could. Norman arrived within a week and went with Perelman to see "the rubicund, smiling, almost excessively polite little" Shawn "at a desk as big as Mussolini's in a huge silent cavern of an office". The interview lasted, Norman wrote, five minutes. Shawn congratulated him on what he had read and told him to let him have the rest of the book, "mentioning what seemed an unbelievable fee for its publication in the magazine".[32]

On 20 July Norman was still writing to James McNeish, asking for information about "the Ruffini matter" and wondering whether Spanish fishermen's aversion to the Catholic Church was something McNeish had "found traces of . . . in Sicily", but between the summer holiday in Ibiza and the autumn the book was finished. Norman went back to New York, checked into the Algonquin Hotel and delivered the typescript to Shawn's secretary; Shawn phoned him the next morning and, inviting him to lunch at the famous and otherwise empty round table, produced the same situation as before, generous words of praise followed by a perspiring agony of silence. Norman knew to keep talking.

Personal events had punctuated the 1963 summer. In July when he was out of the country his friend Malcolm Dunbar had killed himself at a beach on the Hampshire coast. Dunbar had tried before; this time he swallowed a bottle of whisky and aspirins. "It was awful," Lesley recalls, "because he was supposedly frightened of water, but he walked into the sea." The post-mortem routine revealed the magnitude of Dunbar's loneliness: in Norman's absence, only Ito and Frank Allen were available to identify his body. A few weeks later, on 16 August, Norman was away again in Ibiza for the happier occurrence of the birth at the Parsonage of his son Gawaine.

The Honoured Society began serialisation in the *New Yorker* on 8 February 1964. Shawn published the book in six consecutive issues in its near entirety, suppressing, in a surprisingly timorous way, all mention of the mafia's US associations. The magazine nevertheless angered many Sicilians who claimed they had been libelled, and when copies reached Italy Norman found his way strewn with writs. The problem was the ambiguous status of his subject. The two contemporary obstacles for any author who wanted to make the attempt to study the mafia were (1) its frequently disputed existence as a fully structured criminal organism, a secret society, or anything else, and thus (2) a public identity in and out of Sicily that subsisted in a murk of secrecy, denials, rumoured half-truths and perfectly evident violence. Norman had stated his own position in a review he had written the year before of Danilo Dolci's passionate account of Sicily's feudal stagnation, *Waste*.

For two centuries, or more, the Mafia has ruled in Sicily from behind the scenes, through the machinery of the most perfectly designed protection-racket the world has ever known. Its darkest days belong to the era of Fascism, when Mussolini blundered into action against it, gaoling a few hundred small fry, and at least compelling the big chieftains to run for cover. A golden age of new power and prestige followed with the Allied occupation of Sicily, secretly abetted by the Mafia. Presenting themselves as devoted anti-Fascists, the "men of honour" – as they prefer to be known – wormed their way into the good graces of the occupation authorities, and were soon in business as never before. Their most urgent task was the hamstringing of the new laws that gave uncultivated estates to the peasants, and this task they bloodily performed. Dolci's book contains a sombre account of what happened to the peasant leaders who stood up to Mafia power. Six hundred unsolved murders belong to this period.[33]

By the late 1950s a number of (mainly Italian) writers had begun to publish about aspects of the mafia: the scale of "business as never before" was getting hard to ignore both commercially and politically.

Norman had drawn on these writers, in the case of one book too closely. To illustrate the material fact of "the Mafia conspiracy" and its alleged renaissance, and to give himself a good opening, he had written how, in July 1943, a US fighter adorned with a yellow flag emblazoned by a letter "L" had circled low over the town of Villalba in the centre of the island and dropped a packet including a silk hand-kerchief, also yellow and carrying the initial "L". The packet found its way, as intended, to Don Calogero Vizzini, "head of the Mafia of all Sicily" who lived in Villalba; its message was that the US invasion of the island was approved by the individual signified by the "L", Lucky Luciano, then serving a 30–50-year jail sentence in Great Meadows penitentiary, New York, and to be freed and deported in 1946 in recognition of his "war efforts". Once Don Calò had passed the signal to his chieftains across the island they acted, by bribery, blackmail and direct action, to clear the way for US forces to advance unopposed through the island. (This wasn't Don Calò's only service. He also compiled for the Americans a list of candidates for mayor throughout liberated western Sicily, which was immediately found acceptable. "No one seems to have had time," Norman writes, "to investigate his claim that his nominees had suffered for their political ideals, rather than for crimes ranging from armed train-robbery to multiple homicide."[34])

The "Villalba incident", familiar to anyone interested in Franklin Roosevelt's administration's supposed liability for the mafia's revival, had been originally publicised by a well-known Sicilian left-wing lawyer and journalist, Michele Pantaleone, in his book *Mafia e Politica* (1962). "It's something I've been guilty of myself," James McNeish, who knew and liked Pantaleone, says.

After the book was published I happened to be in London and Norman rang me up and said could we have lunch? And we duly did in L'Escargot, we often met there. And we had lunch and Norman said, "I've got a problem. Pantaleone's suing me, what do I do?" He told me what he'd done, and it was the first time I had risen above my station because I was much junior to Norman and I said, "I think you've been very silly." He took it very well. What he had done was to lift not just a paragraph but virtually an entire chapter and he hadn't acknowledged anything. Later I said to him, "What happened?" and he said, "We settled out of court." I think it wasn't deliberate on Norman's part, I think it just left his mind.[35]

A comparison of the two accounts shows that Norman did not lift a chapter at all; his is a legitimate retelling that only touches on Pantaleone's Italian, directly translating the occasional word and phrase. The real offence was to Pantaleone's pride, resulting from Norman's omission of a more gracious acknowledgment than a single line of bibliography.

Norman was rattled by Pantaleone's writ. But in retrospect the twist to his alleged plagiarism of the Villalba incident – a fine story, with the clean lines and pure dimensions of fable – is that we now know that truth sleeps with the fishes. Pantaleone's family were enemies of Don Calogero's, both landowners around Villalba; his account is personally biased and almost certainly untrue. US field forces had passed beyond Villalba by the time Don Calogero gave the alleged command. As elsewhere, the US advance was chiefly aided by Italian forces simply giving up an unwanted fight.

Where Norman was assuredly correct was in his subsequent emphasis on the link between the mafia's post-war rise through political infiltration and the anti-communist policies of both US and Italian governments. "Allied Intelligence agencies were surprised, and in some cases disturbed," he wrote, "at the strength and vitality of the emergent left-wing parties at a moment when, in many places, it was felt necessary to confront the Communist Eastern bloc with an undivided and anti-Communist West."[36] It was these policies that, for example, had sanctioned the mafia-directed massacre at Portella della Ginestra on 1 May 1947, when the people of the towns of Piana dei Greci and San Giuseppe Jato joined forces to celebrate the surprise victory of the Left in the April elections and the application of a new law to end uncultivated land going to waste. Ambushed on a piece of table-land at a pass between mountains, more than 2000 May Day picnickers, two-thirds of them children, were trapped in a spray of machine-gun fire and ricochets that killed sixty-six: an episode Norman related pointedly in *The Honoured Society*, in the direct and bitter style of Giovanni Verga's story "Liberty", as a kind of detailed homage to feudal barbarism.

Beppino Muchetta, a boy who had been looking after the family cart, came with the news that the horse was dead. "We've something more than that to weep about, my boy," his father said, and then Beppino saw his mother and sister lying on the ground, his mother dead and sister screaming in agony. Celestina Alotta, aged eleven, separated from her parents, was carried along on a human panic-wave almost to safety, when a random bullet tore through her back. A father with his dead son in his arms, running first one way and then the other, said years later, "All I wanted to do was to shield him from being hurt again. I didn't realize that he was dead all the time." Bullets ricocheting off the rocks inflicted atrocious wounds. . . . In ten minutes the shooting was over.[37]

The Portella massacre was a savage tragedy, viewed by many Sicilians as the seminal political betrayal of the post-war period and portent of all future betrayals. It also produced Norman's second lawsuit. The mafia's enlistment of Salvatore Giuliano's outlaw band to carry out the killing – a moral devaluation of a romantic, enterprising, socially conscious bandit – also implicated, in Norman's account, some figures in the Christian Democrat party and particularly a Prince Alliata who were supposed to have ordered the massacre and, in Alliata's case, offered the bandits sanctuary on his estates in Brazil. Giuliano's lieutenant, Gaspare Pisciotta, had alleged the involvements at his trial; Norman cited Pisciotta's testimony, not realising that Alliata had already successfully sued another writer, Gavin Maxwell, for repeating it in his account of Giuliano, *God Protect Me from My Friends*. When the writ came down Norman went to Maxwell's lawyer, Michael Rubinstein, who pointed out to him that Alliata was a prince of the Holy Roman Empire, of international reputation and natural authority, as eloquent in spoken English as Italian, and had already won over one judge on similar grounds. A meeting was arranged with Alliata at the Savoy Hotel, for which Norman brushed down one of his now rarely worn Anderson & Sheppard suits (he was more often found in "an extraordinary woolly djellaba", Leila Hadley, Sid Perelman's friend, says). He found Alliata urbane and dignified. Afterwards, Lesley says, "[Rubinstein] looked at Norman and said, 'How do you think you're going to stand up against him? Not well.'"[38] Norman had to agree. The implacable adversary of aristocracy accepted that he would have to fall on a prince's mercy. With lavish apologies he offered amends in the form of settling Alliata's hotel bill and expenses in London and printing his denial of the allegations as a postscript. Alliata accepted.

Norman was rewarded – or diverted – by the book's critical and commercial success, great from the outset. It was translated into fourteen other languages after *The Times* called it "much the best study of the Mafia in English".[39] (Though the *Times* reviewer let slip the Cold

War climate, stupidly describing the Italian Communist Party as having "much in common with the Mafia . . . , being a semi-secret body opposed to the bosses but able to provide useful personal services for the faithful".) The *Times Literary Supplement* praised Norman for "providing the most accurate assessment of the Mafia yet to have appeared in English", the *Spectator* for a book that "has not a dull moment in it", and the *Listener* described him as "one of the finest journalists of his time . . . he excels both in finding material and evaluating it." Negligible dissent came in a piece by Denis Mack Smith in the *New York Review of Books* that dismissed "a traditional if glamorized portrait of the Mafia which leaves much unsaid and unexplained", though Mack Smith's excessive harshness ignored the purpose of Norman's study, which was not to provide a scholarly account but to navigate through turbid alleys of half-truth and sensation for the ordinary reader. *The Honoured Society* was not intended to be ground-breaking, except insofar as Norman intended to raise the level of understanding of his subject. It, like *A Dragon Apparent* and *Golden Earth*, was meant to bring light but also to warm its subject into life, to spread colour and tangible shape and contrast, as much as to illuminate. In the process, however, as his scholarly Sicilian friend Marcello Cimino noted, he had produced a "penetrating and accurate report". He was also among the first, long before the Italians themselves, to define the post-war mafia as a primarily capitalist force or, as Cimino puts it, "a true form of bourgeois capitalism in formation".[40]

He produced one unlikely error, in his translation of the Sicilian concept of *omertà* as "manliness". Its etymology is not entirely safe, but if some dictionaries link *omertà* to *uomo* (man) or *umiltà* (humility), both are attributes of its chief meaning, which is the code of silence that rules the Sicilian conscience. (As the Vicenza writer Goffredo Parise wrote in his story "Italia", "The 'code of silence' was a difficult concept to explain to a foreigner.") At the end of 1964 *The Times* renewed its praise, naming *The Honoured Society* one of "The Year's Best Books".[41] One cloud remained over the book's publication that had nothing to do with it. In the same month, June, Norman learned that his great friend Loke Wan Tho, the bird photographer and reluctant prince of commerce, had been killed with his wife in a plane crash on their way to the Asian Film Festival at Taipei.

In July he drove down to Ibiza with Karen, Gareth and Hester for the last time. He had a new car, having, the previous October, committed his last automobile indulgence with part of his $35,000 fee for the *New*

Yorker's serialisation: a long, low, wide, wafer-shaped, pale metallic green Pontiac Parisienne with a white hood. He had seen it on its stand at the Motor Show at Earls Court and bought it on the spot. As an example of automotive aesthetic it was expressive, but too big to fit in the garage at the Parsonage, which had to be extended to get it in. As a car, it was more show than go because he had mistakenly bought the smallest engine variant. Gareth: "I remember in Spain Dad going along and a Porsche 912 trying to overtake us, and a Porsche 912's basically got a Volkswagen engine in there, and he kicked down for a bit of machismo, to go down into that first gear, and he still couldn't blow it away."

It was the eleventh Ibiza summer, and this year Norman didn't stay but garaged the Pontiac and flew back after a few days to be with Lesley, flying down again to collect the car, Hester and children in September. Up to that summer, he had continued to go to Scotland as regularly as before to see the children. Gareth remembers his efforts to be funny, as children do when their parents' sense of humour is incomprehensible. "He used to send me birthday cards, and they said 'Age 5' on them. He found that funny. I could never understand why he did that." Gareth had started driving and bought his first car for £25. Invited out for a drive, Norman discovered that the car had faulty brakes. His solution, perhaps on the principle that children must make their own mistakes, was to refuse to travel in it and make his son drive home alone. At Gareth's next birthday, he sent another child's card with ten pounds inside it and a message, "Please find enclosed the usual tenner to buy you a bottle of temporary oblivion," with a typically Norman "PS" which this time Gareth appreciated. "And then he wrote, 'By the way, if you're contemplating buying another hideous wreck, be like Mussolini and ask yourself: Am I a collector of deserts?'"[42]

Detached as a father, in Scotland Norman's involvement as a parent had continued to be unusual. The number of middle-class parents who take their children poaching is relatively small. Through their teenage years Norman took Karen and Gareth singly and together, as he had Ito, to the empty roads bordering local estates. With some impatience he had taught Karen to drive the Buick, raised up on cushions, so that she could be the getaway driver while he shot.

It was a fate worse than death to be poaching at that time. If we were caught police would be round to the door and we'd be put in the local *Press and Journal*. That's why he loved it all the more. ... So [one day] we spot a pheasant, and just at that point we think we hear a vehicle coming the other way. But he fires the gun. At that point the dog he's about to release [becomes] gun-shy and starts howling in the back of the Buick. A car appears round the bend and he says, "Quick, go, go." So I put the column change in first and stall the damn thing. He's got now this silenced Beretta stuck in the electric window, trying to get the bloody thing in, there's the dog howling in the back, me trying to start the car up again because it's stalled. [At home] we sit . . . waiting for the police to come round. They never do, so we thought the other car in the other direction must be a poacher too.[43]

At another occasion with Gareth, who had to shoot and retrieve as well (Norman had learned his lesson with the dog), Gareth had put his father's Beretta on semi: "it had telescopic sights, and the hood at the back of the Buick had a [button] flap to it and you just lifted this flap, so you'd put out this silenced barrel . . . and it'd just go dzum–dzum–dzum and the bird was feathers, it was just dancing around and then nothing." A car passed, and they had to drive off in a hurry. "He sent me back at night in my car, in my Opel, to gather the bird, and they were waiting for me." Gareth saw the keepers first and drove on and home empty-handed.[44]

A more human crisis occurred at Banchory that autumn. Karen, at seventeen, was old enough to start to understand the complicated extent of her family's malfunction, and to realise that, as one aspect of it, she would never have her mother's love and esteem. Her answer was to work harder and harder at school and in the face of deepening emotional crisis hold herself together by suppressing every negative feeling. Her resolve to be bright and cheerful had reached the point that if she started to cry, she would slap her face to stop. At school one day she found herself unable to read any of the words on the pages of her schoolbooks, and her constructed self fell in pieces.

Her mother, she recalls, "amazingly rose to the occasion and said, 'I think you're having a nervous breakdown.'" Norman went to Scotland. "Dad came to see me, which was rather concerning because I think the visits had stopped by then. I think he felt totally helpless. I remember him coming up and saying to me, 'You know I love you, don't you?' I said, 'Yes Dad.' I think he probably felt responsibility for it."[45] Together her parents came to a curious solution, for her to go and stay for a time with Oliver Myers and his wife in Nigeria, where Myers was teaching. At Ibadan the Myers' home and marital situation turned out to be no more balanced than Norman's and Hester's – Myers was nursing sexual feelings for his Nigerian secretary and Jill Myers was drinking heavily – but after three months of driving for the family, volunteering on projects and owning a share in a polo pony, Karen found that she was recovering. Flying back to Scotland, she discovered she had enough A-levels to get into Aberdeen University.

She felt her father had been weak in the face of the situation with Hester and prolonged the agony by coming for weekends for so long, "[but] as he said later, he left me there although he knew it wasn't that good where I was, for stability and continuity". A practical continuity only, deficient for all emotional purposes; his daughter's breakdown was the final sign of a torn family that had been pretending it was not for the best part of two decades. No one had emerged from the pretence unhurt; everyone's actions and outlook had been distorted by its unreality. Who, in the end, came out worst? For all her favouritism, negativity, coating of charm and fits of wrath followed by inertia, Hester's position deserves most sympathy. The mother who had wept over her daughter's bed when Karen was a baby was now fifty-six; the whole gamble of her middle years was lost. Karen's impulse to steal the change from her father's coat pockets for her mother reflects an economic fact that Lesley concurs with: Hester was badly done by. "Yes, which is a sad state of affairs. I would think yes. One doesn't know, because Norman was a careful man but he wasn't a mean man. But it clearly wouldn't occur to him to be overly generous to her."[46] More revealing than stolen shillings is the awfulness of the relationship signalled by its literary secrecy: by Hester's exclusion in every guise from Norman's prolific literary reservoir. To write about either it, or her, was beyond even his prose's comprehensive resources of pathos and bitter comedy.

A series of plugging rattles came at them across the water. The sound of the firing alternated with what seemed to Peake long silences. Reasons of economy, he thought. They weren't wasting any bullets. Tracers, threading out of the darkness, converged on the search-light beams and were dissolved.

A white, mist-rimmed eye swivelled and suddenly filled the whole world with its glare. Peake waved back to the Cuban to start up, but as he did so the boat leaped forward, then turned sharply away, throwing both Peake and Varona off their feet.

A Small War Made to Order

An official of The Metal had measured Cross Hands by a novel yard-stick: the egg test. He had always found in any country he had visited that the higher the degree of civilization, the worse the eggs tasted. The only eggs he had ever found to compare with those of Cross Hands were those of a miserable Central American republic where half the population was dying of starvation.

Every Man's Brother

23

PRIVATE DEAD ENDS

"These are just flowers. Berries will come soon"
Russian proverb

DETACHMENT from Banchory, the extraction from Norman's life of a lengthy seam of compromise and unreality, finally allowed an expanding calm to pour into its place. In early 1965 he started a new novel, his first for four years, and as one family replaced two he travelled less. In the summer he drove the Pontiac to Portugal on holiday with Karen and Gareth to discover somewhere new. The undying spell of Ibiza made the Estremaduran coast an anti-climax: the chosen resort of Nazaré was detested, and Norman measured his dislike of Portugal's lushness by how much he missed Spain's unsoftened magnificence, the "sense of the fantastic" it had not failed to produce for him since he had first stood alone in the plain of Castilla–La Mancha in his twenties.

In November he flew to Moscow for the only other journey that year, to enjoy the fruits of the system of payment for foreign writers in the Soviet Union: a tour, with honoured guest status and for as long as he wanted, to whatever destinations took his eye. This was in lieu of royalties for a two-million-copy magazine edition of a Russian translation of *The Volcanoes Above Us*,[1] and he arrived in Moscow aboard a cavernous VIP-fitted Ilyushin, empty but for a clutch of other VIPs, on the eve of its publication and in time to be treated for once in his life, he wrote, to the sight of queues forming to buy a book of his.

The Russian publication had been overseen by Valentina Evashova, a short, energetic professor of English at Moscow University of peasant dress habits and convictions. Norman had first met her in London after she had recommended his fiction for publication to a Soviet state publisher. At the party thrown by Bob Knittel for her at the Ivy restaurant where she was surrounded by the bright talk of "everyone who had done rather well in everything", including Knittel's wife Luise Rainer who had two Oscars, she had been uncomfortable, lacking the necessary social pretences. In Moscow she was in her element. Norman spent four days with her in the city, alarmed at being bundled, Holly Martins-like, into lecturing on English literature – "the only time I ever remember feeling real terror" – and amused by her noisy, stubborn direction of his visit. He was sent first to the obligatory dacha at Sochi on the Black Sea. His much later account of the journey, though very recomposed, catches the rough industrial romanticism of Soviet life, its barely serviceable "luxuries" balanced by warmth, vodka and the constant possibility of adventure. He made the most of Sochi by driving up into the Georgian slopes of the Abkhazskaya mountains 50 kilometres further south with three companions, another two university professors and a Soviet colonel who had requisitioned a military four-wheel drive. The culmination of their exploring was a session of digging up botanical specimens for the garden at Finchingfield, using the colonel's scimitar.

Barred by Evashova from visiting Bukhara on the pretext of an outbreak of plague – the real reason was local unrest – Norman was grudgingly allowed to fly on to Tashkent and Samarkand. The chairman of Samarkand's city council, a former rose grower, offered him a tour of the rose-saturated mountains around the city and a visit to "the simple magnificence" of Tamerlane's tomb, and inevitably a party that, falling on a lesser saint's day, was animated by the minor rituals he enjoyed and readily buried at the back of his memory: "little girls, roused unkindly from sleep, being manacled to the lambs they were to guard during the festivities, and important old men ... moving like chess pieces through the morning mist towards the nearest place of worship".[2] At the party he made the acquaintance of a woman whom he felt must be related to the Uzbeks he had accompanied back to Khorramshahr on HMS *Devonshire*. Known as the Horse Princess, she earned money by dance displays and was the unofficial leader of the mounted Uzbeks of the steppe north of Samarkand. Her people were regarded with distaste by Muscovites, Norman found, their imposed style of dress echoing the Soviet drive for utilitarian uniformity: a gloomy evolution for people who had built mosques of wonderful magnificence and cultivated the world's first rose gardens 5000 years before. For a day Norman succeeded in ditching his interpreter and driving into the steppe to visit the Horse Princess's village: her intelligent fatalism convinced him of a link between her and the fugitives he had returned to a vindictive Soviet regime twenty years before.

His minders at Samarkand had started to sense that he was not a compliant traveller and, claiming a cancellation, flew him back to Moscow. In lieu of his remaining roubles of income Valentina Evashova took him to an antique shop in Moscow (not the Pushkin Museum as he once said) and told him to choose something. The object he chose was a large, fine 18th-century painting of the Bay of Naples. At the Moscow airport customs officials wanted to charge exorbitant duty on the picture; Evashova told him to give it back to her and brought it to him on her next visit, rolled up as a poster. The stout, bundled-up, faintly dotty literature professor remained a friend, visiting Finchingfield several times. Born in 1902, she survived both imperial and Soviet Russias, but in the great inflationary depression of the 1990s her generation, obedient Communists on vanished state pensions, was the most brutally cast aside. She died unacknowledged, in lonely poverty.

Norman came back to England to take up the reins of journalism; another novel; the search for new stories; he wasn't sure. He went on going to R G Lewis on Tuesdays and Thursdays as a duty, often only to pick up pocket money. He had finished the novel he had started at the beginning of the year, a political intrigue set in Cuba, and it was published by Collins the following April. *A Small War Made to Order* is, as his readers knew to expect, well described and well informed. It does not make the shortlist for his best novel – it begins and goes on formulaically, almost carelessly – but manages in the last third to shake off its trudging conventions and become unexpectedly moving. Charles Fane, a *raté* northern Englishman of priggish ideology, has fought on Franco's side and been a Blackshirt but also written an anti-Suez book, *The Banners of Freedom*, that has been so successful in Marxist states that he gets fan mail from enthusiastic proletarians everywhere. The set-up is cursory: a botched US-sponsored Cuban invasion, a decision by the CIA that it needs better intelligence, the recruiting of Fane (including a meeting in a Soho strip club that seems written as a send-up of Graham

Greene), a drop into Cuba via Fane's job on a pink newspaper in Toronto owned by the men of Langley. At a certain point the best thing about the novel is its title, and then, abruptly, after Fane has been involved for some time in a routine narrative of spy-meets-girl, the story is galvanised, as if Norman, without warning, finds in Fane's hunger for his interpreter Clarita – a memory of his own Cuban girlfriend? – something to surprise him and goes back to have another crack at it. (It is on Fane's disastrous second visit to Cuba to get Clarita out that the lazy vessel of the story picks up and at last begins to make way.) In all his fiction it is the things seen, the ground covered, that carry conviction: the authenticity of his action, the photographic mood of his descriptions – "Beyond the taxi's windows he saw a delicate intaglio of night: thin-stemmed trees swaying under their fronds, placid eyes of lamp-lit windows, a group of white-shirted men in languid confabulation at a cross-roads" – and the robustness of his political commentary.

And to the outsider . . . the country would remain much about the same after the brief episode of blood and thunder to come. The Cuban countryman would kill his pig by the roadside, piss in the ditch, go round the town square a dozen times every evening to look at the girls' bottoms, and feed himself on rice and beans. In a few hours' time Philip's private army would be arriving to set him free. To set him free. One by one they would occupy these unchanging villages, blow out the brains of the intelligent minority, tear down all the posters and put up new ones, and go away. And the survivors would be given the right to vote.

Fane could only guess what Philip really stood for, and he did not particularly like it. Philip would have prepared his pose as the champion of democracy, which was the thing Fane most detested in the world. . . . But the gift that Philip would bestow on these harmless farmers and peasants wasn't even Western democracy, but the fake version of it they had always suffered under in the past. On the whole, Fane's sympathies were with the régime doomed so soon to disappear. At least they knew how to keep the mindless mob in its place without any nonsense about elections. He was sorry now that he was Philip's man. Still, there was nothing to be done about it.[3]

Yet the final twenty pages too, an extended action episode of Fane's and Clarita's failed attempt to escape, are moving not just for vividness and pathos. In their element of exploration they are as powerful as almost anything he wrote: as if he had not decided while writing them whether to let Fane die or save him.

The novel probably created few new readers, though most of his reviewers were loyal: Christopher Wordsworth in the *Guardian* said the novel deserved "to rank with the best in intrigue and espionage along with Le Carré and the Ambler of *The Night Comers*", the *Sunday Telegraph* reviewer judged it "cool, most intelligently written and worked out". The *Spectator*, assuredly hostile to his political viewpoint, described it as "ingenious, concise and gripping . . . a very exciting spy thriller and a responsible version of history". But again he was not being edited, and was going down a path with Collins he had followed before, which would fail to produce either consistent success or even consistent loyalty from his publisher.

Looking for something new to write that spring, he had started a further – unusual – exploration of what he could do with fiction. He had come across "a true story of a happening in Llandeilo, South Wales"[4] but didn't yet know what he wanted from it. There was nothing wrong with this: novelists accept drudgery along with the excitement (though a novelist who can't surprise himself before the end will probably have failed). The novel that was published the following year as *Every Man's Brother* would depart completely from the pattern of his writing to be his first and only published novel with a British (or rather Welsh) background. But his attempt to anatomise his own society (perhaps because too close to anatomising his own emotions) was slow to progress.

That spring Oliver Myers came on leave with his wife Jill to stay at Finchingfield. Myers was delighted to immerse himself in Norman's mixed catalogue of the Parsonage's past, its location in an area of significant Roman remains, its early history as the home of the first Earl of Arundel and Anne of Arundel, and paid diligent (fruitless) attention to its alleged poltergeists, but the visit was more memorable to Lesley for Jill Myers' substitution of a case of gin in their luggage in place of her husband's shirts. Myers helped Norman redesign parts of the Parsonage garden, but failed to return to see the plans put into practice, dying of a heart attack before Christmas that year at sixty-three.

While Norman was trying to work out where the new novel was going, he distracted himself with a story about bandits. Its genesis was a mysterious shooting four years earlier in the highlands of Sardinia of a retired English couple visiting the island, murdered while they picnicked outside the town of Orgosolo. He was not just attracted by the theatre of banditry *alla* Salvatore Giuliano: the romantic separatist, at violent odds with feudal oppression. He was deeply drawn by the idea that bandits survived in Europe. Thirty years later, describing his preferred sort of destination, he said, "Generally speaking it has to be a bit horrific. Any place that has a limited atmosphere of suspense and danger is the sort of place I like." He felt more comfortable in those situations, and could write more easily.[5] Another way of explaining such places might be to say that they are not subject to civilisation's bureaucracies, the organising frameworks – civilisation's footings – that begin by bringing order, then move steadily to collect and pinion every experience, every piece of information and human act, and to assign it a value. Because they leave nothing to chance, bureaucratic systems leave no room to be surprised, nor to act (or ultimately imagine) outside their confines. Autonomous, self-perpetuating, self-expanding, as indispensable a partner of modernity as material prosperity, bureaucracy abhors a wilderness.

So places that still existed unruled by bureaucracy, or as if in a time before it, attracted Norman more than any others. His escape reflex was not just a question of getting away spatially: such places appealed to an equal reflex to escape temporally. Adventure, surprise were still possible there. Surprise was a constant element of his pleasure, and he came to believe that bureaucracy and materialism would together be responsible for the eventual assassination of surprise the world over. "People will go where they want, but they won't see anything that surprises or delights them. They will just have a less pleasurable time than I did forty years ago, searching for something they never quite attain. . . . Now all that awaits [them] is a certain amount of exploitation and better food than they'd get at home."[6]

In summer 1966 he felt Sardinia might both surprise him and replicate the adventurous aspect of some of the figures in *The Honoured Society*, particularly Giuliano whom, with some quixotry, he admired. It might possibly provide him with the material for a sequel.

At Cagliari he called on the British consul to ask for the name of any Sardinian journalist who might have been to the site of the murders in the Barbagia mountains and be able to recommend a guide. (A sensible precaution: a Dutch journalist who later travelled alone in the area was shot and seriously wounded.) The consul came up with a contact, advising Norman not to leave the main roads.

When he reached Orgosolo, the bandits turned out to be friendly, mildly flattered that a foreign writer was taking an interest in their latest murders. The back story to the shooting of the English couple, Edmund and Vera Townley, in October 1962 was a dramatic one: 500 men in Orgosolo's population of 4500 had died violently since the war; in Nuoro province alone there had been seventeen killings since the beginning of the year. The Barbagia were a stronghold of the vendetta; there was no time in recorded history when outlaws had not roamed these hills. It had been the Townleys' extreme bad luck to choose for their picnic a bandit duelling ground where the latest round of a feud was about to be settled, and even the men of Orgosolo, most of whom had at one time or another been bandits, had been shocked at their killing. Norman pieced together a fascinating, bloody story of feud between two families, the Muscaus and the Mesinas, but neither it nor the background was enough for a book. He wrote it instead for a piece in the *Telegraph* weekend supplement later that year.[7]

Turning back to his Welsh novel, still finding it hard work, he began thinking of another change of scene. The outcome was that he and Lesley decided to quit Finchingfield for a six-month break to spend the winter somewhere warm away from England together, even to think of settling out of England for good. They chose Tangier. Before they left, Norman had a phone call from the features editor of another colour supplement. Peter Crookston at the *Sunday Times* magazine wanted to run an issue on the subject of heroes. The heroes to be included had all died young: Rupert Brooke was chosen for the cover, Duncan Edwards, Matt Busby's Manchester United prodigy, was another. In a catholic list Salvatore Giuliano's name had also come up.[8] Crookston had not read *The Honoured Society* but Richard West, another *Sunday Times* journalist, had and said, "I know who can write about Giuliano." Crookston invited Norman to lunch; Norman, ardently courteous in professional matters, reversed the invitation and took Crookston to Romano Santi in Soho, one of his favourite restaurants, where his first piece for the paper since Ian Fleming had died, 350 words on Giuliano, delivered to length a few days later, was commissioned.[9]

In November he, Lesley, Kiki and Gawaine left England for Morocco. They rented a house at the bottom of a hill, and at first Tangier was "very amusing" but he rapidly found the city "exceedingly superficial",[10] and amusing turned to sinister, as Kiki, seven years old, remembers. "It wasn't a particularly nice experience. We had to have a minder because it was quite dangerous and we had a woman that used to cook for us." Lesley's mother came out to visit them. "I got very bad food poisoning and my grandmother got ill as well. Dad at the time suggested that it might be this disgruntled woman trying to kill us by poisoning us with whatever she'd put in the cooking."[11] It was also winter in an unheated Mediterranean house. They kept their plans for emigrating alive in the shape of a ruined mosque they had seen at the top of a hill "with a terrific view", which Norman was initially enthusiastic to convert, repeatedly visiting people to see if electricity and water could be connected. But in the end "I couldn't have been more delighted to return [to Finchingfield]. It's the absence of familiar tensions which bores you."[12]

He succeeded in finishing his novel, but as if negativity had become a low-grade infection, his publisher at Collins, Bob Knittel, showed only polite enthusiasm. Norman as usual defended himself with trenchancy, immediately asking his new literary agent, Michael Sissons of the A D Peters agency, to place the book somewhere else. It was sold quickly to Heinemann, with a twist: Norman's solicitor, Hilbery, had advised him to move some of his wealth offshore and the contract with its £1000 advance was in the name of Norman Lewis c/o A D Peters, the Anglo-Bahamian Bank Ltd of Nassau, and William Heinemann Ltd. Norman had a short but friendly relationship with his Heinemann editor, Mark Barty-King. A letter he wrote to Barty-King on 6 May about the production of *Every Man's Brother* revealed another aspect to his conversation with Hemingway.

Dear Mr Barty-King,
    Thank you for your letter of the 4th. . . .
    Biographical material. Unless you feel strongly about this, I would like to omit it.
    On the subject of wrappers, however, I have definite views – arising out of a visit paid to Hemingway shortly before his death. Jonathan Cape, some two years before, had sent him a book of mine he liked very much (The Day of the Fox), to ask H. if he couldn't say something quotable about it. Hemingway received me sitting up in bed with a beaker of what turned out to be Dubonnet in his paw, and within two minutes reached out for the book in a bedside book-case. "This isn't bad stuff, Lewis. Pity about the cover, though. I picked it up five or six times, but the cover always made me feel sick and I had to put it down again. Knocked it off last night hearing you were coming, and if Jonathan wants, I'll call it a masterpiece. Maybe it's kinda late now, though." In view of the above frustrating experience perhaps we could discuss jackets when we meet.[13]

The discussion, whatever it decided, had nil impact. The novel's dust-jacket, white with a cramped sanserif typeface and a feeble bleached-contrast illustration, is awful. The novel itself, published in October 1967, was also without the colour splashes, dramatic surety and ideological confidence of its forerunners. His exploration didn't come off – he didn't ever work out exactly what he wanted from it, and it was a novel that he came to see as one of his least successful. Yet despite considerable confusions of position and purpose, it is a soup of absorbing ingredients for any reader interested in what Britain, or mostly Wales, was like in the mid-1960s.

Bron Owen, imprisoned for five years for crimes he has no memory of and released into the community at the novel's start, takes refuge at his brother's farm in South Wales. The uncertainties of his psychology, faced with rural Welsh Baptist dogma, exclude convalescence or understanding, and his attraction to his brother's kind, sexy wife Cathy triggers a night of violence for which he becomes the scapegoat. Norman's knowledge of the Welsh background – the cloud cuckoo land of his youth, the place of impossible return – is profound, his dramatisation consistently inventive. Cross Hands, a sluggish South Wales village close to Carmarthen, is a cold tropic of savagely applied class distinctions and near stagnation, a place scattered with gin-traps, poison-penners and chapels where reputations are trampled with glee. Its citizens express themselves in a rich vocabulary of obfuscation, determined to betray as little as possible of their true actions and emotions. A submerged violence that is the source of all rumour never surfaces to show its face. There is occasional murder, inevitably, given such suppressions; at any rate, members of the community routinely disappear. They are said to be buried; they are never dug up.

This summary gives an idea of one problem for the reader: that of tone. Is *Every Man's Brother* a thriller? A psychological study of criminal schizophrenia? A satirical tragicomedy? It is hard to know. Norman cannot altogether conceal his antipathy for this environment and instead clothes it in an unforgiving caricature that is incompatible with the portrait of Bron Owen's illness and tragedy. This may have been a mood known to Evelyn Waugh when he was writing the Llanabba Castle chapters of *Decline and Fall* – but Paul Pennyfeather at his most harmless was created for satire. *Every Man's Brother*, swinging between surrealistic elements and fatal realities, is not really at home with either, although Norman's description of the Brynaron police force is comically and delightfully blunt –

Fenn was a Londoner with a bony, urban face and an urban economy of mind, who had reluctantly allowed himself to be exiled to this place because it had been the first inspectorship going . . . he was out of his depth, floundering in a foreign land, among people who concealed their secret thoughts in terrible verbosity. . . .

[Constable] Jones, the one Fenn most despaired of, was classifying the passers-by through the office's fake-Tudor leaded windows on the basis of their heights. The short were the miners, virtuous but damned; those who reached the windows' second row of panes were farmers, also good chaps; the tall were English bastards. . . .

"For instance," Fenn asked him, "do you ever book a Welshman? . . . Don't the Welsh at Cross Hands break the law?"

"Very rarely," Jones said.[14]

– and so is his curtain call of Cross Hands characters at the novel's close. But Norman's emotional self-cauterisation prevented him from exploring the human aspect beyond the comic, and it is hard to disagree (except, if one is being unsparingly honest, with the last sentence) with the reviewer's conclusion in *The Times*:

. . . compare this Wales to the marvellously convincing Cuba in *A Small War Made to Order*. The appalling plight of the saintly, victimized Bron is by no means so compelling as the bones of the community in which it takes place: the suffering rarely comes through. *Every Man's Brother* is highly sympathetic, extremely well written and gives continued pleasure; but greedily one wishes Mr Lewis would do so much more. Because he could.[15]

In the three years since he had detached himself from Banchory, Norman had for the first time watched a family growing up that he wanted to go on living with. Family relations are what only the family's members know, through their prism of viewpoints; the biographer's narrative at such a point is really theirs. The children agree that loving his family did not make their father a modern parent. Lesley brought them up almost singlehanded, as Karen saw. "To some extent Dad was a spoilt man by Lesley, who cushioned him against a lot of the realities of being a parent and of family life, and negotiated for what was needed for the children on their behalf so that he didn't have to have any confrontations with them."[16] Kiki remembers too that "he was quite distant, you couldn't go to him with emotional problems, that was what Mum was for". Limited as they were, his parenting instincts were greater than before and drew him into involvement in often lavish ways. "He was great fun," Kiki says, "and did lots of fun, ridiculous things." He complained in an arch-comic way about having to go on family holidays, but Gawaine remembers "two, sometimes three holidays a year, [and] he may have said they were looming on his horizon, but he was the one who would be organising the holiday". When he travelled without his family, he always came back to Finchingfield with presents heaped up to shower on them; "for us it was almost like Christmas a couple of times a year," Kiki says. What she best remembers are his bedtime stories, a routine that lasted until she was eleven or twelve and started, every night when he was at home, with her father leading a noisy conga of her and Gawaine up the wide Parsonage staircase to bed. "We'd all grip each other round the waist and snake, 'I came I saw I conga'd, da da da da da'. That was the way to get us into bed." The stories he told, "brilliant, brilliant stories", were his own.

He had two stories which I remember really well. One was called Prince Ogon, which was about this African prince who was kidnapped and put onto one of the boats and shipped over to wherever to be in the slave trade, and [Dad told] this fantastic story of his passage on this boat and the hideous conditions that they were all in. He used to go into the details, you know, people having shit fall on them from the bunk above and you know, this disgusting situation, the details that kids absolutely love. That went on in my head for weeks and weeks. And another one was pure fantasy, called "The Scissors Birds", and it was [about] a family who had a father who was a car salesman or a salesman of some sort who loved racing cars, that was it. So he'd spend all the family money on buying these cars and writing them off. And his wife would have to support them, and she had this fabulous tan and she actually had wings, real wings. She had to go into a circus and do an act, so she'd take off her frock and then underneath these wings would sprout and she'd fly around this marquee.[17]

Lesley – the wife with wings, more or less – and he lived harmoniously most of the time. "I clearly provided something for Norman, Norman provided something for me, in emotional and all sorts of terms." As a mother she was "perfectly happy". Her practicality earthed Norman's temperament: she knew for instance that he liked to make a good story and "would in a sense manufacture something so that it fitted his particular image of how the picture would look good."

So if it was necessary to this picture to make it appealing, then he would slant the facts and make them more interesting. In other words the man who was sitting reading his newspaper on the train every morning, because he would do something in a certain way, was really a secret agent. Because suddenly that made that picture look good. There was something about that in Norman's [character] . . . and he used to get quite cross with me because I'm a very down-to-earth person, I'd say, "Norman, that's nonsense, you know, the guy's not a secret agent, or the situation is this", and often he didn't want that. But that was one of the reasons we got on well. I was always direct with him, I didn't attempt to agree with him about everything, and in a funny way, although it didn't suit him, he respected it and liked it.[18]

She accepted her partner's uneasy private nature; motherhood had, if anything, made her more accepting. "I would have said if you looked at our life together, we had a very happy, stable [life] – always better when we were alone, without kids, without people." She was familiar with his mistrustful reflexes. "He always had this suspicion about people. You know, where I would think the best of somebody, Norman would prefer to think the worst of somebody, he would start off on that footing. [He was] very wary of people. And I suppose life had made him that way." She had one regret. "Once he was free of Scotland he wanted me with him all the time – those were the rows we would have – any time I spent away from him he was jealous of, and that I found wearing."[19]

His children were aware of their father's character. Kiki remembers her mother enjoying her father's absence on journeys because they gave her the chance to have women friends down to the Parsonage, "people that Dad wouldn't be that thrilled to see. He was judgmental about a lot of her friends. A lot of that was jealousy, he wanted her really exclusively for himself. And that spilled over with his children as well, the business of 'she's mine, not yours'." It was difficult for her mother, she remembers, "because she'd have to deal with this without offending people. What could she say? 'My husband doesn't like you'? He really was totally irrational about who he liked and didn't like and he just [behaved as if] it was not his problem. 'I don't want to have to see them and that's it.'"[20] Pamela Zargarani, who rented the barn adjoining the Parsonage from 1966 until autumn 1968, was warned by villagers when she moved in that "Mr Lewis walks around the village with his notebook and never says hello to anybody, he's in a world of his own". Although at twenty-three she first thought he was "reserved and looked severe", she found him entirely friendly. When she showed interest in gardening, he offered her the run of the garden; when she thought she might be pregnant, Norman took her sample to the chemist and came back to tell her she was.

Gareth came across a different form of his father's jealousy. He had taken a job at the bar of a hotel in Banchory and had an ambition to fly for BOAC. When one of the hotel's customers turned out to be a BOAC director and offered to write to the company's pilot training school on Gareth's behalf, Gareth told Norman. "He made some comment about [the man's] sexuality [and] wrote back and told him to sling his hook." This sort of turf war was a curious, lifelong commonplace of Norman's psychology, from which I suffered too in the end, though infinitesimally in comparison with, say, Gareth's mother.

I mean, he'd binned my mother years ago, he didn't sleep with her, he'd sleep in the other room and she'd sleep downstairs, but there were people around the village who still thought. . . . She was a very elegant woman, my mother, until the latter years, she could cut a figure, and there were people in the village including the doctor and I think an ex-boyfriend from history who were very keen on her. And the minute you raised their name in front of Dad his lips would become pencil thin and he'd be, you know, "I don't want it but I don't want anybody else to have it either."[21]

Norman's character was even less ready to compromise when he had drunk alcohol. He thought he knew his genetic shortcomings in that area. Karen says, "I remember him saying to me how to a certain extent one is governed by one's genes and 'my father was an alcoholic and I must be very careful around the booze'."[22] His mandarin-like courtesy, unfailing manners, idiosyncratic narrative charm, and sudden outbursts of enthusiasm were all genuine – and were also parts of a presentation of self he had carefully built over years to allow a character driven by subliminally wary, mistrustful, dominating impulses to function socially. Life, or rather childhood, had made him that way too: the temptation to domination is a bleak underside to the insistence on managing one's own life.

Within the family such presentations of self are naturally weaker; alcohol weakens them, inside and outside the family circle, and Norman did not always manage to stop his appetite for enjoyment darkening into what, in him, did not come out as his father's passive babbling but as a less attractive, aggressively autocratic and (rarely) paranoid streak, belittling whoever was his target, usually Lesley, as Ito remembers. "In his relationship with Lesley were what I would call these tropical storms. He would reject her, and this rejection would be almost cyclical. It would happen at dinner, often when there were guests."[23]

However sceptically Norman professed to feel about love, there was no doubt that he loved Lesley in the senses of cherishing her and forsaking all others, but in his alcohol-prompted, uncontrolled unkindness love had no recourse.

He was not an easy man to live with. The children will have probably all told you that. He was not good with too much drink taken. There were occasions, the kids remember them as well, when he'd have too much to drink and then he'd be difficult. No, too much to drink did not suit Norman. It was fine to the point when he'd be telling his stories and it was lovely, but if it went too far then he could become difficult.[24]

PART FIVE

REPORTING

An Engagement in Two Places and Another Time

USA, Latin America, Naples

I have argued with a lot of journalists in my time, and the fault was often not theirs. I could be bad-tempered and erratic, especially in the approach to a big assignment. Friendships with writers sometimes came under strain, and occasionally broke down. While running repairs could usually be effected at the nearest bar, there would always be some legacy of damage.

There was one writer, however, who always brought out the best in me. His name was Norman Lewis, and in a way I became his disciple.

Don McCullin

If you're going to India, the worst possible place a writer could ever go to is Rajasthan. Everybody has written about it, and most of them very badly.

It wouldn't occur to me to go to see the Taj Mahal. I know in advance what the Taj Mahal looks like.

Everybody who goes to Peru goes to Cuzco – we got out as soon as we could.

I knew what was going on in the mountains near Bolivia, and I thought it would be a very interesting area to go and see, because people there behave very naturally; they maybe haven't seen foreigners before.

It's a question of feeling one's way. In some societies, like Cuba, the people are very extroverted. You look for the first opportunity to embrace them around the shoulders and offer them a cigar. But some societies of course are exceedingly withdrawn.

Norman Lewis

I did a trip to California. There was a man called Chavez who was staging a grape-pickers' strike and I went down to see him for the *Sunday Times*. I found that an excessively boring experience. The place, generally speaking, the lack of adventure – everything was standardised, everything was to be expected. I knew that there was no day upon which I would have some new and illuminating experience.

Norman Lewis

. . . not a single sparrow twittered in the eaves of Delano. Nor were there lizards on the dry walls, nor snails in damp places, nor frogs in ditches. Even domestic animals were rare. I remember after several days being stopped in the street by the sight of a wasp crawling out of a post, which by this time seemed extraordinary. A blind and complaisant local patriotism prevents the average citizen of Delano from believing that anything can be seriously wrong with his environment. But while easily swallowing this camel he strains at the gnat of minor perils to his health. Knives and forks in the leading restaurants are enclosed in sanitised envelopes. Butter – considered dangerous – is hard to come by, and a "creamer" composed of eight chemicals replaces milk for one's coffee. These precautions seem excessive under a sky which appears to be burdened with the ash of distant volcanoes, and within sight of ornamental trees being hosed down to prevent their dropping their leaves.

"Slave-Labourers in the Vineyard"

24

WHERE THE GENOCIDE IS

"Cultivate a heart of love that knows no anger"
Cambodian proverb

TWENTY years is a long time in any literary life. It had been that long since Norman had sat down to write his first novel, *Samara*: since then, nine novels and four books of non-fiction. Thirteen times the botheringly mute world of things, images, ephemera, finished processes had been made to speak. He had carried on writing novels, trying to eradicate the frustration he had expressed in his August 1960 letter to Michael Howard. Then he had rationalised his disappointment by blaming his publisher. Eight years later he had had three publishers for his fiction, and none had done any better than the others; yet it didn't matter who published his non-fiction. (In the USA the situation was slightly different. Since Scribner's had published his south-east Asia books in the 1950s, unsatisfactorily in his view, he had been published by five different houses, of whom Pantheon had been the most enthusiastic and William Morrow, his most recent publisher, the least, only staying with him for one book. None had sold his books in any quantity; did the United States just not get Norman?)

What to write about now? Writers put the question to themselves knowing that a book is also a chore, a game of hazard, a flirtation with failure. After the reception of *Every Man's Brother*, the question was a sharp one. For Norman in his sixtieth year, if, as he said he did, he planned to live for ever, a durable answer was needed.

He tried again.

The carbon of a finished novel sits among his typescripts, next to other folders containing drafts that signify the amount of work he put into it. The subject matter is astonishing: an effort, possibly, to modernise radically the content of his fiction. "The Experience" is a narrative, first-person, set in the 1960s, of two English "beats" attempting to get to north Africa on the cheap. One is a speed freak called Jimmy, the other the more or less "clean" narrator. For transport they adopt for the journey a collapsible boat, with initially similar consequences to those suffered by Norman and Eugene Corvaja in 1934. After days of hunger they try to rob a village store, wounding the owner's son; at the next village the narrator picks up a "brass" who is later found murdered. Lacking food, Jimmy reverts to his "minstrels" – speed – and in a paranoia of drugs and near-starvation the pair fall out. The bad trip (in both senses) changes direction, with both protagonists waking up in a French hospital after being picked up by the police, the question then being: which of them, if either, is a murderer? (It turns out in an oddly cheerful conclusion that neither is: the prostitute was murdered by a passing trucker.)

The novel is an outstandingly strange curiosity, shockingly incongruous in Norman's work and revelatory of what happened to his style and tone when they left their usual precinct. With its lucid, wide, sensuous vocabulary and cadences so subtly worked, his language balks at communicating the disyllabic demotic of confused youth. Despite his brave efforts with slang – "minstrels", "stick" (marijuana), "I could see by now that Jimmy and I weren't going to go on grooving together much longer" – the novel's dialogue and narration stand out like a pair of Augustans in disguise at the summer of love. A few sentences reveal the author himself. "My thing was travel – straight and with no trimmings," the narrator says. "Jimmy was the only traveller I knew who could keep up with me, but the great and terrible drawback to hitting the road with Jimmy was the speed. It made him obsessional and sometimes very weird. . . . I liked to cover the distances and keep on the move. I thought of myself as really floating above my scene and outside it, just watching, and sucking something out of it with my eyes."[1] That sentence sounds very like the author describing himself, not unsuccessfully, but profoundly awkward at having to avoid using "difficult" words. "The Experience" may have been submitted to Collins or to Heinemann or both, but was not published.

Afterwards, the answer to his writing dilemma seemed as if it might not lie with books at all. His meeting and friendship with the *Sunday Times* magazine's features editor, Peter Crookston, a converted admirer,

provided an opening for the retrieval of a thread in his writing that
went back to 1957 and his Caribbean reports for Ian Fleming. His
first substantial commission for Crookston was to return to Palermo,
where, on 14 March 1968, a trial of ten high-ranking *mafiosi* arrested
three years earlier was to start. The trial had attracted a blaze of
attention because of the defendants' awesome reputations and the
promise that, with three of them holding dual American and Italian
nationality, the proceedings would uncover the link between the Sicilian
mafia and its American offshoot, in particular with regard to the
international trade in heroin. The legal authorities in Sicily had promised that, unlike former trials, this one would not collapse. Norman
was in his natural realm, his descriptions reflecting his glee at participating.

The prisoners' appearance was the first surprise. Edward G Robinson and
latterly the obsidian features of Danger Man and the television gangsters left
one ill-prepared for the ingrained respectability of these calm faces, this modest
stillness and humility. All of these men seen in the flesh were unrecognisable
from their rogues-gallery portraits published in the newspapers. The difference
was so extraordinary that one wondered if some subjective element could
possibly exist – if one were in fact the victim of some strange suggestive power
that cloaked ferocity in mildness and replaced the famous cold stare of the
mafioso – reported on one well-known occasion to have caused even a bandit
to lower his gun – with a kind of twinkling benevolence.
  . . . Diego Plaia closed his eyes to clutch his small granddaughter to him
and kiss her a dozen times, then fished in his pocket with his free hand for a
packet of sweets. . . . At his side John Bonventre radiated paternalism, looking
like a more than usually unworldly priest.[2]

In his paragraphs of back story about the mafia's post-war golden
age he could not leave out Don Calò Vizzini and Lucky Luciano, whose
alleged humility elicited a sentence of archetypally droll Lewis irony.
"Luciano too was a man of quiet tastes, although he could endure the
trappings of power when thrust upon him." In Palermo, he wrote,
Luciano's memory remained green. ". . . a barman in a hotel he used
to frequent said of him: 'He was possibly the most charming man I
have ever met. Kind and considerate to everyone. Always with the same
lady, and always full of little attentions. An *exquisite* personality.'"
  The court sat for three days and adjourned. Waiting for its resump-
tion Norman made two useful contacts, a northern colonel of the

carabinieri named Giuseppe Russo, and the Palermo head of the Pubblica Sicurezza, the well-tailored Boris Giuliano, who became a friend and later suggested to Norman the basis of his novel *The Sicilian Specialist*. (Both Russo and Giuliano were eventually murdered.) The trial resumed on 30 March, and shortly afterwards Norman returned to England to write the piece, certain that the court proceedings would drag on until they collapsed, as all their predecessors had. They did, and on 25 June the accused men were cleared for lack of proof.

Norman came back to the Easter school holidays and took the family caravanning in Ireland ("very wet, not our kind of holiday"[3]). Returning, he flew to Ibiza for ten days with the idea of solving the holiday-with-children problem by finding an isolated plot of land on the island that he could build on. In the 1950s he had turned down plenty of offers to sell him cheap land on the coast at S'Argamassa near Santa Eulalia, at Portinatx on the island's north-east corner, and elsewhere, but the plot he finally agreed to buy defied logic: on a precipitous hillside by Santa Inès in the north-west, it was gloriously remote but offered steep, almost impossible access to the sea. When a German bought a plot near Norman's shortly afterwards and started to build a zigzag road to the shore, a further drawback materialised when the man was ordered to stop by the municipality because the land had been designated *"zona verde"*. It was so unsuitable, the question arises of whether Norman was subconsciously courting failure. The land was never built on, and his title to it has been lost, though the family did go to Ibiza that summer and stayed in an apartment owned by a business acquaintance of Ito's. Lesley remembers an evening of embarrassment.

This man owned a lot of Ibiza, charming man, and he said to Norman, "I'd like to invite you to dinner. Is there anything that you'd particularly like?" So Norman, who was showing off, said, *"Freixura* is what I like." And *freixura* is the pluck of the animal, it's all the lights, the liver. . . . We'd been out in the sun all day, the children were tiny, they were exhausted and asleep on their feet. We went into this restaurant where the chef greeted us with "You are the honoured guests", then produced a [colossal] fish, that was the starter, and having picked at this, I was finished. And then this poor chef arrived and this great *asaduras* was brought out. [It's] all meat, there's garlic and there's parsley in it. Enormous, enormous . . . and we couldn't start to eat any of it. It was so embarrassing, ghastly. I said to Norman, "You just restrain yourself in future, making these wild statements of what you like."[4]

Norman's account of the mafia trial was published in August. Crookston, pleased with it, asked him for an anniversary essay on Che Guevara a year after Che's murder in Bolivia. The piece Norman wrote underlined with apolitical sensitivity that many who had little sympathy for Marxism had felt a sense of disbelief and loss at the news of his death. (If you were a middle-class *Sunday Times* reader he made it acceptable to identify with the object of your compassion, not your politics.) "The unprecedented gesture of [Che's] renunciation of power and prestige among the leaders of the Cuban government to return to the jungle, and there die, were certain to create a legend and a cult that are without importance. Nonetheless, Che Guevara's teachings and his example are certain to influence deeply that small but determined minority of the young who grow impatient of the confinements of our present system. In the United States a huge frustration grows," he wrote, recalling the grotesque violence at Chicago that August during the Democratic convention, when women and children were tear-gassed on national television. "Young activists in England find it hard to accept a future in which the leaders, whether Labour or Conservative, trot meekly at the heels of the makers of war policies in Washington."[5] How history repeats itself.

Frustration with US policies was not only for the young. In autumn 1968 Norman and Lesley rented their barn to a US serviceman and his English wife (nanny to the daughter of one of Lesley's friends). Norman had disagreed with American involvement in Vietnam since the time of Eisenhower's first deployment of military assistance in 1955. He had disagreed with French occupation, but acknowledged that many of the French had liked and admired the Vietnamese, and that there had been an attachment, however untenable. When the Americans arrived, as he said in a later interview, "I think they just viewed all [the Vietnamese] as the enemy."[6] In early 1969, a few months after his American tenant moved in, he became so angered by the emptiness of Nixon's "peace with honor" promise that he decided he had been wrong to accept US administration dollars for the barn's rent all along and asked the man and his wife to leave. The tenant agreed to go, recognising that it was a matter of conscience, though his wife's connections with Lesley's friend left Lesley picking up the pieces of a "great upset".

In summer 1968, after his return from Ibiza, Norman invited Crookston to lunch for another story discussion. In March, Norman

said, the Brazilian government had suddenly, with little attempt at justification, announced a catastrophe. The country's forest Indians, persisting
in their tribal lands for thousands of years, had abruptly in the last
decade declined so steeply in numbers that many tribes were at the
edge of extinction. Some had already vanished. Their genocide, Norman
told Crookston, had not happened despite the efforts of the government's own Indian Protection Service, but with its routine and eager
complicity. A judicial inquiry was now under way; 1000 employees
would be charged with crimes. Crookston commissioned the piece.

That autumn Norman spent several weeks in Rio de Janeiro and the
forests of the Amazon, and in Brazil, at sixty, his view of what he saw
and cared about when he travelled suddenly changed. He came back
to England with an astonishing story: that, starting in the 1950s, the
Brazilian Indians had begun to be exterminated with the active
connivance and co-operation of the government employees who were
supposed to be preserving them. Thousands of hectares of Indian land,
cleared of entire tribes, was being sold off to *fazendeiros* and mineral
speculators, the proceeds pocketed by Indian Protection Service agents.
In the coils of this Indian calvary he discovered something else. More
extraordinary still than the repetitive mundane details of the murder
of so many was, as an official at the Brazilian Ministry of the Interior
put it, "the disastrous impact of missionary activity".

The missionaries were Protestant fundamentalists, whose demoralising attrition of native cultures Norman had long disagreed with. Now,
as he said, he opposed. Tribes like the Bororos, prototypes for Lévi-
Strauss's principles of structural anthropology, had been robbed of their
livestock by the IPS and made dependent on missionaries, who forbade
their dancing, singing, smoking and all-important funeral rites. The
Bororos had been the more fortunate. Others, Maxacalis, Cintas Largas,
Tapaunas, Patachos, had been made drunk and machine-gunned by
professionals hired by the IPS, attacked with dynamite from the air,
assassinated with gifts of sugar laced with arsenic, injected with smallpox.
Some had disappeared completely. But IPS and missionaries were one.
Norman quoted a *Jornal do Brasil* report of that year. "In reality, those
in command of these Indian Protection posts are North American
missionaries – they are in all the posts – and they disfigure the original Indian culture and enforce the acceptance of Protestantism."[7]

Most telling, when Norman came back and wrote his 12,000-word
article, was its tone. Rarely had he felt the need to fortify his poised

and underplayed irony with contempt. Now he quoted a government report into atrocities committed against Indians that described how Paraná Indians were tortured by grinding the bones of their feet between two stakes driven into the ground. "Why," he wrote, finding a way to keep his anger on the leash with borrowed dispraise, "all this pointless cruelty? What is it that causes men and women probably of extreme respectability in their everyday lives to torture for the sake of torturing? Montaigne believed that cruelty is the revenge of the weak man for his weakness; a sort of sickly parody of valour. 'The killing after a victory is usually done by the rabble and baggage officials.'"[8]

"I never heard Norman say a bad word about anybody. Apart from missionaries. He was always castigating them."[9] The photographer Don McCullin, who worked with Norman, witnessed his opposition many times to the wrong side of Christianity. His hatred was less a hatred of organised religion, Christianity, or even Christian doctrine, than a hatred of any dictatorship of the spirit. He admired the Bororos' extraordinarily intricate funerary rites, agreed with Lévi-Strauss that "Few people are so religious . . . few possess a metaphysical system of such complexity". In a paradoxical way he had reached Kierkegaard's third, religious stage of existence, but all questions of the spirit for him (as for Kierkegaard) were those of freedom, of human equity: the freedom to be like the Indian beyond the reach of civilisation "the perfect human product of his environment . . . at terms with his surroundings, deeply conscious of his place in the living patterns of the visible and invisible universe"; and the equity that was predicated on non-interference and a refusal to use, as the North American evangelists were doing, faith for the ends of power and wealth.

From the time of writing "Genocide" for the *Sunday Times* in the last months of 1968, the observer became the opposer. He had seen barbarity in war, in Sicilian society, and now he saw it irreversibly changing the world – his preferred world – under the shape of religion-driven economics. His anger was deep because, as McCullin puts it, he "idolised those people and those cultures". The change to his writing caused no loss of his gentle drollery or of his compassion for the absurd. It did give him licence to deepen his expression of what he felt. Once asked by the American journalist William Zinsser if he felt some moral compulsion to seek out injustice, he pointed out that like most people's motives his were extremely mixed, admitting that notes of journalistic evangelism sometimes crept in when he wrote about cruelty. He worked hard to detect and correct them (they were a tonal defect, he said, that belonged to his Welshness). His chief reason for not raising his voice was that he felt stridency was always unsuccessful. I asked him about this aspect of his writing several times and had, for Norman, consistent answers.

What I tend to do is, I sermonise, and reading back the day's work or reading it back subsequently I think now this is just a boring sermon on this particular subject, let's either cut it out or cut it down to a paragraph ... if you write this kind of [sermonising] book on the whole a lot of people put it down, they're discomforted or they're bored with it. ... All writers actually want anybody who picks a book up to start reading, they want them to go on and finish it, there's really no satisfaction in putting your readers off by an excessive moral stance about anything. ... It's unconvincing. I provide as I can the facts. Now for example what I'm writing now [about a massacre in Guatemala] – I'm not going to use that word "massacre" more than once. I think that people are repelled. First of all, they really don't want to read about really hideous things, [secondly] I believe it to be more effective in the way I do it.[10]

His allegiance to this tonal restraint (which was not allowed to interfere with often breezily graphic descriptions of atrocities) meant that the eventual impact of "Genocide" was so substantial that, over time, he came to regard it as one of the great achievements of his writing life.

The piece initially ran to about 14,000 words. Crookston was impressed. "I never tried to change his style, but I think I weeded probably a couple of thousand out of that. The beginning needed some editing to speed it up." At 12,000 words it was still going to be the longest piece the magazine had published. Crookston asked Don McCullin, then a young photographer who had made a name in Vietnam and Biafra, to see if he could reach some of the tribes and bring back pictures.

McCullin later respectfully described the assignment as his "apprenticeship before working directly with Norman". Briefed by Crookston with a list of places supplied by Norman, he found the job difficult. "I was treated like shit by the [government] people and then I went to the air force to get a lift to the Xingu[11] where there were two distinguished anthropologists, the Vilas Boas [brothers], and they couldn't have been more unpleasant." But he got the pictures. When Norman saw them, he asked to meet McCullin. It was the beginning of a friendship across a generation between two north London boys, the Forty Hill fugitive and a "very ambitious young upstart from Finsbury Park".

There was an immediate affinity between us. I was young – but this is the irony about Norman at that stage, this was a man who'd spent years working alone and suddenly he came into the magazine/newspaper world and was obliged to go off on journeys with another person, another human being, i.e. a photographer. And Norman had a way about him, he was one of the kindest, most respectful people you'll ever meet, [and] he never ever showed any disapproval [at having] this kind of person around. He respected you for your ability, he didn't expect anything from you. He never expected me to read his books.[12]

McCullin acknowledged a father-figure element to the relationship, but insisted that the most important aspect of Norman's friendship was that he "always brought out the best in me". Norman reciprocated by saying that, whenever he travelled with McCullin, he was amazed by his terrific eye for beauty.

I learnt from him how beautiful the ordinary can be, where previously the only things that attracted me really were non-ordinary things. But travelling with him I would see him suddenly spellbound by the beauty of rain drizzling down the mountainside, where I would normally pass it by, I wouldn't notice it was happening. Trained by Donald, I've developed more observation in these matters.[13]

He paid tribute too to qualities in McCullin that others might have considered less important. "These trips can be very fraught, and you must be able to get on with the person you're travelling with. Don is utterly reliable and fantastically courteous – something of a rarity these days."[14]

"Genocide" was published in the *Sunday Times* on 23 February 1969. The interest was immediate. Extra staff had to handle the copious correspondence and phone calls. One of the people to contact the newspaper was an explorer, Robin Hanbury-Tenison. As a direct result of the article, Hanbury-Tenison that year co-founded Survival International, a campaigning group for the rights, lands and cultures of indigenous people. "The idea of an organisation to represent tribal people was greeted in 1969 with profound scepticism," he recalls. "Most thought the struggle hopeless and the people we cared about doomed to extinction in the near future. We were seen as trying to stop the clock, create human zoos and delay progress."[15] (Today Survival International has supporters in eighty-two countries.)

Although it was not in his nature to express anything stronger than murmured satisfaction, Norman became proud to have triggered a breakthrough in the world's attitude to the predicament, and value, of people whom he regarded as its "supreme humanity". In the penultimate paragraph of "Genocide" he quoted Professor Darci Ribeiro, a leading authority on the Indians who had calculated that if trends continued as indicated by data from the past fifty years, there would not be a single Indian left alive in Brazil by 1980: a prophecy that, because of what Norman wrote, did not get the chance to come wholly true.

In the structuring of his life Norman had chosen the elements he wanted: a form of behaviour that he thought of as managing his own life successfully, and a reaction to the largely awful structural factors of his childhood. Only sometimes to others did it seem a dogmatic, autocratic sort of behaviour; mostly it was presented with charm and spontaneity and hedged with a talent for attentive friendship and hospitality, and that was what those around him saw, and appreciated. He *had* managed his life successfully: done what he wanted, been paid for it, gained a reputation. Not wholly the reputation he desired, but enough of one as a writer, if not a novelist, to let him carry on doing what he wanted, travelling and writing. His life, in fact, had come to seem a powerful affirmation that, whatever the significance of structural factors, they retreat irrevocably to second place when the adult starts to "decide" (that moment may itself define the beginning of adulthood). From 1969 onwards through the decade of the 1970s he discovered that his powers of decision could not always be counted on.

Norman was not in England when "Genocide" was published. It was the English winter and he was in Haiti, having rolled up his family's needs and his own into a Caribbean escape. Arriving in Jamaica on 20 January they booked into a boarding house with a swimming pool in the Blue Mountains above Port Antonio. Five days later Norman left

Lesley, Kiki and Gawaine and flew to Port–au–Prince. His intention isn't clear: the best indication is in the piece he wrote when he got back, in which a bloodied and bruised hotelier, victim of a Haitian army officer's casual beating, tells Norman he is finally leaving. "But I knew him too well, and I knew that next year if I came back he would still be there, a prisoner for life of the charm of this strange and beautiful island."[16]

He went to Haiti because he was contemplating writing a book about the "strange and beautiful island", about its interlacing of violence and charm, its misery and faded relics (but didn't). He stayed for five weeks if his passport stamps are to be believed, and wrote only about a drive into the country to Belladère with his hotelier friend, whom he called Johnson, in his gorgeous, weather-lashed Facel Vega. The narrative delights in radical, just plausible absurdities. At Belladère, a clapboard and tin effigy of nineteenth-century Normandy,

We stopped to watch the approach of a ghostly black version of a French grandee with white Napoleon beard, cutaway coat, panama hat, spats and malacca cane. . . . "This", said Johnson, "is a copy of France as it once was. You won't hear Creole spoken here. These people actually believe themselves to be French. Take that old man with the white beard we just saw. I know him. He has papers to prove he's a descendant of the Duc de Brantôme. There's another family here that goes back to Lamartine. Forget about Papa Doc Duvalier. This is the real Haiti."[17]

Norman flew back to Jamaica on 2 March. The spell of Haiti's absurdity clung on. He drove to the coast one day, parked on the low headland above the beach, and went for a think-walk with his note-book. When he got back, the car had gone. Someone ran to tell him it had fallen over the cliff. He had forgotten to put the handbrake on; rolling over the edge, the car had dug into the sand within a couple of metres of some changing huts. A few days later, he drove the family to a deserted beach where Lesley and the children splashed in the shallows while he swam out to snorkel on the reef. Suddenly Lesley saw him swimming back to her, waving agitatedly, and heard him shout. "Shark, shark." She saw a flash of silver and an eye and grabbed the children from the water. Norman made it ashore and saw that the attacking fish had taken a chunk from his flipper (it was a barracuda, but he said later that he didn't think Lesley knew what a barracuda was). Locals were on hand with the news that two swimmers had been killed by barracudas recently. Norman's near-miss became the source of relentless teasing of Lesley. "He could never let that go. He used to say, 'You were a top-class swimmer, I expected you to come and save me and instead you just grabbed the kids and ran.'"[18]

Still no book was in view. Working on several eventually discarded fragments of fiction, including a story about Haiti, "The Primitives", nothing held his attention for long. The reaction to his novels, and their sales, had made it difficult to think about writing another. Between 1968 and 1972, Lesley says, "he went through a patch where he couldn't think of anything to write". No story was bigger than an article. But journalism filled the gap. "He enjoyed life as long as he had something to write about and the journalism then was enough."[19] It was a time of generous payment for *Sunday Times* contributors so he could survive, although there was less coming from R G Lewis, with more competitors in the late 1960s. More settling occurred at Finchingfield: a swimming pool was put into a corner of the garden, and in May Lesley became pregnant for the third time. If Norman, writing in his red "Silvine" notebooks at the far end of the Parsonage's long, rolling first-floor landing on half a dozen subjects at any one time, was not productive the way he had been without let-up for twenty years, he may have been frustrated but was not dissatisifed.

At the end of the summer he went back to the *Sunday Times* to suggest it send him to cover the Mexican grape-pickers' strike in California, in its fifth year and having reached the point of keeping grapes off American dining tables. Crookston agreed. In late November Norman flew to Kansas City, where he met the strikers' leader, Cesar Chavez, then to Bakersfield where he hired a car and drove north through the San Joaquin valley to Delano. He was impressed by Chavez, a fragile-looking Mexican, and his natural determination that the protest should remain non-violent; "one clears him in one's mind of any suspicion of theatricality". This was more than could be said of pristine Delano, where, he observed, nature had gone and Rachel Carson's silent spring had arrived. "Two hundred and fifty miles away across the border in poverty-stricken Mexico there were butterflies and hummingbirds in the bedraggled gardens of Mexicali, but not a single sparrow twittered in the eaves of Delano."[20] Delano was where, five years before, the strike had begun as a way of protesting the conditions – slave labour and child labour, overwork, poisoning with crop sprays – of migrant grape-pickers. Chavez had told

Norman that he was primarily fighting not for the grape-pickers but for
the dignity of the two and a quarter million Mexicans living in California,
"the niggers of ten years ago" as he called them. California's governor,
Ronald Reagan, had denounced the strike as "immoral" and "an attempted
blackmail of free society", an odd description when, before the strike,
eight-year-old Mexican girls had been working a 70-hour week and adult
pickers with no employment security earned less than half the US poverty
wage.[21]

California alternately horrified and bored Norman. Of nearly 800
Mexicans interviewed by health workers, he wrote, practically all had
signs of toxic spray poisoning. He travelled to Calexico on the US side
of the border and checked into a motel to see the strikebreakers' buses,
full of uncomfortable, penniless Mexicans. He told Pico Iyer later, "I
checked in there and the receptionist understood I was a stranger and
he said, 'I want to tell you something. This city is divided by a river
and there is a bridge over the river and we Americans are on the one
side and the Mexican immigrants are on the other, and if you go over
the other side you may well never return.'" Early on the 26th he drove
his large hired Buick across the bridge to Mexicali. A walk along the
bank of the town's Rio Nuevo – rivulets of glossy congealing black
sewage – presented him with "the worst slum I'd ever seen in my life".
On the way back he took a wrong turning.

I had to back and turn round, and in backing I ploughed through a chicken
wire fence that tangled up with the drive of the car. When I turned round I
had a hundred and fifty yards of fence dragging down the street, with thousands of sparks coming out of it. So I got out and went to the first Mexican
I saw and said, "I've a great problem." I speak a certain amount of Spanish,
and this struck them as very extraordinary. He said, "What is your problem?"
and I said, "I'm going to try and get the fence out." He went round, shouting
at two or three houses, and hundreds of Mexicans came out and they *lifted
this car up, about thirty on each side*, lifted this car up while another man
got underneath it and untwisted the wire. So these were the Mexicans who
are supposed to slit your throat if you're non-Mexican? Instead of which I
went to the nearest bar with all the Mexicans I could find and we drank a
few tequilas and beers, and hugs and kisses all round and I came back.[22]

He had a further destination, nothing to do with his article about
the strike. He had decided to profit from where he was and take *rápido*
buses south to see as much as he could of western Mexico between

the US frontier and Mexico City. After 1400 miles in two days, the seat of his trousers almost worn through, he halted at Guadalajara and booked into a hotel. .

On the last stage of the journey a Huichol Indian had attracted his attention, sitting in aristocratic isolation in his embroidered tunic and pantaloons with his bow and arrows. At his hotel Norman saw a poster advertising an exhibition of Huichol art at the basilica of Zapopan outside the city, and the following morning took a taxi there. The exhibits were chiefly a collection of symbolic textile paintings in brightly coloured yarn and beeswax called *nearikas*, most "painted" by a Huichol named Ramón Medina Silva who was said to have shamanistic powers. The brilliant colours, with the bold glare of peyote visions, and the paintings' insistence on the sacred connections of soul, sex and the animal world moved him. He cut short his Mexican excursion there, determining to come back.

His coverage of the grape-pickers' strike reinforced his standing at the *Sunday Times*. Any frustration he felt at not writing books was soothed into the background by the trips he was making, paid and speculative, and the journalism he was writing. It was a pattern that would continue for a decade: a decade of little urgency, few books, but a chain of long, engaged reports and journeys in which he appeared to be quartering the whole of Latin America. The reports sometimes gave the impression of being about the vanishing of one culture after another; occasionally, as with his return to Mexico, they would celebrate a resistance or a survival, but Norman had begun his "Genocide" piece with a warning that "if you happened to be one of those who felt affection for the gentle, backward civilisations ... then 1968 was a bad year for you", and most years afterwards were, he showed, not much different as modernity continued down its squandering highway. A journey frequently provided him with fuel for the next, as well as plenty of unforced drama. In between, periodically the old itch came back and, ineradicable by other means, was cured by writing another novel. And gradually, despite his ability to break a story and the consistent seriousness of his journalism, his reputation underwent a growing eclipse, his subjects too exotic for an increasingly wan decade.

Before he could get back to Mexico he was caught out by biology. On 13 December his daughter Samara was born two months premature, and he was at home. Lesley went into labour unexpectedly at the Parsonage with a snowstorm blowing outside, so it was impossible to get her to a hospital and Norman was compelled to take part in the birth. The baby was born safely. Her nine-year-old sister Kiki thought she "looked like a little rat". Because her father had helped save her sister, she says, there was always a different bond between them. Afterwards Norman revelled in the story of the doctor finally arriving and telling her parents to prepare for disappointment, that he didn't think the baby "would be any Einstein, Mr and Mrs Lewis".[23] Samara, later shortened to Bubs, went on to qualify as a doctor herself.

The *Sunday Times* agreed to a piece about the Huichol Indians, and on 4 February Norman flew back to Mexico. The Huichols of the Sierra Madre were the only major group north of the Amazon believed to have survived the holocaust of conquest and the invasions of modernity with their traditions and art intact. Cousins of the Aztecs, they inhabited a world governed by occult mystery, "a magic world", as a Mexican anthropological journal puts it, "in which all things are possible and where man may take on the power of the gods by winning their favour. Though command of the supernatural is not reserved for the very few, some individuals possess greater occult understanding and, as powerful shamans, cloud the sun to bring rain, dispel infirmities from men and animals, transform themselves at will or simply disappear."[24]

This time Norman took a photographer with him, David Montgomery, whose pictures had accompanied his California story.

I didn't think I was going off to do anything dangerous, I just thought I was going to Mexico. I think he called me up and said, "Get some hiking boots, we're going to be walking up in the mountains and there are spiders that can jump off trees, and snakes." So right away I was shitting myself, they're two of my favourite things. He just said it in a very droll way, I mean he didn't say it menacingly.

We just met at the airport and this guy that looked like Harold Macmillan or a head schoolmaster turned up and off we went.[25]

Montgomery noticed what Lesley was already familiar with, Norman's tendency to import dramatic elements, in particular secret agents on trains. "I think he was in MI5 or MI6 and he said, 'Oh you know, just before I came into London the most amazing thing happened, old boy. I was standing on the Bishops Stortford train station and there was one of the biggest Russian spies, standing there waiting for a train'

– because I guess Norman knew, these guys know each other, or something like that."

As Montgomery discovered, the Mexico journey needed no decoration. They flew to Guadalajara and called on Father Ernesto Loera, head of the Franciscan mission at Zapopan who had organised the Huichol exhibition Norman had seen. Fr Ernesto advised them to go to Tepic, charter the mission plane, and fly into the sierra from there – though they would have to stay at a mission or they would be killed by the Huichols, who had no reason to trust strangers and were accordingly trigger-happy.

At Tepic they were luckier than they had expected. Ramón Medina Silva, the greatest of the *nearika* artists and alleged shaman, was in town; even more providentially, and as Norman wrote, "It was difficult to believe he meant what he said," when they explained their plans to him he asked if they would like him to go with them.

Norman's most reliable account of the journey is stamped with his admiration for the Huichols' enigmatic rituals, among them their annual expedition to the desert of San Luis Potosí, led by Medina Silva, to collect peyote cactus. He detected a mysterious power in Medina Silva which the anthropologist Peter Furst had witnessed a few years before, when Ramón had demonstrated the meaning of shamanistic "balance" by leaping barefoot across a high waterfall – "'fly' might be more appropriate", Furst wrote – with arms stretched wide and never looking down.

The growing hazards of Norman's and Montgomery's own journey, of bandits, murders and witchcraft, he describes with a quietly gleeful matter-of-factness. (He later said that the war had developed in him a built-in mechanism against fear, telling Colin Thubron that the danger of his subsequent travels was comparatively so much less that he undertook them without trepidation.[26]) After the appearance of his *Sunday Times* account, he expanded on, even sexed up, the journey in two further versions in *The Missionaries* and his autobiography – although he may have been telling the truth when he described it as "the least relaxed three days of my life, by comparison with which the equivalent time spent on the beach-head at Salerno in 1943 seemed relatively calm". David Montgomery certainly saw it that way.

The three flew from Tepic the following day to an airstrip at San Andrès in the only available plane, a commercial twin-engined Beechcraft. "Norman says to me, 'Remember one thing, if this plane goes down, never leave the site where the plane is.' 'Okay Norman.' I didn't realise till later that the place was covered in bandits." At San Andrès they faced a walk of several hours to the Franciscan mission at Santa Clara. (It was here, a few minutes along the trail, that the shaman pulled his 9mm Star pistol from his satchel and asked Norman for proof of his proficiency with a gun.) Montgomery suffered on the walk, although Norman at sixty-two felt no ill effect.

I would say to Norman, "I can't walk, I can't go on, leave me here." He tells the witch doctor, the witch doctor says to me, "Lay down on that rock over there", you know, like big boulders, and I'd lay down on the rock and after ten minutes I feel fantastic . . . they're walking and then the witch doctor would stop and he'd listen to the wind and he'd write whatever the wind was telling him, he'd write it down.[27]

Arriving at the convent at Santa Clara they had a short, freezing night.

Norman explained to me that the Indians really didn't want to have anything to do with the Church but the Church fed the kids so they had no alternative but to let them go to school. As soon as the light came up I bolted for the door, and then Norman came out right after me and he said, "It's a good thing we waited till the dawn came up because the [shaman] would have just seen some movement and plugged us." I said, "Thanks Norman." The next day we played a very fierce game of volleyball with the nuns, really serious, they almost killed us. I've played volleyball, but this was like all their sexual aggression coming out.

In reality, as Ramón told Norman, the instruction the children got at the mission was unimportant. A Huichol soul always remained one and couldn't be transferred to the Christians. The only danger would come if they married out of the tribe; the *mestizo* had no soul. Innumerable details like this of the day spent at the mission are conveyed with Norman's intense scrutiny; at the edge of any scene, he scanned it for everything from the infinitely aspected strangeness of Huichol culture to copious, precise notations of the natural world. The reader is in the middle of every scene, an atmosphere that pays off climactically in his account of the walk back to San Andrès to see the preparations for a fiesta the next day. Montgomery recalls that

We were walking through the forest and another Indian appears. I go over with a cigarette, offer him a cigarette, and Norman somehow, in a very calm, delicate way says to me to get back to him as quick as I could walk in a slow way. I go back, I say, "What's up?" and Norman says, "That guy's a bandit and the shaman was going to plug him."

We keep on walking, and Norman sees a raven.

Norman's own description included, apart from the bandit, two branches crossed over the trail in a *travesía*, as a spell to keep travellers away from the village, which Ramón had to dispel before they could go on. At the village the atmosphere was grimly sinister, and it was clear the fiesta had been cancelled. While they waited for something to happen, a *mestizo* appeared carrying a rifle and a stand-off took place. Eventually Ramón was overruled and the man allowed to go, the bullets for his rifle confiscated, but shortly afterwards Ramón reappeared and announced that he had found the body of a murdered man in one of the village houses. The body had been hidden between the rafters and the roof, and the man had been dead for at least two days.

Montgomery, feeling faint, photographed the body, and, after its consecration in a scratch ceremony, prudence dictated to the three that they turn back to the mission, walking well spaced in single file. When they were clear of the village Norman asked Ramón why had the man been killed? "Because he wanted to be a shaman." The shamans were under threat as leaders of their tribe, he said. The *mestizo* at the village had been a hired killer who had followed Norman's party into San Andrés and had only been thwarted by the villagers' presence from shooting Ramón – a murder that would have been another step in the undermining of the Huichols, the objective being to dislodge them as unwanted nuisances from land rich in mineral rights. Norman was grateful by now to have had a witness to what had happened.

We finally get to the [mission] and I am shattered. Norman keeps saying to me, "See here old boy," he says, "you know I'm Welsh and the Welsh have a reputation for embellishing things." I said, "I don't know what you're talking about, Norman." He said, "Basically lying." He says, "The Welsh have a reputation for this and my wife's never going to believe any of this, so you're going to have to come to the house and tell her the story. No one's going to believe this."

Before they flew out of Santa Clara on the mission plane, Ramón invited Norman and Montgomery to accompany him on the next annual peyote pilgrimage, a twenty-day march to Rial Catorce in the high desert sustained by little apart from virtue.

Several months later, Norman wrote to the Indian Institute in Tepic to contact Ramón about the journey, but had no reply. The shaman had disappeared, as shamans have the power to do; but this disappearance, he discovered later by chance, was final as in June 1971 Ramón Medina Silva had been murdered in a real or staged drunken brawl at his rancho, within months of their excursion together.

At Cuzco we were met by Guillermo, the stout and genial head of the local tourist office, and a beautiful young assistant called Milagros ("miracles"). Two large cars awaited, the second containing two saturnine men in dark glasses and raincoats. (As we were later told that it was unlikely to rain in Cuzco for another five months, I assumed that the raincoats were intended to conceal sub-machine guns.) A score of photographers ran hither and thither like disoriented partridges in the background, and a policeman who wore a peaked cap pulled down so that nothing could be seen of his face above the end of his nose, blew his whistle continuously. It was at this moment that I felt the ball and chain fixed in position around my ankle.

The World The World

I don't think Snowdon really realised what a great man Norman was.

Don McCullin

25

WHERE THE BOREDOM IS

"To whom you tell your secret you surrender your freedom"
Italian proverb

ON his return from Mexico David Montgomery was invited to Finchingfield to confirm that Norman was, for once, telling the truth. He was surprised by one aspect of his reception. "I went to his house for dinner, and he proudly showed me all his wine-making. The whole house was like a brewery." Because a lot of wine was drunk at the Parsonage, Norman had decided to make his own in the bespoke 1970s British way, using a kit from the Braintree branch of Boots. Frank Allen provided him with gallon jars, and he filled the airing cupboard with heaters and tubes. Montgomery recalls that "it was like those kind of comedy films about alcoholics with bottles and chandeliers and everything".[1]

There were family holidays that year at Tenerife and in Catalonia, and in the autumn Sid Perelman was coaxed back to spend two nights at the Parsonage at the beginning of November. He had arrived in London on the SS *France* and moved into the Reform Club, having noisily announced his intention of exchanging New York for London. Norman was fond of Perelman: he was one of the very few people whose conversation and stories Norman would happily acquiesce to listen to; Perelman could match him all the way. "One can see", Abby Perelman, his daughter, says, "why they immediately took to one another. They were two of a kind, both great travellers, both fascinated by language or languages in Norman's case, as I believe I heard my father extol his superior ear for acquiring them; both liking exotic birds and both, perhaps, secretive and suspicious, in my father's case, extremely so."[2] Their alliance may also have lain in a mutual recognition of their vulnerability: the two of them ranged warily against the all too frequent meanness and dullness of the world. But Norman's internal class rebel disapproved of Perelman's migrant Anglophilia (despite going to Anderson & Sheppard for his own suits).

He dressed like an Englishman, he tried to talk like an Englishman, and he knew various members of the British aristocracy, he used to go and stay with some earl in some fearful castle in Ireland whenever he came over here. He tried very, very hard with a fair degree of success to be an Englishman too. Of course he could never divest himself of a slight American accent but he used to go to a leading tailor's in the West End and get his shirts and shoes and all the rest of it.[3]

Perelman had emigrated to quieten a homeless spirit after the death of his wife Laura. Life was souring for him; but London turned out to be less congenial than New York. He had become dependent on recognition, on what Norman called "the spiritual domination of Hollywood", and the daily accostings by eager strangers to praise his writing or a t.v. appearance didn't happen in Britain. "He only stayed about a year. It didn't work. He said he needed to have the stimulation of being somewhere in New York, surrounded by friends [at] Sardi's or somewhere like that, where his cronies all were. It just didn't happen here."

Norman's year ended better than Sid's (who had embarked on an emulation of Jules Verne's *Around the World in Eighty Days* that ran off the rails at Calcutta). His arrangements to evade the winter had been successful. He had persuaded the *Sunday Times* to send him to Guatemala, and this time, on 25 November, he and Don McCullin flew out of London together to make the joint expedition they had been seeking since they first met.

The subject was close to Norman. It was becoming, as if unavoidably, his political decade. He wanted to see Guatemala this time from the perspective of a new crisis, deep even for that bloodstained country, that was being fuelled by a *guerrilla* whose chief grievance was the government's long servitude to US foreign policy. He and McCullin arrived at Guatemala City to find a curfew and state of siege: after nine o'clock the police and army shot at anything that moved. A thorough policy of anti-subversion included shaving the head of any hippy, and McCullin's thick head of hair attracted meaningful glances. The country was on a civil war footing, with *guerrilla* forces, having survived bombs and napalm in the country, moving into the towns, their numbers boosted by university students protesting the government's collaboration with the USA. Extra-judicial executions and disappearances had reached a high tide of intensity.

In part the problem was the same as Cuba's, fifteen years before. Who were the guerrillas? Norman asked at a party. "Sons of middle-class or upper-class families," he was told. "Boys of good education but no money and no hope. While Guatemala remains a banana republic – a supplier of cheap raw materials to the United States – university degrees don't mean a thing." Two or three of his friends, the speaker said, suspected that their sons were involved. The man turned out to be a prominent politician.[4]

Norman enjoyed exploiting his long knowledge of Guatemala, both in seeing what he could and introducing McCullin to it. They drove into the alpine middle of the country to Chichicastenango where McCullin was impressed by his apparent powers of prophecy.

Norman told me before we got to Chichicastenango, "You will go up the steps [of the church of Santo Tomás], there will be pagan fire on the steps and you will go into a totally saintly, kind of Catholicist scene inside. You'll have to pass pagans to get to the Catholics." I could see he was winding me up. And sure enough we got to Chichicastenango, and you could not see a more incredible scene, and he already knew about that.[5]

As Norman had hoped, the Indians of Chichicastenango still presented a paradigm of the resilience of the Indians as a whole.

In fact this Maya-Quiché town offers a unique example of an Indian population that has stood up to, and in the end defeated, the conspiracy of the whites. They survived the original massacres of the conquest, they survived slavery both in its outright form and later in all its fraudulent disguises, but their greatest victory was their rejection of assimilation. In 1824, when slavery was officially abolished, the planters settled in this town six mestizo money-lending families who were also licensed tavern-keepers, and it was their task to make loans and encourage drunkenness in such a way that an Indian would spend the whole of his life working to pay off his debts. ... Still they survived, and not only survived but gradually strengthened their tribal organisation, repaired the breaches, consolidated a little newly-won authority.[6]

The half of Guatemala's population to which Norman's pastoralist values had always attracted him were, he saw, weathering the civil war far better than their "civilised" fellow Guatemalans. He had found himself another pointed example of the twin futilities of Christianity and capitalism.

Western Christian civilisation in Guatemala is in a state of galloping crisis. The half of the population which owns all the fertile land consumes 90 per cent of the national wealth and monopolises literacy, leisure and medical and social services, is seen to be slipping down into the self-destruction of civil war. ... The most startling evidence of the new frame of mind of those who were once so confident that they had brought civilisation to the New World is to be found in a single sentence in Colonel Arana Asorio [Guatemala's new president]'s inaugural speech on July 1, 1970: "Let us now admit that native civilisations have bequeathed to us a superior degree of culture, which we have not improved."[7]

At Chichicastenango he and McCullin stayed in a long, low adobe hotel built around a cool cloistered courtyard garden, where McCullin acknowledged Norman's ability not just to describe the value of the Indians' civilisation, but on occasions to access such things when he travelled. "We stayed in a lovely inn called the Mayan Inn. I had [a] fire and I was writing a letter to my wife and I thought, 'Life isn't so bad after all.' And I thought that travelling with Norman was as if I'd found another key to another lock, and I had." Before they left the town McCullin saw an Indian carving of Christ in the market and observed one of the keys to Norman's sense of humour – that he could suppress completely whatever was comic in a situation, as if there was *nothing* funny at all about it, to the point where he could report it devoid of all emotion.

I said, "Norman, I'd really like that." I wanted this figure of Jesus Christ, and of course the figures in that part of the world were mostly carved in the fashion of Indians themselves, so Jesus Christ is slightly kind of Mayan looking, and so he said, "I'll do this." It didn't go on for long and I said, "How's it going?"

and he said, "Well, this man said to me, he's getting a bit fed up, he said to me, 'Listen, señor, I'm not selling vegetables here!'" Now Norman wouldn't realise that's a real side-splitter, but he delivered it in a totally straight way that made it even more funny.

He eventually got it for me for thirty dollars, and then after I'd got it I said, "Norman, I don't know how to thank you for that, I really love this." He said, "Well, if you ever get tired of it I'd be quite willing to take it off your hands." In other words he wanted it but he didn't push in front of me to get it.[8]

They got back to Guatemala City on 29 November, and over the next week Norman arranged to meet both sides in the latent civil war. A politician – his informant at the party – told him that only open war could follow; a landowner described his kidnapping by Castroite rebels (who went to the trouble of providing him with his favourite whisky); Norman himself was held by guerrillas and interrogated before returning two days later for a briefing on future guerrilla strategy. On 5 December he heard that a notorious killer, Bonachea Leon, had been found dead: Leon was the man implicated as the assassin of Castillo Armas in 1957, whose career had not ended in prison and who had been released from gaol on several occasions, people said, for days at a time to carry out other difficult killings. Norman failed to get firm information on this and several other lines of enquiry for the same reason that it is impossible to get answers in Guatemala today, because truth's vulnerability to the stains of violence remains extreme. (A dozen years after the twenty-five-year civil war eventually ended in 1996, more than 5000 murders still take place every year, the most horrifying component of such statistics reserved for the murders of women, in part a grisly sadism from the habit during the civil war of killing women because they would give birth to rebel fighters.) All that could be said for certain, Norman felt, was that if President Arana turned to further repression the *guerrilla* would deepen, and if he sympathised any more with the Indians, as his inaugural speech had indicated he might, he would be removed as fast as Arbenz Guzmán by the CIA's coup in favour of United Fruit in 1954 and Castillo Armas in 1957.

Norman also spoke to Don Luis Aguilar, governor of Guatemala City and province, who shed some light on the phenomenon of rightist presidents softening towards their countrymen once in power. In Guatemala's case, he said, it could be traced to an increase of solidarity with their fellow Guatemalans against whichever US influence, whether CIA, mafia or Green Berets, happened to be controlling, exploiting, or murdering them by proxy.

Norman warmed to Aguilar's frankness. Not in his *Sunday Times* piece, but remembered in a later account, is his first meeting with Aguilar, just after arriving in Guatemala, at a British Embassy party. Aguilar had read history at Cambridge, and when Norman told him he lived fairly close, "we were instantly joined in one of those shallow but vehement friendships based on a geographical accident. 'Anything I can do for you, dear boy. Any time. Just give me a ring.'" Norman remembered a violent arrest he had seen the previous day of a young man assumed to be a guerrilla. He asked Aguilar if he could fix a meeting

"with one of your political prisoners". Nothing changed in the smile of power that the Indians held in such esteem, as he twirled his glass. Although no fellow guests were in the vicinity, he lowered his voice. "Sorry, dear boy, we have none. A luxury we can't possibly afford."[9]

On 7 December Norman and McCullin flew to El Petén to see what was left of one of the great cities of the Maya, and found it overrun with paratroopers. Two days later they drove together, more for atmosphere than action, to United Fruit's sleazy bastion on the Caribbean, Puerto Barrios, that he had last seen fifteen years before. "The Hotel del Norte awaits the traveller trapped into spending a night in this town. A collector's piece from Somerset Maugham: something to remember and, in a way, to be grateful for, for the rest of one's life. Facing each other across splintered wood in a cage of torn mosquito netting, the toothless Negro reception clerk and I suddenly burst out laughing. He seems amused by the predicament of anybody actually compelled to stay at his hotel."[10]

The following day they returned to Guatemala City for a final meeting Norman had arranged with Dr Adolfo Mijangos López, lawyer and leader of the opposition URD party.[11] Mijangos López, "an agile, vivacious" man in a wheelchair, had just come from the funeral of a murdered friend. He cheerfully admitted to being included on the *ultras*' assassination list – those in the army who believed the rhetoric of anti-Communism. President Arana was already losing control of the army, he told Norman. "The colonels surrounding Arana have fallen in with the US plan of using national armies to do their police work for them. These men have been indoctrinated into the belief that a third world war is inevitable and that they have been chosen to defend the values of occidental culture."[12] Mijangos López felt they might not come after him – "I have one little insurance policy – my wheelchair. They might hesitate before shooting a man in a wheelchair" – but Guatemala was certainly tearing itself into pieces. Norman agreed.

Circumstances bore both of them out. And Mijangos López' insurance policy failed him too. Little more than a month later, on 13 January 1971, twenty-seven shots of a machine-gun volley fired from a taxi as he was leaving his office to go home produced another funeral.

Travelling with photographers, Norman generally enjoyed their company. None became as close to him as Don McCullin. The Guatemala journey changed the direction of McCullin's work. "We'd be going along in the car and [Norman would] say, 'Isn't it extraordinary, can you see those orchids up there?' Well I would never have looked for orchids in the first place." Until he met Norman, McCullin had thought war photography was the only thing he was cut out to do, and what Norman showed him "interfered with my one-track idea of going to war. And this really saved me from myself." Until they went to Guatemala together, he didn't even know what an orchid was. (Norman was able on occasion to match him for ignorance; or dry humour? Waking up on a damp morning in Paraguay in 1974, they smelt breakfast and heard guitar music. What was it? Norman wanted to know. Cat Stevens, McCullin replied. "Oh," Norman asked, "is he a local boy?") The two were never bored in each other's company, and McCullin revered the details Norman elicited from a scene and his eternally unhurried pace, unlike his own. "Norman, you felt, could talk a cobra out of biting you." Norman conversely felt he could always rely on McCullin, for his pictures to express what was happening with clarity and dignity.[13] 1970, in that sense, had been a model year for travelling, Mexico and Guatemala both templates, with their trickle of risk, their openings of adventure and their congenial company, for the kind of journeys Norman liked. The next trip would fracture his expectations.

At Finchingfield in early 1971 the storytelling itch returned. Guatemala had given him more than he could put down for his *Sunday Times* piece, and he began to push and shape what he had seen in November and December into another novel: another mutant shoot from the plant of his unwritten great non-fiction work. On the grounds of discretion and possibly personal safety he set the novel in Colombia, a country described in its eventual jacket blurb as "in the grip of a fierce dictatorship and showing all the signs of an impending revolution". The displaced Guatemala elements don't end there: Robert Howel, the protagonist, has been sent to investigate an alleged massacre of Indians, and once in the country meets a relief worker, Liz Sayers, in bottomless trouble for aiding university students and known urban guerrillas.

Flight from a Dark Equator has, as other Lewis novels do, a slew of storylines: problematic in this case because the reader's interest may easily evolve more towards one subplot than another. One story, of guerrillas marching in from Ecuador, is a superb portrait of passionate idealists attempting to borrow the success of Castro's band of twelve in the Sierra Maestra and avoid the disastrous destiny of Guevara. (They do not.) But another, the central and passionate love affair between Howel and Sayers, does not inflame. Again the question obtrudes that Norman should have been edited and wasn't; more engagement for the reader would have been possible, for example, if Howel had been less well balanced, if he had been opened up a bit, compromised a bit, made to fight a bit on the rebels' side. It was not as if Norman did not want to take the rebels' side. He provided passages of the sharpest description of, for instance, the moral effect of gunfire – "The shots had dignified everyone present. Faces were cleansed of some of their pettiness. Gestures became more composed"[14] – and of lucent revelation about the connection between evangelism and its successor capitalism, anatomised in the Faustian figure of the missionary Grail Williams, ever ready to justify genocide on the religious grounds that a soul, once saved, cannot be lost even if the missionary's other task is to provide Indian labour to work in the murderous conditions of a profitable tin mine. There is a good novel waiting to get out of *Flight from a Dark Equator*, of which the published book was, one concludes, really only the first draft. And that long-standing tension persists: that at their best Norman's "compositions", his non-fiction and journalism, reveal his novelist's instinct at full stretch, while at *their* best his novels attract by an authenticity of action and a sense of reality as political commentary.

Whatever disappointment Norman was feeling at Collins' inability to improve on Cape's publishing record, he stayed with the company and he and Bob Knittel remained friends.[15] Their closeness was slightly lessened by the presence of Knittel's wife, the actress Luise Rainer, who, whenever Norman lunched with his publisher, wanted to join them. Rainer, inseparable from her two small, highly territorial dogs, had starred in Irving Thalberg's last film *The Good Earth* (1937) and in the 1930s been the first actress to win consecutive Oscars, and was a conventional star. Once, after she was robbed in Milan of all her jewellery, left in her car while she prayed in the cathedral for her husband's safe arrival (Knittel was travelling by air), she summoned Norman to her London mews house to demand he write a story about the treatment she had suffered at the hands of the Italian police (which amounted to her being treated as any ordinary tourist victim of a robbery would have been). Norman got somebody at the *Sunday Times* to agree to publish a small piece, but by the time he had the convoluted details he was late for lunch. (And was punctilious about timing.) Rainer, still in her peignoir, jumped into her sports car and insisted on driving him hair-raisingly across the West End.

In July the family went on holiday to Cyprus. In September another rearrangement took place when for the second time Norman felt the urge to discard Finchingfield, suffering a combination of his occasionally recurrent disgust with English class attitudes, the difficulty of finding reasonable non-private education for Kiki and Gawaine, and an accumulation of boredom with Essex. Deciding that Italy should be tried as a place to live (he was also starting to research a new novel with a Sicilian background), within a fortnight he was in Rome. "He was writing . . . anyway it was just an excuse to live in Rome," Lesley says.[16] He found an international school for the children, St George's at La Storta north-west of the city, but accommodation was hard to come by until one of the teachers at St George's directed him to the close-by hamlet of Isola Farnese, a village captured between two rivers and overlooked by a massive escarpment and castle, each of its towers wrapped in its own cloud of mist. Here, in the disused former convent attached to the castle, the family settled on a trial six-month lease.

The setting was extraordinary. The house, all marble interiors, had a main bedroom with one wall that was almost all window through which there was an uninterrupted view of the ruins of Veii, the richest city of the Etruscan League and the size of Athens until sacked by the

Romans in the fourth century BC. The children were happy tenants of a garden that occupied the whole hillside and sloped down to one of the rivers and beyond, where they occupied themselves digging around in the dirt and unearthing shards of painted Etruscan pottery whose colours faded, like the subterranean frescoes of Fellini's *Roma*, inside a few hours of exposure to air. Kiki and Gawaine attended St George's, "a great place" in Kiki's memory. "The Gettys were there, they had two Gettys in my year, the older Getty in the sixth form. We were deeply excited when the older Getty, the one that [had his ear] chopped off, laid a turd outside the headmaster's door. He was dismissed."[17]

Norman's later account of the family's migration to Isola Farnese in a revised edition of *Jackdaw Cake* is a chapter of affectionate or sardonic portraits of moments and Romans[18] – the pillaging of Etruscan fragments from the burial chambers that honeycombed the garden and Kiki's and Gawaine's marauding in village and fields with the local tribe of children; the autumn razzia of sparrow-shooting; the resplendent red SPQR-emblazoned sanitation truck that flytipped the village's garbage into the nearest ravine; the Longobard count who rented the convent to them and kept a herd of creamy white longhorns purely for the sake of animating the landscape; his covertly rebellious maid, Annunziata ("With respect, what does he do? He grows parsley and when it's ready the priest's horse jumps over the wall and gobbles it up"); the doctor Pecorella, proud of his resemblance to Caligula; the saturnine grocer Antonio and barman Primo, both of whom covered all social niceties with the grunted Roman "Eh?"; the men of honour in black Alfa Romeos who glided to the village restaurant with their girlfriends at weekends and had their tyres let down by mutinous villagers while they ate.

The details are lush, splendid, human. They remind the reader of Norman's effortlessness at stuffing and peopling a paragraph, and of his eccentric ability to pour out and connect a fluent stream of both significant and insignificant particulars, without either becoming insipid (the insignificant being the particulars writers often prefer to avoid). In a sense his descriptions are those particulars not just connected, but altered so that it is not so much collections of objects and events that appeal, but collections of *words*: through the rhythm and sound of the words rather than the things they refer to, one enters into the scene.

He did not write about one event. Gareth, who like his sister Karen had not met Lesley, was conducting coach tours around Italy as a guide and visited them at the house; by doing so he broke a taboo and allowed Karen who, from loyalty to her mother, had never visited Finchingfield, to visit the following year.

One known inaccuracy in Norman's account of the months at Isola Farnese exists. The reasons he gives for cutting short the family's *villeggiatura* deliberately stray from the real reason. Instead of, or as well as, problems with the children's schooling at St George's after the discovery of drug-taking there, and the growing feeling that "sober, honest and reliable" village Essex might after all be his Ulubrae, the family's early return to Finchingfield was caused by a sudden crisis in March 1972 in Norman's business affairs.

"I can't remember now whether it was the accountant [who] said, 'Look you really ought to come back and look at things,'" Lesley says. "I can't remember what sparked it off, but it was clear that we had to come and have a look at things. We all came back together."[19]

1972 in any case had started less fulfillingly than it should have done. Peter Crookston, now deputy editor at the *Sunday Times* magazine, had got in contact with Norman at Isola Farnese to tell him that the photographer Tony Snowdon – Lord Snowdon – had been complimentary about Norman's work and would like to travel with him. Norman had suggested Peru, and Crookston and Snowdon had both agreed. Norman flew back to England, and on 23 January Crookston drove him and Snowdon to Heathrow for a Sunday flight to Lima.

Snowdon explained to Norman that he had asked for an early Sunday departure because most people likely to be the targets of press interest didn't fly then. At the airport check-in immediate trouble started. Snowdon, making a bad job of travelling incognito, had his luggage tags – Rt Hon the Earl of Snowdon – immediately recognised; a journalist materialised asking for an interview and, according to Norman, Snowdon asked Norman to persuade her to go away. The airline then insisted on upgrading them to first class, and a limousine appeared to take them to their aircraft.

This foretaste accurately heralded a journey bricked-in by protocol and restrictions and Snowdon's often unconscious need to be in the limelight. Norman was profoundly bored. He was annoyed by an underlying assumption of fealty, characterised by Snowdon's proneness to treat him as his valet, but was more deeply frustrated at being kept away from the places he wanted to see. His dogmatically defended freedom of action carried no weight in the face of diplomatic clucking about a minor British royal's safety. His account in *The World The World* is a sustained, tactfully farcical reconstruction of that boredom and frustration. In a separate interview he described the sequence of the fiasco.

I went to Peru . . . have you ever heard of a man called Lord Snowdon? I was there with him. We were sent by [the *Sunday Times*]. It was a business trip, and we wanted to play this as we would at any other time. So we get there, and the ambassador wants us to have lunch. Snowdon says, "No, I'm not going," because it's a business trip. However we were forced to go, and the first secretary said, "Now where do you want to go while you're here?" So I said that I wanted to go to a place called [Cuyocuyo] in the highlands of the mountains, on the border with Bolivia. That's a place where nobody ever goes, a place where they have the Shining Path. . . . They're Indians who have become communised, and they continue to be attacked by government troops. So I said, "I want to go and see them." So the secretary to the ambassador says, "You won't get permission to go there because it's too dangerous. But if you'd like me to help, I'll get a car for you and a driver, and I'll go with you to the kind of places that can be seen." I withstood this as best I could but it was hopeless. . . .[20]

Norman and Snowdon flew to Cuzco, arranged by the embassy, and got out as fast as they could. Cuyocuyo, the area Norman wanted to go to, inaccessibly alluring as the homeland of a minor but grandiose Indian civilisation, stayed out of bounds and they drove instead to Huaylas in the far north. Meandering around Peru's north-west for a few days, alternating between the bleak landscape of towns wiped off the map by a recent earthquake and the Trujillo Golf Country Club, they straggled back inconsequentially to Lima. Once again the emergent story was of Indian decline, in this case of the Quechua Indians, and their exclusion from the new economy. On a visit to the Lima slums to see the fate of the Quechuas they found a Quechua boy fallen from a building, and Norman gave credit to Snowdon for insisting that he be treated by the hospital they drove him to. Norman did find in Peru an incentive to return; he had picked up signs that areas of Peru's forest were to be carved up among ranchers and mineral prospectors. Snowdon's pictures, too, caught something of the country's many-layered, majestically bleak existences. But the trip was not a success, shackled in obstructions of formality and protocol and with Snowdon's mood swinging between patrician annoyance at the public's attention and a neurotic courting of publicity: a not uncommon phenomenon among royals, as Norman noted. "Tony was the most intelligent, interesting and active member of the Royal family, but even he may not have been wholly able to escape the syndrome consequent upon an over-long exposure to the inanities of palaces."[21] One of those inanities – as Don McCullin, who knew Snowdon, says – is the replacement of respect by rank.

[It] was possibly the worst trip he ever did. He hated that trip actually. Snowdon didn't actually treat Norman with respect. He treated Norman in a slightly contemptuous way and it was unforgivable really that he didn't understand what a privilege it was to be travelling with such a wonderful man, like the rest of us. Another thing about Snowdon was, he went on that trip and he never had any money. Norman said, "He never seemed to have any money, so I had to pay for everything."[22]

Norman would not have registered the offence he felt. The piece was written for the *Sunday Times*, and he did not write the background story of his expedition with Snowdon for another twenty-five years. "There was never a flicker of a piss-take" with Norman, McCullin says. He "never gave any signals away that he was impressed or unimpressed. He had a face that was actually set in stone. It would not divulge any of his inner thoughts, until he was ready to tell you himself."[23]

On his return to Isola Farnese in the second week of February Norman had hardly a month to appreciate the hills, the early spring, his grunted friendships with the grocer and barman, and his children's freedom. By the middle of March the family had packed up and left to return to England. They arrived as *Flight from a Dark Equator* was being published. Its strong title helped sales and it was reviewed appreciatively, if sparingly. "Horrifying and laconic", the *Times* reviewer called it, commending his "taut plotting, exact characterization, and dialogue with all unnecessary fat trimmed off it".[24] Norman was amused that the British ambassador to Colombia, Stanley Fordham, "said he was 'very angry indeed'" about the book, presumably because Norman's prudent distancing of the story from Guatemala had opened a can of worms in its neighbour. Norman had been friends with Fordham during his previous posting to Cuba in 1956–60, although it was in part Fordham's inadequate analysis of Castro's chances of success that had prompted Ian Fleming to send Norman to make his own assessment. Nor did the novel's publication warm Norman's relations with Collins. "This book has a sad history," he wrote in a dedication later. "Undeservedly in my opinion it had the best reviews of any of my books, perhaps because there was a hint of Che Guevara in it. Collins, who admitted that they detested books about Latin America, printed 3500. It sold out in a week and was never reprinted, thus dying an unnatural death."[25]

At Finchingfield the Parsonage's tenants were still in place and he, Lesley, Kiki and Gawaine had to cram themselves into the Barn. From there he set out to investigate what was happening at 202 High Holborn, something he had not seriously done for several years. By the early 1970s R G Lewis had branches at Holborn and Strand plus another six outside the capital. From the profitable specialist small-camera business it had been in the 1950s it had expanded in order to offer a more commonplace range of cameras and products and defend itself against duller but better capitalised competitors. (It had offshoots as a publisher and a processing laboratory with some big accounts, and still offered specialist services – it bought the first MTF lens testing platform – but its chief business was always in retail.) Ito had been made a director and so had Herbert Currey, the business's manager. But somehow, in early 1972, R G Lewis reached the point of collapse.

Norman blamed no one. "Norman's attitude to me about it", Lesley says, "was 'My own fault. I wasn't prepared to put time into the business, I stayed away from it, so what do you expect?'" He and Currey made economies, halving the advertising budget and in August closing the main branch at 202, where it had been for thirty-seven years, and moving to a smaller shop at 217 High Holborn. The profit line recovered, though the crisis did not make Norman more attentive. Richard Colmaine, who worked at High Holborn in the 1970s, remembers that "He didn't pay much attention to the business. He would come in, pick up some pocket money, then disappear for a couple of weeks, sometimes as much as a couple of months."[26] Norman trusted his manager Bert Currey to rein in costs and watch margins. Ito, who became familiar with Currey when he was being trained to work for a stint at his father's processing laboratory, remembers the manager as "quite elegant, rather softly spoken. You would look into his eyes and you would think, This guy's extremely sensitive because he could never look you in the eye, ever."[27]

Another crisis had struck at Finchingfield in the family's absence. The village had been told by the district council that the water-meadows bordering its river were to be turned over to a concrete car park to contain its Sunday trippers, though its surface was to be painted green on grounds of taste. Habitual feudal quietism had given way to unexpected uproar in the village, and a revolt in which Norman joined. The council car park was an obvious act of municipal barbarism, but he couldn't understand why the trippers came anyway. Don McCullin recalls that "what he really detested was, he said, 'You know, on a Sunday afternoon, lines of cars out there, they don't get out, they sit in there reading their *News of the World*, I don't know why they come here.'" Typically he later expanded his private dislike of the scene into a long comparison, of utmost neutrality, between Finchingfield and a similar place of pilgrimage in Asia, where, he wrote, the duck pond would have been surrounded by holy men and hucksters and, far from sitting in silent isolation, "the Indians would have been there for the water, too, but they would have waded into it, sluiced it over every part of their bodies, even drunk a little, their faces imprinted with huge joy".[28]

The village protest was eventually successful and the car park decision reversed. A few years earlier, Norman had persuaded the diocese to let him maintain a large piece of glebe land as a wild bird sanctuary and now, though there was not much cash around, he joined forces with a neighbour to buy the water-meadows and, planting them with matchstick-producing poplars, give them the necessary profitable status. It was only "perhaps half a victory"; but the habitats in the glebe land and the acre of garden he now looked out on, much of it a man-made wilderness of blackthorns and nettles, had started to reverse, in a small way, Essex's clinical agricultural silence and replace it with the rustle and chime of wildlife and birdsong.

The family's cramped existence in the Barn was made worse by Kiki's depression at returning from Italy, where, accepted as an honorary boy, she had been a constant member of the village tribe. She hated her new school and once threw herself downstairs in order not to have to do games. A calmer period followed the move back into the Parsonage in September. In the wake of Gareth's visit to Isola Farnese, Karen arrived at Finchingfield unannounced in dark glasses and a floppy hat, surprising Norman. "He stood there and his mouth was opening and closing like a fish," she remembers, then "he was bawling and yelling up to Les that I'd come to visit." Lesley found herself unprepared because she had just washed her hair, which was in curlers, and at the outset felt instinctively that Karen was staking out her territory with her father, but after she and Norman recovered from their surprise the visit went well. Lesley says, "I wouldn't have said, 'How marvellous.' But now as you know we're the best of friends."

Norman had re-reconciled himself to Essex. He made something of a false distinction between its "country folk" and its "ex-urban settlers" like himself, loading the one with stoic virtues and the other with "fecklessness and incompetences". More truthfully he liked the working-class villagers, "as silent as the Romans, although, unlike the Romans, dragooned by memories of a past that had taught them to keep their opinions on all subjects strictly to themselves",[29] and avoided the local bourgeoisie as far as he could, keeping his reputation for a certain withdrawnness, if not unsociability, in the village.

The reasons for his unsociability went beyond his reflex antipathy to the propertied English middle class (of which he was by now one). He had no small talk and he was temperamentally incapable of functioning at the casual sociable level of consciousness required for mixing with his neighbours. He felt the permanent dilute happiness of the middle classes to be the mortal enemy of his intensely pursued private marvels. When the carceral boredom of a Finchingfield dinner party struck, his reaction was extreme. Accompanying Lesley reluctantly, he would "find myself with somebody like the local land agent on one side and the bank manager's wife on the other, and after half an hour I would physically feel all the power draining out of my body".[30] He fought his boredom with mischief, on one occasion, when the conversation lingered inevitably on the great English subjects of houses and interiors, saying to a naïve female neighbour, "Surely Les has shown you the mirror on the ceiling of our bedroom?", a remark that led within days to an account of the Lewises' erotic mirror spreading around the whole village.[31]

Passionately averting his gaze from Finchingfield's social life, he witnessed as a matter of course Lesley's routine of children, housework and social contacts and was driven on one occasion to a satirical acclamation of her role in an unpublished sketch, "The Busy Day of Mrs

Snodd". From the wife with wings of the bedtime stories he had told Kiki and Gawaine, Lesley turned into a pursued woman with a chaotic schedule of responsibilities and desires. Mrs Snodd is divided, from the moment she wakes, between the martyrdom of motherhood and running a house and her longing for pampered idleness. The sketch is affectionately accurate about the generosity of Lesley's character and her driven nature at home; its gently bickering portrait regularly about-turns into the willing self-mockery of "man", Mrs Snodd's husband.

7.40	[Mrs Snodd] Awakes bleary-eyed and peers with displeasure at the daylight showing through the curtain. She has not slept well, disturbed by thoughts of all the endless tasks concealed in the lap of the coming day. . . .
8.30	Looks in larder. No eggs, no butter, no bacon, no jam. Fortunately two antiquated fillets of kipper turn up at the back of the frig. These will do. . . . Today she will make a cake, weave a basket, paint a hundred square yards of wall, wash a hundred-weight of garments, etc. . . . Must remember not to talk more than the bare minimum – say a total of 50 words. She has read that in most people verbal energy begins to fail after 18,000 words in one day.
8.35	Breakfast over, and children are taken to school by man. She slips into bath to prepare herself for what is to come. . . .
8.50	The telephone rings. It is a friend in Thorpe Le Soken who tells her that, under pretence of soliciting the marital embrace, her husband caused her to lower her guard, and then blacked both her eyes. As she has to function as a marriage counsellor that evening she would like to tidy this up. What does Mrs S suggest? Mrs S says don't waste any more pips dear, and I will ring you back.
8.53	Rings local expert who says raw beef.
9.20	Rings back friend who says, no raw beef, only marinaded beef.
9.50–10.15	The matter is resolved in 3 more phone-calls with recommendation to wear dark glasses.
10.15	Man returns and seems surprised to find her still in dressing gown. A morbid figure, although depressingly healthy – as mutual doctor friend has recently opined: "that bugger is going to live for ever". As about 3,00 words out of daily 18,000 has been used in telephone calls, she decides to communicate with him as far as possible in signs and gestures. . . .
10.50	Mrs Dragnet, the daily, says she could wash if only soap, and Mrs Snodd dashes out for Flash.
11.50	Mrs S returns but has forgotten Flash. She dashes out again.

| 12.35 | Mrs S returns with Flash, but Mrs Dragnet has now gone. Mrs S dashes out again to borrow paintbrush. |
| 1.15 | Mrs S returns with paintbrush. She hears man upstairs going from room to room turning off the lights. Thinks, suppose they all turn that way eventually. Short reverie on the subject of next dinner. Was it Henri Le Ponce in *Estates and Mansions* who published that recipe for Japanese Pigmy Deer cooked in saki? Horrible appearance of man, demanding food. Quickly dusts mouse turds off hamburger and tosses it in frying pan. Says, "I've been picking – must dash now. Appointment with hairdresser. Can I have some money?" |

The day continues in alternately prosaic and surreal episodes. After the hairdresser Mrs Snodd is seized by the desire to help humanity; she phones her friend Angela Wykham-Snoring-Pratt to offer to look after her old uncle over Christmas, "a positive pet . . . but he *is* blind, deaf, dumb and incontinent, and does suffer from Scott-Turner's Pungent Flux, Kleinwurst's Screaming Syndrome, Burke's Flamboyant Ulcer, Hare's Effluent Gout, Kraft Ebbing's [sic] Melodious Petomania, scrofular dermatitis of the lower limbs, foot-rot, glanders, strangulation of the eyeballs, senile spasmodic erection with acute rinitis [sic] of the spermatic cord. . . ."

The list goes on, a reminder of the adolescent verbal performances Norman had once put on for Gwen fifty years before. Once the uncle is sorted out, Mrs Snodd's serious housework consists of promising herself to sew some buttons on one of the man's shirts "one day", throwing fourteen socks needing darning into the Aga instead, and making herself some Earl Grey with icing sugar. At 4.30 another friend calls in distress asking for a reference for her husband as a lay preacher, a man whose felonies run to another fantastic, equally schoolboyish lexicon of

fraudulent bankruptcy, malversion of funds, peculation, issuing of worthless cheques, arson in Her Majesty's dockyards, simony, barratry, abduction of minors, Confusion of the Sacraments, Albigensian Heresy, attempted theft of the Crystal of Lothar, pissing in the font of St Peter's, breaking and entering an enclosure at Whipsnade's Zoo with the intent to commit an act of gross indecency with a Prezhwalsky's Bearded Gnu, inciting the choirboys of St Paul's Cathedral to mutual masturbation, displaying his virile member at the window of the Mother Superior of an order of enclosed nuns, and soliciting the person of the Duchess of Atholl for immoral purposes by greetings telegram, with reply paid for 4/1.

The pleasure in the list, like the pleasure in his descriptions of Isola Farnese, is in a prosody aided by an eccentric roaming eye for which the commission of gross indecency with an ordinary gnu is inadequate. At 5.20 "The rather off-putting and morose figure of man drifts into sight again in garden (did his father really live to 110?)"; at 6.00 as "the Snodds sit sipping their ginger wine" looking out at the garden in the golden evening, Mrs Snodd revealingly reflects that "Only an 88 bus-route cutting across the lawn could do anything to improve what she sees". The climax of her day comes with the evening's last phone call which, while not the funniest episode, reflects both Norman's cutting judgments on those of his wife's friends he couldn't stand and his knowledge that his dislikes made life difficult for her. (He "didn't like me spending too much time with anybody or them getting too much of my attention," Lesley says. "I had this old friend in the village with whom I was very close – it's the Mrs Snodd thing you've got – and I'd pop down and see her and he resented that and he'd be positively rude to her. This happened to me quite a lot. But it was jealousy pure and simple.")[32]

7.50   Mrs "I-I" rings. Mrs "I-I", an ardent social worker, is afflicted with creeping egomania, which makes it necessary to inject "I", or "me" into every three words of her conversation. This involves her in huge syntactical difficulties, and she sounds rather like a reading by a small child out of Book I of "John and Janet" [sic].
Mrs "I-I": "Darling I tired. I work hard. John say me OK? I say him yippee."
Mrs S (looking around nervously. Mimes at man that children upstairs are tearing each other apart): "What is it dear? Do you want us to say the usual?"
Mrs "I-I": "Can I speak?"
Mrs S: "Yes dear, it's quite safe."
Mrs "I-I": "I-I-I-I-I-I-I."
Mrs S: "You-you-you-you-you-you."[33]

"That was the big problem really with Norman," Lesley recalls. The insecurity-shaped gap in his nature, disguised as criticism of her friendships and absences, emerged in intolerance and jealousy. "I would have a trip to London, go up for instance with [my friend] Davina, and when I came back I'd get a cool response. 'You've been gone too long.' So I'd have a shouting match with him and once I've shouted at somebody then it's out of my system. And then he'd be, you know, 'It'll never happen again, I promise, Les, I'm a changed character,' and I'd say, 'It's in your dreams. I've heard it all before, Norman, it'll never change, you're too old to change.'

"So things I might have done otherwise I didn't do because of that. It wasn't a case of unfair or otherwise, it was the way the man was made. That's what he was like. But the sweet point was, I suppose, that he always said, 'I'm going to change, I really am going to change.'"[34]

One of the most characteristic aspects of the two years after the family's return from Isola Farnese in 1972 is apparent by its absence. In December 1972 Norman found funds to take the family to Antigua for Christmas, but apart from the Caribbean, an Easter holiday the following year in northern Spain, and holidays in Spain in 1974 (Easter on the Alicante coast, summer in the north along the Golfo de Gascuña) he didn't travel. For twenty years he had never restricted himself to Europe for so long.

The reason was that he was writing. Nine till one, tea at eleven, no other interruption; in the afternoon a think-walk or a think-drive, note-book in pocket. The book was the novel with the Sicilian background that he had been researching in Rome. The idea for it had come from his friend Boris Giuliano, head of the Pubblica Sicurezza at Palermo, whom he had kept in touch with after his visit to cover the 1968 trial and who had found himself conferring periodically with the FBI when the Sicilian mafia, tearing up its pre-war mandate, had turned to large-scale heroin production. At a stopover on his way to Washington Giuliano and Norman had met at Heathrow for a drink. During their conversation Giuliano put forward the theory that beyond the mafia's core US activities – including production and distribution of a quarter of the world's supply of the drug – it would not have been incompat-ible or implausible for it to have been responsible for the recent assassination of a US president. It had a methodology resting on effi-cient elimination, and had already collaborated with US agencies in the USA and Sicily at the end of, and after, the war (witness the 1947 massacre of the people of Piana dei Greci and San Giuseppe Jato, mafia-organised and carried out with US-supplied weapons). Freebooting elements of the US administration who had been involved in that collab-

oration and others involving, for example, trigger-happy Cuban exiles
in Miami were convinced in the early 1960s that President Kennedy
was selling American power down the river. A mafia hit at the behest
of extreme elements of the CIA was far from fantasy: such was the
premise of Norman's novel. (A premise Fidel Castro himself later lent
support to. "With the expertise I acquired in sharpshooting," Castro
writes, "I can't imagine that with a rifle with a telescopic sight such
as Lee Harvey Oswald had, you can fire, load and fire again in a matter
of seconds. ... Firing three times in a row, so accurately, for somebody who almost certainly didn't have much experience – that's very
difficult. What the official version says is quite simply not possible –
not just like that, bang bang bang.")[35]

Outstanding among Norman's fiction for its length, 345 pages in its
published version, and for its densely threaded and plotted construction, *The Sicilian Specialist* is not just a fictional *summa* of all he knew
about the mafia, or American intelligence agencies. As a novel it surpasses
his journalistic tendency and reflects the long months of novelist's work
that he put into it, and in the end certainly comes closer than any of
his earlier novels to being a work in which *all* the material, descriptive, journalistic, inanimate, active, human, emotional, acknowledges
the importance of composition. As a critic, I still inevitably contemplate its status as a thriller. Too late to think of it as anything else:
even in 1975 we are long past that embryonic time when it might have
been possible to turn Norman's fiction into a branch of *Weltliteratur*.
Yet his compositional aim is remarkably true, and as a novel *The
Sicilian Specialist* conforms closest, I feel, of all his fiction to W H
Auden's retort that "A work of art is not *about* this or that kind of
life; it *has* life". The book's sociology and mafia background are in
that respect irrelevant: the novel is a social form, and to accept that a
novel like *The Sicilian Specialist* can interpret the world widely – repre-
sentatively as well as plausibly – is only to accept the reality of existences
foreign to our experience. The spy, the hitman, the bandit, the renegade are recognisably human so long as the novelist begins with
individuals and not types, without over-darkening or sentimentalising
or forgetting that whatever identity they, and we, have is composed
not merely of ourselves but of others. In that way can a thriller become
more like Goya and less like John Le Carré.

The novel Norman wrote is a linear third-person narrative, the story
of Marco Riccione, a seventeen-year-old in 1943, who escapes on the

opening page from a village in western Sicily that has been overtaken by a platoon of north African Allied deserters. Looting, raping, killing, the Moroccans terrorise the countryside. Understanding that their weak point is lack of food, Riccione finds nine chickens, kills them and injects them with arsenic, then cycles back to his village with the birds dangling from his crossbar. The deserters take him prisoner, sexually abuse him, then the chickens are grilled and eaten. "It was half an hour or more before the venom began its paralyzing work. ... As their intestines boiled, the Moors ran screeching in all directions, tearing at their flesh with their fingernails, vomiting bile and squirting a bloody flux. The dying process was slow, and one Moor crawled a half-mile from the village to the spot where, chewing a cud of earth, he sucked in his last breath eight hours later."[36] For his act of salvation Riccione is embraced publicly by the priest on the steps of the church, and more discreetly invited to join the men of honour.

Admired as a "specialist", for his modesty and silence as much as his cunning, Riccione's rise is watched by interested American liaison personnel as well as other mafiosi. It is initially not clear whether Riccione becomes the target of a vendetta by accident, after organising the suppression of a group of bandits responsible for a massacre (based on the events at Portella della Ginestra), or whether by arrangement with the Americans. Compelled to flee Sicily with his family, he takes up a new identity as a real-estate agent in the east-coast American city of Salisbury. Those who have been watching him, and possibly arranged for his emigration, await the time when they will be able to use him.

Mark Richards, the new Marco Riccione, is married with two children. An unusual thread in *The Sicilian Specialist* is Richards' relation with his wife Teresa, who in her first appearance is a Sicilian child bride, cloistered at home in their third-floor Palermo flat, naked under her frock "as any Sicilian housewife always was about the house in summer" and lovingly submissive. As a bewildered but intelligent immigrant, Teresa begins to change. "She spoke English whenever she could: to the clerks in stores, the delivery men, the cleaning woman, to Mark at home and finally, when her confidence was complete, to the neighbours. By the time a year had gone by, she spoke it perfectly, and with an authentic Salisbury accent unencumbered by the trailing vowels at the end of words that so often betrayed the immigrant Italian. ...

Contact with new friends stimulated her thinking and widened her interests. In Sicily young wives together talked about little but their children or their sexual experiences with their husbands, which they dressed up with wild fantasy. Here, conversation was impersonal. When it came up, sex was discussed at a second-hand level – like something in a television serial, and of little more importance than ceramics, basket-weaving or Republican politics.[37]

The writer's attention to Teresa's accent and conversations and elsewhere to her shopping, baby-sitting, friendships – as well as her prodigious memory and "genuine respect for words" – creates a woman, counterpoint to her husband, whose feelings and views the reader cares to know, and whose husband is right to feel bewildered about her in turn.

In Teresa Mark saw a new restlessness, a new reserve, and a new and almost unfeminine curiosity, and with it there was a change in her physical appearance: a loss of weight, of the gentle, indulgent fat of thigh and bosom, an increase in physical liveliness – even, he suspected, an increase in height.

Moreover, the constant volcano of their sexual life had cooled slightly. The iron routine of the bed imposed by Sicilian custom had been broken by the fact that no one took siestas in Salisbury.[38]

Barred by custom from knowledge of her husband's secrets, Teresa suddenly utters the reality of his world with a shocking intelligence (and respect for the truth of words) after he sets up a killing in Cuba that unravels.

"You've been a man of honour all your life," she said. She paused, startled by her own recklessness, almost as if in fear of a blow.

He stared at the new, unrecognizable face, shaking his head.

"The men of honour are like a monster," she said. "An *orco*, with twenty arms and ten heads. None of you has a separate life. You've never been free to live like other men. First it was Don C., then Vincente Di Stefano. Who will it be when Di Stefano goes? A man who carries out other men's orders. You're not allowed to think for yourself."[39]

Her question, placed almost as an afterthought, is the pivot on which the novel turns: the mafia as an unending cycle not of violence – killing is its symptom, not its origin – but of fealty beyond ethics. (It is a minor but significant part of Norman's moral accounting that he describes

Sicilian fealty as based on honour, while the CIA's version, to which
Mark finally yields, is based on a trick and coercion.)

In Norman's characterisation both Mark's and Teresa's inner lives
retain singularity at the same time as throwing light on their social and
cultural conditions. They are lives that come from a country with a
sympathetic understanding of evil, and Norman's best accomplishment
in the novel is that, while treating a fast-moving stream of action to
equally attentive background (very little is sketchy), he makes Mark's
and Teresa's psychic priority ours, in their failed attempts to escape
their existential prison, to tell themselves the one story that will save
their lives and let them get away.

It is easy to generalise; there are also passages that are slack, not
exactly tidy. But *The Sicilian Specialist* was certainly his best characterised novel so far, his most humanly alive. In the fairly interchangeable
landscapes of the thriller, its informed specificity is remarkable. (It was
not the first large-canvas novel about the mafia: Mario Puzo's *The
Godfather* had come out in 1969.) It is in those details that could not
have come from anywhere but his own observation, that some of its
most moving moments are found. When Mark's blameless brother Paolo,
a garage owner, is blown up in his village in an act of vengeance aimed
at Mark, Mark receives a message that if he returns for the funeral he
will be untouched for the duration of the ceremony. He flies to Palermo
and drives to the family's village, Campamaro, "hardly to be recog-
nized" in the changes of the intervening years. Nothing is left of his
brother: the coffin contains a wax dummy dressed in Paolo's best suit
with an enlarged photograph placed over the dummy's face.

In its authority Norman's description of the funeral leaves the reader
in no doubt of its importance as an expression of family tragedy, and
as a fatal element in the cycle of fealty. In its solemnity the ceremony
has, ironically, Audenesque life, unfathomable, pitiless, serene.

At a signal from the priest the rattle of the drum began, the Isotta crashed
into bottom gear and jerked forward, and the three wailing women following
immediately behind the hearse started to writhe and shriek. Mark walked
alone, followed by Fosca and the leading lights of Campamaro trudging
through the dust six abreast. A long straggling tail of cement workers, who
had been ordered by the local man of honour to attend, plus a sprinkling of
share croppers and goatherds, brought up the rear.

Mark's eyes were fixed on the coffin covered with its purple velvet pall,

Ernestina's scrapbook

Hill climbing in the Type 51
and white shoes

Worn at Motor Racecourse

Sombrero At Brooklands

Mrs. Norman Lewis in a striking fashion at Brooklands yesterday, when practice took place for to-day's meeting, the last of the season.

In Passing

DURING a London daytime alert recently the place was Ludgate Circus, the car, a quick and span "two-three" Alfa two-seater. In that particularly flaming yet highly suitable Italian red. At that instant somehow, it was a car more friendly than it might have done at a more normal moment of an abnormal war-time world. 'Whoa!' one wondered at once, and 'Whither?', the usual chain of recollection flashing briefly through the mind. It gave one a certain sense of pleasure to think that such a machine should still be able to amble along Fleet Street—a very normal-looking Fleet Street—on what happened to be a beautiful November afternoon, more like spring than early winter. An Alfa, a red Alfa, at Ludgate Circus, after three months of all the German has tried to do to London.

Mexican note is struck by Mrs. Norman Lewis watching her husband practising, yesterday, for this afternoon's "Mountain" Championship. Motor Show Meeting, Brooklands.

Precautions at Brooklands

Mrs. Norman Lewis adjusting her husband's helmet during yesterday's practice at Brooklands for the Automobile Racing Club's International Meeting today.

Lying fourth in the second Mountain Handicap at Brooklands, 29 May 1939

Fifth Avenue, July 1939

In Mexico, August 1939

Ernestina and Ito, Havana, a few days after
Norman's departure for England

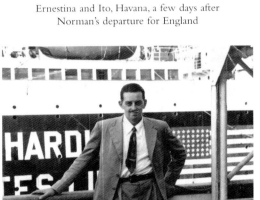

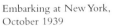

On the beach, Jaimanitas Club,
Havana

Embarking at New York,
October 1939

The view from
4 Gordon Street,
11 May 1941

Private Lewis, Army version

Sergeant Lewis, studio version

Oliver Myers

Norman's diary with photograph of Hester

Hester, St Catherine's Fort, Tenby, 1949

"Tous les hommes sont pareils."
Mme Phuoc, Saigon, 1950

Author, 1950s

Lesley Burley at 19 (above)
and 23 (right)

Karen, Gareth and
Ito in Tossa and Ibiza

"The harbour of Ibiza is full of sailing ships, and the quayside is a permanent exhibition of their jumbled cargoes"

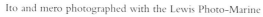
Ito and mero photographed with the Lewis Photo-Marine

Lupita, Ibiza

Guatemala: Burning copal incense offerings to the Maya-Quiché
gods on the church steps, Chichicastenango

Huehuetenango in the 1950s

The Parsonage in the 1960s

Family holiday: Kiki, Lesley, Gawaine, Norman in northern Spain

Africa, two decades apart

Family man

Filming: At Vesuvius (Tristram Powell, director, is on the right)

In the West Papua (Irian Jaya) highlands with Chris Hooke and Yali boys

The gardener

Not understanding the concept of charades

Return to Tossa with
Lesley and Albert Padrol

At Kiki's wedding

At Brighton on his ninetieth birthday with the author, 28 June 1998

In the conservatory at Finchingfield: portrait by Don McCullin of "one of my dearest friends"

from which hung down a black cord with a tassel. Nothing of his brother was being carried to the graveyard. ... This everyone knew but regarded as unimportant, because in the folk beliefs that asserted themselves on such occasions the tassel on the black cord represented the dead man's soul, which at this very moment was present, and would be released only with the interment of the body. In a few minutes' time, when the moment came for the coffin to be lowered into the grave, the dramatic crisis of the funeral would present itself, for simply by taking this tassel in his hand in the presence of the crowd, without so much as a word or gesture, Mark would assume all the obligations of the vendetta. In these ways Campamaro had not moved into the age of Pepsi-Cola and the Gaggia espresso machine.

... Still under its pall, the coffin had been lowered to the ground, the black cord with its tassel now coiled on it like a snake. They were all waiting for him. ... He felt the weight of their willpower, the silent pressure of their determination. The effort to resist these currents of mass suggestion, and the atavistic urge within himself to seize the tassel and clench it for them all to see had started a trembling in his hands. He closed his eyes and thought of his wife and children.

In the great bewildered silence the priest opened his book and began.[40]

He was a kind of gambler in a way, he was gambling, he was going on these journeys and he was willing for these incidents to come up, otherwise he would have come away like a hungry child. He was willing for incidents, and once he'd met Hernando in the British Embassy as the information officer, he knew he had one foot on the ladder, one foot on the first rung, and when you're a writer, it's like being a photographer; when you're a photographer, the moment I put my first roll of film away I feel as if I've put down my first brick for the foundations of a house. It's the same with Norman, once he met Hernando he was on the way.

Don McCullin

I would never laugh in front of him without his consent, but he used to make me laugh because he used to say, "Por favor, man-te-quilla", which was the word for butter, and I used to think, God, this is comical, really, but you would never dare to show your laughter in front of Norman if it was directed towards him. A lot of people must have been around Norman and seen funny sides to him that Norman wouldn't understand. Norman must have realised that there was a dogma about him in a way, like I said to you earlier about doing what you wanted to do.

Don McCullin

I remember one thing that struck me, that he was talking about Ibiza, that he loved Ibiza, he loved Spain, and that's when he said, "You know, we have seen these places at their best and no one can take that memory away from us."

Sergio Viggiani

I never worked with Wilfred Thesiger but I knew him, and there was a certain physical resemblance: both very tall and almost apologetic, quiet, never imposing. They tended to be more observers. Because I didn't speak Italian or Spanish I didn't have any idea of what was going on, but he never imposed himself on a situation. He may well have controlled it to his own satisfaction, but he never ever appeared to be in a rush.

Kenneth Griffiths

Do not thank Neapolitans profusely. It makes them suspicious.

Naples 1977 notebook

26

NAPLES '78

"A worthless parson has a worthless clerk"
Spanish proverb

ON 20 October 1974, after delivering his Sicilian novel and going to the *Sunday Times* with an idea for a new story, Norman landed at Rio de Janeiro and there changed planes to fly north to Asunción in Paraguay, for a second trip with Don McCullin.

He said, "I'm going to go down to the British Embassy, I'm going to check in and see what's going on." He came back and said, "Well, I think I've stumbled onto something rather interesting. The information officer down at the Embassy seems to be a very knowledgeable person. I'm really quite impressed by this young man," I think his name was Hernando, and he said, "In fact he's invited us to his family house", which was some way out of town. So this then turns into a bit of a Monty Python because Hernando turns up, and before we'd even set out on the journey [Norman] says to me, "There's only one drawback to this. I think Hernando's a bit of a plant. I wouldn't be at all surprised if he is working for Stroessner."[1]

Norman's talent for amplification was not new to McCullin, who felt the information officer was what he said he was. Norman also reported that he had accidentally opened the wrong door at Hernando's house and seen him buckling on an automatic pistol; but it took until the end of the journey to change McCullin's mind, when, the night before he was due to have an audience at six a.m. with General Stroessner – an audience the information officer had facilitated – Hernando brought "the most extraordinarily beautiful girl to dinner. And you could see those eyes of his were working with her and he was giving her to me, this beautiful woman. She was only about twenty-two." The typically corrupting move convinced McCullin that "Norman could not have got it more right, knowing the moment he met this man Hernando that he had a double role at the British Embassy".

Yet the information officer found himself playing a triple role, as he too fell under Norman's charm when the visitors drove out to his family house the first weekend. Norman and Hernando, McCullin recalls, spent most of the journey discussing Spanish and Guaraní literature (Paraguay's ancient Indian language), and Norman seemed prepared, in the light of Hernando's poetic leanings and knowledge, to disregard his secret police status. "But at the same time Hernando decided that, whatever his game was – Hernando's game – that was going to get second place because he had this newfound amazing human being [who had] come into his life."[2] Norman himself described his relationship with Hernando as a fluke based on being able to quote one *copla* of García Lorca's *Lament for Ignacio Sanchez Mejías*, about the impact of seeing his friend's blood spilt in the sand and, when Hernando recited "I don't want to see it! / no chalice can contain it, / no swallows can drink it, / no frost of light can cool it", picking up the verse "nor song nor deluge of white lilies, / nor crystal to cover it with silver". "Whatever had separated us could not resist the knowledge that we shared Lorca, and we became freinds."[3]

In governmental eyes – a government like Alfredo Stroessner's – the visitors' objectives were assuredly worth scrutiny. Norman had suggested the journey to the *Sunday Times* after reading an article in *Peace News* by a German anthropologist, Dr Mark Münzel,[4] who had reported that after the completion of an international road to the Iguaçu Falls and Argentina the subsequent land rush had triggered large scale clearance of the surrounding forest habitat of the nomadic Aché Indians. (Norman lapsed on the Achés' name, using "Guayaki", a term with a pejorative connotation, for them in his *Sunday Times* piece. He corrected himself in his 1988 account, *The Missionaries*.) The Indian hunts that followed had been atrocious, often carried out under the direction of professional manhunters by Aché themselves, a group called *señuelos* who, having been captured by white men ("the jaguars"), then believe themselves to be jaguars too, compelled to hunt down more of their kind. Men were shot, women and children as young as five separated and sold as slaves to the farmers of eastern Paraguay at five dollars each.

The official policy of "sedenterisation" intended the survivors to be moved to a small reserve, the Colonia Nacionál Guayaki. There they had continued to disappear. After an assertion of genocide by Paraguayan anthropologists in summer 1972 the Colonia's administrator, himself a manhunter with a criminal record, had been sacked and the administration handed over to a Jack Stolz, an American Protestant missionary. (A Paraguayan army officer told Norman that the missionaries were admired for their efficiency. "When we go in we shoot some, and some get away. They get the lot. When the missionaries clear an area they leave it clean.")⁵

Under Stolz's stewardship Aché went on disappearing. A rancher who attempted to look after a group of them wrote that "I was struck by the fear that this man inspires ... when they noticed he was here, they started to run away into the forest. The women wept."⁶ Missionaries from Stolz's sect, the New Tribes Mission, outnumbered the Aché at the Colonia by August 1973, and around the same time Dr Münzel had a letter from a Paraguayan contact stating that "The New Tribes missionaries are now hunting by motor vehicles for Guayaki in the region of Igatimi in order to reintegrate them [sic] into the reservation". But the Colonia continued to "disappear" Indians.

Norman's and McCullin's contact Hernando, nominally low in the hierarchy, was able to organise immediate access to the Ministry of Defence. The official they saw, a Colonel Infanzón, was courteous and uneasy about a visit to the Colonia headquarters at Cecilio Baez. Waiting for his answer, they visited the ancient Jesuit settlements around Asunción and conducted interviews that confirmed Münzel's account. A bishop, Mgr Alejo Ovelar, spoke of the concern about missionary sects who seemed "indifferent to the spiritual – let alone material – welfare of the primitive peoples among whom they work, but subject them instead to commercial exploitation".

Permission was granted for the visit after several days, under conditions disingenuously agreed to by Norman. The drive to Cecilio Baez in Hernando's Citroën 2CV was a sequence of storms, roadblocks, small Arcadian towns where cows grazed in grassy streets and "aloof horsemen went thudding past under their wide hats, a palm always upraised in greeting", and laterite mud. The town of Caazapá, where Hernando's house stood, "was at the end of the road, and if there was any place in the world to get away from it all, this was it". The next morning, woken, so Norman claimed, by the chords of a harpist "employed by neigh-

bourhood subscription" whose playing was followed by visits from the
local hot meat pie and coffee vendors, the three drove north over worsening roads to Coronel Oviedo. They hoped to avoid the worst of
approaching rain and cut east there to Caaguazú, almost to the Colonia.
Pausing at Coronel Oviedo, Norman visited a woman known as Maria
Calavera ("Mary Skull"), the great witch of Paraguay, an opportunity he
jumped at. In her sixties but eerily girlish in voice and hands, she performed
the same skilful trick with him that had made her famous (General Péron
of Argentina was among her clients) of placing his hand on the skull she
used and making it move. "She told me a great deal," he said later. "The
only thing I wouldn't let her tell me was the date of my death."[7]

At Caaguazú, when they arrived, they found the town and roads to
the Colonia under water, and were forced to return to Asunción.

Another wait loomed. Before they could fill it with an excursion proposed
by Hernando to the Mennonite colony in the Gran Chaco, an English
vet offered them a lift in his Land Rover to Cecilio Baez and the Colonia.
(Norman seems to have trusted Hernando enough not to imagine that
his mission might have been to keep him and McCullin distracted from
the purpose of their journey, but in his later book The Missionaries he
expressed his suspicions about the motives of the vet, who had insisted
they would have to return to Asunción before dark and who he thought
might have been an ally of the New Tribes Mission.)

After the prolonged delays the brief visit to the missionary settlement offered a gloomy, disturbing, all-confirming experience. Jack
Stolz, looking to Norman like "a top sergeant in an American combat
unit rather than a missionary", greeted them coolly, answering Norman's
questions with uncommunicative defensiveness. How many Indians were
there on the reservation? Could he see them at work? What were they
paid? Where had the new arrivals come from? What had made them
come? While Norman put questions, McCullin slipped away to take
pictures. Of the Achés' culture, little remained on the reserve: their
flutes and one-stringed fiddles had not come with them and there were
no chiefs among them or medicine men. Nor were any Aché ceremonies
performed there. How many Aché had Stolz baptised? None, he
answered. He had to be sure that they believed first, but this presented
a difficulty because he had a problem with their language. What, in
that case, was their spiritual fate?

"There is no salvation," Stolz answered, "for those who cannot be
reached."

Of the 300 Indians Stolz said were at the Colonia, Norman counted thirty-five in a campment that stank of human excrement and where the children were visibly malnourished. Some of the adult men who had bows and arrows Norman judged to be *señuelos*, manhunters in the missionaries' pay. Other Aché lay on the ground in attitudes of frozen apathy. At the camp's edge McCullin found two old Aché women close to death and a third younger woman, freshly wounded by a bullet, a tearful boy at her side. Artlessly one of the missionaries' young sons, carrying McCullin's tripod for him, told him that she had been shot while being brought in.

He and Norman waited but no more Aché appeared from the farms where they were supposedly working. Giving a visiting NTM missionary a lift to Asunción, they found out more on the journey back: the missionary, from the Chaco and ebulliently unsympathetic to Stolz's lack of success, told them that Stolz's claim that the men were paid properly was absurd. Because of his role as an Indian catcher Stolz, the man said, had also been shot at by Aché bowmen. The mission received an income from selling goods at its store and agenting the supply of Aché to local farmers, but Stolz was doing it all wrong. In the Chaco they did not have these problems: instead they were allied lucratively in various ways to the activities of American corporations working in the area.

Politically, Norman concluded, the mission at the Colonia functioned as a transitional camp to habituate the Aché to work in the white man's fields. Spiritually, as the bishop had said, concern for the Indians' welfare was nil. They would die unsaved; the mission would shrug its shoulders. On their return to Asunción, Norman described the visit to McCullin as "the most sinister experience of my life".

Norman had wanted to interview General Stroessner before he left but had developed a strictness in his travelling for the *Sunday Times* and locked his airline tickets into a fixed departure date, McCullin remembers.

He said, "If I can't stay, you go and do it," and I said, "Okay." Norman went to see the secretary of the president with Hernando at the palace, and it turned out that no, Norman couldn't be there on the day that they said. While Norman was in the secretary's office a woman came in, a bit of skirt came in, and she wanted to go in and see the president, and – Norman told me all this afterwards – he said it was very curious, "This woman, this tart came in," he says, "and she wanted to see the president and she was talking to the secretary and the secretary said, 'Okay, you can go in but you can't stay long', and then the secretary turned to his secretary and said, 'Let her go in, but don't put her name in the book.'"[8]

McCullin eventually had the audience with Stroessner, the morning after his alcohol-laden dinner with Hernando and the beautiful woman.

The first thing I said [to Norman] was, "It was such a tragedy you weren't there." There were all the cardinals there at six o'clock in the morning, I was reeking of coffee and booze, there were all the generals there, all the lackeys, there were very few women there. I photographed him, Stroessner, I said, "Would you mind stepping outside, sir?" I don't call people "sir" very much in my life, "Would you kindly step out on the balcony where the light is better?" and he said to me, "What do you think of the country?" and I said, "I love the country, blah, blah, blah" . . . he said, "I tell you what, come with me." So he took me over to his generals and he said, "This man has been in Vietnam. You talk to my generals about Vietnam". . . . And I thought, fuck, if only Norman had been here instead of going home, the audience would have given him the most colourful thing he could have witnessed: cardinals in red and the generals over-bedecked with medals and Stroessner himself, the old Austrian [sic]. It was just like something out of a film.[9]

Norman had his story, without the dictator and the cardinals. While McCullin warily accepted the president's invitation to join a group of his bodyguards for a fishing trip, in Finchingfield Norman set about writing his piece as a tripartite combination of political investigation, anthropology and an element of menace – the form he had evolved since his reports for Fleming in the 1950s – in this case in the service of a parable of religious wickedness. It was impact that he was always looking for; but serious impact. The journeys he made for the *Sunday Times* between 1968 and 1975 – to Sicily, Brazil, California, Mexico, Guatemala, Peru and Paraguay – and those he would make for the *Observer* up to 1981 – to Bolivia, Amazonia, Mexico, Honduras and Nicaragua – resulted in a body of writing marked by a quality I would call "loyal detach-ment": a literary tone that was a result of seeing clearly into other cultures without striking a pose of spurious outrage, or passing guilt on to his readers. As a reporter Norman understood that his job was to give life to events and situations, and literary form to their ethical dimen-sions: inequity, suffering, violence. He already knew how hard, and mostly impossible, it was to provide any other form of help after the two years he had spent in occupied Naples. His reporting was dispassionate but its rhetoric was always designed to move the reader in the direction he wanted, towards a passionate reaction.

He enjoyed the anthropology the same way he enjoyed the history; both were ways of "marrying into" his subjects, deepening his relationship with them, rather than skimming the drama off the top. Though he deliberately made no claim to be an anthropologist –

I meddle with it. I dabble in it. As soon as you become a professional anthropologist nobody's going to understand you, and moreover you delve into it so deeply that you finally divide these things up into atoms of knowledge which are not coherent and therefore [the story] escapes the reader to some extent[10]

– he intended to be a kind of intermediary, and routinely pulled in academic source material that would usually only have been read by other anthropologists (he read for example not just Münzel's *Peace News* article but his long 1973 and 1974 documents on the Paraguayan genocide for the Denmark-based International Workgroup for Indigenous Affairs). It satisfied him very much to be able to write in brainy, highly factual detail to publicise anthropological concerns that were the same as his, and the biographer, I think, gives full recognition to his rhetorical and ethical commitment to the anguishing stamp of many of the subjects he covered after 1968; at the same time noting that, even in a writer's mature work, between "to show" and "to show off" is no more than an adverb's difference. (The same, obviously, being true of biographers.) And so the ascetic is reconnected to the dandy he started out as.

Soon after he was back from Paraguay Random House, his New York publisher, published *The Sicilian Specialist*. The plan was for the US edition to appear first, to take advantage of news coverage generated by Norman's account of the JFK assassination, but the tactic backfired. Ruffled plumage in mafia, and possibly CIA, circles led to the novel being un-newsed, with bookstores in major American cities being advised quietly to remove it from their shelves. Norman was left to console

himself with an offer from the *Sunday Times* to serialise the novel in
the colour supplement.

That November he wrote the Paraguay story quickly, and "Manhunt"
was published on 26 January 1975. The Paraguayan ambassador immediately complained, presenting Paraguay as a harbour of racial harmony
with the "fewest problems with the native population" of all Latin
America, and accusing Dr Münzel of unhealthy sexual interest in the
Indians. So did the New Tribes Mission a couple of months later, when
Norman's report was syndicated in the *Miami Herald*. From Woodworth,
Wisconsin, on a letterhead bearing the slogan "Brown gold – Reaching
new tribes until we've reached the last tribe", a Mr Leslie Pederson
wrote on 26 April claiming libel and slander and threatening multi-
million dollar suits, "challeng[ing] any honest person to visit any one
of our Indian camps and see for themselves what we are doing for the
Indians ... in a practical, medicinal and spiritual way". Although
Pederson's letter had no single factual rebuttal to make, Norman wrote
an eloquent three-page reply, reiterating *inter alia* that the charge
against Stolz was not that he personally enslaved Indians "but that he
and his mission are agents in the process by which free Indians, removed
by force from the forest ... are induced to become cheap labour for
planters and ranchers". Stolz had admitted that the mission performed
no evangelical function, as he himself was ignorant of the Aché language;
and

The contention that the Indians can come and go as they please is grotesque.
Why should an Indian who lives happily and well by hunting and collecting
honey submit himself voluntarily to a life of grinding labour? – particularly
when all the activities that give meaning to an Indian's life – his music, his
own religious ceremonies, the use of the lip-ornament by which manhood is
denoted – are denied to him? Moreover, if the Indian is free to come and go,
how is it that ... the Paraguayan Army could deal with Indians "who had
been causing trouble" by putting them on a truck and bringing them to the
colony. What point would there be in carrying out such a deportation if the
Indians were able to escape again?[11]

Asked by the *Sunday Times* for its specific complaints, the NTM
shut up, but Paraguay was the first contact in a battle that would recur
for more than a decade.

Six weekly extracts from *The Sicilian Specialist* also appeared in the

Sunday Times magazine that spring, from April to June. Events in America succeeded in exporting a certain nervousness to the UK, and despite the novel's lavish treatment the magazine did not publicise its serialisation. On 27 May Collins published the UK edition, which made dishearteningly few appearances in the review pages. *The Times* steered clear of reviewing it, though Jeremy Brooks in the *Sunday Times* offered Norman the slightly painful accolade that "his oeuvre is beginning to take on something of the weight and sonority of, say, Graham Greene's". The *Financial Times* was more wholehearted. Martin Seymour-Smith praised the novel's superiority over the factual accounts: "it makes the flesh creep, and all the more so when the author tells us that the three political murders that form an important part of the plot have been 'cleansed of some of their cobwebbing of deceit'. This fiction is worth any amount of documentary." Against expectations, both US and British editions sold 10,000 copies, and Norman was rewarded with foreign editions in France and Germany and the following year, nerves having settled, with a British paperback that sold 100,000, but was disgusted when, despite the paperback's success, Collins' imprint Fontana decided not to reprint.

Another novel, another apparent disappointment. He retreated to reflect. He may have started work on a next novel but put it aside because a friend, probably Bob Knittel at Collins, suggested he break off and write something else. At Easter he took the family on holiday. The strain of relaxing while nursing doubt showed. "We were in Crete," Kiki says,

I guess I was about fifteen and we went out to a restaurant, it was all people dancing with tablecloths in their teeth and we were drinking and eating and having a fabulous time, really my mother was having a great time, and he decided it was time to go. I think we probably moaned a bit, and he really, really got very upset and very angry, you know, fists clenched, teeth like this, quite frightening, [a] slightly mad-eyed look. This was a case of if it wasn't going according to plan, the way he wanted it to go, he could get very angry.[12]

On the same Crete holiday Norman emerged from lunch onto a jetty, missed his step and fell onto the rocks below. Kiki and Gawaine were *Rashomon*-like witnesses: "badly cut hands, wrists, knees – drunk!" Kiki remembers, while Gawaine recalls that "he was completely unharmed (no cuts, bruises) (tipsy after lunch!)."[13] Norman's dogma about doing what he wanted was undeniably accompanied by impatience: Peter Crookston remembers that "He used to get irritable with me if he thought I hadn't pressed hard enough to get a visa for him to go abroad, he would ring every three days and say, 'Have you got my visa yet?' [But] he wasn't at all a prima donna."[14] Both children remember him as impatient, though Gawaine is slightly more forgiving. Norman's short temper when driving was another cause of consternation.

It was all right when you were in England, but when you were driving into Barcelona or somewhere hectic . . . I would be his rear-view mirror and look out of the back to tell him something was coming. It was terrifying, I was reduced to tears on a couple of occasions. But if you ever criticised his driving he'd get terribly upset, he'd say, "I've never crashed, I've been at Brooklands, I've got this incredibly clean record." [And] this is when his impatience came out with other people, with drivers, [he would get] terribly angry. And God forbid you'd ever be put in charge of map reading, that was a nightmare.[15]

He was capable of "effing and blinding" to his teenage children – "Quite often my friends were called 'bloody animals'," Kiki says, "and they were perfectly nice people. Again it was an invasion of his space and he didn't like it." He loved his children, but "it was a different kind of love to the love that other people's fathers would [show], at one remove". He was also oddly overprotective, a residue, possibly, from his mortality-filled childhood. He "was very controlling about certain things, I mean he was obsessed by children falling into rivers and killing themselves and sometimes we felt we were a bit limited. We went out on these rambles in the countryside by ourselves [that] we wouldn't dream of letting our children do now, but he would be worried about us getting into trouble or being hurt in any way." Gawaine agrees about his father's "unnerving" driving and remembers his outbursts and impatience. He feels they were "very minor. . . . I wouldn't say it was often or worrying. It was [just]that sort of flaring anger which would come from a very sort of tranquil moment . . . not directed at us normally, in fact very rarely, but at outside forces which weren't going according to plan. I think it's when you're thinking about stuff the whole time, and then you're worrying, then something else will trip you over the edge."

He and his father were companionable in something of the way Norman had been companionable with his father Richard; fumes of conspiracy, like those that had hung about his excursions with Karen and Gareth, were added to their outings. "I think he wanted a partner in crime to go off and do these little things." He would hear his father coming back from a think-walk "because you could hear his cough before you could hear him, you'd hear the cough, cough, cough of this nervous cough that he had", and says that it seemed normal "to look for Roman pottery or to go birdwatching, or go and sit in a hide for three hours and wait for some strange bird to come in".

I don't think the rest of the family was quite aware what we were up to. We used to do this thing called leaf-moulding, which would be going out to the woods and just digging up leaf-mould for the garden so, and you know, that was good fun. In sacks, stealing it. That was the exciting thing, going to woodlands and . . . we were worried that someone would come in and find us nicking earth. Or going off on a trip to find orchids from the local neighbourhood . . . that was exciting as well because these were all protected species and you'd have to surreptitiously dig away and jump back into the car.[16]

That August for the family's summer holiday they tried Portugal again, the Algarve this time, but the jinx persisted, with everyone bar Lesley falling ill. The event of the autumn took place on 20 September when, after knowing each other for twenty-three years, she and Norman were finally married at Braintree Register Office. She was forty-five, he was sixty-seven. Or non-event. "We only married purely for convenience in the end," Lesley says, "because accountants and solicitors said, 'Really you're much more sensible if you get married.' Ito was our best man." No sentimental journey followed. Lesley flew home to Australia to see her mother, and in December the family, reunited, flew to Agadir for Christmas and New Year.

It had been twelve months of down time. His new novel had failed the test he had set for it, this time to be a transatlantic bestseller, possibly a film – its story drenched in scenes and action had led him to feel the way the narrator of an F Scott Fitzgerald story felt once, the way almost *all* literary narrators feel at least once – "Now if this were a moving picture (as, of course, I hope it will some day be). . . ."[17] He had not begun serious work on anything new, and with no sign of his reputation enlarging except in the evanescent corridors of Fleet Street and Grays Inn Road – in fact the opposite – he was unclear about the future, passionless, stuck.

There was not better news on the business front. R G Lewis continued to drift, not doing as well as it should. As much as he could, he refused to regret, his interview with Hemingway still working its tutelary magic. But he *had* thought about the "something else, something easy" during the year. It was a book he had meditated occasionally, a memoir, its alleged genesis subject to the usual self-deprecating Norman variations whenever he later discussed it: that he waited so long to publish it in deference to friends' pleas to spare them his wartime experiences, or that, being so disorganised, he had only just come across diaries and notebooks that he had mislaid for thirty years.

In spring 1976 he was rereading diaries, making notes, assembling a structure. A memoir in the sense of crowded essay rather than auto-biography, it was meant to be not about him, but about the city of Naples during the eighteen months he had spent there. As sources he had "Army notebooks, which I wasn't supposed to take back" to England, and the personal diary he had written in an unknown Neapolitan's address book. Rereading these, he realised there was a book in them that "I couldn't have written [before], I don't think I'd developed sufficiently as a writer".[18] He often claimed he also had his section reports retrieved from the wastebasket at the palazzo Satriano, but if he did they have disappeared. What he did have was his affec-tion for the city and the period, and the memories both had fed.

What started as a diversion began to turn into something else, accu-mulating the excitement and clarity of a recovered portrait. He worked on the book for most of the rest of the year, breaking off for holidays, Turkey at Easter, Mallorca and Ibiza that summer, the second holiday memorable for Kiki and Gawaine discovering their father's passport and his real age. Kiki had thought he was twenty years younger. Gawaine, at thirteen, was horrified to see that his father had been born in 1908. "He'd somehow managed to tell me that he'd gone into the Army in the Second World War when he was sixteen and had lied about his age, so in my mind I think he was supposed to be twelve or fourteen years younger than he really was. To find out he was sixty-four or sixty-six [in fact sixty-eight] – I thought, Christ, what a nightmare." Both children immediately starting worrying that if their father went away on a journey now, he might never come back. Norman soothed their fears by going nowhere else that year.

At Finchingfield he quickly decided on the book's highly expanded (and composed) diary structure: a choice that, even though the book would always be the view of a stranger, gave the reader the thrill of intimacy. He needed to refresh his knowledge of places and asked the help of a friend of Ito's, Sergio Viggiani, who as a child in Naples had lived through the Allied occupation, to go back to the city with him. Viggiani, invited to Finchingfield at Christmas to discuss making a trip, remembers Norman's "hushed voice, almost classical in the way he spoke". They organised a visit for early March, "a nice time to go to Naples because it's not spring yet but you get the spring light, spring has arrived but hasn't yet made an impact",[19] and flew to Naples via Milan, catching the last connection of the day and getting in just before midnight. "We ate at Ciro a Santa Brigida, on the other side of the Galleria, where the opera house is, and because of that Ciro closes at two o'clock. And we stayed at a lousy dump in the middle of one of the big squares. The intention was to revive his memories, to remember details which he couldn't have picked up from memory." They spent three days in the city, looking at his old boarding house in via Martucci, at Forcella where the black market was centred, and at the gracefully understated palazzo Satriano on the riviera di Chiaia where 312 FSS's headquarters had been. Norman's addiction to coincidences was satisfied by a visit to meet a local Communist politician, Mario Palermo, who turned out to have an apartment in the Satriano on the floor beneath Norman's old office. "He said, 'Oh look, can you see that building there? That's where my office was.' I said, 'That's where we're going.' He said, 'My God, I can't believe it.' So we went up and when we took the lift he said, 'Well, the lift didn't work when I was here. We had to walk four floors.'" Curiously, when Palermo poured drinks and asked Norman the correct thing to say for a toast in English, Norman responded with the least characteristic of all answers. "God bless."

On the last day they went to Orta di Atella, to the scene of the SS massacre at the crossroads in September 1943. Norman's role thirty-two years earlier had been to investigate the imprisonment of a partisan chief named Callisti by the local police chief, *maresciallo* Altamura. Altamura had claimed that Callisti and his partisans were not patriots but thieves who had stolen uniforms belonging to two captured Germans and that, when a German patrol had found the uniforms, assuming their wearers to be dead (they had in fact been freed), they had sparked the murderous reprisals. Although he had arrested Callisti, Altamura said, he had actually been holding him for his own safety, to prevent his being taken in a vendetta. In a bar Norman began talking to people, and a young woman told him that her uncle had been one of the twenty-four who had been machine-gunned at the crossroads. Viggiani recalls, "And she said, 'Well of course those bastards [the partisans] were never punished, and our families are still wounded from what happened.' And she started getting more and more hysterical and crying, trembling and shaking. Norman didn't say anything. He was visibly upset."[20]

By October 1977 he had finished the Naples typescript and delivered it, without a satisfactory title. As soon as the book was with Collins, he packed for Bolivia. He had planned the journey as a "small, reviving evasion" (a typical Normanism for an escape) to coincide with the end of a period of writing, as he had done his 1974 trip to Paraguay with the end of *The Sicilian Specialist*.

The story was another investigation into the Indians and the violently high price of modernity; another report of politico-religious repression, another chapter in his book against exploitation, another entry in his deconstructionist's encyclopedia of civilisation. He flew, as you had to, via Lima, his plane landing at La Paz on 10 October, "engines screaming in reverse and wing-flaps clawing at the thin air" at 3600 metres. The town appalled him as "weird and apocalyptic, infernal, a great ashen hole in the earth under the rim of the Altiplano [that] spreads its suburbs and slums in concentric rings round the walls of this weird amphitheatre".[21] The wind "whine[d] like a persistent beggar at every corner".

He travelled with a photographer, Colin Jones. "The Bolivia story", Jones says, "was 'if we could get it, there was a story'. It was dangerous working with some of his stories, the Bolivian one particularly . . . we were told not to do it and were warned off several times." The danger lay, as in Paraguay, with the political implications of the subject. In Bolivia the Indians' cause had been suddenly threatened in 1977 by the government's bizarre announcement of plans to offer free immigration to up to 150,000 white immigrants, particularly from the beleaguered "white" states of South Africa and Rhodesia (Zimbabwe). White settlers would be given a minimum of 50 hectares of first-class agricultural land gratis; those who wanted to ranch would get much more, plus low-cost labour. Presented as a policy of economic development, the scheme had found objectors among the liberal Catholic Church on the grounds that white South African immigrants "with their violently racial mentality, condemned even in their own countries", would import apartheid. In Norman's view the government's objective was simpler, a quick fix to transform an underperforming nation into a strong – white-dominated, rightist, anti-Communist – state. (Bolivia already had a large, economically burly German-Dutch minority).

In La Paz he met the Bolivian Under-Secretary for Immigration, Dr Guido Strauss, who told him that the trickle of immigrants would become a flood as soon as black majority rule in Africa became a fact, and that Bolivia for the new colonialists would be a promised land. What would happen to the forty-one Indian tribes, numbering 120,000, Norman asked, whose land occupied the areas designated for development? Strauss suggested that if Norman wanted information about the country's Indians, he should talk to the American-backed Summer Institute of Linguistics. He was back with the missionaries.

Fundamentalist, wealthy, officially associated with the government, theologically as hardcore as the New Tribes Mission, the Summer Institute of Linguistics' approach was suave and courteous. Norman "never met a Bolivian who did not regard [it] as the base for operations of the CIA in Bolivia; possibly in South America itself",[22] though he gave credit to its head, Victor Halterman, for his "reticence and modesty", working out of a bare office in a rundown La Paz building. Halterman told Norman that Indian presence on the designated land was a matter for regret: he blamed himself and his fellow missionaries for incompetence on that score at not having harvested all the souls they could. He outlined the SIL's "harvesting" tactics – the building of a shelter in the forest, the cutting of radial paths on which gifts of knives, axes, mirrors were left, the enticing to the shelter and the ensuing breaking of dependency by telling the Indians that now, if they wanted these things, they had to work for money. "We don't employ them, but we can usually fix them up with something to do on local farms," Halterman told him.

Norman saw that this meant the kind of unequal equation with which he was already familiar, and worse: for the sake of one "saved" soul it was justifiable to let 150 others perish, and even if they did not, "something to do on local farms" would condemn them to labour for up to fifteen hours a day and a few cents in wages until illness took them. Norman learnt of debt-slavery, press-ganging and trafficking, of Indian girls sold into white families as unpaid domestics and tame sexual prey, and Indian tin miners who expected to be dead by forty from silicosis.

The assignment "snowballed as we went along," Colin Jones remembers. They were guided by liberal churchmen "who were like plainclothes cops, they said when we were really getting into danger". He and Norman drove south-east out of La Paz to Cochabamba and Santa Cruz, a new town "dizzy with quick profits".

That's where the story really started. There was a big Holiday Inn there, it was the time when the Bolivian government was trying to get Germans, ex-Nazis, they were going to take all the people from South Africa, and they'd started to put street lamps in the middle of the jungle. We burst in there and there were all these fascists, you couldn't believe it, and the hotel was amazingly well run in that Germanic way. I had to walk Norman to his hotel room, because there were these massive frogs hopping about.

In his notebook Norman sketched, dramatically, the Indians' transition.

To the Indians leaving the forest it must seem like a poisoned fairyland. They see the lights. They caress the shining surfaces of the walls, gaze into the incredible shop windows. .... They cough and they die.[23]

Near Santa Cruz Norman was taken to an estate to see cane-cutters and cotton harvesters, all migrant Indians, at work, living in slum barracks without fresh water or medicine. At Santa Cruz on 18 October he found a band of twenty Ayoreo Indians living on waste land, one a young man who had been shot in the head by a policeman (and survived) after trying to help a girl who was being assaulted by two whites. To live, the Ayoreo women in the group had been reduced to selling sex for the equivalent of 13 pence. All the Ayoreos, a tribe known as "the jaguar hunters", had fled from a mission. At their mission three days later, accompanied by his Catholic minders, Norman was confronted by 275 malnourished Ayoreos whose gaze was "emptied by apathy", and a missionary who had recently switched off their water supply to punish them for their children having stolen a small amount of petrol; he excused himself by saying to Norman that he had switched off his own water supply to share their discomfort (Norman noted he had laid on a reserve). The chief problem, for which the man blamed his charges as if they were genetically defective, was that Indians had no concept of punishment for their children.

On the way back to La Paz they halted at a tin mine owned by Rio Tinto, where by now the atmosphere was depressingly familiar. Colin Jones photographed a forbidding desert of grey windowless barracks under a glittering Andean peak. "It was terrible, the altitude and the way they work, but they chew coca and it takes out hunger [so that] they're semi-comatose." Jones was another photographer who came under Norman's charm. He had read *Golden Earth*. "The only country I've ever fallen in love with is Burma, and it was through Norman. He inspired you. Whenever I went on an assignment with him I never knew exactly what we were going to do. He had no definite way of doing it until he hit the ground there." He also admired Norman's professionalism.

He'd been with very, very good photographers, so you had to be careful. If he saw me taking something and said, "That's a load of crap," I'd say, "I know it is, I've got to end the film." But we [photographers] also used to have this fantastic argument with writers, that on the plane coming home from anywhere they'd say, "Oh, you've done your bit, now I've got to go and write it." You'd turn round and say, "So you've got to fucking write it. You can make it up, but if I haven't got the pictures I can't afford to go back and reshoot them." Norman never said anything like that.[24]

On the drive back to La Paz he also met with the writer's desire to get what he wanted. He wanted to reach La Paz, but Norman demanded a stop at a bar on the Altiplano to chase off the horrors.

We stopped at this terrible bar, I was longing to get back, so he goes in and has a very strong drink and he's sitting there and I came out and left him because I didn't speak Spanish. Then he came rushing out the door and said, "Can I have your watch?"

So I said, "What do you want my watch for?"

He said, "Come on, let's have your watch."

I said, "Well it's an expensive watch, Norm."

"I want your watch."

I said, "Well what's it all about?"

"I've just seen some Inca or Mayan pottery that these blokes have got and they don't want dollars, they want your watch."

So I had to give him the watch.[25]

The episode of the watch chimes with a story, "The Bolivian Treasure", that Norman included later in a collection of journalism,[26] in which he is introduced to a *huaquero*, a professional grave robber on the shore of Lake Titicaca. He writes that he had gone to the town of Achacachi to look at its grim one-man tin mines, and in a village 160 kilometres to the north had tracked down the man, who had apparently found gold funerary items, one a jewel in the shape of a butterfly. But the necessary preliminary of sacrifice of a llama's foetus to Tio, the god of the mines, went wrong, so Norman was not permitted sight of the jewellery and could only be offered the consolation prize of an, as it turned out, stupendously interesting and valuable ceramic jaguar the man also carried. For payment the grave robber wanted a watch, but Norman's was too small. The alternative of £50 (way more than the price of a watch) was refused "with a contemptuous smile". Colin Jones is not mentioned in the story of the failed acquisition of the jaguar, nor does Norman's notebook have a source for the treasure story although he noted the sacrifices to Tio and the conditions endured by the miners (they "went into a hardly visible hole in [the] mountainside . . . walked or half-crawled for 2 km [and] came out dragging tin on [their] back"). He had a habit of writing short pieces of fiction that drew from his reservoir of experiences: I would place the treasure story in his own category of "Leave anything to my imagination and nobody could recognise the facts after a few years".

Recomposing thirty-five-year-old experiences through the medium of that imagination and his notebooks, *Naples '44* was published on 28 February 1978. Needlessly Collins made it look like a half-hearted thriller, white-jacketed with lettering in loud Princetown type and a boring pen-and-ink illustration of a rifle with two flasks of wine slung from it. It sold badly. By the end of the year it had only sold 3206 copies in hardback, about half what his book about the mafia had achieved (and several hundred less than his next novel would sell). Collins had indicated that they would publish a paperback edition in their Fontana imprint, then welshed on their promise. Norman must at last have begun to doubt whether Collins were capable of publishing him.

The book's reviews, at least, did not reflect its supposed lack of popularity. After first reading it five years later, I must have run my eye a hundred times down the laudatory review extracts on the back cover of my Eland Books reissue as a promissory note of the pleasure that awaited.

"Uncommonly well written, entertaining despite its depressing content, and quite remarkably evocative." (Philip Toynbee, *Observer*)

"His ten novels and five non-fiction works place him in the front rank of contemporary English writers ... here is a book of gripping fascination in its flow of bizarre anecdote and character sketch; and it is much more than that." (J W Lambert, *Sunday Times*)

"A wonderful book ... Norman Lewis exactly catches the strange excitement I felt in that first acquaintanceship with a country even more fascinating and lovable than Vietnam." (Richard West, *Spectator*)

"Sensitive, ironic and intelligent." (Paul Fussell, *New Republic*)

"One goes on reading, page after page, as if eating cherries." (Luigi Barzini, *New York Review of Books*.) In his review Barzini noted the small, but significant, signifier that Norman "writes very well, inconspicuously well".[27] But it was the half-page piece by Jack Lambert, the *Sunday Times*' former literary editor, that best responded to the book's restorative portrait: to its feat of unvanishing the past.

There are perhaps ten active English-language writers whose books I make haste to read as soon as possible. Ever since his first novel, *Samara*, appeared in the late 1940s, Norman Lewis has been one of them.

... His particular qualities as a writer are all present [in *Naples '44*]: swift narrative readability, intense pictorial evocation, sardonic curiosity coupled with detached sympathy. So are the qualities in life which seem to stir him most: passionate alienation, revolutionary egotism, tribal loyalties and implacable vitality.

... the horrors of war, Mr Lewis soon realised, are only a top-dressing on the volcanic soil of Naples and its hinterland. It is the people of this alarming and exuberant world, not the military intruders, who supply the rich, often dreadfully funny, substance of *Naples '44*.

It is an unblinking celebration of the splendours and miseries of a fiery way of life by a man responding to it with all his senses but without ever being submerged; all the time groping for understanding.[28]

Such appreciation by readers came later, and not by itself. *Naples '44* is an accidental masterpiece like all masterpieces – and in any case the epithet is premature in 1978. Fuller valuing of the book's worldly insights, its political clarity, its rhetorical grasp of, and compassion for, its own times and its humanity, its tone, would occur, and its reputation be refined, with a commendable slowness. The American edition was published by Pantheon the same year, with a huffing puff from Sid Perelman ("If this book shouldn't get the critical and public acclaim it deserves, all of us might just as well box up our typewriters. Lewis's reconstruction of the disorganization, the despair, and yet the will to live, by any means, of the population, his compassion and humor, are just plain terrific"). Possibly as a result of a definite winnowing of American glory in Norman's account of Fifth Army's conduct in Italy, the book did no better than it had in Britain.

Norman worried about his lack of impact: as he had under different conditions in the 1950s and 1960s, he watched his output, the work he was putting in, the reactions of critics and readers, and the absence of a breakthrough. He cared and was disappointed; but it was part of his self-construction to exercise a modest stoicism and not allow himself to be soured by the fact that, as J W Lambert had it, he had not "broken through the mysterious barrier separating the admired from the famous". His retort to fame was to stay interested. Returning from Bolivia the previous November he had written his report, not for the *Sunday Times* but the *Observer* where Peter Crookston was now the magazine's editor. (Donald Trelford, the *Observer*'s editor, allegedly demonstrated the point about fame when Crookston told him he had a great writer for the magazine, "Norman Lewis", and Trelford replied, "Who the hell's Norman Lewis?") He had also that winter started work on a novel set in Bolivia, and was thinking about a new long piece of journalism sparked by the journey.

In spring 1978 he faced a more immediate problem. R G Lewis was failing. For five years he had continued to keep it going, and for the last four had tried several times to revive its stuttering trajectory by extending, then cutting back its activities, closing or selling branches when profits were threatened. By autumn 1977 five of its eight branches had gone, including 125 Strand. The only shops left were at High Holborn, Worcester and Bristol. He disliked the business as much as ever. "It was like a kind of dead weight around his neck," Ito says. "He said to me, 'Whenever I have to go into town and go to R G Lewis, I'm so depressed.'" Now it had reached the stage where the company's poor performance could no longer continue. None of the directors, Norman, Ito or Bert Currey, or the company's accountant had any public explanation for the mess the business was in.

Norman decided to seek a buyer. He found one in another photographic business, Dollonds, and by early summer 1978 "Britain's Scientifically Minded Camera Firm", which Norman had started and owned for more than forty years, was no longer in his hands. He remained philosophical about it, knowing that he hadn't run it properly because he was bored with it. But the sale also caused a family falling out when Norman had his accountant ask Ito to make his shares over to Norman. "Norman had run the business, but it had to be settled," Lesley recalls, feeling that it brought to a head the poison Ito had been fed by his mother as a boy, that Norman had failed to send money and failed generally to support them both.[29] The truth, from Ito's point of view, was simpler: he was deeply hurt that his father had not asked him in person to give up the shares but got the accountant to do it. Ito stopped seeing his father, and though Norman wrote to him and he came to Finchingfield the quarrel was not resolved.

Norman's decision about the sale's proceeds however seems to indicate that he didn't much care about benefiting personally. He told Lesley that Hester had always maintained that she wanted to open a nursing home, and so when the sale was concluded he felt Hester should have first call on the monies.

But Hester, now sixty-nine, turned down the offer. Gareth remembers that his mother had no zest for new projects. "I can't remember the last time she saw [Norman] but it would have probably been in the mid-1970s. Her sister who owned the house was a senile diabetic, and Mum's life was in fact looking after her. She always had this fantasy that when she didn't have that around her neck, she would then free herself and go and do the things she'd always wanted to do. In fact the death of her sister, who fell in the bath and cracked her ribs and died from pneumonia, was really the beginning of my mother's decline. She lost interest in everything."[30]

The incidents he collected were treasures, they were things that he could bring away and then make them grow.

Don McCullin

He said, "I'll take you to a place where they do something that will make your eyes pop out." It was a bar at this place in Mexico which he seemed to know, it was full of flies, and the waiter used to go "phhttt" like that and he'd end up with a whole handful. Norman said, "You try it." So everybody was trying it. Norman knew about this bloke doing this, but he was great at all those stories.

Colin Jones

He was a good man, a funny man, a really good journalist, meticulous in note taking. In the evenings we'd go out to a bar and talk, we were drinking Cuba Libres then, he was very good company. Norman influenced a lot of people. One of them was my friend David Blundy, who always said that he admired Norman Lewis immensely.

Alain Le Garsmeur

AMAZONIA AND OTHER
DISAPPEARANCES

"It is more culpable to destroy an oasis
than to kill seventy prophets"
Saharan proverb

IN the notebook he brought back from Bolivia, Norman's notes included this.

In the last 10 years the number of days of high winds [per year] has increased from 100–140 (due to deforestation).

In the ten years he had been reporting from Latin America, his contacts and the Portuguese and Spanish newspapers he read had started talking of a new phenomenon. Deforestation of the rainforests of Amazonia in order to use the land for extensive cattle ranching offered instant, short-term economic gain and was accelerating. In a single year, 1975, the forest had lost 11 million hectares, 4 per cent of its trees. In Brazil, Paraguay and Bolivia Norman had viewed forest clearances from the perspective of the "harvesting", dispossession and murder of forest Indians; now he was starting to collect data on their effect on the balance of nature and future weather. In December 1978 in England he read an article in *New Scientist* that put forward an increase in sunlight reflectivity and a build-up of carbon dioxide as consequences of tropical deforestation. He called Peter Crookston at the *Observer* and told him the background. "He told me that he thought it could have worldwide implications, that burning the forests in the Amazon would be like the world losing a lung. I'd never heard anyone say this before and I was bowled over by the idea."[1] Crookston agreed to the piece and "bust the *Observer*'s budget" to pay for the travelling.

Norman put aside his almost completed novel and landed with Colin Jones at Manaus in northern Brazil on 4 January. They had been able to take a direct flight from London because Manaus was a freeport, afloat on duty-free money at the edge of the jungle. He spoke first to ecologists at INPA, the National Institute of Amazonian Research, who were trying as fast as they could to fill the gaps in their knowledge of an ignored ecosystem. Most of the large-scale burning of the forest had been done by foreign multinationals, companies like Volkswagen do Brasil, Liquigas and King Ranch of Texas, but a potential new wave had just been revealed in a government deal to sell 40 per cent of the forest in concessions to pay for Brazil's balance of payments deficit. Widespread protests had begun, but the scheme remained on the table. Smaller-scale burning went on permanently. Norman had heard rumours that landowners were using napalm to fire the forest. He and Colin Jones chartered a plane. "I managed to get an aeroplane hired," Jones remembers. "Norman wouldn't go up in it, he said, 'I'll never go up in a single-engined plane in the rainforest, two engines only.'"[2] He eventually did, and enjoyed painting the flight luridly to Leila Hadley when he got back. "Flew over 1000 miles of Amazon forest in 1-engine seaplane piloted by Brazilian high on cocaine and with only half a face (rest a plastic surgery reconstruction, very unsuccessful, after several crashes)."[3] The obverse of such exaggerations was his ability to switch off the world's tedium. "The other thing about Norman", Jones says,

is it never got boring, because we'd started in Manaus – Manaus is one of the most boring places on earth, oh fuck is it boring! – the Amazon there is so wide [and] it's one of the most boring rivers. But he'd come up with, he'd say, "Well, you know it flowed the other way." I said, "I didn't know that," and he said, "Well you've been up in the Andes, and when we went up into the Andes there were seashells." It was that information that he always used to entertain you with. I shall never forget him showing me the seashells just before the snowline.[4]

He and Norman flew north along the route of the BR174 highway at 300 metres over "one of nature's exaggerations . . . one third of the world's trees",

having from this height the appearance of sparkling moss. . . . Fires appeared as blue smudges here and there, and there were never less than a half-dozen in sight, and many charcoal scrawls and flourishes showed on the green pages of the jungle where others had burnt out. . . . Land here costs too much to attract ranchers thinking in terms of 20,000 to 30,000 hectares, whose operations would show up on a satellite photograph. Close to Manaus it was a matter of 100 hectares here and 200 there, but it was sad to think just how many small fires must have been alight all over the Amazon basin on a fine day like this.[5]

They saw the desertification of already abandoned fields, their skin of humus exhausted. Later they drove out on the highway to see estates "sometimes furnished with a swimming pool by which the *fazendeiro* and his friends could have sat to enjoy the view across a wasteland resembling the aftermath of the battle of the Somme". They stopped at a fire in progress where the manager explained his methods. Napalm was expensive; it was cheaper and easier to cut down the big trees, strew piles of lorry tyres at intervals through the forest, douse them with petrol and set them alight.

We were startled by the speed of the fire's advance, dodging and leaping into the branches, clinging to lianas, turning into small bonfires the bundles of orchids and ferns lodged in the forks and axils. The noise, as wood exploded everywhere under pressure of boiling sap, was terrific.

Leaving Manaus they travelled upriver to Iquitos and Belém. At Iquitos they stayed on the Spanish promenade – "A beautiful promenade, but the hotel was rough," Jones remembers, "the food was rough, the hotel had no light bulbs, just blown bulbs with flies, no shades, full of cock-roaches and rats" – before he persuaded Norman to move to the Hilton. From Belém they tried to visit Daniel Keith Ludwig's Jari Forestry project. The secretive Manhattan billionaire had bought 4 million hectares of the forest in 1967 to set up a pulp lumber business. On the estate he had built airstrips, a private railway and a deep-water port: he had floated a 60,000-ton pulp mill from Japan. "Larger than Belgium," Norman noted. "Ludwig concentrates but does not distribute money."[6] Jones recalls that Ludwig "had his own army. He wouldn't let you anywhere near his place. If you were on the river and you went to his bank, maybe twenty miles [long], someone would come out and tell you to piss off."

At Finchingfield in February Norman supplemented what he had seen for himself with the now famous research by Harald Sioli of the Max Planck Institute for Limnology,[7] showing that the Amazon biome contributed through photosynthesis 50 per cent of the world's production of oxygen and that its destruction would sacrifice not only that oxygen but its capacity to absorb the carbon dioxide exhaled by the world's oil-based societies – both factors capable of altering the world's climate. As a naturalist and champion of Indians Norman might have condemned deforestation purely for its local devastation of rare habitats, tribes, species. Instead, the first mainstream writer to do so, he wrote how destruction of the rainforest would inevitably provoke unpredictable change in the world's weather.

The biographer should no doubt officiously refrain from erecting partisan monuments to his subject. But there is surely a margin of the remarkable in the prophetic quality of Norman's concluding paragraphs. A new threat to the forest's existence was also approaching, he wrote, "this time one that is far more likely to bring about the final solution". Brazilian public opinion, he felt, could to an extent keep the appetites of the ranchers at bay. The new menace would come from a demand for biofuel.

Two barrels of petroleum substitute can be made from a ton of wood, and the Amazon forest is estimated to contain 415 billion cubic feet of timber. The Brazilian press ... signalled the opening of a new battle front by quotations from an article in *Data Shell*. Ethyl alcohol and methane, commonly substituting for petrol in the last war, said the article, were now easily and cheaply produced from vegetable matter. Technical difficulties hampering Amazonian production in the past had been overcome, and with the decrease in reserves and constant increase in petroleum prices, substitutes were about to come into their own.[8]

Few readers would have equated the content of Norman's *Observer* article when it appeared in April 1979 with the situation that would face them thirty years later. The stir created by his report was chiefly among television production companies wanting to exploit his research, though nothing came of their interest; Norman let the *Observer* deal with them, retreating to the Parsonage to revise his Bolivian novel. With R G Lewis disposed of, he felt emancipated from a tyranny; with a break from his cycle of Latin American journeys, he drew breath with the family. He had taken Lesley and the children to Greece again for Easter, and at the end of June to northern Spain to "botanise" in the Pyrenees, according to Gawaine, and to visit Santiago de Compostela.

At sixteen Gawaine was beginning to see his father, in his seventy-first year, with unconstrained eyes, appreciating his willingness to provide pleasure, critical of his fussiness when travelling with his family.

A lot of money was spent on family holidays, and we had a lot of them [but] he hated travelling, absolutely hated the process of going to the airport. He was the world's worst traveller. The man would panic if we weren't out the door on time. This pressure cooker would build up. A point always of friction and potential blow-up was failing to get to the airport on time, and until we were in the hotel at the other end it was a stressful experience.

Some of our Greek family holidays were very, very enjoyable, perfect weather, beaches for the kids, windsurfing and that kind of thing, a family holiday in the most normal sense – you know, if you don't want to piss your kids off don't put them in the back of the car for five hours going plant-hunting, because you know it's not a lot of fun, although nostalgically you can look through rose-coloured spectacles at how great it was to find these plants.

The good thing about the holidays was he could speak the language, so we'd be a step above the average holidaymaker. Dad [also] had this expression, his "traveller's instinct". We'd go out for the family meal in the evening and he would have to find us the right restaurant for the family meal, and he would say, "My traveller's instinct tells me this restaurant is the right one." Basically his traveller's instinct had to have a clean white tablecloth, the waiters had to be attentive, but he didn't want any sort of sycophanting or fawning, no ponciness at all, just very basic, straightforward. And he would never go to a restaurant where there were other tourists. Once he'd found this place – which we'd find occasionally – we would order a local fish dish or whatever; if there was *mero* he'd say, "I'll have that," and he'd always say, "That was the finest *mero* I've ever had in my life." It would be the finest paella, the finest this or the finest that, and this used to bug us intensely. "How could it be the finest? You had this last holiday. Is it better than last time?" But it would always be the finest.[9]

Back from Spain on 2 July, he left again on the 15th for four days in Naples to do a story as part of a series for the *Sunday Times* magazine. Ken Griffiths, the photographer, noticed his unassertiveness.

We just walked around. [Other writers] used to say things like, "We're going to do this, we're going to do that". . . . But Norman never said that, he just said, "Oh I've got an idea, this might interest you." Or he would follow along and I would get ready to do some pictures on location, he'd come along and he would just start talking. Because I worked with a plate camera, it takes a bit of setting up, so he would just disappear, come back, it didn't seem to worry him, I think it amused him more.[10]

The piece Norman wrote on his return, "Surviving with spirit", is infected by the leniency of his affection to the Naples that he remembered, of corruption and marvels, and found intact: its sea, "beyond a bordering of intense pollution . . . as brilliant and translucent as any in the world", its best restaurants vulnerable to bandit raids "but a Neapolitan friend involved in a hold-up had been stimulated rather than alarmed". He observed the "tremendous chuckle of twin 230 Mercury engines" as a cigarette smuggler's launch from the port's fleet of forty or so fired up in broad daylight and shrank towards its rendezvous on the horizon with a Tunisian freighter, and quoted the city's mayor, Maurizio Valenzi, describing the trafficking as "not a crime, an illegal solution".

He toured the *bassi* again and the scoured crimson façades and the saints, in particular Santa Maria del Carmine and the embalmed Blessed Egidio, whose speciality was transforming "off" fish to saleable life, the atheist in him judging not their sanctity but their encouragement of human solidarity, and he concluded, "The income per capita is only a third of that in Milan; but, for me, Naples will always be the better place to live in."[11] He did *not* ever live in Naples in peacetime. But the city's vitality and its population's sense of belonging, its emotional unity and oriental rejection of change, preserved it as a prime symbol of his personal topography: a city that had first helped construct that topography and his understanding of what he, the vagabond de-adherent, was always looking for. He regretted staying only four days, Ken Griffiths recalls, "because he didn't know me, he was very shy in some ways, but he did say, 'I really wish I'd stayed longer.'" Leaving, he missed a definitive moment: the attempted kidnap of Griffiths and his assistant by their (armed) driver. The photographers escaped by persuading the driver to drop them at the hotel and meet them for dinner, gambling that he would agree because it would give him an opportunity to return with back-up. Instead at their hotel on via Partenope they rapidly packed, checked out and drove themselves to Rome.

"James Maxwell was in Bolivia partly for the money." The opening sentence of the dustjacket blurb for *The German Company* announces another Lewis hero, a not entirely mercenary character for whom defeat is the only possible outcome in his struggle against the political and commercial power of the Gesellschaft für Forstkultur, the German company of the title. Maxwell, the British owner of a trucking company, is a romantic; is he enough of one to carry the reader? For any Robert Louis Stevenson-loving reader, the novel's subject has strange echoes of Stevenson's confrontation with a German copra plantation in Western Samoa in the 1890s, and is a comprehensive lexicon of Norman's own targets: Indian exploitation and environmental plunder, tourism and American evangelism. It may be the first novel with a reference to climate change.

"We need the road," Adler said. . . . "It would take two years and two million dollars to do it, and even then it would remain subject to flooding. This is a problem that gets worse every year. Something has happened to the climate."
"It's got wetter," Maxwell said. "Wetter in the wet season and drier in the dry."[12]

It is not dogged by some of the habits of Norman's novels – lack of engagement, bloodless love affairs, a preference for action and atmosphere over human complexity – and its interesting parts, about the politics of forest clearance and the corruptions of foreign involvement, are as knowingly conveyed as the tone of daily life and behaviour. ("The German company", a novelist's hybrid of Ludwig's Jari Forestry project managed by Bolivian ex- and neo-Nazis, operates in a country sketched with elaborate flavour by Norman after spending only three weeks there.)
But Norman's twelfth novel does not work. Its Romanticism is not

large or tragic enough, its personal stakes not high enough, its form not wrought enough. You could say that no novel that ends with a hero's polite deportation, unharmed, can be satisfying. Waged within too limited a dramatic scope, Maxwell's defeat is too small.

It was Norman's first novel since 1950 not to find a US publisher. He was getting used to his novels being published and going out of print rapidly, although *The German Company* was published on 3 September and in its one edition sold 3595 copies before the end of the year, more than *Naples '44*, probably as a result of its title. It amused him that the indefinite appeal for anything connected with Nazis kept the novel available and borrowed in British public libraries.[13]

At the same time as writing diminishingly successful novels, he had also begun writing, as non-fiction, memoirs in which his novelist's process was at work. The following month to coincide with an exhibition at the Royal College of Art, "The Amazing Bugattis", the *Observer* reunited him with his Type 51, now owned by a Hertfordshire farmer, and to the photograph of Norman, Bugatti and a herd of Friesians added 2000 words of his highly composed reminiscences about the Bugattis he had owned. The article began with his detailed description of a drive he had made to the Black Sea and back in his Type 40 – the journey with Ernestina of May 1938 – which he made elsewhere in both a Ford and a Buick. It went on in the same sportive and highly adaptive vein.[14] This was new. Or not completely new. *Naples '44* had been tentatively personal, and adapted from his real diaries. But the seeds of this style are from earlier. We need to go back to late 1949 or early 1950 and what he wrote comically-frustratedly then in his diary. "I'm not a liar, countrymen, but my imagination sometimes takes control. Let it go a few years and I'm never sure myself what happened."

Once an excuse for what he claimed was an involuntary process, impossible to date but probably beginning in his childhood as soon as he realised the power of sentences, at the end of the 1970s that statement was changing into a virtual declaration of method. The kind of autobiography that he had viewed thirty years before with condescension had turned into the substantiation of a subject he was now choosing intentionally: himself. In future he would publish fewer novels (three still to come in the next ten years) in favour of writing more openly about his own life as an observer of so many lost events and places, in a series of memoirs initiated by *Naples '44*.

That is certainly how it seems. Biographically speaking.

Yet as biographer I feel bound to throw out this analysis as false: false in the sense that it is not the analysis that matters. In biographical or personal terms it *might* matter. In literary terms (the terms – I'm repeating myself, I know – that make Norman worth writing a biography about), it doesn't. What matters instead is the shift in the literary object, the shift that makes the handover of subject and approach *formally* interesting. What had Norman been writing until 1975? Novels, thrillers of exotic and/or revolutionary stamp; travel-compositions of different kinds; journalism, some with remarkable political impact. He was now starting to write fewer novels; more re-creations of the past (his past); autobiographical journalism. What makes this changeover interesting is not its shift of subject but its deepening, its making ambiguous, of Norman's narration.

The literary object now *seems* to be more himself, which would certainly be an interesting shift into the spotlight. If it were true. But it is not, because Norman isn't writing about *himself*. Leaving aside for a moment his inhibition at writing at any deeply emotional level, a key quality of *Naples '44* and the books that would follow it is that he is not a *self* in any of them nearly so much as he is a rhetorical agent. His being present enables him to handle his material, and that is all. If he were not there, he would not be able to handle the material narratively in the way that he does. What he has begun to give his readers with *Naples '44* is not, finally, the story of the life of Norman Lewis, displaced child, compensatory dandy, natural businessman, competent photographer, three times husband and father, racing driver, soldier, spy, traveller, writer, hedonist, etc. etc.; but a new set of entries in his personal encyclopedia in which *the past is a place* as much as any of the places he has been to and written about. What it was like, this past, is as much a matter of the words' textures and richnesses, of invention's textures and richnesses, as any other place is. The force of living in it – of presence, tone, gesture, fullness, evanescence – needs to be represented: the reader needs "the active presence of absent things".[15] How do Norman's "restored" autobiographies represent that force? By framing it inside the significant verbal landscapes of fiction; landscapes of words borrowed from the novelist, borrowed from a Welshman's imagination spontaneously taking control.

What caused him to make the change, make the past his literary object? On a journey with Colin Jones to Mexico in early 1980 he revealed a vein of his feelings he rarely talked about: his feeling of being left behind. The 1960s had given him recognition and reputation with one book, *The Honoured Society*; the 1970s, despite his hurling himself again at the bastion of novelistic success, and his ample exposure in his reporting for the *Sunday Times* and the *Observer* – two of the world's finest newspapers at the time – had left him feeling less recognised than before. By 1980 he was seventy-one, and as he looked around him, feeling that he should have some acceptance by now, instead he felt he was disappearing. He was stoical about it; he remembered Hemingway's Faustian contract; he was allowably disappointed. The Romantic still willed a breakthrough, the pragmatist had nothing to say (he continued to make a reasonable living and now had the capital from the sale of the photography business). But after nearly thirty years, the author was hurt to see the beginnings of his own eclipse.

He and Jones had landed at Mexico City on 29 February with an unusually unformed idea of their assignment. "We went to Mexico because he'd got this bee in the bonnet that there was a race of Indians that can run up mountains ... and Crookston let him go." Norman had made enquiries, but after two days journalist and photographer found themselves in Mexico City without a story. "He said, 'Leave it to me, I've heard about this place, Villahermosa, which is continually under water, sounds interesting.'"[16] They flew to Villahermosa and there hired a Mexican Volkswagen to explore the state of Tabasco, 60 per cent of which was swampland (in autumn 2007 swamp deteriorated to floodland, trapping 300,000 in their homes). Serendipity intervened; he located a community of Chontal Indians, marsh dwellers since they had been chased there by the Spanish, who charmed him by their subversion of a government project to turn the fertility of the marshes to profit, resisting with stubborn conservatism and sly humour. Norman reported with glee an Indian grinningly dismissing the Tarzan scene on his own T-shirt, "These are the legends of a primitive people."[17] He and Jones drove south into Chiapas, climbing into the sierra to San Cristóbal de las Casas, aiming for the Guatemalan border.

Norman said to me, "You've really got to see this, it's just like Walt Disney, all these mountains," but there was too much fighting going on and we could easily have been in trouble because whites were being taken for Americans everywhere. All the borders were crossable, not in the official way, but we didn't go.[18]

During the drive, according to Jones, Norman aired his anxiety about his reputation. He told Jones he was worried about the popularity of writers like Paul Theroux, who had been getting fulsome coverage for an account of a railway journey from Boston, Massachusetts through central and south America, *The Old Patagonian Express*. "He said to me he was very sort of worried about Paul Theroux ... he said that there was a scene when [Theroux] got to the Mexican border, this woman came in, a prostitute, came into the compartment while the train was standing there and gave him a blow job. Norman said to me, 'Do you think that really happened?' And I said, 'I doubt it, I doubt it.'" It did not really happen in Theroux's account either: the worst that happened was that in cruising Nuevo Laredo's red light area a girl hitched up her skirt at him. But the success of the attention-calling style of the new generation of writers represented by Theroux cast him down.

He had this chip about Paul Theroux, you know, worrying about "Why, how do I get better known?" He thought he was doing everything wrong, he didn't think he was modern enough, he didn't think he was in the Weidenfeld set. He resented that he wasn't a member of these literary groups. He asked, had I ever been to a Weidenfeld party?[19]

In these conversations lies, I suspect, a part of the answer to why he started to take the past as his literary object. Of course there are other reasons for looking back. He was in his early seventies, when retrospection becomes enjoyable. Nothing says it was not an accidental evolution either: witness the conception of *Naples '44*, stumbled on after he finished *The Sicilian Specialist*. But it is reasonable to argue too that he had started to glimpse what a repository of the irrecoverable, strange and *sui generis* his past was, to understand that his past had a value that had not been revealed so far – and, even more, that to have lived such a life was in itself a sort of resistance and victory, a successful counter-attack against the epiphenomena of media success and fame, against the method of the Therouxs of the world. No judgment of Norman's style allows us to call it simple, exactly; his apparent modesty in print was also his device for delivering the best fruits of his prose, and always underplaying the encrustations of the bizarre and the extreme that enriched it allowed him to exaggerate by appearing to do the opposite. "Whatever I tell you, cut by a half or two thirds," he admitted to an interviewer.[20] But apparent modesty was real modesty too, and from a real desire for invisibility (go back to Forty Hill for the reasons), he shrank by reflex from self-projection. In 1980 he may have begun to see that to write about his past, to re-create, not himself, but the freedom, adventure and surprise that nourished the primitive sense of happiness he lived for, was the weapon with which he might retaliate.

In a curious way the Mexican journey echoed such thinking. Some 40 kilometres or so into the mountains above the hippy-overrun San Cristóbal, he and Jones visited, with an Indian guide, the isolated villages of Chamula, Tzinakantán and Amatenango, all displaying a militant re-emergence of Indian culture. Tourists had had their cameras smashed and been beaten; vigilantes defended their sacred places violently against the outsiders' rolls of film and permissiveness. Norman was told by sign to put his notebook away. Outsiders had a reason to be interested: at Chamula, Jones recalls, the interior of the church was

unbelievable. Norman said – he went in first – "Wait till you see this." There were massive statues of Sebastian, made of wood and all bleeding and nails. There were no church benches. They sat around on straw on the stone floor and they were drinking, boozing in groups. And the light! It was all stained glass and it was pouring in in pools. I thought, This is the most spectacular. . . . Even Norman said he'd never seen anything like it.

I could have paid them a thousand quid and they still wouldn't let me do it. It was the only [picture] I never got.[21]

Whether Norman made the connection between himself and the Chamul Indians or not, he would have seen a purity to the Indians' resistance to every way of doing things but their own. We may also pause and reflect that the point about resistance is not to defeat the enemy, but to last longer than he does.

For the next three years Norman nursed a retaliation that evolved, probably unpremeditated, but with its own energy. This is another way of saying of course that I don't know what happened, or how the alteration in his writing came about (perhaps no more than he did), but I am sure that without energy – the kind of contrary energy that wants to overturn the state of things – neither Norman nor his writing in the 1980s would have had the vitality that they both showed and went on showing. It was also always a primary reflex of his to fight back in his own way.

Outwardly not much changed. In spring 1980 he began another novel. On 5 October he left his desk for Seville to research another "city" piece for the *Sunday Times* magazine, again with Ken Griffiths as photographer. The city seemed "dirty, depressed and anarchistic", and Norman's memory of its Fascist undercurrent revived.

Sevillians had shown themselves at a loss to know what to do with civil liberty, and some excesses had stirred up a sullen reaction. The walls were covered with resentful graffiti. . . . Franco's face had been stencilled everywhere, accompanied sometimes by the supplication, *Come back to us. We can't carry on without you. All is forgiven.*[22]

The atmosphere got to him. For two nights he was alone at the grandiose Hotel Alfonso XIII before Griffiths arrived. Untypically he found a bar and started drinking on his own. The second night he had so much Anis del Mono that, returning to the hotel, when he asked for the key to his room no words came out. Seville in the end showed itself so dour that the *Sunday Times* did not run the article until 1985, by which time Norman had been back and found a city transformed by renewal.

Three months later, in mid-February 1981, he flew to Egypt to research a piece for the *Observer* magazine. The magazine was commissioning a series of river journeys and he had been asked to go down the Nile, or, in the event, up it. He reversed his trajectory in the finished article, descending from Khartoum to the delta instead of, as happened, starting in Cairo. He was again with Colin Jones; for a night they organised themselves among the city's "convulsive, despairing crowds [and] entangled traffic" and then drove into the delta, "beautiful in all its parts", where naked boys stalked moorhen and delved for catfish in the mud, though 90 per cent of the children, he thought, suffered from bilharzia.[23] They then travelled up through El Minyah and Luxor to Aswan where Norman observed the mixed blessing of Lake Nasser, noting that the disruption of the river's annual floods had cut its fertility downstream, holding back the silt and allowing salt to build up.

His account, an admiring-lamenting panegyric to the "river of life", points out that its 5000-kilometre "ribbon of fertility" had once been responsible for the existence of 25 million people "which, ruling out China, would probably have exceeded the number of the inhabitants of the rest of the globe". His own interest lay, typically, in its two extremities. Skipping through its longest section, he and Jones flew back to Cairo. They had tickets for Khartoum and Juba, capital of Sudan's south. They told an acquaintance at the British Embassy they were flying on Sudanese Airlines and were told they were in for a surprise. "And when we landed at Khartoum airport," Jones recalls, "the plane hit the ground with such a force that the oxygen masks all came down like confetti. As soon as we got to the hotel Norman got back [on the phone] to the embassy and said, 'I now know what the surprise is.'" At Khartoum they found that their tickets for Juba, sold to them in Oxford Street, were useless because there hadn't been a flight for eighteen months, but Norman nevertheless found himself seduced by the Sudanese – and well placed for a leisurely attack on the barbarities of one of his great hate figures, Lord Kitchener, who eighty years before had dug up the Mahdi's body and taken the head for carving into a drinking cup, restrained finally by Queen Victoria's shocked protest.

He and Jones eventually found a Land Rover for hire and drove south to the Jebel Aulia dam, then east across the confluence of Blue and White Niles and downstream to the sixth cataract and above it "wide, tranquil waters ... beanfields and birds and butterflies galore, and little girls ... tugging goats by the ear, one by one, down to the water and actually persuading them to drink". They had enough fuel for three days' driving. They reached Meroë and slept in the desert in the lee of the Land Rover among the 200 pyramids of the Kushite kings.

"He was tough," Jones says. "We had to sleep out in the desert for two nights. We only had bedrolls, blankets. He said to me, 'If you've got a blanket, sleep on it, don't put it over you.'" Jones was photographer on two of the *Observer*'s other river journeys, with Bruce Chatwin and Paul Theroux.

I went down the Volga with Chatwin and I didn't really get on with him. He was much more an aesthetic type of writer. Norman loved writing about danger and death whereas Chatwin wouldn't go near those things. [The Yangtse journey with Theroux] was hideous. Norman is very sympathetic to who he's with, and if I had to stay an extra day because something was happening Norman would stay with me. Some writers call you "my photographer". A lot of them, like Paul Theroux, would say, "I can't wait, I've got to go on," and never had any sympathy. Norman treated you equally.[24]

Not much changed, outwardly; but between shortening stints of work at Finchingfield on his novel, the pace of Norman's journalism accelerated.

On 16 April, two months after he got back from Cairo, he landed in Honduras for a trip that would produce two articles, almost a diptych of US involvement in central America. He and Alain Le Garsmeur, the photographer who accompanied him, landed at Tegucigalpa, finding it closed for the Easter holiday in an "opulent silence".[25] They met the *Sunday Times* correspondent David Blundy before driving to investigate the fate of a Honduran banana co-operative on the north coast, the only workers' co-operative in a country dominated by dollar banana corporations. They found workers cutting and packing diligently, but economically on their last legs after being on strike; Standard Fruit had engineered the peasant takeover as a means of getting the plantation back on its feet in the wake of a hurricane, at no cost to itself. Norman offered his scenario, the only scenario, he implied, that the country's powerful northern neighbour understood.

On 13 February 1981, plainclothes gunmen under army orders put an end to the strike . . . now, after the years of wasted effort, the Isletas peasants were to learn that their income as independent producers had actually fallen below the wages paid to workers on other plantations. . . .

What Honduras suffers from is not communist subversion but hunger. . . . [But] the scene is set for what is becoming a traditional American involvement. Secret lease-lend arms agreements are concluded, the advisers and the "Green Beret" training teams arrive, Alexander Haig resurrects the old Vietnam domino theory, and warns the world that unfortunate Honduras is number one on the hit-list (with Guatemala and Mexico to follow) for a communist takeover of Central America.[26]

Drawn always by Guatemala, Norman with Le Garsmeur drove up from the Isletas plantation to the border. Le Garsmeur remembers, "One time he got nervous on our trip, when we were on the border and I was photographing [it] and the people on the border, and Norman suddenly got very edgy and said, 'We've got to get out of here, Alain.' And I saw one border guard start walking towards us, and he went for his revolver and we turned the jeep round and high-tailed it out of there."[27]

On 24 April he and Le Garsmeur flew south to Nicaragua. The 1980s was seeing the brew of military dictatorship come to the boil across central America, everywhere stirred with the black pitch of US covert support and weapons. US policy in the region was not so much anti-Communist (no energy was expended advertising the benefits of democracy, or capitalism, to a receptive *demos*) as simply pro-army. Armies kept US investments dry, US shareholders warm, by keeping the poor without power, keeping them from rising above their status so close to the earth. In Honduras, the United States returned the compliment by choosing the country as its base for supporting anti-Sandinista Contras fighting the Nicaraguan government and Salvadorean troops fighting FMLN guerrillas. Norman wrote, "We have seen it all before." He had. The Ronald Reagan who would preside over the coming Iran–Contra affair was the same politician who a decade and a half earlier had denounced Mexican grape-pickers in California as "immoral" and blackmailers of "free society".

At the Nicaraguan capital, Managua, the other panel of the diptych presented itself: a country congratulating itself on its liberation from the US-backed leadership of Anastasio Somoza two years before and heading into a new season of right-wing violence, with former members of the National Guard "training alongside Cuban exiles in camps in Florida. . . . Such reports elicited from Fidel Castro the comment, with reference to the fiasco of the Bay of Pigs: 'Man is the only animal capable of stubbing his toe twice on the same stone.'"[28] Norman and Le Garsmeur arrived on a Friday evening, in a country "scrupulous and watchful" about the presence of gringos. On Saturday morning Le Garsmeur went out to take some pictures and was arrested. He spent the morning being ineffectually interrogated, and the soldiers quickly realised he had nothing to tell them. The courteous interrogating officer drove him back to the hotel in his own car. "I strolled into the hotel and there was Norman. He asked me, 'What have you been doing, Alain? Where have you been?' He was amused to hear that I'd spent the day in prison, but he was concerned and showed it by making some calls to our contact to check that everything was okay and that nothing else was going to happen."[29]

Nicaragua was, again, Norman's kind of place: a country of long vitality and short rancour, a stubborn underdog that would not allow harassment by a juggernaut to interfere with pleasure or poverty with happiness. He and Le Garsmeur toured Managua and the cities around it in the only car for hire, an embarrassing Cadillac, once the property of a National Guard officer; they found a beautiful, shell-holed landscape, flattened in the capital by the recent earthquake; but playgrounds had been made, a literacy campaign was under way, and meat, a policeman promised him as if he almost believed it, would replace bean stew by the end of the week.

All Nicaragua's problems stemmed, Norman thought, from a century of being in the wrong place – the trigger being that it was so close to Panama that the USA was unable to resist taking it over, for fear that some other nation might beat it to building the Canal. Occupied by a force of US Marines from 1912 to 1933, the country's only defender had been the skinny, frail Augusto César Sandino ("The sovereignty of a people must not be discussed, but defended with gun in hand"). On Sunday Norman visited Sandino's house and noticed a photograph of him with Somoza, taken after they had made peace and shortly before Somoza – "Sure he's a son of a bitch, but he's *our* son of a bitch," in Franklin Roosevelt's impudent phrase – had Sandino assassinated.

"You only have to glance at [the photograph]", Norman wrote in his notebook, "to know who is to be the killer and who the victim. Sandino slightly Chaplin-ish. Bow-legged, unsubstantial, a little man's hero. Somoza fleshy and confident, a crooked politician or banker."[30] The Sandinistas, a third of them women, had thrown out Somoza's son in 1979 but known tyranny for so long that freedom had "had to be studied before it could be understood", and now the nation faced the long, wearing chivvying of an offended superpower, of aid packages cancelled on spurious grounds, of the courting of neighbours who wished them ill, of routine destabilisation.

Raids and random massacres across the Honduran border by exiled Nicaraguan National Guards were also commonplace. Norman and Le Garsmeur drove north to Ocotal and spoke to some American nuns who supplied medical services and were "overflowing with enthusiasm for the [new] regime". Borrowing the nuns' Land Rover, they drove up the mountain tracks and ravine beds to Lascañas and Santa Maria, "on as raw a frontier as ever existed . . . a straggle of bullet-scarred buildings up a hillside . . . decorated by magnificent propaganda posters".

The Sandinista troops had got used to repelling the incursions, were bored stiff, and just wanted to get back to their farms and jobs – echoing the feelings of a May Day editorial in the normally conservative *La Prensa* that Norman read on his return to Managua, and of Norman himself.

Why always the military men? Why always the dictatorships? What's wrong with a little support for democracy, for once? . . . They talk about the dangers of a Moscow–Havana axis, but it's the crimes these generals and their armies commit that prepare the ground for Communism. . . . Washington always makes the same costly mistake in Latin America. It only wants to talk to the military, and then it throws away more and more aid to pull them out of the mess of their own making.[31]

Back in Essex, he added to the articles that came out of the Honduras–Nicaragua trip that November with two significant pieces about his past. One was the first version of the story of his recruitment by Ian Fleming, the other his first account of his part in the repatriation in 1944 of Soviet prisoners. Over four Sundays, from 1 to 22 November, Norman had a long essay every week in the *Observer* magazine. He had raised his feelings of neglect with Peter Crookston, who made efforts to help, quoting as part of a generous strapline for the Ian Fleming article Jack Lambert's comment about Norman's being admired rather than famous, adding that his self-effacing nature and "commitment to family life in the depths of Essex" kept him "far from the literary salons of London, where to be seen is often more important than to be published".[32]

On the subject of his felt eclipse: in common with those driven by feelings of exclusion, as Norman had been since he stood sixty years before on the edge of the Forty Hill games, he found it hard to believe people thought of him when he was not present (one of the reasons he was scrupulous about keeping in touch with his small circle of friends). If recognition is a due, he had not had it. But he had not been as forgotten as he thought. Working for the *Sunday Times* and the *Observer*, he was certainly unaware of the warmth and admiration in which he was held by other journalists. This was particularly true at the *Observer*. "One of the nice things", Alex Frater, an assistant editor at the magazine who commissioned the series of river journeys, says, "is that when Norman came to see us, word would go out around the newspaper that 'Norman Lewis is in the building'. The news that Norman was arriving created a buzz of excitement, even among the hard cases on the news desk, you know, the guys who never wanted to show that they were impressed. When Norman came, they would come up and find some excuse to pass by my desk or Peter [Crookston]'s and get themselves introduced to Norman."[33]

Egypt, Sudan, Honduras, Nicaragua. His travelling that year was not finished: in mid-November he flew to Libya for a week to see Karen, now married, qualified as a nurse and living outside Tripoli with her husband who worked for a US drilling contractor. The atmosphere was febrile, of secret police and hotheads patrolling chaotic streets with AK47s; Norman's daughter lived in fear of her father taking out his notebook.

Back at Finchingfield he had an unexpected glimpse of a world from which he had not disappeared; or at least his books had not. An admirer had approached his agent with a request to buy rights to *A Dragon Apparent* and republish it, though the person in question, a tyro publisher in his mid-thirties, did not know any of his other books or if he was alive or dead.

Somebody very warmly recommended *A Dragon Apparent* to me and it was indeed the first Eland book that I did. I read it and completely loved it, and what was completely bizarre about it was that I didn't know he was alive at that stage. I went to the agent's and bought it, and I remember that I did not know that he had written the wonderful *Naples '44*, nor did his agent tell me. It wasn't until another person said, "There's a book called *Naples '44* by a man called Norman Lewis," [that] I thought, Well I'd better just check just in case it's the same person. So you can imagine how the poor man was suffering in a way, being in an abyss at that stage. I bought the world English language rights to *A Dragon Apparent*, if my memory's correct, for £250.[34]

The speaker, John Rickatson-Hatt, a public-school and Oxford graduate conscripted into the City who had caught reading like a contagion in his twenties, gone on to work as a publisher's sales representative, taken a sabbatical to write a well-informed book of advice for travellers and, in the writing, decided to republish books that he felt had been forgotten, started Eland Books from his house at Eland Road, Battersea, in August 1982 with a reprint of Norman's thirty-year-old account of south-east Asia. Hatt's appearance belied his rigour as a selector of titles for his list. He later claimed that he read "about 165" books for every one he reprinted, but, wearing spectacles that changed colour with the light, he looked more like a coach courier who supplemented his income by arranging excursions to phonily historic places, whose history he fabricated.

Having found that Norman wasn't dead, Hatt invited him to lunch at the Polish Club in Knightsbridge to settle the details of publication.

"He wanted to go to the lavatory," Hatt recalls, "so I took him downstairs to show him where it was. The Polish Club was a pretty shambolic place then and I went outside and there was a fruit machine rather typically and so I put in some money and I got the jackpot, and as Norman came out money was pouring, clunk, clunk, clunk, clunk clunk, money absolutely pouring out of this thing, and I remember Norman saying, 'Oh dear, when I get home they're going to say, "Norman, you're lying again." ' "[35]

Norman and Hatt got on well over a mild intake of vodka, though Hatt had expected an "effete, Chatwinesque sort of writer, because he writes in a very highly cultivated way, doesn't he? He was completely different from what I expected." He found him not wary, but stubbornly against publicity and defensive about his status. "He said to me that he wouldn't go into a bookshop and look for his books because he knew they would never be there. He sort of couldn't bear to look."

As soon as Eland's first title was published, a former British ambassador to Laos, in a review in the *Times Literary Supplement* of a length normally reserved to first publications, vindicated Hatt's judgment. "Norman Lewis's visit to Vietnam, Cambodia and Laos in 1950 resulted in a vivid and thoughtful book, which has acquired additional significance over the past three decades. . . . Eland Books deserve a garland of coriander and a toast of 'Mekong whisky' for republishing *A Dragon Apparent*."[36]

Awoken to Norman's work, Hatt exercised his foresight to acquire publishing rights to *Naples '44*, *Golden Earth*, *The Honoured Society* and *The Changing Sky* on similar terms. Norman later did not hesitate to acknowledge Hatt's role. "Until John dug my books up, I had been forgotten as a travel writer."[37] (Or not known. A friend of Hatt's, Bruce Palling, wrote to Graham Greene asking him if he would consider writing an introduction to the Eland edition of *A Dragon Apparent*, and Greene wrote back – though it's impossible to rule out Nabokovian game playing in his reply – a "puzzled A5 letter saying, 'Dear Palling, Yes, I have fond memories of Indo-China. *A Dragon Apparent?* I've never heard of it. What is it?'")[38]

The *TLS* review of *A Dragon Apparent* however came on the heels of another review in the same paper of Norman's latest novel, to which it typically contrasted. *Cuban Passage*, published that May by Collins, is a novel of parallel fortunes set at the time of Castro's rebellion, in which an expatriate British adolescent living in Havana rebels to the tempo of Batista's downfall. The *TLS* reviewer, Nicholas Shakespeare, found serious fault with both Norman's characters and "focus", observing that "the author tends to make effigies of all his characters" and that the novel's situation needed to be mediated by a "less dyslexic" character than a delinquent sixteen-year-old.[39] Both criticisms probably have to be accepted but, again, the novel's faults are so mechanical that Norman cannot have been edited properly beyond first draft stage; this time too he had the bad luck to be published, as he wrote, "by Collins in a moment of extreme crisis brought about by a sudden illness (from which he shortly died) of Bob Knittel, the managing director". The typescript was handed to a crime editor who wanted a slicker ending, which in Norman's view made a nonsense of it. "I believe that even copies were not sent out for review, and it was the worst-produced book I have ever seen. . . . I recommend the first bit which gives a good idea of Cuba at the time."[40] John Hatt agrees. He tried to collaborate with Collins, "who published [Norman] very badly, almost as samizdat. Though Collins was a huge company, I used to send out many more copies of Norman's books, both for reviewing and promotion."[41] On the novel's publication the *Observer* magazine bestowed an affectionate profile by his friend Peter Crookston, "The novelist as adventurer", and it sold in the USA to Pantheon, a house that had published two of his novels in the 1950s, where it had appealed to his editor, André Schiffrin. On its (rather better produced) American appearance, the *New Yorker* judged it "an unusually trim and plausible thriller". In June in the British *Spectator* Patrick Marnham, in a late combined review, adamantly disagreed with the *TLS* and congratulated Norman on the reissue and the novel.[42]

Now, after two decades of being published by Collins plus much of one feeling increasingly that he was not being recognised by his publisher or any other arbiters, Norman was not consoled. The threatening crisis came when, soon after *Cuban Passage* was published, he telephoned

Collins' publicity department and asked to speak to the publicity director.
He was asked who was calling.

"Norman Lewis," he answered.

"Norman who?" the young woman at the other end asked.[43]

Blithe, unconscious, it was a reply of inspired destructiveness.

PART SIX

REWRITING

A Revision in Two Restorations

A reputation, a past

When I'm in Norman's presence I immediately become younger, because there's a gaiety about him. His great passion is the beautiful, vanishing people of the world. I've learned a great deal of etiquette from the way he presents himself in their presence. He allows them to grow into dignity. They see it in each other's eyes.

Don McCullin

We stayed in the Vesuvio Hotel on the old harbourfront, looking towards the Castel dell'Ovo, and we went down into the restaurant, La Bersagliera. We went there a couple of nights and then I thought, Oh well it must be a bit boring for him, and I said, "Shall we go into the town and find somewhere?"

"Oh no, when you've found a good place, stick with it."

We did once have lunch at the restaurant on the far side and I said I might have spaghetti con vongole. Norman said, "Well, make sure it's tinned." So he called the waiter over and said, "Vongole fresche?"

"Si, si, signore, fresche."

"Don't touch it. Don't touch it, Tristram."

Tristram Powell

I'm probably one of the few people, certainly that I know, that can actually enter a room and leave it, and nobody will know that I've been there. I can just come in completely silently, I can turn the handle of the door, I can let myself in, I can sum up the situation and retreat, and nobody will know that I've been there. This is an acquired knack which I've never lost. I've just kept out of the way, behaved myself, kept quiet, in that way deflected wrath as much as I possibly could.

Norman Lewis voiceover, 1986

ANOTHER COUNTRY

"A man is only as old as his arteries"
English proverb

THIS is not the end of his story: Norman's acceptance of invitations to adventure in a century of converging conformity will go on for another twenty-one years, very nearly without cease. It is the beginning of a lusher time, of fewer contrasts, biographically suaver. For the biographer the sermon of chronology beckons – one of Norman's feats in the last two decades of his life was that he just went on and on – but it is a chronology whose boredom he himself foiled by staying interested, and whose fascination he hunted down with apparently indestructible toughness. "*El viejo qui quiere vivir para siempre*", he signed himself in a dedication to a Spanish friend,[1] and alongside the absence of self in his writing is an almost complete absence of complaint. Only the rarest mention of a setback, a fractured skull or another bout of malaria, suggests the physical cost of his journeys.

In August 1982 he was in the middle of a novel and had had an idea for another autobiographical book when he and the family flew to Corfu for the summer holiday. Returning to write and to think about the Collins situation, he happened to see a BBC t.v. film about the Panare Indians of southern Venezuela. The film set off his Indian-admiration, and he contacted the anthropologist who had been consultant to the expedition, Dr Paul Henley, and with Don McCullin visited Henley at home in Cambridge.

Henley was returning to Venezuela at Christmas, and the three agreed to meet at Caracas. Henley suggested that Norman and McCullin plan their visit for the best chance of seeing a Panare dance and initiation ceremony, in the dry season around the end of February. "The trip to Venezuela", Norman wrote later, "was planned as a kind of spiritual antidote to the creeping depression produced by the experience of tribal people. . . . Unreached tribes still existed."[2] The Panare, living in the savannah south of the Orinoco, were not unreached. As Henley says, "One thing that is attractive about the Panare . . . is that in the dry season you could drive in your Land Cruiser up to the front door of the longhouse."[3] But they had a reputation for self-confidence, physical beauty, and artistry that Norman could not resist.

The *Sunday Times* agreed to commission a piece. On 19 December he, Lesley and the children flew to Sri Lanka for Christmas and New Year. In January, discovering that the Venezuela visa situation was impossible, he and McCullin decided to travel as tourists.

They landed at Caracas on 20 February and met Henley. The bureaucracy of a mildly Marxist state temporarily quenched adventure. To get to the Panare territory south of the town of Caicara del Orinoco, they needed a permit from Ciudad Bolívar, the state capital, as Henley recalls. "Unless we had this bit of paper we could have been stopped at any moment because there were a lot of military people around and they were just longing for something to do. To arrest people like us would have been a diversion." So instead of driving directly south from Caracas they had to travel three-quarters of a square: east, south, then back again west.

The journey was faintly burlesque. They left Caracas in Henley's Land Cruiser and stayed the night on the coast at Barcelona. Turning south, they were arrested for speeding on the evidence of non-existent speed cameras and told they would be put on trial. Henley succeeded in bribing their way out of a trial – McCullin claimed he had "never seen such bare-faced bribery in all my life" – and reaching Ciudad Bolívar they had to spend several days courting a local politician for his support for their venture and the essential permit. At Ciudad Bolívar Norman discovered to his displeasure that his long standing enemy, the New Tribes Mission, had become entrenched in the Panare area.

They reached their destination in the untouched savannah beyond Caicara six days after they set out. Henley recalls, "I was so impressed by the way that [Norman] sat in the back of that Toyota Land Cruiser – it was very uncomfortable in the back and he and Don took turns – without complaint. He was remarkably resilient." He found Norman a natty adventurer – "He wore this khaki safari suit with short sleeves with a cravat. He left the cravat off when we got into the rural areas, but he always wore the safari suit. The image I have in my mind is of him sitting in my Land Cruiser with his cravat on" – and he was amused by his relationship with Don McCullin, "this kind of banter between him and Don all the time. [It was] partly Norman pulling Don's leg, and from time to time he would turn to me and say an aside about Don in Spanish to further tease Don. For example, Don was often complaining about how much tax he paid, and he would turn to me and say, 'Don is a very rich man' in Spanish. '*Es muy rico*.'"⁴ For McCullin the journey stood out for its conviviality: in addition to their friendship, and the feeling they both had when they travelled that they were getting away with something, its obstacles introduced a note of irresponsibility somewhere short of hysteria.

We were hot and we sat in this river and Norman said, "Cor blimey, what's that?" I said, "What's your problem?" and he said, "Something's attacking me." We started talking again and he said, "Do you know something? I think something's attacking my scrotum. There's some little fish," he said, "we'd better get out of here quick," and we both started being nibbled. And there was a woman on the bank of the river, on the other side, and there were huge butterflies and I said to Norman, "Do you think because she's using that detergent it's attracting the butterflies?" Our conversations were almost like two people in an old people's home sometimes.⁵

McCullin would begin a conversation to set Norman talking because he "was always afraid of putting my foot in it". He was also capable of adding unexpected value to Norman's experience.

With the Panare Indians we had to sleep in hammocks. One night in the jungle I said to him, because I always carry things in my suitcase or my bag, "Norman, would you like a vodka and tonic?" And he said, "Vodka and tonic?" I said, "Yes." He said, "Well, where's it going to come from then?" and I said, "I've got it." He said, "Well, I mean if there's enough to go round." He was always, always apologising, always searching for proof that he's not inconveniencing somebody.

Journey and story turned out all right in the end, but Norman's approach to writing about the Panare produced dissent between anthropologist and journalist. Henley, in his early thirties, had studied the tribe for more than five years, "trying to really be as precise as possible about what they meant by a particular word or what their customs actually were", and he had got close enough to one group in the Colorado valley for them to adopt him. Norman was charmed by the Panares' dignity. At the first Panare village he saw men in "scrupulously woven loincloths ... moving springily like ballet dancers", who offered them hot mango juice. They went on, meeting the group who had adopted Henley. No festival was imminent because "God did not like it"; they hung around, driving the Indians to gather mangoes and the following day to go fishing. Henley felt that Norman's view of missionary intrusion – as in their discouragement of the initiation festival – as the root of all evil was simplistic.

His eyes really lit up when I explained to him that the missionaries disapproved of these things or at least they disapproved of the drinking that was associated with them. In the Panare language they refer to their sugar-cane beer with charming economy as "o?" which is "o" with a glottal stop, and they use the same word to describe their festivals, so if you take the beer out of the festival you've literally got nothing left. Ostensibly all sorts of ritual business was going on, like dressing the boys in their loincloths for the first time, [but] they reasoned that if you take away the beer you can't have these events any more. So Norman was in a bit of a cleft stick because on the one hand he was pleased that he could report another iniquity of the missionaries, but on the other hand he was disappointed because he did have a kind of Romantic interest in this, with a capital "r", like all of us.

When it was clear the Panare had no plans for an initiatory festival, or even a dry-season "for nothing" dance, interest was salvaged by a fishing expedition at which a band of men temporarily poisoned a stretch of the Tortuga River, hauling in several hundred kilos of stunned fish. (Those that were left quickly recovered.) McCullin's photographs of the Panare fishing are a visual cornucopia of grace: river, tense Indian physiques and the flash of fish flanks. But with not much else to see he and Norman made plans to return to Caracas, and Henley drove them as far as Caicara before returning to his field site. They stopped en route at a diamond mine, attracted by its name, Tiro Loco ("Crazy Shot"), and by the presence of a new settlement of Panare on the outskirts. No Panare worked at the mine, but instead supplied "excellent vegetables" to the miners from their gardens, which they bartered for tools and necessities. Norman made unfavourable comparisons between the missionaries and the "villains in big hats and spectacular

whores" of the shanty town. "Tiro Loco prided itself on being tough.
. . . In Tiro Loco you could actually see the swing-doors of a bar fly
open and an unwanted customer pitched through them headfirst into
the street. . . . The miners supplied [the Panare] with all they needed,
with no strings attached. In Tiro Loco the Panare could drink, dance,
paint themselves and perform their ceremonies to their heart's content."[6]

They parted from Henley at the truck ferry at Caicara at dawn on
7 March. "Don photographed some melon sellers in the early morning
light, unloading their stock by chucking them from one to another,"
Henley recalls. The setbacks were not over, McCullin says.

It was a gruelling long journey by road after the Orinoco, several hours, and
I said to Norman, "Look, why don't we just jump in a Cessna and we'd be
back in town in an hour and a half?" And he said, "I have an aversion to
small aeroplanes, they fall out of the sky with regularity. If you'd like to go,
by all means." One of his favourite things was "by all means". "By all means,
you take the Cessna but I prefer to stay in the taxi." This is another thing
about Norman: you always allowed him to do what he wanted. [So] we came
across the river, and just prior to the boat leaving the bank he walked straight
into an iron bar which would knock most men down and keep them down.
He had a huge bloody great egg on his head and I was really concerned. I
said, "Okay, sit down, Norman, take it easy. I'm really sorry this has happened."
He said, "Oh, all right," and he sat and was very quiet. [Then] I helped to
push the boat off and slipped, and skinned all the front of my shins. I was
bleeding down my shinbone, and he was sitting there with a bloody great egg
on his head, and I felt in a way it was worth me losing the skin on my leg
just to have the privilege of knowing that I'm sitting with this wonderful man.

Their wounds sparked their one conversation about books and
disclosed Norman's view of the limits of truthfulness, possibly spiced
by jealousy.

I told Norman once when I was in Cambodia and I walked into an ambush
and got injured and I was lying in this darkened hospital and I could hear the
crunch of the mortars on the outskirts of Phnom Penh. This very nice girl
from the British Embassy used to come round and bring me cakes and things,
and she said, "Oh, the First Secretary wondered if you'd like to read this
book?" and it was called *As I Walked Out One Midsummer Morning*. . . .
And Norman said, "Oh, yes I know. That was written by Laurie Liar." I said
I enjoyed it, and he said, "Er, we-e-ell."[7]

At Finchingfield Norman wrote the *Sunday Times* piece quickly, impatient to deal with other projects. When he read the published version, Paul Henley was critical. Attacking the missionaries, Norman had cited a translation of a text about the Crucifixion that New Tribes Mission personnel had distributed to the Panare. It was the key to Norman's article and to its title, "The Tribe that Crucified Christ" –

> The Panare killed Jesus Christ
> because they were wicked
> Let's kill Jesus Christ
> said the Panare.
> The Panare seized Jesus Christ.
> The Panare killed in this way.
> They laid a cross on the ground.[8]

In Henley's "probably pedantic, scholarly" view, it was a serious mistranslation.

You've probably come across this a lot, it's very common – every tribe in the world, every ethnic group in the world has a word which means "people", which they refer to themselves by, and everybody else is something else. But the generic word when you use it in the language for "people say this" or "people do that", or when a person has a pain in his foot, the word that they use for that generic person is also the word that they use for themselves as opposed to anybody else. So in translating the phrase for biblical purposes the evangelicals would use this generic term because they wanted to suggest the idea that it was Everyman who did this, so they used the generic word [i.e.] "the people crucified Christ". They *weren't* specifically saying "the Panare crucified Christ". So on what I would consider a flimsy mistranslation a rather substantial edifice is built.[9]

This wasn't Henley's only objection. He also felt that Norman's mind had been decided before he came. "I remember him saying to Don, when we were discussing how brief their visit had been compared to their original plan, 'Oh don't worry old boy, I've written most of it already anyway,' and it was sort of true, I think he was kind of looking for local colour to flesh out an argument he'd already rehearsed." Henley took the step of writing a long, "naïve" letter to the *Sunday Times* when the article appeared. A coldness followed between him and

Norman that was gradually repaired, though even when it was, Norman's tendency towards suspicion would not let him believe in a simple difference of approach. "Paul is rather mysterious," he wrote to a friend five years later. "He was with us in Venezuela, but I suspected a certain amount of behind the scenes contact with the enemy."[10]

Thirty years later Henley didn't recant but conceded that "academic specialists qualify every statement with a footnote or an 'if' or a 'but', but don't change the world. It's people like Norman who are prepared to be a little bit imprecise, shall we say, about associations and consequences. They're the people who change the world in the sense that they're the people who cause outrage – which might then be tempered by an encounter with the facts."[11]

A further, species distinction might be that "the truths which we travel so far to seek", in Lévi-Strauss's phrase, differ between anthropologist and writer. Where the anthropologist seeks to do "effective work" stripped of the "dross" of adventure, the writer is *married* to adventure, united with his or her quest – he or she *is* his or her quest – and cannot help disputing humanly on paper about its object. The dispute is all a part of composition, of truthfulness. For a writer a journey is not the anthropologist's "weeks or months lost in travelling", the "negative aspect of our métier". A writer's journey is a vociferous polemic against standing still.

A month after he came back from Caracas, Norman had finished writing and thinking. The armaments of his next move were assembled. On 5 May he wrote to his agent, Richard Scott Simon.

Dear Richard,

You will remember that I have spoken to you about projects for several books. I have now decided to give priority to an autobiographical episode based on several years spent in the immediate post-war period in a Spanish fishing village, working off an[d] on as a fisherman.

This would be a sequel in time and mood to *Naples '44*, although I should aim at a greater poetic content, and although the war element would not be present, as in the previous book, there would be no shortage of bizarre and sometimes exciting occurrences. Many of the ancient Mediterranean customs

I witnessed have disappeared for ever. .... This is a book I'm going to enjoy writing, and if I'm not enticed away to somewhere like the Gran Chaco I could hope to finish within 9 months.[12]

Richard Scott Simon phoned Christopher Sinclair-Stevenson, the publisher of Hamish Hamilton, and put Norman's case.

(Christopher was my employer but it was a good call. I witnessed his merited reputation if not for fancy salaries, then for editorial shrewdness, loyalty to authors (and employees), and building writers' careers: Peter Ackroyd, William Boyd, James Buchan were three novelists whose first books he took on around this time. From intellectual and worldly slants, it would have been hard in the one-tracked 1980s to find a publisher who interpreted more broadly the perpetual wager.)

Sinclair-Stevenson was interested. On 9 May Scott Simon sent two submissions, one the crunchingly titled novel, "Pharaoh Becomes Osiris", that Norman had been working on the previous year, the other a proposal for the "autobiographical episode" in the fishing village, "Codalar – the village of cats". "I hope you like it all," Scott Simon wrote. "Once I hear from you I could get him unravelled."

(Christopher did. I remember the afternoon editorial meeting when he first talked about Norman as a lost, now found, master. Over my remembered recomposition of this discovery of a Rembrandt in the loft hovers a mythical, if faintly humble, figure suspended between greatness and forgetting. To a young man as I was, trying obtusely to nail the traits of literary success, something incorrigibly immodest seemed to hang about his name.)

Sinclair-Stevenson passed me "Pharaoh Becomes Osiris" for a reader's report. An adaptation of world news like *The Sicilian Specialist*, it was a sceptical analysis of the early 1980s struggle for Arab leadership clothed in a story of political murder: the attempted assassination of Gaddafi, cooked up and financed by the CIA. (History knows the plot failed, and that instead of the Libyan demon it was the USA's Egyptian ally Sadat who was killed.) Set in Cairo and Tripoli, the novel's fall guy was Ronald Kemp, a gentle escapist of the same family as many Lewis heroes, particularly *A Single Pilgrim*'s sad company man, Crane. When he later gave a copy of the novel to a friend, he signed it "(Great secret – the hero is me)".[13]

I see I wrote about the first draft that Norman "has a very sure hand with description, but never gets to grips with describing Kemp,

who becomes the anomaly of being a subsidiary character centre stage",
and that it was at times difficult to know where the "frantic" atmosphere was leading. I wrote to Norman less bluntly, arguing that Kemp
deserved a more central role and expressing admiration for his portrait
of Libyan expatriate life; by return I had a letter thanking me for my
"most generous appreciation" whose tone indicated that he was philosophical about editors' cavils. He may have been in a positive frame
of mind: Pantheon in the USA were also enthusiastic about the novel,
Eland Books had just republished *Naples '44*, a *Times Literary
Supplement* review had cheered its pleasures, calling it an "illuminating
portrait of that much-occupied city",[14] and Graham Greene had broken
cover to John Hatt expressing his "tremendous" enjoyment of it.[15]

Sinclair-Stevenson's agreement of terms on the novel and the Catalonia
memoir – £2000 advance for one, £5000 for the other – led to the
lunch at the Grange I have described, at which Norman's wariest self
was succeeded by a performance of one of his impromptu symphonies
of stories. That is what they seemed like: confidential music, brought
out, breathed on, played and put away again, storytelling as a form of
ritual magic in which he turned the tables on his audience so that he,
silent at the start, finished by reducing it to silence. Alex Frater remembers a similar lunch at the *Observer* around this time, when Norman
at first sat eating and saying nothing.

Norman always seemed hungry and he sat eating hunched over, looking slightly
like an old turtle. Then he started telling a story in that odd voice of his, about
how he had recently come back from talking to monks at a monastery in
[Sicily] who had recently brought in a monk they disapproved of, and after
talking to him for a time had knocked him out and laid him on the refectory
table and cut his throat. Norman was surrounded by senior *Observer* management, all talking newspapers with each other, and as he talked they gradually
stopped, and there was a deepening silence and then total silence around the
table.[16]

Being published by Hamish Hamilton led to a summer of editing.
In the course of several exchanges of letters and notes he was infal-
libly obliging and pleasant. There was a drawn-out choosing of a title
for the novel acceptable to author and UK and US publishers (which
did not happen: it ended up with two different titles, *A Suitable Case
for Corruption* in the UK, *The Man in the Middle* in the USA. It was

also the book in which he first deliberately concealed his age, giving his date of birth as 1918 in the cataloguing in publication data). To soften the deluge of editorial mail I and others in America were sending, I posted him a present of a copy of Gerald Hanley's novel *Noble Descents*. He replied with a postcard of Santorini.

Thank you very much indeed for sending me "Noble Descents". . . . I am much enjoying it, particularly as a respite from Alonso de Barros' "Moral Proverbs" (8,000 of them) which I feel I ought to go through before finishing my Spanish book. The postcard, by the way, is a fraud, which is to say I'm staying in Parga in the north of Greece, which is provincial and unmemorable in its facilities, for which reason it offers the huge benefits of being spared from package-deal pressures.

All the best, and again thanks, Norman[17]

On 21 September he wrote from Finchingfield that "The alterations have been without end. I hope you will be pleased with the result."[18] His next plan was that he and Don McCullin were going to Vietnam in the autumn to "go over the old itinerary of *A Dragon Apparent*, which covered the most interesting parts of the country, and comment on the inevitable changes". The trip turned out to be less certain than he had thought. Following "an introduction to the Ambassador by the veteran Australian Communist, Wilfred Burchett" he had had "tea with HE (a highly oriental occasion, this, when the teacups slid hither and thither over the table's richly lacquered surface), and the Ambassador was sufficiently enthusiastic to say he would write to his brother, who is Minister of Culture. So far, however, the visas have not come through."[19]

He carried on working on his Spanish memoir and broke for a week's half-term flight to Madrid with Lesley and Bubs. On 14 November a finished typescript of "Cat People and Dog People" was delivered – a reference to the contrast between the fishing villagers of "Farol" and their inland neighbours. Assuming that he had not started writing when he submitted the proposal, he had finished it in a quick seven months. I read it that weekend.

Saturday disappeared in the reading of Norman Lewis's Spanish period, fishing and observing the last two years of an expiring Catalan way of life. Villagers stop fishing, abandon taboos and servitude, realise the power of money, lose their pride. Norman prefers eccentrics and makes the reader prefer them too.[20]

"Cat People and Dog People", which eventually became *Voices of the Old Sea*, was in first draft similar to his other books, as I began to understand: loose, replete with anecdote, vignette, tableau, starved sometimes of cohesion or stranded in inconclusion. This managed to seem insignificant: it *felt* extraordinary, acting on me, I remember, almost physically across a spectrum of emotions and sense impressions. Despite the austerity of its subject, the effect was like putting my head into a box of aromatic drugs, a sensation that went on peculiarly long after reading. At its most comic it bounced on a bed of sadness, at its most elegiac (and it was one of the saddest books I had ever read) it remained absurd. It was clear that Norman was the kind of author for whom an editor – a young editor, conspiring with himself to be something else, seeking a tutor in the ways of writing – of making the world legible – could feel a deeply fortunate bond of respect. It was clear too that he couldn't be seventy-five, as rumoured.

Vietnam was going to take time to come off, he said at El Vino's ten days later, and before he and Don went there he was thinking of spending some time in – living in – Nicaragua; he was also contemplating an autobiography. I told him I would want to buy his autobiography in slight preference to his book on Nicaragua. A week later Sinclair-Stevenson made an offer: £2500 for the autobiography, £5500 for the book about Nicaragua. An element of miscalculation entered into these sums partly because Hamish Hamilton were cautious, not having published him yet. Word came back that Norman was "at a loss to understand the logic behind the offer" for an autobiography for which, in his mind, his Spanish memoir was only a curtain-raiser. Twenty-four hours later, "an untitled autobiographical work" was contracted for £7500. Satisfied, Norman flew with Lesley and Bubs to Tenerife for Christmas.

Something had happened, was happening for him. This was the sequence of publishing-related events after Christmas:

In January 1984 Eland republished its third Norman Lewis title, *Golden Earth*. It was celebrated by reviewers, few more than Auberon Waugh, who felt strongly enough to make the uncomfortable journey to Finchingfield to interview him.

In April Eland's edition of *The Changing Sky* appeared, as did Waugh's interview – Norman's first – in *Tatler*. On the 22nd the BBC began a fortnight of readings from *Naples '44*. There was talk of a dramatisation to be scripted by Alan Bennett. On the 26th *A Suitable Case for Corruption* was published.

In May I bought a short story from him for a collection of travel stories.

At the end of June Hamish Hamilton bought publication rights to *The Sicilian Specialist*, sold paperback rights to Penguin the same day.

On 2 July Norman was back in Spain for three days "to pay a visit to, and report on the present condition of Farol" for the *Sunday Times*, which also wanted to run an extract from the forthcoming *Voices of the Old Sea*.

On 3 September Hamish Hamilton published *Voices of the Old Sea*.

In November Eland republished *The Honoured Society*, and on the 16th Norman won the Angel Literary Prize.

Five books published or republished; a year he had started mistrustful of strangers, of publicity, and by whose end he was submitting, for a short time, to daily interviews (three print and six radio interviews when *Voices of the Old Sea* appeared). Nervous of the mordacious Waugh, he had been primed by John Hatt to provide a decent bottle of wine to smooth the meeting; he did, and reported that when Waugh spotted the bottle on the table – a single vineyard Chambolle Musigny 1971 – "those little eyes grew very much larger".[21] By the time the World Service interviewed him in September, after a publication lunch, he could write, "Dear Christopher, I have made a discovery, namely that you <u>can</u> go away and do a lucid broadcast after an excessive lunch, <u>if</u> the wine is good."[22] Waugh's description of their meeting sang the kind of praises he reserved for few and dwelt on the reasons for Norman's lack of recognition, identifying his enthusiasm as one.

The name Norman Lewis somehow slips the memory, existing in its own compartment. Practically none of us has any idea what he looks like, how old he is, whether he is married – or not, like the Akond of Swat. . . . Bit by bit I began to understand why the name Norman Lewis has never appeared in neon lights on the London literary scene, why we never see him on any of the fatuous literary television programmes, why no Sunday editors ask him what books he has most enjoyed at Christmas time. Despite his highly sophisticated awareness of the world about him, he is basically a simple man . . . he also shuns the company of the London literati, seeing himself as the exact opposite of writers such as C P Snow and Paul Theroux in this respect. . . .

Theroux writes with well-bred scorn, Lewis is always consumed with ill-bred enthusiasm.[23]

Even his fiction benefited from the radiating interest. When *A Suitable Case for Corruption* was published, reviewers who had not mentioned his work before began to write sentences like "I have been a fan of Norman Lewis since his earliest travel books, and his novels are no less interesting." He was doing well out of a boom in travel books, new and reprinted by publishers wanting to capitalise on John Hatt's success, but it was a return to vogue over which, by growing accord, he was presiding. He had one setback, when the *Times Literary Supplement* turned down an extract from *Voices of the Old Sea* for its travel supplement for curious reasons of consistency – that it "read like chapters from a novel".

Away from the epiphenomena of publishing and publicity he was restless, his writing energy as high as it had been in the 1950s. He produced a draft programme of three more books to follow his auto-biography: on Vietnam, Nicaragua, Sumatra. After a three-week holiday in July and August on Skiathos,[24] in September he, Lesley and Bubs moved temporarily to Cambridge to be close to Bubs' new school, The Perse. They had bought with some of the capital from the sale of R G Lewis a terraced house at 37 Bateman Street, near the station, where they planned to live Monday to Thursday. That October I was invited to Bateman Street for lunch. The journey from London was made gloomy by clouds and the filthy train up from King's Cross, and behind damp trees the language schools and secretarial colleges on Station Road nourished by the university's reputation radiated more gloom. Welcomed by Lesley, I felt the impression dissipated but unrest remained. Norman shifted his tall, angular frame from room to compact room, as if he couldn't reconcile himself to something: Cambridge, being indoors, the weather. What I was seeing was his restlessness in miniature, his unease with England, with having nothing to observe. Lunch, his foil, went on till five as he earthed his unease in an output of fresh stories – north Vietnam before the French defeat, Peru with Snowdon, plant-hunting in the Abkhazskaya with a scim-itar. The freshness was remarkable, as the journalist Bruce Palling concurs, "I don't know how many times I went and had lunch with him. . . . Every time there'd be a two-hour, three-hour talk after lunch, and nothing would be repeated."[25]

The year of readers' discovery of Norman seemed to falter with the reception of *Voices of the Old Sea*. Sinclair-Stevenson had to write to the literary editors to remind them it had been published. John Hatt wrote around too, shocked the book could be overlooked. "Almost at the same time Eric Newby's *On the Shores of the Mediterranean* came out [Newby's book was reviewed widely, appearing on bestseller lists]. "And his book was a potboiler *de la* potboiler, you know. I personally wrote to every single literary editor, saying, 'This is unbelievable, how can you do this?' I just remember how shocked I was that this great book should have been ignored."[26]

"Farol was lucky . . . to have its last old days described by this wonderful, tough, gentle, poetic writer," Geoffrey Wheatcroft eventually wrote in the *Spectator* of 8 December, three months after the book's publication.[27] "A haunting book [that] encapsulates a whole social revolution," Colin Thubron agreed on 16 December.[28] "This book testifies to Lewis's continuing concern with cultures under threat of extinction," the *TLS* commented three weeks later, ". . . with a novelist's eye for a rounded story as well as an anthropologist's nosiness. . . . The only mystery to remain unresolved is that of Lewis himself."[29] Only three reviewers, Nicholas Wollaston in the *Observer*, Bill Greenwell in the *New Statesman* and Peter Lewis in the *Daily Mail*, had rallied to the book on its appearance, Wollaston remarking that "His book should be under every tourist's pillow in Spain, to show what went on before corruption and monotony set in and hot dogs drove out the cats."[30] Peter Lewis had spoken to Norman about his return to Farol/Tossa before writing his review. He found him "still nursing his disgust. . . . 'It now has 250 hotels and an illuminated sign that flashes "Let's Go Play Cowboy Games". I never felt so distressed at anything in my life as the prospect of having to spend the night there,'" he told Lewis.[31]

In the article Norman had written for the *Sunday Times* about his return, 1500 words that echo with the scrape of the writer's dragging footsteps, he had sketched the contrast between ancient austerity/poverty and modern comfort/tawdriness created by thirty-five years' development. He found his one-time fishing comrade, Sebastian, now sixty, rich and apparently happy after building himself a hotel on a once valueless chicken run he had owned in the village, but admitting (as Norman had it) that "something this place used to have is gone". What was missing, Norman asked him, among all these bright lights, this music, this laughter, this seemingly successful search for instant joy? What was it that had turned its face away, withdrawn its magic, that had died?

Sebastian was ready with the answer. "Poetry," he said. "It's abandoned us."[32]

Whether that is exactly as Sebastian spoke it, as an answer it can hardly be disbelieved – even by his Catalan publisher who says, "When I read *Voices of the Old Sea* I'm not sure it's my country. I find things which are certainly Mediterranean but not Catalan, and then I wonder if Norman did not include things from Sicily that he knew so well. I told him once, politely."[33] Or by critics who accused him of glorifying the fishermen's poverty and of claiming "more than he really knows" (*Sunday Times*) or saying less than he really knew (a *New York Times* reviewer who wanted to know more about Norman's "love life" and finances). The poetry of the coast had shrunk to nothing. As late as 1959 Norman had written that he still went to Spain "to get away from the insipidity of modern times".[34] By 1984 insipidity, by Norman's calculation, had overrun its shore, where the pursuit of life – whose poetry mostly lies somewhere close to its capacity for unmediated uncertainty – had been shrunk to a pursuit of money.

His narrative had set out to restore uncertainty, and poetry. He himself hardly figured in it, functioning instead as that rhetorical agent, intermediary between his interior life and his past; encyclopedist. It offers the sense of loss that is present in all time that passes, and at the same time the intensest pleasure in time in its passing. As in *Naples '44*, he restored the past as a place that was constructed of experience, knowledge, and *words*; his remembered pleasure in diving, the changes of sea and weather, the bloodstained spasm of the tunny season and the daily routine is undiminished.

The fish hit bottom, and the men took the lines and hung on with agony in their faces as the line cut into their hands, opening old sores, and the blood began to flow.

Almost in the same moment all the other boats had hooked fish, and a great confusion began, because some small boats were being dragged in all directions, even gyrating like leaves in a whirlpool, and the proper sickle-shaped tunny fishing formation had broken up. To this disorder was added the fouling and crossing of lines and the extravagant underwater knots tied in them as the tunny twisted and turned, shot under the boats and encircled them as they came closer to the surface with the loss of their first ebullient energy. Now they came into sight; great gliding metallic shapes, appearing strangely inanimate although still possessed of great reserves of power.

In our boat a kind of demented ballet was being performed, with Simon the dominator who should have restored order distracted by his struggle with a monstrous fish.[35]

Not through collections of events and objects does the reader enter into the place he creates, but through the sudden appeal of verbal landscapes.

Sharp variations exist in the climatic patterns of the Mediterranean area. Unlike Italy, when October provides a succession of faultless days, this is the month along the Spanish coast when a prolonged summer suddenly collapses, and the year is gone. What follows for the fishermen when the winds calm, the rain ceases and the sun shines once more, is a lifeless parody of the lost summer. The sea's currents change direction and turn cold, and the big shoals of fish, like migrating birds, move away southwards. The fellowship, the shared excitements and frustrations of men working together in the big boats, is at an end.[36]

Sebastian had tied up his boat in a cove near the spot where we had seen the big fish, and we walked there together along a cliff path with changing vistas of the sea. After the furrowed grey wastes of water surrounding our islands the huge vivacity of the Mediterranean never ceased to astonish. Here it was splashed all over with plum-coloured stains of weed-beds among which bald rocks just beneath the surface were brilliant uncut emeralds. Light-scaled water thrashing about in the deep coves rose and fell, uncovering and submerging great shining boulders like wallowing buffaloes. Wherever there was a beach it was spread with black membranes of drying nets, and here and there a small wedge of colour showed where a woman was at work closing up the holes left by the dolphins.

All Sebastian's expressions seemed accentuated by the thin pencilling of moustaches that rose or fell in sympathy with the elation or depression of a sensitive mouth, and on this occasion he was in low spirits.[37]

Norman continued to be restless and productive. Before flying to Tunisia for Christmas and New Year, he delivered the typescript of his autobiography to Hamish Hamilton. *Jackdaw Cake* was an extension of his current subject, taking his past from the moment he was pushed into the presence of his three aunts at Carmarthen up to his post-war discovery of Farol/Tossa. He participated in the text as autobiographer in his customary, scantest way; through the drollery and fine screens of surrealism it was almost impossible to identify the emotional wounds of his childhood or any other admission about himself. (Though writing in the first person, he gave the impression that he was writing about himself, like the book's every other character, in the third person. It was also impossible to calculate his age, which he concealed with deliberate vagueness and diversion.)

Sinclair-Stevenson wrote to him on 2 January, "Dear Norman, I read your autobiography over Christmas and laughed long and loud. It's tremendously readable and entertaining and full of all sorts of joys and delights. . . . The only thing that slightly worries me about the book is the fragmentary nature of it."[38] Norman was led through a round of editing and additions, and persuaded to add an epilogue. The editing was "harsh in places", I wrote in my diary, "sentences changed round, lines cut, wholesale tense sequences altered. I hope Norman's trust is an elastic thing."[39] He seemed happy with the process – "And thank you in advance for all your efforts," he wrote[40] – but I wonder whether I read his reaction closely enough. The work cost him time and effort he possibly knew to be necessary, but behind the mask of his delightful politeness his impatience (with hindsight) is detectable, "The alterations have been without end", about *A Suitable Case for Corruption*, "Well here it is again. A lot of work", about *Jackdaw Cake*. They were small indicators.

That February he published a curiosity in a collection of stories I had edited, stories about travel that were intended to show in the sudden vogue for travel writing that it was, generally, all fiction. Norman's contribution, "A Weekend in Havana", had originally been an episode in *The Sicilian Specialist* about a visit incognito by President Kennedy to Havana; it had not been published before because his US publisher had panicked at its account of Kennedy's taste for *amor internacional*. In its portrait of the President's appetite for rum and Cuban womanhood it also offered, in a more interesting form and with Norman's customary political subtlety, his own analysis of the dilemma the President had wanted to duck over the Bay of Pigs.[41]

In April he and Don McCullin made their fourth trip together, to Sicily. They visited Corleone and Ficuzza and had lunch at the straitened estate of Caltavuturo, where land reform had left the *barone* with only 500 hectares of his original 2000 and where Norman met the grandson of the leader of the Sicilian Separatists, who remembered, as a young boy, being kidnapped and then ransomed by Giuliano. It poured with rain most of the time, and he was more fascinated than McCullin, who "wasn't terribly impressed" except by Norman's friend, the journalist Marcello Cimino, about whom he said to Norman afterwards that he was "the only man I've ever known who to me is like a saint must have been".[42] The true atmosphere of the journey is probably in the unusually aimless account that Norman wrote for the *Sunday Times* which was not published; though it sparked another thought, as he wrote to Cimino. "You will be staggered, and probably horrified to learn that I have decided to write a novel having a Sicilian background. This, I realize, is an impertinence, but it is a country which fascinates me endlessly, and the treatment will be sympathetic, as most people will agree was my treatment of Naples."[43]

Returning the corrected proofs of *Jackdaw Cake* to Hamish Hamilton a month later he wrote, "While respecting your views on the subject of punctuation I've quietly slipped ba[c]k a comma here and there. . . . Again thanks for all your work, I'm sure that this will be another disti[n]guished H[amish] H[amilton] production."[44]

It wasn't. An atrocious mistake was made with the dustjacket, a lettered design in yellow with a jackdaw silhouette below dreary type – one reviewer said the book had the worst jacket he had ever seen – and it was inexplicably printed on the cheapest possible paper. Norman, away for most of the summer filming an hour's documentary for the BBC arts strand *Arena* and then on holiday on Lesbos, remained publicly cheerful and uncritical. He had enjoyed filming for *Arena* in and around Naples. He and the director Tristram Powell had begun with a preliminary visit, stayed at the Vesuvio on via Partenope, eaten at La Bersagliera.

"I had a really splendid time in Naples," he wrote, "which remains my favourite city, and" – typically – "I only hope that the BBC people enjoyed it half as much." The cameramen were charming. "Colin [Waldeck, cameraman] is also a wine buff, and the only time I came really unstuck was when I tried to assert my authority in the matter of Italian wines, and was compelled to concede immediate defeat. All this team were so nice and so <u>interesting</u> that it was like being back in the Army in the Intelligence Corps, but with a far better type of man."[45] In the filming Powell found him "very easy because he didn't really modify his behaviour too much between when he was being filmed and when he wasn't being filmed. He was a natural." Powell opened the film with scenes of a Neapolitan police chase and raid that ended at a Naples *autostrada* interchange. Blue and white Alfas put on showy handbrake turns, klaxons shrieked, officers in jeans sprinted to a brown BMW deserted under the flyover, its doors flung wide. Norman, edge of shot, stonily watchful, is unnoticeable until he walks towards the camera. "He looked so ordinary, he just looked like a military man on holiday in his flappy-sleeved shirt and his cotton trousers," Powell recalls. "He was very good at just having casual conversations with people and asking them questions, and he was very unthreatening."[46]

The crew filmed at Paestum and Pozzuoli, at the cavern of the Sybil at Cumae and at Poggio Reale where, at a criminal trial of a hundred or more alleged Camorra members, Norman "just drifted over to this couple who had their hands linked between their two cages and they told him their story. I was very pleased with that, it was just a gift." To camera, he was oddly more candid about himself than he generally was in print, connecting, on the temple steps at Paestum at sunset, his loneliness as a child to his writing. "Possibly because I was an only child, possibly because I was extremely lonely, it was a great consolation to write about things and to solidify them in my imagination, to assist me to remember the pleasant experiences I'd had."[47]

The performer emerged. Powell says, "There were one or two occasions where I got him to sort of act a little moment which he'd done spontaneously and we hadn't been filming." Leaving Cumae he had enthused over the view of the site of the first Greek settlement in Italy, then noticed some fennel growing on the path. "That was a perfect piece. 'Oh, fennel. Very good with broad beans.' He'd done it naturally when we weren't filming and I said, 'Oh Norman, could you just do that again? It was so nice,' and he did it beautifully."

Jackdaw Cake was published on 16 September. The reviews were prompter, interviews more numerous (ten radio appearances), book and writer praised warmly with an odd residue of unsatisfied curiosity that sometimes amounted to frustration. Auberon Waugh in the *Spectator* described Norman as "revered by his many admirers as the greatest travel writer alive, if not the greatest since Marco Polo",[48] but could not explain the book's title (John Hillaby answered that: "very Welsh. It's the bible-thumpers' repudiation of earthly lusts").[49] The *Daily Telegraph*'s David Holloway was disconcerted that "one of the most accomplished of all travel writers, a foreign correspondent of distinction, a novelist of standing" had written a book that was "in no proper sense an autobiography . . . not hot on dates . . . very sparing in [its] information" and left the reader at the end "asking almost more questions about Norman Lewis than one did at the start" but conceded "For all its lack of documentation it is a wonderful read."[50] Gavin Young described it as "hilarious, tender . . . certainly one of Norman Lewis's best books" and noticed that "As much as its predecessors, *Jackdaw Cake* is a travel book tinged with the most delicious fantasy. . . .

Norman Lewis is a London Welshman . . . and it strikes me that these tangy reminiscences have a good deal of the Welshness, the especially robust South Walian enchantment of Dylan Thomas's best prose. It strikes me, too, that it is not merely the title *Jackdaw Cake* that calls similarly to mind the author of *Peacock Pie*. Lewis shares the shiver-inducing power of Walter de la Mare to make the reader view the world as if through a stained-glass distorting mirror, a power particularly in evidence when he writes of the sad, hilarious eccentricities of the three Carmarthenshire aunts. . . . Although there is nothing really *nasty* in this most engaging book, Mr Lewis is undoubtedly possessed of the quick inner eye that can spot at once the fantastical in the everyday.[51]

Norman was applauded for the fertility of his childhood remembrance, for his horror stories about the French in north Africa (slightly missing his point that the British were ready to follow suit), for his eye for comedy in Enfield and tragedy in Philippeville. His modesty was described as "excessive" and "sublime", and in the *Sunday Times* Philip Oakes observed that "In any cult of personality he would be a nonstarter. But as a witness to his own times – the good, the bad and the ludicrous – he is unmatched."[52] Many reviewers replicated the conclusion of the *Times* reviewer Allan Massie. "This superior chronicle of corners of lunacy is undeniably fascinating. It is, though, an uncommonly reserved memoir, telling us little directly about the author. I am sure he meant it that way, for he has acquired a truly Sicilian fastidiousness about personal revelation."[53] Julian Rathbone in the *Guardian* hoped he would return to autobiography, slightly overestimating Norman's frankness in his judgment of the book's contents as "the undiluted experience of a writer whose wonderfully concrete descriptions . . . so directly and accurately suggest the realities beneath"; but

Rathbone's reading also evoked in a useful insight the seriousness with which Norman had once been read, when statements of policy and political absolutes mattered to readers of novels.

Thirty years ago, on the trains to the Suez demonstrations, we earnestly debated whether fiction could be or should be *engagé*. Sartre was the name we bandied; *The Volcanoes Above Us* and *The Day of the Fox* were the books we had read. This "autobiography" concentrates on four extended episodes which shaped the committed and engaged writer Lewis was to become.[54]

(Less interestingly, the book touched off Enfield loyalties when the *Enfield Gazette*, playing its role as opium of the suburbs, inflamed readers with the headline "Did Enfield's 'mafia' squire have a three-girl harem?"[55] The story about Sir Henry Bowles, his supposedly homosexual brother Gussie, and the ugliness of Jesus Church produced a page of letters decrying the alleged slurs – "Bowles book an 'outrage'", "Withdraw book!" Norman did not respond.)

Norman returned to work on the novel he had mentioned to Marcello Cimino. He was also scratching an annoyance of his own. (It is difficult sometimes to avoid feeling that Norman's contentment was predicated on having a target of dissatisfaction or impatience close by.) This time the blow fell on his agent Richard Scott Simon's head, as in November Norman moved his business from Scott Simon's to the larger Anthony Sheil agency, citing a falling-off in his overseas sales. On 20 December he stopped work to spend Christmas week with Lesley and Bubs on a short tour across Andalucía, driving from Valencia to the Algarve and back to Seville for two days on the 27th. From January onwards he did little but write: the novel was costing him effort – he referred to it in a letter as "the present crushing task". Halfway through the month he escaped to meet his Russian promoter, Professor Evashova, and beforehand to have a reunion lunch with a fellow sergeant from 91 FSS, Derek Wise, who had written to him after reading *Jackdaw Cake*. Wise, a retired lawyer whose career had been spent in Paris, and his wife Nancy gave Norman lunch at L'Escargot. "He didn't look his age," Wise says, "I remember seeing him walk away when we said goodbye, he was very brisk."[56] Norman wrote to thank them and gave over most of the letter to an account of his post-lunch meeting with Valentina Evashova.

After leaving you the other day, as you know I went to see the Russian professor, and I simply cannot describe the high comedy of the interview. I tried to make my wife Lesley an excuse for being unsatisfactory in one way or another, saying that she was ill (as she was slightly) with a pain in the chest. "This," she said, roaring with fury, "is no more than nerves." I told her that Lesley did not suffer from nerves. "In that case it is cancer," she said. The meeting became all the more fantastic because I am slightly deaf, and she is totally so. Misunderstandings flew like flocks of pigeons through the air. In the end she dismissed me with a cry of "My dear Norman, I have concluded that you are <u>med</u>, you are a perfect fool." To which I replied, my dear professor, that is precisely my opinion of you.[57]

In the third week of March he broke off again for a week in Spain, and in April finally posted a completed typescript of the Sicilian novel to his agent at Anthony Sheil, Gill Coleridge.

As reviewers observed when it was published, *The March of the Long Shadows* did not read greatly like a novel; mutedly coloured in pages of twilit description of a Sicily abandoned by both the war and post-war recovery, its story was almost free of plot or development. What happened next was, I think – as biographer I am at my most subjective here – a combination of inexperience and lack of sensitivity on my part, and a fragility of person on Norman's. Always appreciative, always enthusiastic, punctiliously courteous, he was also – though as the result of those qualities you almost never noticed – always prickly and quick to be offended. This was less the effect of ego than of locked-away childhood anger (and some Welsh volatility): his trenchancy and unstable temper were, I feel, self-defences against any future hurt or efforts by others to impose their will. Over the years of managing his existence, he had developed a deep but always fragile structure of happiness that was easily disturbed and wonderfully concealed.

I finished reading the novel and phoned him at Finchingfield to tell him how much I had enjoyed it and – I cringe at my unbridled officiousness – to talk about where it would benefit from editing. I suggested that he, Christopher Sinclair-Stevenson and I might meet. A few days later he wrote asking to postpone the meeting until his agent was back from America and could be included. His letter was subdued, and he returned to the subject of editing.

Dear Julian,
Gillian Coleridge seemed reasonably enthusiastic about the book, but I must
say that I suspect her of being a very polite lady. This was only a day or two
before she left for the States, and she intended to read it again, so I can only
hope that there will be no modification of rapture.

The thing is I particularly asked whether she envisaged tinkering – the
reason being that I wanted to know if I could safely get down to something
else. She said no. . . .[58]

I reread the typescript, which I still liked and still thought did not
read as a novel, and looked at Norman's income from the previous
three books. I phoned him again to ask more tentatively (I had realised
by now he was unhappy) whether he might agree to it being published,
more or less unedited, as non-fiction. This probably seems aberrant,
but it was not just the novel's open-endedness but its more than emblematic authenticity of description that made it possible to read it as
non-fiction. The sales were certain to be better, I said. He replied that
he felt he had greater earning power as a novelist. I assured him that
the reverse was true. He said it was an interesting proposition and
asked to think about it before we met.

Whether he was just irritated by the suggestion that the novel
needed editing, or offended that Hamish Hamilton saw it as no more
than fine descriptive non-fiction, the category he had always found
easier to write than fiction, the meeting didn't take place. He was in
Spain from 2 to 11 June. On the 12th, the day after he got back,
Gill Coleridge phoned Sinclair-Stevenson to say that Norman was
looking for another publisher. I was horrified. I wrote to Norman
that it had been the worst news of the year, that I didn't know how
to express my disappointment because I was unused to being so
disappointed. Editing his books, I added truthfully, had "given me
almost more pleasure than anything else in the last three years"
(given how little he'd liked being edited, I need not have said that).
The guilt was not all mine. Hamish Hamilton had not helped itself:
at the critical moment on her return from the USA, Gill Coleridge
had tried to buy a copy of *Jackdaw Cake* and could not find one at
any London bookstore or the publisher's warehouse. And I could not
have known then that Norman's novels had throughout his career
been by far the most sensitive area of his literary pathology, all the
way back to his 1951 letter to Michael Howard in which, advancing

then furiously hedging, he had set out his "ultimate" ambition to be "a good novelist".

Gone: but in person he let me off the hook as graciously as ever. "Dear Julian, I cannot tell you how relieved I was by the tone of your most generous letter. Be sure you will always remain more than a professional friend so far as I am concerned. . . . Best wishes, as ever, and see you soon, Norman."[59]

And a coda: neither to exonerate nor incriminate, but almost simultaneously Norman received a letter from someone else who wanted to correct him, after reading a book of his that I hadn't edited, *A View of the World*, a paperback collection of his journalism recently published by Eland Books.

> La Résidence des Fleurs,
> Avenue Pasteur,
> 06600 Antibes
>
> 9th June 1986

Dear Norman Lewis,

There is always the tiresome reader who corrects an error, and this time I am the tiresome reader as it gives me the excuse for expressing my great admiration for your works.

And the error? In *A View of the World* you have Jaurès assassinated in the Chambre des Députés – he was killed in the Café d[u] Croissant in Montmartre. You speak of the assassin Villain being "quietly released". He was tried for murder in 1919 and acquitted by a packed bourgeois jury and 150,000 people met, urged on by Anatole France the next Sunday to protest against the verdict.

Forgive this tiresome reader and admirer. Our paths seem strangely similar – Laos, Vietnam, Belize, Goa, Liberia, Cuba, Panama.

> Yours sincerely
> Graham Greene[60]

In July the Lewises left Cambridge and moved back to Finchingfield, then flew to the Adriatic coast south of Trieste for the family holiday. On 3 August Norman was the guest on *Desert Island Discs*. He had recorded the programme in May and seemed to enjoy it: he had sought John Hatt's advice about the choice of records but chose his own, among them, apart from the Mozart clarinet concerto in tribute to Malcolm Dunbar, Stravinsky's *Petrushka* for its iconoclasm, "being a bit of an iconoclast myself", the Cuban "Guantanamera" for its reminder of "a place of such stupendous beauty, such drama, such music everywhere", and the austerest *saeta* he could find by La Niña de los Peines.[61] He indulged in brief gamesmanship about desert islands, pointing to his visit to one – Kamaran in the Red Sea – fifty years before and offering the expert's view that the diet faced by a castaway who was not a fisherman ("You can grope around the place and you can get squid and you can get octopus: this can be done because I've done it") was "not attractive in flavour". His chosen book was Herodotus' *Histories*, his luxury a spirit stove.

The BBC had broadcast Norman's *Arena* film at the end of January, widening his celebrity, but these forty-five minutes of Sunday morning radio conversation, lightened with snatches of eight favourite records, are the most British of public recognitions. Even if only in terms of Norman's own fears of having been forgotten, the fifteen-year eclipse was passing.

Here you're in Alice's Wonderland. Everything's turned upside down. You mustn't be surprised at anything. The police chief's a robber, the archpriest runs the bank, and a bandit raises funds for the poor. It's the local brand of normality.

The March of the Long Shadows

After that I stopped writing fiction. I think there was some sort of submerged morality that struggled against the falsity of fiction. It wasn't quite life as I saw it and experienced it.

Norman Lewis

I don't like to go to five-star hotels. I enjoy the simple life, the simple pleasures, things which are reasonably accessible. And I enjoy an adventure. My life has been exceedingly adventurous, much of which you have never heard about.

I'm devastated at this moment as I listen to myself, an inexorable smugness, I hope you'll forgive me that. No, no, this is a fact, I lead a heady life even these days.

Norman Lewis

HEADY ROAD

"Work, the drug of life"
Spanish proverb

NORMAN never crossed Jack Lambert's barrier separating the admired from the famous, but he didn't want to be drinking half-pints of Dubonnet in his pyjamas or escort movie stars who cared not to wear knickers. Recoiling from small talk, he didn't want to spend his evenings at Lord Weidenfeld's either. He wanted his books to sell, to travel to whatever wilderness he chose, and when not there to dictate the writing timetable and summon the company he liked. He was not forgotten, and had found new literary renditions of his subject: the journey that was about staying put (*Naples '44*, *Voices of the Old Sea*), the past's conversion into another form of journey (*Jackdaw Cake*). In *The March of the Long Shadows* he had succeeded in converting the novel into another sort of travel-composition – as Sterne had done the opposite two hundred years before, in *A Sentimental Journey*. The countless places of his life had made his existence more gazetteer than chronicle, and with considerable artistic suppleness he had managed to make travel, his drug, his reflex, also his capital literary metaphor.

Personally, a level of dogma had always been involved. Frank Allen, visiting him that summer, discovered his unforgiving side. Allen and Norman had been friends for thirty-five years, the Allens and Lewises for thirty. Allen had a habit, when he was free, of driving over from Whipps Cross to visit Norman at the Parsonage unannounced, "Because he [Allen] didn't mind anyone popping in and he was terribly insensitive," Lesley says.

Frank was a member of the Sherlock Holmes Society . . . these were not areas of interest to Norman as you can imagine, but Frank had a tremendous breadth of knowledge and so from a conversational point of view he interested Norman to talk to. . . . Frank was a great, great reader, had always wanted to write himself and therefore was almost insistent that he read everything that Norman wrote, and Norman couldn't stand it in the end. Because Frank had no literary talent at all. [And he] said, "I can't take it any more, Les, I can't relax because this man will appear on my doorstep." And as you know Norman liked best just to see people occasionally.[1]

When Frank Allen arrived again unannounced in summer 1986, Norman refused to see him. The only explanation Lesley could think to tell him was that her husband had gone mad.

The March of the Long Shadows was sold to Secker & Warburg, along with a new book that by October was "going well". Norman had thought about returning to Burma that autumn but the Burmese, like the Vietnamese, appeared not to want him back and a visa did not materialise. He went on working. The book, provisionally called "The Indians", was more than a skilful piece of recycling. It was a logical synthesis of his Latin American journeys and the journalism that had resulted from them: an expression of his admiration for the Indians as his ideal human beings and his concomitant hatred for the Protestant missionaries who hunted and detribalised them. He framed the narrative inside a brief partisan history of missionary impact worldwide, and the book's eventual title was *The Missionaries*, although as Graham Greene wrote, reproving him when reviewing the book, because its target was Protestants rather than Catholics it should properly have been called *The Evangelists*.

He was in Spain again in September and at Christmas, happy with his new publisher, and with their jacket for his novel. By March he had practically given up hope of a Burmese visa and consoled himself with another visit to Spain, to Seville in April. On 11 May he wrote to his publisher, David Godwin, announcing the despatch of a revised version of the book about the Indians. Godwin had suggested that he make the book more autobiographical, which he said he had tried to do.

The autobiographical element has been strengthened throughout, and a long passage which I think links up quite well added with episodes gathered in Vietnam. . . . At the moment I am a little punch-drunk and nervous at the possibility of having perhaps repeated myself. I should have read through it once more and ma[d]e sure that nothing like this has happened, but am now committed to going off to Spain tomorrow to do something about bull-fighting, and find it hard to concentrate.[2]

Madrid, Tenerife, Seville in autumn, Tossa, the Costa Blanca and Alpujarras, Seville in winter, the impoverished roads of Extremadura, Barcelona and Empordà, Ronda, Andalucía in spring, Santiago de Compostela and Gerena: it was his eleventh visit to Spain in five years. Most had produced an article for a Sunday supplement or *Harpers & Queen* (where John Hatt was travel editor) or the lushly produced subscription magazine *Departures*, edited by Lucretia Stewart. He nevertheless still believed in the worst sort of destinations, Hatt recalls. "I said, 'Norman, where would you like to go?' and he said, 'I'd like to go anywhere with a vicious dictatorship, a very cruel country ravaged by poverty, and a particularly malignant variety of malaria' – which was not going to immediately appeal to *Harpers* readers."[3] In June Hatt had published a careful selection of Norman's journalism, *A View of the World*, and many of Norman's inclusions conformed to the description, but in a new foreword he repudiated his "theories about the protective properties of bad government, bad communications etc. ... Bad governments preserve nothing, and even good ones have a mediocre record in this direction."

Reviewing the collection, Patrick Marnham called it "a triumph" and rejected the description of Norman as a travel writer in favour of "a pure writer ... who uses fiction, non-fiction and journalism, whatever comes to hand, to record his experiences and depict his world".[4]

But Spain was his recurring and default destination. He enjoyed the great cities, Seville most of all, and creeping out of them into their hinterlands "to discover whether, despite the lamentable profanation of much of Spain's coastline, the Spain of old is still to be found off the beaten track". The Spanish possessed too, he said, similarities to the kind of English who he felt had once existed. "A good Spaniard caught off the beaten track, not in Barcelona or Madrid or somewhere like that, reminds me of what I've read of a really good upright Englishman maybe two generations back."[5] He wrote about Spain with the undifficult quickness of fifty years' knowledge, so that most of the time a glimpse or impression was enough for him to read a paragraph's worth of observations into the landscape. His notebooks, decreasingly legible from the mid-1970s onwards, reflect this lazily vigilant rapidity of assimilation, catching details as a chameleon catches crickets, as well as reflecting the smoothings of age, his notes reduced to their constituent squiggles, almost meta-notes. He continued to find things to say about Spain; in return Spain kept his escape reflex under control, the emotions that fed his prose balanced. Spain had been the country that first calibrated his reactions: fifty years later it almost seems as though he keeps going back to see if it still exists, to see if *he* can still feel. Could the old Spain still be found? The answer was a qualified yes. An hour from Torremolinos you could turn your back on the world in the remaining Berber villages of the Alpujarras. Vultures still nested on the southern flanks of the Serranía de Ronda, and there were "many small Lorcas tucked away ... where the pungent flavour of provincial Spain persists, and the dignified procrastination implicit in the word *mañana* continues to be held in respect". But the solitude was often of desertion, of villages abandoned by their populations – an emptiness that, as he nosed through inland Spain year after year, seemed specifically to supply a favourite cadence in its "piercing melancholy that clings to places where a way of life is at an end, and about to be forgotten", and to fill a place in his own sentimental spectrum.[6]

The "something about bull-fighting" was the conclusion of two visits to the Albacerrada bull-breeding farm at Gerena north of Seville and the Alcalá de Guadaïra bullfighting school. They brought about a near recantation of the dismissal of tauromachy in his 1959 essay "The Bullfight Revisited" – and in particular of his previously ironic evaluation of the "noble" bull. He spoke to the master of the bullfighters' school, Señor Ballesteros. "Above all we teach our boys to master fear," Ballesteros told him.

"That's the most important thing of all." Almost plaintively he added: "You see, the horns are very sharp. It's bad for them if they get scared."

The more I saw of these Spaniards of the deep south the more it became clear to me that it was a misapprehension to believe that their feeling for bulls was anything less than an almost obsessional admiration and respect.

Where he didn't believe Hemingway, he almost believed a Spaniard.

Noble is the adjective almost never out of Spanish mouths when they speak of the bulls, to whom they frequently attribute such human qualities as candour and sincerity. This is F. Martinez Torres, himself a bullfighter, on the subject of courage: "The bull is the only animal in creation that is not daunted by any wounds he receives. He does not possess the treacherous or bloodthirsty instinct of other animals that crouch unseen and spring on their prey from behind. He attacks nobly from the front. Face to face, there is no animal that can beat him."[7]

The March of the Long Shadows was published while he was away and its wide reviews, from the *London Review of Books* to the *Sunday Mirror*, indicated that most reviewers hardly cared whether it was fiction or non-fiction. Its account of an ex-Field Security soldier, John Philips, returned to a creaking Sicily in 1947 to observe whether its Separatist movement might really, given Allied help, be moving towards creating a British, or American, dependency, gave Norman the chance to write again "about his old, obsidian, basic Sicily".[8] The march of the long shadows of the title, a ceremony to celebrate the arrival of spring and the time when "Whatever is to happen, we shall soon know", is one of the details that "impress themselves on the story, giving it a fuller meaning, creating a very particular resonance. Without any fuss or stridency, Lewis celebrates a unique mixture of the rarefied and earthy while composing a sort of swan-song for it all, set at a moment just before it becomes impossible to savour it as before."[9] It was "a fine evocation of an atmosphere compounded of the arid dust of crumbling masonry, highly seasoned horse stew, rough red wine, oil lamps and urine – the ancient smell of Sicilian feudalism".[10] Its affective elements – Philips's love affair with the fadingly gorgeous Marchesina, his friendships with Avvocato Crispi, the local lawyer (shadow of Lattarullo), and Moscato, the bibulous museum curator, hooked on embalming fluid – supplied no outcome bar a conviction that "Sicily is a preposterous island ... but enslaving as well", which its reviewers were unanimously content with. As a whole the reviews showed little impulse to analyse; their mood was affectionate admiration. Yet the novel is unusual not only in its taxonomy. One of its most enigmatic aspects is its blurred modernity – blurred in its formal resemblance to two different genres, thriller and plotless lyric, superimposed on one another but slightly out of register, modern in its nearly post-modern substitution of mood for action.

Whether this reflected some alteration of Norman's focus – a seventy-nine-year-old's paring down of sequence in favour of contemplation –

or not, the book would be his last novel, a quitting of fiction for which he later gave several reasons. He was not ready yet. On 18 July he was interviewed on BBC radio's arts programme *Kaleidoscope* and still described himself as "first a novelist and then a travel writer. I've written far more fiction than non-fiction" (true: *The March of the Long Shadows* was his fifteenth novel). He was currently writing short stories that he wanted to put into book form – one, "Girls in May", in which the economics of Sicilian heroin production enact an interesting theme of teenage boredom and addiction, had appeared in the *London Daily News* in June – and added that "There is a definite, a different, if you can use the word, emotional feeling about writing fiction, which by the way I find a little bit harder." Asked about his journalism he also (watch the armoured self-deprecation) claimed to be

certainly a very bad journalist . . . I don't give the bare facts stripped of all the surrounding background, I put everything in. As a result, very few papers [will] look at my stuff. I usually manage to get into the colour supplements, I have contributed fairly frequently to the *New Yorker*, but on the whole I have tried in the past to sell my work to other publications [and] usually they don't find it sufficiently journalistic. In fact, from their point of view, not good enough journalism.[11]

He may just have been feeling playful. He had been enjoying accolades and privileges: on 12 June he and Lesley had dined at High Table at St Antony's College, Oxford, as guests of Redmond O'Hanlon, and two days before the interview, 16 July, he had been awarded an honorary doctorate by the University of Essex. Complex feelings about the academy, a sensation of inferiority combined, as his friend Nathan Keyfitz says, "with a sense that it was full of self-satisfied professors who had nothing to offer him, nor he them",[12] did not show at the presentation, although in the group photograph he is characteristically at odds with the other doctorands. His brown Hush Puppies disrupted a glossy line of black footwear, and his mortar board was pushed back on his head the way his felt hat had been pushed back in the photograph Ernestina had taken of him, elbows resting on the edge of their Mercury's windshield, in Mexico in 1939.

However "not good enough" as a journalist, he was in demand. He was writing a long essay about Essex, one of his very few accounts of England, for *Granta*, and that summer the *Sunday Times* telephoned

him to ask where was the one place in the world he had not been and
would like to go. On a whim he answered, "Tahiti", not expecting
they would come up with the air fare, but they did. On 10 September
he flew to Greece to research a short story (a mystery about island
women in the Cretan Sea who dumped their unwanted spouses down
dry wells), and was back at Finchingfield the night of the October 1987
storm.

We are only minimally devastated here, but passed a few dramatic moments.
Eleven big trees went, and rising soon after dawn on Friday I was in time to
see the top of one carried away like a black albatross, and managing to wing
20 yards or so before coming down.[13]

After selling the Cambridge house he and Lesley had bought another
in Islington, north London, at Dagmar Terrace, and they moved into
"winter quarters" in early November. On the 19th Norman landed at
Papeete's Faaa airport. He spent ten days in the Windward and Leeward
Islands, most of it slightly bored. There was not enough to do, once
the first impression of post-Gauguin indolence and a landscape more
or less exclusively in the service of high-end tourism was described. He
went to Raiatea first, where he noted that Uturoa, its main port, was
"a beachcomber's hangout of a place from the turn of the century
patched and stained with corrugated iron". Stores "selling [a] wild
miscellany", open-fronted bars, an abandoned Panhard "under a mulch
of leaves and blossom", a "splendid pompous notice of [a] restaurant
that is no longer there" and a tide of forgotten anchors and ropes "only
held in check by the road's metalled surface" pleased him, and the
Raiatean women "in exquisite local printed pareus" held his boredom
in check.[14] He crossed briefly to Bora Bora and was irritated at the
monopoly of activities – fire-walking, desert island boat trips, shark-
feeding – by the grand hotels. As usual, in avoiding them his tolerance
revived. "Waitresses in small hotels giggling and affectionate and liable
to add a pat and a squeeze to normal service," he noted: like the other
"Gauguin faces" he saw, they were "less melancholic than those of the
master who probably repressed their smiles". He had a misgiving, "Do
Tahitian girls copy Gauguin pictures?" and rejected it, "In reality they
have more spirit and style." (It was a custom, or he made it one, that
the young women he met wrote their names in his notebook: Isabel
Pakarati Tepano, Marie-Jo, Éliane.) On the 23rd he sailed to Huahine

where with his contact, Bruno Saura, he observed a family reconcilia-
tion between the man's favourite nephew and his wife, who was
demanding expensive home improvements as the price of staying with
him. "Huahine is like a face pressed against a window pane separating
it from the consumer display," he noted. "To buy these things you must
go to Papeete, work, suffer." The Leeward Islands' taboos ("You never
go out fishing if you've had a row with your wife – because a shark
will get you") and the islanders' belief in communal activity and natural
magic interested him, but island life lacked edge. "The centre of social
life on Huahine is the booze store with its fish tanks and flowers and
the entertainers playing and singing endlessly what sounds like 'Show
me the way to go home'."[15]

On Tahiti he tried to inject some drama by recalling the destruc-
tions of the London Missionary Society in the early 1800s (which in
his *Sunday Times* piece occupied him longer than the destructiveness
of the French government's eighty-eight nuclear tests at Mururoa), and
the upheaval brought by the imported wealth that had come in train
of the nuclear programme. The materialist glamour of the capital failed
to provide an object for his restless eye, and he spent his afternoons
riding a borrowed bicycle in search of interest beyond "the implacable
elegance" of the high island's single peak, dense forests and long sashes
of black sand.

Garlanded, he left Tahiti on 29 November. At Islington on his return
he was still in demand. Editors wanted chips from the growing crystal
of his memoirs: he worked on the Tahiti piece and the Greek island
story, and was commissioned by the *Sunday Times* to revisit Thailand
in the New Year. Commissions as a rule went smoothly – tidy couplings
of professionalism and respect – but conflict blew up over his essay
about Essex. "In Essex" was supposedly a memoir for a *Granta* edition
entitled "Home", but Norman was recomposing it heavily, to the point
of fiction – in common with his inexistent Cretan island there was no
"Long Crendon" in "the ugliest county" and he never lived at a farm
called (self-referentially?) Charmers End, as the narrator did – which
may have added fuel to the dry fire of fury caused when it was edited.
Granta's editor, Bill Buford, had been keen to commission an original
essay; before, he had only published extracts from Norman's books.
Norman had accepted but remained wary of him in person. "I think
he's got a heart of ice beneath that friendly exterior," he told a friend.
Buford was also a known megalomaniac in his editing: it is alleged

that writers often did not recognise their work after a Buford rewrite. In January Norman received the edited version of "In Essex" from *Granta*, and after reading it was so incoherent with anger that it was left to Lesley to speak to Buford. She told him he must withdraw the piece, that he couldn't treat Norman, with his reputation, in this way, and that either the piece went in as Norman had written it or it didn't go in at all. Buford retreated.

Norman flew to Bangkok on 20 February. He sought, as he had at Tossa, some sign of preservation. He had last seen Thailand in 1952 after, as he reported, the surreal modernisation of the country by its leader, Marshal Plaek Pibulsonggram, whose team of experts had flown to the USA and there concluded that the USA's "moral and material superiority" was based on whisky-drinking, men and women dancing together in public, and the ceremony of striptease. Thirty-six years later, to travel hopefully was better than arrival: Bangkok, "the Babylon of our days", still had its water-city of "splendid wooden houses, verandas, staircases and balustrades ... fretsaw wonders", but at its end lay "tourist confusion" at a floating market of depressing slatternliness.[16] Old Chiang Mai's curling roofs and dawn fishermen-archers pleased him more, and from Chiang Mai he drove up to the opium gateway of Mae Sae, recalling its Shan warlord's partnership with the CIA and deploring the Thai and Burmese governments' treatment of their hill tribes, persecuted for a deforestation that was inevitably the work of large corporations. At Phuket, its inexorable development begun, he wrote, one relic of charm had survived "at Mai Khao – a long and deserted beach north of the airport. ... The beach is feathered by the mossy shade of huge casuarinas, from which fishing owls as large as eagles come planing down [and] the turtles come ashore at night by the hundreds to deposit their eggs." The once most seductive land of Siam, he realised without much surprise, had changed by as much as its ancient religious art of healing by massage, now practised by roughly 750,000 Thai women working in the parlours of its tourist centres from the age of twelve upwards.

The Missionaries was published on 3 May 1988. A week before it went on sale, Peter Ackroyd judged it "the story of a religious tragedy"[17] that had started in Tahiti in 1797 with the arrival of the first brick-layers and butchers of the London Missionary Society, who, in the name of God's love, had forbidden the Tahitians to sing, dance, surf, tattoo their bodies or adorn themselves with flowers. Two days after its publication the *Listener* called Norman "a pocket Herodotus".[18] On Saturday 7 May Graham Greene had "no hesitation in calling Norman Lewis one of the best writers, not of any particular decade, but of our century".[19]

Other reviews called the book "superb ... rare and formidable" (*Sunday Times*),[20] "a judicious exercise of personal courage" (*Guardian*)[21] and "compulsive, deeply upsetting and unforgettable" (*Financial Times*).[22] In the *Times Literary Supplement* Paul Henley, putting away his reservations, paid homage to Norman's "unrivalled personal experience" and was reminded by his portraits of rural Latin America "of Gabriel García Márquez at his best. As with García Márquez, it is hard to know whether to laugh or cry."[23] In the week of 19 May, when Norman attended a publication dinner with Lesley, David Godwin, John Hatt, Gill Coleridge, Nicholas Shakespeare and others, it was one of the most reviewed books. Dissent was sparse. The *Spectator* carried a review by Philip Glazebrook describing Norman as a writer whose scenes he "cannot forget", but accusing him of false syllogisms and using unnamed sources and concluding that "An unbiased reader, whilst fascinated by the book, will perhaps judge that Mr Lewis attributes too many evils to Evangelical Christianity." (Glazebrook also raised the undeniable point that "Even to visit [the Indians] is to endanger them, whatever our intentions."[24]) The *New Statesman* also condemned Norman's "unswervingly romantic" portrait of tribal cultures as an "unsustainable" trope of colonial discourse.[25] The *London Review of Books*, in an informed essay by John Ryle, put forward the inevitab-list's view of the implacability of global penetration, acknowledging Norman's account as impeccably unsentimental but criticising it as buttressed by wishful thinking.[26]

There is no question that *The Missionaries* is partisan. Its survey of Christian evangelism does not seek to be balanced: as how could it? Norman was an idealist, a pastoralist, a hippy *avant la lettre*, a Romantic (however sceptical), a militant in the cause of the noble savage. In a short treatise that he wrote on the philosophy of work in one of his 1950s notebooks, in which he compared the ways of life of Moïs and Mexican Indians, he made his belief clear. "In spite of the reaction to

the late 18th century 'noble savage' it still remains a fact that from
Columbus to British officers parachuted into Borneo in the last war,
comment on the happiness of uncivilised people is universal."[27] *The
Missionaries* is not judicious or fair. In its journey from Norman's first
encounter with Rafael Aparicio's mother's servants in Guatemala City,
"clean and respectable" Indians selected for her by a mission at
Quetzaltenango, through his acquaintance with the Moïs of Vietnam
to his visits, often brief, to rural Guatemala, Mexico, Bolivia, Paraguay,
and Venezuela, it is throughout and above all a *polemic* (Greek,
polemikos = war). It is difficult to characterise passages like the following
from Caicara on the Orinoco, where Norman saw detribalised Indians
on the streets, any other way.

One – pointed out as a Panare – lounged on a corner. His relative prosperity
was advertised by the flowered shirt, jeans, trainers, short haircut, and the
cigarette in a long holder. This he waved about between puffs in a manner
copied from an old film. His wife, who crouched in an angle of the wall just
out of sight, was for sale for a cupful of sugar. His prosperity, I was assured,
would be short-lived, for he was in an advanced stage of tuberculosis. . . .
   These in Ayacucho and Caicara are the reached. Where is the light they
were promised?[28]

It is a sad picture, delivered with anger, and unverifiable. The detail
of the wife for sale seems as though it might have come from another
journey when, in Bolivia, he met the band of Ayoreo fugitives, the
"jaguar-hunters" with their wives forced into prostitution by the roadside at Santa Cruz. He is also inconsistent, writing that he refuses to
carry a gun, calling it "a murderer's tool", belying his own long fascination with firearms. None of these unverifiables or inconsistencies
matter. Polemics don't need to be consistently true: their moral justification is nowhere near as important as their aesthetic justification. A
good polemic is, above all, *a good text*, liberating, exhilarating, a
provider of intense reading pleasure. If unjust, its injustice gives us the
opportunity to understand better those it attacks. The New Tribes
Mission and the Summer Institute of Linguistics were not without the
resources to defend themselves; and even in its injustice Norman's
account was drawing on his long resources, his years of encountering
Protestant evangelists and holding surreal conversations with them about
the fires of Hell that awaited the unsaved because their missionary

keepers could not speak their language, and of witnessing the one consequence of the Indian harvests that he could not endure, the destruction of their sense of belonging.

He did not need the radical scepticism of the ethnographer to tell the story. His story, as he had first formulated it in Vietnam, was the soul of a situation as he saw it; his polemic had a *human* target to attack in the shape of the Bible Belt, pre-modern descendants of the Protestant revolution whose equation of capitalism and Christianity as parts of the same work ethic he detested. To that extent also his ideas echoed Weber's, loathing the evangelists more for their capitalism (enshrined in the title of the NTM's journal *Brown Gold*) than for their Christian faith, because it is their capitalism with its perpetual counting – souls saved, funds raised, income generated by workers – that typifies their assault on what he considered the paramount human values: belonging, balance with nature, freedom, joy. The Indians' incarnation of those values made them, in his view, supreme examples of humanity. The Indians were his avatar, and his admiration of them a form of ritual paying of respect. By their attacks on Indian ways of life, the evangelists were, in an important way, infringing Norman's ritual space. The lapsed Calvinist de-adherent was as ferocious in defence of his admired Indian adherents as ever. The ferocity of his polemic was the most human thing about it.

The missions, and others, protested when the book appeared but the only protest Norman acted on was a phone call and letter from General Dynamics in St Louis, Missouri cordially denying that it had ever been involved in funding the evangelists. (References to General Dynamics and another company, Westinghouse, were omitted from the paperback edition.)

On 2 June he and Lesley were in Spain again, to research a story about conditions in the Cantabrian north-west for the *Sunday Times*. It was a landscape of ancient rural Europe, of bears dwindling and wolves on the increase and a Celto-Iberian past; an addition to his lexicon of old Spain. In the village of Arbeyales in the National Reserve of Somiedo he was delighted to be told by the local priest-mayor that he was the first foreigner in the man's memory to have visited the village.[29] The trip was "outstandingly successful", he wrote to Gill Coleridge, "more like Central Asia than Spain".[30] He and Lesley returned to dine at St Antony's with O'Hanlon again on the 25th, and on 3 July Lesley threw a surprise party at the Parsonage for Norman's eightieth birthday. On the Sunday morning he was invited out to drinks by Josie and Wendy, friends in the village, while Lesley laid tables at speed and Ito's wife Katherine materialised lunch. The day was hot. Either side of lunch guests drank and talked in the Parsonage garden: the ordinary birthday lunch of an octogenarian, loved by family and friends, and something renascent about the day too, marked by his enjoyment of the attention of a new generation of friends, there because they admired his writing.

That Norman could be eighty, few of his guests believed. He nearly ignored the fact. Standing talking on the lawn, we got on to the subject of Tahiti. Bruce Chatwin, he said, had phoned him to ask whether Norman thought he should go to the Pacific. "I advised him against it as extremely boring."

I said surely he must have found something interesting about Tahiti. On one of his bicycle rides, he said, he had stopped to rest and after a few minutes an "exceptionally beautiful" young Polynesian woman walking along the road had also stopped and talked to him. They had sat by the roadside and chatted in French for some time, Norman enquiring about her life, she asking him where he had come from. Confidentially he finished up, "And I'm sure that if I'd been forty-five years younger I could have scored."[31]

He responded to his new generation of writer-friends by often admiring, spontaneously encouraging, reliably advising them. Ian Thomson, who had reviewed *The Missionaries* and was writing a travel guide to southern Italy, was one. Redmond O'Hanlon was another. On 10 May Norman sent a copy of *The Missionaries* to O'Hanlon, already notorious with his second book for finding it difficult to finish a book, with the inscription

Dear Redmond – Congratulations on having put the Amazon and Orinoco behind you – and now forward to the Congo! I am moved to quote Lorca's *Lament for the Death of a Bullfighter*: the passage in which the poet calls for pall-bearers worthy of his friend.

"*Yo quiero ver aquí los hombres de voz dura.*
Los que doman caballos y dominan los ríos lejanos [sic] –
(I want to see here men with hard voices.
Breakers of horses and dominators of distant rivers.)"

Love to you all – I hope shortly to invite you to share with us a traditional missionary pie.

Norman[32]

On 8 August, back from the family holiday, he told O'Hanlon that he had been reading his book. "It is magnificent – a true Peter Fleming style adventure, but better. I'm now starting on it again." O'Hanlon, an irrepressible celebrant at the cabinet of curiosities that is his house near Oxford, invited Norman and Lesley to a party for the publication of *In Trouble Again* on 8 October, where they met the broadcaster Terry Wogan and, for the first time, the undeceivable reporter Martha Gellhorn. (The eclectic guest list was partly the result of O'Hanlon's sociability, partly due to his having recently appeared on Wogan's t.v. chat show.) Late in the evening Norman and Lesley left behind the whisky-drinking Gellhorn, still drinking whisky, and went back to their shared b & b, "but there she was at breakfast the next morning because I drove her to the station, and she was in fine form", Lesley recalls.[33] Two days later Norman wrote to say he had enjoyed himself hugely and discovered an unexpected likeness in one of the other guests.

Dear Redmond
Both party and Wogan <u>the best</u>. Amazing to find that Martin Amis is the look-alike of the Algerian I saved from the guillotine in Philippeville. Martha Gellhorn most entertaining and witty. In all, a splendid evening. Now off to S Spain and endless paellas. Love to you all. . . .

Norman[34]

He and Lesley were in Valencia for ten days. When they came back at the end of the month they were visited at Finchingfield by Gill Coleridge. (Coleridge had left Anthony Sheil Associates earlier in the year to join Deborah Rogers' smaller literary agency.) The visit was to light a slow fuse in relations between Gill Coleridge and John Hatt, and eventually Norman, over the arcane complexities of publishing licences, methods and loyalties. In short, John Hatt was a small publisher with poor distribution in the USA (he had US rights in four of his five Lewis titles) and would always be a small publisher. However much effort Hatt had put into reviving Norman's fortunes – and it had been passionately substantial, from delivering review copies by hand to spending large sums of his own money on advertising – Norman was anxious to find a bigger audience in the USA and also wanted "good quality hardback editions of those books" available in the UK.

On 2 November Coleridge wrote to Hatt pressing him to change his

US distribution and asking him to confirm that he was ready to let an appropriate UK publisher have the necessary hardback licences in return for "appropriate and fair percentages" to him. Hatt replied that he was "perfectly happy" with the idea of the hardbacks and thanking her for her suggestions about US distribution.

Norman *was* anxious, though not strictly the way his agent expressed it. There was a reason for him wanting the good-quality hardback editions. He was profoundly grateful to Hatt, but his gratitude did not override misgivings about Eland as a publisher. In May that year he had already written to his agent about poor sales. Before you yourself have published a book, it is probably impossible to comprehend authors' sensitivity to the non-availability of their work; afterwards, nothing is easier to understand than this deep, personal-seeming slight. The difference was that Norman kept it so well hidden. Under the guise of not wanting to offend Hatt, he hid behind his agent.

30th May, 1988

Dear Gill . . .

A very sketchy research on the John Hatt front produced nothing much for one's comfort. The leading book shop in Upper Street[, Islington] had not heard of Eland. Dillons had but no longer carried them in stock. Heffers in Cambridge stocked 3 titles but Bowes and Bowes had nothing to offer. No small Essex towns such as Braintree and Saffron Walden carry stocks. It took the lady who looks after my dog 6 weeks to obtain *Golden Earth* to order. . . . I would certainly not dream of hurting John's feelings by confronting him with these facts, but I thought I would pass them on to you for your tactful approach on the subject.

Or perhaps not dream of confronting Hatt because temperamentally he always feared confrontation. In autumn 1988 the situation was unsettled. Hatt owned the contracts, and Coleridge could not move without his consent. (An irony to the tension between the two was that Coleridge owed her role as Norman's agent to Hatt, who had suggested her to Norman when he wanted to leave Richard Scott Simon.)

Norman's annual plans for travel seem to fall under a different light in such a situation: leaving his agent to work on his publisher, he moved to escape. He had planned first on a longish trip to Borneo (he had signed a contract with Secker & Warburg for a book with the working title "Indonesia") but deferred it in favour of a less demanding journey to Goa and Kerala. He was putting together a collection of recent pieces; he told his agent there would be a novel finished by late summer.

But it turned out to be impossible to get away from publishing annoyances. That spring, as *The Missionaries* was published, Secker had moved from its battered, companionable offices in Poland Street to the renovated Michelin House, a windy address at Brompton Cross, south Kensington. His editor David Godwin had left and moved to Jonathan Cape. On 5 December Norman packed all his annoyance into a letter to Gill Coleridge.

Dear Gill,

I thought I should write to tell you of my feelings about Secker, which have been slowly simmering to the boil for some time. Like other authors on their list to whom I have spoken I was dismayed by the move to Michelin House with its markedly industrial environment just when I had settled in at Poland Street, which was not only pleasant but accessible, which Michelin House certainly is not . . . I am afraid that I have reached the stage in my life when such minor embellishments have become important.

These are my lesser grievances. Far more important is the chaos to which I was subjected at the time of the move, which happened to coincide with the publication of my last book. For days on end I was unable to reach Secker on the phone. Messages that should have reached me never did. In the case of two major interviews . . . the journalists were only able to finally track me down by a species of detection. On one occasion, when I finally got through and asked for Serena Davies [publicity], it was to be told that no-one of that name worked in the building. . . .[35]

His solution was to move back to Cape, with whom he said, flirting with nostalgia, "I had a long and happy relationship". Coleridge agreed. On 20 December Dan Franklin, who had taken over from David Godwin as publisher at Secker, wrote that "as a long-standing admirer" he was disappointed by Norman's wish to move to Cape but, as Norman said to his agent on the 29th, "he is resigned to the inevitable".[36]

Despite the frustrations Norman maintained a high level of activity. He had recently written about Thailand twice; Extremadura (the *sierra* country off the road he had taken with Ernestina in summer 1936, on the eve of the Civil War); his meeting with the young Loke Wan Tho in his 500K Mercedes; and was researching a sequel to his "Genocide" article based on new information about New Tribes Mission activity in Paraguay and a recent investigation by Luke Holland of Survival

International. Four of his novels were being reprinted, and *Voices of the Old Sea* had been optioned for a film by Mike Radford. He was faced by a last problem before he left for India: more *Granta* editing. He had sent the magazine 2500 words on "Siam and the Modern World", and two days before his departure the magazine had returned the copy "with at least 100 alterations".

He spoke to a *Granta* staff editor, Angus MacKinnon, who was "full of apologies, and ... incident[al]ly said that he wholeheartedly agreed with me and thought that the piece had been grossly over-edited".[37] MacKinnon says, "Typically Buford had made a terrible hash of editing the piece and left me to deal with Norman, who was (a) absolutely furious with Bill and (b) about to go off to India. Once Norman had got everything off his chest, we sat down and decided what we were going to do."[38] Norman asked for the piece to be sent back, then after discussion agreed to let MacKinnon handle it and *Granta* publish it. On 6 February, three weeks after Norman had left for India, Bill Buford also apologised over two pages, not for his own editing but, at length, for the magazine's maladministration (though not exactly by him). It was a letter of some charm, and a week later Norman, after recovering from the jet lag of his return flight, accepted the offered explanation.

In his eighty-first year Norman was blessed with a sort of fusion, and subsequent crystallisation, of travelling energy and writing energy. Very little was inevitable about his next decade and a half: he did not get more famous, as he might have done, he did not get honoured, as he might have been, and he did not slow down. John Hatt recalls, "He could go off for three weeks and one would be sitting here having a very dull life reading the *Daily Mail*, and you'd pick up the phone and say, 'Norman, when are you going?' And he'd been and come back. Three weeks had gone in nothing and he'd been through as many adventures as people would have in a lifetime."[39] At the beginning of 1989 he had no book to write: the novel he had mentioned – supposedly about the Quixote-like excursion of a second-rate group of musicians across Spain – was not being written. Needing to write, incapable of not writing, he found his subjects in journalism, going, coming back, writing, going again. On 16 January he flew to Goa and on to Kerala

for three weeks with Lesley, Kiki and Bubs. Three unusually gentle
pieces came out of the journey (it isn't customary to find sentences like
"Sightseeing is comfortably done by buses which wander everywhere
along the country roads. There is no better sample run than to take a
trip from Dabolim airport to one of the northern resorts" in Norman's
writing).[40] The tone was not repeated in his memoir *The World The
World*, in which he described the building of the holiday villas on Goa's
north coast, where he and his family had stayed, by bonded child
labourers – slaves – mostly young girls imported from Rajasthan and
crammed into low plastic shelters to sleep.

From Goa there were no Air India seats to Kerala; the family had
to take long-distance taxis to Cochin and back, stopping first at the
Casino then the Malabar Hotel in early February. Kerala he found
Communist, fertile, "the East at its tidiest", healthy, literate, lacking in
all the defects of socialist states, its fishermen of the Arabian Sea living
in an idyllic reminder of the men of Tossa ("These people are not understanding money," his guide told him. "When there is a good catch they
are buying jewellery for their wives").[41]

Despite the ideal tone, and so the lack of writing edge, Norman
found something about India stimulating, and kept in mind the idea
of continuing with the material and returning to the sub-continent.
In April he flew to Barcelona for the *Sunday Times*, sufficiently short
of money to ask the features editor at the magazine, Julian Browne,
for a £1000 advance. India had been very expensive, and though
he was paid well for his journalism and, contractually separated
from Secker, had just agreed a £10,000 advance for his collection of
pieces with Cape, his travel budget was never small. "We spent all
our money on travelling," Lesley remembers. "That's what we gave
the children too. I used to buy all my clothes at charity shops or the
local village dressmaker. We didn't spend money on the house then
[either]."[42]

At the end of April Norman met David Godwin to discuss a possible
book about India. He was concerned about Cape's ability to provide
enough of an advance for him and Lesley to live while he was writing
it. "It seems possible to me that David, in a first flush of enthusiasm,
may have been guilty of hinting at the kind of figure which he later
had second thoughts about. As I know we both agree, I am facing two
years of work on this book," he wrote to his agent, "and it seems likely
to be my biggest literary endeavour for many years – or at any time."[43]

In the event his inference that he could earn more from journalism did not need to be tested. A week later Cape agreed to pay him £60,000, plus £10,000 expenses, for "India".

He had been planning to go to Corsica for a story about the island's flora, but his appetite was roused by hearing about an Italian snake-cult celebrated in the small town of Cocullo in the Abruzzo hills. Like Naples, Abruzzo is a place where Catholicism and natural magic are by long local practice inseparable. The festival of San Domenico paid tribute to the local saint's continuation of the pagan ritual, a survival from pre-Roman times in which, on the first Thursday in May, dozens of snakes gathered six weeks before in the surrounding mountains were carried through Cocullo's streets not just by the *serpari* or snake-men but the townspeople and children. On 2 May Norman flew to Rome. He drove north-east to L'Aquila in Abruzzo and booked into the Hotel Duca degli Abruzzi. Edward Burman, a writer living at L'Aquila, gives a rare account of the observer observed.

I was told that an English "journalist" was coming to the area. My friend, who was director of the local tourist authority, begged me to show him around. My first impression was of a dull old man bent over the bar, [an] elderly bank-clerkish looking man wearing a cardigan under a suit, and of a very boring couple of days ahead – I suppose it was easy to misread his modesty and self-deprecating humour at first sight. I think he was tired, but he seemed both boring and uninterested in me.

The next day we set off in my car, and already at lunch in Santo Stefano di Sessanio things were better. We had an excellent lunch cooked to order by an old lady beside a beautiful mountain lake. I had rung in advance (she knew me) and ordered some pasta – which she began to mix and roll only after I'd called – and lamb. Santo Stefano was an important meeting point for the beginning of the annual transhumance to Puglia, where shepherds gathered and made huge flocks to travel together. This is important because the transhumance to the north from Puglia began in May exactly when vipers awake from their hibernation. The problem of snakes was always the loss of sheep (*pecus* = sheep = pecuniary), not men. Without understanding that, I explained to Norman, the snake festival would have no meaning.

Norman impressed me with his astonishing appetite for strong red wine, and we had a marvellous conversation. Even after a bottle each at lunch, he walked up a steep hillside (the starting point was the lake at 1450 m above sea level) like a mountain goat.

We stopped at Navelli [and] in Scanno, which we walked around together after dinner. In the morning we drove to Cocullo. Those two days remain in my mind, as he talked to shepherds, old ladies, priests [and] I watched him coax information from stubborn interviewees with the most innocent-sounding questions. But the most important was Alfonso di Nola, a marvellous Italian anthropologist and one of the leading experts on [pagan cults]. Most of the interesting things in Norman's article came from him.[44]

Norman sent Edward Burman a signed copy of *Naples '44* and invited him to visit. He did several times and was impressed again by Norman's

attitude (or lack of attitude) towards ageing. . . . I remember his son, then around 25, pushing him into the swimming pool at Finchingfield and his laughing as if he were fifty years younger.[45]

Norman was not finished with travel for the year, going to Scotland in July to visit "an estate in the middle of a wild-life reserve" as background for his India book and to Sicily in September to write more explicitly than before about the island's domination by mafia control and the social disintegration that followed any power struggle. "I went out with a reporter from *L'Ora* interviewing people at the end of their tethers in wholly Mafia dominated villages (and towns). The situation in these places when state control has been completely abolished – even to the extent of the police's withdrawal – is something that beggars belief."[46] Nor was he finished with journalism. He wrote a tribute to his beautifully suited friend Boris Giuliano, head of Palermo's Pubblica Sicurezza, on the tenth anniversary of his murder,[47] and inaugurated the "Villains" half of the *Independent* magazine's "Heroes & Villains" column with an energetic condemnation of Lord Kitchener as a looter and retributive sadist. (We stray into the typical here – Norman could hardly have held another view – but Winston Churchill concurred, writing to his mother after the battle of Omdurman, "Omdurman was disgraced by the inhuman slaughter of the wounded, and Kitchener was responsible for this.")

He expected to be "off at the beginning of November" to India but did not get away as quickly as he wanted to. His friend Marcello Cimino, the journalist from *L'Ora*, died at the end of October from liver cancer. Norman had visited him in Palermo in September, when Cimino had told him he was ill. His later valedictory description of the visit is an oblique tribute to Cimino's friendship over twenty-five years –

the taxi from Punta Raisi airport dropped me at Marcello's home, 110 via
Maqueda, and once again I climbed the staircase wandering through the lower
parts of this ancient building, arriving finally at the top-flat rooms and roof
garden where I knew that my friends would be waiting. They were there, as
I had seen them so often before, each in his or her favourite place in sun or
in shade. It was one of those environments that suppressed evidence of change.
There were the little trees in their pots, the trellis drooping its honeysuckle
among the tiny blue butterflies. . . . Marcello announced that he had just
returned from the family's vineyard. The harvest, he said, had been the best
for years. "The rain came at the right time. It makes all the difference," he
told me.

"How many bottles?" I asked.

"Fewer than usual. About three hundred. But that's the trouble with the
good smaller grapes, you have to expect it. Still it's worth it. We're quite
happy."[48]

Cimino's death six weeks later, without drinking that year's wine, "was
like the loss of a family member".

At the end of October his collection of recent pieces, *To Run Across
the Sea* was published, and admired with force for the "lyrical brilliance" of its author's style[49] and his "admirable anger . . . the grinding
wheel on which he sharpens" his prose. His prescience was recognised.
"Mr Lewis was a pioneer, one of the first to realise what was happening,
and to sound the alarm."[50] Victoria Glendinning wrote that "He has
probably done more than anyone else to alert the world to the accelerating destruction of the rain forests, the commercial greed of the
destroyers, the wanton loss of animal and plant species, and the irreversible consequences for climate and rainfall."[51] The book's apparent
disarrangement, beginning totemically with "Another Spain", continuing with "In Essex", with the remaining nineteen pieces at random,
provided no continuity but offered cross-references of mood and concern,
from Essex to south America, Tahiti to Amazonia, Cantabria to Paraguay.
The one piece that might have been omitted was the recent article about
Goa. The author himself was at his most self-deprecatory where his
collections were concerned. "Bruce," he signed a copy to Bruce Palling,
"herewith the last of my *estafadas* [frauds], I promise."[52]

The book's reception underlined its author's return to favour, as
other signs did: several radio readings that autumn, a 3000-copy reprint
of a paperback *The Missionaries* that made it the imprint's bestselling
title for the year, a $40,000 advance sale of US rights in "India" to

Gary Fisketjohn at Atlantic Monthly Press, a request to translate forty
pages of *Naples '44* in a German anthology of eye-witness accounts of
the war, *Europa in Trümmern*, edited by Hans Magnus Enzensberger,
and in January – a sort of consecration – an offer from Adelphi in
Milan for the Italian translation rights to *Naples '44*, twelve years after
its first publication.

He landed at Delhi on 10 January 1990 with less fixed intentions
than he had claimed in the proposal he had given his publishers.
Ambiguity crowned the project: Norman knew that there was an
underlying expectation from his publishers, and agent, that he deliver
an account of a super-Indian journey, a saturation of pageantry,
colour, and perfume, of fragrant ghats and undiscovered Taj Mahals.
He had written with typically deflecting charm to reassure Gill
Coleridge of his intentions the previous June. "I thought I detected
the faintest perturbation in your tone when the subject of Indian tribal
peoples came up the other day. This is to assure you that these will
not be featured except in relation to dramatic episodes, and probably
rarely even then. I realize that this book has to be supercharged with
general appeal."[53]
    It was, as such assurances generally are, a writer's promise. He
would write what he wanted. His first destination and the book's
starting point was Patna in the state of Bihar. It was John Hatt who
had painted Bihar to him as an extraordinary place of political anarchy,
"a third of its MPs having been to prison, some of them MPs *from*
prison, a huge murder rate". Hindu and Muslim fundamentalism that
had fuelled cycles of reprisal after the storming of the Ayodhya mosque,
caste wars and bonded labour were also its lot. In the 1989 elections
around 2000 voters had been murdered, some buried in mass graves.
Even today the Tourism of India website promotes Bihar beseechingly
as "The state that represents every thing good and bad within the
country[,] waiting to be explored and rediscovered". In planning the
book Norman had been put in touch with the journalist Ian Jack,
who had travelled and lived in Bihar in the 1980s, and Jack had
invited him to lunch at his house in north London. He lent him some
standard histories of India, but, he says, "It seemed to me impossible

that Norman could get 'inside' it, without any Indian language, little
experience of India, and on such a short trip."

Perhaps there was envy in this attitude: I, after all, had spent years researching
a book on India and written very little of it. Maybe I even thought Norman
was too blithe, too inconsiderate of his own ignorance. What I didn't understand was that he had a very realistic approach to book-making – what he
saw he would describe, he would never know everything, the important thing
was to set down a particular experience sympathetically, wisely, wittily – maybe
even accurately. No point worrying about incompleteness, the larger picture.[54]

John Hatt had suggested that Norman confine himself to Bihar, "but
in actual fact of course I spent rather a short time there, I drove about
1200 miles across it and that was it".[55] He arrived at Patna on the
evening of 13 January and spent a week in the state. His first impression stepping off the plane into "the shed which serves as an airport"
was of being besieged, and in the streets towering ramparts of advertising hoardings dwarfed the rickshaw pullers and the homeless who
worked and slept at their base, but as a foreigner he admitted feeling
"better off in P[atna] than Delhi. By comparison with the great cities
there are relatively few beggars – this public cannot afford them."[56]
He saw the burning ghats and "a dismal shed" that was the new electric crematorium, publicised by a leaflet made to order for his sense of
the absurd.

*Low rate burning for families. Discount satisfaction. Ashes for river in 45
minutes.*[57]

He was more impressed by Bihar's civic abuse, in the shape of a Patna
housing estate of 3000 flats for low-income tenants, of which 90 per
cent had been occupied by those who could afford to bribe the state
housing board. On the 15th he drove east along the Ganges to Bhagalpur,
still smoking after the worst violence of the November elections. The
police had a particularly bad reputation at Bhagalpur, with stories circulating about their blinding those they disliked with syringes of acid,
and he and his driver Amresh left the sinister, burned-out town in the
morning to avoid police questions, reaching Ranchi later that day. The
India of pageantry was eluding him, and he it; he passed dozens of
truck wrecks, "a village moated with flowing shit", and through country

whose poverty he recognised by the thinness of its dogs. He was based at Ranchi for three days in a failed attempt to bypass prohibitions on travel to the south; he filled in time with a fairly dull drive to the tiger reserve at Palamau, a visit to Ranchi's large asylum – a British legacy – and a long discussion of sati and dowry deaths with Amresh.

From Ranchi his mood changed as he approached Calcutta, skirting the edge of the Santal tribal area, where the villages were "a Brueghelesque scene of hundreds of figures occupied in every possible activity. . . . The Santals vote Communist," he reported happily. "A Santal can build a bamboo house in 2 days."[58] At Calcutta he met Lesley, whom he had not wanted to take to Bihar with him; she had arrived on the 21st after spending two days at Delhi with friends.

Calcutta aroused his ambivalence. Despite his stomach for violence, his first contact with India, at Calcutta in 1950 on his flight back from Saigon, had repelled him so much, he told me later, that he had not returned to India for thirty-five years.[59] (Not quite true; but when he had travelled to Karachi and Bombay in 1952 he had skipped around and across the sub-continent as far south as he could.) In 1950, after eating at the Great Eastern Hotel with his friend Gautam Chautala, the Reuters' Saigon correspondent also flying back to Paris, he had walked out into Calcutta's streets. Not far from the hotel, among the human bundles of rags lying across the pavement, "A woman who had covered her face with a scarf so that none of it was visible lay legs apart, vagina exposed." He had been more shocked than he had ever been before. "The war in Vietnam had imposed instant anaesthesia. . . . I had permitted a hardening of the tissues of sensitivity. This was different. The exposed vagina within twenty yards of a doorman dressed like a maharajah in turban and scarlet coat was no part of the protocol of peace. I was not ready for Calcutta."[60]

On the 24th he and Lesley left Calcutta's Howrah station on the 6 a.m. express to Bhubaneswar, a seven-hour journey, which "leaves and arrives more or less on time but otherwise ignores all corporal satisfactions".[61] Despite protestations to Gill Coleridge, he was gravitating towards the India he most wanted to see. Effortful days had to be spent (by a Mr Bose, the agent Norman had found) organising a driver and permission to enter southern Orissa state, and filled in by Norman and Lesley with temple-visiting done with a certain laconic resignation, implied by notebook entries such as "Scenes of buggery were rather high up, in corners and not very obvious positions. A crowd of middle-aged Georgian women were inspecting what was on offer." On the 26th he and Lesley moved to Puri. Unable to stay at Mr Bose's and everyone else's recommendation of the Raj-era South Eastern Railway Hotel, they had to put up with a smily tourist shake-down at the mausoleum modernity of the Marina Gardens. All of this, despite Puri's wide shallow beach, its waters sagging with fish, despite the Sun God's temple at Konarak ("Families seem to speed up passing the vast display of erotica, slow down to admire [the] horse and chariot, the young visitors reverse this process"), was a chafing place till Norman could get moving again. On the 29th he and Lesley made a last diversion to the bird sanctuary at the Chilika Lake, but the nesting season was over and they made do with a packed boat trip to the shrine of Kali Jai, a Hindu version of the archetypal girl drowned on her wedding day.

Next morning at seven they finally left, passengers in an Ambassador laden with bottled water, with guide and driver, Forsterian pilgrims to the heart of India. Having seen so much, Norman had acquired a tendency to be reminded wherever he was of somewhere else: India at first like Mexico, "brilliant blue houses under black rocks . . . the nasal membrane-tingling odour of toasting chilies, the peons asleep with their hats pulled over their eyes, the fighting cocks, and the silent, evasive dogs".[62] The journey was comfortable, the vintage motoring notwith-standing, and contributed to his feeling that "all the accidents of travel just sort of came together without really much effort on my part". One lay in the Lewises' guide's motive for accompanying them, a man in his twenties named Sarat (Norman called him Ranjan Prasad) and who "said to me an almost incredible thing, and almost too romantic: that he [just] wanted a free trip plus something of a reward, down to see a tribal girlfriend who he'd seen the year before".[63] They stopped the night on a Dalat-like hilltop at the spa of Taptapani, whose scalding springs were "inhabited by [a] fertility god to whom all pray". Tribal women came to immerse themselves and grope for seeds that dropped from overhanging pods into the pool and its mud floor. "The air is full of anxiety and hope," Norman noted. Was it successful? Of course, Sarat said, but only the tough tribal women could stand the tempera-tures.

In the Orissan hills next day, Mexico was replaced by the "softer splen-dours of one of the countries by the China Sea". What was unexpected about tribal India was its lushness and loneliness, full of appeal for Norman but not entirely idyllic. That day "and succeeding days we drove all day without encountering, except in an occasional small town, a single private car ... there is virtually no travel in the interior of India. There is nowhere to stay, nowhere to eat, and it is not particularly safe."[64] The village of Saora people whom they came across that day, one of the most populous and long-established groups, offered immediate insight into situations he was familiar with: the tribe's hospitality and tidiness (outside the caste system, they had to clean up for themselves), the village as "a hive of every type of activity", the importance of ceremonial drinking, a self-sufficiency based on cow's milk, pulses and the sale of tussore cocoons – and the interference of a governmental "tribal development" programme, in this case a project to store all the village's cow dung, previously dried and burned for fuel, in a concrete bunker and pipe the resulting gas to village houses (no gas resulted and they no longer had dung for fuel).

They drove on towards Gunupur and found further familiar interference in the form of Christian missionary effort, which, though Catholic, at one village, Potasing, conformed to Norman's template of evangelical tragedy: the loss of tribal icon painting and carving, religious confrontation with Hindus, the cutting of trees that produced the villagers' palm wine, the replacement of festivals with hymns on Sunday. But the future for the Saoras was not bright for another reason, Sarat told him. They did not understand money; they were cheated, first by merchants, then moneylenders, and ended by having to sell their land and work as labourers. "Now we have industries more labour is wanting. Also politicians and landowners are desirous of obtaining more land. This is happening thousands of times every day."[65]

In the next week this picture expanded. The Dongria Kondhs at Badpur, also proto-Australoids and ruled by a cheerful and artistic feminism, were in monetary thrall to the sinister Dombs who inserted themselves as middlemen. The nomadic Kutia Kondhs outwitted exploitation with military ferocity, their women wearing daggers in their hair, their babies "g-strings [and] anklets with bells".[66] The Parajas at Koraput, having avoided missionary contact, were gloriously drunk in the throes of a wedding festival. At the same Paraja village Norman discovered the reason for Sarat's eagerness to come along on the journey: that the previous year, at another Paraja village, he and a Paraja girl had fallen for each other. The girl's father had approved the marriage, even renouncing the bride-price. As a lapsing Brahmin with a pantheistic streak, Sarat had let distance lend ardour to the prospect of seeing the girl again. At Jeypore, southern Orissa's entertainment capital ("Our propaganda is travelling 10 kms anywhere for your pleasure. Say yes to life", a cart full of musicians proclaimed), Norman learned that the long memories of tribal people were valued for the longest parts of the *Mahabharata* and that every local village had a "theatre field" set aside. Norman was as usual fascinated by the implicit definition of culture as being the way a tribe found to solve its problems – like the Mirigans' elder who had saved his vegetarian village from starvation by decreeing that the ibis, numerous in local swamps, did not count as an animal and could therefore be eaten.

From Jeypore he and Lesley made daily excursions to tribal areas. A visit to the Kondh market at Kundili made the reality of the Dombs' violent parasitism visible, the market's entries blocked by "trading" points where Dombs fleeced Khond farmers with mounting aggression. One of their last visits was to a village of toga-wearing, matriarchal Koyas, whose hospitality and dignified drunkenness engaged Norman's sympathy and whose marriage custom – the capture of adolescent boys by mature women – he savoured for its outlandishness. Another, to the territory of the Bondas east of the Malakangiri Hills, led to another depressing sighting of missionaries and of the Bondas themselves, a still naked group of belligerent males and females dressed only in jewellery but apathetic.

A return journey was made to Kangrapada, the Paraja village where Sarat had apparently met his tribal girlfriend; though factual uncertainty surrounds it. It did not happen when Norman placed it, at the finale of his account, and in his notebooks no account follows of Sarat meeting his girlfriend again as he does touchingly in the finished book (although at the moment of commitment his Brahmin caste status reasserts itself and he makes an ashamed retreat). Norman prepared himself in his notebook for something worth noting at, as Sarat described it, "the last village where girls have big earrings and dance. Saturated with leisure, standing on the threshold of the Eden from which they will be driven. People gossip, drink, sleep and dance." In the event, although he admired the Parajas' round houses and an old lady who "wears [a] necklace of heavy silver that cannot be removed until death", his only other observation was that the "girls' earrings [are] now smaller".[67]

To judge from notes may be an injustice, especially when Norman's were becoming more spidering and economical (he still managed to fill five small spiral-bound Silvine notebooks en route). Whatever the extent of the alterations he made in composing the journey as a book on his return, the latter corresponds more closely than usual to the sequence and mood of his notebooks. It is also certain that he enjoyed the 4000-kilometre journey, writing to John Hatt from the Hotel New Kenilworth International at Bhubaneswar on 8 February,

We did 1,300 miles in BIHAR – some of them memorable – Lesley joined at Calcutta and we have since covered 1,500 miles in Andhra Pradesh & Orissa – where little can have changed for a century or two. In all these miles – about a quarter of which were through jungles – the only wild animal seen was an enfeebled looking jackal – still I am probably the only person who ever visited Laos, once known as the country of a million elephants, without seeing one. Otherwise it has all been most interesting, and occasionally dramatic – we passed through one village in Orissa where they had just recovered the bodies of 3 people killed by a single sloth bear, which would appear to be the most ferocious of local animals.[68]

Enjoyment not being the *sine qua non* of authorial success, there were reviewers who, when the book came out, would have liked it more composed than it was. The temples-and-gods middle section was criticised, and Hatt himself felt the book was not what it could have been: that

it didn't come together, quite frankly it didn't have enough work in it. And a book's not just a book because you've got 250 pages, a book is more than that. And I think it was probably also, to be brutal, too comfortable going with Lesley. You need to be alone and to talk to people for hours and hours in the evenings. [In Bihar] there's more than enough for five books by Norman. Or he should just have done Orissa and the tribals. . . . One of the great paradoxes, I think, of his life, is that when he was producing masterpieces quite often they were ignored, then he built this terrific name and [wrote] some books of the second line – for him – [that] he knew would be respectfully reviewed and they were.[69]

In mid-September he was "still bashing away" at the book after a family holiday on the Ionian island of Zakynthos that had been "a bit of a farce. Not wanting to hold up the work I was stuck at a table drinking retsina and eating peaches all day, and as a result put on half a stone."[70]

The typescript that he delivered in early October with the working title "Into India" was his first full-length account of a journey since *Golden Earth* in 1952: a remarkable fact for an author described as a travel writer. Did he feel it was a book of the second line? *A Goddess in the Stones*, as it was published in June the following year, started out with the intense verbal photography he had always been able to summon since *A Dragon Apparent*, photoflooding the scene of his arrival at Patna with the notations of maturity, a brilliance part stylistic, part experiential. He had seen more than most UN officers and World Bank experts of the distinction between tolerable rural poverty and the urban version inexorably replacing it.

Floodlit faces radiating joy through the twilight and thickening fog praised Japanese stereos, Scotch whisky, wise investments, luxury footwear and packaged food. Nearing the city the gap left between the bottom of the hoardings and the earth provided glimpses of the homeless, scattered like the victims of a massacre, singly and in groups, who had claimed these uncontested spaces to settle for the night.

The discretion with which he picked out the contrast was great. "There was no room here for the luxury of privacy," he continued. "Men defecated candidly, without effort or concealment."[71] Such an observation was as incidental as the other elements of the scene, a medieval maelstrom transposed to the twentieth century, but few other writers could remind their reader so well of the true contrast, between the Indian homeless and him or her, and "the luxury of privacy". He had read to deepen his account, citing twenty titles in his bibliography from Ibn Battuta and the Portuguese Manrique to the latest surveys of the Anti-Slavery Society. He shaped its tone, and to the accusation that he had been hard on India confessed later that he had "continually found myself leaving out accounts of [caste] atrocities . . . the overall view is one of a baneful sort of civilisation. By comparison with Burma and Thailand, for me it is a sad place."[72] If the book suffers in places from narrative shapelessness, it is perhaps because for all of his writing life Norman had been in love with adversity, his writing, however lyrical, steeled by the struggle; now, at eighty-two, he was also in love with his survival. His great adversary had ceased to be the evanescence of success or the elusiveness of recognition and become merely the evanescence of time, to be battled by writing.

On 15 October he wrote to Gill Coleridge that he had heard from David Godwin, "who rang up on Saturday to say that he liked the book. Enthusiasm expressed in this way by a publisher in the middle of a weekend is a new experience for me, and I was greatly impressed."[73] In July Coleridge had told him that both his UK and US publishers were happy for him to travel "anywhere you like" for another book. He had mentioned Indonesia or Papua New Guinea. On an early November afternoon I visited him at Finchingfield to interview him for a magazine. He was dealing with Cape's suggested revisions to the India book – he had finally inclined himself to the need for editing – and reading the *Indonesia Handbook*, planning a first visit to Indonesia in January. I promised to send him Robert Mitton's photographic study, *The Lost World of Irian Jaya*, which he hadn't been able to get hold of. Enjoyment was a repeated motif of our conversation. The India book had been "extremely" enjoyable to write, the trip "much more enjoyable than I expected it to be". I asked him about the novel he had planned to write the year before. He answered that to write novels required a certain ability to be introspective, which at the moment he seemed to lack. "I find them on the whole for temperamental reasons less enjoyable. You see, I don't really look into myself very much, I really look at the scene around me and that's what gives me immense pleasure, examining these glorious surfaces."

I feel I really ought to write a novel now but I'm becoming self-indulgent and I really want some more. [There has been] Burma, Indo-China, India, three real travel books. The fourth one is an indulgence. I feel I really have to go back to Asia. And the problem of course was to find a place equalling the others in interest, history, unspoilt situations, all the rest of it. It seemed to me I really couldn't think of anywhere else.[74]

He didn't feel misdescribed as a travel writer ("I feel no sense of grievance or neglect") or wish that he could reach a wider public. In his drill sergeant's rasp and with a characteristic sweep of his large hand, settling the matter, "I am, really, extremely happy to have achieved the degree of recognition I have achieved," he said. "I'm delighted with it."[75] Before I left I asked him to sign a copy for me of his recent collection of pieces, *To Run Across the Sea*. He wrote in his choppy script, the three lines at random angles,

For Julian
from NORMAN
Nov. 1990

below, in parentheses, adding

(Semi-invisible man)

About having something to say: I once went to Spain on a week's el cheapo holiday and I remember going to a particular castle, which was quite interesting. By coincidence Norman and Lesley were going quite soon after that, southern Spain, same airport, Malaga, and I wrote them two or three pages on what I thought was worth seeing and what would be fun to do, and they went to this castle, and I had a conversation with them afterwards on the telephone with Norman describing it to me. It was absolutely wonderful, his description of this castle that I had been to. He brought such value added to it in how the noblemen or the servants would have opened this window, seen this extraordinary view. So there was no Celtic fantasy on this occasion, this was his describing what I saw. I had been there but he was just much better at looking.

John Hatt

I don't regard myself as a travel writer, I just happen to be a writer and a traveller at the same time. But eventually you develop, with luck, a certain amount of visual and physical feelings which you previously didn't have. A great influence on me has been Donald McCullin. I learnt from him how beautiful the ordinary can be, ordinary things where previously the only things that attracted me were non-ordinary things. But travelling with him I would see him suddenly spellbound by the beauty of rain drizzling down the mountainside, where I would normally have passed it by.

Norman Lewis

The rain is white with a soft metallic sheen. It suppresses obstinate colours. The country women camouflage themselves against this in blues and reds, big flowered prints that offer some resistance. Floods flow softly carrying orange and white blossoms down the street. The rain cleans the city of unsympathetic outlines: the City Hotel disappears behind the downstrokes of water, the river across the road opposes it successfully with its swirl of white curves. The footballers are undeterred, chasing a ball that floats away from them.

Sulawesi and Irian Jaya notebook

ONE MORE EMPIRE

"Truth is twelve years old"
Goan proverb

"JUST back from 5 days in Barcelona which is excellent at Christmas time; weather like a goodish English April," Norman wrote on New Year's Day 1991. A week later on a drizzling afternoon Pico Iyer visited him at Finchingfield, one of the first of many younger writers to make the pilgrimage to interview him. Iyer had flown from California to meet him, and his erudition made their conversation an interesting fencing match as the American writer made a play to pin Norman's style to that of the Jacobean playwrights because "some of the things that you've written seem almost extremely apposite, I mean especially the wartime stuff, where [you describe] the most unspeakable happenings and atrocities I've read about since Shakespeare's day". Such content was novelistic, he suggested. Norman demurred, replying that it was just a question of phases and that, just as in the 1950s he had "decided to write no more travel" and write novels instead, at present he had "this travel phase on". His Indonesian journey was "a piece of self-satisfaction. I enjoy travelling so much, and I feel that if I leave it much longer I may get arthritis or a bad heart or something. I'd better go while I'm all in one piece, then I'll come back and write a novel or two."[1]

He and Lesley flew to Singapore on 15 January. Lesley flew on to Australia, Norman to Jakarta to meet his son Gawaine who had been travelling in Nepal. The two were to join up to travel together to Irian Jaya first, then to the territory of Aceh in northern Sumatra. They flew to Ujung Pandang on Sulawesi, where Gawaine encountered his father's ability to read and then write a place in only a few hours. It was raining; Sulawesi's capital is a dull paragon of the modern Orient. Next morning, after a night at the Makassar Golden Hotel, Norman told his son he had enough. Gawaine did not believe him. They strolled together down the road. "What do you see?" he asked his son. "Nothing," Gawaine replied. Norman immediately indicated a wedding store where a full-scale rehearsal was taking place, pointing out the couple, wearing ersatz medieval gowns, being photographed in a white plaster stagecoach and a pocket-size Greek temple, and peering through a plaster castle's tower window.

They reached Irian Jaya (West Papua) that evening, 22 January. This western half of New Guinea had been Dutch New Guinea for seventy years when, in 1969, it was annexed by Indonesia. It was an automatic candidate for self-determination – its people's Melanesian cultural roots gave them nothing in common with their Indonesian neighbours – but again Eisenhower's anti-Communism, covetously married to portents of large mineral, oil and gas deposits, fortified Indonesian and US resolve to prevent independence. West Papua is the first instance we have of a UN interim administration. It did not portend well. An "Act of Free Choice" in 1969, with sixteen UN observers for a territory the size of Spain, produced a unanimous "vote" by 1026 Papuan representatives to integrate with Indonesia, at which the Papuans were detained and threatened violently until they assented. Some UN officers, notably U Thant's deputy, knew the vote was a sham and raised no objection.

Ninety per cent of West Papua's land mass is highlands, jungle and swamp and largely unmapped. For a week Norman did little more than mooch around the horror of the coastal settlement of Jayapura, a patched-together territorial centre whose overlay of civilisation fails to mask chasms of squalor, and Wamena, the main settlement of the central highlands. The highlands, watered by the fat bends of the Baliem river and discovered by white men only in 1938, are peopled by 100,000 Neolithic tribesmen who were headhunters before Protestant missionaries began arriving in 1946. (In 1985 I hiked alone for three weeks in the central highlands, living in Dani tribal villages. From the air then you saw the Baliem valley as Richard Archbold saw it in 1938, an 80-kilometre cradle of green, the sun sparkling back from the irrigation channels in village gardens, the stockaded villages everywhere like tidy mushroom clumps: a scene of lush peace belied by the military transports and hefty Indonesian garrison at ground level, there to suppress the long-standing OPM independence movement. At least 100,000 Papuans have died as a result of the occupation and violent repression.) Norman visited various villages of the Dani, stocky, athletic agriculturists addicted to ritual warfare, and was befriended by one, Namek, who had a few words of English, when doing the tourist sights of visiting the villagers' smoked ancestors. He received an invitation to a pig feast at Namek's village; he also observed the hapless behaviour of guests at the Wamena Palace Hotel, attempting to buy black market spirits in a dry town, and tried to discover more about Indonesian Army activities. "Josephus says that 4 bombers and 7 helicopters used in DANI operation," he noted, referring to one of the regular reprisals against those suspected of OPM affiliation or even found to be flying Papua's Morning Star flag. It had been, as Gawaine says, "a fairly hard-core journey", but this time it was clear that thirty-six hours, or even a week, were inadequate for much more than a reconnaissance.

On the 28th they flew back to Sulawesi, and on the 30th were in Aceh. A long-standing separatist movement and the Indonesian military's manoeuvres to crush it had reportedly made travel difficult, and when they reached Medan they were informed by the government tourist office that no buses were running. They had not wanted to take a car, feeling it would insulate them from whatever Acehnese life they could locate, but had no alternative, and, initially surprised that they should be allowed to take a car into a war zone, were less so when they found that with the Toyota that was delivered to them also came a minder, "Mr Andy". Gawaine viewed the journey through its boredom and restrictions and the annoyances of Mr Andy. The journey's surprise for him was what his father saw.

We had to drive along the coast of Sumatra and try and conjure up some facts. And this is what always amazed me about Dad. That trip, I'd have thought nothing happened, we just went from place to place and it was just this horrible mixture of grim. . . . There was obviously a fair bit of poverty about but not poverty in the African sense of poverty, just poor people mixed with karaoke bars in the middle of really weird fishing villages and places.

We'd drive along for hours over pretty rough old roads with Andy trying to tell us what we should and shouldn't do and where we should go and getting it all wrong and saying, "This'll be interesting for you." And I was thinking, What are you going to write about? There's nothing seems to be happening here. And we got to Banda Aceh which is just like a nice, big bustling town, it was perfectly pleasant, we stayed in a nice hotel and we went out and saw a few bars and restaurants, we saw a few things, we met some people, I can't remember there was much focus or purpose to it. It amazed me that he could get so many pages out of this. Obviously to make it interesting the chronology was reversed, and certain things happened at the same place which didn't happen in real life. It didn't really matter, these things occurred. But I just found it boring and I thought, Christ, what are you going to write about here? This is a boring trip.[2]

Norman did not find much excitement in Aceh – military and separatist activity, for one thing, was always just unseen – but was still able to paint a journey of verbal landscapes, of Banda Aceh, "birthplace of Muslim fundamentalism", with its atmosphere of "Franco's Spain immediately after the last war", of Lame and its "aroma of baffled expectations and stagnation" and the Lauser National Park, "a billowing Sahara doodled over with patterns of ash". He continued to have trouble with the Indonesian diet – in Aceh far more limited and badly cooked than he had expected – and survived mainly on packets of biscuits he had brought with him.

He was back in England in mid-February, having been away for a month, putting the journey in a positive light.

Just got back. Irian Jaya was excellent, although difficult in the matter of internal travel. I also went to the northern tip of Sumatra, where a separatist insurrection had been going on for some time. The Indonesian guide I took along stayed a week then took off after one of the locals had significantly drawn a finger across his throat, having learned where my friend was from. An interesting place – all the more so through the demise of tourism.[3]

Part of the plan for the next leg of the journey was to learn Indonesian. "It seems to [be] prone to surrealism," he wrote to Gill Coleridge on 22 March. "I've just mastered a list of phrases, one of them being 'Holding three orchids the man kicked the dog repeatedly'."[4]

While writing a piece about Namek and the Danis' survival for Justine Picardie, his loyal editor at the *Independent* magazine, he faced up to another moment of megalomaniac editing, this time from Gary Fisketjohn, now at Knopf, who having taken seven months to offer his editorial comments was suggesting extensive rewriting for the US edition of *A Goddess in the Stones*. Among the hundreds of pink file copies of letters Gill Coleridge wrote tirelessly on Norman's behalf is an unsent fax to Fisketjohn in which she noted that "I really am appalled. . . . It's almost as though you haven't read his books before and didn't know what to expect . . . he is regarded as one of the world's best travel writers and you just don't do this to him. He's not 18 – he's 81, for heavens sake!"[5] Another publisher was not hard to find: Jack Macrae of Holt bought the book as soon as the Knopf contract was cancelled and the Indonesia book too, which Cape had just contracted for £50,000.

Norman's publishing record was at a general high. *A Goddess in the Stones* appeared on 4 June, and Jonathan Keates wrote that "There is something uncanny about Lewis's endless ability to deliver. He pronounces no sledgehammer verdicts, thunders no warnings or prophecies, yet it is hard to imagine any more effective threnody for India."[6] Disappointment came from Geoffrey Moorhouse that "it's not particularly good Norman Lewis, who can be very good indeed" (though bizarrely placing Norman as "not one of the great stylists, certainly not a Morris or a Raban"),[7] and from William Dalrymple who called the middle section "dull" and caught Norman, he thought, on his panic whenever he was faced with beauty; but Dalrymple still called his prose "a joy to read . . . he can make the most boring things interesting".[8] The *Sunday Telegraph* published his portrait of Calcutta from the book, and on the front of the same section ran a full-page interview by Nicholas Shakespeare entitled "The Spellbound Scrutineer", which drew an amused response from Norman.

Dear Nicholas
A note to say that your various misrepresentations of our chat went down well here. Despite my description of this village as a terrible place, the gardener now turns up in the mornings ten minutes earlier than formerly, and it has been reported that some approval has been voiced in the local re my alleged brothel-creeping activities. Using an Essex recommendation of the kind, alas, in these days hardly every heard, one regular is supposed to have remarked "well at least it shows he's some blood in his shins". I'm accepted at last – and only you to thank![9]

Publishing a new book did not divert him from the fate of his earlier books, which he returned to regularly. Any practising writer is aware that he or she is positioned in the public mind at the value level of his or her last book, and at the same time keeps a strictly private archive of the values of its precursors. He was "sad and bewildered", he wrote to his agent in early July, about the near disappearance of *Voices of the Old Sea* and *Jackdaw Cake*, which he blamed on

Hamish Hamilton,[10] although, the biographer feels bound to say in both a confusion of roles and self-defence, both had been published in paperback by Penguin, and it is the paperback not hardback edition that carries a book's life after publication. His Eland Books editions preoccupied him too. Gill Coleridge had already suggested to John Hatt that he allow hardbacks to be published, and now suggested that Penguin take over his Lewis titles as mass market paperbacks, with appropriate compensation to him; she also reminded him of the poor state of his US distribution.

On 9 August Hatt replied passionately, defending his work and Eland's record. Penguin would never be as vigorous as he had either in promoting or keeping the books in print, he wrote. "Where were these paperback companies, when I went through the initial struggle? They then took the view that it was impossible to promote these authors. I even went to see the head of Penguin ... but he told me there was no commercial prospect for selling any of our titles."[11] He pointed to the reprint policies of larger publishers, to let books go out of print and build up "dues" from bookstores for months, even years, while Eland reprinted as soon as an edition was exhausted so that its list was always available. It was something of a vindication of his argument that as he was replying to Gill Coleridge, Penguin, having been offered *A Goddess in the Stones* for a paperback edition, withdrew in the face of a higher offer from another house, Picador. Coleridge acknowledged the irony and gently suggested that should Picador show itself worthy in future, she would suggest that it offer him "an outrageously generous advance" for his backlist titles. Again the matter rested.

Norman was away during this renewed engagement. In early July he flew to Jakarta on the second leg of his Indonesian journey. The plan was to meet his daughter Bubs and from there descend eastwards with her to Bali and then to East Timor. Access to Timor turned out to have been made lengthy and hard: the half of the island that Indonesia had invaded in 1975 had been open to foreigners for a year but at Denpasar a non-facilitation policy, clearly imposed from above, operated at the ticket office. It took father and daughter eight days to get seats on a flight to Dili on 13 July. Flying across the Flores Sea, Bubs made friends with three nuns, two returning to an orphanage that they ran in the mountains and the third just arrived from Rome to join them. The Lewises had a lift from the nuns into town, and both put up for the first night at the Hotel Turismo.

Borne from airport by tiny, chortling Salesian sisters. Can it be possible that devotion and a celibate life can generate this outflowing of joy?[12]

The verbal photographer began hoarding images: the hotel, by reputation under constant watch but in reality more shabby than sinister; the unemployed seafront; dusk.

The hotel's wide wooden staircase has taken on that special dry and dusty look of staircases from which the carpeting has long since been stripped.

The trees here with thin, sharp leaves, sprout from bare earth, polished here and there by erosion.

Beached craft display a desolation that no terrestrial building can match (banished by the sea and rejected by land).

Evening scene a bedraggled romanticism. Families searching the wide sand at low tide. Small boys climbing the coconut palms. Strewn wreckage backlit in an incredible sunset.[13]

Travel's accidents came together in Dili when next morning the Salesian nuns invited Norman and Bubs to travel with them and stay at their orphanage. His account of their stay at Venilale, paralleled by his retelling of the landings and atrocities of the 1975 invasion, made the East Timor section, though short, the centre of gravity of the eventual book: a holocaust and its aftermath, veiled in concealment and remoteness. (Even the story of the "Balibo five", two Australian, one New Zealand, two British journalists murdered at the border town of Balibo by Indonesian parachutists in April 1975, their bodies then dressed in Portuguese uniforms and propped up behind machine guns, is barely known and remains uninvestigated by their governments. This is not to forget the at least 200,000 Timorese deaths in the occupation and conflict.)

Norman developed an unreserved respect for the sisters at Venilale: as who could not? They had survived the Indonesian invasion, and then the mountain bombings and clearances intended to sweep Xanana Gusmao's Fretilin resistance from its forest refuges, they retained an arrangement with the Indonesian Army that somehow did not touch their pastoral role – one of the orphanage's residents he met was Gusmao's wife, Justina, with one child by her husband and one by her gaoler in prison – and they defended their piety with as much bounty as strictness. The window onto Timorese life that they provided, and the excursions they enabled to other missions, Norman could not have found elsewhere. He fully acknowledged the complete contrast between them and the arrogant "affection for materialism" displayed by Protestant fundamentalists. Their poverty and charity was a resounding proof of the Weberian hypothesis that capitalism could never have been invented by Catholics.

[At] the beginning of our friendship, there was something slightly daunting about the Salesian religious uniform, its archaic style hinting at a repudiation of the physical world. For the first moments in the striking presence of the 32-year-old Sister Marlene in her immaculate habit, I was touched by the memory of medieval austerities, of the visions and voices of such as Teresa of Avila. Within minutes I was to see her demonstrating a vigorous Portuguese folk-dance to a class of orphan girls, and the original impression faded out with an article by a journalist who had smuggled himself into East Timor at the time of the worst trouble, and depicted her struggling through the thickets of the Soul Mountain to the assistance of children under attack by the planes. Thereafter I was reminded less of Teresa of Avila and more of Villon's "bonne Jeanne" (que les Anglois brûlèrent à Rouen).[14]

Physically East Timor knocked him out. While he was away John Hatt had written to him disquietedly about the attempts to persuade him to sell mass market rights in Eland titles. From Finchingfield he wrote to Hatt on 15 August to "Be sure I shall never underestimate the great effort you put into the discovery and promotion of my books – and of course I owe you an eternal debt of gratitude on that account. If BOTH of us can benefit by any modification of present publishing arrangements, that is another matter. . . . The trip on the whole was strenuous and I have been in bed with what the doctor terms 'exhaustion' since getting back. Otherwise quite exciting."[15]

The final part of his Indonesia research, a new incursion into Irian Jaya, was held over till the following year for several reasons: he was writing; the best time to go was the English summer; interest in filming the journey had been shown by a television production company, and television, plus the inevitably sluggish Indonesian permission to film, took time to arrange. Additionally a very slight suspicion that his health needed time to recover, and that he was finally tiring of the atmosphere if not the effort of violent places, surfaced just before Christmas in a letter to his and Sid Perelman's mutual friend, Leila Hadley (now Hadley Luce).

Dear Leila,

I was really enchanted to hear from you and to be given an opportunity to tap away with the old worn-down finger in reply. . . . Good to know that you're going as strong as ever, and able to gather up the last of the places everyone should see before they surrender to the final depravity of our times. I still manage to collect a few topographical rarities. This year has been a little better than average, with Banda Aceh, the northern tip of Sumatra, and the interior of Irian Jaya. A second trip was to East Timor. . . . If the permit comes through – which is by no means certain – I shall be going back to Irian Jaya with a television crew in June. This will be the last of Indonesia so far as I am concerned. Alas all these very interesting places tend to be hard going – many mosquitoes, too much plain rice, and too many police with their hands on their guns.[16]

At the end of the year complicated publishing questions came up again. Penguin had surrendered the rights to *Jackdaw Cake*; Gill Coleridge hoped that David Godwin and Norman's new paperback publisher, Peter Straus, could between them include a new edition as part of a deal that Straus had suggested for an omnibus edition of Norman's three Asian books. The proposal was an interesting one, but would make another itch for scratching, as Eland Books held rights in two of the three Asian titles. And it contained a paradox, in the form of a sort of tacit denial, or at least lack of acknowledgment in the discussions so far, that Norman, despite the esteem he was held in, was not a fastselling or bestselling author and had not been since the 1950s. Despite – because of? – the quality of his writing, and despite the enthusiasm of publishers like Godwin and Straus, he occupied the generally shunned outer area of the commercial publishing map whose heart is represented by the decisive principle of economies of scale: an author who sold slowly, in modest numbers. With care and attention he would never gravitate to the centre of the map, but he could sell steadily. The truth is that in one respect what Norman wanted – his books generally available in good-quality editions – had so far not been achieved better by anyone than Eland Books. What continued to damage John Hatt's case was that in eight years he had not succeeded in making Norman's books similarly available in America.

In mid-February 1992 *A Goddess in the Stones* won a Thomas Cook Travel Book Award jointly with Gavin Young's *In Search of Conrad*, an accolade that rebounded on sales, with Picador reprinting its paperback edition. (It went on to sell more than 23,000 that year.) Paper preparations went on for the television film. Would Lesley go? Filming was first timed for March; on 9 March Bernard Clark Productions and Gill Coleridge were still negotiating Norman's fee. (Other film interest, in the form of requests for options for *The Honoured Society* and *Naples '44*, was still, half welcome, half nuisance, rife. Mike Radford's film of *Voices of the Old Sea* had not progressed.) On 20 March Norman wrote to say that Don McCullin was "very keen to come to Irian Jaya" and that the film's director was equally enthusiastic for McCullin to participate. Lesley was able to withdraw. Fees were agreed, but in June the filming slipped to September, then to October.

Norman continued writing the rest of the book; seeing friends; always stimulated by signs of life on his behalf or others'. He had evolved, in his own way, a circle among that younger generation of writers. Colin Thubron remembers his attentiveness, "After reading my first book on Russia, he wrote me a letter which I still cherish ('I only read two books a year' ...),", and a sense that "His (deceptively) simple style, his irony, his way with dialogue, and his sharp observation of the anomalous – not to mention his political seriousness – would appeal to a younger generation more easily than any of his contemporaries."[17] A good review, or bad, of a book by a younger writer he had corresponded with produced a note, as did any article he liked. To Ian Thomson whose *Bonjour Blanc*, about Haiti, had been panned by a reviewer he wrote,

I read the review on Sunday and thought it so atrocious I noted bits of it to Lesley. Did you by any chance make an enemy of this girl? I had an even worse one by Geoffrey Moorhouse in the *Guardian*. ... This will be overlooked in the general impression created by all the excellent reviews you have had – for example the Ballard one.[18]

I remember the kindness and quickness of his reactions. The previous September I had finished a book about a journey to the US nuclear test range at Kwajalein atoll in the mid Pacific. I asked him if he would read it. When I sent it he wrote back within a day after reading twenty pages, and wrote again a few days later when he had finished it, offering a quotation for the jacket. In his notebooks I came across three pages filled with tryouts for the grossly indulgent quote he eventually sent.

He liked to see visitors, as Lesley says, "occasionally". Angus MacKinnon, his editor at *Granta*, recalls that "On more than one occasion he'd send you a rare edition of one of his books, quite unprompted. Norman and Lesley were wonderful hosts. Saturday lunch at Finchingfield was always great fun, although no one was ever entirely confident in Norman's abilities to get the chemical mix in the swimming pool right. 'It might feel a little sharp,' he'd say with a shrug."[19] Ian Jack remembers

sitting in the car with the window down as we were about to leave one Sunday evening and asking Lesley if there was a way of reaching the M11 without going down the crowded Bishops Stortford–Colchester Road. A highly detailed solution followed. "Don't turn right at the Cock and Bull, go straight and then turn right at the house with the bouncy castle, then take the second left when you see the old railway bridge" and so on, with me nodding as though I could remember what she was telling me. Norman came over and said something like, "That's right. Pretend to understand while not really understanding – the predicament of the traveller down the ages."[20]

Pico Iyer, who published a long profile of Norman in *Traveler* magazine in June, was invited to lunch when he came back to England that July. "I took the train in and had lunch with him and spent most of the afternoon just chatting in the garden – I remember his being very proud about having a bird in the garden that could whistle 'What shall we do with the drunken sailor?'"

After that, I felt he had better things to do than entertain me, but I remember, in between his offers to come up to London and collect me any time I wanted to visit, his reading a book I wrote about Cuba, and saying something like "Glad to see fewer ophthalmologists' conventions from North Korea" (in reference to an earlier piece I'd written about the island at least two years before), I was surprised that a man in his eighties would take any time at all to read the work of fumbling apprentices.[21]

"Shrieks [of] reptilian ecstasy" met him and McCullin at the Mansapur Rani Hotel at Sentani, Jayapura's airport, on 19 October.

A wistful dog calls at regular intervals. The minder snoozes lightly through a breathless snoring. At night tree frogs enclose the compound with their low pitched barks.[22]

After a day of negotiation with the MAF – Missionary Aviation Fellowhip – office he, McCullin and the television crew flew directly to the village of Endoman in the highlands. The people there were not Dani but Yali, who in some cases still dressed in the traditional mass of bamboo hoops around their middle that they combined with a Dani-like penis gourd. Neither helped in keeping out the cold and damp of a forest village at 1750 metres, but their way of life, structured around poor cultivation in barren mountain landscape and limited ritual warfare to keep their numbers down, provided no luxuries. They burned fires constantly in their huts and proudly clung to a complicated system of ancestor-worship and taboo. Inevitably they had been got at by evangelists: in an early conversation the chief, Yurigeng, seemed to parrot phrases about the benefits the Lord Jesus had brought, until Norman asked him how many men he had killed in wars. "[Suddenly] there was an unmistakable flicker of interest – perhaps even the ghost of a patrician smile. ... 'Twenty-seven,'" he told Norman through the interpreter, Catan.[23] Whatever Norman's inclination to romance the tribal people he encountered, there is no doubt about the Papuan highlanders' keen-ness for a fight. (In 1985, during a lull in fighting between two villages, I watched bands of young men taking up positions for the next skir-mish: a series of battles that led three years later to a climax in which more than a dozen were killed.)

Norman spent ten days at Endoman. He was welcomed by the Yali who were bored and restless and happy to defy the Indonesian decree banning tribal conflict and stage a battle for the film crew. He was also able to satisfy the needs of the director, Chris Hooke, while gath-ering what he needed. Hooke thought "the Endoman section went very smoothly and was very good . . . he was extraordinarily amenable, there was nothing he wouldn't do". But the diet of Cup-a-Soup and Endoman's misty, drizzling climate brought serious problems out of a clear sky when the crew flew down to the Baliem valley. No special arrange-ments had been made for Norman, and at eighty-four he had by a fraction overstepped his constitution's limits. Around Wamena he did more filming, interviewing the chief, Obaharok – who in the 1970s had briefly married the American anthropologist, Wyn Sargent, before the Indonesians expelled her – and the chief's present wife, Aku, a calm, genial Dani woman who had lost six fingers and both ears to the custom of lopping as a ritual mark of grief.

Three days after arriving at Wamena, Norman showed symptoms of the bronchitis endemic among the Yalis. He could not walk far, so as a point of practicality the crew had the equivalent of a sedan chair made so that he could be carried. McCullin thought this a "prattish" idea, but it aided mobility. The mistake, Hooke realised, was to film him being carried.

"I think it was with a kind of mixture of bemusement and fear and annoyance that he went along with that. I got the feeling in the end that he felt he shouldn't have done that. I think he felt humiliated." Unintentionally the director had triggered one of Norman's fiercest sensitivities, to any suggestion that he was vulnerable or old. At the interview with Obaharok, relations worsened. Norman began having difficulty hearing, despite having a hearing aid.

Finally I think I said to Norman, "Maybe you should check the battery on your hearing aid, Norman."

And he got really cross. He said, "Oh I suppose your camera batteries never run out. They seem to run out all the time, actually, if I remember correctly." It was, "Don't talk about batteries, you run out of batteries all the time." Anyway he checked his battery and sure enough it was flat and he put a new battery in and away we went.

That was really the first sign of irritation from him and we were all looking at each other, and we didn't quite know whether he was joking or not. I remember we all discussed it later and [were] wondering "Is this a sea-change, is something going on here?" And then of course it just got worse after that.[24]

Norman's annoyance was a function of his illness; in normal circumstances, and still to those he trusted, his courtesy remained impeccable. McCullin brought him "cups of tea, and you'd say to Norman, 'Would you like a cup of tea, Norman?' 'Oh, as long as it doesn't inconvenience anybody.' And here was he, half-dead." The bronchitis weakened him to the point that the crew stopped filming for three days while he went to bed. The next stage of the journey was to be the most challenging, and now looked doubtful. Norman was adamant that he wanted to continue as soon as he recovered. There was a reason. The crew had got permission to film at the Freeport copper mine, 150 kilometres west of Wamena and 4000 metres above sea level. Freeport was a place to which very few outsiders had gained access – it was also a synthesis on a huge scale, amounting to an archetype, of Norman's founding conflict: the confrontation between tribal people and the capitalist model. West Papua possesses the third largest reserve of copper and the largest reserve of gold on the planet. To this wilderness came Freeport-McMoRan in 1967. No mine on earth moves as much rock each day as its Grasberg mine (production in the first years of this century was between 200,000 and 300,000 tonnes of ore a day). At night from the coast the mine's floodlights hang glowering amber in the sky, 4 kilometres up, but nothing seen from sea level can prepare the eye for the mine itself. The spectacular access road drives up through mountains without foothills, and where the blue peaks of the Jayawijaya range burst vertically out of freezing silken mists, Freeport's engineers simply shaved the crest off one knife-edge ridge after another until the surface was wide enough for two 40-tonne trucks to pass. At Mile 68 is Tembagapura, the mine's all-American township; at Mile 74 a cable tramway transports the visitor the last 1500 metres through the clouds to the Grasberg's summit. Sliced like a boiled egg, the huge inverted cone at its centre is deepening year by year as the ore is blasted out and carried to the surface in a never-ending caravan of 200-tonne trucks. The OPM and local people have attacked the mine in retaliation for land expropriations. The army has retaliated, bombing, rocketing and strafing villages with US-supplied warplanes. In 1999 when I went up to the mine, Freeport were still sufficiently worried by OPM activity to send their explosives up in dummy convoys, with only one truck in the line loaded. For the highland Amungme tribe, on whose land the Grasberg stands, the mine was, and is, a cultural and spiritual cataclysm. The earth they walk on is their ancestral mother, the mountain her head: in the past, whenever someone died, they used to be taken to the Grasberg's summit. The mine, in their belief system, is gouging out their mother's brains before their eyes.

"He was absolutely insistent, because Tembagapura was the place he wanted to go to all along. And by the time he got to Tembagapura he actually was on the mend. When we were driving into Tembagapura I remember he was right on the edge of the seat, watching everything."

But another point of friction abraded Norman's relations with the film's director, that the visit had been set up on a strict "no awkward questions" basis. Hooke had decided any such questions would be addressed in commentary afterwards.

"Charlotte [Moore, the assistant director] and I really set that up, that was the other thing that Norman got very annoyed at. We set it up through John Cutts [in charge of the Tembagapura Community Development Project] and there were all sorts of provisos, but Norman had just got there and he just wanted to do his thing, and here was this film crew telling him, 'Norman, let's cool it.' He didn't really appreciate that." The restrictions Norman was suffering were hardly worse than those on any comparable television film, but, used to working things out his own way, and running out of strength, they angered him. He insisted on accompanying the crew in the mine's cable car to the highest plateau, at 3960 metres – another demanding journey – where they spent the morning. When he came down he went to Tembagapura's medical clinic. There the Australian doctor told him he had pneumonia, and told him he should leave immediately for his health's sake. Privately he thought Norman was very lucky to have survived the day. Don McCullin volunteered to leave with him. They faced several plane journeys and more than 30 hours' flying to get home. By the time Norman arrived back at Heathrow he did not know where he was.

It was a hell of a long journey back to Jakarta. At Jakarta I checked him in at British Airways and he had a Club ticket, I was in animal class. I said to the purser on the plane, "Can you do me a favour? This man's very sick, he's a distinguished writer in England. Can you call me if anything goes wrong?" I went downstairs to my seat and he came down and said, "Why don't you sit with your friend and care for him?" So I got him home and they were all waiting for him at the airport, and later I got these wonderful messages from his children, saying, "Thank you for saving my father's life." I didn't save his life, he saved his own life because he had that willpower.[25]

Through the summer and in Norman's absence, long publishing negotiations were slowly turning to ancient enmities. Cape had made an offer to publish an omnibus of Asian books, and Gill Coleridge had written to John Hatt pointing out that Norman would be "thrilled" and asking if he would have any objections. In September Hatt refused. Any Cape/Picador omnibus would sit on bookstore shelves next to Eland editions and seriously reduce their sales. Coleridge conciliated, and in the face of pressure, mainly that it was Norman's wish, Hatt relented, but asked for at least £10,000 to cover lost sales – a near colossal amount for an omnibus. Before leaving for Irian Jaya Norman had written to Coleridge with a generous offer to cover Hatt's losses from the edition personally, but with his final sentence – "Thus he could not lose anything but face" – Norman pointed to exactly the reason why generosity was not likely to be enough. Very much face was involved (and face was something of whose importance Norman was himself highly sensible). The curiosity in the clash between Hatt and Coleridge is that on one side an agent was conscientiously and insistently looking after her client's interests; on the other a small publisher was underlining in each letter he wrote (and Hatt wrote passionately long letters) that "After all my struggles, it is only fair that I am now allowed to look after what I perceive to be *my* interests".[26] Hatt and Norman, in fact, shared an intriguing concert of values. Hatt's present struggles were scarcely any different from what Norman's had once been; and nor was the trenchancy of his defence. Both were upset by the ending of their friendship. On 3 December Gill Coleridge finally, with what feels like almost mesmerised weariness, handed the matter over to Godwin and Straus, writing to Hatt that "we've aired this matter long enough, so unless we hear improved terms from Cape and Picador we should let it drop".

With two weeks of bed rest at Finchingfield and Lesley's care, Norman recovered enough to get on a plane with her and fly to Madeira for three weeks in January, where he was able to finish writing the second Irian Jaya journey and his account of his visit to the Freeport mine. The cadences of its last pages were forcefully similar to those of *A Dragon Apparent*.

Legal quibbles, evasions and the manipulations of the law are used against tribal people like the Amungme who have been ousted from their lands. . . . This perhaps is the one area in which Freeport, whose engineering achievements have amazed the world, may be said to have revealed an Achilles heel of ineptitude. ... But perhaps the government is at the back of its refusal to make reparation. ... All these minority people who have populated the innumerable islands of Indonesia and have developed their own separate languages and culture, are now to be persuaded or compelled to surrender to the central government the resources upon which they and their ancestors have lived. At best they will become unskilled labourers working in mines, or in the plantations that are to replace the vanishing rainforests, or growing rice for the surplus population of Java dumped in their midst. Those like the Amungme who refused to accept this future can expect to be shoved away out of sight and forgotten. In this way the empire is consolidated.[27]

He delivered *An Empire of the East* on 8 February. The achievement – the largely uninsured flourish – of the journeys to Indonesia made an adventurous book. If they were an indulgence, as he called them, they were an indulgence of a specific Lewisian sub-category: asceticism as hedonism, the pursuit of harmony in the bare minimum, hedonism as a masterfully self-denying discipline. His survival of them in his mid eighties made the journeys outstanding reclamations of the land of adventure, a response of his unceasing escape reflex supplemented by all the sharpness of escape from physical ageing's insuperable "less" and "without". He was, I think, satisfied with the result. His mood all year was more than relaxed; what the French call *désinvolte*. On 28 January he broke the silence with John Hatt, assuring him that he quite understood his decision but that "it would be a pity if small differences over publishing attitudes were to be allowed to interfere with our friendship" and he hoped to hear from him. He would probably have been feeling cheerful that day. The *Guardian* newspaper in its "Centipede" column, that each week sought to mediate "the best of the 20th century", had named him its travel writer, with

that precious gift ... of lifting the curtain on a brilliantly coloured world which has vanished or is unattainable.

This, surely, is the secret. ... No one has exploited this gift more memorably than Norman Lewis. He has written conventional narratives, among which *A Dragon Apparent* – about south-east Asia – is outstanding. Even better, however, are the books in which he hardly travels at all: *Naples '44*, his account of wartime chaos in Italy, and *Voices of the Old Sea*, a record of his life in a village on the Costa Brava in Spain just before mass tourism was invented.

Little enough happens in the book. They fish for tunny and sardines. There is a feud over cork trees. A fiesta takes place, a storm breaks. The first hotels are built, foreigners arrive. Of the narrator, we learn little. He blends into what he describes with such subtle, elegiac passion. This is the Lewis way, which makes him the master.

For the rest of winter and spring he dealt with the new book's demands: revisions, an introduction, final rewriting of the Irian Jaya section, commentary for the film. In the text he hardly mentioned his pneumonia, except in a typo that, uncorrected, gave him a "long infection", but writing to a friend he described it in one of his typical sentences of sly crescendo as "some very mild bug, no more than a nuisance, but which kept me in and out of bed for some months".[28] (The construction is Pythonesque in its use of an understatement that turns out to be absurd inverted exaggeration.) He remained negative only about the film, writing to Gill Coleridge after he had seen the rough cut that he thought the right word for it would be "ordinary". "A slight coolness", he said, had developed between himself and Chris Hooke over Hooke's "lengthy" use of interviews with the mine's public relations person, John Cutts, whom Hooke had allowed to unbalance the film (another way of putting this might be that the director had not allowed Norman's view to prevail: Norman's reaction was a proof that he saw no difference between a travel film, which this had been commissioned as, and a documentary).

Coolness underestimated the temperature: his reaction had been icy when he saw that Hooke had also included an interview of him in bed with bronchitis at Wamena. Hooke recalls, "I got a letter from him. The main thing I remember was [him saying] 'I think this is an absolutely un-artistic film.' That stuck in the stomach, coming from an artist like Norman. [Then] Lesley rang us up and said, 'Norman really is objecting to this scene.' I said, 'Well it's not a problem, Lesley, we'll just cut it out, if it's upsetting him. It's not crucial.' 'Would you? *Please* do that.' We [had] put it in with great intentions because we thought it showed his fortitude and humour and strength, you know, 'Norman, you're ill, do you really want to go to Tembagapura?' And, 'Nothing will stop me.'"[29]

In May he wrote to Gill Coleridge about his next book, mentioning a novel "about which I have been thinking on and off for years". In June he signed a contract with Picador for a new extended edition of

Jackdaw Cake. "Peter Straus came for lunch. I am interested in the pauses in the conversation while (I suspect) he schemes."

He is interested – apparently very much so – in my doing a book for him of eleven pieces of 20 pages each, but this wants thinking about. Peter is very clearly travel-book orientated. The question is should I take a break from non-fiction at this point?

He is also putting an omnibus proposition up to John – which I am sure will not take off.[30]

Unforeseeably, it did. Hatt and Straus had lunch in July, and without warning Hatt agreed to the omnibus, against an advance of £3500. Other arrangements, including American distribution, were put up for possible collaboration. Coincidentally, with one disturbance settled another surfaced as Norman's publisher at Cape, David Godwin, quit. Godwin's career at Cape had begun at Bedford Square – Norman had liked the return to Heartburn House – and for a time Godwin had been able to run Cape as his own domain within Random House, its group owner. Moving subsequently to Random House's group building south of Victoria, he had seen more changes than he cared for. He was succeeded by Dan Franklin – a succession that Norman, after his courteous exchange of letters with Franklin before he left Secker five years before, greeted with his best cautious approval.

Franklin felt the force of his and Lesley's warmth as well as his (well disguised) literary presence. "I'd never met anybody like him. I'd read *Naples '44* so I had the idea of this godlike figure, the funniest, this funny, funny, funny, brilliant writer, the best, the Graham Greene quote and all that, and then you met this figure who so wasn't that at first sight. And then half an hour later he was that. And once one had become significant in their lives, they were kinder than anyone I've ever met. To give you an example, for six months I had a slipped disc in my neck which nobody diagnosed and it made it incredibly difficult to read. I scarcely knew them at that stage, but I got a call from Lesley saying, 'Come to the house in Islington at six o'clock on Friday, we've got something for you,' and they had got their local carpenter in Finchingfield to make a bookstand so that I didn't have to bend my head to read manuscripts."[31]

At the end of July Gill Coleridge wrote that the question of what Norman might write next was closer to being answered, as she was about to lunch with Franklin. "I wanted to hear whether he's keen to commission you to do a novel next, or, like Straus, would want more travel. Then I can advise which would be financially the most lucrative."[32] These encounters at the crossroads where writing and money meet, a standard (if not always sufficiently frequent) feature of a practising writer's life, don't tell the whole story of Norman's feelings about writing another novel. He had gone on writing stories, including the last one he had published two years before, "After the Earthquake", and an unpublished but haunting sketch of loss, "The Autobahn Back to Stalingrad", in which a German pensioner at intervals of years receives unaddressed cards from her lost wartime fiancé bearing the same message, "*Ich komme wieder*" ("I'll come back"). But he had, or had developed, a reserve about fiction. He didn't enjoy it as much, and gave his interlocutors an impression of mistrusting its truthfulness. There are other traces here too, of the youngish Cape writer who in 1951 intended to be "a good novelist" but mistrusted himself.

On 16 September *An Empire of the East* was published. The combination of admiration and affection was widespread, noting Norman's age (mainly wrongly), his courage, his "modest, self-effacing humour" that "never prepares you for his calm indictments of butchery",[33] "his resolve, his integrity",[34] "infinitely sure touch",[35] "delight in the picturesque, the quirky, the beautiful".[36] The book was "witty, erudite, always enthralling . . . vintage Lewis",[37] "one of his best books since *A Dragon Apparent*",[38] not "a book to rank alongside his classics [but] an astonishing work of great range",[39] "a powerful work, made brilliant by its simplicity".[40] Anthony Burgess, echoing Luigi Barzini, wrote that "His prose is almost edible. In old age he is writing better than ever."[41] Most reviewers said, or implied, that only Norman "would have travelled to find . . . out [what he did]; only he would have reported it".[42] Most wished for more. Norman wrote to Ian Thomson that his "was a wonderful review not only from the ego-restorative point of view but because it was professional. I had several of the other kind, very nice in their own way, but like the (probably last) one by Anthony Burgess who spent much space on telling us about Malaysia in his days. . . . [PS] You are entirely wrong about my mellowing. I am as ferocious as ever – but in a more subterranean way!"[43]

It had been a year of celebration by reviews, and wasn't over. Adelphi had published *Napoli '44* in July: *La Stampa* had called Norman "more mature, more experienced about the affairs of war than Burns, and more clear-eyed than Malaparte",[44] and *La Repubblica* "a stranger whose infallible perception misses nothing";[45] *Corriere della Sera* called the book "an extraordinary document of the time".[46]

On an early Monday evening in November Norman and Lesley made a rare trip to London together. The occasion was a birthday party at the Groucho Club for Martha Gellhorn, a few months younger than Norman. Both were now eighty-five. Lesley recalls that the dinner was "fascinating. Her coterie of young men [was there], John Simpson, Jon Snow, Nicholas Shakespeare, John Hatt. It was predominantly a male occasion."[47] Gellhorn had been asked, as had Norman, by the *Daily Mail* to write a piece about her best of all time travel book for its New Year's Day edition, and told him she had chosen *Naples '44*.

A month later Norman tried again to restore his friendship with John Hatt, moved to write by the book's endurance.

6 Dec

Dear John,

I think that the sudden quite extraordinary upsurge of interest for *Naples '44* calls for the exchange of congratulations. Collins originally proposed to issue this in Fontana but welshed on the understanding, so there was no paperback. The hardback printing was probably about 2,000, and they gave me a few appallingly produced copies left over that were too few even to remainder. The fact that it has survived all these years, that Geoffrey Wheatcroft recently described it as "the best single memoir of the war", and that our mutual friend Martha Gellhorn has written an eulogistic piece for the Daily Mail after all this time testifies to your success as a publisher. . . .

I remember when I last wrote I was hoping you might have a meal with us at some time; and I hope this is still possible if you feel like venturing out in this direction. . . .

Perhaps we can both brush variations of opinion about such things as omnibus volumes aside – I am extremely sorry that this thing ever seemed worth considering. Life is too short!

Yours,
Norman[48]

Hatt replied a week later, also "sorry that the omnibus saga caused such ill-feeling", promising to visit in the new year, and on New Year's Day Gellhorn's short, eloquent review of the edition of Norman's book that Hatt had kept in print for a decade appeared. "With no briefing, no orders, [his] small marooned British unit developed – and maintained throughout – its own interesting freelance lifestyle. Lewis understood the Italians' misery, admired their fierce will to live, was surprised by nothing and enjoyed their society. ... We oldies who remember the war in Italy", she finished up, "know that *Naples '44* is the real thing, pure gold. It has all the qualifications to become a classic: the ring of truth, superb writing and the magical lure of a book you cannot put down."

"The novel is well under way and I hope to show you several chapters quite soon. Happy New Year and love! Norman."[49]

"Norman has decided to write another travel book, about Southern Italy."[50]

"Dear Dan, Here are some pages from Norman outlining the possible contents for his next book. He has written very little about any of these, and in most cases nothing at all. Possibly the Bugatti story, and the mission to Castro are doubtful; we can discuss."[51]

Between January and mid-March Norman started on and abandoned a novel and a book about southern Italy. He broke off from the travel book on the physical grounds that it wasn't practical and because in researching he hadn't found "enough new interesting material". The novel vanished for unspecified reasons – for the unspecified reasons novels do. "Mostly, we authors must repeat ourselves – that's the truth," as F Scott Fitzgerald, in "One Hundred False Starts", had it. "We have two or three great and moving experiences in our lives – experiences so great and moving that it doesn't seem at the time that anyone else has been so caught up and pounded. ... Then we learn our trade, well or less well, and we tell our two or three stories – each time in a new disguise – maybe ten times, maybe a hundred, as long as people will listen."[52] If it didn't work, it was "not very difficult to run back and start over again – especially in private". The novel Norman had begun made forty-two pages, but I think his efforts to apply a spark (changing from the first to third person, changing names and motivations) failed. By far the best of "The Airship", the fragment's working title, is the opening scene of the boy, an asthmatic single child, curiously watching his mother weep as a burning Zeppelin crumples out of the sky. Fitzgerald in his essay names two kinds of fictional stalemate, "Plots without emotions, emotions without plots". Norman's case was the latter.

He started over with a proposal for a second volume of autobiography (when Gill Coleridge had his less than perfect typing retyped he thanked her assistant, "I am reminded of William Shawn of the *New Yorker*, who once said to me, 'I only have to take a look at the ms to realize that a contribution has come in from you'") and spent most of the year writing it. The previous year he had extended *Jackdaw Cake* in a chapter describing the family's emigration to Isola Farnese and return, but that book had effectively ended in 1946. The new one opened with his meeting Oliver Myers on a train in 1937 and dovetailed into the post-Guatemala years and 1950s. He interrupted the writing with regular journalism and occasional celebration: after flying to La Gomera in January for an article ("no tourists yet apart from a few earnest Germans & people are as they were in Spain 50 years ago"[53]) he accepted an invitation to Étonnants Voyageurs, a festival held annually in May at Saint-Malo in Brittany, to receive the Prix de l'Astrolabe, awarded for his work and for a French edition of *The Day of the Fox*, *Torre del Mar*, which had just been published. "The French do book fairs very well, and if you are a glutton you have a wonderful time. I was bewildered when someone pointed out a newspaper headline which said 'Festival Re-Discovers English Masterpiece', more so later to be extravagantly fêted on the score of a novel of which I remembered so little after the passage of the years."[54] If Norman was a glutton for anything it was the pleasure of the applause that, for two days, he absorbed with an expression of delighted serenity. At the restaurant where he received the prize, and a cheque for 10,000 francs, he was presented to his French audience in an introductory speech, but the room was packed with French writers and journalists who already admired him. The queue at the following day's signing session snaked out of the marquee.

Bad, expected news followed a fortnight after his return. On 6 June Hester died at a nursing home in Surrey. She had developed dementia at Banchory and despite being cared for by a network of neighbours had deteriorated. "She found it difficult to dress herself, she couldn't cook any more, she couldn't watch television, she couldn't read, she just sat there staring into space." Gareth had arranged for her to move into a nursing home at the foot of his garden, where she had lived for two years "and thrived in a bizarre sort of way". Norman expressed a wish to go to the funeral. He and Lesley drove down and spent the night at Gareth's, and the next morning Lesley stayed at the house to look after Gareth's daughter. The cortège was unusual due to Norman's son's inherited interest in cars, the hearse followed by Gareth "in a Renault Alpine V6 turbo in red and behind that a Nissan 200SX turbo also in red, sitting with their hazards flashing". In the front seat of the Renault Norman, his children remember, could not face Hester's coffin.

"Karen was behind me in the Alpine, and Dad's eyes were dropped, he didn't look at the hearse or the coffin that sat in the back. She said to him, 'The coffin's there, Dad,' and he said, 'I don't want to look,' and she said, 'Look at it. *Look at it*.'"[55] Karen remembers that her father looked and "broke down and cried, 'I loved her so much.'"[56]

He went back to work, briefly observing publication in July of *I Came I Saw*, the extended edition of *Jackdaw Cake*, in a Picador Travel Classics series alongside books by Robert Byron, Redmond O'Hanlon and Apsley Cherry-Garrard. ("Iconic", "splendid", "excellent", "permanent" were the reviews' gratifying epithets.) At the end of July the family holiday, always well populated even after the children grew up – and Kiki married – swelled to a group of eleven flying to Skopelos in the Aegean. Norman's quest for the places undepraved by tourism failed this time, and he felt "we were several years too late . . . everything gets worse. It either gets worse faster, or it gets worse slower."[57]

A consistently pessimistic posture on the planet's evolution was part of Norman's antinomic indulgence of frequent air travel *and* belief in preserving the world's glorious surfaces from development, conformity, insipidity, dilution, and so on. It did not disturb him that at the same time as observing those surfaces he couldn't help participating, even infinitesimally, in their destruction – as it didn't disturb him that one of his sons worked as a director of Thomson's at the height of the package holiday boom, and another at Owners Abroad: as why should it? The antinomy of travel in a fragile world does not so much demand a guilty verdict, or special dispensation, for the writer as that we recognise – or not – a justification that is solely aesthetic. Norman's relation to the world's wilder landscapes is fundamentally a relation to its *verbal* landscapes: to the multiple, detailed, exhilarating, ripe co-ordinates of his prose and to the bright haze of meaning that enshrouds it. For so long as he was able to *write*, travel's paradoxes were immaterial. An indication of as much is audible in his own answer in an interview three years earlier. Did it depress him, Nicholas Shakespeare asked him, that things were continually getting worse? "I can't say that it does, actually."[58]

He and Lesley spent two weeks in Spain in September, and by Christmas when he returned there for the holiday a large part of the book was written. He had finished accounts of Cuba and north Vietnam and a long account of his journey through Peru with Snowdon; in January he wondered "if what might be seen as an attack on Snowdon shouldn't be toned down. After all, I got on quite well with the man."[59]

Correspondence flowed between Norman and his agent, and agent and American publishers, about whether the book *was* a travel book or an autobiography; Jack Macrae at Holt, who wanted a travel book, was showing caution because of Norman's slow American sales and the uphill process of establishing him. "I suspect that when this book reaches its final form it will be no more satisfactory than now from Jack's point of view," Norman wrote in December, insisting that "it is an autobiography".[60] At the end of January Dan Franklin at Cape phoned to say he was delighted with the excerpts he had seen.

Norman had planned fairly idly a winter trip to Guatemala, but a recurrence of bronchitis forced him to put it off and work instead on getting the new book finally done. In January 1995 the long discussed omnibus appeared. One reviewer, noting that Norman saved himself from high-mindedness by a preference for communicating his enjoyment of a "richly unexpected" world, wrote that time and we were making such situations semi-extinct. "Lewis, where another writer would dish them out with moralising linctus or a fake spirit of adventure, has given us them page after page, year after year, as the most delicious of unageing wines."[61] There was no toasting of the book's success with John Hatt however, and in another publishing discussion that month about who would republish *Voices of the Old Sea* which Penguin had recently surrendered, Norman revealed to Gill Coleridge his sadness about the loss of Hatt's friendship. "My contact with John is tenuous these days. I have written 2 exceedingly conciliatory letters but not much by way of reply."[62]

As he usually did when he was unable to travel, he diverted his energy Voltaireanly into the Parsonage's garden. To Colin Hamilton, an antiquarian bookseller who shared his botanical enthusiasm, he wrote that he was "looking forward as usual to spring and the hope that my meconopsis will flourish". But it was an unusually wet winter and spring, with three times the usual rainfall. The cold damp was felt by Bill Zinsser, who flew from New York to interview Norman in early March. Zinsser, a friend of Perelman and a former GI in Italy, enquired what Norman meant by leading a monastic life at the Parsonage. "Well, it's monastic in that —"

Zinsser: It's got electricity.
Lewis (laughing hard): Just a few modest conveniences to please my wife.
Zinsser: If it could be a little colder you'd appreciate it more?

"The room where I interviewed him", Zinsser says, "actually had a fire going and was minimally warm, but the others that I saw downstairs were kept unheated."[63] Three months later Norman told Colin Hamilton the spring had been so wet it

practically wiped out my meconopses and primulas. I lost some rare unnamed primulas given me by the curator of the Moscow Botanical Gardens, plus desert irises, which have no problem dealing with the Caucasus and Central Asia, but have succumbed to ESSEX.[64]

He asked Hamilton for advice about disposing of his collection of books on central America bought in the 1950s and in his next letter on 30 May, thanking him, added that he was now

heavily involved with Cape in editing the latest "autobiography" and straining to supply no more than the minimum of personal details, which they point out are normally accepted as essential to such a work.[65]

The following day Dan Franklin went up to Finchingfield to talk about the addition of "personal details" (and discuss cutting down the Snowdon material) before Norman and Lesley left for a plant-collecting trip to Andorra. Peter Straus had written in similar vein: Norman thanked Straus profusely for his "various suggestions", "wholly in agreement" with them, then deployed a new swerve about Straus's request for more about himself.

When it comes to personal reflections on my life I may find myself in slightly deep water, because being by nature prone to extremes and statements that might be considered wild I am rather careful about this area. We do not want to put too many readers off.[66]

The general implausibility of this statement (though it underlines a certain self-mistrust) offers one clue to the reason behind his reticence: there was *no* explanation for it. He liked to observe, describe, stay in the background; out of the way of harm. Scratch him, and he was still the boy standing on the edge of the games in the Freehold, surviving a childhood whose ruling motif was disappearance: of one brother after another, of his sense of belonging, of his parents' rationality and, finally, of himself as the only means of countering boredom, or horror, or misery, or wrath. His childhood over, disappearance had remained his life's motif, escape its expression, writing – re-materialising in words – its salvation. But not about himself. Norman, Normie, Lewis, Dickie Dwl, the boy they didn't have to teach, did not forget that to reveal himself either to his peers or his overseers could only bring down trouble on his head, because he had never had to remember it. It was what he was stamped with.

In consequence, parts of the finished autobiography have the truth stretched over them to cover those reticences. Norman brings forward, for instance, his visit to Ernestina in Guatemala to spring 1946 to avoid having to say anything about the most intense period of his life with Hester (who doesn't appear); he avoids the acutely transitional year of 1949 and its Italian experiment, bringing forward the Tossa and Ibiza years. As its title suggests, *The World The World* is composed as an autobiography not of the self and time, but of place. Reviewers noticed. The following April when it was published, Colin Thubron wrote that Norman "turn[ed] uneasily to autobiography";[67] another reviewer described it as "not so much an autobiography as a photograph album",[68] another that his diffidence "is indistinguishable from secrecy. . . . The reluctance of the author to provide readers with even the basic facts of his personal life has hamstrung the autobiographical venture as efficiently as if he had set out to avoid using the first personal pronoun."[69]

He satisfied readers in one respect, with rewritten final pages that closed the book on a remembered, or composed, conversation with his Indian guide to Orissa, Sarat, about the reason why he travelled. It was not quite freedom, he wrote.

It's just a compulsion I've always felt. It's the pull of the world. I spent most of my childhood on my own, and some of it was in the mountains of Wales. I would go exploring with the idea in my head that the farther I was from home the better it would be. The next valley would always be wilder. The lake would be bottomless, and I would find a mysterious ruin, and there would be ravens instead of crows in all the trees. Now it's not just the Black Mountains of Dyfed, but the world.[70]

A compulsion as potent, and as granitic, as the compulsion not to reveal himself.

PART SEVEN

FINISHING

An Ending in Three Beginnings
Guatemala, Sicily, Spain

Lewis's only rival as a travel writer whose modesty has made him almost invisible is the French naturalist Victor Jacquemont (1801–32) whose posthumous three-volume *Voyage in India* gives the best account there is of the sub-continent and its English rulers. It is gentle, humorous and entirely persuasive. His great friend Prosper Mérimée remarked that whenever he found himself in a difficult situation he asked himself what advice Jacquemont would give.

A fan of Lewis might well feel the same way.

John Bayley

31

TO THE VOLCANOES

"Three things give us hardy strength: sleeping on
hairy mattresses, breathing cold air, and eating dry food"
Welsh proverb

NORMAN had been in contact with a young Guatemalan writer who
wanted to translate *The Missionaries* into Spanish. The last time he
had visited Guatemala, with Don McCullin in 1975, the country had
been at the edge of an abyssal decade. From the late 1970s to early
1990s abuse of power became endemic, and the army's suppression of
opposition had caused uncounted thousands of deaths. Twenty years
later, negotiated agreements on human rights, resettlement and indigenous rights secured a brittle peace. Norman had immediately taken the
hint. He had had to postpone the idea of the trip the previous winter,
but in late 1995 began to ask his Guatemalan correspondent, Rodrigo
Rey Rosa, about conditions and hotels.

He spent the rest of the autumn reading and gardening in his own
way at the Parsonage. "At least I am doing a little to improve things
here by doubling the size of the pond and that of the ditch (which is
all it is) that provides the water," he wrote to Colin Hamilton. There
had been surprises. "We have accidentally cut through an ancient
refuse pit which has yielded up most of a floor dating back about
3000 years ago. This is 10 yards from the spot, before we moved in,
where the old gardener of those days dug a number of unbroken
Roman vessels (now in the Colchester Museum)."[1] He was again
suffering frustration with his publisher. Though he liked Dan Franklin,
he felt it not right that Cape should be a successful house and have
an editorial department that was understaffed and delaying him from

making plans; to this he added the recalled annoyance of having arranged to be in England on publication day of *An Empire of the East* and found that Cape's promotional activity seemed to amount to a single trip "accompanied by a junior employee" to a BBC radio interview (at this point his complaint became as much about the BBC as Cape).

I was placed to await this [interview] in a narrow passageway in the bowels of the building, and with me was Dervla Murphy who had been dragged hundreds of miles from some Celtic place of refuge to take part in the lugubrious process in which we were involved. Although a woman evidently capable of great resignation all she could say to me as employees hurried past, tripping over our feet, was, "This is the end of the road."[2]

Gill Coleridge reassured him that the past promotional problems had been to do with the handover to Dan Franklin and that his present editing was in hand, soothing him with an offer from the *New Yorker* to commission a 6000-word piece about the town of Corleone in western Sicily. Norman accepted, but anticipation of a return to central America had gripped him. Guatemala had to come first, and at the end of November he wrote to Rey Rosa that

we'll almost certainly come to Guatemala in late January or early February and we much look forward to seeing you. We shall have a car and travel round as much of the country as possible. I would particularly like to go to Quiché and Huehuetenango again, and perhaps find something to write about.[3]

After the Christmas break in Barcelona he and Lesley flew to Miami on 28 January, pausing for two days to see Gawaine, working in Florida, before reaching Guatemala City on the 31st. The first plan had been to take the rough road from Santa Cruz del Quiché, beyond Chichicastenango, to the town of Chisec north of Cobán. An army patrol had committed a massacre at a farm at Chisec in October, an act of intimidation against returning refugees that had resulted in eleven Indians, aged from 7 to 56, being executed. Then Norman changed his mind: he wanted to revisit the Huehuetenango of his 1955 visit and Chisec was too far to be able to do both. He and Lesley wound first out of the traffic inferno of Guatemala City down into the old architecture of Antigua, a procession of seventeenth-century houses sprinkled with the silhouettes of churches and monasteries beheaded by the 1773 earthquake. In two comfortable days at the Hotel Santo Domingo, he tracked the country's continuing violence in the newspapers. At Antigua itself regular armed robberies still took place, one of them outside the police station a few days earlier. From Antigua he and Lesley joined the highway north to the shabby town of Panajachel at the edge of Lake Atitlán. The view has changed at Atitlán since Aldous Huxley in 1933 judged it beyond "the limit of the permissibly picturesque".[4] Nothing prepares you for the sprawling, mysteriously lit tract of wild blue water encircled by the concave slopes of volcanoes; but by 1996 the lake's level and purity were coming under threat from sheer human numbers. Atitlán had been vandalised by both civil war and tourist development, Norman felt. Only the village of Santiago on its far side had preserved its independence, its Tzutuhil Indians dignified, pugnacious resisters of the army, militias and modernity.

Rodrigo Rey Rosa met them two days later at Chichicastenango. They stayed another two days at the town, and after a supper at the Mayan Inn, where Don McCullin had thought life wasn't so bad twenty years before, the three carried on northwards the next morning in Rey Rosa's borrowed 4 x 4 through alpine orchards dotted with vultures and terraces hanging from the hillsides. Norman had a new destination. Beyond Huehuetenango and into the Cuchumatanes, where cactuses take over from orchards and the sheep are the blue of the rock, was the Ixchil triangle. (Staying a decade later at a finca at 3000 metres in the Cuchumatanes, where a good mule still fetches twice the price of a horse, I felt that the remoteness and silence probably came closest to what Norman had experienced on his initiatory visit fifty years before.)

Norman had read about another massacre at an Ixchil village named Chajul in 1979 in Rigoberta Menchú's book I, Rigoberta Menchú: an Indian Woman in Guatemala: the story of how, during a "model operation" by the army, Menchú had seen her brother and other villagers tortured then set alight in front of the church and an audience of hundreds of Indians trucked in to watch.

In the event they did not pass through Huehue but took a direct road through Sacapulas into the highlands as far as Nebaj, a sprawl of grey adobe streets (now a small hikers' Kathmandu) where the triangle begins. They stayed at the Las Hermanas inn, one of only two in town, "cleanish" as Rey Rosa remembers but uncomfortable, cold. "It was

eerie, there was no army any more, but the atmosphere was there."[5]
Descending again on unsurfaced roads, they finally entered the country
of the *guerrilla*, of forests, ravines and hideouts, and between Nebaj
and Chajul the way was cool, depopulated and silent, the meadows
apparently abandoned, the place purged of human animation.

Rey Rosa afterwards wrote a short novel, *Que Me Maten Si* ...,
painted in the violences and abuses of power of the civil war. One of its
characters is Lucian Leigh, an eighty-five-year-old English writer revealed
subsequently to be a spy, who he admits is based wholly on Norman.
(Leigh's transceiver for coded messages is in his hearing aid. ...) In the
novel a young man named Ernesto, a reformist former army officer,
drives Leigh to Chajul: its white church gleams at the end of a long
straight stretch of road. He and Leigh visit the church.

At the back of the church, to the right of the altar, was a crude contemporary painting showing piled-up Indian bodies, bloody and mutilated, in the
middle of a semi-circle of uniformed soldiers. "Blessed are the persecuted" was
written at the bottom of the frame.

The two speak to an old and a younger villager: the old man confirms
that twenty-three were killed.

The younger man interrupted. "Yes, but they didn't kill them here."
"No," the old man said. "They took them over there."
The two exchanged a look. The younger man said, "I was a firefighter then.
We fetched the bodies from the pine forest." He gestured behind him at the
place where past the church the tops of some pines could be seen. "They were
scattered here and there, they were dead, their guts spilled open."
The Englishman was listening impassively. "So it wasn't here it happened."
The former firefighter pointed back at the pines past the church again.
"Can we see the place?" Ernesto asked.
The firefighter said yes, and led them around the church to where a muddy
track climbed to the edge of the village. ... The Englishman came up slowly,
taking careful steps in the mud, and Ernesto couldn't help admiring him. He
must have been well over eighty, and still going strong. ...
"It's just up there," the Ixchil said, but the pines were at the top of a steep
slope.
"Go on," the Englishman said. ... At the top of the slope the firefighter
said to Ernesto, "They killed them in the middle of the night, at three in the
morning. They had tied them up on the square and they led them up here.

They chucked a grenade in among them, then went in with machetes to finish them off. They said to us firefighters, 'You men burn and bury the remains.' We put their guts back, sewed up their wounds and took them all to the cemetery together. There were so many of them that there weren't enough boxes – coffins – we had to bury some of them in plastic bags."[6]

"Lesley was cross with me for taking Norman up the muddy path," Rey Rosa remembers, "but Norman said he could make it." Two footnotes surface from Norman's visit: that fifteen years after the atrocity the villagers were still wary of cars and ran away at the sight of Rey Rosa's Toyota; and that his fictional account, with all its discrepancies from Menchú's (which Norman more or less used), is as factual a recall, he says, of the conversation he had with the old man and the former firefighter on the square as he could make it.

Chajul, "impossibly remote", certainly represented the best as well as the worst of the circumstances of Guatemala that Norman was drawn to: its houses an early Indo-Spanish mixture of adobe, tiled roof and *terraza española*, its villagers' weaving practices uncompromised by contact, their bearing and manner more handsome than that of urbanised Indians. High in the sierra, overlooking the Mexican border and pillows of forest mist to the horizon, the village appears to demonstrate both the cost and possibilities of resistance. (When a tarmacked road, already begun, reaches Chajul as it is scheduled to, its powers of resistance will be tested again.) "We had a fairly rough and tough few days," Lesley recalls, but returning to Nebaj and then Antigua via Cobán and Uspantán, Norman was happy with what he had seen.

At Finchingfield in late February he started writing immediately, wanting to put together a sketch of Guatemala's continuing vulnerability and remaining beauty. When I saw him at the Parsonage a month later he had finished a draft, a reshuffled itinerary that closed on a newspaper story of an event that had occurred on the outskirts of Antigua during his absence in the sierra. The newly elected president, Álvaro Arzú, out for a ride on horseback had found his way blocked by a weaving Suzuki pickup. Arzú's bodyguards had attacked the car and shot the driver, and the story had been presented as a well-foiled plot against the president's life. Norman was delighted by its absurdity. He had read "about ten versions of this," he said, "all of which are substantially different, but what comes out of it is that

the driver was probably drunk at the time. He was delivering milk
. . . a drunken milkman who couldn't drive a car."[7]

To William Zinsser the previous year, he had rationalised his non-
writing of fiction as the result of having pleased himself without giving
his motives much thought –

The fact of the matter is this: like most people's my motives are exceedingly
mixed. I'm not even myself when I'm talking to you. You make a point and
I think, well that may be right. I know a certain amount about myself in a
superficial situation . . . but even then I may be a bit off. . . . I used to regard
myself as a novelist, but I gradually sort of slipped away – sort of truancies.
I said, I'll clear off and go somewhere and then I'll come back and write
another novel. But obviously travel writing seems to have taken over[8]

– and he now decided that the story of the drunken milkman could
stand for why he was no longer interested in writing novels. "In the
short time of this trip to Guatemala I've experienced new sensations
by the thousand, and had I been writing a novel during that time I
would have had no new sensations . . . instead of trying to drag things
up from inside me all the time I want my life to be full of incidents
like that to think about, rather than worry about my own reactions
to everything . . . every now and again I have different ideas on myself
and I have come to the conclusion that whatever posture I may put
up or defence or veil, basically I am an adventurer."[9] He had realised
too, possibly, that at eighty-seven he no longer had fair years to waste.

After we talked that morning in March, I suggested we go out for
lunch: I wanted to try to find out what was in Norman's makeup, or
England's, that made one unable to write about the other. We drove
south off the downland onto the mute Essex plain, and as we passed
through Braintree's suburban estates his travelling eye was as enthusiastic and acute in disenchantment as in pleasure: swivelling to point
out a long line of low, morose 1930s villas he said with satisfaction,
"Now this is midway to hell. There, look. Pure *Kulturbolschevismus*,
you see."

"There's plenty to observe here, Norman."

"I admit it. But I'm afraid I could not foresee spending three months
in an estuarial slum here in order to get the atmosphere."

"What's the difference between an Essex slum and one in central
America?"

"Here I would not be serenaded to sleep. I wouldn't be woken by a harpist who would fetch me a fresh roll from a trolley for breakfast. I love old witches; I can't imagine I would find one anything like as good here as the one I found in Paraguay."

We plumped for Maldon on the Blackwater estuary as a destination: a view, something ancient and picturesque, riggish marine smells. The town when we reached it was a Dantesque spiral of a one-way system that spewed us out into a pub in the high street where the other drinkers squinted at us from their stools.

We ordered sandwiches and talked about Lorca and Norman's love of coincidences, and his affinity with brutal people. "I get on terribly well with them. I offer them no competition." I was anxious about his sandwich, had warned him against prawns. These, when they arrived, were colour-enhanced supermarket corpses reanimated with bottled dressing, but in the car park afterwards he thanked me. "Do you know, that must be the best prawn sandwich I've had in fifteen years." On the return journey he asked conversationally, "Do you ever have problems with this car?" (A twenty-year-old Mercedes.) "No," I said. Before we had reached the next bend on the flat, reed-edged country road a chilling bang came from the back of the car's chassis, signalling the differential's permanent expiry.

Unusually Norman found it difficult to finish the piece about Guatemala as he wanted. He asked me to look at it, which I did, suggesting that it suffered from a slight Roman gloominess and that he might take out some material about missionaries and reorganise the end. On 15 April, before he and Lesley flew to Crete for ten days, he wrote punctiliously as always to thank me "for all your help which is most valuable", adding a p.s. in respect of the Mercedes and his ability to attract coincidences, "Do remind me to tell you of another Lewis coincidence, which may strengthen your feeling that witchcraft must be involved." Two weeks later, on 1 May, there was "Dinner with Norman tonight [a publication dinner for *The World The World* at Dan Franklin's]; fit and fantastic-looking. We should all give up writing novels."[10] Yet he had not. To Rodrigo Rey Rosa that July, after Rey Rosa and his girlfriend had visited, he insisted that he was "now at work on my new novel"[11] which he hoped to finish that winter.

The reviews for *The World The World* were as good as he could have wished, aside from reservations about his discretion. Professor John Bayley even decided that his substitution of "self-effacement for the appearance of innocence" was a superior quality in writing that was usually about flamboyance "or flamboyant understatement". Norman, Bayley wrote, made "Lawrence of Arabia or Bruce Chatwin, even Wilfred Thesiger and Freya Stark, look like the most tremendous show-offs". His skill instead was

to show how dull travel is while making it interesting. Oh the dullness and monotony of Angkor Wat, of the stupendous stones of Cuzco, of those innumerable Mochica-Chimu effigy pots, exquisitely depicting every conceivable kind of sexual intercourse. How dull the world is, but how fascinating to read about in a book as good as this. When he left Trujillo Lewis was presented with an effigy, in the form of a frog, stylised to the point of becoming an amphibious abstraction. "There remained a face wearing a tolerant, quizzical expression, and the slyest of smiles."[12]

When he was faced in public by efforts to prise open his discretion, it was almost possible to hear the synchronous *thunk* of a central locking device as self-effacement switched to concealment. At the Hay-on-Wye festival at the end of May he was interviewed by the historian Felipe Fernández-Armesto. Outside the weather was cold and squally; inside the tent Norman was bundled in a bulky borrowed white anorak. A witness in the audience recalls that he was "unforthcoming", and that the less forthcoming he became the longer and more rambling and excited Fernández-Armesto's questions became. Apparently clutching at straws, he put it to Norman that an anecdote in his latest book could have found a place in *Voices of the Old Sea*: why had he not included it? "Lewis stirred in his nylon swaddling clothes and replied laconically, 'Incompetence, I suppose.'"[13]

In the last two weeks of July Norman went with Lesley to Scotland, staying at Tarbert and taking in enough of Argyll and its "almost Mediterranean" landscape "with tiny white cottages set in the most brilliant fields" to turn in a short piece on his return.[14] In September he was shortlisted for the *Esquire*-Waterstone's Non-fiction Awards, but at the black-tie hotel dinner at the Inter-Continental in London on the 25th he did not win. Colin Thubron says that "it was sad that Norman had come all the way to London for what must have seemed a glitzily alienating event to him, unless he had won it (which neither of us did!)". He had also written an essay about Enfield and Sir Henry Bowles and, at the suggestion of an American magazine, a piece titled "Should tourism be rationed?", a question to which he knew there was no real practical answer – and which like all "shoulds" carried an unventilated whiff of piety. (If he was going to be honest, there were his own, mainly unsuccessful, efforts at liberating antiquities also to consider.) Developers, he concluded, were the worst offenders for defacing the culture of ordinary people and inducing "well-meaning" tourists to "participate in the trivialization of the countries they visit". But it was not an argument he could care strongly about.

At the end of October he told his agent that he had "already written at least ⅛ of my novel about awful things in unexpected places",[15] rather little, if he was serious, for a book he had started in July. He seemed to have been captured by journalism, hypnotised even, at a time when a magazine culture of a far softer kind than he had once practised was in the ascendant. He was in demand and well paid, but in the three years since 1993 had written little better than his essay about the Yali, "Standing on the world's edge" – and that had been an extract from *An Empire of the East*.[16] There had been *interesting* pieces, various, rich, entertaining; but he was getting into the journalist's habits of routine production and self-plagiarism. In his diffident way he wanted to stay in the public eye – he wrote several times to his agent during the 1990s suggesting "it would be a good thing" to write a regular piece for this or that magazine – forgetting that, the quality and impact of his *Sunday Times* journalism of the 1970s notwithstanding, that decade had been the period when he was most forgotten. The trouble was, as Flaubert has it, that "The strongest have perished there. . . . You first make one little concession, then two, then twenty. You delude yourself about your integrity for a long time. Then you don't give a toss and then you turn into an idiot." Or as Norman's admirer Cyril Connolly adds, "To put our best into [journalism] is another folly, since thereby we condemn good ideas as well as bad to oblivion. . . . Writers engrossed in any literary task which is not an assault on perfection are their own dupes."[17] Norman hadn't lost his integrity but he had left his path; he had also let himself be trapped in administration, referring to himself as "Norman the Chaotic" in one of the frequent letters he sent asking for clarification of another unpaid newspaper invoice (he may have had furious reactions to business affairs, but was far more fastidious about his writing income than he had been about R G Lewis income). The article about Corleone for the *New Yorker* was the only one he didn't write: having intended to interview Totò Riina, the current mafia "boss of bosses", then in prison serving several life sentences, he had discovered that Riina could no longer be visited and had to excuse himself from the contract.

One substantial contract was signed in autumn 1996: a new film option on *Naples '44*, the third, taken up this time by the Walt Disney subsidiary Miramax. But an air of aimlessness hovered, extending through the winter. What was he doing? Journalism had depleted his reservoir of ideas if not his energy, and there seems, from the biographer's bloodless perspective, a hint that the indefatigable producer, after twenty-nine books (fifteen novels, fourteen non-fiction) in sixty-one years of publication, the writer who switched without fuss or loss of impact between genres, was for the first time not so resilient; nowhere near fading or declining but, without a book being written (or only a shadowy one, very slowly), suddenly indistinct.

On 24 January he and Lesley travelled to Cancún and the Yucatán – he had wanted to go back to central America but a *Daily Telegraph* travel editor, Michael Kerr, had asked him for two articles on Mexico – and on their return went almost immediately to southern Spain. Nothing seemed amiss when I saw him for a weekend at the end of April, except that it was not clear what he was writing. A letter to Leila Hadley in June seems to shed light.

19.6.97

Dear Leila

An enormous delay, I'm afraid, in replying to your charming and most welcome letter. We were staying about the time you posted it with my son [Gawaine] in Miami where, of all things, he makes a living advising people how to invest their money. On the whole it was a rather dreary experience, however from Florida we went straight to Andalusia (near Ronda) which was pleasant and unspoiled. Back from these journeys there were further delays over a mysterious infection, but happily that's cleared up. Thank you very much indeed for sending me Pico Iyer's cuttings. My wife found them over-enthusiastic to the point of absurdity, and laughed long and loud at certain flattering references made by you from about 30 years ago, occasionally raising her eyes from the letter to confront the wasted reality of the lean and slippered loon facing her across the table. . . .

The "mysterious infection" was recurrent stomach pain and black stools that were investigated by endoscopy: a duodenal ulcer was diagnosed, which he had probably been aggravating for years with an Alka-Seltzer habit. But it was also writer's licence, extended into a metaphor for his non-writing malaise. On 23 May he and Lesley were at Aberdeen for Gawaine's wedding, where Gareth remembers his father as distracted.

The last time I saw him was at Gawaine's wedding, and he came over to me and said to me, "Smoked salmon, my boy, what about that?" and I said, "Great Dad, eh?" He put his hand on my shoulder and he said [whisper], "What kind of car are you driving now?" and I said, "A Mercedes Benz," and he said, "A Mercedes Benz, eh?" and with that he wandered off.

Later Gareth walked over to his father and kissed him on the forehead. "I knew that was the last time I was ever going to see him."[18]

In June he and Lesley, who had also been unwell with her back, flew to Samos for a short holiday. Finally, after their return, a new book was decided, a collection of recent journalism to which he would add some unseen/unwritten pieces. He was rehearsing some of them when I stayed at the Parsonage on the last weekend of July.

Norman at 89, lapsing into Spanish after drinking a lot at dinner, retains an extraordinary interest in the remembered dramas of life. Peculiarly, his sense of action and narrative seems to have got wholly honed by the war, encouraging him to see everything afterwards, fiascos like the battle of Salerno and experiences like interrogating an SS major for 5 days (or letting another go who held up a hand with a bullet hole clean through it), in those terms of raised reality and pronounced meaning. Much invented, of course. But enough to make tears come into his eyes at the telling of the story of the interrogation.[19]

The book of journalism was commissioned by Cape; he had, finally, got his mojo back. Afterwards, when the journalism was done, he wanted to write a book on Sicily, he wrote to Giuliana, Marcello Cimino's widow, that autumn. "As I told you on the phone I have now decided to write a book – which has been commissioned . . . – about Sicily, which has always, by reason of its culture, history and great natural beauty, been my favourite. Above all I am determined not to make this a superficial travel account, but to get as near as I can to producing something approaching a classic work." He had hoped to return to Sicily before Christmas but been delayed until January at the earliest because he needed a cataract operation. "I shall never forget the few all-too-rare occasions", he wrote, "when we have been together. Marcello was the best, and most admired, of my friends. . . . Naturally I am looking forward, most of all, to seeing you and hopefully Gabriella too, on this occasion."[20]

Despite claiming to be the poorest of correspondents, he kept up a habit of lengthy letter writing that year, expressing always in his sub-decipherable handwriting some combination of warmth and affection, congratulation, pleasure, offers of copies of his books the recipient might not have read, the desire to meet, versions of stories that occurred to him as he was writing. In a letter that December he included a revealing addendum to his account of youthful reading of Enfield's Carnegie Library collection of Russian literature. I was recently back from the Crimea and had written a piece in the *Guardian* about Chekhov's last years at Yalta, which he read and immediately wrote to say he had enjoyed.

Dear Julian

A neighbour just brought in your *Guardian* article "The Seagull's Last Cry" – which is really excellent – pity you don't do a regular feature for the paper.

Did I ever tell you about the days in my father's shop when – through lack of any other reading – I read through possibly a complete collection of Russian literature someone had given the local Carnegie library. What stood out for me was a short story by Chekhov about a man who experiences a number of hallucinations in a train, and finally realizes he's got typhus.

Les sends love.

Norman[21]

The story, called "Typhus", is about a young lieutenant going home to Moscow after serving in Petersburg. It begins on a train with the soldier, Klimov, irritable at the prattle of a fellow passenger, then starting to feel sick and run a temperature. In Moscow he goes straight to bed. After two weeks of fever and hallucination he wakes to a bright morning, feeling wonderfully well after having survived typhus. In his moment of euphoria he discovers that his eighteen-year-old sister Katya, with all her life and beauty ahead of her, has caught typhus from him while nursing him and died. "And his joy gave way to the boredom of everyday life and the feeling of his irrevocable loss." No Chekhov story, however dazzled Norman was by Chekhov, could match the impact that the story of a prematurely dead sister made on him for other than literary reasons.

Norman worked on the collection of journalism, "A Mess of a Battle", through summer and autumn 1997. It was delivered by the end of November and contained six unpublished pieces, some longer than others and some reworkings: of his Nicaragua and Honduras experiences, and his landing at Salerno. Four pieces stand out – his rebellion in prose against Sir Henry Bowles and his class, "God Bless the Squire"; a memoir of his days as an Intelligence interrogator of suspected Nazis; a highly recomposed but delightfully credible account of his meeting with Enrique Carreras; and his recent essay on Guatemala. His publisher suggested organising the collection in the order in which the events described had happened, implicitly emphasising his literary endurance; it was given a new title, *The Happy Ant-Heap*; and by January Norman was free to concentrate on Sicily.

He had hoped the island might have changed for the better. "Arriving in Palermo after nightfall" in mid-February, he wrote to his agent,

we found that the hotel staff had gone home and there was no food. Here in the Piccadilly Circus of Palermo [the Quattro Canti] every restaurant but one was closed and to reach it involved us in a couple of hundred yards walk through streets that were totally empty. We were the only customers in this restaurant and the owner thanked us with tears in his eyes for coming. "If you are approached on your way back," he said, "stop and let your arms fall to your sides. Better to stay off the streets after sundown." . . . <u>Not</u> recommended for your next family trip to the continent.[22]

He and Lesley decided to leave Palermo quickly, hired a car and chose routes inland to areas that he promised he had bypassed before. (His agent had lectured him on avoiding the temptation of self-plagiarism, an injunction that was inevitably impossible to obey.) Lesley drove, and they headed first into the bandit country, now deserted, of "sparkling grasslands . . . pyramidical mountains spreading soft purplish lagoons of shadow into the valleys". (Norman *had* been here before: this was the torn-off, lonely skyline between Portella della Ginestra and Corleone.) They stayed at a remote house, Il Rifugio, in the forest of Ficuzza in the most ancient mafia heartland, which operated as a hotel only if you were recommended. The people seemed of a different race from Italians: Il Rifugio's owner Antonio "was constantly in physical action, sawing up branches to feed the enormous fire or preparing meals for which the ingredients were cut up with a kind of surgical skill. There was an absence of laughter inherited perhaps here in the unchanged countryside from the Islamic days when it was avoided by persons of orthodox breeding."[23] They went on to "the notorious mafia places", Corleone, Piana degli Albanesi, then drove to Mazara del Vallo on the coast, an agreeable, permissive town that is so far south it seems to have taken in north Africa by osmosis: even here "cars using the autostrada running through the town's outskirts had been under attack by bandits on two successive days".[24] They returned via the coastal town of Trapani, a new locus of Sicilian fashion thanks to drug-profit investment in strings of boutiques, and the magnificent broken triangles of the mountains between San Giuseppe Jato and Partinico. Back at Palermo he changed his mind about the city in daylight, won over to "its Islamic monuments, the tottering baroque palaces (some housing a dozen families) crowded into its centre, the immaculate schoolchildren disgorged in the morning from its slums, even the municipality's toleration of love by the light of day in the cars parked in the bushes of the Parco della Favorita or all along the via Filangieri, down by the port".[25] From Finchingfield he wrote to Gill Coleridge that the trip "went even better than hoped". To Rodrigo Rey Rosa a month later he said, unusually straight, that Sicily's appeal had more to do with his attraction to the edge of things than with pleasure. "It is not a place I actually enjoy, but the drama is constant – so much so that the book practically writes itself. The pages of *Giornale di Sicilia* are stuffed with the most dreadful stories."[26]

I drove out to see him at Finchingfield on 23 May. About to be ninety, he was almost jumpy with enthusiasm, describing the Sicilian book as "a snapshot of Sicily at this moment. . . . I have to be very careful not to put too much in of the past. Anyway the point is it gives me something to write about." In a Voltairean mood, he talked about joy, gardening and good fortune. The outlook for the next ninety years was getting worse and worse. "I'm in a hurry to make the most of what is left."

I suppose by nature I am philosophically pessimistic and yet somehow or other I derive intense joy from being alive. That is why I propose to live longer than most people do. This is a thing that I have studied, how to keep alive and enjoy yourself, but as regards the rest of it, the pessimism is total. I mean anybody coming back here in a hundred years time who had known this – they would find it difficult to believe that such horror had descended upon them. The whole of this country will be covered by concrete and paint. People will require a special pass to go on a visit to the country. I put it all down to the love of money, the seeking of money, rather than other things.

Writing for me is not really comparable. It's in the same sphere as drinking good wine. I write because I enjoy it. I am indescribably lucky. I'll tell you something: I will suddenly stop Lesley or one of our children in the middle of a conversation and say how lucky we are. They get tired of this, they don't see it properly. I am lucky. I am incredibly lucky. My appetite is satisfied by writing, drinking good wine, and wandering around in a well-kept garden, or better still of course an untouched landscape.[27]

Of which Sicily had been the most recent.

I took a course through a place which had been until recently infested with bandits, and what struck me and Lesley was that in some ways this was the most beautiful place we had ever seen. And the reason was, everywhere, *nothing* was touched. There were fantastic lakes and mountains, no dirt, no miserable people – the reason being that the bandits had gone away a long time ago and left it, and the people hadn't come back, so what we got there was nature as it used to be two thousand years ago. So I'd certainly prefer that to my garden, which comes maybe second or third.[28]

In May he heard he had won another prize, the Duke of Devonshire's Heywood Hill Prize for a lifetime's contribution to literature, though it continued to seem that only the French felt he was worth a prize to himself. As with the Thomas Cook award he had won jointly, this one was to be shared with Richard Ollard, the biographer and historian. Before collecting it he and Lesley returned to Sicily for ten days to finish his research: to not so untouched places, including the village of Aci Trezza which he had last visited during the war on his father-in-law Ernesto's behalf, and where Ernesto had intended to buy a house when the war was over. He described his pain at the return to his friend James McNeish.

How glad I am that Giovanni Verga [born at Catania close by] and you are unlikely to go back. At the entrance to the beach where all the painted boats used to be readying themselves for the waves was a large notice with usual illustration saying that all cars illegally parked there will be towed away. . . . A bar in Catania has just been closed by police for inviting couples to come in, <u>strip off</u> and have a free drink on the house. What is happening to us all?[29]

He travelled by train with Lesley and friends to Chatsworth on 19 June to receive the Heywood Hill Prize, presented by P D James on behalf of the Devonshires to the joint winners. Norman's lack of fame went before him. "I am ashamed to say," Baroness James said, "that until Mr Saumarez Smith sent me a copy of *Golden Earth* and *Naples '44* I had not read Norman Lewis." After a marquee lunch that flashed with a large number of mayoral chains of office assembled from the surrounding Derbyshire countryside, the duchess gave Norman a goody bag of Chatsworth gift shop items as he left. On the station platform as we waited for the train I pointed out to him that his signed guide to Chatsworth was addressed "To Richard Ollard".

"That sort of thing is always happening to me," he said.

The next Saturday, on the eve of his ninetieth birthday, Lesley gave a party for him at Bubs' house in Brighton. Karen had driven from Cornwall, and it was a surprise. Norman was delighted and after he had endured the singing of "Happy birthday" saluted his guests and told them, "I haven't had a better birthday party since I was four."

On Sunday morning – a fresh English Sunday – we walked down to the seafront. Norman wore a sweater with his blue cotton trousers and jacket. The long wisps on top of his head danced, his expression was still, observing, internalised, halfway between blankness and serenity, until he leaned over the rails and pointed out the stretch of tarmac below on which he had competed in a standing half-mile in his Le Mans-winning Alfa in 1938, "coming second to last" in his class. At ninety he still insisted he had never won anything, never discovered anything, had no distinction; an inverted conceit that time had not changed. Perhaps his only positive conceit was that time had not changed *him*. He never referred to his age in his writing, locating himself notion-ally always somewhere around the high point of the arc of human vitality, between the ages of thirty and fifty. On the front at Brighton, that apparent agelessness, the willed part of his literary and personal character that ignored the passing of his own time, acquired for as long as the moment lasted a quality of epic and of pathos. For, to paraphrase Beckett's narrator, he had to go on. He would go on. He could not go on for ever.

There are some people who don't operate with rules. They think everything belongs to them; it doesn't. And Norman felt like that. He felt that everything he had, had to be respectfully and duly earned by appreciating his good fortune being there in the first place. And in the end that's another thing I learnt really, because I learnt that there was still enough of the tapestry that hadn't fallen apart, of the globe that we live on.

Don McCullin

I had these long, long telephone calls with him. He was the master of the good telephone conversation, there would always be interesting or wise things to come out of it. And the thing was, I might as well just say it now, in my life he was one of the most remarkable people I ever met. I think often one's interest in somebody or affection or whatever can be gauged by how often you say to yourself, "Oh I'd like to tell somebody that, it would interest them or make them laugh or they would be able to top it with something interesting themselves." And very very often I thought, Oh I must tell Norman that. He was completely unlike anybody I've ever known and a tremendous addition to my life.

John Hatt

When the tree is gone, we appreciate its shade.
Sicilian proverb, *The March of the Long Shadows*

Between a kiss and a betrayal – what?

1960 diary

32

FINCHINGFIELD

"Death is a black camel that lies down
at every door. Sooner or later you must ride the camel"
Arabian proverb

THE *Happy Ant-Heap* was published on 20 August. "I particularly want you to have this book," Norman told James McNeish, "because the reviews are far and away the best I have ever had. This, to me, is inexplicable. It's OK but I'm stunned to get nearly a whole page (cover) on one of the *Observer* supplements. It's just a collection of pieces – about one third of which have already been published."[1] The young came out in numbers to admire their senior. "Wherever he lands, he has a sharp eye for beauty, oddity and human idiosyncrasy. ... He knows how to camouflage himself with calm. ... For him, the world is never done."[2] "The subtle exactitude of his prose – curiously formal, sometimes Latinate – is a delight to read."[3] "As a triumphant declaration of literary longevity, *The Happy Ant-Heap* must be virtually unparalleled in modern literature."[4]

Norman had contacted McNeish to ask his permission to quote from his published work about Sicily and to ask him for "a few words about life in Cammarata", where McNeish had lived in the early 1960s. McNeish's replies reopened a correspondence that should have primed Norman's memory. In reality working for Dolci, his recording for the BBC had been a blind, he reminded Norman, though a functioning one that he had adopted in order to be accepted in the village. Cammarata had been run by a friendly *capomafia* named Mangiapane who toured his fief on a white horse and, when McNeish presented himself, sent a message to his cousin ordering him to play the proscribed silver jaw's harp for him (proscribed because the Church claimed that its tone made young women swoon and become infertile).

I found Cammarata under his benign tutelage to be morally bankrupt, besides superstitious. The local witch advised mothers to hang fox-toothed amulets round a baby's neck so its teeth would grow evenly. No group society or human association existed. It was found impossible to start a football team. An attempt had once been made to form a musical band from the sister villages of Cammarata and San Giovanni Gemini, but the idea collapsed from mistrust. Illiteracy and unemployment in Cammarata were around 70%.[5]

On 25 January 1999 Norman thanked him for a "marvellous letter" with a scribbled note: unusually scribbled, even by Norman's standards. When I stayed at the Parsonage at the beginning of February, a reason for his haste appeared. He had started writing with high expectations but Lesley said that he was having trouble with the book, feeling it had become "too episodic".[6] Recovering from his doubts, he worked quickly enough to be able to write to Gill Coleridge six weeks later with a promise to "get the Sicilian book off to you tomorrow". With the provisional title "The Dark Princes of Palermo" it had taken him just over a year to write; but the second half of March delivered bad news on two fronts. Giuliana, Marcello Cimino's widow, who had given him and Lesley considerable research help the previous year (and long-standing hospitality at the palazzo on via Maqueda), died of cancer; and Gill Coleridge phoned him with reservations about his manuscript. She wrote the following day to couch these in the tactful encouragement of a loyal agent – "I want to assure you that the book is full of wonderful writing and fascinating stories, and all it needs is a thorough going-over." Norman replied the same day, with gratitude explaining that he was "a born muddler and am dazzled by the somewhat [sic] detective skills with which you have dealt with this matter!".[7] Better news followed. Again a film version of *Naples '44* looked possible – the project was being developed for an independent television production, a first script had been written – and there had been enquiries about options on both *The March of the Long Shadows* and *The Honoured Society*. (Another appeared that September about *The Sicilian Specialist* from the French division of Warner Bros.) He and Lesley flew to the Ionian island of Lefkas and, putting up at the small town of Nidri, he worked every day at revisions of the manuscript. "I've actually found the last Mediterranean unspoiled places [sic]," he told McNeish, "and we are going back (it was so good) in September."[8]

Barely a month after their conversation, he returned his typescript to his agent on 3 May. He was always a rapid rewriter (with Lesley's typing help), but this urgency was curious – and general. There was his hasty letter to McNeish, followed by others that presented him as highly busy ("I've been dashing round the country coping with emergencies," to McNeish enigmatically in March); his rapid rewriting of a book that needed considered, substantial attention; and within ten days of sending off the typescript, another letter to his agent in a tone of pre-emptive insistence.

13.5.99

Dear Gill

I am now in the mood to tackle a new book, and in view of the modest acclaim for *The Happy Ant-Heap* propose something along those lines but with a somewhat more dramatic – and even occasionally sensational content.

Soon after Castro came to power in Cuba I visited on behalf of Ian Fleming's governmental department, plus much of Central America, including Haiti, the Domenican Republic [sic], El Salvador. Some of the material gathered on these expeditions was extraordinary indeed, for the agent with whom I worked also dealt with President Kennedy on his secret visits in search of pleasure in Cuba, and I have a file on certain of his activities,* along with accounts of other happenings which might not be too delicate to include in the narration. . . .

*He was mad on laundresses, for their fresh odour of soap.[9]

What was he feeling? Why the hurry? To the second question he had given his answer, "to make the most of what was left". The most of the last good places. Of seeing. Of writing. Of time. For what he was feeling, no intelligent guess will do. After his death Don McCullin felt that he was "a man who walked in much darker shadows than the ones we normally walk in, he was in the shadow of the shadow. Norman was like one of those eels that come from the Sargasso."

In early 1999 he was beginning to sink slightly deeper in the waters of every day. He was experiencing minor memory lapses. His working memory, in particular the part dedicated to ordering larger units of information and chronology, seemed weaker. His deafness had become pronounced and his hearing aids sometimes could not cope. When friends phoned him, they sometimes found it hard to keep a conversation going.

In February, staying at the Parsonage for a few days, I heard him tell the story of the repatriation of the Soviet soldiers twice within half an hour; he reprised other stories too, and for the first time it was easier to talk to Lesley. After the February visit I phoned regularly. When Norman answered, it was often difficult to deal with the silence, or shriek, of one or other of his hearing aids; then Lesley would come on the line. In retrospect, I didn't consider Norman's side of the battle to hear, and be heard.

"Of course the trouble was, you didn't pick up the signs with Norman. His Alzheimer's was very slow, so that one realised it latterly, because he was not an easy man and could take umbrage about certain situations with people, and then there was this very unforgiving thing and that was 'finish', he didn't want anything more to do with the person."[10]

Spoke to Norman three days ago. "How are you?"

"Adequate."

A silence.

"I was just calling to see how you and Les are. Are things all right?"

"Moderate."

Silence.

"Was it my wife you wished to speak to?"

"I'd love to have a word with Les."

The sound of his walking away. Silence. The sound of his coming slowly back. "I'm afraid she is not in the house."

The line goes dead.

Norman has always, without fail, found something positive to say in the sixteen years I've known him. I phoned Bubs in Brighton and left a message. She phoned back next morning, saying Norman had probably had a series of small strokes. Yesterday I wrote to Les, this morning she phoned. Norman has had a small heart attack, shown by an ECG, and his doctor says there may be an onset of mental . . . she found it hard to say the word. She said that his paranoia "which has always been there" was coming out more, he got depressed when she wasn't there, and he had been depressed. He is writing as well as ever, but personally he is sometimes there, sometimes not. They can only wait and see. I suspect it is much harder than she is saying. She suggested I don't call the house. They're going to France.

Should I have included this? Am I violating the limits of biography or of friendship? (A diary entry of 5 June 1999, it refers to a phone call I made three days earlier, on the 2nd.) I have identified myself in the likeness of Norman's biographer in these pages; in that likeness it seems right to question the inclusion of this piece of quoted material, as it does to say that it is the piece of quoted material I've thought hardest about including. I could have described the onset of Norman's Alzheimer's a hundred other ways, many of them more tactful, and spared myself this internal discussion. Another writer naturally would have – I'm not sure I would have shared the diary extract with another biographer – and might also have found a way to account for Norman's last four years by other means. Feeling called on to justify myself, my only answer is that in any piece of subjective narrative, any story, you make your own leap between events and their envisioning in prose; so once this episode was in place in my mind, once it had happened *there* as part of an understanding of Norman's situation, and had become part of the composition of understanding, it was impossible to suppress it.

The biographer and subject were at war: two subjective views, two antagonists. In his mind Norman had written a story about me. The phone call ended our friendship and all contact. I had got too close to Lesley (in his mind his suspicions went further than that). When Lesley had invited me to stay at the Parsonage that February, she had done it without consulting him. When she told him I was coming he hit the roof, although he showed nothing of his anger when I was there. His reaction, in one sense, was a reflex to a perceived threat – from his youngest days he had always been self-effacing for a reason, always wary, armoured in that complicated, courteous, generous, entertaining, story-laden presentation of self that travelled hand in glove with a habit of hypersensitivity to any apparent peril. In another sense, since all questions of character come down eventually to a question of balance, his reaction was simply a clinical outcome triggered by his illness.

Perhaps illness co-determined his sense of urgency. In June he had written to Sarat, his Indian guide of a decade before, asking when he

might be available for a tour to Bastar in Chhattisgarh state, deeper
inside tribal India, later that year. More reasonably, the rewritten
version of "The Dark Princes of Palermo" had gone to Cape, and Dan
Franklin worked on a first edit and wrote to Norman on his return
from France. (By their close attention to Norman's work in the 1990s,
both Franklin and David Godwin rehabilitated fully the editorial record
of the Cape of the 1950s). The book, Franklin wrote, remained too
short. It read like sketches, its form and chronology were confusing.
Norman replied immediately, almost abjectly,

to say how terribly impressed (as well as a little shamefaced) I am at the terrific
amount of work you have put into this – I cannot thank you enough.[11]

In early September he and Lesley returned to Lefkas and Nidri. When
he started working on the typescript he saw his editor's work in a less
appreciative light, remaining grateful but objecting a month later to "the
extensive cancellations – without explanation – of things that are a matter
of my personal opinion and that I regard as important".[12] Another month
passed and the feeling of interference, and his defensiveness, grew: Franklin's
editing had become "schoolmasterly ... editorial intrusions".[13] James
McNeish and his wife were in England from New Zealand and stayed
at Finchingfield that autumn. McNeish's chief memory is of

a slight feeling of panic. We'd come the night before, we'd had a good meal,
we'd gone to bed and Norman had said, "Okay, so we'll see each other at
breakfast", and we came down to breakfast and there was just Lesley. And
she said, "Norman will be along in a moment." In about ten, fifteen, twenty
minutes he appeared and he had a very short breakfast, and "You'll excuse
me. I'm having trouble with my last chapter", and he vanished.[14]

Struggling to cope with the mental effort of amplifying and ordering
the text as well as the intensity of the editorial exchanges, he was helped
by Gill Coleridge who went through the script with him again at the
end of November. By Christmas Franklin was satisfied. The rewriting
which Norman had thought might take him two months had taken
four. He made light of it to others: to John Hatt he wrote that "I've
only yesterday finished 18 months' work on a book dealing with my
Sicilian adventures – most of it rewritten at least 3 times. I've never
got the knack of writing anything comfortably at the first go!"[15] Hatt

had finally come to lunch that July ("Make it the 4th, if you like. All the lilies will be vulgar by then except for the odd pure white species")[16], and Norman and Lesley saw other friends, including Charlotte Moore, the young assistant director on the Irian Jaya film, whom Norman had become fond of despite his falling out with the director. The writer and historian on India, William Dalrymple, visited in late September and talked all day with him until the light died in the autumn garden. He found Norman "frail but entertaining, wry and modest". Don McCullin, living in Somerset, phoned him from time to time. To begin with, Norman carried on answering the phone,

and then Lesley would answer the phone and we'd chat and I'd say, "How's Norman?" and she'd say, "Oh he's fine, darling," and call him, "Norman, Norman," and he'd pick up the phone. "Ah hello Don, how are you? Where are you going?" And I'd tell him and he'd say, "I'd give my eye teeth to come on the next one." And then one day I rang and it was just Lesley and he didn't pick up the phone any more.[17]

They flew to Barcelona for Christmas and were entertained by Norman's Catalan publisher, Albert Padrol, and his wife Teresa. His unstinting courtesy to friends remained. He sent the Padrols a thank-you copy of Don McCullin's *Sleeping with Ghosts* and wrote a second time a few days later that "Our stay in Barcelona is certainly destined to provide the highlight of the year, and we remember your lavish hospitality with the utmost gratitude."[18] The symptoms of his condition came and went: he developed sudden dislikes for people, mainly men (such as his daughters' partners), was rude to old friends and would then approve of them once they'd gone, and reacted disproportionately. His daughter Kiki one day touched him unexpectedly with her hand; he threatened to break her fingers. His memory did not improve. Lesley watched, cared for and felt the inexorable fall and scattering of the pieces of his character.

We used to have, particularly with a bottle of wine between us, long long discussions on all sorts of things. And that was what at the end of course was missing. A sudden death is dreadful but Norman had just gone so long before, you had no conversation at all with him for years really. It slowly slowly had gone, really it was very slow in its progression but that's what disappeared first. He could sustain it for a short while, he'd go into one of his stories, but he couldn't [keep it going].[19]

Simultaneously Kiki, living in the village, felt the opening of an emotional channel that had not been present before.

I got the feeling that because he was getting more scared as the Alzheimer's got worse, you got that feeling of fear, and I think because of that he was really trying to pull you towards him. He was very loving as well.[20]

He continued willingly to submit to the discipline of writing; his ability to go on writing, to hold the line of his character by writing, was paramount. He really enjoyed it, he told the journalist Ian Jack who visited him the following August. "It may be, he says, the only thing he does enjoy: 'It is my salvation.'"[21] Climbing the Parsonage's wide staircase, walking along the long rolling landing after breakfast, staying in his study till lunchtime, producing in black or blue ballpoint pen 400 words a day. "His best sentences come to him at 4 a.m.," Jack wrote, "when he will get out of bed and get them down 'before they have time to be misshapen by current thought'."

The new collection he had written to Gill Coleridge about the previous May was gathered together, reprints of five longer pieces (four about Indians), and two long new pieces, one about his mission to Aden with Ladislas Farago in 1937, "A Voyage By Dhow", the other about his wartime repatriation of the Uzbeks and Tajiks and subsequent return to the Soviet Union at the invitation of Valentina Evashova. Both are softer versions than their predecessors, and both demonstrative of Norman's continued command of his composing hand, which seems patchy in its output only by comparison with his earlier works. Neither essay is entirely original, or consistent with earlier versions. Both contain new elements, some factual, some less so, some conflicting, as well as instances of paragraphs lifted from earlier books and articles, and they produce, apart from their other effects, a curious heightening of the sense of stories as performance. The effect on the reader is of scenes and events told before and now restaged under different lighting and with modified direction and the odd extra bit of business (the preparations for a public execution on the waterfront at Hodeida) by a narrator claiming full storyteller's rights as Samuel Johnson in 1735 had defined them: that "he who tells nothing exceeding the bounds of probability, has a right to demand, that they should believe him who cannot contradict him".[22]

Dan Franklin read "A Voyage by Dhow" that August and found it "fascinating, very mysterious (in a good sense) and occasionally very funny". He wished Norman "a good summer".[23] Norman replied, "I am going on 2 weeks holiday but alas to Gascony – try as I might to get out of it. However next year I will see to it that we have an adventure at all costs!"[24] Since Norman had sold the photographic business Lesley had invested some of the proceeds in property; the holiday to Gascony was to a house she had recently bought for the family to gather in, a comfortable brick country villa between a maize field and a trout stream outside Ciadoux, north of Saint-Gaudens in the Midi-Pyrénées. While they were at Ciadoux that August Norman started to talk in loops. The symptom passed, but what had been until the holiday a collection of the symptoms of age was recognised as something seriously wrong.

In October he sent the second of the two original pieces, "Into Russia". "You will be astounded to hear that I took nearly three months to write this. Let's hope you find it worth the trouble,"[25] he wrote to Dan Franklin. Franklin did. What was slightly more astounding was that Norman also had another full length book in mind, in fact had had for some time, but he did not tell Franklin yet.

In Sicily, as the Sicilian book now was, was finally published on 2 November. As Norman's books had been for the past five years, it was celebrated for extra-literary as well as literary reasons. Its sketches – a word Norman had rejected as he struggled to write a more encompassing book – "ring with the restless melancholy of old age", one reviewer wrote;[26] it was generally regarded as not his most important book but greeted with accumulated respect by reviewers who knew his work and the extent of his association with Sicily. It was admired too by one reviewer who seemed not to have heard of him; the writers who had were unambivalent in praise. "It is a pleasure to share the addiction of such a stylist as he once more feeds his habit," one wrote.[27] *The Times* offered him its best bouquet, commenting that "reading Lewis on Sicily is like reading a modern Homer or Pausanius".[28]

Cape went back to press only six days after publication. The one cloud over the book was in a letter Norman received from Marcello Cimino's sister-in-law, Gabriella, after she received a finished copy. Conscientiously Gabriella had sought to help by correcting a dozen minor mistakes, but had also gently taken issue with Norman over his portrait of her brother-in-law and Norman's inference that he had been on close terms with senior mafia figures. Lesley knew that Gabriella was right, but Norman refused to answer her, she says. "She wrote wanting changes to the book, and Norman wouldn't have it. He was already having these mini strokes and he was too far gone. I knew there were mistakes in the book as I was typing it, but there were these small battles every day and I couldn't fight him on this. So Gabriella was right."[29]

By spring 2001 Norman's mental condition was labile. At Easter, on the way to the airport to fly to the French house, he tripped over a bag in the drive of the Parsonage and gashed his leg. At Toulouse airport Lesley suggested that he sit down while she and Kiki fetched the luggage, and while he sat, in pain, a thief stole his hand luggage containing all his medicine. Lesley found a doctor and by calling Karen, a French speaker and qualified nurse, was able to arrange for new prescriptions. At the end of the holiday they planned to return from Carcassonne, but walking around the walled city Norman fell again full length over a kerb, gashing his head and the side of his face. In no condition to travel, he had to be taken back to the house for several days to recover.

He still gave the impression, when necessary, that all was well. On 25 April he thanked Gill Coleridge for her reaction to a first draft of the new book he was working on, telling her it was a delight "as a chronic sufferer from doubt in the matter of my literary turn-out, to gulp the reassuring draught of your approval". (Only the substitution of "turn-out" for "output" might have raised suspicion.) Three weeks later he travelled to London for a lunch with Harold Pinter, who wanted to meet him and had asked Peter Crookston if he could arrange it. Crookston "arranged lunch for the three of us at the Groucho Club for Wednesday 16 May".

Norman was then 93 and just beginning to have problems with his memory, though he was very lucid and amusing while we drank a glass of wine in the bar. He told me he had entered the wrong door at the Groucho (it was the one used for large parties) and had been wandering around in the unlit corridors and empty rooms until he came to a room full of people having a conference . . . he explained that he was up from the country and had become lost in the big city. He was then led down to the bar.

[Pinter] arrived a few minutes later, dressed as usual all in black, including a black silk shirt open at the neck. He was totally charming and immensely complimentary about Norman's writing. He said he had just been rereading *The Empire of the East* that morning. "We are all in your debt for the brilliant way you exposed corruption in Indonesia and the part the Americans played in supporting Suharto's terrible regime," he said. . . . Then he went into a rant against American foreign policy, which I joined in. Harold was particularly exercised about the suppression of the independence movement in East Timor, which he said had begun the day after Nixon and Kissinger had visited Jakarta – suggesting that they had given Suharto the go-ahead for the crackdown in which several students were killed.

Norman told him he was working on a new book [and] Harold expressed great admiration for Norman's book on the Sicilian mafia. . . . By now we had been talking for nearly two hours and Norman was tired and his speech was becoming slurred, though he had not taken more than one other glass of wine since we left the bar. . . . It was a very convivial and successful lunch [but] I wish I had taken Harold more seriously when he had told me two years ago that he would like to meet Norman.[30]

To Sara Wheeler, another writer who met him that summer, he contained every physical and mental deficit with charm. "In a small way," he told his visitor, after apologising for not being able to hear her, "none of the bits of me quite work any more."[31]

He still felt that the bit of him that mattered most worked, and believed the book he had sent to his agent in draft in April was now finished. It was on a subject he had long contemplated, its bones the same as his first published book, *Spanish Adventure*: the journey that had taken him, Ernestina and his brother-in-law Eugene to Madrid and the insurrection of October 1934 and then, via the length of Portugal, to Seville. There were differences of method (no canoes), personnel (no Ernestina), chronology and telling. In *Spanish Adventure* he had gone on to north Africa, and where his earlier book veered from France into Spain and out again, he had constructed the new account around a quest, on behalf of his father-in-law Ernesto, to find the tomb of his Corvaja ancestors in the marvellous city of Seville. There was also much recomposition of the story, notably in the addition of his and Eugene's long walk to Zaragoza and of the events in Madrid.

Most importantly to Norman, the subject was Spain: "incorruptible" Spain, Spain as it had first overwhelmed his emotions, Spain that had first demoted him to a stain under the sun in its arid immensity, Spain and "its combinations of desert, forest and mountain" that contained "an element of the fantastic", and with it a perfect Romantic aesthetic. We can never return, except in memory; and this was his own Spain come full circle, his expression of every writer's quixotic denial of the impossibility of return, Spain as a feat of remembrance and reliving.

But memory, and the feat, were eluding him. He wrote twice to Gill Coleridge at the end of June and again in mid-July to say that the book was done; in mid-August he accepted that he needed to return to it after his agent read his second draft and suggested it was not yet a final version. In October *A Voyage By Dhow* was published – *The Times* described the two new pieces as "worth the price of the book alone"[32] – and he took heart from the reviews. They did not help. At the end of November he wrote to Coleridge again, chiding her for not visiting during the lily season in July as she had promised and telling her that "I'm getting fairly close to the finish of the Sevillian campaign (thank God) which should be put to bed by Christmas".[33] It was not: he could not summon the concentration necessary. Lesley recalls, "On the whole he wasn't [unhappy], I don't remember him really being either frightened or really unhappy,"[34] but during his struggle to write the book she gave up offering criticism because he took it badly. "He believed in himself. Despite his mother treating him harshly, she also told him very regularly he was wonderful. From this he possessed a very strong belief in himself. Even if [his writing] didn't seem to make sense, he was sure that was how he wanted it to be."[35]

In the New Year they flew to France for a short holiday. Lesley had sold the villa at Ciadoux and on impulse bought a smaller house nearby, close to L'Isle-en-Dodon. It was more or less a ruin with a spectacular view of a medieval village and thirteenth-century church, and builders had been contracted to restore it who had assured Lesley that, though not completed, enough work had been done for it to be habitable for their arrival. When they arrived they found a building site. Norman could not settle and stayed up all night, and Lesley had to keep showing him her passport to prove who she was. They flew home next day.

Norman wrote to his agent again in May 2002 in a letter a little more untidy than usual that "I hope to be able to show you the book within two or three weeks". He did not send the letter until the end of July, with another letter announcing the book's end, the letter this time also showing signs of struggle.

25.7

Dear Gill,

Delighted to hear from you and will much look forward to seeing you shortly. I believe we'll be here until September – so come whenever you can.

The Tomb in Seville – provisional title, comes to an end this week and I'll

get it off to you as soon as the most of the corrections have been looked into.
    Please come and see us forthwith.
    Love from us both
    Norman[36]

His typescript, finally sent with as much tidying as could be done
to Cape on 10 October, was accepted by Dan Franklin in early December
against a modest advance of £5000, and scheduled for publication the
following November. Franklin did not know how ill his author was.
He had been aware since publishing *The World The World* that each
new typescript necessitated more editorial work, but professionally and
loyally felt that the music lingered on. Norman's later reuse of parts
of older books "was slightly maddening" for an editor.[37] With *The
Tomb in Seville* he felt it did not matter, and much of the un-reused
typescript read remarkably well, in both pictorial and dramatic senses.
As humane and quizzical and coolly warm as always, in places it seemed
as if Norman's verbal landscapes had rubbed flat with age, leaving an
impression that was indistinct and faded. As a whole, the book had
achieved the virtuous contrasts of a Gobelins tapestry hanging on a
château wall, of sharp and brilliant dyes that draw the eye and mingle
with vaguer areas where the colours have submitted to the erosions of
age. The race against time's grim "It was" was won, just.

By December Norman still wrote, Lesley recalls, "or there were always
notebook and pen at his bedside but what he wrote was gobbledy-
gook. He drank less. He ate less."[38] In his papers is an undated scrap
of writing, apparently from his last efforts at *The Tomb in Seville*, that
has an Eliot-like quality in his repeated grappling for description rooted
in physical images, the disintegration of whole sentences leaving isolated
images high and dry, and something touching in its repeated desire to
call Ernesto and the realisation that there is no longer any time.

This was Britain by the sea with the moon mysteri. . . . . . y seabirds
the delivery of newspapers and milk
the yawning customs men
So what next
Just in time to catch the 8.15 if we're lucky

if we're lucky to call Ernesto
mewing seabirds and the soft patter of rain smell of fish
the sea smell captured like a trapped animal in the rain
the groan of fog horn and rattling of chain
A bus goes in half an hour
if we're lucky with customs
we'll just have time to call Ernesto on the phone, we'll have time to call
Ernesto on the phone
Well here we are, all in one piece and time is no longer our own.
Bus goes in 12 minutes not really time even to call Ernesto on the phone
seagulls' melancholy excitement and melancholy sea
the gulls' excited melancholy
the fish-smell in nets – the excited melancholy repeated endlessly by the
gulls[39]

He continued to have periods of a kind of lucidity, sometimes saying to Lesley, "I'm mad, aren't I?" Sometimes he was convinced he was in Enfield, sometimes in France. His nights were disturbed, and his doctor prescribed Risperdal for his anxiety, which he had been prescribed during the early paranoid stage of the illness. He remained anxious and was always calling for Lesley if she was out of the room for more than a few minutes. His weight went down to 57 kilos and he began to hide things. (His credit cards, Lesley's purse with £100 in it.) With his other problems – arrhythmia, angina, and a faulty heart valve – his doctor thought he would not last beyond Christmas. When he did, the doctor conceded that he had not reached ninety-four for nothing. He clung to the remnants of his toughness through January, sometimes rebelling, not sleeping and staying up much of the night: one morning Lesley came downstairs and found an empty box of chocolates and a half-drunk bottle of wine on the kitchen table. Occasionally he even seemed to turn his illness to his advantage: on Lesley's birthday, after a family lunch, he asked to go for a drive, a favourite activity. Lesley told him she had had too much to drink, and Gawaine's wife Ginny offered to take him out. As they drove through the Essex downland he decided that he was in India and was astonished that the Indian countryside looked so much like England.

By March he had become thinner and was eating very little, in bed almost all the time. A will still resisted. In early April Lesley took him for a drive in their new car, from Finchingfield to Kiki's house in north London. Norman slept most of the way, and when they arrived Lesley put him to bed. He woke up and announced he would commit suicide if he had to wait any longer. When they arrived back at the Parsonage he said, "Well, that was a very pleasant afternoon," and suggested to Lesley they go for a drive in the new car, not remembering he had just driven to his daughter's.

In June Lesley, who for months had been under a version of house arrest – Norman continued to be anxious and call her if she was out of the house or room for more than a few minutes – arranged to go to France for a few days to move some belongings into a house Kiki and her husband had bought. She left on a Wednesday, 11 June; Norman took her departure well. Gawaine arrived with his family from London, and on Thursday morning Norman's carer came and Gawaine took Norman into the garden, by the swimming pool where a young local man was doing some weeding. When he and his father got back to the conservatory Norman told Gawaine, "Thank you very much for your work. I'll pay you when I can."

"I'm your son."

"If you don't take your foot out [of the door], I'll call the police."

The carer was locked inside with Norman, Gawaine was locked out. The doctor was called, but said that with Norman's heart condition, an injection to calm him might kill him. Bubs drove up from Richmond where she was living and "worked a miracle" calming her father down. Norman was nevertheless up most of the night, walking up and down, and Lesley was forced to return on Friday. When he saw her Norman told her it had been "the worst experience of my life, I was about to commit suicide".

His power of recognition continued to decline and he sometimes asked his wife who she was. Once, coming downstairs, he asked her, "Are you the queen?"[40] He became incontinent and Lesley found it difficult to stop him falling out of bed. His doctor told her that there was no alternative to hospitalising him. On 11 July he was admitted to Saffron Walden Community Hospital, a small cottage hospital with only two wards. "By that time he was really almost unaware that he'd gone to hospital. They took him by ambulance and luckily they gave him the side ward which was bright and sunny. One of the nurses came up to him, and he held her hand and squeezed her hand, and she said, 'I think he thinks I'm you.'"[41] Well cared for, he was no longer aware of very much and barely knew anyone. Karen came. "I was so glad that when they called me he was unconscious because he always said to me, 'If I'm ill and you come I'll know it's going to be the end, you've come to bump me off.' I spoke to him in Spanish so that it would be something that might trigger off pleasant memories, I quoted him his favourite poems of García Lorca."[42] She disapproved of the nurses' routine of sitting her father in an armchair, where he sat with his head slumped, and that they would not give him a catheter because he had pulled catheters out, and drew herself up and, with the resolve of the girl who had demanded of her father in Ibiza fifty years before that he "Yield the bottle" of Anis del Mono, insisted he have a catheter. The doctor acquiesced.

Norman was comfortable again, but he was ill with pneumonia, unconscious, and his organs were failing one by one. In his last hours he called out, "Monty, Monty," trying to reach the beloved older brother he had not seen since he was seven, and died early in the morning of 22 July of bronchopneumonia and heart failure, with Lesley at his bedside.

It was the end of the lily season. He had made himself scarce for the last time.

The Tomb in Seville, Norman's account of his first adventure, was published in November 2003. Spain, when he travelled there in September 1934, was Europe's antithesis and his own, a country of extremes and hallucinations and straight-backed vitality, an escape from Enfield's nothingness. The book is a double reconstruction, of a journey and of a memory of a journey, into a double time, a twentieth century that precurses the twentieth century: surviving Moorish Spain, pre-industrial Spain, Spain on the edge of Africa. This place and time, afterwards, became more than a subject for him. They were a pole, a magnetic South, its flag planted in the city of Seville, to which he was drawn back repeatedly and by which he thereafter set the compass of his escapes. He began travelling as a Romantic hedonist; continued as a more worldly one (to the extent of including spying among his pleasures, as a kind of anti-007 who was the real thing); and ended in his own self-denying sub-category, pleasing himself in observation, addicted equally to the words he found and the places they portrayed. "If this is your land, where are your stories?" the Indians of British Columbia are said to have asked state officials when the government demanded to appropriate their territory. Norman, an outsider from nowhere, made it his pleasure to tell stories about places that still had them (by implication, of course, the places he knew but didn't write about were damned).

But beneath his pleasure were a lifelong desire, and inability, to belong. In pursuit of the happiness and humanity that belonging offered, neither available in his formative life at Forty Hill and Carmarthen, he found them in his written life, and beginning and ending in Sevillian Spain what he communicated – and what had gone, it seemed, immediately after he died – was a whole way of seeing the world through that lens. So his writing, like Swift's (another essayist and polemicist) or Defoe's (another writer, journalist, businessman and spy), accumulates into a makeshift encyclopedia, and he himself into the encyclopedist. His encyclopedia is of belonging and loss; not one with any pretence at objectivity, but with a theme – the theme of his century – and a first-person bias that are matched by the ubiquity and superiority of his focusing eye: an encyclopedist's subjectivity, in fact, that far from partially witnessing the world's wholeness, samples it with a gaze so intense that the world itself changes before the reader's eyes.

All of which is said with a final qualification: in person, so constant were his curiosity and enthusiasm that his concern for everything that was being lost in the world was forever overruled by his interest in what came next.

ACKNOWLEDGEMENTS

I could not have written this account of Norman's life without the unfailing encouragement and kindness of Lesley Lewis, who gave me unrestricted access to Norman's notebooks, diaries, letters and other papers. Her generosity, warmth, wonderful company, and relaxed but constant support in the face of my five years of enquiries and, ultimately, of my version of the man she shared her life with for half a century are inadequately recognised by any praise I can offer.

Norman's children, Norman "Ito" Lewis, Karen Holman, Gareth Lewis, Kiki Wood and Gawaine Lewis, all offered me similar kindness and candour.

Among those who knew Norman well, I want to pay a particular tribute to Gwen Merrington, Norman's childhood friend who grew up with him in Forty Hill and who, as this book moves towards publication, is approaching her ninety-ninth birthday. She has submitted with grace and amused good humour countless times to my descending on her in Devon, and asking her if we could just go over that again. Without her, Part One would have been vastly the poorer.

Norman made a bonfire of a large quantity of his papers in the 1990s. Careless of his place in posterity, he may have turned fire-starter to remove traces of his private life but the fire was principally lit to clear his study of rubbish. The remaining Norman Lewis archive, including his seventy-odd notebooks and diaries, is with the Lewis estate, represented by the Rogers, Coleridge & White Ltd agency, London. For access to other sources of Norman's papers and related material, I am indebted to Frances Wollen, Jim Palma and the Victor Gollancz archive at the Orion Publishing Group; Verity Andrews and the George Routledge & Sons and Jonathan Cape archives at Reading University

Library; Juliette Mitchell at Penguin Books, Nicholas Lee and the Hamish Hamilton archive at Bristol University Library; Jean Rose and the Random House archive, Rushden; *Granta* magazine; Gill Coleridge at Rogers, Coleridge & White Ltd; and Rose Baring and Barnaby Rogerson at Eland Publishing Ltd.

I want to express my immense thanks to those who offered me letters, diaries, recordings and unpublished manuscripts: Edward Burman, Guiditta Cimino Nicosia, Peter Crookston, Leila Hadley Luce, Colin H Hamilton, Nathan Keyfitz, James McNeish, Barrie Nicholls, Redmond O'Hanlon, Bruce Palling, Abby Perelman, Tristram Powell, Rodrigo Rey Rosa, Gabriella Saladino, Michael Sells, Nicholas Shakespeare, Ian Thomson and Julie Varnals. For allowing me access to unedited transcripts of their interviews I am deeply grateful to Pico Iyer, John Keay, and William Zinsser, and to James Owen and Nicholas Wroe for permission to quote from their published interviews.

Many of the above named also shared their memories of Norman in conversation, and my composition of Norman's life would have been impossible without their generous stories and those of: Jean-Luc Benard, Malcolm Borthwick, Richard Colmaine, Joyce Dale, William Dalrymple, Basil and Marion Davidson, Alex Frater, Charles Glass, David Godwin, Ken Griffiths, Paul Henley, Chris Hooke, Ian Jack, Colin Jones, Pauline Kenway, Alain Le Garsmeur, Len Lyons, Angus MacKinnon, Don McCullin, Tom Maxwell, Peggy Milton, David Montgomery, Nicholas Murray, the late Eric Nicholls, Albert Padrol, Joan Puckeridge, Luise Rainer, Dudley Reed, Christopher Sinclair-Stevenson, Colin Thubron, the late Sergio Viggiani, the late Derek Wise and Nancy Wise, and Pamela Zargarani. For their time and generous hospitality I would also like to thank: *Britain*: Lorna Bedford, Michael Bracewell and Linder Sterling, Alex and Monique Lifschutz, Redmond and Belinda O'Hanlon, Nicholas and Gillian Shakespeare, Gloria Ward, Nick Whiting; *Naples*: Francesco Durante, Sergio Lambiase, Carlo Knight, Raimondo di Maio, Paolo de Marco, Xan Smiley; *Sicily*: Laura Long, Renata Pucci Zanca, Pasquale Marchese and Elena Vincenzo, Gabriella Saladino, Mary Taylor Simeti; *Guatemala*: Andre Cloutier, Ana Cofiño, Fernando Mejia Flores and Pauline Décamps, Oscar Perén; *Vietnam, Laos and Cambodia*: Peter Murray, Vo Ngoc Thu, Sengphone Chanthala; *Cuba*: Elizabeth and Joseito, Estudios Areito.

I am indebted to the following for help in many forms: Tom Alban, the late Constance Allan, Richard Beswick, Alex Bowler, Stephen Corry,

Marleen Daniels, Peder W Eriksson, Alan Greer, Robin Hanbury-Tenison, Lisa Harrison, Bryan J Hewitt, Zoe Hood, Lucy Hughes-Hallett, Alastair Kenneil, Michael Kerr, Stuart Miller, Peter Moseley, Penelope Phillips, Juliet Pickering, Simon Prosser, Josep M Romero, John Ryle, Linda Shaugnessy, Sarah Spankie, Peter Straus, Nikolai and Alla Yerynyak; the staff of the Newspapers Reading Room, British Library; Bob Light, Bugatti Owners Club; Richard Day, David Morys and Julie Bridcutt, Bugatti Trust; Graham Dalling, Enfield Council; M C Weeks, Enfield Grammar School; Elaine Camroux-Maclean, Foreign & Commonwealth Office Library; Diane Wilcocks and Richard Yarwood, Forty Hill School; Catherine Armstrong, Alasdair MacInnes and Felicity Windmill, HarperCollins UK; Toby Haggith and the staff of the Collections, Imperial War Museum; Alan Edwards, Fred Judge and Jonathan Baker, Intelligence Corps Association and archive; Miles Gallant, Motorbooks; the staff of the National Archives; Brian Liddy, National Museum of Photography, Film and Television; Sara Beaugeard, Royal Photographic Society; Paul Smith, Thomas Cook UK Ltd; Pat Davy, The Vintage Motor Cycle Club; Guy Walker, Tim Walker Restorations.

My father Jack Evans deserves especial gratitude for, among very many things, the weeks he spent transcribing my interviews.

I would like to thank Lesley Lewis, Ito Lewis, Kiki Wood, Samara Lewis, Don McCullin, Gwen Merrington, David Montgomery and Albert Padrol for the loan and use of photographs from their private collections. Thanks are also due to *Amateur Photographer*, The Klemantaski Collection and the Orion Publishing Group for their permission to use copyright images. Efforts have been made to trace all proprietors of copyright material, and where this has not been possible (as in the case of the translation of Herodotus between chapters 10 and 11) I regret any omissions, which will be rectified in future editions.

My profound thanks go to my publisher, Dan Franklin, for his exemplary levels of patience and enthusiasm; to my agent, Derek Johns, for his seamless encouragement; to Norman's agent, Gill Coleridge, for her warm support; and to John Hatt for our many discussions, and for keeping Norman's books in print.

My least specific appreciation goes to Natasha, for everything.

Julian Evans, Clifton Down, 2008

ILLUSTRATIONS

NL = photographs taken by Norman Lewis

First section

"Self, washed and polished for the occasion" (Lesley Lewis)

David Warren Lewis, tea tycoon. With Norman's grandmother and
   father (Lesley Lewis)
The Lewises of Forty Hill: Richard, Monty, Norman and Louisa (Lesley
   Lewis)
Aunts Polly (standing) and Annie (Lesley Lewis)

343 Carterhatch Lane (Julian Evans)
Life after Forty Hill: the Beacon of Light Spiritualist church (Julian
   Evans)
Forty Hall (Julian Evans)

On the roof of 343 Carterhatch Lane (Lesley Lewis)
First vehicle (Lesley Lewis)
The Arab of Enfield: self-portrait with headdress, dagger and hand-
   guns (NL, Lesley Lewis)

At 17 with Louisa and one of Sir Henry Bowles' maidenly "visiters",
   possibly Miss Phoebe Tupperton (Lesley Lewis)
At 19 with unknown Welsh attendants (Lesley Lewis)

First motorcycle, a Reading-Standard (Lesley Lewis)
The dust roads and orchards of Forty Hill (Lesley Lewis)
Family, and Carmarthen relations (Lesley Lewis)
Gwen Nicholls in British East Africa, holding off another suitor (Gwen
    Merrington)

Levantine swell, Nice, March 1930 (Lesley Lewis)

Studio subject, by his friend Alex Hagen (Ito Lewis)
In Paris with Ernestina, 1933 (Ito Lewis)

Driver: Bugatti dual-cowl Type 30 (Lesley Lewis)
Driver: Bugatti Type 40 (Lesley Lewis)
Driver: road-race FWD Alvis (Lesley Lewis)

Tea with mother (Lesley Lewis)

Hotel breakfast, late 1930s (Lesley Lewis)

Ernestina and her Moroccan kestrel by Norman, Epping Forest, 1936
    (NL, Ito Lewis)
Norman by Ernestina (Ito Lewis)

Writer: dustjacket of his first book, *Spanish Adventure* (photograph
    NL, jacket by permission of the Orion Publishing Group Ltd)
Businessman: advertisement from *Amateur Photographer*, 19 October
    1938 (courtesy *Amateur Photographer*)

Spy: "The sambuk was a small one without colour or carving, but
    graceful of line . . . . The negro waved his arm irritably and shouted
    in Arabic that it was improper to photograph him undressed" (NL,
    Lewis papers)
Suakin, "a habitation of dragons and a court for owls", 1937 (NL,
    Lewis papers)

Milan Grand Prix, 1937 (NL, Ito Lewis)
London garage, 1937 (Lesley Lewis)

Iver Heath, spring 1939 (Ito Lewis)

Ernesto Corvaja with grandson Ito (NL, Ito Lewis)
Father and son at Pine Cottage (Ito Lewis)

Second section

Hill climbing in the Type 51 and white shoes (Lesley Lewis)
Ernestina's scrapbook (Ito Lewis)
Lying fourth in the second Mountain Handicap at Brooklands, 29 May
    1939 (© The Klemantaski Collection)

Fifth Avenue, July 1939 (Ito Lewis)

In Mexico, August 1939 (Ito Lewis)

Ernestina and Ito, Havana, a few days after Norman's departure for
    England (Ito Lewis)
On the beach, Jaimanitas Club, Havana (NL, Ito Lewis)
Embarking at New York, October 1939 (Lesley Lewis)
The view from 4 Gordon Street, 11 May 1941 (NL, Lesley Lewis)

Private Lewis, Army version (Lesley Lewis)
Sergeant Lewis, studio version (Ito Lewis)
Oliver Myers (Ito Lewis)

Norman's diary with photograph of Hester (Lewis papers)
Hester, St Catherine's Fort, Tenby, 1949 (NL, Lewis papers)
"Tous les hommes sont pareils." Mme Phuoc, Saigon, 1950 (NL, Lewis
    papers)

Author, 1950s (Lesley Lewis)
Lesley Burley at 19 and 23 (Lesley Lewis)

Karen, Gareth and Ito in Tossa and Ibiza (NL, Lesley Lewis)

"The harbour of Ibiza is full of sailing ships, and the quayside is a
    permanent exhibition of their jumbled cargoes" (NL, Lewis papers)
Ito and mero photographed with the Lewis Photo-Marine (NL, Ito Lewis)
Lupita, Ibiza (NL, Lewis papers)

Guatemala: Burning copal incense offerings to the Maya-Quiché gods on the church steps, Chichicastenango (NL, Lewis papers)

Huehuetenango in the 1950s (Julian Evans)

The Parsonage in the 1960s (NL, Lesley Lewis)

Family holiday: Kiki, Lesley, Gawaine, Norman in northern Spain (Lesley Lewis)

Africa, two decades apart (Lesley Lewis)

Family man (Lesley Lewis)

Filming: At Vesuvius (Tristram Powell, director, is on the right) (Lesley Lewis)

In the West Papua (Irian Jaya) highlands with Chris Hooke and Yali boys (© Don McCullin)

The gardener (Lesley Lewis)

Not understanding the concept of charades (Lesley Lewis)

Return to Tossa with Lesley and Albert Padrol (Albert Padrol)

At Kiki's wedding (Lesley Lewis)

At Brighton on his ninetieth birthday with the author, 28 June 1998 (Samara Lewis)

In the conservatory at Finchingfield: portrait by Don McCullin of "one of my dearest friends" (© Don McCullin)

NOTES

Prelude: The reluctant biographer

1 Norman Lewis interviewed by John Keay, *Kaleidoscope*, BBC Radio 4, transcript, 17 July 1987.
2 Milan Kundera, *The Art of the Novel*, London 1988, p127.
3 Paul Delany, *British Autobiography in the Seventeenth Century*, London 1969, p141.
4 E H Gombrich, *In Search of Cultural History*, Oxford 1969, p39.
5 Kundera, op. cit., p145.

Part One

Becoming
A Youth in Eight Tendencies:
Exclusion, madness, mistrust, boredom, escape,
dandyism, hedonism, speed

Chapter 1: Arabia

1 Letter, 31 March 1937, National Archives, FO371/20780.
2 Norman Lewis interviewed by the author, 13 March 1996.
3 Interview with Eric Nicholls, 3 December 2003.
4 Interview with Joyce Dale, 3 December 2003.
5 *South from Granada*, London 1957.
6 "Blessing the squire and his relations", unpublished TS, Lewis papers.
7 *The Happy Ant-Heap*, London 1998, p6.
8 "Blessing the squire and his relations", loc. cit.

9   Interview with Gwen Merrington (née Nicholls), 25 March 2003.

10   Gwen Merrington, "Memories of Lewis", unpublished MS, March 2003.

11   *Jackdaw Cake*, London 1985, p29.

12   Ibid., p35.

13   Interviews with Gwen Merrington, 25 March and 13 May 2003.

14   Interview with Gwen Merrington, 25 March 2003.

15   *The Happy Ant-Heap*, op. cit.

16   Norman Lewis interviewed by the author, loc. cit.

17   Until the 1950s school heads had, by statute, to keep a log. Despite being advised in the "Code of Regulations" to make "the briefest entry" and that "No reflections or opinions of a general character are to be entered", despite the log's being inspected by the vicar and squire, and then by bureaucrats from town halls, head teachers were recklessly human in their entries, glorying in their triumphs, grumbling about their pupils, vituperating about parents, colleagues and the heating system. Surviving logs like Frederick Eastaugh's are a fascinating glimpse into educational and social history. At least one English novel is based on a school log: Byron Rogers in his biography of J L Carr notes that Carr's novel *The Harpole Report* is largely based on the school log he kept for fifteen years at Highfields primary school in Kettering.

18   Norman Lewis interviewed by the author, loc. cit.

19   Bill Nicholls recorded memoir, 20 September 1994.

20   Ibid.

21   "Airship on fire. Bodies falling", unpublished TS, Lewis papers.

22   Gwen Merrington recorded memoir, December 1993.

23   Ibid.

24   Bill Nicholls recorded memoir, 20 September 1994.

25   Phone conversation with Gwen Merrington, 2 March 2005.

26   Phone conversation with Gwen Merrington, 14 February 2005.

27   Norman Lewis interviewed by the author, loc. cit.

28   Ibid.

29   Norman Lewis interviewed by William Zinsser, unedited TS, 7 March 1995.

30   Quoted in interview with James Owen, *Daily Telegraph*, 27 June 1998.

31   Letter from Gwen Merrington, 29 July 2007.

32   *The World The World*, London 1996, p293.

33   Bill Nicholls recorded memoir, loc. cit.

Chapter 2: China

1   *Jackdaw Cake*, London 1985, p4.

2   Ibid., pp4–5.

3   Ibid., p8.

4   Ibid., p6.

5   Norman Lewis interviewed by Pico Iyer, unedited TS, January 1991.

6   *Jackdaw* Cake, op. cit., p13.

7   23 February 1931.

8   "Blessing the squire and his relations", unpublished TS, Lewis papers.

9   *Jackdaw Cake*, op. cit., p24.
10 Ibid.
11 Ibid., p25.
12 "A season in Tenby castle", unpublished TS, Lewis papers.

Chapter 3: Rejected worlds

1   Phone conversation with Lesley Lewis, 10 May 2006.
2   Interview with Eric Nicholls, 3 December 2003.
3   Phone conversation with Gwen Merrington, 14 February 2005.
4   Acceptance speech at the Thomas Cook Travel Book Award, 30 January 1992.
    A more accurate translation is "To the limit of my ability".
5   *Jackdaw Cake*, London 1985, p42.
6   Interview with Eric Nicholls, loc. cit.
7   Norman Lewis interviewed by Nicholas Wroe, *Guardian*, 11 November 2000.
8   Thomas Cook Travel Book Award speech, 30 January 1992.
9   *Jackdaw Cake*, op. cit., p39.
10 Loc. cit.
11 *Jackdaw Cake*, op. cit., p38.
12 Interview with Gwen Merrington, 25 March 2003.
13 *Jackdaw Cake*, op. cit., p40.
14 *Gargantua and Pantagruel*, Book Four, chs 55 and 56.
15 Norman Lewis interviewed by the author, 13 March 1996.
16 Gwen Merrington, "Memories of Lewis", unpublished MS, March 2003.
17 Norman Lewis interviewed by William Zinsser, unedited TS, 7 March 1995.
18 An association for supporting and spreading the principles of the Conservative
    Party.
19 *Jackdaw Cake*, op. cit., p57.
20 "God bless the squire", *The Happy Ant-Heap*, op. cit., pp1–3.
21 *Jackdaw Cake*, op. cit., pp45–6.
22 "Blessing the squire and his relations", unpublished TS, Lewis papers.
23 *Jackdaw Cake*, op. cit., p47.
24 "Your description of Sir Henry Bowles' infatuation with women seems to
    correlate with the invitation of my parents and the gifts that he gave to my
    mother such as a pair of earrings and also a silver cigarette case. ... My
    mother was a rather attractive and vivacious woman" – letter from Peder W.
    Eriksson, 13 March 1997.
25 "Blessing the squire and his relations", loc. cit.
26 Bill Nicholls, Gwen's father, had been a founder of the Enfield Labour Party.
27 Interview with Norman ("Ito") Lewis, 5 May 2004.
28 Norman Lewis interviewed by the author, loc. cit.
29 Ibid.
30 Ibid.
31 *Jackdaw Cake*, op. cit., p56.
32 Quoted in Mea Allan, *E A Bowles*, London 1973, pp165–6.
33 Interview with Gwen Merrington, loc. cit.
34 Gwen Merrington, "Memories of Lewis", loc. cit.
35 Interview with Joyce Dale, 3 December 2003.

36 Gwen Merrington recorded memoir, July 1998.

37 *Jackdaw Cake*, op. cit., p54.

38 Ibid., p61.

39 In October 1924 the Conservatives were returned to power when a letter purportedly from Grigori Zinoviev, president of the executive committee of the Comintern, to the Communist Party of Great Britain was published in the *Daily Mail*. The letter, urging British Communists to stir up the proletariat in preparation for revolution, was a forgery, possibly by British secret service officers. Its invention was an act of political thuggery that ensured Ramsay MacDonald's Labour government lost the election four days later.

40 Bill Nicholls recorded memoir, 20 September 1994.

41 Letter, undated, 1980s.

42 In *Jackdaw Cake* his school-leaving takes place an unexpected decade later, after "the ice-age following the great American slump had set in". When the book was published in 1985 Norman was in his late seventies, but few people knew his real age. His last three children believed he was much younger. The first hundred pages of his autobiography are scattered with false and improbable dates to throw readers off the scent.

43 Norman Lewis interviewed by Nicholas Wroe, *Guardian*, 11 November 2000.

44 Interview with Gwen Merrington, 13 May 2003.

Chapter 4: Mrs England's Dining Rooms

1 Norman Lewis interviewed by Pico Iyer, unedited TS, January 1991.

2 Norman Lewis interviewed by the author, 13 March 1996.

3 Interview with Joyce Dale, 3 December 2003. The Nichollses were nowhere near wealthy enough for the girls to buy the latest fashions. Gwen and her sisters made most of their own clothes.

4 Gwen Merrington, "Memories of Lewis", unpublished MS, March 2003.

5 Gwen Merrington recorded memoir, July 1998.

6 Ibid.

7 Ibid.

8 Gwen Merrington, "Memories of Lewis", loc. cit.

9 Ibid.

10 Ibid.

11 Gwen Merrington recorded memoir, loc. cit.

12 Ibid.

13 Gwen Merrington, "Further memories of Lewis", March 2003.

14 Gwen Merrington recorded memoir, loc. cit.

15 "In view of how lightly such an escapade would be viewed today, [telling the story now] is more of a way of at last revealing rather than concealing the truth". Ibid.

16 Gwen Merrington, "Further memories of Lewis", loc. cit.

17 Norman Lewis interviewed by the author, loc. cit.

18 The Goat tavern sat on Forty Hill green next to the now filled-in duckpond. At the time of writing it is closed and boarded up.

19 *Jackdaw Cake*, London 1985, p65.

20 Ibid.

21 See Chapter 6.

Chapter 5: Sicily

1   *Jackdaw Cake*, London 1985, p69.
2   Interview with Joyce Dale, 3 December 2003.
3   Interview with Gwen Merrington, 25 March 2003.
4   Interview with Gwen Merrington, 13 May 2003.
5   Phone conversation with Gwen Merrington, 8 December 2003.
6   Interview with Gwen Merrington, 13 May 2003.
7   Interview with Gwen Merrington, 25 March 2003.
8   Interview with Gwen Merrington, 13 May 2003.
9   *Jackdaw Cake*, op. cit., p74.
10 Ibid., p82.
11 Ibid., p79.
12 Ibid., p81.
13 Ibid., p82.
14 Ibid., p107.
15 Interview with Ito Lewis, 24 February 2005.
16 Interview with Ito Lewis, 17 March 2004.
17 Norman Lewis interviewed by the author, 13 March 1996.
18 *Vile Bodies*, London 1930, p112. (Page numbers refer to the 2000 Penguin edition.)
19 Ibid., p158. There is of course also a Speed King, a "dirt-track racer" whose activities are followed in the novel.
20 *Society Racket*, London 1933, p65.
21 Ibid., p172.
22 Interview with Gwen Merrington, 25 March 2003.
23 Interview with Eric Nicholls, 3 December 2003.
24 Phone conversation with Joyce Dale, 22 November 2003.
25 *Jackdaw Cake*, op. cit., p90.
26 *Amateur Photographer*, 5 April 1933.
27 *Amateur Photographer*, 14 February 1934.
28 *Jackdaw Cake*, op. cit., p95.
29 Ibid., p96.
30 Ibid., p100.
31 *Vile Bodies*, op. cit., p162.

Chapter 6: Spain

Inter-chapter material referring to Victor Gollancz Ltd is reproduced by kind permission of the Orion Publishing Group.

1   "The first experience can never be repeated. The first love, the first sunrise, the first South Sea island, are memories apart, and touched a virginity of sense" – *In the South Seas*, Tusitala edition, London 1924, p4.
2   *Spanish Adventure*, London 1935, p3. (Page numbers refer to the Henry Holt & Co. US edition.)
3   Ibid., p4.
4   Ibid., p5.

5   Ibid., p9.
6   Ibid., p12.
7   *Don Quixote*, trans. Edith Grossman, London 2004, p652.
8   *Spanish Adventure*, op. cit., p33.
9   Ibid., p42.
10 Ibid., p66.
11 Ibid., p87.
12 Quoted in Gerald Brenan, *The Spanish Labyrinth*, Cambridge 1943, p275.
13 *Spanish Adventure*, op. cit., p101.
14 Brenan, op. cit., p281.
15 *Spanish Adventure*, op. cit., p110.
16 Ibid., pp114–6.
17 *The Tomb in Seville*, London 2003, p44.
18 *Spanish Adventure*, op. cit., p127.
19 Ibid., p131.
20 Ibid., pp137–8.
21 Ibid., p143.
22 Norman Lewis interviewed by the author, 13 March 1996.
23 Edward Conze, quoted in Brenan, op. cit., p271.
24 Brenan, op. cit., p271.
25 Ibid.
26 *Spanish Adventure*, op. cit., p179.
27 Ibid. He may not have been aware that Toledo was not all tourists and touts.
    In the province of Toledo as many as 100 agricultural collectives had been
    established by the workers and UGT officials on land formerly managed by
    large landlords. The industriousness Norman witnessed may have been some
    of those collectives at work.
28 Interview with Don McCullin, 13 July 2004. McCullin admits he now himself
    uses the same yellow filter in his anthropological work. "I always want the
    black sky and the black people."
29 *Spanish Adventure*, op. cit., p234.
30 Ibid., pp237–8.
31 Ibid., p255.
32 Not to be confused with the post-impressionist Viktor Borisov-Musatov (1870–
    1905) – if Norman gave the Russian his real name.
33 "Bousbir" in colloquial Moroccan still signifies a brothel. The original Bousbir
    was closed down in 1953.
34 Norman obscured his identity. Quazim's "real" name, the one he gave Norman
    at any rate, was Osman. Norman photographed Osman but for libel reasons
    the photograph was not included and is now lost.
35 *Spanish Adventure*, op. cit., p273.

Chapter 7: Anywhere but here

1   *Amateur Photographer*, 1 May 1946.
2   Victor Gollancz archive, Worthing. Material from the Victor Gollancz archive
    is reproduced by kind permission of the Orion Publishing Group.

3   Norman Lewis interviewed by the author, 13 March 1996.

4   About £6000 at today's rates.

5   Letter from Norman Collins to Norman Lewis, 4 February 1936, Victor Gollancz archive, loc. cit.

6   Quoted in a letter from Norman Collins to Dr Pallares, 11 February 1936, Victor Gollancz archive, loc. cit.

7   *Jackdaw Cake*, London 1985, p103.

8   Ibid., p104.

9   *A Voyage by Dhow*, London 2001, p1.

10 Foreign Office minute of 22 May 1937, National Archives, FO371/20778.

11 "Strategic Importance of the Yemen", report by the Committee of Imperial Defence, Chiefs of Staff Sub-committee, 19 February 1937, National Archives, FO371/20780.

12 *A Voyage by Dhow*, op. cit., p2.

13 Norman Lewis interviewed by Pico Iyer, unedited TS, January 1991.

14 *A Voyage by Dhow*, op. cit., p8.

15 *The Riddle of Arabia*, London 1939, p99. Farago's claim that this 120-kilometre plain was part of the Empty Quarter, hundreds of miles to the north, is pure fantasy.

16 *A Voyage by Dhow*, op. cit., p7.

17 *The Riddle of Arabia*, op. cit., p69. This passage attracts a marginal line of crosses in Norman's copy of Farago's book.

18 Ibid., p94.

19 "Farago wrote an autobiography which I have been trying for years to get my hands on. This has been finally hunted down by a friend and . . . helps to confirm my opinion that both in Abyssinia and later in Aden under the [British] government's protection he was a spy in the service of the Italians" – letter from Norman Lewis to his agent Gill Coleridge, 8 May 2000, Rogers, Coleridge & White Ltd archive, London.

20 *Jackdaw Cake*, op. cit., p119.

21 *Sand and Sea in Arabia*, London 1938, p30.

22 Ibid., Foreword.

23 Ibid., p57.

24 Ibid., p61. This paragraph reappears, with one word changed, in "A Voyage by Dhow".

25 Ibid., p67.

26 Ibid., p89.

27 Ibid., p105.

28 *A Voyage by Dhow*, op. cit., p45.

29 *Sand and Sea in Arabia*, op. cit., p118.

30 Norman Lewis interviewed by the author, loc. cit.

31 *Sand and Sea in Arabia*, op. cit., pp119–20.

Chapter 8: To the edge

1   And rarest. Only twenty-five 500Ks were built between 1935 and 1936.
2   Norman Lewis interviewed by the author, 13 March 1996.
3   "There I was, at Brooklands, in the fastest Bugatti", *Observer* magazine, 7 October 1979.
4   With the marginally eccentric title of *African Majesty: a Record of Refuge at the Court of the King of Bangangte in the French Cameroons*, London 1938.
5   Letters of June 1938, George Routledge & Sons archive, University of Reading.
6   Letter from Julie Varnals to Gwen Merrington, 17 April 2003.
7   Routledge archive, loc. cit.
8   *The World The World*, London 1996.
9   R G Lewis advertisement, *Amateur Photographer*, 5 October 1938.
10 Ibid.
11 *The World The World*, op. cit., p6.
12 *Amateur Photographer*, 26 October 1938.
13 British Automobile Racing Club.
14 *The Autocar*, 17 March 1939.
15 Ibid., 2 June 1939.
16 Barry Eaglesfield, *The Bugatti Book*, London 1954, p133.

Part Two

Being
A Life in Three Wars:
Ernestina, the Axis, himself

Chapter 9: From a war to a war

1   Quoted in Greg Dening, *Performances*, Melbourne 1996, p105.
2   Norman Lewis interviewed by Pico Iyer, unedited TS, January 1991.
3   *Jackdaw Cake*, London 1985, p122.
4   *The World The World*, London 1996, p8.
5   Norman Lewis interviewed by James Owen, *Daily Telegraph*, 27 June 1998.
6   *The World The World*, op. cit., pp8–9.
7   *Jackdaw Cake*, op. cit., pp123–4.
8   Ibid., p124.
9   Ibid., p123.
10 Ibid., p126.
11 Ibid., p127.
12 *Amateur Photographer*, 15 November 1939. He later misplaced the date of his return, writing in *Jackdaw Cake* that, leaving Havana on 10 November, he reached Tilbury on the 29th.
13 *The World The World*, op. cit., p11.

14 *Jackdaw Cake*, op. cit., p134.
15 Mark Honigsbaum, *Financial Times* magazine, 3/4 February 2007.
16 *The World The World*, op. cit., p12. Another account of the evening appears in a letter of 7 December 1994 to his agent, describing "the direction in which the current book [*The World The World*] is heading". The date is given as 10 May 1941, "the day before we both went overseas in the war", though Norman did not receive his call-up papers until early September. He may have been confusing the dinner with the night of the Gordon Street bombing. The Madeira is said to have been 1823, the Yquem 1887 – but he was very likely correct in writing that "we finished that night insanely drunk but irrationally hopeful of the future".
17 Interview with Gwen Merrington, 13 May 2003.
18 Ibid.
19 Interview with Gwen Merrington, 25 March 2003.
20 Phone conversation with Gwen Merrington, 14 February 2005.
21 Gwen Merrington, "Memories of Lewis", unpublished MS, March 2003.
22 Interview with Gwen Merrington, 25 March 2003.
23 Gwen Merrington recorded memoir, December 1993.
24 Bill Nicholls recorded memoir, 20 September 1994.
25 Interview with Gwen Merrington, 13 May 2003.
26 Lewis papers.
27 *In Sicily*, London 2000, p6.
28 Papers of Captain D M Jacobs, OBE, Imperial War Museum (IWM) 5947 67/254/1.
29 Papers of J R T Hopper, IWM 6342 97/3/1.
30 Quoted in Bob Steers, *FSS*, Heathfield, E Sussex 1996, p221.
31 Interview with Fred Judge, Intelligence Corps archivist, ICHQ, Chicksands, Bedfordshire, 15 November 2005.
32 Interview with Derek Wise, 22 February 2004.
33 *Jackdaw Cake*, op. cit., p136.
34 Quoted in Steers, *FSS*, op. cit., piii.
35 "Notes on Field Security, MEF", National Archives, WO204/10315.
36 *Jackdaw Cake*, op. cit., p137.

Chapter 10: North Africa

1   Interview with Derek Wise, 22 February 2004.
2   *Jackdaw Cake*, London 1985, p139.
3   Interview with Derek Wise, loc. cit.
4   Ibid.
5   Ibid.
6   Ibid.
7   "Memoirs of a Massacre Town", *The Changing Sky*, London 1959, p190.
8   *Jackdaw Cake*, op. cit., p143.
9   His real name may have been Cassar, Castellano or Cianfarani.
10 Greg Dening, *Performances*, Melbourne 1996, p104.
11 "Generous", Old French from Latin *generosus*, from *genus, gener-*, "stock, race".

12 *Jackdaw Cake*, op. cit., p158.
13 Interview with Derek Wise, loc. cit.
14 Ibid., p174.
15 John Horne Burns, *The Gallery*, New York 1947, p118.
16 *Jackdaw Cake*, op. cit., pp173–4.
17 In his autobiography he refers to it as a "car accident". He may have been hit by a car.
18 Interview with Derek Wise, loc. cit.
19 Interview with Gareth Lewis, 22 October 2004.
20 Interview with Karen Holman, 7 October 2004.
21 *Jackdaw Cake*, op. cit., p175.
22 Interview with Derek Wise, loc. cit.
23 Notebook, Lewis papers.
24 Letter of 1943 quoted (or "quoted") in *Jackdaw Cake*, op. cit., p190; no original.
25 Interview with Derek Wise, loc. cit.
26 *Jackdaw Cake*, op. cit., p193.
27 Saturday in his autobiography, but it must have been a day earlier, for reasons which become clear.
28 *Jackdaw Cake*, op. cit., p199.
29 Notebook, loc. cit.
30 *Jackdaw Cake*, op. cit., p189. In his autobiography he situates his return to Philippeville in June 1943, but so far as I have been able to situate the massacre accurately, it took place in July and he would not have been able to hear about it in June.
31 Interview with Lesley Lewis, 1 October 2005.
32 Notebook, loc. cit.

Chapter 11: Naples '43

1 From a *Havana Post* cutting sent to Norman by Ernestina in late 1939, Lewis papers.
2 *Naples '44*, London 1978, p11.
3 *The Journey Man*, dir. Tristram Powell, *Arena*, BBC2, 28 January 1986.
4 *Naples '44*, loc. cit., p13.
5 Notebook, Lewis papers.
6 Ibid.
7 Ibid.
8 Ibid.
9 *Australian Dictionary of Biography*, supp. vol., Melbourne 2005, pp187–8. After the war this soldier became the founding editor of the *Australian Financial Review* and a respected journalist.
10 Notebook, loc. cit.
11 Ibid.
12 John Horne Burns, *The Gallery*, New York 1947, p220.
13 Notebook, loc. cit.
14 *Naples '44*, op. cit., p25.

15 "Military Police and War Department Constabulary" notebook I, Lewis papers.
16 *Naples '44*, op. cit., p32.
17 Interview with Sergio Viggiani, 4 May 2004.
18 Notebook, loc. cit.
19 During the Allies' bombardment, the *scugnizzi* – street boys – rose up against the occupying Germans. They were encouraged by being told that "at Torre del Greco the Americans have already prepared hot spaghetti". Building barricades and firing on the Germans with stolen weaponry, hundreds died, but the Germans retreated.
20 *Naples '44*, op. cit., p34.
21 One evening on via Toledo, the street of crowds that leads from the old centre to the Santa Lucia waterfront, I watched a small girl in a buggy, no more than two years old, practising her future role as she was pushed through the press of people. Mouthing gossip to no one, pushing her palms forward simultaneously, she hunched her shoulders in an already perfectly captured gesture of wry despair.
22 Notebook, loc. cit.
23 *Naples '44*, op. cit., p44.
24 Quoted in John Gatt-Rutter, "Naples 1944: Liberation and Literature", in *Italy and America 1943–44*, Naples 1997, p82.
25 Ibid.
26 "Military Police" notebook I, loc. cit.
27 *Naples '44*, op. cit., p56.
28 Notebook, loc. cit.
29 *Naples '44*, op. cit., p53.

Chapter 12: Naples '44

1   At the time of writing it is hard to disregard the echoes from this Allied occupation to that of a coalition successor 60 years later.
2   *Napoli 1940–1945: quarantaquattro*, Milan 1978.
3   He recalled later that when he wrote *Naples '44* he had also had the benefit of his Intelligence reports (now lost). "What saved me in Naples is that we were obliged to produce a daily report. I would hand my report over, and my superior would read it over and chuck it in the waste paper basket and I'd just get it [out] again. I came back with a staggering amount of information" – Norman Lewis interviewed by William Zinsser, unedited TS, 7 March 1995.
4   Diary, entry of 1 January 1944, Lewis papers.
5   Lewis papers.
6   Diary, loc. cit.
7   Named Salerno in *Naples '44*, London 1978.
8   Allied Military Government for Occupied Territories, the military rule administered by Allied forces during and after the Second World War in Europe.
9   Rufo brothers in *Naples '44*.
10 Diary, entry of 9 February 1944, loc. cit.
11 *Naples '44*, op. cit., p150.

12 "Military Police and War Department Constabulary" notebook IV, Lewis papers.
13 Diary, loc. cit.
14 "Military Police" notebook IV, loc. cit.
15 *Naples '44*, op. cit., pp100–1.
16 Ibid., p102.
17 *Forces Françaises Libres*, the army of General de Gaulle's government in exile.
18 Diary, loc. cit.
19 *Naples '44*, op. cit., p138.
20 *The Journey Man*, dir. Tristram Powell, *Arena*, BBC2, 28 January 1986.
21 Virgil, *Aeneid* VI, 43 ff.
22 *Naples '44*, op. cit., p156.
23 Diary, entry of 25 July 1944, loc. cit.
24 *Naples '44*, op. cit., p187.
25 Diary, loc. cit.
26 Ibid.
27 Ibid.
28 "The Cossacks Go Home", *A View of the World*, London 1986, p232.
29 Diary, loc. cit.
30 "The Cossacks Go Home", op. cit., p233.
31 Diary, loc. cit.
32 Ibid.
33 Ibid.
34 Ibid.
35 Ibid. "Time hath, my lord, a wallet at his back, / Wherein he puts alms for oblivion, / A great-sized monster of ingratitudes: / Those scraps are good deeds past; which are devour'd / As fast as they are made, forgot as soon / As done: perseverance, dear my lord, / Keeps honour bright: to have done is to hang / Quite out of fashion, like a rusty mail / In monumental mockery" – Ulysses in Shakespeare's *Troilus and Cressida*, Act 3, scene 3.
36 Ibid., entry of 15 December 1944.

Chapter 13: Naples '45

1 Diary, entry of 5 January 1945, Lewis papers.
2 Ibid., entry of 26 April 1945.
3 *Naples '44*, London 1978, p199.
4 Diary, entries of mid-May to 7 June 1945, loc. cit.
5 "A year among the Italians had converted me to such an admiration for their humanity and culture that I realize that were I given the chance to be born again and to choose the place of my birth, Italy would be the country of my choice" – *Naples '44*, op. cit., p203.
6 "If I lose you I'm lost."
7 "Military Police and War Department Constabulary" notebook V, Lewis papers.
8 Ibid.
9 *Works and Days*, lines 582–96.
10 *Jackdaw Cake*, London 1985, p208.

11 "96 FSS Security Intelligence Report, 1–16 July 1945", WO170/7115, National Archive.

12 Ibid.

13 Diary, undated, loc. cit.

14 Conversation with Norman Lewis, 13 March 1996.

15 Ibid.

16 Diary, entry of 21 April 1950, loc. cit.

17 "Denazification: Ultima Verba", J R Tempest papers, Imperial War Museum, IWM 12841 03/50/1.

18 J R T Hopper, "Figures in a Fading Landscape", IWM 6342 97/3/1.

19 "The Private Secretary", *The Happy Ant-Heap*, London 1998. The man's name, Poldau, does not appear in Norman's notebooks.

20 Diary, undated, loc. cit.

21 Diary, entry of 29 July 1945, loc. cit.

Part Three

Narrating

A Structuring in a Storm of Alterations:
Demobilisation and disentanglement,
furious evasion and literary objects

Chapter 14: "Keep moving"

1 "Extract of letter from Norman Lewis – 28.6.51", Jonathan Cape archive, University of Reading.

2 His Alfa Romeo 8C. Alfa's race cars were developed under Enzo Ferrari's direction until 1937.

3 Interview with Derek Wise, 22 February 2004.

4 *The World The World*, London 1996, p22.

5 Notebook, Lewis papers.

6 In *The World The World* the de Szecsys became Lazlo and Lena Papas.

7 *Granta 20: In Trouble Again*, December 1986.

8 Interview with Ito Lewis, 17 March 2004.

9 Norman Lewis interviewed by Nicholas Shakespeare, unedited TS, 4–5 May 1991.

10 Interview with Karen Holman, 30 June 2005.

11 Alan Thompson, *The Day Before Yesterday*, London 1971, p45.

12 Mass Observation file report no. 2468, *Fuel Crisis*, May 1947, Mass Observation archive, University of Sussex.

13 Interview with Gwen Merrington, 25 March 2003.

14 Interview with Gwen Merrington, 13 May 2003.

15 *The World The World*, op. cit., p35.

16 "A season in Tenby castle", Lewis papers.

17 Ibid.

18 Interview with Derek Wise, loc. cit.
19 "A season in Tenby castle", loc. cit.
20 Diary, entry of 23 January 1949, Lewis papers.
21 Letter, 5 December 1947, Jonathan Cape archive, loc. cit.
22 Dedication to signed copy, Michael Sells collection.
23 *The World The World*, op. cit., p49.
24 R G Lewis advertisement, *Amateur Photographer*, 13 November 1946.
25 Hester died Hester Mary Lewis on 6 June 1994.
26 "A season in Tenby castle", loc. cit.
27 Diary, entry of 17 January 1949, loc. cit.
28 "'After I had bundled in my things ... the thought that I was done with the earth for many many months to come made me feel very quiet and self-contained as it were. Sailors will understand what I mean.'
   "Marlow nodded. 'It is a strictly professional feeling'" – *Chance*, London 1914, p28.
29 Diary, entry of 29 March 1949, loc. cit.

Chapter 15: Just going

1 Notebook, Lewis papers.
2 Diary, entry of 2 April 1949, Lewis papers.
3 Notebook, loc. cit.
4 Diary, entry of 4 April 1949, loc. cit.
5 Notebook, loc. cit.
6 Ibid.
7 Ibid.
8 "The Promontory of Gargano", *The Cornhill*, no. 980, autumn 1949.
9 Notebook, loc. cit.
10 "The Promontory of Gargano", loc. cit.
11 Diary, entry of 11 April 1949, loc. cit.
12 *Reflections on Blue Water*, London 1999, p191.
13 *The World The World*, London 1996, p50.
14 Conversation with Malcolm Borthwick, 24 June 2005.
15 "A season in Tenby castle", Lewis papers.
16 In *Jackdaw Cake*, *The World The World* and the unpublished "A season in Tenby castle".
17 "A season in Tenby castle", loc. cit.

Chapter 16: A narrative empire

1 1950 diary, Lewis papers.
2 *A Dragon Apparent*, London 1951, p17.
3 "Memoranda" entry, 1950 diary, Lewis papers.
4 *A Dragon Apparent*, op. cit., p18.
5 Norman Lewis interviewed by William Zinsser, unedited TS, 7 March 1995.

6   "Indo-China" notebook, Lewis papers.
7   Ibid.
8   There is always another mismatch too, of course: between the moment that happened and the outline given to it in tiny handwriting in a notebook afterwards: the mismatch between existence and the fact that the notebook does not exist that is big enough to contain every moment. But that is a difference that can be left to theoreticians of consciousness.
9   *A Dragon Apparent*, op. cit., p20.
10   Introduction to Miguel de Cervantes, *Don Quixote*, translation by Edith Grossman, London 2004.
11   "Indo-China" notebook, loc. cit.
12   Ibid.
13   Ibid.
14   Ibid.
15   Norman Lewis interviewed by the author, 13 March 1996.
16   Ibid.
17   Comptoir Saïgonnais de Ravitaillement, a supply company.
18   "Indo-China" notebook, loc. cit.
19   Conversation with Lesley Lewis, 17 March 2007.
20   "Indo-China" notebook, loc. cit.
21   Ibid.
22   Ibid.
23   *A Dragon Apparent*, op. cit., p208.
24   "Indo-China" notebook, loc. cit.
25   *A Dragon Apparent*, op. cit., pp227–8.
26   1950 diary, loc. cit.
27   *A Dragon Apparent*, op. cit., p286.
28   "Indo-China" notebook, loc. cit.
29   *A Dragon Apparent*, op. cit., p.316.
30   Ibid.
31   1950 diary, loc. cit.

Chapter 17: The land of the Brain-fever bird

1   *Times Literary Supplement*, 24 March 1950.
2   Diary, entry of 12 April 1950, Lewis papers.
3   Interview with Gwen Merrington, 13 May 2003.
4   Interview with Karen Holman, 7 October 2004.
5   Interview with Karen Holman, 30 June 2005.
6   Interview with Gareth Lewis, 22 October 2004.
7   Interview with Karen Holman, 7 October 2004.
8   *Wonderful, strange and adventurous journeys by ship and other means.*
9   Letter from Norman N Lewis to Norman Lewis, 1 December 1996.
10   Nathan Keyfitz memoir, undated.
11   Norman Lewis interviewed by the author, 2 November 1990.
12   "1951–Burma" notebook, Lewis papers.
13   *Golden Earth*, London 1952, p42.

14 Ibid., p41.
15 "1951–Burma" notebook, loc. cit.
16 Ibid.
17 Ibid.
18 *Golden Earth*, op. cit., p66.
19 "1951–Burma" notebook, loc. cit.
20 Ibid.
21 Op. cit., p113. After the publication of *Golden Earth* the Fire-Tank Whisky company sent him a case of their best product in thanks.
22 "1951–Burma" notebook, loc. cit.
23 Ibid.
24 Ibid.
25 Ibid.
26 Ibid.

Chapter 18: A world of intentions

1   Diary, entry of 4 July 1951 (notes for 30 April onwards), Lewis papers.
2   Interview with Ito Lewis, 17 March 2004.
3   Diary, entry of 20 May 1951, loc. cit.
4   Diary, entries of 20–25 June 1951, loc. cit.
5   *The World The World*, London 1996, p67.
6   Ibid.
7   Diary, entry of 20 July 1951, loc. cit.
8   Michael Howard, *Jonathan Cape, Publisher*, London 1971.
9   "Extract of letter from Norman Lewis – 28.6.51", Jonathan Cape archive, University of Reading.
10 Diary, entry of 21 February 1952, Lewis papers.
11 "1952–Bombay Hanoi" notebook, Lewis papers.
12 Ibid.
13 Ibid.
14 The earliest people of Sri Lanka, forest-dwelling hunters now mostly assimilated with the Sinhalese.
15 "1952–Bombay Hanoi" notebook, loc. cit.
16 *The World The World*, op. cit., pp85–6.
17 Notebook, Lewis papers.
18 Ibid.
19 *Operation Vulture*, the US plan to save the French, involved delivering nuclear bombs from B29 bombers based at Clark in the Philippines or from Navy jets operating from Seventh Fleet carriers offshore. It was vetoed by the British, and by the French commander who did not wish to annihilate his forces along with the Viet Minh. The Americans' longer aim was not to aid French colonialism but "to provoke a reaction from Peking, bringing the United States and China to war before China had a chance to become strong enough to threaten US interests in the future": Arthur Radford, US Joint Chiefs of Staff Chairman, quoted in Hayes, Zarsky, Bello, *American Lake*, London 1987, p55.

20 Notebook, loc. cit.
21 1952 diary, endnotes, loc. cit.
22 Interview with Karen Holman, 7 October 2004.
23 *The Changing Sky*, London 1959, p202.
24 Norman Lewis interviewed by the author, 13 March 1996.
25 Interview with Ito Lewis, 17 March 2004.
26 Nathan Keyfitz memoir, undated.
27 Diary, entries of late 1952, loc. cit.
28 Interview with Lesley Lewis, 5 October 2004.
29 Interview with Peggy Milton, 25 February 2005.

Chapter 19: To the wicket gate

1   From the Prologue to John Bunyan, *Pilgrim's Progress*, London 1678.
2   Letter, 17 February 1953, Jonathan Cape archive, University of Reading.
3   *Ways of Escape*, London 1980, p127.
4   *A Single Pilgrim*, London 1953, p230.
5   Letter, 7 April 1953, Jonathan Cape archive, loc. cit.
6   Letter to G Wren Howard, 17 May 1953, loc. cit. He would publish another
    twenty-six books, thirty-three in all.
7   *Naples '44*, London 1978, p62.
8   Interview with Lesley Lewis, 4 October 2005.
9   Interview with Peggy Milton, 25 February 2005.
10 Interview with Gwen Merrington, 25 March 2003.
11 Interview with Lesley Lewis, 5 October 2004.
12 Interview with Lesley Lewis, 22 January 2006.
13 Letter, 22 September 1959, Lewis papers.
14 Interview with Karen Holman, 7 October 2004.
15 Ibid.
16 Interview with Ito Lewis, 17 March 2004.

Part Four

Loving
A Reclamation in Two Decades:
1950s, 1960s

Chapter 20: Spanish earth

1   Conversation with Ito Lewis, 22 May 2005.
2   "Foreword", *The Changing Sky*, London 1959, p7.
3   "Tossa 1953" notebook, Lewis papers.

4   Notebook, Lewis papers.
5   Letter from Peter Moseley, 13 September 1996, Lewis papers.
6   "Tossa 1953" notebook, loc. cit.
7   Jonathan Cape archive, University of Reading.
8   "Tossa 1953" notebook, loc. cit.
9   Ibid.
10 Ibid.
11 Ibid.
12 Interview with Karen Holman, 7 October 2004.
13 "Amour de vivre", *L'envers et l'endroit*, Paris 1937.
14 Interview with Ito Lewis, 17 March 2004.
15 Interview with Karen Holman, 30 June 2005.
16 Interview with Ito Lewis, 17 March 2004.
17 "Ibiza", *The Changing Sky*, op. cit., pp196–8.
18 Ibid., pp198–9.
19 Interview with Karen Holman, 7 October 2004.
20 Interview with Karen Holman, 30 June 2005.
21 Conversation with Ito Lewis, 22 May 2005.
22 Interview with Gareth Lewis, 22 October 2004.
23 Conversation with Ito Lewis, 22 May 2005.
24 Ibid.
25 Santa Eulalia notebook, 1954–5, Lewis papers.
26 Interview with Ito Lewis, 5 May 2004.
27 Interview with Ito Lewis, 17 March 2004.
28 Conversation with Ito Lewis, 28 January 2007.
29 Santa Eulalia notebook, 1954–5, loc. cit.
30 Norman Lewis interviewed by William Zinsser, unedited TS, 7 March 1995.
31 Interview with Karen Holman, 17 October 2004.
32 Interview with Karen Holman, 30 June 2005.
33 "Ibiza", op. cit., pp224–5.
34 Interview with Karen Holman, 7 October 2004.

Chapter 21: Several revolutions

1   Conversation with Lesley Lewis, 22 May 2005.
2   Conversation with Norman Lewis, 13 March 1996.
3   Interview with Lesley Lewis, 1 October 2005.
4   Interview with Lesley Lewis, 22 January 2006.
5   Conversation with Lesley Lewis, 22 May 2005.
6   Interview with Lesley Lewis, 1 October 2005.
7   *Don't Tread on Me: The Selected Letters of S J Perelman*, London 1987, p147.
8   Letter copy, 26 December 1953, Lewis papers.
9   Conversation with Ito Lewis, 22 May 2005. Norman chose *Petrushka* as one of his *Desert Island Discs* in 1986.
10 Conversation with Ito Lewis, 28 January 2007.
11 Interview with Ito Lewis, 17 March 2004.
12 Ibid.
13 Interview with Ito Lewis, 5 May 2004.

14   Ibid.
15   "A Bookman's Jottings", *The Bookman*, October 1957.
16   Conversation with Lesley Lewis, 22 May 2005.
17   *The Times*, 14 November 1953.
18   *Times Literary Supplement*, 27 November 1953.
19   *The Tablet*, 21 November 1953.
20   G S Fraser, *The Modern Writer and His World*, revised edition, London 1964, p169.
21   *The World The World*, London 1996, p130.
22   *The Changing Sky*, London 1959, p74.
23   "Belize Guatemala Feb. March 1955" notebook, Lewis papers.
24   Ibid.
25   *The World The World*, op. cit., p133.
26   21 July 1956.
27   Notebook, Lewis papers.
28   Ibid.
29   Ibid.
30   Eric Hobsbawm, *Interesting Times*, London 2002, p363.
31   "A Letter from Cuba", *The Changing Sky*, op. cit., p125.
32   Conversation with Lesley Lewis, 23 August 2007.
33   *The Times*, 7 July 1955.
34   *Times Literary Supplement*, 15 July 1955.
35   Interview with Lesley Lewis, 1 October 2005.
36   Interview with Basil Davidson, 16 December 2003.
37   Diary, entry of 25 April 1956, Lewis papers.
38   Interview with Gareth Lewis, 22 October 2004.
39   Interview with Basil Davidson, 16 December 2003.
40   *The Volcanoes Above Us*, London 1957, pp216–7.
41   *The World The World*, op. cit., p147.
42   Interview with Basil Davidson, 16 December 2003.
43   "A Few High-Lifes in Ghana", *The Changing Sky*, op. cit., pp21–2.
44   "French West Africa 1957" notebook, Lewis papers.
45   Norman Lewis interviewed by the author, 2 November 1990.
46   "The Bullfight Revisited", *The Changing Sky*, op. cit.
47   Interviews with Lesley Lewis, 5 October 2004 and 1 October 2005.
48   *The World The World*, op. cit., p188.
49   *The Bookman*, September 1957.
50   *Evening Standard*, 8 October 1957.
51   *Sunday Times*, 6 October 1957.
52   *The Volcanoes Above Us*, op. cit., p21.
53   *New Statesman and Nation*, 19 October 1957.
54   Reprint Society broadsheet, August 1957.
55   Norman Lewis interviewed by William Zinsser, unedited TS, 7 March 1995.
56   Letter, 3 October 1957, Lewis papers.
57   "Guatemala – the mystery of the murdered dictator", *The Changing Sky*, op. cit., pp100–8.
58   Norman Lewis interviewed by Nicholas Wroe, *Guardian*, 11 November 2000.
59   Norman Lewis interviewed by Nicholas Shakespeare, unedited TS, 4–5 May 1991.

60 Graham Greene, *Our Man in Havana*, London 1958, p40.

61 "A Letter from Cuba", op. cit., p134.

62 "How Ian Fleming recruited me for a mission to Havana", *Observer* magazine, 15 November 1981; also "Mission to Havana", *A View of the World*, London 1986, pp239–50.

63 *The World The World*, op. cit., p171.

64 Ibid.

65 Ibid., p174.

66 *Sunday Times* magazine, 23 February 1969.

67 Interview with Basil Davidson, loc. cit.

68 Lewis papers.

69 Letter, 2 November 1958, Lewis papers.

70 Interview with Lesley Lewis, 1 October 2005.

71 "Cuba in Process of Transformation" and "War Clouds in the Caribbean", *Sunday Times*, 12 and 19 April 1959.

72 Fred Majdalany was a writer and *Daily Mail* film critic, Sheila Majdalany was a journalist and, briefly, a pre-war girlfriend of Norman's. She had written to him in the 1950s in the manner of those surprised by their ex-partner's success, saying, "I didn't know you could write, we must meet up." Lesley had asked Norman what she was like and recalls that he was vague, just saying that she was "a plain, rather dumpy figure". "What arrived for a visit at Orchard Street was instead an incredibly elegant visitor, despite her pregnancy with her first child rather late in the day, wearing a monocle" – conversation with Lesley Lewis, undated.

73 Quoted to Pico Iyer, January 1991.

74 *The World The World*, op. cit., p189.

75 Norman Lewis interviewed by the author, loc. cit.

76 Horace, *Epistles* 1/11:27.

77 *The Times*, 30 July 1959.

78 *Times Literary Supplement*, 11 July 1959.

79 *New Statesman and Nation*, 11 July 1959.

80 Letter from Ernestina Corvaja, 22 September 1959, Lewis papers.

81 Ibid.

82 Letter, 2 February 1960, Lewis papers.

83 Letter, 17 November 1959, Jonathan Cape archive, University of Reading.

84 Letter, 19 December 1959, Jonathan Cape archive, loc. cit.

85 Interview with Gareth Lewis, 22 October 2004.

86 Interview with Karen Holman, 7 October 2004.

87 Letter to Tristram Powell, 27 August 1996.

88 Norman Lewis interviewed by Nicholas Wroe, loc. cit.

89 Norman Lewis interviewed by Pico Iyer, unedited TS, January 1991.

90 *The World The World*, op. cit., p160. In Chapter Eight, where the story of the 1957 mission to Havana is recomposed with embellishments, Fleming's contact Edward Scott is out of town when Norman arrives. He occupies himself with a visit to the two generals, a meeting that took place two years later.

91 Ibid., p162.

92 "High Adventure with the Chocos of Panama (six hours required)", *A View of the World*, op. cit, p294.

93 Dedication to signed copy, Michael Sells collection.
94 Ted Willis in 1959, quoted in Michael Bracewell, *England Is Mine*, London 1997, p62.
95 *Darkness Visible*, London 1960, p181.
96 Ibid., pp196–7.
97 Ibid., p42.
98 *The Times*, 26 May 1960.
99 Letter, 12 August 1960, Jonathan Cape archive, loc. cit.

Chapter 22: Secret states

1   Lewis papers.
2   Letter, 19 March 1960, Lewis papers.
3   Lewis papers.
4   Ibid.
5   Interview with Karen Holman, 30 June 2005.
6   Interview with Karen Holman, 7 October 2004.
7   Interviews with Karen Holman, 7 October 2004 and 30 June 2005.
8   Interview with Gareth Lewis, 22 October 2004.
9   Interview with Karen Holman, 30 June 2005.
10 Letter, 1 May 1961, Jonathan Cape archive, University of Reading.
11 Letter, 1 March 1961, Lewis papers.
12 Conversation with Ito Lewis, 22 May 2005.
13 See "Alligators in the Swamp", *The Happy Ant-Heap*, London 1998, pp75–81.
14 Interview with James McNeish, 11 April 2005.
15 Conversation with Lesley Lewis, 22 May 2005.
16 Phone conversation with Lesley Lewis, 10 May 2006.
17 *The Tenth Year of the Ship*, London 1962, p244.
18 Ibid., pp23–5.
19 Phone conversation with Lesley Lewis, 30 November 2005.
20 *The Times*, 29 March 1962.
21 Interview with James McNeish, 11 April 2005.
22 Ibid.
23 Conversation with Gabriella Saladino, 12 October 2005.
24 "Sicily project" in a letter to Dan Franklin, 29 January 1988, Random House Group archive, Rushden.
25 Ibid.
26 ". . . En este mundo traidor / nada es verdad ni mentira; / todo es según el color / del cristal con que se mira" – Ramón de Campoamor, *Cantares, Dolores y Humoradas*.
27 *Border Ballads*.
28 Alfred de Vigny, "Le cor", *Poèmes antiques et modernes*.
29 Federico García Lorca, "Canción de Jinete", *Canciónes*.
30 Interview with Karen Holman, 7 October 2004.
31 Interview with Lesley Lewis, 1 October 2005.
32 *The World The World*, London 1996, p208.

33 "Dolci and the Great Conspiracy", review of Danilo Dolci, *Waste*, London 1963; Lewis papers.
34 *The Honoured Society*, London 1964, p20.
35 Interview with James McNeish, 11 April 2005.
36 *The Honoured Society*, op. cit., p145.
37 Ibid., p160.
38 Interview with Lesley Lewis, 5 October 2004.
39 *The Times*, 4 June 1964.
40 Epilogue to Eland Books edition of *The Honoured Society*, London 1984, p253.
41 *The Times*, 31 December 1964.
42 Interview with Gareth Lewis, loc. cit.
43 Interview with Karen Holman, 7 October 2004.
44 Interview with Gareth Lewis, loc. cit.
45 Interviews with Karen Holman, 7 October 2004 and 30 June 2005.
46 Interview with Lesley Lewis, 1 October 2005.

Chapter 23: Private dead ends

1 *Vulkanii nad Nami* in *Roman-Gazeta* no.11 (335), 1965, Moscow.
2 "Into Russia", *A Voyage By Dhow*, London 2001, p208.
3 *A Small War Made to Order*, London 1966, pp167–8.
4 Dedication to signed copy, Michael Sells collection.
5 Norman Lewis interviewed by James Owen, *Daily Telegraph*, 27 June 1998.
6 Ibid.
7 "Bandit Stronghold", *Telegraph* weekend supplement, 18 November 1966.
8 Giuliano was murdered on 5 July 1950, four months before his twenty-eighth birthday.
9 "Salvatore Giuliano", *Sunday Times* magazine, 29 January 1967.
10 Norman Lewis interviewed by Nicholas Shakespeare, unedited TS, 4–5 May 1991.
11 Interview with Kiki Wood, 16 March 2004.
12 Norman Lewis interviewed by Nicholas Shakespeare, loc. cit.
13 Random House Group archive, Rushden.
14 *Every Man's Brother*, London 1967, pp20–3.
15 John Forster, *The Times*, 4 November 1967.
16 Interview with Karen Holman, 30 June 2005.
17 Interview with Kiki Wood, loc. cit.
18 Interview with Lesley Lewis, 5 October 2004.
19 Interview with Lesley Lewis, 1 October 2005.
20 Interview with Kiki Wood, loc. cit.
21 Interview with Gareth Lewis, 22 October 2004.
22 Interview with Karen Holman, loc. cit.
23 Conversation with Ito Lewis, 22 May 2005.
24 Interview with Lesley Lewis, 5 October 2004.

Part Five

Reporting
An Engagement in Two Places and Another Time:
USA, Latin America, Naples

Chapter 24: Where the genocide is

1   "The experience", unpublished TS, Lewis papers.
2   "All honourable men", *Sunday Times*, 11 August 1968.
3   Conversation with Lesley Lewis, 7 September 2007.
4   Interview with Lesley Lewis, 5 October 2004.
5   "How much does Che Guevara matter?", *Sunday Times*, 6 October 1968.
6   Norman Lewis and Don McCullin interviewed in conversation by Angus MacKinnon, *Condé Nast Traveller*, October 1997.
7   "Genocide", *Sunday Times*, 23 February 1969.
8   Ibid.
9   Interview with Don McCullin, 13 July 2004.
10 Interviews, 1990–8.
11 At Xingu the Vilas Boas brothers had succeeded in creating a refuge for several tribes free from missionary contact.
12 Interview with Don McCullin, 13 July 2004.
13 Norman Lewis interviewed by Pico Iyer, unedited TS, January 1991.
14 *Telegraph* magazine, 4 December 1993.
15 http://www.cabilla.co.uk/robinsbooks/documents/4.html
16 "A Smart Car in Haiti", *To Run Across the Sea*, London 1989, p81.
17 Ibid., pp86–7.
18 Phone conversation with Lesley Lewis, 6 September 2007.
19 Ibid.
20 "Slave-labourers in the vineyard", *Sunday Times*, 1 February 1970.
21 Governor Reagan wrote a three-page letter to Norman after his *Sunday Times* article appeared, now lost.
22 Norman Lewis interviewed by Pico Iyer, loc. cit.
23 Interview with Kiki Wood, 16 March 2004.
24 "Mitos, ritos y Hechicerias", *Artes de Mexico* no.124, 1969, p65.
25 Interview with David Montgomery, 8 December 2004.
26 Email, 20 October 2007.
27 Interview with David Montgomery, loc. cit.

Chapter 25: Where the boredom is

1   Interview with David Montgomery, 8 December 2004.
2   Letter from Abby Perelman to the author, 5 February 2006.
3   Norman Lewis interviewed by Pico Iyer, unedited TS, January 1991.

4   "Guatemala: Banana republic on the brink of doomsday", *Sunday Times*, 14 March 1971.

5   Interview with Don McCullin, 13 July 2004.

6   "Guatemala: Banana republic on the brink of doomsday", loc. cit.

7   Ibid.

8   Interview with Don McCullin, loc. cit.

9   "Guatemala revisited", *The Happy Ant-Heap*, London 1998, pp170–1.

10   "Guatemala: Banana republic on the brink of doomsday", loc. cit.

11   Unidad Revolucionaria Democrática.

12   "Guatemala: Banana republic on the brink of doomsday", loc. cit.

13   Don McCullin and Norman Lewis interviewed in conversation by Angus MacKinnon, *Condé Nast Traveller*, October 1997.

14   *Flight from a Dark Equator*, London 1972, p72.

15   It is impossible to go deeper into Norman's editorial relationship with Bob Knittel because the files are lost.

16   Interview with Lesley Lewis, 1 October 2005.

17   Interview with Kiki Wood, 16 March 2004.

18   "Isola Farnese", *I Came I Saw* (revised edition of *Jackdaw Cake*), London 1994.

19   Interview with Lesley Lewis, loc. cit.

20   Norman Lewis interviewed by William Zinsser, unedited TS, 7 March 1995.

21   *The World The World*, op. cit., p259.

22   Interview with Don McCullin, loc. cit.

23   Ibid.

24   *The Times*, 16 March 1972.

25   Dedication to signed copy, 20 August 1986, Bruce Palling collection.

26   Interview with Richard Colmaine, 7 June 2005.

27   Interview with Ito Lewis, 5 May 2004.

28   *The World The World*, op. cit., p202.

29   "Isola Farnese", loc. cit.

30   Conversation with Norman Lewis, 13 March 1996.

31   Conversation with Lesley Lewis, 30 January 2007.

32   Interview with Lesley Lewis, 5 October 2004.

33   "The Busy Day of Mrs Snodd", Lewis papers.

34   Interviews with Lesley Lewis, 5 October 2004 and 1 October 2005.

35   Fidel Castro with Ignacio Ramonet, *My Life*, London 2007.

36   *The Sicilian Specialist*, London 1975, p8.

37   Ibid., pp92–3.

38   Ibid., p93.

39   Ibid., p279.

40   Ibid., pp244–6.

Chapter 26: Naples '78

1   Interview with Don McCullin, 13 July 2004.

2   Ibid.

3   *The Missionaries*, London 1988, p148.

4   "Manhunt", *Peace News*, no. 1902, 22 December 1972, pp9–12.
5   Quoted in Don McCullin, *Unreasonable Behaviour*, London 1990.
6   Quoted in "Manhunt", *Sunday Times*, 26 January 1975; also "Manhunt", *A Voyage by Dhow*, London 2001.
7   Conversation with Norman Lewis, 13 March 1996.
8   Interview with Don McCullin, loc. cit.
9   Ibid.
10 Norman Lewis interviewed by William Zinsser, unedited TS, 7 March 1995.
11 Draft reply to Pederson letter, Lewis papers.
12 Interview with Kiki Lewis, 16 March 2004.
13 Communicated to author, 2006.
14 Interview with Peter Crookston, 28 October 2003.
15 Interview with Kiki Lewis, loc. cit.
16 Interview with Gawaine Lewis, 22 January 2005.
17 "Dice, Brassknuckles & Guitar" (1923), *The Short Stories of F Scott Fitzgerald*, New York 1989, p238.
18 Norman Lewis interviewed by Pico Iyer, unedited TS, January 1991.
19 Interview with Sergio Viggiani, 4 May 2004.
20 Ibid.
21 "Bolivia" notebook, Lewis papers.
22 "The white promised land", *Observer*, 5 March 1978; also *A View of the World*, London 1986.
23 "Bolivia" notebook, loc. cit.
24 Interview with Colin Jones, 7 December 2005.
25 Ibid.
26 *To Run Across the Sea*, London 1989, pp99–104.
27 *New York Review of Books*, 7 February 1980.
28 *Sunday Times*, 12 March 1978.
29 Interview with Lesley Lewis, 5 October 2004.
30 Interview with Gareth Lewis, 22 October 2004.

Chapter 27: Amazonia and other disappearances

1   Conversation with Peter Crookston, 16 October 2007.
2   Interview with Colin Jones, 7 December 2005.
3   Letter, 7 February 1979.
4   Interview with Colin Jones, loc. cit.
5   "The rape of Amazonia", *Observer* magazine, 22 April 1979; also "Burning the trees", *To Run Across the Sea*, London 1989, pp152–69.
6   "Brazil" notebook, Lewis papers.
7   Now renamed the Max Planck Institute for Evolutionary Biology.
8   "The rape of Amazonia", loc. cit.
9   Interview with Gawaine Lewis, 22 January 2005.
10 Interview with Kenneth Griffiths, 13 December 2004.
11 "Surviving with spirit", *Sunday Times* magazine, 6 April 1980; also *A View of the World*, London 1986, pp180–193, and *A Voyage by Dhow*, London 2001, pp161–179.

12 *The German Company*, London 1979, p114.
13 "This is the book with my best library borrowing record – on account of its title. Interesting, eh?" – dedication to signed copy, Michael Sells collection.
14 "There I was, at Brooklands, in the fastest Bugatti . . .", *Observer* magazine, 7 October 1979.
15 Paul Valéry, quoted in Greg Dening, *Performances*, Melbourne 1996, p116.
16 Interview with Colin Jones, 7 December 2005.
17 "Mexican mosaic", *Observer* magazine, 19 October 1980.
18 Conversation with Colin Jones, 9 February 2006.
19 Interview with Colin Jones, loc. cit. George, later Lord, Weidenfeld co-founded the publishers Weidenfeld & Nicolson, and by the 1970s was at least as well known for throwing sedulously attended parties at his flat on the Chelsea embankment, a hub of Leftish cultural and political networking.
20 *The Times*, 23 July 2003.
21 Interview with Colin Jones, loc. cit.
22 "Travelling back in the city of perpetual light and motion", *Sunday Times* magazine, 2 June 1985.
23 "Khartoum and back", *To Run Across the Sea*, London 1989, pp46–66.
24 Interview with Colin Jones, loc. cit.
25 Notebook, Lewis papers.
26 "Enslaved to the banana", *Observer* magazine, 8 November 1981.
27 Interview with Alain Le Garsmeur, 15 March 2006.
28 "Life without Uncle Sam and his son-of-a-bitch", *Observer* magazine, 1 November 1981.
29 Interview with Alain Le Garsmeur, loc. cit.
30 Notebook, loc. cit.
31 "Life without Uncle Sam and his son-of-a-bitch", op. cit.
32 "How Ian Fleming recruited me for a mission to Havana", *Observer* magazine, 15 November 1981.
33 Phone conversation with Alex Frater, 26 October 2007.
34 Interview with John Hatt, 1 February 2005.
35 Ibid.
36 Alan Davidson, "The promise of chaos", *Times Literary Supplement*, 13 August 1982.
37 Quoted in Nicholas Shakespeare, "A traveller's companion", *The Times*, 14 June 1986.
38 Interview with Bruce Palling, 2 November 2007.
39 *Times Literary Supplement*, 14 May 1982.
40 Dedications to signed UK and US editions, Michael Sells collection.
41 Email, 3 November 2007.
42 *Spectator*, 12 June 1982.
43 Conversation with Norman Lewis, undated.

Part Six

Rewriting
A Revision in Two Restorations:
A reputation, a past

Chapter 28 : Another country

1   Dedication to signed copy of *The Missionaries*, Albert Padrol collection.
2   *The Missionaries*, London 1988, p179.
3   Interview with Paul Henley, 19 January 2006.
4   Ibid.
5   Interview with Don McCullin, 13 July 2004.
6   "The tribe that crucified Christ", *Sunday Times* magazine, 15 May 1983.
7   Interview with Don McCullin, loc. cit.
8   "The tribe that crucified Christ", loc. cit.
9   Interview with Paul Henley, loc. cit.
10 Letter to Redmond O'Hanlon, 1988, undated.
11 Interview with Paul Henley, loc. cit.
12 Letter, 4 May 1983, Hamish Hamilton archive, Arts and Social Science Library, Bristol University.
13 Dedication to signed copy, Redmond O'Hanlon collection.
14 *Times Literary Supplement*, 24 June 1983.
15 Letter, 25 April 1983.
16 Phone conversation with Alex Frater, 26 October 2007.
17 Postmarked 5 August 1983, Hamish Hamilton archive, loc. cit.
18 Letter, 21 September 1983, Hamish Hamilton archive, loc. cit.
19 Letter, 6 October 1983, Hamish Hamilton archive, loc. cit.
20 Author's diary, 22 November 1983.
21 Author's diary, 13 February 1984.
22 Letter, 6 September 1984, Hamish Hamilton archive, loc. cit.
23 *Tatler*, April 1984.
24 The island of another overlooked writer, the father of modern Greek fiction, Alexandros Papadiamandis.
25 Interview with Bruce Palling, 2 November 2007.
26 Interview with John Hatt, 1 February 2005.
27 *Spectator*, 8 December 1984.
28 *Sunday Telegraph*, 16 December 1984.
29 Tony Lambert, *Times Literary Supplement*, 4 January 1985.
30 *Observer*, 9 September 1984.
31 *Daily Mail*, 2 September 1984.
32 "Farol 1984: profits and losses", *Sunday Times* magazine, 2 September 1984.
33 Email from Albert Padrol, 18 January 2007.
34 "Foreword", *The Changing Sky*, London 1959, p7.
35 *Voices of the Old Sea*, London 1984, p35.
36 Ibid., p67.

37 Ibid., p90.
38 Letter, 2 January 1985, Hamish Hamilton archive, loc. cit.
39 Author's diary, 22 March 1985.
40 Letter, 3 February 1985, Hamish Hamilton archive, loc. cit.
41 Julian Evans (ed.), *Foreign Exchange*, London 1985, pp29–42.
42 Letter to James McNeish, 6 January 1999.
43 Letter to Marcello Cimino, 3 September 1985.
44 Letter to author, 28 May 1985, Hamish Hamilton archive, loc. cit.
45 Letter to Nicholas Shakespeare, 4 September 1985.
46 Interview with Tristram Powell, 16 August 2005.
47 *The Journey Man*, directed by Tristram Powell, *Arena*, BBC2, 28 January 1986.
48 *Spectator*, 28 September 1985.
49 *London Standard*, 9 October 1985.
50 *Daily Telegraph*, 4 October 1985.
51 *Literary Review*, October 1985.
52 *Sunday Times*, 15 September 1985.
53 *The Times*, 14 November 1985.
54 *Guardian*, 27 September 1985.
55 *Enfield Gazette*, 10 October 1985.
56 Interview with Derek Wise, 22 February 2004.
57 Letter, 31 January 1986.
58 Letter, 19 May 1986, Hamish Hamilton archive, loc. cit.
59 Letter, 16 June 1986, Hamish Hamilton archive, loc. cit.
60 Lewis papers.
61 "She was regarded as the greatest of flamenco singers of our times, with an
    extremely pure and classical style. Saetas are invocatory verses sung during
    the passing of the image of the Virgin in the processions of Semana [Santa]
    at Seville and elsewhere. They must be spontaneous. My most moving expe-
    rience in this direction happened in Córdoba two years ago, at the end of a
    procession when they were taking the images back to their churches [and] the
    procession, on the point of breaking up, happened to pass a bus queue. This
    set off a sensational saeta from a woman in the queue" – letter to Ian Thomson,
    22 June 1987.

Chapter 29: Heady road

1   Interview with Lesley Lewis, 5 October 2004.
2   Letter, 11 May 1987, Random House Group archive, Rushden.
3   Interview with John Hatt, 1 February 2005.
4   *Literary Review*, July 1986.
5   Norman Lewis interviewed by Bruce Palling, *Eothen* 6 (newsletter of Western
    & Oriental Travel), spring 1996.
6   "Costa Blanca", unpublished, Lewis papers.
7   "Among the Bulls", *To Run Across the Sea*, London 1989, pp78–9.
8   Andrew Sinclair, *Sunday Times*, 24 May 1987.
9   Neville Shack, *Times Literary Supplement*, 5 June 1987.
10 Patrick Skene Catling, *Sunday Telegraph*, 17 May 1987.

11 Norman Lewis interviewed by John Keay, *Kaleidoscope*, BBC Radio 4, transcript, 17 July 1987.

12 Nathan Keyfitz memoir, undated.

13 Letter to author, 21 October 1987, Hamish Hamilton archive, Arts and Social Science Library, Bristol University.

14 "Raiatea" notebook, Lewis papers.

15 "Tahiti 1987" notebook, Lewis papers.

16 "Bangkok etc" notebook, Lewis papers.

17 *The Times*, 28 April 1988.

18 Robert Fox, *The Listener*, 5 May 1988.

19 *Daily Telegraph*, 7 May 1988.

20 Paul Taylor, *Sunday Times*, 8 May 1988.

21 Biba Kopf, *Guardian*, 13 May 1988.

22 Robin Lane Fox, *Financial Times*, 14 May 1988.

23 *Times Literary Supplement*, 1 July 1988.

24 *Spectator*, 7 May 1988.

25 Olivia Harris, *New Statesman*, 6 May 1988.

26 *London Review of Books*, 13 October 1988.

27 Untitled notebook ("Notes, Poetical", crossed out), Lewis papers.

28 *The Missionaries*, London 1988, p218.

29 "The last of the old Europe", *Sunday Times* magazine; also "The Last of Old Europe", *To Run Across the Sea*, op. cit., pp203–12.

30 Letter, 13 June 1988, Rogers, Coleridge & White Ltd archive, London.

31 Conversation with Norman Lewis, June 1988.

32 "*Lejano* (distant)" is an addition of Norman's.

33 Interview with Lesley Lewis, 1 October 2005.

34 Postcard, 10 October 1988.

35 Letter to Gill Coleridge, 5 December 1988, Rogers, Coleridge & White Ltd archive, London.

36 Letter to Gill Coleridge, 29 December 1988, loc. cit.

37 Letter to Gill Coleridge, 14 January 1989, loc. cit.

38 Email, 22 September 2007.

39 Interview with John Hatt, loc. cit.

40 "Goa", *Marie Claire*, August 1989; also *To Run Across the Sea*, op. cit., pp105–11.

41 "The happy ant-heap", *Independent* magazine, 2 September 1989; also *The Happy Ant-Heap*, London 1998, pp129–39.

42 Interview with Lesley Lewis, 1 October 2005.

43 Letter to Gill Coleridge, 20 April 1989, loc. cit.

44 Email, 24 November 2005.

45 Email, 17 November 2005.

46 Letter to Gill Coleridge, 29 September 1989, loc. cit. See "Peace of the godfather", *Independent* magazine, 13 January 1990; also "Where the mafia brings peace", *The Happy Ant-Heap*, op. cit., pp140–50.

47 "Life and death with the mafia", *Independent* magazine, 22 July 1989; also "Boris Giuliano – The Man Who Might Have Smashed the Mafia", *The Happy Ant-Heap*, op. cit., pp82–93.

48 *In Sicily*, London 2000, pp33–4.

49 Ian Thomson, *Sunday Times*, 12 November 1989.

50 Trevor Fishlock, *Daily Telegraph*, 30 December 1989.
51 *The Times*, 9 November 1989.
52 Dedication to signed copy, Bruce Palling collection.
53 Letter to Gill Coleridge, 26 June 1989, loc. cit.
54 Email, 12 December 2007.
55 Norman Lewis interviewed by the author, 2 November 1990.
56 Notebook, Lewis papers.
57 *A Goddess in the Stones*, London 1991, p10.
58 Ibid.
59 Conversation with the author, undated.
60 *A Goddess in the Stones*, op. cit., p109.
61 Notebook, loc. cit.
62 *A Goddess in the Stones*, op. cit., p197.
63 Norman Lewis interviewed by the author, loc. cit.
64 *A Goddess in the Stones*, op. cit., p207.
65 Ibid., p222.
66 Notebook, loc. cit.
67 Ibid.
68 Letter, Eland Books archive, London.
69 Interview with John Hatt, loc. cit.
70 Letter to Gill Coleridge, 15 September 1990, loc. cit.
71 *A Goddess in the Stones*, op. cit., pp3–6.
72 Letter to Clare Roberts, 21 June 1991, Rogers, Coleridge & White Ltd archive, London.
73 Letter to Gill Coleridge, 15 October 1990, loc. cit.
74 Norman Lewis interviewed by the author, loc. cit.
75 Ibid.

Chapter 30: One more empire

1 Norman Lewis interviewed by Pico Iyer, unedited TS, January 1991.
2 Interview with Gawaine Lewis, 22 January 2005.
3 Letter to the author, 17 February 1991.
4 Letter to Gill Coleridge, 22 March 1991, Rogers, Coleridge & White Ltd archive, London.
5 Fax from Gill Coleridge, 16 April 1991, loc. cit.
6 *Observer*, 16 June 1991.
7 *Guardian*, 30 May 1991.
8 *Spectator*, 25 May 1991.
9 Letter to Nicholas Shakespeare, June 1991. "Blood in his shins" is a Welsh, not an Essex, phrase.
10 Even to the extent of accusing his biographer of designing the "moribund crow" on the horrible dustjacket.
11 Letter, 9 August 1991, Eland Books archive, London.
12 Notebook, Lewis papers.
13 Ibid.
14 *An Empire of the East*, London 1993, p118.

15 Eland Books archive, loc. cit.
16 Letter to Leila Hadley Luce, 3 December 1991.
17 Email, 20 October 2007.
18 Letter, 3 March 1992.
19 Email, 22 September 2007.
20 Email, 12 December 2007.
21 Email, 25 October 2005.
22 Notebook, Lewis papers.
23 *An Empire of the East*, op. cit., p157.
24 Interview with Chris Hooke, 15 May 2007.
25 Interview with Don McCullin, 13 July 2004.
26 Letter from John Hatt to Gill Coleridge, 9 November 1992, Eland Books archive, loc. cit. My italics.
27 *An Empire of the East*, op. cit., pp230–1.
28 Letter to Leila Hadley Luce, 12 February 1994.
29 Interview with Chris Hooke, loc. cit.
30 Letter to Gill Coleridge, 28 June 1993, loc. cit.
31 Interview with Dan Franklin, 15 May 2007.
32 Letter from Gill Coleridge, 26 July 1993, loc. cit.
33 Linda Grant, *Literary Review*, September 1993.
34 Roger Clarke, *Sunday Telegraph*, 3 October 1993.
35 Michael Thompson-Noel, *Financial Times*, 9 October 1993.
36 Geoffrey Wheatcroft, *Daily Mail*, 13 November 1993.
37 Soumya Bhattacharya, *The Times*, 19 November 1993.
38 Ian Thomson, *Daily Telegraph*, 1 January 1994.
39 Roger Clarke, loc. cit.
40 Michael Fathers, *Independent*, 23 October 1993.
41 *Observer*, 17 October 1993.
42 Geoffrey Wheatcroft, loc. cit.
43 Letter, 3 January 1994.
44 Masolino d'Amico, *La Stampa*, 10 July 1993.
45 Corrado Augias, *La Repubblica*, 9 July 1993.
46 Raffaele La Capria, *Corriere della Sera*, 28 August 1993.
47 Interview with Lesley Lewis, 1 October 2005.
48 Eland Books archive, loc. cit.
49 Letter to Gill Coleridge, 6 January 1994, loc. cit.
50 Memo from Gill Coleridge to Amanda Urban, International Creative Management, New York, 16 February 1994, loc. cit.
51 Letter from Gill Coleridge to Dan Franklin, 16 March 1994, loc. cit.
52 *Afternoon of an Author*, London 1958, p168.
53 Letter to Leila Hadley Luce, 12 February 1994.
54 Letter to Gill Coleridge, 27 May 1994, loc. cit.
55 Interview with Gareth Lewis, 22 October 2004.
56 Conversation with Karen Holman, November 2007.
57 Quoted in *Sunday Times*, 18 September 1994.
58 Nicholas Shakespeare, "The spellbound scrutineer", *Sunday Telegraph*, 2 June 1991.
59 Letter to Gill Coleridge, 14 January 1995, loc. cit.
60 Letter to Gill Coleridge, 21 December 1994, loc. cit.

61 Julian Evans, *Guardian*, 31 January 1995.
62 Letter, 3 February 1995, loc. cit.
63 Norman Lewis interviewed by William Zinsser, unedited TS, 7 March 1995.
64 Letter to Colin Hamilton, 11 May 1995.
65 Letter, 30 May 1995.
66 Letter to Peter Straus, 26 June 1995, Rogers, Coleridge & White Ltd archive, loc. cit.
67 *Sunday Times*, 21 April 1996.
68 Christian Tyler, *Financial Times*, 27 April 1996.
69 John David Morley, *Times Literary Supplement*, 26 July 1996.
70 *The World The World*, London 1996, p293.

Part Seven

Finishing
An Ending in Three Beginnings:
Guatemala, Sicily, Spain

Chapter 31: To the volcanoes

1   Letter, 31 October 1995.
2   Letter to Gill Coleridge, 29 October 1995, Rogers, Coleridge & White Ltd archive, London.
3   Letter, 21 November 1995.
4   Aldous Huxley, *Beyond the Mexique Bay*, London 1934, p139.
5   Interview with Rodrigo Rey Rosa, 21 March 2006.
6   Rodrigo Rey Rosa, *Que Me Maten Si . . .*, Barcelona 1997. Author's translation.
7   Norman Lewis interviewed by the author, 13 March 1996.
8   Norman Lewis interviewed by William Zinsser, unedtited TS, 7 March 1995.
9   Norman Lewis interviewed by the author, loc. cit.
10 Author's diary.
11 Letter, 17 July 1996.
12 *London Review of Books*, 18 July 1996.
13 Email from Nicholas Murray to the author, 17 November 2005.
14 *GQ*, December 1996.
15 Letter, 20 October 1996.
16 *Independent on Sunday*, 12 September 1993.
17 "Palinurus", *The Unquiet Grave*, London 1945, p1.
18 Interview with Gareth Lewis, 22 October 2004.
19 Author's diary, entry of 27 July 1997.
20 Letter to Giuliana Saladino Cimino, 15 November 1997.
21 Letter, 11 December 1997.
22 Letter to Gill Coleridge, March (undated), Random House Group archive, Rushden.

23 Enclosure to letter from Gill Coleridge to Dan Franklin, 7 April 1998, Random House Group archive, loc. cit.

24 Letter to Gill Coleridge, 2 March 1998, loc. cit.

25 Letter to Gill Coleridge, 30 March 1998, loc. cit.

26 Letter, 10 April 1998.

27 Norman Lewis interviewed by the author, 23 May 1998.

28 Ibid.

29 Letter, 28 February 1999.

Chapter 32: Finchingfield

1   Letter, 10 November 1998.

2   Kate Kellaway, *Observer*, 19 July 1998.

3   Ian Thomson, *Evening Standard*, 10 August 1998.

4   William Dalrymple, *Sunday Times*, 9 August 1998.

5   Letter from James McNeish, 2 January 1999.

6   Author's diary, 1 February 1999.

7   Letter to Gill Coleridge, 1 April 1999, Rogers, Coleridge & White Ltd archive, London.

8   Letter, 28 April 1999.

9   The "file" has not come to light.

10 Interview with Lesley Lewis, 5 October 2004.

11 Letter to Dan Franklin, 20 August 1999, Rogers, Coleridge & White Ltd archive, loc. cit.

12 Letter to Gill Coleridge, September (undated), loc. cit.

13 Letter to Gill Coleridge, 26 October 1999, loc. cit.

14 Interview with James McNeish, 11 April 2005.

15 Letter, 19 November 1999.

16 Letter, 22 June 1999.

17 Interview with Don McCullin, 13 July 2004.

18 Letter, January 2000 (undated).

19 Interview with Lesley Lewis, 1 October 2005.

20 Interview with Kiki Wood, 16 March 2004.

21 *Condé Nast Traveller*, November 2000.

22 "The Portuguese traveller ... has amused his reader with no romantick absurdity, or incredible fictions; whatever he relates, whether true or not, is at least probable; and he who tells nothing exceeding the bounds of probability, has a right to demand, that they should believe him who cannot contradict him" – from Johnson's preface to his first prose work, a translation of the Portuguese Jesuit Lobo's *Voyage to Abyssinia*.

23 Letter to Norman Lewis, 21 August 2000.

24 Letter to Dan Franklin, 23 August 2000, Random House Group archive, Rushden.

25 Letter to Dan Franklin, 27 September 2000, loc. cit.

26 Sara Wheeler, *Daily Telegraph*, 11 November 2000.

27 Peter Hughes, *Daily Mail*, 20 December 2000.

28 *The Times*, 25 October 2000.

29 Conversation with Lesley Lewis, 1 November 2005.
30 Peter Crookston, diary memoir, May 2001.
31 Norman Lewis interviewed by Sara Wheeler, *Literary Review*, October 2001.
32 James Eve, *The Times*, 1 December 2001.
33 Letter to Gill Coleridge, 28 November 2001, loc. cit.
34 Interview with Lesley Lewis, 1 October 2005.
35 Conversation with Lesley Lewis, 22 May 2005.
36 Letters to Gill Coleridge, 9 May and 25 July 2002, loc. cit.
37 Interview with Dan Franklin, 15 May 2007.
38 Conversation with Lesley Lewis, 23 May 2005.
39 Lewis papers.
40 Phone conversation with Lesley Lewis, 17 June 2003.
41 Interview with Lesley Lewis, 1 October 2005.
42 Interview with Karen Holman, 7 October 2004.

SELECT BIBLIOGRAPHY

ADDISON, Paul, *The Road to 1945: British Politics and the Second World War* (Jonathan Cape 1975)

ALLAN, Mea, *E A Bowles* (Faber and Faber 1973)

BOTTING, Douglas, *In the Ruins of the Reich* (George Allen & Unwin 1985)

BRACEWELL, Michael, *England Is Mine* (HarperCollins 1997)

BRENAN, Gerald, *The Spanish Labyrinth* (Cambridge University Press 1943)

– *South from Granada* (Hamish Hamilton 1957)

BURNS, John Horne, *The Gallery* ((USA) Harper & Brothers 1947)

CAMUS, Albert, *L'Envers et l'Endroit* ((Algeria) Éditions Edmond Charlot 1937)

CASTRO, Fidel with RAMONET, Ignacio, *My Life*, trans. Andrew Hurley (Allen Lane 2007)

CERVANTES, Miguel de, *Don Quixote*, trans. Edith Grossman (Secker & Warburg 2004)

CHEKHOV, Anton, *The Early Stories: 1883–8*, trans. Patrick Miles & Harvey Pitcher (John Murray 1982)

CLAYTON, Anthony, *Forearmed: a History of the Intelligence Corps* (Brassey's 1993)

COE, Jonathan, *Like A Fiery Elephant: the Story of B S Johnson* (Picador 2004)

CONNOLLY, Cyril ("Palinurus"), *The Unquiet Grave* (Hamish Hamilton 1945)

DALLING, Graham, *Enfield Past* (Historical Publications 1999)

DALLOZ, Jacques, *La Guerre d'Indochine 1945–64* ((France) Éditions du Seuil 1987)

DAVIES, Martin (ed.), *Eivissa / Ibiza: Island Out of Time* ((Spain) Barbary Press 2005)

DE MARCO, Paolo, *Polvere di Piselli: la vita quotidiana a Napoli durante l'occupazione alleata (1943–44)* ((Italy) Liguori Editore 1996)

DELANY, Paul, *British Autobiography in the Seventeenth Century*, (Routledge & Kegan Paul 1969)

DENING, Greg, *Performances* (Melbourne University Press 1996)

EAGLESFIELD, Barry & HAMPTON, C W P, *The Bugatti Book* (Motor Racing Publications 1954)

FARAGO, Ladislas, *The Riddle of Arabia* (Robert Hale 1939)

FITZGERALD, F Scott, *The Great Gatsby* (Charles Scribner's Sons 1925)
 – *The Last Tycoon* (Charles Scribner's Sons 1941)
 – *Afternoon of An Author* (Charles Scribner's Sons 1958)
 – *The Short Stories of F Scott Fitzgerald: a New Collection* (Charles Scribner's Sons 1989)

FRASER, G S, *The Modern Writer and His World* (Derek Verschoyle 1953)

FREUD, Sigmund, *On Metapsychology* (vol.11, The Penguin Freud Library, Penguin Books 1984)
 – *Art and Literature* (vol.14, The Penguin Freud Library, Penguin Books 1985)

FUSSELL, Paul, *Abroad: British Literary Traveling Between the Wars* (Oxford University Press 1980)

GOMBRICH, E H, *In Search of Cultural History* (Oxford University Press 1969)

HENNESSY, Peter, *Never Again: Britain 1945–51* (Jonathan Cape 1992)

HERRMANN, Dorothy, *S J Perelman: a Life* ((USA) G P Putnam's Sons 1986)

HOBSBAWM, Eric, *Interesting Times* (Allen Lane 2002)

HOWARD, Michael, *Jonathan Cape, Publisher* (Jonathan Cape 1971)

IYER, Pico, *Tropical Classical* ((USA) Alfred A Knopf 1997)

JACOBS, Norman & BROADBENT, Chris, *Speedway's Classic Meetings* (Tempus 2005)

KIERKEGAARD, Søren, *Either / Or: a Fragment of Life*, trans. Alastair Hannay (Penguin Books 1992)
 – & POOLE, Roger, STANGERUP, Henrik (eds.), *A Kierkegaard Reader* (Fourth Estate 1989)

KUNDERA, Milan, *The Art of the Novel* (Faber and Faber 1988)
- *The Curtain* (Faber and Faber 2007)

LEWIS, Norman, *Spanish Adventure* (Victor Gollancz 1935; (USA)
Henry Holt & Company 1935)
- *Sand and Sea in Arabia* (George Routledge & Sons 1938)
- *Samara* (Jonathan Cape 1949)
- *Within the Labyrinth* (Jonathan Cape 1950; Robinson Books 1984;
(USA) Carroll & Graf 1986)
- *A Dragon Apparent* (Jonathan Cape 1951; (USA) Charles Scribner's
Sons 1951; Pan Books 1957; Eland Books 1982)
- *Golden Earth* (Jonathan Cape 1952; (USA) Charles Scribner's Sons
1952; Eland Books 1983)
- *A Single Pilgrim* (Jonathan Cape 1953; (USA) Rinehart & Company
Inc. 1954)
- *The Day of the Fox* (Jonathan Cape 1955; (USA) Rinehart 1955;
Penguin 1958; Robinson Books 1985; (USA) Carroll & Graf
1986)
- *The Volcanoes Above Us* (Jonathan Cape 1957; (USA) Pantheon
1958; Penguin 1958; Arrow 1987)
- *The Changing Sky* (Jonathan Cape 1959; (USA) Pantheon 1959;
Eland Books 1984)
- *Darkness Visible* (Jonathan Cape 1960; (USA) Pantheon 1960;
Foursquare Books 1963)
- *The Tenth Year of the Ship* (William Collins 1962; (USA) Harcourt
Brace & World 1962; Vintage 1992)
- *The Honoured Society* (William Collins 1964; (USA) G P Putnam's
Sons 1964; Penguin 1967; Eland Books 1984)
- *A Small War Made to Order* (William Collins 1966; (USA) Harcourt
Brace & World 1966)
- *Every Man's Brother* (William Heinemann 1967; (USA) William
Morrow 1968)
- *Flight from a Dark Equator* (William Collins 1972: (USA) G P
Putnam's Sons 1972; Vintage 1992)
- *The Sicilian Specialist* ((USA) Random House 1974; William Collins
1975; (USA) Ballantine Books 1975; Fontana 1976; Hamish
Hamilton 1985; Penguin 1985; (USA) Carroll & Graf 1986)
- *Naples '44* (William Collins 1978; (USA) Pantheon 1978; Eland
Books 1983; (USA) Pantheon 1985)
- *The German Company* (William Collins 1979)

- *Cuban Passage* (William Collins 1982; (USA) Pantheon 1982)
- *A Suitable Case for Corruption* (Hamish Hamilton 1984; (USA, as *The Man in the Middle*) Pantheon 1984; Penguin 1984; (USA) Carroll & Graf 1985)
- *Voices of the Old Sea* (Hamish Hamilton 1984; Penguin 1985; (USA) Viking Penguin 1985)
- "A weekend in Havana", *Foreign Exchange*, ed. EVANS, Julian (Hamish Hamilton 1985)
- *Jackdaw Cake* (Hamish Hamilton 1985: (USA) Viking Penguin 1986; Penguin 1987; Picador 1992)
- *A View of the World* (Eland Books 1986)
- *The March of the Long Shadows* (Secker & Warburg 1987; Arrow 1989)
- *The Missionaries* (Secker & Warburg 1988; (USA) McGraw Hill 1988; Arrow 1989; Vintage 1992)
- *To Run Across the Sea* (Jonathan Cape 1989; (USA) Random House 1989; Vintage 1991)
- *A Goddess in the Stones* (Jonathan Cape 1991; Picador 1992; (USA) Henry Holt & Co.: a John Macrae Book 1992)
- *An Empire of the East* (Jonathan Cape 1993; Picador 1994; (USA) Henry Holt & Co.: a John Macrae Book 1994)
- *I Came, I Saw* (revised ed. *Jackdaw Cake*, Picador 1994)
- *The World The World* (Jonathan Cape 1996; Picador 1997; (USA) Henry Holt & Co.: a John Macrae Book 1997)
- *The Happy Ant-Heap* (Jonathan Cape 1998; Picador 1999)
- *In Sicily* (Jonathan Cape 2000; Picador 2001; (USA) St Martin's Press: Thomas Dunne Books 2002)
- *A Voyage By Dhow* (Jonathan Cape 2001; Picador 2003)
- *The Tomb in Seville* (Jonathan Cape 2003; (USA) Carroll and Graf 2003; Picador 2004)

Selected journalism:

"The promontory of Gargano", *The Cornhill*, no.980, autumn 1949

"The señores" (short story), *New Statesman and Nation*, 7 January 1950

"The road from Hoa-Binh", *New Statesman and Nation*, 19 April 1952

"The adopted son" (short story), *New Statesman and Nation*, 12 July 1952

"Letter from Belize", *New Yorker*, 15 October 1955

"Socialism and Don Erminio" (short story), *New Statesman and Nation*, 25 February 1956

"Letter from Ibiza", *New Yorker*, 10 March 1956

"A quiet evening in Huehuetenango", *New Yorker*, 21 July 1956

"A high life or two in Ghana", *New Yorker*, 23 November 1957

"Haiti – the Caribbean Africa", *Sunday Times*, 16 February 1958

"Tubman bids us toil", *New Yorker*, 11 January 1958

"Cuban interlude", *New Yorker*, 3 May 1958

"Cuba in process of transformation", *Sunday Times*, 12 April 1959

"War clouds in the Caribbean", *Sunday Times*, 19 April 1959

"Two generals", *New Statesman and Nation*, 2 July 1960

"Fidel's artist", *New Statesman and Nation*, 17 December 1960

"Bandit stronghold", *Weekend Telegraph*, 18 November 1966

"Salvatore Giuliano", *Sunday Times*, 29 January 1967

"Where is Mr Istiqlal?", *New Statesman* (short story), 25 August 1967

"All honourable men", *Sunday Times*, 11 August 1968

"How much does Che Guevara matter?", *Sunday Times*, 6 October 1968

"Genocide", *Sunday Times*, 23 February 1969

"Slave-labourers in the vineyard", *Sunday Times*, 1 February 1970

"The survivors", *Sunday Times*, 26 April 1970

"The last trip to Marmalade", *The Cornhill*, no.1067, spring 1971

"Guatemala: Banana republic on the brink of doomsday", *Sunday Times*, 14 March 1971

"Peru: the problems of staying alive", *Sunday Times*, 12 September 1972

"Manhunt", *Sunday Times*, 26 January 1975

"The white promised land", *Observer*, 5 March 1978

"The rape of Amazonia", *Observer*, 22 April 1979

"There I was, at Brooklands, in the fastest Bugatti", *Observer*, 7 October 1979

"Surviving with spirit", *Sunday Times*, 6 April 1980

"Mexican mosaic", *Observer*, 19 October 1980

"The tribe that won't surrender" (with Jean-Pierre Dutilleux), *Observer*, 25 January 1981

"Life without Uncle Sam and his son-of-a-bitch", *Observer*, 1 November 1981

"Enslaved to the banana", *Observer*, 8 November 1981

"How Ian Fleming recruited me for a mission to Havana", *Observer*, 15 November 1981

"Voyage to certain death on Stalin's orders", *Observer*, 22 November 1981

"The tribe that crucified Christ", *Sunday Times*, 15 May 1983

"Farol 1984: profits and losses", *Sunday Times*, 2 September 1984

"Wanderlust", *Departures*, April 1985

"Travelling back in the city of perpetual light and motion", *Sunday Times*, 2 June 1985

"The shaman of Chichicastenango", *Granta* 20, winter 1986

"That ol' black magic", *Time Out*, 7 January 1987

"Life's rich tapastry", *Departures*, May 1987

"Girls in May" (short story), *London Daily News*, 8 June 1987

"Essex", *Granta* 23, spring 1988

"Looking down the wells", *Condé Nast Traveler*, May 1988

"Loke's Merc", *Independent*, 24 December 1988

"Siam", *Granta* 26, spring 1989

"Among the bulls", *Departures*, March/April 1988

"A harvest of souls", *Independent*, 1 April 1989

"Life and death with the mafia", *Independent*, 22 July 1989

"Goa", *Marie Claire*, August 1989

"Secrets of the sierra", *Departures*, September/October 1989

"The happy ant-heap", *Independent*, 2 September 1989

"Lord Kitchener", *Independent*, 23 September 1989

"Snakes of San Domenico", *Independent*, 21 October 1989

"Peace of the godfather", *Independent*, 13 January 1990

"Castro's days of glory", *Independent*, 20 April 1991

"Of guides and gods", *Departures*, May/June 1990

"After the earthquake" (short story), *Independent*, 9 March 1991

"Back to the stone age", *Independent*, 8 June 1991

"Yule among the Celts", *Independent*, 21 December 1991

"Namek and the smoked ancestor", *GQ*, September 1993

"A most sinister war", *Independent on Sunday*, 6 March 1994

"Hemingway in Cuba", *Granta* 50, summer 1996

"Aphrodisiacs I have known", *Granta* 52, winter 1995

"A harp, a witch and a friendly shark", *Sunday Telegraph*, 9 June 1996

"Peace offering", *GQ*, December 1996

"God bless the squire", *Granta* 56, winter 1996

"Hope in the land of eternal spring", *Punch*, 11 January 1997

"Cancun's virtual reality", *Weekend Telegraph*, 29 March 1997

"Mysteries of the men behind the masks", *Weekend Telegraph*, 5 April 1997

"See Naples and die", *Observer*, 11 January 1998

"Travelling in Burma was harder than I expected...", *Observer*, 12 July 1998

"Addicted to flesh", *New Yorker*, 23 & 30 August 1999

"An amateur spy in Arabia", *Granta* 75, autumn 2001

McCULLIN, Don, *Unreasonable Behaviour* (Jonathan Cape 1990)

McKIBBIN, Ross, *Classes and Cultures: England 1918–1951* (Oxford University Press 1998)

MAGEE, Bryan, *To Live In Danger* (Hutchinson 1960)

MALAPARTE, Curzio, *The Skin*, trans. David Moore (Alvin Redman 1952)

MOMMSEN, Wolfgang J, *The Age of Bureaucracy: Perspectives on the Political Sociology of Max Weber* (Basil Blackwell 1974)

MOWAT, C L, *Britain Between the Wars, 1918–40* (Methuen 1955)

NORMAN, Frank, *Stand On Me* (Secker & Warburg 1959)

PEARSON, John, *The Life of Ian Fleming* (Jonathan Cape 1966)

PERELMAN, S J & CROWTHER, Prudence (ed.), *Don't Tread On Me: the Selected Letters of S J Perelman* (Viking 1987)

PLANT, Sadie, *Writing On Drugs* (Faber and Faber 1999)

POND, Hugh, *Salerno* (William Kimber and Co. 1961)

POOLE, Roger, *Towards Deep Subjectivity* (Allen Lane 1972)

REY ROSA, Rodrigo, *Que Me Maten Si...* ((Guatemala) Del Pensativo 1997)

ROSS, Alan, *Reflections on Blue Water* (Harvill Press 1999)

SALMON, Lorraine, *Pig Follows Dog: Two Years in Vietnam* ((Vietnam) Foreign Languages Publishing House, Hanoi 1960)

SCHNEIDER, Jane C & Peter T, *Reversible Destiny: Mafia, Antimafia, and the Struggle for Palermo* ((USA) University of California Press 2003)

SHENG, Lanling Xiaoxiao, *Chin P'ing Mei (The Golden Lotus)*, trans. F C C Egerton (George Routledge & Sons 1939)

SIMETI, Mary Taylor, *On Persephone's Island: a Sicilian Journal* ((USA) Alfred A Knopf 1986)

STEERS, Bob, *FSS: Field Security Section* (Robin Steers 1996)

STILLE, Alexander, *Excellent Cadavers: the Mafia and the Death of the First Italian Republic* (Jonathan Cape 1995)

THOMAS, Hugh, *The Spanish Civil War* (3rd ed., Hamish Hamilton 1977)

THOMPSON, Alan, *The Day Before Yesterday: an Illustrated History of Britain from Attlee to Macmillan* (Sidgwick & Jackson 1971)

[Various], *Italy and America 1943–44: Italian, American and Italian-American Experiences of the Liberation of the Italian Mezzogiorno* ((Italy) Istituto Italiano per gli Studi Filosofici / La Città del Sole 1997)

TRILLING, Lionel, *Sincerity and Authenticity* (Oxford University Press 1974)

VERGA, Giovanni, *Little Novels of Sicily*, trans. D H Lawrence (Basil Blackwell 1929)

　– *Mastro Don Gesualdo*, trans. D H Lawrence (Dedalus 1984)

　– *I Malavoglia: The House By The Medlar Tree*, trans. Judith Landry (Dedalus 1997)

WAUGH, Evelyn, *Vile Bodies* (Chapman and Hall 1930)

WEBER, Max, *Selections in Translation*, ed. W G Runciman, trans. Eric Matthews (Cambridge University Press 1978)

INDEX